The Political Battle over Congressional Redistricting

The Political Battle over Congressional Redistricting

Edited by William J. Miller
and Jeremy D. Walling

LEXINGTON BOOKS
Lanham • Boulder • New York • Toronto • Plymouth, UK

Published by Lexington Books
A wholly owned subsidiary of The Rowman & Littlefield Publishing Group, Inc.
4501 Forbes Boulevard, Suite 200, Lanham, Maryland 20706
www.rowman.com

10 Thornbury Road, Plymouth PL6 7PP, United Kingdom

British Library Cataloguing in Publication Information Available

Library of Congress Cataloging-in-Publication Data Available

ISBN 978-0-7391-6983-4 (cloth : alk. paper)—ISBN 978-0-7391-6984-1 (electronic)
ISBN 978-1-4985-1545-0 (pbk : alk. paper)

♾ ™ The paper used in this publication meets the minimum requirements of American National Standard for Information Sciences—Permanence of Paper for Printed Library Materials, ANSI/NISO Z39.48-1992.
Printed in the United States of America

To my parents and stepparents

W. J. M.

To Meme and Pawpaw

J. D. W.

Contents

List of Figures

List of Maps

List of Tables

Preface

Last year, we assigned our students in U.S. political systems to play the "Redistricting Game" as part of our discussions on Congress. We expected that some students would play the game while others would simply ignore the game and try to answer the survey questions we had provided. What happened, however, was different than either of us could have predicted. Students came to class angry. Some had spent hours working all of the possible scenarios to determine how many different ways they could draw the lines. Others had failed to ever get the lines drawn in a manner that would be accepted by all necessary parties. And perhaps most impressively, students began to ask about how Missouri conducts redistricting. Once that question was answered, they followed up by asking how their procedures compare to other states. And that is where this book becomes valuable. By focusing on states that either gained or lost congressional seats as a result of the decennial census, we present case studies that help demonstrate how different states handle redistricting. Despite having the same task before them (and computer programs capable of drawing theoretically perfect districts), there is still a winner-take-all mentality amongst majority parties in state legislatures when the time comes to draw the lines. Through this book, we hope to share myriad of struggles faced across our nation as states strive to draw district lines.

In preparing this book, we have been fortunate to have had the assistance of many individuals whom we need to take time to thank. First, we would like to thank everyone at Lexington Books for making this book possible. Melissa Wilks, Lenore Lautigar, and Justin Race have been invaluable as editors. Likewise to Erin Walpole, Alison Northridge, and Alissa Parra for answering our frequent questions related to graphics and formatting. Next, we have to thank the individuals who really made this book everything that it is—our contributing authors. While we had established relationships with some authors, others were solicited especially for this project. We appreciate their willingness to invest their time and effort to help us tell the story of Congressional redistricting in the past two years. All of our authors assisted us more than they know by sending in chapters that were true to the goals of the book and only in need of minor edits. Rick Althaus, our colleague at SEMO, also deserves a special thank-you. Rick regularly sent stories and links to us in an effort to improve the quality of all chapters. We would be remiss—if not in trouble—if we did not thank our wives. Both academics themselves, Jill and Breanna patiently allowed us to become absorbed in this work as it progressed and assisted with proofreading chapters. Most important, they tolerated our seemingly endless conversations regarding the latest chapter we had received or the most recent piece of news that we had to include. Without their patience and support, this volume would have never been proposed, let alone produced.

William J. Miller
St. Augustine, Florida

Jeremy D. Walling
Cape Girardeau, Missouri

December 17, 2012

1

Tom and "Gerry"?

The Cat and Mouse Game of Congressional Redistricting

William J. Miller

Critiques of redistricting by those familiar with the process have varied throughout our country's history. Writing in the midst of the 2001 redistricting battle in his state of Michigan, Governor John Engler took time to remark that redistricting is one of the purest activities any legislative body can undertake. Designed to be neutral and allow for the greatest degree of representation possible for citizens, redistricting—as Engler describes—allows the legislature to redraw district lines after each decennial census. But not everyone takes Engler's cheery approach toward redistricting. Charles Bullock deemed redistricting "the most political activity in America" without offering judgment of whether that is good or bad.[1] Newt Gingrich, former Speaker of the House, discussed in 2006 how "[Democrats] get to rip off the public in the states where they control and protect their incumbents, and [Republicans] get to rip off the public in the states [where they] control and protect [their] incumbents, so the public gets ripped off in both circumstances. In the long run, there's a downward spiral of isolation."[2] As opposed to Engler, who highlighted the pure intentions of redistricting, Gingrich focused on the actual process. And much like making sausage, he found that redistricting is something that is better not observed going through the process. Samuel Issacharoff goes a step further and discussed how political parties become cartels when it comes to redistricting—making deals for the simple purpose of self-preservation.[3] But perhaps Pamela Karlan gives us the best idea of what redistricting is all about when stating that "redistricting, like reproduction, combines lofty goals, deep passions about identity and instincts for self-preservation, increasing reliance on technology, and often a need to 'pull [and] haul' rather indelicately at the very end. And of course, it often involves somebody getting screwed."[4]

As the title of this book indicates, political parties gear up at the state level for pre-census elections, knowing that the party in power will have some extra sway when it comes to redrawing legislative district lines. Why does redistricting matter?

As the Brennan Center for Justice explains, there are various ways that redistricting can alter the political dynamics within a state and within Congress.[5] First, politicians in power at the time of redistricting will be able to ultimately choose their voters. For incumbents, this is the opportunity to create a safer district for themselves. In a bizarre way, this is one area where Democrats and Republicans seem to be in complete agreement and willing to assist one another. Second, incumbents can actually be sacrificed through the process. Members of the minority party leadership can have their districts carved in a way that they become vulnerable in their next election. Third, politicians have the chance to pack their opponents together in districts. In this way, they sacrifice certain districts in order to increase their odds of winning in all of the surrounding districts. Fourth, politicians can eliminate challengers by drawing lines that alter their bases of support. Lastly, those who draw the lines can dilute minority voters through a number of mechanisms and split communities in a way that impacts representation. For all of these reasons, redistricting matters.

THE FOUNDATIONS OF REDISTRICTING

When an individual attempts to remodel a house, the ultimate success of the project is oftentimes tied to the understanding of the original structure; likewise, before we can begin to understand the modern redistricting process, we need to understand the originally pure intentions. Even in the early years, it became clear that there are no neutral lines for legislative districts.[6] As decided in the Great Compromise of 1787, each state would have two senators (elected from the states prior to the Seventeenth Amendment) and then the seats for the House of Representatives would be allocated according to the population of each state. Per Article I, Section 2, clause 3, "Representatives and direct Taxes shall be apportioned among the several States which may be included within this Union, according to their respective Numbers, which shall be determined by adding the whole Number of free Persons, including those bound to Service for a Term of Years, and excluding Indians not taxed, three fifths of all other Persons." Furthermore, Article I states that "the Number of Representatives shall not exceed one for every thirty Thousand, but each State shall have at Least one Representative." Using these equations for guidance, the initial United States House of Representatives had 59 seats in 1789. Today, each state is still apportioned the number of seats it deserves through roughly the same method. A state gets approximately a number of seats equal to its percentage of the entire U.S. population (minus the District of Columbia and other federal territories). The Constitution does not, however, tell states how they must divide those seats within their own borders.

Redistricting is the redrawing of district lines in states that have more than one member of the House of Representatives. For states with only enough population to justify one representative, the entire state serves as the congressional district. Per the Constitutional mandate described above, fifty seats are automatically apportioned (one to each state) to assure representation. The provision that seats are to be apportioned among the several states according to their number ultimately leaves all seats above the required one per state ambiguous in nature. Throughout our nation's history, we have used five different mathematical appropriation methods. At present, the selected method is the Method of Equal Proportions. The method is based on the idea that proportional differences in the number of persons per representative should be kept to a minimum and near equal. As a result, the method creates a priority scale for each seat after the first 50 are automatically assigned. These scales tell us which state is most deserving of the next allocable seat. Deservedness is determined by which state needs the seat most to allow for near equality in representation for all citizens of the country.

Every ten years when the census is taken, congressional seats are reapportioned based on population gains and losses. Public Law 62–5 in 1911 set the number of members of the House of Representatives at 433, while also allowing for the addition of two seats when New Mexico and Arizona were admitted to the Union in 1912. In 1929, the Reapportionment Act locked the number of members of the House at 435. Despite leading to more constituents per representative than had been originally mandated by the Constitution, 435 members was deemed to be the largest working group size that would allow for efficiency and effectiveness in the workings of our national legislature. The cap can be adjusted by Congress, however, if deemed necessary. In the past ten years there have been efforts to add voting districts for the District of Columbia and the state of Utah but neither has been successful.

Politicians and citizens alike have not always viewed the apportionment process positively. Charges of malapportionment have been levied after most census tabulations. Before the 1960s, many districts were extremely uneven with regards to population—even getting as high as 8 to 1 in some states. Yet ultimately, many of the issues have arisen due to the devolution of districting powers to state governments, who can seemingly do as they please. To this point, we have not discussed how the states then decide to actually draw the lines within their states. There are three architects of drawing lines within states as part of redistricting: state legislatures, politician commissions, and independent commissions. In the 42 states where legislatures are able to redraw the lines, district lines pass just like other pieces of legislation with a majority vote in each house. Some states, however, choose to impose a supermajority while others utilize joint resolutions to prevent the potential of a gubernatorial veto. Of these 42 states, seven use advisory commissions to assist the legislature or governor in determining where lines should go. In these states, legislative committees work on lines first while non-legislators from the advisory committees assist. The key is that the legislature is not bound by any recommendations from the advisory commission. In actuality, they do carry weight since most members are appointed by legislative leadership in the states. Two states have backup commissions. Whereas advisory commissions held in the initial drafting of lines, backup commissions are put in place in case the legislature fails to agree on a plan. There is typically a deadline provided for in the state constitution that indicates when backup commissions will begin working. New Jersey and Hawaii are the only states to use politician commissions. In these bodies, legislators are permitted to serve on redistricting commissions, but the legislature at large does not carry the ability to redraw lines on their own. Six states use independent commissions to draw their lines. These commissions do not permit active politicians or public officials to participate in the redistricting process. Some states go as far as to bar legislative staff or lobbyists from being active on independent commissions. For a complete list of states in their categories, see table 1.1.

There are numerous arguments for and against each type of redistricting method. Using the legislature alone is viewed as being the most political process (which seemingly is a positive or negative depending on how you align with the majority party in your state at the time of redistricting). While many will argue that allowing the legislature is appropriate since it is largely a legislative function, others contend that politicians lose sight of the true intent of representation and instead fight for gains for their own party. Advisory commissions are typically seen as helpful, but they do not always have to be listened to and are largely appointed by members of the legislature. Further, they are typically only active in the early goings of the process. Backup commissions are helpful in ensuring states meet deadlines to accomplish new lines when there is contention within the legislature and an eventual stalemate. Yet they too fall victim to being overly political at times. Political commissions are at times more efficient since they are made up of smaller numbers than the entire legislative body, but they are still—in name and spirit—political. Independent commissions are the least political of the methods, but there are still political tie-ins. When states worry about partisan leanings of commission members, they are acknowledging the concern. But, on the whole, these bodies are better suited to separate themselves from incumbency and politics while negotiating successfully and agree on reasonably imperfect plans.

The goals of redistricting today are for legislators to be as transparent as possible and to seek citizen input as much as is practical. In past years, many citizens have voiced concerns that redistricting resembles back-room politics where negotiations between partisans ultimately trump the simple application of fairness and equality. If secrecy breeds distrust, redistricting has clearly been negatively impacted. With new technologies available, citizens have been able in recent years to begin working to draw their own maps and trying to apply the same standards as commissions and legislatures across the country. States during the last round of redistricting began to willingly make available the same demographic and political data they used to decide on districts. But it was only 26 states (or barely over 50 percent). Eighteen states went further in 2002 and allowed the public to utilize expensive redistricting software to help mimic the process and allow citizens to see the difficulties in drawing maps. In some cases, states are even proposing lines and then holding meetings to gauge citizen response and then making adjustments. The hope is even more transparency and citizen involvement in the future.

Table 1.1. How States Conduct Congressional Redistricting

Legislature	Politician Commission	Independent Commission
Alabama	Hawaii	Alaska
Arkansas	New Jersey	Arizona
Colorado		California
Delaware		Idaho
Florida		Montana
Georgia		Washington
Illinois		
Kansas		
Kentucky		
Louisiana		
Maryland		
Massachusetts		
Michigan		
Minnesota		
Mississippi		
Missouri		
Nebraska		
Nevada		
New Hampshire		
New Mexico		
North Carolina		
North Dakota		
Oklahoma		
Oregon		
Pennsylvania		
South Carolina		
South Dakota		
Tennessee		
Texas		
Utah		
West Virginia		
Wisconsin		
Wyoming		

(continued)

Table 1.1. (*continued*)

Legislature	Politician Commission	Independent Commission
Advisory Commission		
Iowa		
Maine		
New York		
Ohio		
Rhode Island		
Virginia		
Vermont		
Backup Commission		
Connecticut		
Indiana		

KEY COMPONENTS OF A
SUCCESSFUL REDISTRICTING EFFORT

While the key requirements of redistricting have been touched on throughout, it is important to highlight the key requirements of congressional districts impacted by the redistricting process. Districts should be made up of equal population, fair to minorities, contiguous, compact, and respectful of traditional political boundaries. In this section, we will discuss these key ideals behind successful redistricting.

Equal Population

The idea of equal population within districts comes back to the ideal of one man, one vote so often espoused in American politics. Each district across the country should have as close to the same number of citizens within its boundaries as other districts as is possible. Within a state, there should be an even more minimal difference between district populations. According to the United States Constitution, there can be no variance greater than 10 percent between the largest and smallest districts—and even in these cases there must be a justifiable reason for such disparity. States have the option through their state constitutions or statutes to set an acceptable variance of less than 10 percent. Iowa, for example, only permits a less than 1 percent variance between district populations. In such states, line drawers are faced with many more challenges (such as trying to keep counties or towns in tact in the same district).

Fair to Minorities

The Voting Rights Act of 1965—and its subsequent amendments—has done much to protect minority voting rights. The original act barred districting plans that intentionally or inadvertently dilute the voting power of racial minorities—in short preventing the cracking of districts. Since the 1982 amendments were added, states have been encouraged to pack districts to ensure the election of minority officeholders through so called majority-minority districts. In 1986, the Court determined (through its decision in *Thornburg v. Gingles*) a set of questions to help ascertain whether a minority group's ability to select representation had been violated. The Court would look at whether the group was large enough, compact enough, and cohesive enough to select a representative if they were put into one district and if evidence of racially polarized voting by the majority existed when determining if a redistricting plan was constitutional. The Voting Rights Act went so far as to require particular states to submit their redistricting plans to Bush's Department of Justice in 1990 or a federal district court to ensure compliance given their particularly discriminatory past. Ultimately, many of the districts drawn to ensure majority-minority outcomes became the most blatant cases of intentionally manipulated, discontinuous boundaries recorded in American electoral history.

Section 2 of the Voting Rights Act applies to all states in our country. This section works to protect a minority's right to vote. It mainly concerns itself with potential causes of vote dilution, of which redistricting is one. Redistricting could dilute a minority's voting power if:

- A minority community can fit reasonably in a geographically compact district;
- Voting-age minorities would represent a majority of the voters in that district;
- The minority population would usually vote for the same candidate;
- The white population would usually vote for a different candidate; and
- The minority vote is not otherwise protected given the totality of the circumstances.[7]

Section 5 of the Voting Rights Act, on the other hand, only applies to covered jurisdictions that have historically attempted to limit the voting rights of minorities. In these nine states (and seven others, partially), all district line changes must be approved by the Department of Justice or a federal court. To receive the necessary pre-clearance, district plans cannot intend to dilute minority voting power and make minority voters no worse off than the previous lines.

Contiguous

Nearly all states require that the districts that are drawn be contiguous. This means that all parts of the district are physically adjacent to one another. The only real exceptions made are for the presence of large bodies of water which may be used in some areas to connect districts.

Compact

Most states require districts to be reasonably compact. Unfortunately, there are myriad explanations as to what exactly qualifies as compact. As a result, judging compactness is typically quite subjective (and consequently political). Measures to look at compactness include examining the contortions in a district's boundaries, the distance from center to outer boundaries, and the location of the population core of a district compared to the boundaries. Ultimately, a general idea of compactness involves the fact that districts where citizens live near each other in somewhat geometric shapes are more compact than those with tendrils of citizens who do not fit the typical geometric shape we would expect.

Respectful of Traditional Political Boundaries

A majority of states require line drawers to pay special attention to traditional political boundaries. If a county, city, town, or ward does not need to be split into multiple districts, there is no reason to do so. Likewise, if such a traditional boundary does need to be split, it should be split into as small a number of districts as possible. More than the other issues raised above, traditional political boundaries are supposed to be protected whenever it is practical to do so.

Other

Different states include other various requirements for the line drawers within their control. Some, for example, seek the protection of communities of interest. These groups can be based on any number of factors (such as social, racial, ethnic, cultural, or economic interests) but ultimately share the same legislative concerns and benefit from solidarity in representation. Other states directly discuss the idea of protecting incumbents through redistricting and ban the drawing of districts which unduly favor any candidate or political party.

GERRYMANDERING

As we said previously, not all redistricting is done fairly. From this idea, the political buzzword of gerrymandering has come to be. Originating in the *Boston Gazette* in 1812 in response to the actions of Massachusetts Governor Elbridge Gerry when creating a salamander-shaped district within the state to benefit the Democratic Party, the term signifies the decision to draw district lines to directly benefit one group. By 1812, politicians had realized the ways the redistricting process could be utilized to deliver electoral victories as opposed to merely trying to fairly draw lines to be fully representative. Gerrymandering is often noticed due to the oddly shaped districts emerging from the process.

There are three major methods to gerrymandering: cracking, packing, and tacking. When cracking a district, an area of partisan strength is split into other districts to dilute the buildup of power and influence. This method denies a group a sufficiently large voting bloc in any district. Packing, on the other hand, involves combining as many of one party's voters as possible into one district, attempting to ensure electoral success. Tacking, lastly, involves reaching out from the center of a district to include a further away geographic area populated by voters with desired characteristics. While there are three main techniques to gerrymander, there are also three different types of gerrymandering that tend to occur. Pro-incumbent gerrymandering occurs when a state legislature is closely divided and unable to give an advantage to one party or another. In this case, the members instead move to protect their own self-interest by reinforcing the present power structure. Second, with partisan gerrymandering we find redistricting efforts that attempt to maximize the possible seats that the party in power could win. This may involve splitting a traditionally conservative district into two weak conservative districts, for example. Lastly, racial gerrymandering occurs when district lines are drawn to favor or disadvantage a racial or ethnic group. Again, this could involve either packing all members of a group into one district or spreading them out so thinly that they may not receive representation.

Given that redistricting ultimately occurs as a result of reapportionment, which is based on the decennial census, it should come as no surprise that political actors have debated how to conduct the census. While Census Bureau statisticians are largely recognized as being nonpartisan, many political actors (particularly of the nonpresidential party) note that they are controlled by the extremely political Commerce Department. Per the Constitution, the census is supposed to be an "actual enumeration." Yet it is impossible to actually count every member of such a diverse and large population. While accountants use methodologies that they believe do the best job possible at properly counting the population, after the 1990 count the bureau found through a recount that their initial estimations had missed nearly 5 million residents (2.1 percent of the entire population). More troubling, however, was that a majority of these individuals were minorities from low-income areas and that the Republican secretary of commerce ultimately decided to use the original census numbers, effectively determining that 2.1 percent of the population did not exist. Sampling techniques became a major point of contention during the 2000 census as Democrats called for a method that would allow statisticians to better estimate hard-to-count populations, such as the homeless, less wealthy, immigrants, and transients—all who tend to be Democratic voters. Ultimately, the census estimated that it missed 6.4 million individuals and double counted 3.1 million. As in previous attempts, blacks and Latinos were most likely to be undercounted while non-Latina whites were most likely to be overcounted. Ultimately, in *Department of Commerce v. U.S. House of Representatives* (1999), the Supreme Court found that statistical estimates could not be utilized, even if they allowed for a more accurate count, given that the Constitution clearly calls for an actual enumeration. Thus, if Democrats wish to see their voting blocs more accurately counted to allow for potentially more representatives in states where they constitute a higher percentage of the population, they will need to help statisticians determine ways to better achieve higher count rates in these areas.

REDISTRICTING AND THE COURTS

Moving from concerns on how the way the population is counted plays a role in districting, we turn toward the history of policy and court decisions related to the process of reapportionment. Most policies that have been enacted related to apportionment focus on attempting to ensure that malapportionment does not occur or is corrected. Congress began regulating House districts as early as 1842, when it added a requirement that representatives should come from districts composed of contiguous territory and that each district should elect one representative only. The 1872 Reapportionment Act added even finer language, claiming that districts should be as close to equal in regards to population as possible. These two clauses were eventually combined in 1901 when the Apportionment Act stated that districts were to be made of contiguous and compact territory and should consist of an equal number of citizens. This clause was last included in the Reapportionment Act of 1911. All of these previous laws, however, would lapse and not be included in the Reapportionment Act of 1929, which has become the permanent reapportionment bill thus far in America's history. To place the 1929 act in context, we must revert to 1920 when Republicans retook the House from Democrats. After gaining power, Republicans violated the Constitution and refused to reapportion the House on the standards of equally populous, contiguous, and compact districts given that many of the newly elected representatives were aware that they would have been redistricted out of their current seats. Motivated purely by self-interest, the Reapportionment Act of 1929 ultimately did away with the provision for districts, allowing the parties and the representatives (in this case Republicans) to elect representatives at large or to draw districts in politically beneficial shapes and sizes. At this point in history, political parties in control of the state legislatures were able to draw districting lines at will.

The Supreme Court, in *Wood v. Broom* (1932), acknowledged that the provisions last stated in the 1911 act had immediately expired in 1912, given that the provisions of each apportionment act were valid only for the apportionment for which they were written. After 1929, not until 1941, when Congress enacted a law for redistricting contingencies if states failed to redistrict in a timely manner after a census, did the United States have any national standards for redistricting. Aside from the *Wood* decision, the Supreme Court avoided an active role in districting and apportionment; but in 1962, in *Baker v. Carr*, the Warren Court opted to overturn *Colegrove v. Green* (1946) and declare reapportionment issues to be judicial questions, not merely political, in a wrenching case that involved one justice abstaining based on his inability to decide and two other justices altering their decisions at the last minute.

While many questioned the Court for potentially violating the separation of powers and becoming entwined with legislative power, cases began to appear on the docket only two years after the *Baker* decision. At this point in history, districts of grossly unequal sizes and populations often existed side by side. Since the 1929 Reapportionment Act, states had been free to do as they pleased, allowing inequality to flourish. Take for example the state of Vermont, where one district had 36 people while another had over 35,000 (a ratio of roughly 1,000 to 1). In 1964, the Court ruled on its first apportionment case, finding in *Reynolds v. Sims* that state districting schemes that fell short of assuring Fourteenth Amendment protections of equality within state legislatures were unconstitutional as they were unrepublican in bicameral states, thereby violating the Article IV, Section 4, constitutional requirement that states have republican governments. From this point forward, districts *would* need to be roughly equal in population. That same year, the Warren Court in *Wesberry v. Sanders* extended the principle of one person, one vote to the U.S. House by highlighting the intentions of Article I, Section 2, of the Constitution. Hugo Black, writing for the majority, reminded states that as nearly as practical, one person's vote in a congressional election should be worth as much as someone else's, regardless of the state in which they live. While asking for equality in district populations was easily done, achieving equality has proven to be much more difficult. Consider the 1983 Supreme Court case *Karcher v. Dagger*, in which the Court struck down a New Jersey plan in which districts were not permitted to vary in size by more than 1/7 of 1 percent. William Brennan, in the majority opinion, noted that allowing for any variance in district size would ultimately go against the Constitution's idea of equal representation.

To fully understand the policy influence the Court has had since its decision in 1962 to enter the quandary, we need to more fully examine the three types of gerrymandering mentioned earlier. The most common form of gerrymandering is partisan in nature. This variety can occur only when one party controls the process within a state. While the goal is to pad the numbers for a particular party statewide, scholars Bruce Cain and David Butler have found the process to be an inexact science.[8] Ultimately, the net effect nationwide tends to be a wash as different parties control redistricting in different states at different times. The Supreme Court has not been overly active with regard to partisan gerrymandering—in many cases viewing the right to partisan gerrymander as a spoil of electoral victory. In *Davis v. Bandemer* (1986), however, the Supreme Court did determine that gerrymandering was a judiciable issue when the gerrymandering was substantial, long-standing, and harmful to the political minority. To the present day the Court is yet to hear a case based on the problem of measuring partisan inequities, however, and in *Hunt v. Cromartie* (1999), it went as far as to allow states to engage in constitutional political gerrymandering. By 2004, in *Vieth v. Jubelirer*, the Court claimed that partisan gerrymandering claims were nonjusticiable because there was no discernible and manageable standard for adjudicating such cases.

Ultimately, representatives are allowed to choose their constituents. Another area of gerrymandering that the courts have largely left untouched revolves around pro-incumbent gerrymandering-often referred to as sweetheart gerrymandering. In these circumstances lines are redrawn to protect incumbent legislators. Typically this occurs in split-party states where partisan gerrymandering is out of the question so legislators instead opt to protect their own. With gains and losses split fairly evenly among both parties, there is considerably less resistance to this method of gerrymandering. In the aftermath of reapportionment in 2000, large states such as California, Ohio, Illinois, New York, and Texas all protected the present legislature through pro-incumbent gerrymandering. Again, the Supreme Court has stayed away from intervening with pro-incumbent gerrymandering.

While the Court has steered away from the first two forms of gerrymandering, it has been extremely active in attempting to assure equality for all ethnic and racial groups by curbing the practice of racial gerrymandering. Throughout history, the Deep South has drawn district lines to ensure that African Americans could not get a majority in any district and consequently could not send a representative to Congress. Not till long after the passage of the Fifteenth Amendment did the Supreme Court step in to assure equality for African Americans, however. In the *Gomillion v. Lightfoot* (1960) case, the Court found that the 28-sided boundary of Tuskegee designed to exclude African Americans was unconstitutional and in violation of the Fifteenth Amendment. With this decision, the Supreme Court had inserted its foot into a political battle that continues to this day.

Throughout the 1990s, the Supreme Court has heard numerous cases and ultimately presented two main guidelines for states to follow when navigating through the redistricting process with race in mind. First, the Court found that race cannot be the predominant factor in districting, unless a compelling reason can be shown for this decision. As a suspect classification, race-based districting is subject to strict scrutiny when used to treat citizens differently. As such, laws that relate to the subject matter must fulfill a compelling state purpose, be narrowly tailored to fulfill that purpose, and be the least restrictive means to fulfill that purpose. In *Shaw v. Reno* (1993), the Court ruled that nonminority citizens had legal standing to sue a state over racial gerrymandering. The *Shaw* case dealt with the 1st and 12th districts in North Carolina, which white citizens claimed were so blatantly gerrymandered that it violated their own right to equal protection by diluting voters. Likewise, in *Miller v. Johnson* (1995), the Court rejected two districts in Georgia due to race being the predominant factor. To challenge districts on racial grounds, the majority of the Court found that the plaintiff must show that race was the predominant factor in placing individuals either in or out of a district and that race-neutral means of redistricting, such as contiguity and compactness, were ignored. In response to the *Miller* decision, at least 10 districts were found to be unconstitutional and sent states back to the drawing boards.

While saying that race could not be the sole factor in districting, the Court did leave open the possibility that race could be used as one of many factors. In *Hunt v. Cromartie* (1999), the last redistricting case of the twentieth century, the majority found that where black voters tend to be Democrats, it is extremely difficult to separate race from politics, consequently allowing race to be a legitimate concern with redistricting. This decision was upheld by *Easley v. Cromartie* (2001), which more directly stated that race often correlates with political behavior. As an ending reminder, it is important to remember that every state handles districting in its own manner. While districting state legislatures, many of the same topics—particularly gerrymandering—arise and need to be handled at the state level. Given the scope of this article, however, it proves impractical to discuss the varying methods that states utilize when districting their state legislatures.

When looking at the effects of redistricting, numerous topics immediately emerge as powerful consequences of the procedures employed to draw districts. First, we must note that partisan gerrymandering in particular has reduced competition, increased the incumbency advantage, and reduced voter turnout in many areas across the country. Ultimately, the individuals who are playing the game make the rules while they are still playing. Second, we have witnessed prolonged court battles as a direct result of the districting decisions of states. As the previous discussion demonstrated, the Supreme Court decided in 1962 that districting was a justiciable issue, and, ever since, it has been an active player in the legislative task of redistricting. At times the Court has been extremely active in its approaches, while preferring at other times to be more permissive and hands-off. It appears that many Courts have borrowed Potter Stewart's take on pornographic materials and claim to simply know bad districts when they see them. Given the rash of 5–4 decisions, it should be clear that redistricting will not be leaving the Court's docket anytime soon. Lastly, we have seen redistricting in recent years benefiting the Republican Party. Migration patterns have led to a loss of seats for traditional Democratic areas (the Northeast and Upper Midwest) while the Republican-leaning South and Southwest have seen an increase through apportionment. Through Republican control in the past decade we have also witnessed the stacking of minorities in safe districts as Republicans have attempted to assure victories for themselves in outlying areas. Racial redistricting itself helped contribute to the GOP domination of the South that emerged throughout the 1990s. With such effects present, numerous questions existed as we entered toward the 2010 decennial census and the assuredly contentious reapportionment and redistricting that will follow.

First, we must look at what the main goal of redistricting should be: providing equality or maintaining political and geographic boundaries. Gaining equality in number has led to the violation of political divisions, city and county lines. The districts that ultimately emerge are merely artificial creations that lack, as Alan Ehrenhalt explains, any sense of geographical community.[9] Equality in number leads to less descriptive representation. What needs to be determined is what we view as more important to ensure proper, equal representation. Is my voice heard louder and counted any more or less if all districts are equal in size or if the boundaries of my geographical community are respected and maintained?

Second, we again have to determine the best way to handle minority rights. Are we better off assuring minority voting rights through majority-minority districts or through influence districts? While majority-minority districts assure representation for minorities, it has led in many ways to a paradox of representation, according to David Lublin.[10] There are more minority lawmakers, but at the same time it makes it so that surrounding legislators have fewer minorities in their districts, making them less likely to consider minority needs and wants when considering policies. Ultimately, majority-minority districts increase descriptive representation but evaporate minority leverage over legislative outcomes. An alternative that has been suggested involves the creation of influence districts, which would consist of substantial minority members, but not quite a majority. By doing so, minorities would have a higher chance of seeing a minority elected, but they would not sacrifice their say in numerous other districts to simply gain one representative. Once again, the Courts will need to ascertain opinions on determining how minority voting rights and representation can best be served as cases continue to appear on the docket.

Two changes occurred in the latter half of the first decade of the twenty-first century that may change the lay of the land for redistricting in the future. First, in 2006, the Supreme Court held in *League of United Latin American Citizens v. Perry* that states were free to mid-decade redistrict as often as they please. As a consequence, the door is now open for parties to begin redistricting procedures as soon as they take control of a legislative chamber. In reality, states could find themselves being redistricted in a partisan fashion up to five times a year depending on electoral outcomes. Whether states would ever choose to redistrict more regularly than once a decade is a question that is yet to be answered. Second, the District of Columbia Voting Rights Act of 2007 passed the House and only failed in the Senate due to Republicans utilizing a filibuster despite Democrats having 57 votes in favor of the bill. With Democrats in control of Congress and President Obama stating he would sign the bill, it is possible that the size of the House will move from 435 to 437. The District of Columbia would receive a voting seat in the House while a second seat would go to Utah (which is the next state in need according to the Method of Equal Proportions). Despite passing the Senate, House leadership has appeared reluctant to move forward with the bill to this point.

THE 2010 CENSUS AND DECENNIAL REDISTRICTING

Continuing recent trends, states in the Sun Belt region of the country continued to gain seats after the 2010 census while states in the Rust Belt lose them. After the 2000 census, the average House district contained 646,952 voters. In the wake of the 2010 census, the national average district will be approximately 710,767. The smallest districts will be approximately 527,624 (Rhode Island) while the largest will be in Montana (994,416).

As expected with demographic trends between 2000 and 2010, there were a number of states that gained or lost seats after reapportionment from the decennial census. Overall, 12 seats among 18 states shifted. Illinois, Iowa Louisiana, Massachusetts, Michigan, Missouri, New Jersey, and Pennsylvania have all lost 1 seat; New York and Ohio each lost 2 seats. Arizona, Georgia, Nevada, South Carolina, Utah, and Washington gained 1 seat; Florida gained 2 seats, and Texas gained 4. In this book, we will be focusing on these 18 states. While the redistricting battle is one worth studying in all states, we have chosen to concentrate our efforts in areas where states are forced to either remove or add districts. By doing so, we believe we can see the most political decisions possible. Table 1.2 presents a breakdown of the data related to each of the states we are examining in subsequent chapters.

In the following chapters, readers will learn about the redistricting process in these 18 states and how politics impacted the ultimate lines that were drawn. Each chapter presents a unique contribution that helps show how redistricting is largely left to each state. As long as they follow a set of guidelines, they are largely free to choose how they wish to draw lines that will separate voters and ultimately decide who becomes a member of the United States House of Representatives.

Table 1.2.   Apportionment Data and Information Related to the States Included in the Book

State	2000 Population	Seats in Congress 2000	2010 Population	Percentage Change from 2000	Seats in Congress 2010	Seat Change from 2000	2010 Average District Population
AZ	5,140,683	8	6,412,700	24.74	9	1	710,224
FL	16,028,890	25	18,900,773	17.92	27	2	696,345
GA	8,206,975	13	9,727,566	18.53	14	1	691,975
IA	2,931,923	5	3,053,787	4.16	4	−1	761,589
IL	12,439,042	19	12,864,380	3.42	18	−1	712,813
LA	4,480,271	7	4,553,962	1.64	6	−1	755,562
MA	6,355,568	10	6,559,644	3.21	9	−1	727,514
MI	9,955,829	15	9,911,626	−.44	14	−1	705,974
MO	5,606,260	9	6,011,478	7.23	8	−1	748,616
NJ	8,424,354	13	8,807,501	4.55	12	−1	732,658
NV	2,002,032	3	2,709,432	35.33	4	1	675,138
NY	19,004,973	29	19,421,055	2.19	27	−2	717,707
OH	11,374,540	18	11,568,495	1.71	16	−2	721,032
PA	12,300,670	19	12,734,905	3.53	18	−1	705,688
SC	4,025,061	6	4,645,975	15.43	7	1	660,766
TX	20,903,994	32	25,268,418	20.88	36	4	698,488
UT	2,236,714	3	2,770,765	23.88	4	1	690,971
WA	5,908,684	9	6,753,369	14.30	10	1	672,454

NOTES

1. Charles S. Bullock III, *Redistricting: The Most Political Activity in America* (Lanham, MD: Rowman & Littlefield, 2010).

2. Juliet Eilperin, "The Gerrymander That Ate America," Slate 2006, www.slate.com/articles/news_and_politics/politics/2006/04/the_gerrymander_that_ate_america.html (accessed January 13, 2013).

3. Samuel Issacharoff, "Gerrymandering and Political Cartels," *Harvard Law Review 116* (2002): 45–53.

4. Pamela S. Karlan, "The Fire Next Time: Reapportionment after the 2000 Census," *Stanford Law Review 50* (1998): 731–63.

5. Erika Wood and Myrna Perez, "A Media Guide to Redistricting," Brennan Center for Justice (2011).

6. Robert G. Dixon Jr., "Fair Criteria and Procedures for Establishing Legislative Districts," in *Representation and Redistricting Issues*, ed. Bernard Grofman, Arend Lijphart, Robert B. McKay, and Howard Scarrow (Lexington, MA: Lexington Books, 1982), 7.

7. Wood and Perez, "A Media Guide."

8. Bruce E. Cain and David Butler, "Redistricting Myths Are at Odds with Evidence," *Public Affairs Report 32* (1991): 6.

9. Alan Ehrenhalt, *The Lost City: The Forgotten Virtues of Community in America* (New York: Basic Books, 1996).

10. David Lublin, *The Paradox of Representation: Racial Gerrymandering and Minority Interests in Congress* (Princeton, NJ: Princeton University Press, 1997).

2

Utah

Pizza Slices, Doughnut Holes, and One-Party Dominance

Adam R. Brown

Republicans dominate Utah in every way. Republicans have controlled Utah's House since 1975 and its Senate since 1977. Republicans also control all four elected executive positions, including state auditor (since 1969), treasurer (since 1981), governor (since 1985), and attorney general (since 2000). Four of Utah's five current Supreme Court justices were appointed by Republican governors; all were confirmed by Republican senates. Of the seven Utahns to serve in the U.S. House since 1995, only one has been a Democrat. Without question, Utah is an overwhelmingly Republican state.

When the legislature convened in late 2011 to adopt new district maps, Republicans controlled over three-quarters of the seats in each legislative chamber. In most states, redistricting is a fierce process that pits Republicans and Democrats against each other. With Republicans controlling such an overwhelming majority of seats, the casual observer might expect Democrats to have little or no influence over the process. Instead, Utah's Republicans were surprisingly accommodating to legislative Democrats, almost to the point of magnanimity—but only with regard to state legislative maps, which received near-unanimous legislative approval.

When it came time to draw congressional maps, however, the narrative changed from consensus to conflict. Utah's lone Democratic member of Congress, Representative Jim Matheson, had managed to survive a highly-criticized 2001 gerrymander attempt. To the dismay of Utah Republicans, Matheson continued to win reelections throughout the subsequent decade. In 2011 he was still in office, a lone blue dot in an otherwise red state. Utah acquired a fourth House seat following the 2010 census as a result of its rapid population growth. Drawing this new district would require a wholesale redrawing of district lines, creating the perfect opportunity to revisit the Matheson gerrymander and try, once again, to draw Rep. Matheson out of office.

The results of Utah's 2011 redistricting process largely affirm the existing political science research literature. The process was controlled by a single party, one that has long dominated every branch of government. Unsurprisingly, the new congressional maps do few favors for the state's Democrats. Legislative Republicans chose to follow what Cox and Katz[1] termed a "microcosm strategy," creating four districts that equally reflect the state's Republican dominance. Moreover, they also removed familiar Republican areas from Matheson's district and replaced them with unfamiliar ones. This decision to replace one set of Republicans with another was probably not an incidental artifact of the redistricting process. Rather, Yoshinaka and Murphy[2] have argued that introducing this sort of "population instability" during redistricting often reflects an intentional effort to break up a minority incumbent's "personal vote."[3]

Before assessing Utah's redistricting process in the light of the political science literature, I will begin by describing the demographic trends that led Utah to acquire its new congressional seat. After describing Utah's general redistricting process and giving some background on the 2001 redistricting round, I will examine the most recent redistricting effort and assess its effects.

DEMOGRAPHIC TRENDS FROM 2000 TO 2010

Between 2000 and 2010, there were three major demographic changes relevant to the 2011 redistricting process. First, and most importantly, the state grew rapidly, giving rise to a fourth congressional seat. Second, the Hispanic population grew extraordinarily fast, and in a manner that may force Utah's mapmakers to pay greater attention to the Voting Rights Act in future years. Third, Utah's voters became even more Republican, making a gerrymander even more attractive and attainable for the state's Republican legislators.

Population Growth

Utah has seen tremendous growth in recent years. The 2010 census reported population growth of 530,716 residents, resulting in a total population of 2,763,885. Only Nevada and Arizona surpassed Utah's 23.8 percent growth rate. Utah remains only the 34th most populous state, but it continues to grow rapidly. With its new seat, Utah's four congressional districts will have an average population of 690,971.

Most Utahns live along a narrow north-south corridor (the Wasatch Front) that follows Interstate 15. This corridor spans 4 of Utah's 29 counties—Utah, Salt Lake, Davis, and Weber. These four counties are home to 75.4 percent of the state's population despite containing only 4.4 percent of Utah's dry land. There are enough people (2,083,934) in these four counties alone to fill three of Utah's four House districts, with 11,020 people to spare. The 381,484 new residents in these four counties (72 percent of the state's total growth since 2000) are sufficient to fill more than half a congressional district.

At the political, economic, cultural, and demographic center of the Wasatch Front lies the state's most populous county, Salt Lake County. With 1,029,655 residents—37 percent of the state's population—the county could fill one and a half congressional districts on its own. Whether Salt Lake County would receive its own congressional district turned out to be a major dispute. Democrats insisted that the state's preeminent "community of interest" should remain intact. Meanwhile, Republicans had little interest in creating a relatively safe Democratic district. I discuss this matter later in this chapter.

With the state's population growth concentrated along the Wasatch Front, Utah's existing three districts became imbalanced between 2000 and 2010. During this decade, the first district covered the northern part of the state, the second district covered the state's vast eastern and southern expanses, and the third district covered the central and western parts of the state. Together, the three districts formed a pinwheel shape converging on Salt Lake City, as seen in map 2.1.

The state's fastest growth between 2000 and 2010 occurred in the third district. The third district's population base lies in the Provo-Orem metropolitan area of Utah County, just south of Salt Lake County. Utah County added more residents (148,028) during this decade than any other county in Utah. The third district also takes in the western half of Salt Lake County, which is where most of that county's growth took place. Increasingly, growth in Salt Lake County and Utah County has occurred outside the historic population centers such as Salt Lake City and Provo. Indeed, Salt Lake City grew at a sluggish 2.6 percent during this period, while Provo grew at only 7.0 percent. Instead, growth has occurred in historically rural and suburban areas in southern Salt Lake County and northern Utah County. West Jordan, in southern Salt Lake County, grew at 51 percent. The nearby city of Lehi, in northern Utah County, grew at a whopping 149 percent. Both of these cities—as well as the other high-growth parts of Salt Lake County and Utah County—were located squarely in the third district from 2000 to 2010.

The state's other major growth area, Weber and Davis counties (just north of Salt Lake County), sat entirely within the first district. Together, Weber and Davis counties added 102,188 residents to the first district between 2000 and 2010. Meanwhile, the second district was left behind. Although the second district did reach into the eastern half of Salt Lake County, the cities there are older and mostly full. As such, the second district's only major growth area was in far-off Washington County in the state's extreme southwest corner, but even Washington County added only 47,761 residents.

These county-by-county growth patterns are apparent in map 2.2. Of the five counties that added 30,000 or more residents between 2000 and 2010, four are along the Wasatch Front. Utah's population has long been concentrated along this narrow corridor. These growth patterns have reinforced that trend. This increasing

Map 2.1. Utah Congressional Districts, 2001–2011. National Atlas of the United States.

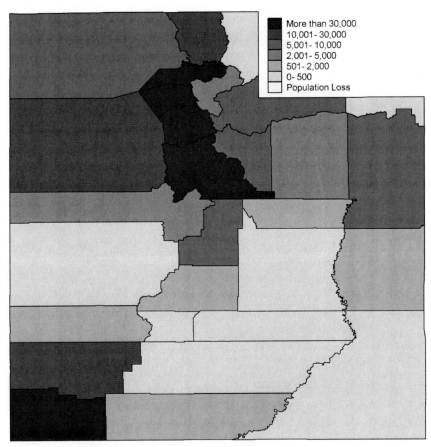

Map 2.2. Population Change by County, 2000–2010. U.S. Census Bureau.

concentration of population in a small part of the state forced the legislature to think carefully about how the new 2011 district maps should treat rural areas, a matter discussed in greater detail below.

As a result of these growth patterns, population growth in the first and third districts (held by Republicans) outpaced growth in the second district (held by a Democrat) between 2000 and 2010. Table 2.1 shows that the addition of a fourth district after the 2010 census forced the third district to shed approximately 275,261 residents. The first and second districts also needed to shed over 200,000 residents apiece. From these numbers, one might have expected the legislature to keep the second district mostly intact while taking a sharper knife to the third district. Instead, it was the second district that saw the most drastic changes in 2011.

Table 2.1. Utah District Populations

District	2011 Incumbent	2010 Population	Target Population	Difference
1	Rob Bishop (R)	906,660	690,971	+215,689
2	Jim Matheson (D)	890,993	690,971	+200,002
3	Jason Chaffetz (R)	966,232	690,971	+275,261
4	—	—	690,971	−690,971

Hispanic Growth

Utah has long had a white supermajority, but the state's Hispanic population has grown rapidly in recent years. Of Utah's 530,716 new residents in the 2010 census, 156,781 (30 percent) are Hispanic. Statewide, the Hispanic population grew by 78 percent (from 201,559 to 358,340) in the 2000s, bringing it to 13 percent of Utah's total population in 2010. By contrast, Hispanics represented only 9 percent of the population in 2000 and 5 percent in 1990.

Almost every county saw its Hispanic population grow during the 2000s, but the most dramatic Hispanic growth has occurred in Utah's older cities. For example, Salt Lake County's Hispanic population grew by 68 percent (from 106,787 to 176,015) in the 2000s. Of 131,268 new residents in Salt Lake County since 2000, 69,288 are Hispanic, accounting for almost 53 percent of the county's overall growth. Indeed, the state's Hispanic population has grown increasingly concentrated within Salt Lake County. Nearly half of the state's Hispanics reside there.

Within Salt Lake County, Hispanic growth has been concentrated mainly in the northern areas, in the older population centers in and around Salt Lake City. Salt Lake City and its neighbors have large Hispanic minorities, ranging from 19 percent to 33 percent of their total populations. In fact, several cities would have lost population between 2000 and 2010 if not for Hispanic growth. Taylorsville, for example, gained 3,909 Hispanics, offsetting a decrease of 3,250 whites. Salt Lake City gained 7,383 Hispanics over the last decade, offsetting a decrease of 3,853 whites. As Hispanics move in and whites move out, these traditional population centers are becoming more Hispanic.

As recently as the 1980s, there were large tracts of undeveloped land in the 45 miles between Salt Lake City and Provo. As mentioned earlier, these areas experienced the most rapid population growth between 2000 and 2010. But unlike the traditional areas, where growth has been driven by Hispanic immigration, growth in these new cities has been driven mostly by white immigration. These new population centers have had some Hispanic growth, of course. South Jordan, for example, more than tripled its Hispanic population between 2000 and 2010, growing from 962 to 3,008, but its white population grew much larger, expanding from 28,115 to 46,145. With whites moving into the suburbs and Hispanics moving into the traditional population centers, Utah's Hispanic population is becoming increasingly concentrated in the older urban areas.

The 1965 Voting Rights Act prohibits states from drawing district maps in a manner that dilutes the voting power of a racial or ethnic minority. Utah has never had enough concentrated minority voters to cause mapmakers to worry about this sort of lawsuit. As traditional population centers become increasingly Hispanic, however, Utah's mapmakers may need to begin taking care not to divide up Hispanic populations. The areas where Hispanic growth has been most concentrated also happen to be the most heavily Democratic areas in the largely Republican state, making them prime targets for any attempted partisan gerrymander. If a partisan gerrymander had the incidental effect of splitting up a concentrated Hispanic population, the Voting Rights Act could become relevant.

Throughout the 2011 redistricting process, these sorts of concerns about minority disenfranchisement did not come up. Simply put, the large Hispanic population in Salt Lake City, Taylorsville, West Valley City, and other nearby cities is not large enough yet to raise this concern. Still, if northern Salt Lake County's Hispanic population continues to grow as rapidly over the next decade as in the previous one, then matters may be very different in 2020. The 2011 redistricting effort may have been the last in Utah to be relatively immune to a lawsuit alleging disenfranchisement of a racial or ethnic minority.

Partisan Shifts

As the state has grown in population, it has also grown more Republican. Figure 2.1 shows the GOP advantage in Utah since statehood. For each presidential election

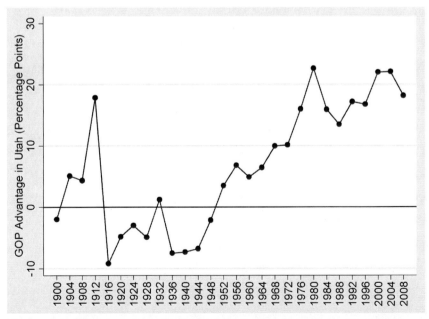

Figure 2.1. GOP Advantage in Presidential Elections in Utah. Created by the author.

year, this figure plots the difference between the Republican presidential candidate's vote share in Utah and his vote share nationally. By plotting the difference between Utah's vote and the national vote, this figure draws out the GOP advantage in Utah while holding national partisan tides constant. From 1916 until the 1960s, Utah's vote share was consistently within 10 percentage points of the national tally. This began to change in the 1970s, when Utah shifted rapidly toward the Republican Party. From 1984 to 1996, Utah's Republican vote share exceeded the national Republican vote share by 13.5 to 17.2 percentage points. The gap widened further in the 2000s. In presidential elections held in 2000, 2004, and 2008, Utah's preference for the Republican Party (relative to the nation) was stronger than in any year in Utah's history with the singular exception of 1980. Although the Republican advantage decreased mildly in 2008, each of the estimates from the 2000s is higher than any estimate from 1984 through 1996. The Republican advantage in Utah relative to the nation was stronger in 2000, 2004, and 2008 than in the preceding four presidential elections.

Utah's increasing preference for the Republican Party is confirmed by survey data collected by the Utah Colleges Exit Poll. This exit poll, administered biennially since 1982 by political scientists at Brigham Young University and other Utah universities, reaches a large, statewide sample of Utah voters. Exit polls from 1992 to 2000 found an average of 58.5 percent of respondents calling themselves Republican, but exit polls from 2002 to 2010 found an average of 62.8 percent calling themselves Republican. That comes out to a rise of 4.3 percentage points in the 2000s as compared to the 1990s. Moreover, every exit poll estimate from the 2000s is higher than any estimate from the 1990s or 1980s (except 1994).

This statewide trend has been reflected in almost every county. I calculated a partisanship score for each county by averaging its presidential and gubernatorial votes for every election since 1980. (Utah's gubernatorial elections occur in presidential election years.) Using this metric, there was not a single Democratic-majority county in 2008; the most Democratic county was 57 percent Republican. This represents a pronounced change from 1992, when two counties gave a majority of their averaged presidential-gubernatorial votes to Democrats, and another four counties gave between 45 and 50 percent of their votes to Democrats.

Using this metric, only one county (rural Kane County) decreased its share of Republican voters between 1992 and 2008, dropping slightly from 81 percent Republican to 77 percent. This minor retreat was more than offset by a huge shift in rural Carbon County, which changed from 34 percent Republican in 1992 to 61 percent in 2008, a 27 percentage point shift. Table 2.2 lists GOP support in 1992 and 2008 for Utah's 10 most populous counties. The table is sorted by the right-most column, which shows how many percentage points each county moved to the right between 1992 and 2008. The table illustrates Utah's significant rightward shift in a state that has already been a Republican stronghold for decades.

Table 2.2.   **Republican Vote Share in Utah's 10 Largest Counties
(Average of Presidential and Gubernatorial Votes)**

County	1992 GOP	2008 GOP	Change
Utah	82%	85%	+3
Iron	81	85	+3
Washington	79	82	+3
Cache	76	81	+5
Davis	72	78	+6
Salt Lake	54	60	+6
Box Elder	79	86	+7
Summit	49	57	+8
Weber	61	72	+11
Tooele	55	73	+18

For simplicity, I have presented a comparison of only 1992 and 2008. It is possible that 1992 was an unusually Democratic year in Utah, or that 2008 was an unusually Republican year in Utah. This possibility seems remote, given that Democrats nationally fared better in 2008 than in 1992. Still, similar patterns obtain when I compare 1988 to 2004. The precise numbers are, of course, different, but the general pattern is the same. Between 1988/1992 and 2004/2008, every county but one moved toward the Republican Party in presidential and gubernatorial elections.

Using three different approaches, I have shown that Utah became even more Republican in the 2000s compared to the 1980s and 1990s. The areas that lean Democratic are fewer and smaller than they were in 2000. During the 2011 redistricting session, this increasing Republican dominance made it even easier for legislative Republicans to draw maps that favor Republican candidates.

I have discussed three important demographic changes that took place between 2000 and 2010. First, the state's population grew sufficiently to procure a fourth congressional seat for Utah, with most of that growth concentrated along the urbanized Wasatch Front. Second, the Hispanic population grew rapidly in a concentrated area around Salt Lake City; by 2020, this minority population may be large enough to raise Voting Rights Act concerns. Third, Utah became even more Republican over the past decade.

THE PROCESS OF REDISTRICTING IN UTAH

Utah's constitution and statutory code have little to say about redistricting. The Utah constitution sets only two constraints on the process. First, it sets a loose deadline, stipulating that redistricting be completed by the end of the first general legislative session after the census results are received.[4] Since the 2010 census results were received in spring 2011, this language would suggest a deadline of March 8, 2012, the last day of the legislature's 2012 general session. Second, the state constitution also gives rules for how many districts will be drawn for each chamber of the state legislature[5], a stipulation that is irrelevant when considering congressional districts.

Statutory code adds a few minor rules to these constitutional constraints. Once the redistricting process has been completed, for example, statutory code requires that the maps be written into state code, with official maps sent to the lieutenant governor's office to be used as a basis for legislative intent.[6] State code also specifies how county clerks should deal with maps that inadvertently omit parts of the state.[7]

Other than these constitutional and legal guidelines, the details of redistricting are left up to the legislature to handle through the standard legislative process. Utah's constitution limits the legislature to a 45-day general session held each winter from January to March. Although the constitutional language prevents either chamber from convening and holding a vote outside of session, however, it does not prevent committees from holding hearings and considering proposals. These interim committees cannot pass a bill into law, but they can conduct preliminary work on a bill, so that it will be ready for floor debate when the legislature convenes. Legislative rules contain provisions for the appointment of joint House-Senate interim committees. They are led by two co-chairs, one from each chamber. The legislature routinely appoints interim committees at the close of each general session with jurisdictions parallel to each chamber's standing committees, so this process is familiar to legislators.

Given the severe time constraints imposed by Utah's 45-day legislative session, legislative leaders typically appoint a joint House-Senate interim redistricting committee to meet during the interim (summer) months to prepare maps. Generally, the committee consists of about five state senators and about fifteen state representatives, with Democrats and Republicans represented according to their seat shares in each chamber. After a few months of hearings and debate, the committee sends final proposals to the legislature. Rather than wait until the winter's general session, the legislature typically asks the governor to call a special session in the autumn to vote on the committee's recommendations. Nothing in the constitution, code, or legislative rules requires the state to use the interim process followed by a special session for redistricting. Rather, it has simply become tradition to use this mechanism.

In recent decades, the redistricting committee's first order of business has been to agree on a set of "procedural guidelines" and "redistricting principles." The procedural guidelines adopted April 25, 2011, are mostly innocuous, containing, for example, a reaffirmation of the state's existing open meetings law: "Redistricting Committee meetings will be open to the public." The most ambitious of the procedural guidelines declares that "political data should not be shown to or discussed with redistricting committee staff." Note, though, that this restriction applies only to non-partisan legislative staff; it does not apply to lawmakers themselves, who are free to consider political information. The 2011 redistricting committee adopted the same procedural guidelines as were used in 2001.

In contrast to the "procedural guidelines," the "redistricting principles" lay out a set of substantive criteria that the newly drawn districts should meet. On May 4, 2011, the redistricting committee formally adopted the same principles as had been used in 2001 (except as noted below), which I quote verbatim:

1. Congressional districts must be as nearly equal [in population] as practicable with a deviation not greater than +/– 0.1 percent [0.5 percent in 2001].
2. State legislative districts and state school board districts must have substantial equality of population among the various districts with a deviation not greater than +/– 3.5 percent [4 percent in 2001].
3. Districts will be single member districts.
4. Plans will be drawn to create four congressional districts [three in 2001], 29 State Senate districts, 75 State House districts, and 15 State School Board districts.
5. In drawing districts, the official population enumeration of the 2010 decennial census will be used.
6. Districts will be contiguous and reasonably compact.

As far as U.S. House districts are concerned, these principles do not say anything that is not already required by the federal courts, with only one exception: The vague suggestion that districts will be "reasonably compact." The committee explicitly rejected more stringent principles, most of which were proposed by minority Democrats. For example, Democrats proposed that district competitiveness be considered as a redistricting principle. Democrats made this proposal for political reasons; Republicans rejected it for equally political reasons.

Democrats also proposed that the committee's "redistricting principles" state an intention to preserve "communities of interest," such as cities and counties. This proposal was a transparent attempt to keep Salt Lake County together. As the state's Democratic stronghold, any Republican gerrymander would almost certainly slice Salt Lake County up. Republicans rejected this proposal. The House chair of the redistricting committee, Republican Representative Ken Sumsion, explained that he preferred to keep the list of redistricting principles brief and broad.[8] In his view, more detailed redistricting principles might provoke lawsuits claiming that the committee had failed to follow its own principles. Broad principles were his way of preserving legal flexibility. Clearly, they would also preserve political flexibility. In the end, the 2011 redistricting committee kept the same principles as had been used in 2001.

THE 2001 REDISTRICTING PROCESS

Before delving into the 2011 redistricting process, let us pause to look back to 2001. After the release of the 2000 census redistricting data in March 2001, legislative leaders assembled an interim committee of fifteen representatives and five senators, with seven Democrats and thirteen Republicans. The two committee chairs, one from each chamber, were both Republicans. In its first meetings, the committee adopted the procedural guidelines and redistricting principles discussed above.

Utah had expected to receive a fourth congressional seat after the 2000 census. If the census had found just 857 more people in Utah in 2000—or 857 fewer in North Carolina—the state would have received a fourth seat. Instead, North Carolina gained a thirteenth seat, and Utah held steady with three. Utah filed suit, claiming that the census had underestimated Utah's population by overlooking the 11,176 Latter-day Saint missionaries living temporarily outside Utah, and that the census should not have imputed the occupancy of non-responding houses based on the occupancy of neighboring homes. Federal judges ultimately ruled against the state on both issues. The Supreme Court did not issue its final ruling until June 2002, however, long after Utah's constitutional redistricting deadline had passed. Foreseeing this possibility, the redistricting committee drafted two separate congressional plans. One had three districts, the other had four. Both plans were passed by the legislature and signed by the governor, with language specifying that the four-district map would automatically become law if the Supreme Court ruled in Utah's favor.

Despite the complications caused by this ongoing litigation, the 2001 redistricting process was otherwise routine. The redistricting committee met throughout the summer of 2001. Of the first eleven public hearings (held between April 26 and July 16), seven were held away from the capitol, allowing the committee to hear comments and suggestions from residents throughout the state. The meetings heard comments from a variety of political, civic, and community leaders.

Some hearings featured presentations by Utah's members of Congress, Jim Hansen (Republican, 1st district), Jim Matheson (Democrat, 2nd district), and Chris Cannon (Republican, 3rd district). The two Republicans urged the committee to create districts that evenly blended rural and urban areas, so that all three districts would have a similar mix of interests. Jim Matheson, Utah's lone Democrat in Congress, opposed this idea, which would have required a complete redrawing of his urban Salt Lake County district. Giving each district a similar rural-urban balance would, Matheson argued, require splitting up Salt Lake County's residents, who shared more in common with each other than with rural residents. These competing positions came to define the committee's debate, with the Republicans favoring the former and Democrats endorsing the latter.[9]

Ultimately, the committee sided with Republicans, producing a map that spread rural areas evenly across all three districts. The legislature met in a special session from September 25 to October 5, 2001, adopting the committee's proposals with only minor changes. The governor approved the maps a week later.

The new maps could not have differed more starkly from the old ones. When the dust settled, 684,000 Utahns found themselves in a new district.[10] Nothing in the 2000 census demanded such radical change. Indeed, population growth during the 1990s had been fairly stable across the three districts. To equalize the districts' populations (at 744,390 per district), the redistricting committee needed to remove

20,766 residents from the first district, add 42,288 to the second district, and re- move 21,521 from the third district. The legislature could have corrected these mod- est population imbalances with minor changes to the map. Had they done so, only 6 percent of the state's population would have been moved into a new district. Instead, the committee chose to completely redraw the lines so that every district would have a rural-urban mix. Instead of moving 6 percent of voters into new districts, they moved 31 percent into new districts.

In the process, the second district went from being the state's smallest to its largest. In the 1980s and 1990s, the second district had been an urban district contained mostly within Salt Lake County. Now, it included vast expanses of wilderness and a large number of far-flung towns and cities. Only a small portion of Salt Lake County—mostly the older cities along the county's eastern half—remained in the district. The map in map 2.3 depicts the maps adopted in 1991 and 2001 in panels (a) and (b). In all panels, district 1 is light gray, district 2 is white, and district 3 is dark gray. From 1991 through 2001, the first and third districts surrounded the small, urban second district, located entirely within Salt Lake County. This map contrasts sharply with the map adopted in 2001. Matheson suddenly lost half his (urban) constituents, who were replaced with mostly rural voters.

To defend these new maps, the committee emphasized the need to balance rural and urban areas within each district. Many observers saw it differently, criticizing the new map as a flagrant attempt to gerrymander Jim Matheson out of office. Even high-profile Republicans joined in this criticism. Utah's junior senator, Republican Bob Bennett, called the plan "one of the worst examples of partisan gerrymandering he had ever seen." U.S. Representative Jim Hansen said, "If there was ever an argu- ment for letting someone other than the legislature do redistricting, this is one."[11] The *Wall Street Journal* took notice, running an editorial calling the Utah redistrict- ing plan a "scam" to defeat Matheson.[12] The *Journal* further warned that this new map could lead to "effective disenfranchisement."

Throughout the redistricting process, Matheson threatened repeatedly to sue if his district were gerrymandered. As early as April 2001, when the redistrict- ing committee had scarcely been appointed, he declared that the only reason Democrats had not filed a lawsuit after the 1991 redistricting was that the party lacked the funds. By contrast, "I have the ability to raise the money and I would" if necessary, he warned.[13] When the committee presented its final map, Matheson condemned it, saying it "makes no sense," giving rise to new reports that he was considering filing suit.[14] Ultimately, Matheson chose to run rather than litigate, saying, "I'll put my energies into being a candidate and running a good campaign in my new district."[15] To Matheson's withdrawn threat, the executive director of the state Republican Party responded, "We never thought he would sue. It just appeared to us to be a public-relations stunt."[16]

Although he retreated from his threat, Matheson's subsequent campaign was hard fought. Matheson struggled to win reelection in 2002, his first race with the new map. Two years previous, in his first race, he had won with a comfortable 15-point

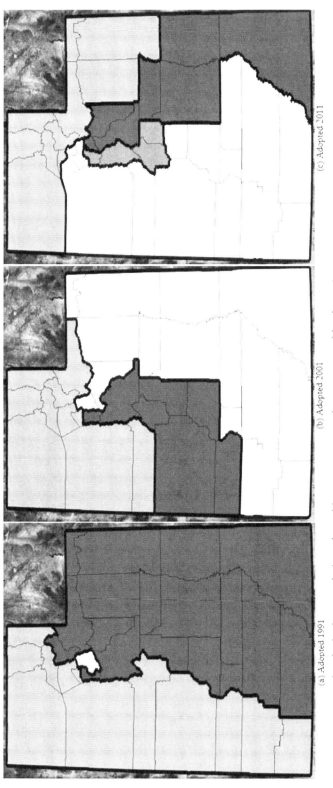

(a) Adopted 1991   (b) Adopted 2001   (c) Adopted 2011

Map 2.3.   Congressional District Boundaries Adopted in 1991, 2001, and 2011. Created by the author.

margin in an open race. In 2002, using the new map, Matheson won by only 1,641 votes in a near-tie. Nevertheless, Matheson recovered in ensuing years. By 2006 and 2008, he was winning by larger margins than he had enjoyed under the old map. The legislature's attempt to gerrymander him out of office failed. By the time the 2010 census results came out, Matheson was still in office. As the state's only Democrat in federal or statewide office, he once again found himself a prime target for gerrymandering.

FROM "PACKING" TO "MICROCOSM"

Whenever a single party controls the entire state government, we would generally expect the legislature to follow a strategy that promotes the majority party's interests. "Under unified control, . . . whichever party controls the state should simply impose a plan in its own interests."[17] There are two general ways to pursue a partisan gerrymander. The "packing" strategy entails sacrificing one or two seats to the minority party. By packing as many minority party voters as possible into a small number of districts, mapmakers hope to inflate the number of districts that lean even slightly toward the majority party. By contrast, the "microcosm" strategy entails making every district mirror the state's partisan balance. Rather than cede a handful of "packed" districts to the minority party, legislators might try to control every district through this microcosm strategy. This strategy becomes more attractive as a party's electoral dominance grows.[18]

What Utah witnessed in 2001 was a groundbreaking shift among legislative Republicans from a packing strategy to a microcosm strategy. Back in 1991, the state's legislators had the first opportunity in decades to draw maps under unified partisan control. The most recent experience with single-party redistricting had been fifty years previous, when Democrats held the governor's mansion as well as decisive majorities in both legislative chambers. By 2001 Utah was growing increasingly Republican, but Democratic majorities remained a recent memory. Indeed, the 1990 legislative elections had seen a minor correction to the state's rightward drive. Republican control of the Utah House fell from 64 percent of seats to 59 percent; control of the Utah Senate fell from 76 percent to 66 percent. When a single party controls the entire state government, Cox and Katz expect the party to pursue the microcosm strategy only if it "is confident that it will get a majority of votes cast in its favor over the life of a redistricting plan."[19] Lacking this confidence, Republicans in 1991 chose to cede one district to Democrats by pursuing a packing strategy rather than a microcosm strategy.

By 2001, Republicans had expanded their electoral majorities sufficiently that they could safely pursue a microcosm strategy rather than a packing strategy. Legislators, of course, used different terminology, claiming that they wanted to see "rural-urban balance" in every district. No matter what words we use, one thing was clear in 2001: it was no longer necessary to cede one district to Democrats in order to preserve two safe Republican ones. The result was the pinwheel map shown in map 2.1, one intended to create three Republican-majority districts.

THE 2011 REDISTRICTING PROCESS

Once the census released redistricting data in March 2011, the Utah legislature began anew to follow the same process it had employed ten years previous. Legislative leaders appointed a joint interim committee of fourteen representatives and six senators, with fourteen Republicans and six Democrats. Democrats were granted 30 percent of committee slots despite holding only 23 percent of the legislative seats. The two committee chairs, one from each chamber, were both Republican. In its first two meetings, the committee adopted the procedural guidelines and substantive principles discussed above.

After two preliminary meetings to handle organizational matters, the committee embarked on an ambitious statewide tour soliciting public comment. Between May 20 and July 26, the committee held 17 public meetings, each in a different venue. Seven of these meetings were held within the four heavily populated Wasatch Front counties. The remaining 10 meetings reached into more distant parts of the state. In total, the committee held hearings in 14 of Utah's 29 counties, including 10 of its 25 rural counties.

In early June, while these hearings were in progress, the state also launched a first-in-the-nation website, RedistrictUtah.com, where citizens could draw district maps of their own. The website was preloaded with census information. As citizens moved their proposed boundaries, the website would count the number of people within each district. If a citizen's map included the right number of districts, covered the entire state, and maintained equal population across districts, then the map's creator had the option of publishing it on the website and submitting it for the committee's consideration.

Of course, holding committee hearings throughout the state and allowing Utahns to create their own maps does not help unless Utahns choose to participate. Toward that end, a coalition of good government groups formed the "United Citizens' Counsel" to raise awareness of the process. Members included the League of Women Voters, the Utah Education Association, AARP, RepresentMe Utah, and others.[20] Their efforts seem to have paid off. Committee hearings were well attended, and many Utahns undertook the extraordinary effort of creating and submitting complete maps.

As early as July 12, 67 different people had gone to the effort of creating and uploading a map. Many had uploaded several maps. Looking over the submissions, I found that 44 users had uploaded one map, 12 had uploaded two, 5 had uploaded three, and 6 had uploaded four or more, for a total of 112 distinct maps. Of the 67 contributors, 5 were current legislators, 4 of whom served on the redistricting committee. The remaining 62 contributors were (apparently) civilians.

By the end of the month, the number of maps submitted through the website had grown to 160. Some maps dealt with state legislative districts, but most dealt with congressional districts. The senate co-chair of the joint committee, Senator Ralph Okerlund, assured Utahns that the maps "are really helpful," promising that "we will continue to use them" as part of the process.[21] Indeed, the legislature relied heavily on a citizen's map in drawing state school board districts. Of course, the state school board map was the least political part of the committee's job. The *Salt Lake Tribune* wryly observed, "Virtually no one expects a citizen map to be adopted for . . . legislative and congressional boundaries."[22]

Representative Ken Sumsion, the House co-chair of the committee, was less sanguine about the role of public input. Speaking of the 14 public hearings held to that point, he said, "I'm not sure what we've learned really [from public hearings]. . . . Most people want a representative who lives in the neighborhood," but not everybody can have that.[23] Following up on this statement, the *Salt Lake Tribune* reviewed the minutes of the first 14 hearings and found that keeping communities intact was brought up by more than half of those who testified.[24] One such comment came from Summit County Democratic Chairman Glen Wright at the Park City hearing: "The county should be split as little as possible. . . , [but] you are probably tired of everyone saying 'keep us together and divide the other guy.'"[25]

Throughout this process, most debate was framed around "doughnut hole" and "pizza slice" options. Those advocating a "doughnut hole" approach favored a return to the type of map adopted in 1991, preserving one or two urbanized "doughnut hole" districts along the central Wasatch Front, with rural areas combined into two or three surrounding districts. Those advocating a "pizza slice" plan wanted to continue the approach introduced in 2001, in which rural areas would be evenly divided across four districts that would converge on Salt Lake City, as if Utah were a giant pizza sliced four ways. Despite the toothsome rhetoric, this was merely a rehash of the 2001 redistricting battle, with the same battle lines as before. Republican advocates of the "pizza slice" approach were pursuing a microcosm strategy; Democratic advocates of the "doughnut hole" approach were pleading for the relative mercy of a packing strategy.

After almost five months of work, the committee released its six congressional finalists via RedistrictUtah.com on September 22, 2011. All six maps had been created and published through the state's redistricting website. Two had been drawn by members of the redistricting committee, including a map from the committee's House co-chair, Rep. Ken Sumsion, and another from its Senate co-chair, Sen. Ralph Okerlund. Two had been drawn by legislators unaffiliated with the committee, including House Rules Committee Chair Wayne Harper and freshman Rep. Fred Cox. The remaining two were submitted by citizens, Steve Clark and David Edward Garber.

The six congressional finalists appear in map 2.4. Districts are shaded the same as in map 2.3, with district one in light gray, district two in white, district three in dark gray, and district four in medium gray. Four of the finalists (panels a, d, e, and f) were obvious pizza slice plans, with the center of the pizza generally located

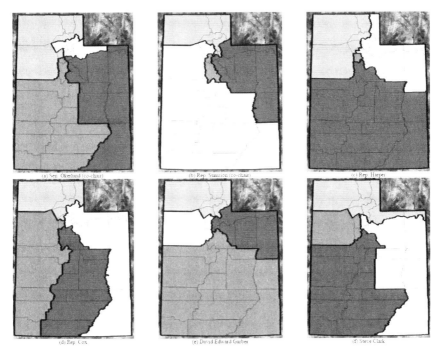

Map 2.4. Six Congressional District Finalists. Created by the author.

in Salt Lake County. Rep. Harper's plan (panel c) was a doughnut hole, but with a twist. Democrats wanted a doughnut hole centered around Salt Lake City and the surrounding (Democratic-leaning) cities, but Rep. Harper drew his doughnut hole in Salt Lake County's rapidly growing (and generally Republican) southwestern portions; the more Democratic parts of the county would have been grouped with conservative rural voters in the state's northeast. Rep. Harper's map served as a reminder that a doughnut hole map, though preferred by Democrats, could still be used to favor Republicans. Rep. Sumsion's plan (panel b) struck something of a middle ground, adopting a broadly "pizza slice" approach while integrating Rep. Harper's idea of a Republican-leaning doughnut hole along the western edge of the Wasatch Front. Any of these proposals—including the two doughnut hole plans—would have created four Republican-majority districts.

Within a few days, the committee approved Rep. Sumsion's map, albeit with minor changes. Once again, the most drastic changes concerned the second district, the only one held by a Democrat. Utah's first district remained mostly intact, preserving its population base along the northern Wasatch Front. Utah's third district changed shape considerably, but that change was mostly restricted to its rural areas; Rep. Chaffetz maintained most of his Utah County population base, including the deeply conservative Provo-Orem corridor. To the extent the third district did change, it still remained overwhelmingly Republican.

Rep. Matheson, meanwhile, lost a significant portion of the second district's population base. In the decade since his narrow 2002 victory, Rep. Matheson had made significant headway in winning over rural Republicans in eastern and southern Utah. In 2011, legislative Republicans rewarded him by taking away these "Matheson Republicans" and giving him a mostly new set of rural Republicans in western and southern Utah. He did not pick up additional Democrats; as with the 2001 map, Salt Lake County's Democrats were divided across all the state's districts.

Democrats were enraged. Upon learning of the committee's decision, Jim Dabakis, chair of the state Democratic Party, said, "Pass this map; we'll see you in court!" Echoing Jim Matheson's words from ten years earlier, he added that "it makes no sense." "There's nothing fair, there's nothing honorable about this map. These maps are a giant insult to all the people of the state of Utah."[26] The left leaning *Salt Lake Tribune* called this "pizza slice" treatment of Salt Lake County "a libel against pizza lovers everywhere," adding, "anyone looking at this monstrosity for the first time is likely to scratch his head and wonder, 'How did they come up with that?' The only reasonable explanation is that they are trying to create a Republican advantage in each of the four districts."[27] One legislator, Carl Wimmer, had made it known months earlier that he planned to run for Congress. The *Tribune* editorial observed that "these boundaries [for the new fourth district] fit perfectly with the congressional aspirations of Carl Wimmer."

A week later, the legislature convened in a special session to consider the committee's recommendations. Protestors organized by the Fair Boundaries Coalition, RepresentMe Utah, and the Democratic Party ate pizza and doughnut holes as they urged the legislature to reject the maps. At the rally, Salt Lake County Mayor Peter Corron complained, "We asked for a doughnut, expected a pizza, and were given instead a plate of scrambled eggs." He added, "This is a lawsuit waiting to happen."[28]

These complaints and legal threats failed to elicit a serious response from legislative Republicans. However, the special session rapidly encountered problems from an unexpected direction: a sharp dispute between House Republicans and Senate Republicans. Most of this battle played out behind closed doors. Still, the seriousness of the disagreement quickly became obvious. After only a day in special session, the legislature moved to adjourn for two weeks so that the two sides could negotiate a compromise. Despite all the public hearings, despite all the citizen maps submitted through RedistrictUtah.com, the mapmaking process moved behind closed doors as Republicans met privately to resolve their differences.

Those left out of these closed-door discussions were quick to note the two-faced nature of the process. The committee had spent months holding public hearings, and the state had invested significant resources launching RedistrictUtah.com to solicit citizen impact. But once the House-Senate conflict arose, Republicans went behind closed doors to sort things out. Democratic state senator Karen Morgan complained, "As we sit here, maps are being drawn in secret behind closed doors."[29] Jim Dabakis, the state's Democratic Party chair, said, "If the public were here, it would be outraged."[30] Meanwhile, Republicans stressed the need to move slowly and carefully. House Speaker Becky Lockhart justified the delay: "What we don't want to do is rush this. . ., so we decided to take a step back, let the committee do more work, and have the public involved."[31] House Majority Leader Brad Dee concurred, saying, "We feel the public needs to review some of the things we have discussed."[32]

In part, this battle erupted over Jim Matheson, the only Democrat to represent Utah in Congress since 1995. Legislators in both chambers wanted him gone.[33] The desire to gerrymander Matheson out of office ran into two obstacles, however, which contributed to the House-Senate spat.

First, legislators worried about citizen backlash. These worries were enhanced by the memory of a very sour experience from the previous spring. During the previous winter's legislative session, legislators privately prepared a bill revising the state's Government Records Access and Management Act (GRAMA), Utah's version of the federal Freedom of Information Act. This bill, HB477, would have made it more difficult for outsiders to request certain government records, and it would have made some records inaccessible entirely. Perhaps legislators anticipated that the bill would be unpopular; they pushed it from introduction to final passage in only three days, faster than 95.8 percent of the bills that passed that year.[34] A strange coalition of Tea Party groups, liberals, good government activists, and media lawyers formed an awkward alliance to fight the bill. Their pressure led the governor to call a special session after the general session ended so that the legislature could repeal the bill, which he had signed shortly after its initial passage. The uprising over HB477 made legislators hesitate to provoke a similar backlash over redistricting.

Second, legislators worried about what Matheson would do if he were gerrymandered out of office. No Democrat has held any statewide office in Utah since 2000; Jim Matheson has been the only Democrat to represent Utah in Congress since 1995. As such, Jim Matheson is the only Democrat capable of frightening Utah's highest elected officials. If Republicans drew Matheson out of office, observers expected him to challenge either Governor Gary Herbert or Senator Orrin Hatch. As such, legislators felt pressure from Gary Herbert and Orrin Hatch not to force Matheson out of office. As much as legislators wanted Matheson out of the House, they did not want to push him into the Senate or into the governor's mansion.

These two factors rendered legislative Republicans unsure of how to deal with Matheson. The House-Senate gridlock also arose as a result of certain legislators seeking to produce maps favorable to their own congressional aspirations. Rep. Carl Wimmer had formed a congressional campaign exploratory committee months earlier, with a desire to run in the new fourth district. As the special session broke down in gridlock, Rep. Dave Clark told reporters that he was "very, very involved in the exploratory stages" of a congressional run.[35] After the redistricting process concluded, one more legislator (Rep. Stephen Sandstrom) announced his intention to run for Congress. With so many legislators interested in running under the new congressional maps, the special session's breakdown may have been inevitable.

Eventually, legislative Republicans completed their backroom discussions. When the special session resumed two weeks later, the legislature promptly passed a revised congressional map (map 2.3, panel c) that strongly resembled the committee's recommendation (map 2.4, panel b). The new map gave the new fourth district additional rural lands and made some changes to the immediate Salt Lake City area, but otherwise it preserved the general flavor of Rep. Sumsion's proposal.

In an editorial, the conservative *Daily Herald* called the new map a "crime against humanity," saying its "idiocy" would "border on the laughable if it didn't hurt so many communities. . . . Many cities have been illogically split. . . . To divide the state's natural communities in this way . . . is enough to bring James Madison howling from the grave."[36] Dismissing the committee's public hearings and public mapping website as "little more than a charade," the *Herald* complained that the real maps were drawn in secret by House and Senate Republicans: "Closed meetings make for closed minds, as proved by this outcome."

The left-leaning *Salt Lake Tribune*'s editorial was more direct: "Gov. Herbert should veto this monstrosity."[37] The editorial called concerns about rural-urban balance "a fig leaf to cover their desire to subdivide Democratic strongholds." Citing a Democratic consultant, the editorial estimated that every district was at least 62 percent Republican. The *Tribune* editorial went on to claim that legislators had ignored public input, despite putting on a show of soliciting it: "While you are at the [RedistrictUtah.com] website, . . . you will search in vain for a [citizen] map that resembles the one the Legislature finally adopted. The citizens who devised maps on the interactive website and submitted them in good faith wasted their time."

Ignoring these complaints, Governor Gary Herbert signed the new maps into law on October 20, 2011, a week after the legislature passed them. He praised the legislature for "engag[ing] members of the public in an unprecedented way" to produce a "reasonable" outcome that "followed the law."[38]

AFTERMATH OF THE 2011 REDISTRICTING

Following Governor Herbert's signature, Jim Dabakis, the state's Democratic chair, repeated his threat to sue: "The chances are very good that we will let a judge decide if the Legislature did a fair job on congressional redistricting."[39] As of this writing, no lawsuit has materialized. Filing may have been delayed because of a standoff over government records, a rehash of 2011's battle over HB477. In preparation for a possible lawsuit, both state parties submitted requests for records related to the redistricting process. When public records requests arrived, legislative staff estimated how much it would cost to fulfill them. The Republican Party was assessed $2,000 to fulfill its request, which it promptly paid. The Democratic Party was assessed $5,000 to fulfill its broader request. For several weeks, Democrats refused to pay, contending that redistricting is so important to the public interest that both parties' requests should have been fulfilled free of charge. Eventually, on January 23, 2012, the Democrats relented and paid the $5,000 fee. By that time, the annual seven-week general session had begun, and the legislature's barebones staff was fully engaged in

assisting legislators and committees with legislation. As a result, Democrats are unlikely to receive the materials they requested before March 2012, making a lawsuit
unlikely until that time.[40]

Meanwhile, Rep. Jim Matheson chose not to pursue reelection in the second
district (where he lives), declaring instead his intention to run in the new fourth district. Jason Chaffetz has represented the third district since 2008 despite living in the
second district (a problem corrected by the new maps), so Republicans would find
it difficult to accuse Matheson of carpetbagging. Early polls showed him beating all
likely Republican candidates in head-to-head matchups, including state representatives Stephen Sandstrom and Carl Wimmer.[41]

It is not clear that legislators made Matheson's district any more Republican than
it already was. After all, legislators pursued the same microcosm strategy in 2011
that they followed in 2001. In both cases, rhetoric about pursuing rural-urban balance in every district had the additional implication of making every district mirror
the state's overall partisan balance. As shown in table 2.3, the second district gave
68 percent of its two-party vote to George Bush in 2004 and 59 percent of its two-
party vote to John McCain in 2008. These percentages are slightly less overwhelming than the corresponding percentages in the first and third districts, but they still
indicate Republican dominance. After the 2011 redistricting session, a Democratic
consultant estimated that the first district was 72 percent Republican, the second 65
percent, the third 74 percent, and the fourth 62 percent.[42] These estimates suggest
that the legislature did not make Matheson's district more hostile. Indeed, Matheson
himself said that the new district was "no tougher than my district is now."[43]

However, the legislature did find a way to threaten Matheson without making his
district more Republican. As Yoshinaka and Murphy have noted, gerrymandering is
as much about creating "population instability" as it is about district partisanship.[44]
They define "population instability" as "altering the composition of a district's 'geographical constituency' in a way that may not necessarily alter the district's underlying partisan balance."[45] Even if legislators did not make Matheson's district more
Republican, they might have complicated Matheson's reelection efforts by replacing
Republicans familiar with his conservative ideology with Republicans who know
him only as a Democrat.

By taking "Matheson Republicans" out of the second district and replacing
them with Republicans unfamiliar with Matheson, the legislature might reverse

Table 2.3.   Utah District Partisanship

District	2004 Vote for Bush	2008 Vote for McCain	2011 Estimated Percent Republican
1	74%	66%	72%
2	68%	59%	65%
3	79%	70%	74%
4	—	—	62%

Matheson's successful efforts to cultivate a personal vote. The fruits of these efforts are apparent in figure 2.2. Matheson entered office in 2000 under the 1991 map with a comfortable 56 percent-41 percent victory. Under the new 2001 map, he eked out a narrow win in 2002 by only 1,641 votes. In subsequent years, however, his victory margin grew steadily. By 2008, he was winning by a 30 percentage point margin, claiming 65 percent of the vote in a district that gave only 41 percent of its vote to Obama.[46]

Although the legislature did not make Matheson's district more Republican in 2011, it did take actions to break up Matheson's personal vote. A Democratic consultant estimated that only 30 percent of Matheson's former constituents remained in the new second district, with 39 percent in the third district (held by popular Republican Jason Chaffetz) and 25 percent in the new fourth district.[47]

At first glance, it may not be obvious why Matheson chose the fourth district over the second, where he lives. Both are similarly Republican (65 percent in the second, 62 percent in the fourth), and both contain a similar percentage of Matheson's former constituents (30 percent in the second, 25 percent in the fourth). After taking a closer look at how the maps divide Salt Lake County, Matheson's decision makes more sense. It appears that the 30 percent who remained in the second district are mostly concentrated in the heavily Democratic eastern portions of Salt Lake City. These Democratic neighborhoods would probably vote for Matheson in a general election even if he were a stranger to them. Meanwhile, the 25 percent who moved from the second district to the fourth are in the more politically diverse communities

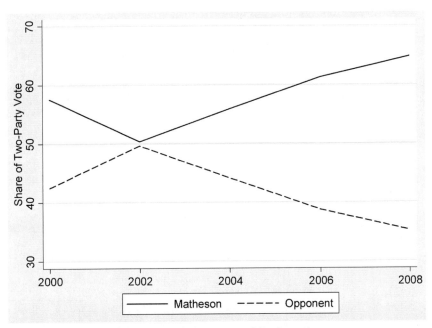

Figure 2.2. Matheson's Electoral Margins. Created by the author.

of Murray, Lehi, Sandy, and Draper. Many of these voters would be Republicans, but they would be Republicans who are familiar with Matheson. If Matheson ran in the second district, he would retain 30 percent of his former constituents, most of whom would be Democrats likely to vote for him anyway; by moving to the fourth district, he retains 25 percent of his former constituents, many of whom are "Matheson Republicans" willing to cross party lines for him.

CONCLUSION

Utah's redistricting process played out roughly as the political science literature would have predicted. Legislative Republicans seized the opportunity presented by unified government to draw a map favorable to Republican candidates. Recognizing their electoral dominance, they continued to use a "microcosm" strategy rather than cede a safe Democratic seat with a "packing" strategy.[48] Legislative Republicans further complicated Matheson's reelection by breaking up his personal vote, moving Republicans familiar with Matheson out of his district and replacing them with Republican strangers, the "population instability" strategy discussed by Yoshinaka and Murphy.[49]

Perhaps the greatest lesson to be learned from Utah's experience is the importance of this population instability strategy. Utah has grown so Republican that it would be difficult for it to draw maps that do not favor the Republican Party. If somebody attached chalk to a cat's tail and let it draw random district lines around the state, odds are good that each district would have a Republican supermajority. Somehow, Jim Matheson has managed to win by decisive majorities despite living in an overwhelmingly Republican district. Recognizing his resilience and the strength of his personal vote, Republicans resorted to this "population instability" strategy to weaken him. Based on November results, it appears Republicans still have work to do to win in the district as Matheson kept his seat.

NOTES

1. Gary W. Cox and Jonathan N. Katz, *Elbridge Gerry's Salamander: The Electoral Consequences of the Reapportionment Revolution* (Cambridge: Cambridge University Press, 2002).

2. Antoine Yoshinaka and Chad Murphy, "Partisan Gerrymandering and Population Instability: Completing the Redistricting Puzzle," *Political Geography* 28 (November 2009): 451–62.

3. Bruce E. Cain, John A. Ferejohn, and Morris P. Fiorina, *The Personal Vote: Constituency Service and Electoral Independence* (Cambridge: Harvard University Press, 1987).

4. Article IX, Section 1 of the Utah Constitution.

5. Article IX, Section 2 of the Utah Constitution.

6. Utah State Code sections 20A-13-102, 36-1-103, and 36-1-202.

7. Utah State Code section 20A-13-103.

8. Lee Davidson, "Utah GOP Downs Dem Redistricting Proposals," *Salt Lake Tribune*, May 4, 2011.

9. Bob Bernick Jr., "This Map Won't Fly, Matheson Says," *Deseret News*, September 21, 2001; Bob Bernick Jr. and Zack Van Eyck, "Stephens Sees a Fair Redistricting," *Deseret News*, September 25, 2001.

10. Bernick, "This Map Won't Fly."

11. Greg Burton, "Bennett Blasts GOP Redistricting Plan; State's Junior Senator Calls the Reworking 'Gerrymandering'," *Salt Lake Tribune*, April 11, 2002.

12. *Wall Street Journal*, "The Gerrymander Scandal," November 7, 2011.

13. Bob Bernick Jr., "Don't Mess Up Boundaries, Matheson Tells Legislators," *Deseret News*, April 18, 2001.

14. Bernick, "This Map Won't Fly."

15. Bob Bernick Jr., "Matheson to Run, Not Litigate," *Deseret News*, November 5, 2001.

16. Bernick, "Matheson to Run."

17. Cox and Katz, *Elbridge Gerry's Salamander*, 39.

18. Cox and Katz, *Elbridge Gerry's Salamander*, 33.

19. Cox and Katz, *Elbridge Gerry's Salamander*, 33.

20. Richard Piatt, "Utah Group Urges Public Input in Political Redistricting Process; Propose Map of New Boundaries," *Deseret News*, May 16, 2011.

21. Lee Davidson, "Public Hearings Bring Redistricting Compromise," *Salt Lake Tribune*, July 26, 2011.

22. Lee Davidson, "Lawmakers Endorse Citizen Map for New School Board Boundaries," *Salt Lake Tribune*, August 22, 2011.

23. Davidson, "Public Hearings Bring Redistricting Compromise."

24. Davidson, "Public Hearings Bring Redistricting Compromise."

25. Davidson, "Public Hearings Bring Redistricting Compromise."

26. Chris Vanocur, "Utah Democratic Chairman: 'Pass This Map, We'll See You in Court!'" *ABC 4 News*, September 28, 2011.

27. *Salt Lake Tribune*. "Congressional Pizza," September 28, 2011.

28. David Montero, "Protestors Vent against Utah Redistricting Maps," *Salt Lake Tribune*, October 3, 2011.

29. Lee Davidson and Robert Gehrke, "Talks to Redraw Congressional Map Put on Hold," *Salt Lake Tribune*, October 4, 2011.

30. Davidson and Gehrke, "Talks to Redraw Congressional Map."

31. Davidson and Gehrke, "Talks to Redraw Congressional Map."

32. Billy Hesterman, "Lawmakers Say Taking Time on Maps Is a Good Thing," *Daily Herald*, October 6, 2011.

33. Multiple legislators have confirmed this to me in private conversations.

34. Adam R. Brown, "How Rushed Was HB 477, the GRAMA Bill?" *Utah Data Points* 2011, www.http://utahdatapoints.com/2011/03/how-rushed-was-hb-477-the-grama-bill/ (accessed January 26, 2012).

35. Lee Davidson and Robert Gehrke, "Behind Redistricting Breakdown: Backlash Fear, Congress Hopes," *Salt Lake Tribune*, October 7, 2011.

36. *Daily Herald*, "Utah Legislature Commits Crime against Humanity," October 18, 2011.

37. *Salt Lake Tribune*. "Veto District Map," October 20, 2011.

38. Lee Davidson, "Governor OKs New Utah Congressional Maps," *Salt Lake Tribune*, October 21, 2011.

39. Davidson, "Governor OKs New Utah Congressional Maps."

40. Billy Hesterman, "Dems Pay Records Fee While Maintaining Documents Are in Public Interest," *Daily Herald*, January 23, 2012.

41. Dennis Romboy, "Rep. Jim Matheson Leads All Comers in Utah's New 4th Congressional District, Poll Shows," *Deseret News*, December 25, 2011.

42. Lee Davidson, "Redistricting Fallout: Matheson Looks at Other Districts," *Salt Lake Tribune*, October 19, 2011.

43. Davidson, "Redistricting Fallout."

44. Yoshinaka and Murphy, "Partisan Gerrymandering and Population Instability."

45. Richard F. Fenno Jr., *Home Style: House Members in their Districts* (Boston: Little, Brown, 1978).

46. Matheson experienced a setback in 2010, winning by a much narrower 5 percentage point margin in a year when the Tea Party was extremely successful in Utah.

47. Davidson, "Redistricting Fallout."

48. Cox and Katz, *Elbridge Gerry's Salamander*, 33.

49. Yoshinaka and Murphy, "Partisan Gerrymandering and Population Instability."

3

Incumbency, Influence, and Race

Redistricting, South Carolina Style

Christopher N. Lawrence and Scott H. Huffmon

In this chapter, we give an overview of the key events in the 2010 redistricting cycle in South Carolina, particularly as they affected the districts created for the U.S. House of Representatives. The 2010 cycle was particularly noteworthy for the state as it was the first time the state had gained a U.S. House seat since the 1880 census; it was also the first redistricting cycle in which the House, Senate, and the governor's office were controlled by the Republican Party since the Reconstruction era.

HISTORICAL BACKGROUND

The Impact of Reapportionment

As one of the original 13 states, South Carolina has been continuously represented in Congress since 1789. In the initial apportionment set out in the Constitution (Article I, Section 2, Paragraph 3), South Carolina was entitled to five representatives in the U.S. House; rapid population growth entitled South Carolina to a sixth seat after 1793, eight seats after 1803, and nine seats after 1813. A change in the apportionment method after the 1840 census, from the "Jefferson method" to the "Webster method," resulted in the loss of two seats in 1843, with further losses after the 1850 and 1860 censuses resulting in an all-time minimum of four representatives.

After the Civil War South Carolina's representation in Congress recovered somewhat, reaching seven representatives again from 1883 through 1933, when the state lost a seat after the 1930 reapportionment. From 1933 to the present, South Carolina has had six representatives in Congress; however, due to population gains reflected in the latest reapportionment, a seventh seat will be re-created as a result of this redistricting cycle, effective in 2013.

The Impact of the Voting Rights Act

South Carolina is one of 16 states covered in part or full by the preclearance provisions in Section 5 of the Voting Rights Act, requiring its redistricting plans and other laws pertaining to voting be approved by either the U.S. Department of Justice (DOJ) or a three-judge panel of the U.S. Court of Appeals for the District of Columbia before they can go into effect. As DOJ was under the control of Democrats in 2011 (unlike in previous redistricting cycles), supporters of increasing black representation in South Carolina's congressional delegation might have come in with some optimism that the administration would use the preclearance process to push for a second majority-minority district in the state; as events came to pass, however, that was not the case.

Since the Supreme Court's ruling in *Northwest Austin Municipal Utility District No. One v. Holder* (*NAMUDNO*),[1] voting rights advocates have been concerned that a denial of preclearance might lead to a state challenging the constitutionality of Section 5 as currently applied; accordingly, the Department of Justice may have been reluctant to block redistricting plans it may have otherwise objected to let the Court take an early opportunity to strike down Section 5. Indeed, South Carolina is one of the states widely believed to have been considering such a challenge,[2] echoing its role as the initial challenger of preclearance in *South Carolina v. Katzenbach*.[3] Despite this speculation, however, South Carolina has yet to join the state of Texas and the city of Kinston, North Carolina, in filing its own case directly challenging the constitutionality of Section 5, even though the Department of Justice recently failed to preclear a Voter ID bill passed by the legislature in 2011.[4]

The Results of the 2000 Redistricting Cycle

Although the South Carolina House and Senate, both controlled by the Republican Party, were able to agree on a redistricting plan for the state House, Senate, and Congress (H. 3003, 2001), their plans were vetoed by Democratic Gov. Jim Hodges and the legislature was unable to override his veto. Accordingly, a three-judge panel enacted a redistricting plan for all three chambers in March 2002 (*Colleton County v. McConnell*, 201 F. Supp.2d 618, 2002). Hodges sought reelection in 2002, but was defeated by Republican Mark Sanford; the legislature subsequently passed a redistricting plan covering the state House and Senate, but not the congressional delegation (S. 591, 2003), which Sanford signed into law and which was precleared by the U.S. Department of Justice. As a result, South Carolina went into the 2010 redistricting cycle with court-ordered maps for the congressional delegation but legislatively-passed maps for the state legislature.[5] The map adopted by the Court in 2002 is illustrated in map 3.1.

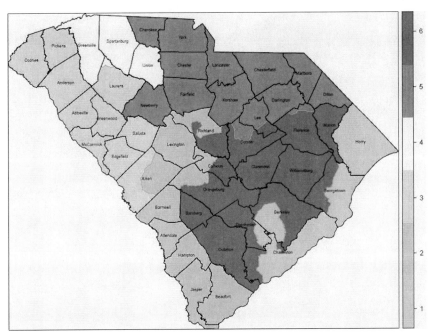

Map 3.1. Map Adopted by the Court in 2002. Created by the author.

POPULATION CHANGE FROM 2000 THROUGH 2010

Using the corrected 2000 census tabulations, South Carolina grew 15.3 percent between 2000 and 2010, increasing from a population of 4,011,832 to 4,625,364. As is typical, however, growth was hardly uniform across the state; these trends are illustrated in map 3.2.

Among those counties that grew, some experienced growth at a much higher rate than others. By contrast, 12 of South Carolina's 46 counties experienced population loss.[6] Those 12 counties lost an average of 4.21 percent of their population. Williamsburg County experienced the greatest population loss with a growth rate of –7.52 percent. An additional seven counties experienced stagnant growth with a growth rate of 3 percent or less.[7] Seven counties experienced a growth rate of over 20 percent, 4 of which had growth rates that exceeded 30 percent.[8]

It is traditional to overlay geography onto discussions of South Carolina politics. Historically, the state has been informally divided into regions when discussing its politics. Students of South Carolina history will be very familiar with these four

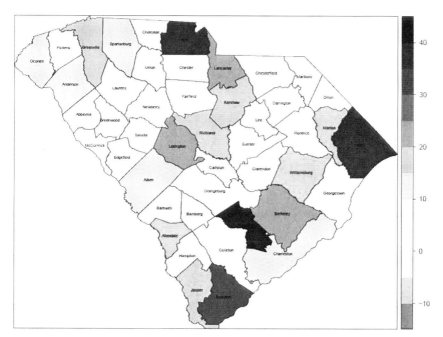

Map 3.2.   County Growth between 2000 and 2010. Created by the author.

traditional designations: the Low Country, in the southwestern portion of the state bordering Georgia; the Pee Dee, named after the Pee Dee River, which itself was named for a Native American tribe, comprising the northeastern section of the state bordering North Carolina; the Midlands, the central portion of the state; and the Upstate, spanning the Appalachian foothills in the northern portion of the state. Counties near the "edge" of the informal line distinguishing these regions may "migrate" depending on who is defining the regions, but table 3.1 represents one possible list of South Carolina counties defined by traditional region.

However, metropolitan growth patterns have suggested other possible regional definitions. These current regional definitions may be more meaningful for the current discussion. The informal list of regions considered here include the four traditional regions—the Low Country, the Pee Dee, the Midlands, and the Upstate—plus the Savannah River Region, the Charleston Metro Region, and the Charlotte (NC) Region (South Carolina counties near the city of Charlotte, North Carolina, that have experienced significant growth as suburbs and exurbs). Counties falling into these seven informal regional designations may be found in table 3.2, and are illustrated in map 3.3.[9]

As can be seen in table 3.3, the Savannah River Region, Upstate, Pee Dee, and Midlands all lagged statewide average growth while The Charleston Metro Region, the Low Country, and the Charlotte Metro Region all had growth rates in excess of 20 percent. In general, large geographic swath of South Carolina grew moderately, at best, while the majority of growth happened in three comparatively compact regions.

Table 3.1. South Carolina Counties by Region—Traditional Groupings

Upstate	Low Country	Midlands	Pee Dee
Abbeville	Allendale	Aiken	Chesterfield
Anderson	Beaufort	Bamberg	Clarendon
Cherokee	Berkeley	Barnwell	Darlington
Chester	Charleston	Calhoun	Dillon
Greenville	Colleton	Edgefield	Florence
Greenwood	Dorchester	Fairfield	Horry
Lancaster	Georgetown	Kershaw	Lee
Laurens	Hampton	Lexington	Marion
Oconee	Jasper	McCormick	Marlboro
Pickens		Newberry	Williamsburg
Spartanburg		Orangeburg	
Union		Richland	
York		Saluda	
		Sumter	

Metropolitan regional growth in the Charlotte and Charleston areas was the largest engine of growth. Even though the Low Country experienced slightly higher growth than the Charleston Metropolitan Region, it represents far fewer people than the much more densely populated areas of either the Charleston or Charlotte areas. However, even this map masks some trends.

While the Pee Dee region overall showed moderate growth, Horry County, the most populous county in the region and the home to Myrtle Beach, experienced

Table 3.2. South Carolina Counties by Region—Current with Metro Areas

Upstate	Low Country	Midlands	Pee Dee
Abbeville	Beaufort	Bamberg	Chesterfield
Anderson	Colleton	Calhoun	Clarendon
Cherokee	Hampton	Fairfield	Darlington
Greenville	Jasper	Kershaw	Dillon
Greenwood		Lexington	Florence
Laurens		Newberry	Georgetown
Oconee		Orangeburg	Horry
Pickens		Richland	Lee
Spartanburg		Saluda	Marion
Union		Sumter	Marlboro
			Williamsburg

Savannah River Region	Charleston Region	Charlotte (NC) Metro Region
Aiken	Charleston	Chester
Allendale	Berkeley	Lancaster
Barnwell	Dorchester	York
Edgefield		
McCormick		

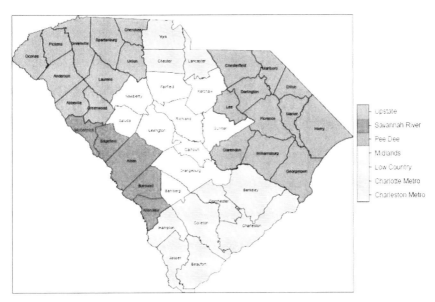

Map 3.3.   Contemporary Regions. Created by the author.

the third-highest growth rate of any county at 36.93 percent and the second-highest growth rate of any county with a population greater than 200,000. When Horry County is lumped in with the rest of the Pee Dee, a region of great poverty since the end of the Civil War, its dynamic growth is masked. Every other county in the Pee Dee region experienced below-average growth including three counties that lost population, one of which—Williamsburg County—had a greater percentage point loss of population than any other South Carolina County. In short, the Pee Dee Region with both one of the fastest-growing, heavily-populated counties and the county experiencing the greatest population decline was easily the region subject to

Table 3.3.   Growth by Region

Region	Growth
Charlotte Metro	29.16%
Low Country	22.72%
Charleston Metro	21.06%
Midlands	13.95%
Pee Dee	13.55%
Upstate	11.6%
Savannah Rover	8.78%

the most dynamic change. This region would ultimately become the heart of the newly-drawn 7th Congressional District.

While geographic differences in rates of growth dominate questions about locating a new Congressional District, geography was not the only dimension that exhibited differential growth rates. Both age and race play into the story of differential growth. According to the 2010 census, those ages 65 and older make up 13.6 percent of the population, up one and a half percentage points from 2000. However, the two counties that anchor South Carolina's metropolitan regions, Charleston County for the Charleston Metro Region and York County for the Charlotte Metro Region, both have populations of residents age 65 and older that are below the statewide average. The story along South Carolina's coast is somewhat different.

The South Carolina coast has experienced much growth due to an influx of retirees. An analysis of tax filings shows that much of the migration to non-metro region coastal areas is coming from the northeastern and midwestern regions of the United States.[10] While both Colleton and Jasper counties can claim thin slices of South Carolina's coastline, easily more than nine-tenths of the coastline is within Horry, Georgetown, Charleston, and Beaufort counties. Population statistics bear out this influx of retirees: Horry, Georgetown, and Beaufort counties, the three major coastal counties not in the Charleston Metro Region, each have 65 and older populations at or near 20 percent, significantly above the state average. Horry and Beaufort counties are also two of the four fastest-growing counties in the state.

With respect to race and ethnicity, the white, black, and Hispanic populations all grew at notably different rates. While the white population increased 13.52 percent, the black population only increased by 8.9 percent. Growth in the Hispanic population seems dramatic at 147.89 percent, but while that is an impressive growth rate, it is helpful to keep those numbers in context, as this growth (as in most states other than Florida, New York, and those bordering Mexico, all of which historically have had many Hispanic residents) started from a very low baseline. Only 5.1 percent of the state's population is Hispanic according to the 2010 census.

Digging a little more deeply, we can see even more dramatic differences in the geography of population change. The South Carolina House of Representatives has 124 districts. Based on the 2010 census, the ideal size of each district should be approximately 37,301 individuals. However, fewer than a quarter of those districts remained within 5 percent of the ideal population based on the existing district lines adopted in 2003. Sixty-one districts were more than 5 percent below ideal size while 33 districts were more than 5 percent above ideal size. At the low end was House District 74, on the north side of Columbia, which was 24.63 percent below ideal size. On the high end was House District 118, southwest of Hilton Head, which was 81.12 percent above ideal size. Of the 5 districts that were more than 20 percent below ideal size, all were majority-black districts. Of the 14 districts that were 20 percent or more above ideal size, 10 had white populations that were higher than the state average.[11]

ADOPTING THE CONGRESSIONAL MAP

As a result of the reapportionment process and population gains realized in the 2010 census, South Carolina was entitled to an additional seat in the House of Representatives effective with the 113th Congress to take office in January 2013. Accordingly, to comply with federal and state mandates to equalize populations between districts, the boundaries of the six existing districts required substantial changes to allow for a reformed 7th District, while at the same time attempting to follow other principles that the state legislative committees had sought to follow, including incumbent protection and the preservation of existing communities of interest.[12]

The creation of a new district was seen by Democrats and African Americans as an opportunity to create a second district likely to elect an African American Democrat—or, at the very least a Democrat—to Congress, joining the existing 6th District's veteran representative James Clyburn (D-Columbia). Until the November 2010 election, which saw African American Tim Scott of Charleston, a Republican, elected in the 1st District, while South Carolina's population was 27.9 percent African American,[13] only one of the state's six representatives in Congress was black. While many African Americans welcomed Scott's election, nonetheless the vast majority of black South Carolinians—like most black Americans—are Democrats and presumably would prefer to be represented by a Democrat themselves; hence, Scott would not qualify as a minority representative under the definition advanced in *Thornburg v. Gingles*.[14] If two of the seven newly-created districts were "majority-minority" in nature, such a plan would correspond almost exactly with the share of African Americans in the statewide population in 2010.

The state's Democrats also saw the redistricting cycle as an opportunity to reverse the erosion of their position in national and state politics. All six U.S. representatives from South Carolina were Democrats well into the 1960s, with Democrats retaining a majority of the state's representatives until the elections of November 1980, but after the defeat of the 5th District's John Spratt in November 2010, only one Democrat—Clyburn—remained. A favorably-constructed open seat might allow Democrats the best opportunity to reverse this trend, particularly in the upcoming November 2012 election when high participation from the party's African American base could be expected due to Barack Obama seeking reelection to the presidency.

On the other hand, Republicans saw the redistricting cycle as an opportunity to consolidate the gains they had made in the past decade. In the November 2010 elections, Republican candidate Mick Mulvaney of Indian Land had dispatched long-serving Democratic representative John Spratt, whose reputation as a fiscal conservative and ability to build a coalition incorporating the 5th District's African American population (approximately one-third of the total district population) had historically protected him against Republican challengers but who was increasingly challenged by a district that was becoming more suburban and Republican over time. Mulvaney and his party sought to protect the first-termer from a likely Democratic challenge in November 2012 (when Democratic and African American turnout would likely be higher due to the presidential contest). Republicans also needed to protect first-term incumbent Scott, although his reliably Republican district would require less effort to shore up. Beyond protecting existing Republican incumbents, the party also had an interest in ensuring Democrats would not successfully gain a toehold in a newly-created 7th District seat. They would be assisted in these goals by having a friendly governor; unlike in the 2000 redistricting cycle, when the Republican-controlled legislature's plan was vetoed by Democrat Jim Hodges, newly-elected Republican Nikki Haley was unlikely to veto any plan adopted by Republicans in the House and Senate.

Further complicating matters for Republicans, however, the 2010 redistricting cycle was also the first time that preclearance decisions would be made when the U.S. Department of Justice was controlled by Democrats, who might be more aggressive in blocking preclearance of Republican-friendly plans than the Republican-controlled Department of Justice had been in previous redistricting cycles, when Republican interests and the interests of African American representatives had often coincided to produce maps at the expense of Democrats' partisan and ideological interests.[15] Regardless, satisfying five incumbents and creating a sixth favorable seat would be a challenge for mapmakers operating under the constraints of the Voting Rights Act and the need to develop contiguous districts.

As in most states, while official action on redistricting would need to wait for the release of redistricting data from the U.S. Census Bureau (known as the "P.L. 94-171" data, after the 1975 federal law requiring the Census Bureau to tabulate data meeting states' redistricting needs), political actors were already aware of general population trends due to between-census population estimates. The legislature formally began considering the redistricting legislation on March 30, 2011, when the congressional redistricting bill H3992 was introduced in the House of Representatives.

Robert W. "Wes" Hayes Jr. is a Republican state senator who represents the 15th Senate District. This district includes Rock Hill, the largest population center of the 5th Congressional District, and a majority of York County, the second-fastest growing county in the state and the fastest growing county with a population over 200,000. Having served in the South Carolina House of Representatives from 1985 through 1991 and in the South Carolina Senate from 1991 until the present, this is the third round of post-census reapportionment and redistricting that Senator Hayes has been through.

Despite the partisan wrangling surrounding the redrawing of congressional district lines after the 2010 census, Sen. Hayes noted that, relative to the redistricting process after the census of 1990 and 2000, the process this time was "the smoothest of them all."[16] Hayes attributed much of this to unified party government. In 1990, Caroll A. Campbell Jr., only the second Republican elected to the South Carolina governor's mansion since Reconstruction, held the chief executive position while both the SC House and Senate were under Democratic control. In 2000, the governor's office was held by Democrat James "Jim" Hodges while both the state house and senate were controlled by Republicans, although the Senate just barely so. Republicans were able to gain control of the state senate by one vote after the 2000 election left the body tied 23–23; although Republicans would have had effective control of the chamber anyway, due to the tie-breaking vote of Republican Lieutenant Governor Bob Peeler, Democrat J. Verne Smith of Greer switched parties, giving the Republicans a slim but definitive 24–22 majority in the Senate for the first time since Reconstruction.

Hayes noted that there were repeated partisan clashes between the governor and the legislature over reapportionment in 1991 and 2001 and that the federal government had to intervene both times. The post-1990 reapportionment fight ended up in the federal courts, which required the gerrymandering of the 6th Congressional District to create the state's only majority-minority district.[17] After the 2000 census, Democratic Governor Hodges vetoed the plan created by the Republican legislature. The legislature failed to overturn the governor's veto and the process again went to the federal court system.[18] Although the state did ultimately adopt a locally-passed redistricting plan for both chambers of the state legislature in 2003, when Hodges was replaced by Republican Mark Sanford, the court-ordered plan remained in place for the U.S. House delegation throughout the decade.

Although the relationship between Republican Governor Nikki Haley and the Republican controlled legislature has been quite rocky at times,[19] unified party control seems to have made the 2011 process much smoother than the dramas of 2001 and 1991, which came in eras of divided government. This is not to say that the process has been free of controversy this time around, however. There have been partisan clashes over the drawing of the 7th district that have centered mostly around the dilution of the black vote in the Pee Dee region and an intra-party fight among legislative Republicans over whether the new 7th district should be centered around Horry County or Beaufort County. The argument over the dilution of black votes in the Pee Dee region was destined to be lost by Democrats who are minorities in both legislative chambers. The intra-party fight among Republicans came down to three considerations: incumbent protection, drawing a new safe Republican seat, and who got to set the agenda and draw the final lines.

Congressman Tim Scott is the first African American Republican to be elected to Congress from South Carolina since the end of Reconstruction.[20] Scott was swept into office as part of the Tea Party wave that swept over South Carolina in 2010. Scott won 61.49 percent of the vote in his native county of Charleston and 68.94 percent of the vote in Horry County, home of Myrtle Beach, one of the Tea Party's strongholds in 2010. Although he ran very strong in Horry County, his strong showing in, not to mention his residence in, Charleston meant that he would have a nearly insurmountable incumbent advantage over a Republican challenger from the Beaufort area, in the Low Country region of the state, if redistricting combined those counties into the same district. If the new 7th district cut the heavily populated Horry County out of the 1st district replacing it with the quickly growing Beaufort County (in the 2nd district prior to redistricting) would be a logical choice. Only a plan that left both Horry and Charleston Counties in the 1st district would allow a Beaufort County-centered district to be created that excluded Congressman Scott's home county of Charleston.

Two Low Country state senators, Sen. Tom Davis and Sen. Larry Grooms—both of whom were widely speculated to be eyeing a congressional bid if the 7th district were centered around Beaufort County and both of whom adamantly denied any such aspirations[21]—backed plans for a 7th district that was centered around Beaufort County. Before redistricting, quickly-growing and comfortably Republican Beaufort County was wholly in the 2nd Congressional District represented by Columbia-area Republican Joe Wilson. While it may seem odd that a Republican incumbent might consider giving up a comfortably Republican county, Beaufort County was only connected to the heart of the 2nd Congressional District by way of Allendale, Hampton, and Jasper counties. According to the 2010 census, Allendale County is 73.63 percent black, Hampton County is 53.86 percent black, and Jasper County 46.03 percent black. Wilson lost all three of these counties handily in 2010 and was willing to give up his access to the Republican stronghold of Beaufort County if it meant he could shed three of the counties where he ran the weakest from his district. The formal plan submitted jointly by Congressmen Mulvaney and Wilson (see map 3.4) clearly demonstrate that Congressman Wilson was willing to make this trade-off. Their proposal slices Allendale, Hampton, and Jasper counties out of the 2nd district and places them in Democrat Jim Clyburn's majority-black 6th district.

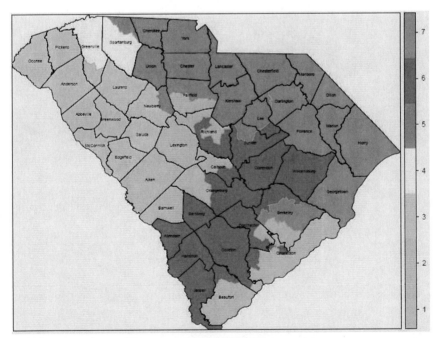

Map 3.4. Mulvaney Districts. Created by the author.

Davis would publicly accuse a fellow Republican, State Rep. Alan Clemmons of drawing a congressional district that Clemmons planned to run for.[22] Alan Clemmons is a representative from Myrtle Beach in Horry County and the chair of the Election Laws Subcommittee of the House Judiciary Committee. This is the subcommittee in charge of drafting the official congressional redistricting plan for the South Carolina House of Representatives.

The proposal for a 7th district centered on Beaufort County may be seen in map 3.5. As table 3.4 shows, based on Black Voting Age Population (BVAP), the Beaufort-centered plan achieves the goal of making six relatively-to-very-comfortable Republican districts and leaving one majority black district.[23] However, it failed on three critical points. First, it was opposed by the president *pro tempore* of the SC State Senate, Republican Glenn McConnell, who worked to get the votes to adopt an official SC Senate plan that was close to the Horry County-based plan for the 7th which was favored by the House[24]; it was also opposed by the Chairman of the SC House subcommittee tasked with drawing the House proposal for congressional redistricting. Thirdly, it failed to account for the preferences of two established congressional incumbents: Republican Joe Wilson and Democrat James Clyburn.

While one might argue that, in the abstract, Representative Wilson should have been indifferent to a Beaufort-based 7th district since it still would have allowed him to shed the part of his district where he runs the weakest, the facts point to a tacit agreement between congressional incumbents to protect their interests. Wilson

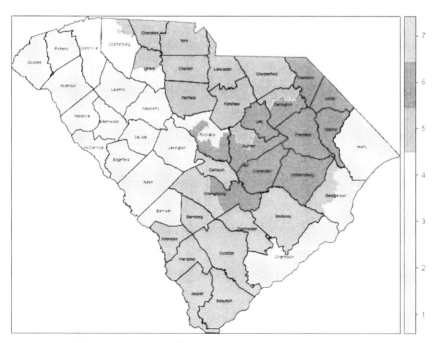

Map 3.5.   Staff2 Districts. Created by the author.

Table 3.4.   BVAP by Congressional District for
Proposal with Beaufort Co. Based 7th District

District Number	BVAP (DOJ definition)
First	21.06%
Second	21.34%
Third	18.34%
Fourth	17.89%
Fifth	24.56%
Sixth	53.46%
Seventh	28.84%

formally signed on to a plan that moved the heavily African American counties of
Allendale, Hampton, and Jasper to Clyburn's district. According to 5th district Republican Congressman Mick Mulvaney, he discussed the Mulvaney-Wilson plan with
Congressman Clyburn and Clyburn was amenable to the part of the plan that moved
Allendale and Hampton counties from the 2nd to the 6th district.[25] Additionally,
both of the proposals submitted by Congressman Clyburn demonstrate his amenabil-
ity to taking Allendale and Hampton counties into the 6th district, reluctance to take
on new area in the northeastern Pee Dee (something any Beaufort-based proposal
for the 7th district would necessitate), and a preference for a new 7th district based
around Horry County (see maps 3.6 and 3.7). With intra-party opposition from

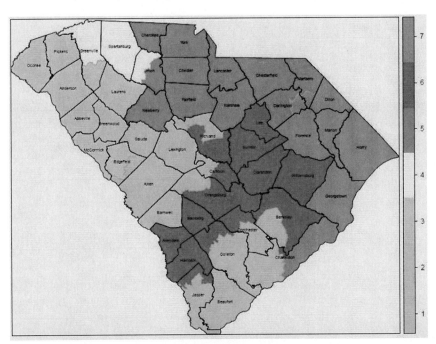

Map 3.6.   Clyburn First Districts. Created by the author.

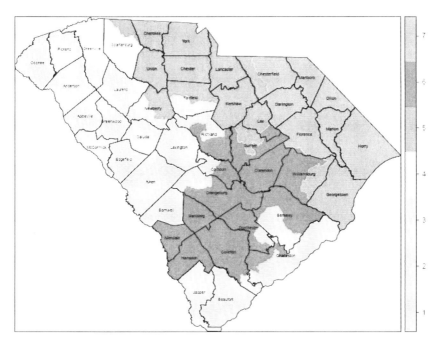

Map 3.7.   Clyburn Second Districts. Created by the author.

powerful Republicans in both the South Carolina House and Senate, and opposition form influential key congressional incumbents from both parties, the proposal for a Beaufort-based 7th district stood little chance of coming to fruition.

In addition to the plans developed by incumbent representatives and those developed by the legislative committees, three additional proposals were submitted: one plan was drafted by the South Carolina chapter of the American Civil Liberties Union (map 3.8); a second was drafted by the state chapter of the NAACP (map 3.9); and the third was the product of a private citizen, Matthew Kuhn, who appears to have been a student in a law school course on redistricting at Columbia University (map 3.10). The plans proposed by the ACLU and NAACP are noteworthy in that both attempted to create two majority-minority districts; both would have created a new 7th district in straddling the Upstate, Charlotte Metro, and Midlands regions, either of which barely would have had an African American voting age majority but presumably could have resulted in the election of an African American candidate with support from other non-whites and a smattering of white support. While the ACLU plan was the more compact of the two proposals, it had a much higher variation (over 4 percent) in district population than is generally considered acceptable in congressional plans.[26] The NAACP's proposal for a 7th district, while maintaining equal populations between districts, attempted to string together black neighborhoods in the Upstate cities of Greenville and Spartanburg and connect them to the rural Midstate to create a viable majority-minority district; their plan in many respects strongly resembled the initial,

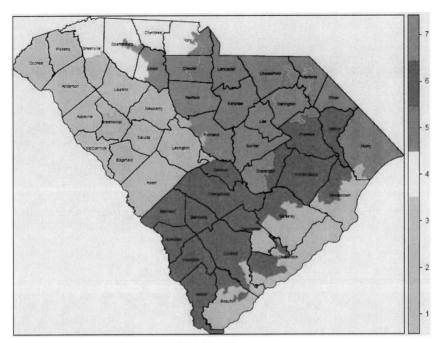

Map 3.8. ACLU Districts. Created by the author.

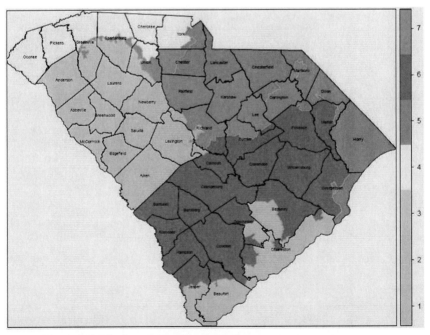

Map 3.9. NAACP Districts. Created by the author.

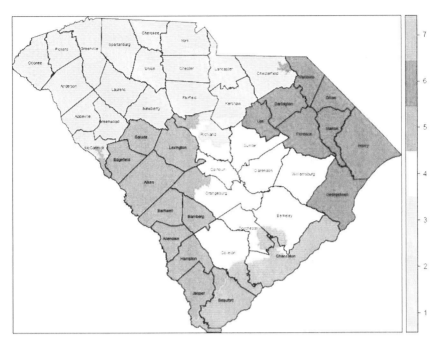

Map 3.10.   Kuhn Districts. Created by the author.

1992 version of North Carolina's majority-minority 12th Congressional District, notorious for stretching 120 miles along Interstate 85 to collect small pockets of black voters in every community between Charlotte and Durham, sometimes no wider than the highway itself, the creation of which launched a saga of redistricting litigation in the 1990s and was ultimately struck down in *Shaw v. Reno*.[27] In case the parallel to the infamous NC-12 wasn't clear enough already, the NAACP even used the same highway to construct their proposed district!

However, the most serious dispute over the creation of the new 7th district came from within the legislature itself, in the form of protest from state legislative Democrats over the dilution of black voter strength, particularly in the Pee Dee Region. Senate Democrats supported a plan that would create a mostly Horry County based 7th district (see map 3.11). However, it was a 7th district that would have over 30 percent Black Voting Age Population (BVAP), thus giving a moderate Democrat with decent name recognition a fighting chance to win the district. BVAP of over 44 percent is usually considered the point that gives African Americans the opportunity to elect a "minority-preferred candidate"—in this case, an African American candidate, while a BVAP of approximately 33 percent offers a black population good chance at "substantive representation," usually in the form of a white Democrat; notably, the 5th district in the 2000 cycle had been such a district, electing moderate white Democrat John Spratt until the 2010 Republican surge swept him, and the Democratic majority in Congress, from office.[28] A new district with 30 percent BVAP would certainly be considered a minority-influence district and could defi-

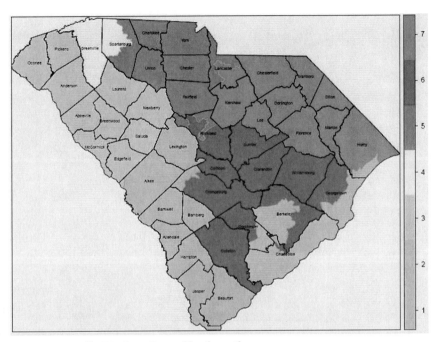

Map 3.11. Staff1 Districts. Created by the author.

nitely offer a shot at a Democratic win with a competitive candidate. Republicans supported this plan because, even though it gave a certain kind of Democrat a chance at winning the district, it wasn't a very good chance.

Through legislative maneuvering, however, the president *pro tempore* of the South Carolina Senate, Republican Glenn McConnell, managed to substitute the South Carolina House drawn plan, via a motion of concurrence. This move was strongly opposed by several Senate Democrats because it lowered the BVAP of the proposed 7th District by nearly four percentage points when BVAP was already at the low end of a critical potential tipping point for Democrats. Table 3.5 compares

Table 3.5. Comparison of BVAP (DOJ Definition) by Congressional Districts

District	Existing Districts: 2000 census	Existing Districts: 2010 census	Newly Adopted Districts (Act 75)	SC Sen. Judiciary Comm. Staff Plan 1 (Supported by Sen. Dems)
First	18.52%	18.21%	18.18%	19.28%
Second	23.95%	25.43%	21.48%	22.06%
Third	19.01%	18.59%	17.93%	18.31%
Fourth	18.17%	18.75%	18.23%	18.57%
Fifth	29.99%	29.45%	26.46%	23.10%
Sixth	53.55%	52.08%	55.18%	52.70%
Seventh	—	—	27.64%	31.26%

BVAP for the existing six congressional districts after both the census of 2000 and 2010 as well as the BVAP under the adopted plan and the first South Carolina Senate plan that had Democratic support.

South Carolina Sen. Gerald Malloy, an African American Democrat from Hartsville in Darlington County in the Pee Dee Region, and South Carolina Senator Vincent Sheheen, a white Democrat from Camden in Kershaw County (a county in the Midlands Region that borders the Pee Dee Region) both rose to oppose concurrence with the South Carolina House proposal. Both counties would have been in the new 7th district under the South Carolina Senate proposal that passed with support by Democrats. The following exchange between the two gentlemen, recorded in the (SC) Senate Journal outlines their opposition based on diluted BVAP and the creation of a safer Republican district.

> Senator MALLOY: [. . .] But I will speak to what happened in the Senate Judiciary plan. In the Senate Judiciary plan—and I'm going to focus primarily on the 6th and the 7th Districts—the 7th District that was drafted initially, and these matters are part of the record that we have, the African American voting age population was 31.26 percent on this Senate staff plan number 1.
>
> Senator SHEHEEN: Senator, what you are saying is—our Republican colleagues have led the African American vote out of the 7th Congressional District under the amendments that occurred?
>
> Senator MALLOY: I'm giving the numbers. It has gone down from my initial proposal. And basically we started out with the first proposal of 31 some odd percent and it's now down to 27.64 percent.
>
> Senator SHEHEEN: Senator, I want you to look at this map with me. Look at Florence County there. Florence County is split. In the lower half of Calhoun County, Darlington County, Florence County—do you know the demographic makeup of that county at all? Do you know why that was split like that?
>
> Senator MALLOY: I do not know why it was split. But I know looking at the plans and looking at the resulting numbers, it appears that the numbers on the new plan have 27.64 percent where the earlier plans had a more African American population.
>
> Senator SHEHEEN: And that would dilute African American voting in the 7th Congressional District?
>
> Senator MALLOY: I think it would.
>
> [. . .]
>
> Senator SHEHEEN: [. . .] What's going on is our Republican colleagues want to have six of the seven congressional districts likely electing Republicans, is that right?
>
> Senator MALLOY: I don't know what their end game is, but I'll tell you that's what's likely to happen.[29]

In the end, the will of several powerful Republican members of the South Carolina House and Senate, combined with Republican control of the governor's mansion and both South Carolina legislative chambers, and the preferences of powerful Congressional incumbents from both parties meant the creation of the new 7th district could only favor the election of a 6th Republican. The facts that the new district contained only one county that was not traditionally defined as part of the Pee Dee Region, and that the majority of the traditional Pee Dee Region was now in a single district rather than split, would help the state argue that the new 7th district constituted a "community of interest." When this is combined with the general understanding that a BVAP of 27.64 percent is still considered a "minority-influence" district,[30] preclearance by the Department of Justice was hardly surprising, at least based on past precedents under Republican administrations.

As discussed above, unlike in 2001, the Republican legislature faced a friendly, Republican governor and thus there was no risk of the congressional plan being vetoed; Governor Haley signed the redistricting bill H3992 into law on August 5, 2011, upon which it became Act 75 of the 2011–2012 South Carolina General Assembly, and referred it for preclearance to the U.S. Department of Justice, who cleared the plan on October 28, 2011 (see map 3.12).

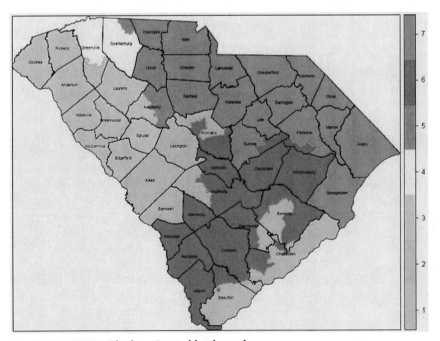

Map 3.12.   H3992 Districts. Created by the author.

LEGAL CHALLENGES AFTER PRECLEARANCE

Although all three plans were precleared by the U.S. Department of Justice in October and November of 2011, plaintiffs representing Democrats and African Americans filed a lawsuit (*Backus v. South Carolina*) on November 11, 2011, in federal court challenging the congressional districts as illegally using racial gerrymandering; specifically the plaintiffs allege that the legislature illegally "packed" black voters in the 6th Congressional District, denying them the opportunity to elect candidates of their choice in other potential districts; the plaintiffs amended their complaint on November 23, 2011, to also include similar allegations regarding the state House and Senate plans. As of this writing, these challenges have not been resolved.

CONCLUSION

At the outset, the 2010 redistricting cycle in South Carolina had the potential to be highly contentious; however, a number of factors seem to have contributed to making it a relatively low-key affair. Unified Republican control of the legislature and the governor's mansion produced an environment that would downplay partisan concerns on both sides of the aisle: unlike in 2001, Republicans could reasonably expect that a plan that they adopted would be signed by the governor, rather than vetoed, while Democrats clearly had no expectation of being able to seriously obstruct a plan favored by the majority. At the same time, however, the threat of a Democratic administration withholding preclearance may have restrained more radical plans on the part of majority Republicans, particularly any effort to weaken incumbent Democrat James Clyburn.

Another factor that seems to have made the process operate smoothly is the apparent understanding between the incumbent representatives, across party lines, to avoid radical proposals that Republicans in the legislature would be unlikely to accept. Clyburn, for example, might have been expected to advance plans that were similar to those proposed by the ACLU and NAACP that would have favored the election of a second African American representative (and would have led to serious reconfigurations of the existing 4th and 5th districts in the Upstate and Metro Charlotte regions); instead, Clyburn advanced two incumbent-protection plans that served his own reelection interests rather than partisan interests; similarly, Joe Wilson favored adopting a more compact district that consolidated his support and ceded Beaufort County to the districts of Clyburn and Tim Scott.

The third factor appears to have been the broad agreement among the congressional incumbents, state Democrats, and many state Republicans to center the new district on Horry County (Myrtle Beach/Conway); even though Democrats would have favored a more competitive district configuration than that which was ultimately adopted, with the apparent exception of a few politicians who might have benefitted from the opportunity afforded by an open seat focused on Beaufort County, a new Pee

Dee district seems to have been broadly supported, reducing the potential for conflict. Interestingly, this district configuration simultaneously produced a district with heavy Tea Party support and a large population of Republican-leaning voters who migrated from out-of-state, but also a district with the potential for a conservative Democrat to succeed if he or she could assemble the right black-white coalition (a Beaufort-centered district, on the other hand, probably would have favored a "country club Republican" and might have also been less susceptible to a Democratic challenge), perhaps satisfying the interests of more politicians on both sides of the aisle.

Finally the decision by the U.S. Department of Justice not to intervene in the districting process—despite outside plans from the ACLU and NAACP being submitted that demonstrate that the state could have created an additional majority-minority district, albeit one which would have raised serious questions about its compactness and contiguity, which under the *Gingles* standard the state would arguably be obliged to do, particularly given the apparent underrepresentation of the state's black population under current arrangements—is a noteworthy development, perhaps reflecting an ongoing concern by the Obama administration to avoid, in the light of *NAMUDNO*, potential Voting Rights Act cases where the fact pattern would be difficult for the administration to defend before the Supreme Court. It is unclear at present if this apparent strategy, also visible in the Department of Justice's recent efforts to render the Kinston case moot by withdrawing its objection to preclearance before it reaches the Supreme Court,[31] will successfully forestall a successful VRA challenge over the long term, but at the very least it is clear that the administration has not chosen to intervene in this particular instance.

NOTES

1. 557 U.S. 193, 2009.
2. See, for example, Richard L. Hasen, "Holder's Voting Rights Gamble: The Supreme Court's Voter ID Showdown," *Slate*, December 30, 2011. www.slate.com/articles/news_and_politics/jurisprudence/2011/12/the_obama_administration_s_risky_voter_id_move_threatens_the_voting_rights_act.html [Retrieved February 27, 2012].
3. 383 U.S. 301, 1966.
4. Richard L. Hasen, "The Modest South Carolina Suit against DOJ's Blocking of Its Voter ID Law," *Election Law Blog*, February 7, 2012. http://electionlawblog.org/?p=29430 [Retrieved February 27, 2012].
5. "Senate and Congressional Redistricting since 2000," http://redistricting.scsenate.gov/redistrictingprocess.html [Retrieved February 9, 2012].
6. Those counties that lost population include: Abbeville, Allendale, Bamberg, Barnwell, Calhoun, Chester, Hampton, Laurens, Lee, Marion, Union, and Williamsburg.
7. Those counties exhibiting stagnant growth include: Colleton, Darlington, Fairfield, McCormick, Marlboro, Orangeburg, and Sumter.
8. Those counties that experienced growth rates above 20% include: Beaufort, Berkeley, Dorchester, Horry, Lancaster, Lexington, and York. Among these, those counties that experienced growth greater than 30% include: Beaufort, Dorchester, Horry, and York.

9. This designation of county by region comes from Exhibit 8 from the South Carolina House of Representatives 2011 Judicial Preclearance Submission: http://redistricting.schouse.gov/PreclearanceSubmissionH3991.html.

10. See www.forbes.com/special-report/2011/migration.html.

11. For more data on this size disparity between districts, see Exhibit 6 from the South Carolina House of Representatives 2011 Judicial Preclearance Submission: http://redistricting.schouse.gov/PreclearanceSubmissionH3991.html. After reapportionment of SC House Districts, no district was more than 2.5 percent above or below the target ideal population size.

12. The Senate Judiciary Committee's redistricting guidelines are in the following document: http://redistricting.scsenate.gov/Documents/RedistrictingGuidelinesAdopted041311.pdf; the House Judiciary Committee adopted a similar set of guidelines, listed in this document: http://redistricting.schouse.gov/6334-1500-2011-Redistricting-Guidelines-(A0404871).pdf.

13. 2010 U.S. Census QuickFacts for South Carolina, http://quickfacts.census.gov/qfd/states/45000.html.

14. 478 U.S. 30, 1986; see also *League of United Latin American Citizens v. Perry*, 548 U.S. 399, 2006, in which the Supreme Court invalidated a plan that resulted in the election of a Hispanic Republican from a district in which 46 percent of adults were Hispanic.

15. See, for example, L. Marvin Overby and Kenneth M. Cosgrove, 1996, "Unintended Consequences? Racial Redistricting and the Representation of Minority Interests," *Journal of Politics* 58: 540-50.

16. Personal interview (Huffmon) with SC State Senator Robert W. "Wes" Hayes, Jr. (R-15th), February 14, 2011.

17. See *Leonard v. Beasley*, Civil No. 3:96-CV-3640 (D. S.C.).

18. See *Colleton County Council v. McConnell*, 201 F. Supp. 2d 618 2002.

19. See, as one example of many, www.thestate.com/2011/12/18/2083880/i-sleep-eat-and-breathe-jobs-every.html.

20. http://dailycaller.com/2010/11/02/tim-scott-first-black-republican-elected-to-congress-from-the-south-since-reconstruction/.

21. www.southcarolinaradionetwork.com/2011/07/25/sc-house-senate-to-work-out-congressional-district-plan/.

22. Opinion piece printed in the *Island Packet* newspaper on July 7, 2001, and formally inserted into the July 26, 2001, Journal of the (SC) Senate: www.scstatehouse.gov/sess119_2011-2012/sj11/20110726.htm#p34.

23. See http://redistricting.scsenate.gov/StaffPlan_Congressional/StaffPlan%202/StaffPlan2_DistStat.pdf.

24. www.southcarolinaradionetwork.com/2011/07/25/sc-house-senate-to-work-out-congressional-district-plan/.

25. Personal interview (Huffmon) with Congressman Mick Mulvaney (R-SC 5th) February 22, 2012.

26. The exact legal standard for population inequality in congressional redistricting is unclear. However, with modern GIS technology, redistricting plans adopted for Congress can be developed with deviations well within the likely margin of error of the census itself.

27. 509 U.S. 630, 1993.

28. David L. Epstein and Sharyn O'Halloran, 2006, "Trends in Substantive and Descriptive Minority Representation, 1974–2004," in *The Future of the Voting Rights Act*. David L. Epstein, Richard H. Pildes, Rodolfo O. de la Garza , and Sharyn O'Halloran, eds. Russell Sage Foundation.

29. July 26, 2001 Journal of the (SC) Senate: www.scstatehouse.gov/sess119_2011-2012/sj11/20110726.htm#p34

30. David L. Epstein and Sharyn O'Halloran, 2006, "Trends in Substantive and Descriptive Minority Representation, 1974–2004," in *The Future of the Voting Rights Act*. David L. Epstein, Richard H. Pildes, Rodolfo O. de la Garza, and Sharyn O'Halloran, eds. Russell Sage Foundation.

31. Richard L. Hasen, "Big Developments in LaRoque Voting Rights Case (Kinston)," *Election Law Blog*, February 27, 2012. http://electionlawblog.org/?p=30604. [Retrieved February 28, 2012].

4

Swimming against the Tide

Partisan Gridlock and the 2011 Nevada Redistricting

David F. Damore

Entering the 2011 reapportionment and redistricting process, Nevada Republicans had much to fear. Regardless of the final boundaries for the state's U.S. House and state legislative districts, changes to Nevada's political demography between 2000 and 2010 ensured an outcome that would benefit the Democrats. Rather than accepting this fate and working with the majority Democrats to minimize the damage to their party's electoral prospects, Republicans dug in their heels and forced redistricting into state court in hopes of getting a better result.

This did not happen. Instead, the final maps drawn by a panel of special masters resulted in a redistricting plan for the Nevada Legislature that was more favorable for the Democrats than either of the plans that Republican Governor Brian Sandoval had vetoed during the regular session of the Nevada Legislature. And while the Republicans were able to gain some concessions in the drawing of the boundaries for the state's four U.S. House seats, the special masters and the supervising state court judge rejected the party's claim that one of the seats must be drawn as a majority Latino district. As such, the outcome of the 2011 redistricting provided a fitting coda to a decade that saw the Nevada GOP deteriorate from the state's dominant political force to an internally divided minority party that only now appears to be recognizing what changes to Nevada's political landscape means for the Republican Party's future in the Silver State.

In this chapter I investigate the demographic and political origins of Nevada's 2011 redistricting that facilitated this change in fortunes for the two parties. While my primary focus is on the state's four U.S. House districts, I also consider the maps for the Nevada Legislature to assess at a finer level of analysis how Nevada's continued urbanization and diversification is reshaping political representation in the state. In so doing, my investigation highlights how a once sparsely populated state that had long been dominated by rural interests has been transformed into one of the most densely populated and ethnically diverse states in the nation.

The chapter is organized into five sections. Section one draws on U.S. census data to examine key changes to Nevada's demographics between 2000 and 2010. Next, I briefly summarize the process by which Nevada conducts its redistricting. This is followed by a review of the state's 2001 redistricting process, which despite a number of similarities to 2011 had a very different outcome. In section four, I examine the 2011 redistricting in detail. The chapter concludes with a discussion of the implications that the 2011 maps and continued demographic change are likely to have in the coming decade.

A DECADE OF TRANSITION

Between 2000 and 2010 no state experienced anything like the political and demographic changes that occurred in Nevada.[1] With a population increase of 35.1 percent, Nevada had the largest percent population gain in the country, and the state grew at rate that was over three and a half times faster than the national average of 9.7 percent. In terms of raw population, Nevada increased in size from roughly 2 million residents in 2000 to just over 2.7 million in 2010 (see table 4.1). As a consequence, after the 2010 census, the state was awarded its fourth seat in the U.S. House of Representatives.

The impact that such rapid growth has on political representation is significant. The maps that were implemented after the 2000 census populated each of Nevada's three U.S. House seats with 666,088 residents. By the end of the decade the districts had swelled to 820,442 (NV–1), 835,896 (NV–2), and 1,044,213 (NV–3).[2] At the time of the 2010 midterm election, Nevada's 3rd was by far the largest House district in the country. Growth created even more severe deviations for Nevada's state legislative districts. In 2010 the most populous Assembly and state Senate seats varied from their ideal populations by 299 percent and 175 percent respectively.[3]

More consequential to Nevada's internal political dynamics are the asymmetries in growth between the state's rural and urban spaces. As is summarized in table 4.1, between 2000 and 2010 virtually all of Nevada's population increase occurred in

Table 4.1.   Change in Nevada's Population Density, 2000–2010

Geographic Space	2000 Population	2000 Population Share	2010 Population	2010 Population Share	Growth 2000–2010	Change in Population Share (+/–)
Clark County	1,375,765	68.8%	1,951,269	72.3%	41.8%	+ 3.41%
Washoe County	339,486	16.9%	421,407	15.6%	24.1%	–1.3%
All Other Counties	283,006	14.3%	327,875	12.1%	15.8%	–2.2%
Total	1,998,257	—	2,700,551	—	35.1%	—

Note: Data from U.S. Census Bureau "Nevada State & County QuickFacts," http//:quickfacts.census.gov/qfd/states/32000.html (accessed January 5, 2012).

the state's two urban counties with 11 percent of the growth occurring in Washoe County (Reno) and 83 percent occurring in Clark County (Las Vegas), which increased in size by roughly 42 percent during the decade. In contrast, the combined population increase in the state's 15 rural counties was just 6 percent of the total growth or less than 45,000 residents. Despite its large land area, Nevada now has one of the country's most urbanized populations in the United States as nearly nine out of ten residents live in the state's two population centers and Clark County is now home to approximately three-quarters of the state's residents.

Thus, regardless of the underlying partisan dynamic, reapportionment of the state's U.S. House and state legislative districts meant that Nevada's new House seat would be located in southern Nevada and state legislative seats would be shifted from northern Nevada to Clark County. For southern Nevadans, the 2011 redistricting was a day of reckoning that had been a long time in coming. Prior to the mid-1960s, Nevada, like many states in the Mountain West, had a long history of malapportionment whereby rural interests were over–represented at the expense of urban residents. By one such metric, prior to the reapportionment revolution (e.g., *Baker v. Carr*, 396 U.S. 186, 1962; *Wesberry v. Sanders*, 376 U.S 1, 1964; and *Reynolds v. Sims* 377 U.S. 533, 1964), a majority of the upper chamber of the Nevada Legislature could be elected with just 12 percent of the population.[4] In contrast, after the 2011 redistricting, all or parts of 47 of 63 state legislative districts and three of four U.S. House seats were to be located in Clark County.

If increased urbanization was one pillar of demographic change in Nevada during the prior decade, as is detailed in table 4.2, increased diversification surely was another. Between 2000 and 2010, Nevada's minority populations increased by over 11 percent, and today nearly 46 percent of Nevadans are classified as non–white. The vast majority of this growth occurred in the state's Latino community, which as a share of the population increased from 20 percent in 2000 to over 26 percent

Table 4.2. Change in Nevada's Population Diversity, 2000–2010

Ethnic/Racial Group	2000 Population Share	2010 Population Share	Change in Population Share (+/−)
White	65.2%	54.1%	−11.1%
African American	6.8%	8.1%	+1.3%
Latino	19.7%	26.5%	+6.8%
Asian and Pacific Islander	4.9%	7.8%	+2.9%
Non-White Population[a]	34.8%	45.9%	+11.1%

[a]African American, Latino, Asian, Pacific Islander, and American Indian and Alaskan Native.

Note: U.S. Census Bureau, "DP-1. Profile of General Demographic Characteristics: 2000," http://factfinder.census.gov/servlet/QTTable?_bm=y&-geo_id=04000US32&-qr_name=DEC_2000_SF1_U_DP1&-ds_name=DEC_2000_SF1_U) and "State and County QuickFacts for Nevada," http://quickfacts.census.gov/qfd/states/32000.html (accessed January 5, 2012).

in 2010. In addition, Nevada recorded significant gains in its Asian American and Pacific Islander populations, which now constitute around 8 percent of residents; a share that is equivalent to Nevada's African American population.

Politically, the combination of increased population density and diversity created an environment that was advantageous for Nevada Democrats. To make the most of these opportunities necessitated significant investments in resources and talent by U.S. Senate Majority Leader Harry Reid's extensive political organization in the state.[5] In particular, early in the decade Reid's organization made outreach and mobilization of the state's Latino community its top priority. In 2008, Democrats also received a significant boost from Nevada's status as the "first in the west" presidential nominating event. In contrast, other than maintaining the governorship, the Nevada Republican Party's most notable developments during the decade were the introduction of Sharron Angle to the national political stage, the resignation of scandal plagued U.S. Senator John Ensign, and a continual turnover in the leadership of the state party organization. As a consequence, Nevada Democrats flipped the state from Republican to Democratic leaning by decade's end. Figure 4.1, which summa-

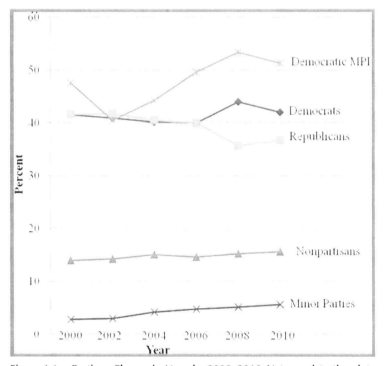

Figure 4.1.   Partisan Change in Nevada, 2000–2010. Voter registration data from Nevada Secretary of State's webpage http://nvsos.gov data (accessed January 5, 2012). Data for Ceasar and Saldin's Major Party Index (higher values indicating greater Democratic strength in the electorate) from http://scholar.harvard.edu/saldin/data (accessed January 5, 2012).

ries Democratic electoral strength using Ceaser and Saldin's Major Party Index and presents voter registration figures between 2000 and 2010, captures the Democratic rise in Nevada during the prior decade.

REDISTRICTING IN NEVADA

As noted above, the historic norm for redistricting in Nevada was malapportionment whereby each county, regardless of population, was awarded one Assembly and Senate. Because Nevada did not gain a second U.S. House seat until after the 1980 census, U.S. House members were elected at large for the state's first 118 years. After the reapportionment revolution of the mid-1960s, Nevada adopted redistricting requirements akin to those used in other states: equal population of U.S. House districts; population deviations for state legislative seats less than 10 percent; boundaries that are compact, contiguous, and preserve political subdivisions (e.g., counties and cities) and communities of interests; and compliance with Section 2 of the Voting Rights Act (VRA) of 1965. In addition, Nevada's redistricting guidelines allow map drawers to preserve the core of existing districts and consider the residency of incumbents.[6]

Beyond these judicially recognized redistricting principles, redistricting in Nevada has some unique features. Unlike many states that have removed state legislators from overseeing the process, redistricting in Nevada is under the purview of the Nevada Legislature.[7] Also, although the Nevada Constitution caps the total size of the Legislature at 75 and constrains the ratio of Senate and Assembly seats, the size of the state legislature is set by statute.[8] Presently, there are 42 Assembly members and 21 state Senators. The small size of these chambers coupled with the state's immense geographic area (Nevada is the seventh largest state in the country, but only the 35th most populated) means very large and increasingly fewer standalone rural state legislative districts.[9] Despite the present two-to-one ratio between Senate and Assembly seats, Nevada does not require that two Assembly districts be nested in a Senate district, and the state still allows multimember Senate districts, which are represented by two members (who run in alternating cycles) and have twice the population of the comparable single member districts. These two considerations can provide map drawers a great degree of latitude in drawing state legislative boundaries. Finally, despite its significant concentration of minorities, redistricting in Nevada, unlike its southern neighbor Arizona, is not subject to Department of Justice pre-clearance.

Reapportionment and redistricting in Nevada begins with the creation of a Committee to Study the Requirements for Reapportionment and Redistricting, which consists of state legislators from both chambers and political parties who meet during the interim. The purpose of the committee is to examine reapportionment and redistricting requirements in coordination with the collection and release of the decennial census data. Once the post-census biennial legislative session begins, the process is turned over to the Assembly and Senate Committees on Legislative Operations and

Elections, who are charged with holding public hearings throughout the state and developing preliminary maps for the state's U.S. House districts and state Senate and Assembly, as well as for the Nevada System of Higher Education Board of Regents and the State Board of Education. These activities are assisted by the Legislative Counsel Bureau, which also maintains the state's redistricting website.[10] Although some of the state's previous redistricting plans have been challenged in the courts, prior to 2011, the state's political branches had always completed redistricting during either regular or special session.

THE 2001 NEVADA REDISTRICTING

Many of the issues that affected the process in 2011 had their origins in the state's 2001 redistricting.[11] Specifically, between 1990 and 2000 Nevada was again the fastest growing state in the country (during the decade its population increased by an astonishing 66.3 percent) with the vast majority of the growth concentrated in southern Nevada. As a consequence, Nevada was awarded its third U.S. House seat after the 2000 census, and reapportionment of the Nevada Legislature required shifting seats from northern Nevada to Clark County, which in 2000 was home to roughly 7 out of 10 Nevadans (refer to table 4.1). In addition, for the first time in the state's history, representation of the state's Latino community (20 percent of the population) was at issue.

Despite these similarities between 2001 and 2011, the process went fairly smoothly in 2001. This was the case for a number of reasons. First, politically, at the time of the 2001 redistricting, voter registration was evenly divided between Democrats and Republicans (refer to figure 4.1) with Democrats drawing their strength primarily in southern Nevada and the GOP dominating the state's rural counties, most of Washoe County in northern Nevada, and pockets of Clark County. As a consequence, partisan control of the Nevada Legislature was split with Democrats in the majority in the Assembly and the Republicans holding the Senate, an arrangement that precluded either party from trying to implement a partisan gerrymander. Second, other than calling a special session to complete redistricting, Republican Governor Kenny Guinn stayed out of the process, allowing legislative leaders to compromise among themselves without fear of executive meddling or a gubernatorial veto. Third, because of the latitude that Nevada affords map drawers (e.g., multimember Senate districts and un–nested Assembly and Senate seats), party leaders of each chamber were more-or-less able to accommodate one another's preferences. Thus, while southern Nevada did gain two Assembly seats and one Senate seat, the displacement of rural legislators was limited as some rural Senate districts were stretched to include parts of the state's urban centers instead of being eliminated altogether.

The final product was a redistricting plan that avoided any legal challenges and yielded the most typical redistricting outcome—incumbent protection for both parties—that maintained the state's political status quo. The only real hitch in the process was bickering over the partisan composition of the state's new U.S. House district. A Republican state Senator, who would go on to hold the seat until 2008, forced a special session in hopes of gaining a more favorable drawing of the seat. In exchange for shifting the boundaries to lean Republican (the district had initially been drawn with an even partisan split), the Republicans dropped their expansion proposal. In their initial maps the Republicans had increased the size of the Nevada Legislature by adding two Assembly seats and one Senate seat to offset the shifting of seats from northern to southern Nevada in order to preserve safe Republican districts in northern Nevada.

Because geographic and partisan considerations dominated the process in 2001 and the state was not obligated to accommodate minority voting interests beyond the requirements stipulated in Section 2 of the Voting Rights Act, Latinos received little representation in the final maps. Specifically, while Latinos constituted one in five Nevadans at the time of the 2000 census, after the 2002 midterm election, just 5 percent of state legislative seats were held by Latinos and there were no Latinos among the state's congressional delegation.

THE 2011 REAPPORTIONMENT AND REDISTRICTING

The decision of both Democrats and Republicans to file placeholder lawsuits early in 2011 signaled that redistricting negotiations were going to be less amicable this time around. Because Republicans were in the minority in both chambers of the Nevada Legislature, they feared that Democrats would use their clout to implement a partisan gerrymander. Nevada Democrats were leery of Republican claims that one of the state's U.S. House districts must be drawn with a majority of Latinos; an outcome that would dilute Democratic strength in the other districts. To add further rancor to the process, Republican Governor Brian Sandoval vowed to veto any plans that he thought were unfair.

In addition to Nevada's Democratic shift in the intervening ten years (at the time of the 2010 census Democrats had a 7.5 percent registration advantage; refer to figure 4.1) and a more engaged governor, two other factors that had not been present in 2001 complicated negotiations in 2011. First, after the 2008 electoral cycle term limits for state legislators went into effect. Prior research indicates that term limits can erode legislative professionalism and undercut legislators' capabilities.[12] To some degree, this was the case in Nevada as many of the leaders in both parties and chambers were in their first and only terms in those positions. In addition, because term limits alter state legislators' time horizons and career paths,[13] term-limited legislators may use the process to position themselves to compete for other offices, typically those with broader constituencies.[14] As is noted below, these dynamics were certainly in play on the Democratic side given that the state was gaining a new House seat and Democratic incumbent (NV-1) Shelley Berkley was giving up her safe seat to run for the U.S. Senate.

A second factor that hindered negotiations was the resignation of Republican Senate Leader Bill Raggio just prior to the 2011 session. Raggio, who was the longest serving member of the Nevada Legislature, had a significant hand in the 1981, 1991, and 2001 redistricting negotiations. However, after crossing party lines to endorse U.S. Senate Majority Leader Harry Reid during Reid's 2010 reelection campaign against Sharron Angle, Raggio was stripped of his leadership position in the Nevada Senate. Subsequently, he resigned from office despite having two years left in his term. Many observers speculated that if Raggio had remained in the Senate that he would have tried to engineer a deal to expand the legislature and preserve safe, rural Republican seats in exchange for an extension of taxes that were due to sunset in 2011.[15]

Absent their most skilled and experienced negotiator, the Republican effort from the start was uncoordinated and ham-handed. Instead of presenting one set of state legislative maps, Republicans in each legislative chamber drew their own. However, because the plan drawn by Assembly Republicans did not comply with the Voting Rights Act, legislative lawyers advised against releasing the maps. As a consequence, Assembly Republicans were forced to rely on maps drawn by a Senate Republican consultant. The GOP Senate maps, however, drew the ire of Assembly Republicans because of the manner in which rural counties were divided into multiple districts. In contrast, legislative Democrats presented one set of state legislative maps that eliminated the existing multimember districts, nested two Assembly seats inside state Senate districts, and used city and county boundaries (instead of census tracts as the GOP plan did) to keep communities intact.

Concerns about the boundaries for state legislative districts, however, were secondary to partisan differences in how the state's four U.S. House seats should be drawn. The initial maps produced by Assembly and Senate Democrats sought to create three seats favorable to the Democrats and one safe Republican seat. Particularly odious to the GOP was the Democratic Assembly plan that placed Republican incumbent Joe Heck (NV–3) into a seat that had a 15 percent Democratic registration advantage. Not coincidentally, termed-out Assembly Speaker John Oceguera was planning to run in that district against Heck in 2012. Similarly, the Senate Democratic maps sought to shift the lines for the safe Democratic seat (NV–1) northwards in order to provide an electorally advantageous district for Senate Majority Leader Steven Horsford, who too was planning a 2012 congressional bid.

The Republican proposal was no better as it sought to create two Democratic districts and two Republican districts. To create two Republican seats required splitting the state's rural counties in half and then linking each half to GOP enclaves in Washoe County in the north and Clark County in the south. More troubling for the Democrats was the Republicans' plan for Nevada's new House seat (NV–4), which poached a chunk of voters from NV–1 to create a district with a Democratic registration advantage of nearly 37 percent and that was majority Latino.

Indeed, political representation of Nevada's booming Latino community became the hill upon which Nevada Republicans let redistricting negotiations die. In vetoing both redistricting bills passed on party line votes during the regular session, Governor Sandoval cited the lack of a majority Latino district in justifying his actions. Sensing that legislative Democrats were unlikely to compromise on this point, Governor Sandoval refused to call a special session to complete the process. Thus, for the first time in the state's history, a state court would oversee the completion of Nevada's 2011 redistricting.

The Republicans' vigorous defense of Latino voting rights (it became the party's sole talking point throughout negotiations) was met with a great deal of skepticism, if not outright hostility and derision in the broader political environment. Putting aside the obvious partisan advantage that such a district would provide the GOP in Nevada's other three U.S. House seats, Democrats and many affiliated Latino organizations and activists were quick to point out that this was the first time that Nevada Republicans had shown any interest in the political aspirations of the state's Latino community. Andres Ramirez, a leader of The Nevada Latino Redistricting Coalition, a group organized to lobby for Latino interests during redistricting negotiations, summed up the feelings of many Latinos by noting that Nevada Republicans would "have us believe they have our best interests in mind, yet they never reached out to talk to us" and then added, "we Latinos can speak for ourselves. We don't need anyone to speak for us."[16]

On this count, the evidence could not be clearer. Despite Nevada's rapidly growing minority population, the sum total of diversity in the Republican legislative caucus in 2011 was three white women—a point succinctly summarized by the headline of a *Las Vegas Review Journal* story assessing the composition of the Nevada Legislature: "GOP Legislators Look Old, White, Male."[17] In contrast, the Democratic caucus in the Nevada Legislature featured eight Latino and eight African American members, a Native American, and 14 women.

More generally, Republican claims that Nevada was required to create a majority Latino U.S. House district rested on a dubious application of Section 2 of the VRA and subsequent Supreme Court decisions. As the Nevada Republicans own redistricting website explained,[18] Section 2 of the VRA (as interpreted in *Thornburg v. Gingles*, 478 U.S. 30, 1986 and *Bartlett v. Strickland*, 556 U.S. 1, 2009) only allows the creation of majority-minority districts when three conditions are present: members of the minority group vote for the same candidates; the minority group votes for a candidate that is different from the candidate preferred by the white majority and the white minority always defeats the minority's preferred candidate; and the minority group is of sufficient size and compactness that it would constitute the voting age population in a single member district.

Support for any of these conditions in Nevada is non–existent. For instance, while Latinos in Nevada generally support Democrats 70 percent to 75 percent of the time,[19] the preferences of Latinos are far from monolithic, particularly as compared to African Americans, the group whose voting rights the VRA had originally been created to protect. Also, there is no indication that the white majority (which given the state's demographics barely constitutes a majority at all) were voting to deny

Latinos representation of their preferred candidates. In 2010 Nevadans reelected two Latinos to statewide office from different political parties (Democratic Attorney General Catherine Cortez Masto and Republican Governor Brian Sandoval) and elected eight Latinos to the Nevada Legislature, half of whom represented districts with Latino populations of less than 40 percent.

Lastly, because it is impossible to draw a compact U.S. House district in Nevada that has a voting age population that is majority Latino (Latinos constitute just over 22 percent of the potential electorate in Nevada and roughly 15 percent of Latinos reside outside of Clark County), the Republicans sidestepped condition three by constituting NV–4 with a majority Latino population. And to accomplish this (see map 4.1) necessitated combining Latino communities in North Las Vegas, Las Vegas, and unincorporated Clark County with three fingers snaking around McCarran International Airport, Interstate 15, and Interstate 515 and reaching to the border of the state's second largest city, Henderson; all the while being surrounded on three sides by another district (NV–1), with both of these districts then encircled by yet another district (NV–3). As such, it was difficult to argue that anything besides race had motivated the drawing of the map; an outcome that was clearly at odds with the holding in *Shaw v. Reno* (509 U.S. 630, 1993), which forbids race from being the primary factor in drawing boundaries.

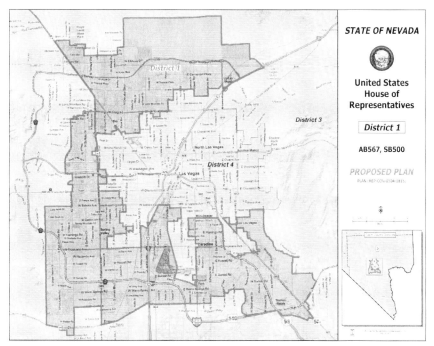

Map 4.1. Republican Proposal for Majority Latino U.S. House District (NV-4). Nevada Legislative Counsel Bureau.

Not surprisingly, then, the House maps drawn by Republican and Democratic legislators were driven by partisan considerations. But because the judiciary had never overseen a redistricting in Nevada, it was uncertain if any of the proposed plans would even be considered by the state court. The presiding judge, Carson City District Judge Todd Russell—himself the son of a former Republican governor—did little to quell these concerns when he suggested that he would approach the process by "trying to think outside of the box."[20] After a lengthy hearing, Judge Russell appointed three special masters to draw the maps, but offered no legal direction about how to proceed, as Russell refused to rule on any of the legal questions surrounding the case including the issue that had nominally forced redistricting into the court to begin with: the applicability of Section 2 of the VRA to Nevada.

The situation was then exacerbated by Nevada Supreme Court Chief Justice Nancy Saitta, who in late September 2011 sent Judge Russell a letter questioning his ability to handle the redistricting case in a timely manner given the March 2012 candidate filing deadline and time needed to process any appeals to the Nevada Supreme Court or to federal court.[21] Democratic Secretary of State Ross Miller, whose handling of Nevada's first special election for a U.S. House seat had earned a strong rebuke from Judge Russell earlier in the spring, then added more fuel to the fire by filing a writ of mandamus with the Nevada Supreme Court requesting that the high court either direct Judge Russell to decide the legal questions surrounding the case instead of "referring those questions to a panel of non-jurists" or simply decide the questions itself.[22]

All of the legal handwringing, however, was for naught as the special masters completed their initial maps just 23 days after receiving their orders from Judge Russell. After a mid-October 2011 hearing, Judge Russell made one of three changes to the boundaries for a state Senate district that had been requested by Republican lawyers, and then on October 26 he signed off on the final maps. By choosing not to draw a majority-minority U.S. House seat, the special masters implicitly sided with the Democrats on the VRA question; a view also shared by Judge Russell who finally tipped his hand by noting in his closing comments that "I don't believe the (Voting Rights Act) is even an issue."[23] With no legal issue upon which to mount an appeal, Nevada Republicans quietly acquiesced, which, in turn, led the Nevada Supreme Court to deny Secretary of State Miller's request to intercede in Judge Russell's handling of the process. Thus, with no pending legal challenges, Nevada's redistricting was completed in early December 2011.

The final map for Nevada's four U.S. House seats does not tilt as favorably to the Democrats as those that were vetoed by Governor Sandoval. At the same time, the fact that the Democrats did not request any changes to the special masters' plan is telling. By simply coupling the state's natural population distribution with basic redistricting principles (boundaries that are compact, contiguous, and recognize political subdivisions and communities of interests), the special masters drew districts that were consistent with the expectations that many observers had entering the process: two Democratic seats (NV–1 and NV–4), one of which is ironclad (NV–1), one Republican district (NV–2), and one swing district (NV–3).

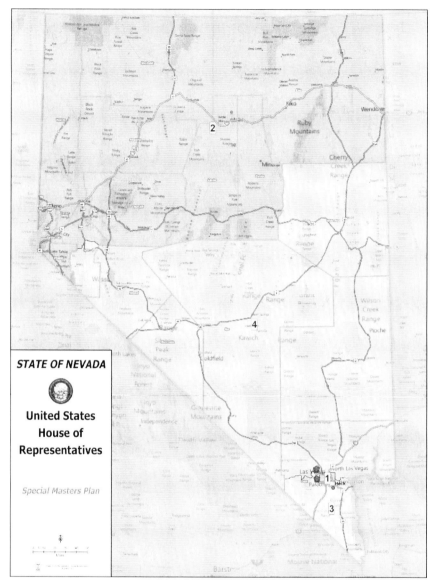

Map 4.2. Nevada's Final U.S. House of Representatives Map. Nevada Legislative Counsel Bureau.

Inspection of the final boundaries for the state's congressional seats (see map 4.2) suggests at first blush that Nevada's new House seat (NV–4) is a hybrid rural/urban district. The district extends over 260 miles north from the middle of Clark County to the border separating White Pine and Elko Counties; picking up along the way five rural counties and part of another. Despite the district's massive geographic area (well over half of the state), only 11 percent of the district's constituency lives outside of Clark County—an indicator of just how thinly Nevada's rural spaces are populated. The geographic imprint of the second district is also quite large as it contains Washoe County, nine rural counties in their entireties, and part of another. However, less than 40 percent of the district's population resides outside of Washoe County. The other two U.S. House seats (NV–1 and NV–3) are both contained within Clark County and, reflecting the density of southern Nevada's population, the footprint for NV–1 is one of the smallest in the country.

Table 4.3 summarizes each U.S. House district's demographic and political characteristics. Inspection of these data reveals some interesting dynamics. Most notably, while the special masters did not create a majority Latino House district per se, because of the heavy concentration of Latinos in the core of Las Vegas, NV–1 is 43 percent Latino (with a Latino voting age population of 37 percent) and has a total minority population of over 66 percent. The district is also the most Democratic of Nevada's U.S. House seats with Democrats holding a 27 percent registration advantage. The ethnic and partisan composition of NV–4 is akin to that of NV–1. Specifically, over half of the state's new House district is composed of minorities, and the district has the largest share of African Americans of any of the seats and the second largest number of Latinos. The Democrats hold a registration advantage of nearly 13 percent; not quite the Democratic stranglehold as NV–1, but a district that will be difficult for the Republicans to contest.

In comparison, the minority population in the state's northern district (NV–2) is less than half of the total for NV–1 and 60 percent of the minority population of NV–4. The variation in the ethnic compositions of NV–1 and NV–4 and NV–2 reveals one of the most significant distinctions between northern and southern Nevada: the state's two regions are inhabited by people with very different demographic, and to a lesser extent, political characteristics. Yet, despite being the district with the smallest minority population, the GOP registration advantage is only 7 percent. At the same time, since it was created after the 1980 census, the seat has never been held by a Democrat.

Far and away, however, the district that will be the state's most competitive throughout the coming decade is NV–3. Originally created after the 2000 census to lean Republican, the district swung in near simpatico with the national political environment. The GOP won the seat easily in 2002 and 2004 and barely in 2006. In 2008 the seat went Democratic for the first time before shifting back to the Republicans in 2010 by less than 2,000 votes. Even after shedding a third of its population, the district remains evenly divided and will be one of a handful of suburban districts across the country where partisan control of the House of Representatives will be determined in the coming decade. The district has the smallest concentration of Latinos, the largest Asian and Pacific Islander populations, a slight Democratic registration advantage, and the largest share of nonpartisan or minor party affiliates of the state's four U.S. House seats.

Perhaps where the special masters had the most significant impact is in the maps for the Nevada Legislature. In drawing these lines, a number of changes were made

Table 4.3. Demographic and Partisan Composition of Nevada's U.S. House Districts, 2011

District	Democratic Registration	Republican Registration	Nonpartisan and Minor Party Registration	Latino	African American	Asian and Pacific Islander	Total Non-White[a]
1	52.3%	25.2%	22.5%	42.8%	11.6%	10.6%	66.5%
2	35.3%	42.8%	21.9%	20.4%	2.6%	5.8%	32.1%
3	39.9%	37.2%	22.9%	15.7%	7.8%	16.4%	41.3%
4	45.9%	33.2%	20.9%	26.6%	15.8%	8.1%	53.6%

[a]Latino, African American, Asian, Pacific Islander, and American Indian and Alaskan Native.

Note: Data from "United States House of Representatives Plan - Special Masters - October 14, 2011 Population Report," www.leg.state.nv.us/Division/Research/Districts/Reapp/2011/Proposals/Masters/CON-Masters-Tables.pdf (accessed December 29, 2011).

to the manner in which these districts traditionally have been constituted. In so doing, the special masters produced plans that differ significantly from those that were proposed by both parties' legislative caucuses. Most notably, the special masters eliminated the two remaining multimember Senate districts and, as the Democrats had proposed, nested two Assembly seats inside a single Senate district despite no requirement to do so. Thus, the practice of stretching state Senate seats across the boundaries of as many as ten Assembly districts was ended. As is noted above, this technique was used in 2001 to preserve the seats of rural, Republican Senate incumbents in order to maintain the partisan status quo in the Nevada Legislature. In addition, the special masters virtually eliminated cross-district population deviations. After the 2001 redistricting, the overall range of deviations for the Assembly and Senate maps were 1.97 percent and 9.91 percent respectively. In 2011, these deviations were reduced to 1.33 percent for the Assembly and 0.80 percent for the Senate.

However, the decision that will have the most significant partisan implication is how the special masters reapportioned state legislative seats. Because of Nevada's asymmetric growth, southern Nevada was assured of gaining one Senate and Assembly seat, as well as parts of another district in each chamber. The maps proposed by both parties called for moving seats located in and around Washoe County (Reno) to southern Nevada, while preserving two stand-alone rural state Senate districts. Instead, the special masters drew only one stand-alone rural Senate district that stretches from the Idaho border into the northern portion of Clark County and moved the other rural state Senate seat to southern Nevada. Moreover, the Senate seat in Washoe County that the parties had originally agreed to move south was drawn with a Republican registration advantage of less than 1 percent. Thus, instead of being ensured of two safe rural Senate seats in the coming decade, the GOP will have only one and the party will need to win one seat in urban Clark County in 2012 and hold a closely divided district in Washoe County just to stay even.

More generally, as the data in table 4.2 suggests, for Nevada Republicans to gain the majority in either chamber of the Nevada Legislature in the coming decade will require that Republican candidates consistently win an overwhelming share of the nonpartisan vote (16 percent of the electorate). In the state Senate, 12 seats have a Democratic voter registration advantage in excess of 5 percent as compared to only 5 seats for the GOP. And in only one of the four competitive Senate districts do Republicans have a registration advantage greater than 1 percent. The GOP's prospects are even less favorable in the Assembly where the Democrats now have 25 seats with registration advantages in excess of 5 percent. In contrast, there are only 8 seats that favor the Republicans to this degree and 9 seats where neither party enjoys a registration advantage greater than 5 percent

IMPLICATIONS AND CONCLUSIONS

Despite months of legal maneuvering and bitter partisanship, the new maps for the Nevada Legislature and the state's four seats in the U.S. House of Representatives accurately reflect the tremendous changes to Nevada's political demography between 2000 and 2010. The fact that the final product tilts in favor of the Democrats is the new reality in a state that at some point in the coming decade is likely to have a population that is majority-minority and will be even more concentrated in its urban spaces. As I note throughout, the traditional image of Nevada as a Republican stronghold dominated by the preferences of its rural inhabitants is no longer accurate as the state is one of the most urban and demographically diverse in the country. In this regard, Nevada serves as a microcosm for many of the trends reshaping broad swaths of the county. And just as Nevada's zeitgeist is being updated to account for these dynamics, so too will the nation's broader social identity.

For Nevada Republicans, the 2011 redistricting was not their finest hour and instead served as an appropriate endpoint to a decade highlighted by incessant intra-party squabbling and leadership turnover, middling electoral performance, and an inability to either recognize or adapt to the state's changing demography. Perhaps because the Nevada GOP planned all along to force the judiciary to set the rever-sion plan for the 2011 redistricting, there was little interest in negotiating with the majority Democrats. Indeed, because the party lacked any legislators as skilled as the deposed Bill Raggio and the party's caucus, including Governor Sandoval, entered the 2011 legislative session unified in their opposition to extending taxes that were to sunset, the party had little with which to bargain.[24]

In the end, the party miscalculated on both redistricting and taxes. By allowing redistricting to be put in the hands of the special masters, the GOP ended up los-ing forever a safe, rural state legislative district in exchange for an even drawing for NV–3. While this may buy Republican incumbent Joe Heck one or two more terms in the seat, given the trajectory of the state's political demography and that district's history of swinging in concert with the national political environment, NV–3 eventually will tilt blue. In terms of taxes, late in the legislative session the Nevada Supreme Court handed down a ruling that the taking of local tax revenue from some locales (and hence, treating local governments unequally) by the state government was unconstitutional. Because the decision effectively created a $600 million hole in Governor Sandoval's proposed budget,[25] Sandoval was forced to abandon his prior position and advocate for extending expiring taxes, a decision that facilitated a bi-partisan budget compromise and allowed the governor to extricate himself politically from his party's most reactionary and conservative elements.

If Republicans and their rural allies were the losers, the winners were Latinos and by extension the Democrats. It is this point, more than any other, which captures the changes in Nevada in the last decade. Despite significant organization and lobbying efforts throughout the 2001 redistricting negotiations, Latino interests received no serious consideration. Fast forwarding to a decade later, the representation of Latinos became the main source of partisan contention that resulted in the judiciary setting the state's redistricting plan. Certainly, Latino activists may have preferred to have mem-bers of their community distributed more evenly among the state's U.S. House districts (refer to table 4.3). At the same time, except for NV–2, the northern Republican seat, the Latino population is larger than the Latino voting age population in the other

Table 4.4. Partisan Composition of Nevada's State Legislative Districts, 2011

Chamber	Number of Districts	Safe Democratic[a]	Safe Republican[b]	Competitive[c]	Latino Friendly[d]
Senate	21	12	5	4	7
Assembly	42	25	8	9	15

[a]Democratic registration advantage greater than 5%.
[b]Republican registration advantage greater than 5%.
[c]Partisan registration differences less than 5%.
[d]Latino population in excess of 30%.

Note: Data from "Senate Plan—Special Masters V2—October 26, 2011 Population," www.leg.state.nv.us/Division/Research/Districts/Reapp/2011/Proposals/Masters/SEN-Masters-V2-1026_Tables.pdf and "Assembly Plan—Special Masters V2—October 26, 2011 Population," www.leg.state.nv.us/Division/Research/Districts/Reapp/2011/Proposals/Masters/ASM-Masters-V2-1026_Tables.pdf (accessed December 29, 2011).

three U.S. House districts. Thus, as the ranks of voting age Latinos swell and Latinos continue to become more politically engaged, their electoral clout will only increase. In the near term, this impact is likely to be most evident in the Nevada Legislature. As table 4.4 indicates, over a third of all state legislative districts have Latino populations in excess of 30 percent. Coupling these demographics with the effects of term limits means that the number of Latinos in the Nevada Legislature in the coming decade will surely increase from the present eight. The only question then is if these politicians will all have D's next to their names or if some will be elected as Republicans.

In this regard, there is some evidence that Nevada Republicans are starting to come to grips with the state's changing political landscape. Heading into the 2012 electoral cycle, the party hired a Latino outreach coordinator,[26] some eight years after the Democrats began their extensive Latino outreach and mobilization efforts. Still, the GOP's insistence that one of Nevada's U.S. House districts must be majority Latino engendered little good will among the state's fastest growing demographic group. As a former federal judge, Governor Sandoval had to have known that the law was not on his party's side. But by choosing to cling to such a tortured interpretation of the VRA to justify his vetoes of the Democratically passed redistricting plans, he and his party were perceived not as standing on principle, but rather as using the representation of Latinos as a fig-leaf for partisan gain. The fact that Nevada Republicans were so adamant about this point during redistricting negotiations, but then failed to appeal the final maps because they did not include a majority Latino district only served to reinforce this cynicism.

NOTES

1. All demographic and population data cited in this chapter come from the U.S. Census Bureau, "DP-1. Profile of General Demographic Characteristics: 2000," http:// factfinder.census .gov/servlet/QTTable?_bm=y&-geo_id=04000US32&-qr_name=DEC_2000_SF1_U_DP1& -ds_name=DEC_2000_SF1_U) and "State and County QuickFacts for Nevada," http://quick facts.census.gov/qfd/states/32000.html (accessed January 5, 2012).

2. Legislative Counsel Bureau, "United States House of Representatives Districts – 2010 & 2000 Populations," www.leg.state.nv.us/Division/Research/Districts/Reapp/2011/Tables/PopulationCongressionalDistrictsInNevada2010.pdf (accessed December 28, 2011).

3. Legislative Counsel Bureau, "Nevada State Assembly Districts—2010 & 2000 Population," and "Nevada State Senate Districts—2010 & 2000 Population," www.leg.state.nv.us/Division/Research/Districts/Reapp/2011/Tables/PopulationPercentChangeAssemblySenate-DistrictsInNevada2010.pdf (accessed December 28, 2011).

4. Manning J. Dauer and Robert G. Kelsay, "Unrepresentative States," *National Municipal Review* (December 1955): 571–75, 581.

5. See David F. Damore, "Reid vs. Angle in Nevada's Senate Race: Harry Houdini Escapes the Wave," in *Cases in Congressional Campaigns: Storming the Hill,* 2nd ed., eds. David Dulio and Randall Adkins (New York: Routledge, 2011): 32–53, and David F. Damore, "The Tea Party Angle in the Nevada Senate Race," in *Tea Party Effects on 2010 Senate Elections,* eds. Will Miller and Jeremy Walling (Lanham, MD: Lexington Books, 2011): 47–66.

6. Legislative Counsel Bureau, "Reapportionment and Redistricting Newsletter," Volume 2 No. 1 (February 2010), www.leg.state.nv.us/Interim/75th2009/Committee/Studies/Redistrict/Other/Vol2No1.pdf (accessed January 3, 2012).

7. As part of the legal maneuvering surrounding the process in 2011, the Nevada Supreme Court indicated that it would be willing to consider if the Nevada Constitution required redistricting to be approved by the executive branch or if the process could be decided unilaterally by the Nevada Legislature. On this point, the Nevada Constitution is vague as the relevant section (Article 4, Section 5) reads: "It shall be the mandatory duty of the Legislature at its first session after the taking of the decennial census of the United States in the year 1950, and after each subsequent decennial census, to fix by law the number of Senators and Assemblymen, and apportion them among the several counties of the State, or among legislative districts which may be established by law, according to the number of inhabitants in them, respectively." Because the Nevada Supreme Court did not wade into the legal disputes surrounding the 2011 redistricting, the issue was never litigated.

8. Article 4, Section 5 and Article 15, Section 6, *The Constitution of the State of Nevada,* www.leg.state.nv.us/const/nvconst.html (accessed January 3, 2012).

9. Excluding Nebraska (because of its unicameral structure), the average size of the lower and upper houses of the other 49 state legislatures are 110 and 39.22 respectively.

10. Legislative Counsel Bureau, "Nevada Reapportionment & Redistricting 2011," www.leg.state.nv.us/Division/Research/Districts/Reapp/2011/ (accessed January 3, 2012).

11. For an extended discussion of the 2001 redistricting in Nevada, see David F. Damore, "The 2001 Nevada Redistricting and Perpetuation of the Status Quo," *American Review of Politics* 27 (Spring and Summer 2006): 149–68.

12. Thad Kousser, *Term Limits and the Dismantling of State Legislative Professionalism* (New York: Cambridge University, 2005).

13. John M. Carey, Richard Niemi, Lynda W. Powell, and Gary F. Moncrief, "The Effects of Term Limits on State Legislatures: A New Survey of the 50 States," *Legislative Studies Quarterly* (February 2006): 105–34.

14. Jennifer A. Steen, "The Impact of State Legislative Term Limits on the Supply of Congressional Candidates," *State Politics and Policy Quarterly* (Winter 2006): 430–47.

15. Because of the economic downturn and the state's unstable tax base, Nevada's budget has been cut significantly in the last four years. To alleviate some of the most drastic cuts, in

2009 Raggio negotiated a set of temporary taxes that were to expire in 2011. Like any good deal-maker, Raggio had a history of using one negotiation to set up another. In this regard, his insistence that the taxes be temporary was widely viewed as leverage that could be used in the ensuing session's redistricting negotiations.

16. Delen Goldberg, "Latino Leaders Come Up with Their Own Redistricting Plan," *Las Vegas Sun,* www.lasvegassun.com/news/2011/may/20/latino–leaders–come–their–own–plan –redistricting (accessed December 30, 2011).

17. Ed Vogel, "GOP Legislators Look Old, White, Male," *Las Vegas Review Journal,* www .lvrj.com/news/gop–legislators–look–old–white–male–110786804.html (accessed December 30, 2011).

18. "Nevada Republican Legislators Redistricting Plans," www.nevadarepublicanlegislators .com (accessed December 30, 2011).

19. Estimating the vote preferences for minorities is a difficult endeavor. For instance, a 2010 election eve poll produced by Latino Decisions estimated Latino support for U.S. Senate Majority Leader Harry Reid at 90 percent (*n* = 400 with a margin of error of +/– 4.9 percent for the 95 percent confidence interval) in his reelection bid against Sharron Angle. In contrast, the National Election Pool Exit Poll for Nevada indicated that Reid won 68 percent of the Latino vote and Angle 30 percent (*n* ~ 570 with a margin of error of +/– 2 percent for the 95 percent confidence interval). For an extended discussion of exit polling in minority communities, see Matt Barreto, Fernando Guerra, Mara Marks, Stephen Nuño, and Nathan Woods, "Controversies in Exit Polling: Implementing a Racially Stratified Homogenous Precinct Approach," *PS: Political Science & Politics* 39(July 2006): 477–83.

20. Anjeanette Damon, "Who Wants the Most Political Task Out There? Apparently No One," *Las Vegas Sun,* www.lasvegassun.com/news/2011/jul/12/who–wants–most–political –task–out–there–apparently (accessed January 2, 2012).

21. Letter from Nancy M. Saitta, Chief Justice, Supreme Court of Nevada to First Judicial District Court Judge Todd Russell, September 20, 2011, media.lasvegassun.com/media/pdfs/ blogs/documents/2011/10/03/saitta.pdf (accessed January 5, 2012).

22. *Miller v. First Judicial Court of the State of Nevada,* Emergency Petition for Writ of Mandamus Pursuant to NRAP 27(e), October 3, 2011, nvsos.gov/Modules/ShowDocument .aspx?documentid=2093 (accessed January 5, 2012).

23. Anjeanette Damon, "Judge Signs Off on New Congressional Districts," *Las Vegas Sun* www.lasvegassun.com/news/2011/oct/27/judge-signs-new-congressional-districts (accessed January 5, 2012).

24. In the short term, all is not lost for Nevada Republicans. The twin consequences of term limits for state legislators and the bounty of Democratic electoral opportunities have created a leadership vacuum, particularly in the state Senate where no fewer than three sitting Senators, none of whom is termed out, expressed interest in running for Congress.

25. To prevent even more drastic budget cuts and avoid the political fallout for raising taxes, Governor Sandoval's budget proposed taking over $300 million in school bond reserve funds and redirecting sales tax from Clark and Washoe Counties among other budgetary gimmicks.

26. Data made available to the author by Latino Decisions suggests that Nevada Republicans have a steep hill to climb. Pooling tracking poll data for 2011 indicates that among Nevada Latinos just 7 percent feel that the Republican Party is currently doing a good job reaching out, while 58 percent think that the GOP does not care and 21 percent see the Republican Party as being hostile toward Latinos.

5

Redistricting the Peach State[1]

Charles S. Bullock III

During the first decade of the twenty-first century, Georgia continued to grow as it had for more than a generation. The growth from 2000 through 2010 exceeded that for the nation sufficiently to earn the Peach State a fourteenth seat in Congress. This addition came after having gained two seats in the 2000 census and one seat a decade earlier. The census showed Georgia to be the nation's ninth largest state poised to overtake Michigan for eighth place early in the next decade. Atlanta, the transportation and economic center for the South, provided most of the impetus for growth. The Atlanta metro area, which with 28 counties is the largest in the nation, contains the bulk of the state's population with almost 5.3 million residents at the time of the census. Atlanta's growth, which slowed but did not cease with the onset of the recession, came, in part, at the expense of other parts of Georgia. The southwest corner of the state and portions of the old cotton belt between Athens and Augusta actually lost population during the decade. More generally, the southern half of the state, the area below the fall line that extends from Augusta through Macon and on to Columbus, continued the trend more than half a century old and accounted for less and less of the state's population.

The Republican Party has grown apace with the state's population with much of the impetus for the GOP coming from outside Georgia. At the time of the 1990 census, aside from presidential contests, Georgia remained an azure blue state. Democrats held all of the statewide offices, all but one of the congressional seats, and 80 percent of the state legislative positions. A decade later, Republicans filled one Senate seat, eight of the eleven House seats, two statewide constitutional offices and more than 40 percent of the state legislative positions. The 2010 election saw Republicans complete their takeover of what had become a scarlet red state. Republicans controlled all 15 statewide partisan offices, eight of 13 congressional seats, and almost two-thirds of the state legislative seats.

As a result of their ascendance, 2011 marked the first time Republicans redrew the state legislature's districts. Republicans had crafted new congressional districts in 2005 immediately after taking control of the state house which gave them majorities of both legislative chambers and the governorship.

2001 REDISTRICTING

The Republicans who had their fingers on the redistricting mouse in 2011 found themselves in a very different position than Democrats had been a decade earlier. Following the 2000 census, Democrats desperately sought to prolong their control of the state legislature, a dominion they had ruled for 13 decades. With the state becoming increasingly Republican and with the most dramatic growth coming in Republican-leaning areas, Democrats in 2001 resorted to exceptional tactics. Democrats approached redistricting with goals that seemed extraordinary in light of the changes clearly underway. They hoped not simply to arrest their slide; they set their sights on taking seats away from the GOP.

Democratic goals for the congressional map had implications beyond Georgia. GOP control of the U.S. House rested on a paper thin margin of 221. If Georgia Democrats could win the two new seats and pick off a pair of sitting Republicans then the state might have reversed the partisan control of the House. That kind of success could breathe life into the whispers that Georgia Governor Roy Barnes had presidential ambitions.

To bolster Democratic prospects, the two new congressional districts were given substantial minority populations. The 12th District was configured as a bacon strip anchored in the north by the reliably Democratic college town of Athens. It then reached all the way to the coast to include the African American portion of Savannah. Along the way it picked up most of Augusta and also included several rural Black Belt counties. This district's population was 42.3 percent African American. Republicans, at this time, could usually win districts that were less than 30 percent black, but as districts became increasingly black, Republican prospects faded. Typically districts more than 40 percent African American elected Democrats. The other new district was placed in metro Atlanta and had a population almost evenly divided between blacks who composed 40.7 percent and whites who had 42.1 percent of the population. The authoritative *Almanac of American Politics* said of this district that it "can rightfully be depicted as the most geographically grotesque district in the country" (Barone with Cohen 2003, 491). This district, as shown in map 5.1, which some christened the "dead cat on the expressway" district, had its head in south Fulton. Clayton County provided the body with one front leg extending down to Griffin while the other front leg went all the way to Jackson in Butts County. One rear leg reached out to Lawrenceville in Gwinnett while the other leg extended all the way to Monroe in Walton County.

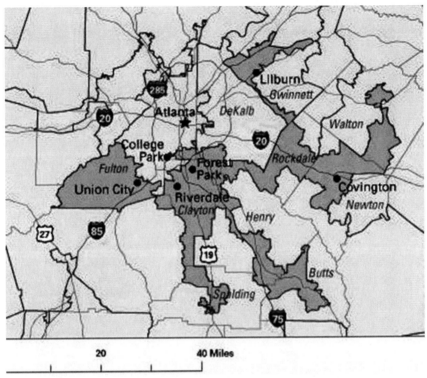

Map 5.1.   Georgia 13th Congressional District—2002. National Atlas of the United States, http://nationalatlas.gov/printable/images/preview/congdist/GA13_109.gif.

Not satisfied with creating two districts with black populations usually sufficient to elect a Democrat, those in charge of redistricting set out to eliminate two Republican incumbents by pairing them. The 1st District, which Jack Kingston had represented since 1993, was extended westward with a finger punched out to include the home of Saxby Chambliss who had represented the 8th District for eight years as shown in map 5.2. On the north side of Atlanta, John Linder and Bob Barr were also placed in the same district. These pairings resulted in two additional open seats. One of these, the 3rd District, filled much of the middle part of the state. With its population almost 40 percent black, it stood a good chance of electing a Democrat. The other district without an incumbent, the 11th, was another strange configuration. It extended along about half of Georgia's western border with Alabama but then also picked out parts of the northwestern and southwestern Atlanta suburbs including Marietta, the home of Lockheed Georgia. This 28 percent black district had supported George Bush in the 2000 presidential election but with only 51 percent of the vote. However, its average partisan vote for the three previous election years indicated support for Democrats below the presidential level. The most recent

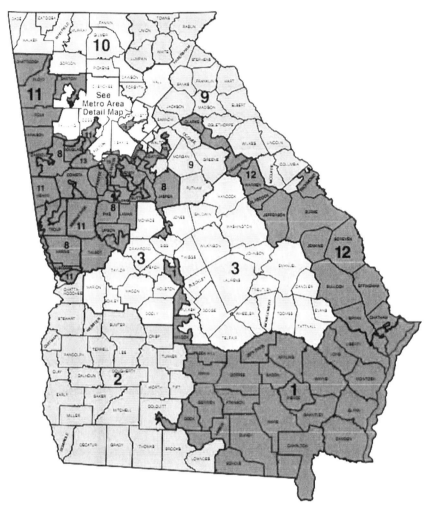

Map 5.2.   2002 Georgia Congressional Districts. Carl Vinson Institute of Government, University of Georgia.

election for statewide constitutional officers, 1998, showed this district casting 55 percent of its votes for Democrats, which encouraged Democrats to believe they could win this open seat.

Democrats went into the 2002 election with high hopes since there was no liberal member of their party heading the ticket in a presidential campaign. Moreover, Roy Barnes would be seeking reelection as governor, and Democrats had won the governorship in each of the last 50 elections. The 13th District performed as expected and David Scott won easily with 60 percent of the vote to become Georgia's fourth

African American in Congress. The 3rd District turned out to be surprisingly close, but Democrat Jim Marshall did eke out a 1,528 vote victory.

Republicans, however, won the other two open seats. Contributing to the GOP success were poor decisions made by Democrats in their primaries. In the 11th District Democrats rejected former member of Congress, Buddy Darden, who was hoping to restart a career interrupted in the Republican sweep of 1994. Darden, a moderate conservative, had served as district attorney and in the Georgia House before embarking on an eleven-year career in the U.S. House. Although Darden would have been a stronger general election candidate, he lost to wealthy, free-spending novice Roger Kahn. Kahn spent $2.8 million of his own money in an effort that outspent his opponent by two to one, but he managed only 48 percent against Republican Phil Gingrey.

The situation in the 12th District was bizarre. On the Republican side, college professor and rural county commissioner Max Burns narrowly defeated Barbara Dooley, the wife of legendary University of Georgia football coach Vince Dooley. Seven candidates entered the Democratic contest including one state legislator but with the winner being the son of the majority leader of the state Senate. Champ Walker, however, proved to be anything but a champion. Although not discovered by his primary opponents, it came out very early in the general election campaign that Walker's arrest record was far longer than his political record. He had been arrested multiple times for offenses including leaving the scene of an accident, driving without a license, and shoplifting. Although Walker pointed out that he had never been convicted, that explanation did not reassure voters. He did not help himself by avoiding debates against his Republican opponent. As a result, even though Al Gore had defeated George Bush by nine percentage points in the district and the Democratic vote figure for the 1998 elections showed the district to be 61 percent Democratic, Burns handily defeated Walker taking 55 percent of the vote.

Democratic hopes of winning a seven-six majority in the delegation came up short. Republicans retained their eight seats, but Democrats did gain two. The decision to put Chambliss and Kingston into the same district backfired badly on Democrats. Chambliss opted not to contest the Republican primary against his colleague and instead ran for the U.S. Senate where he unseated Democrat Max Cleland.

To appreciate fully the lengths to which Democrats went in their 2001 redistricting efforts, consider their plans for the state legislature. Democrats consistently over-populated Republican districts in order to absorb as many of their opponents in a minimal number of districts. At the same time they under-populated Democratic districts trying to stretch their limited resources. In addition, the new Democratic maps paired approximately half of all Republican incumbents thereby creating numerous open seats where Democrats would have better prospects for success than if they had to challenge sitting Republicans. In the state House plan, Democrats resurrected multi-member districts, a traditional practice that had ended in 1992. The multi-member districts illustrate stacking, one of the classic gerrymandering tactics as they combined one Republican district with two or more Democratic districts in order for Democrats to win all of the seats in the multi-member district.

In the 1990s, Georgia redistricters had learned how to string together distant populations at the behest of the Department of Justice (DOJ), which had ordered the state to maximize the number of majority black districts.[2] Georgia refined these skills at drawing districts having extraordinary shapes with narrow necks and long arms and fingers reaching out to capture designated populations in 2001 with the objective of linking geographically distant populations that shared a partisan tie. The plans often victimized Republicans by giving them districts that spread across multiple split counties making it difficult to campaign and almost guaranteeing that in the distant corners constituents would have little contact with their legislator. One congressional district, the new 13th, linked African Americans on the south side of Atlanta with black pockets in several of suburban county seats.[3]

2005 REDISTRICTING

Republicans completed their sweep of state government in 2004. Shortly before the primary filing date for that year's election, a three-judge federal court invalidated the state legislative maps. The court objected to the Democrats' decision to under-populate Atlanta and South Georgia districts at the expense of North Georgia and the suburbs. The judges pointed to the 1964 *Reynolds v. Sims* decision that required both legislative chambers to be based on population and not on geography. When the Democratic House and Republican Senate proved unable to agree on new maps, the judges hired Nathaniel Persily, a law professor at Columbia University well versed in redistricting, to serve as a consultant and devise new maps. Persily was provided with no political data and did not even know where the current incumbents lived. Moreover he was blocked from talking with Linda Meggers who had headed the Legislative Reapportionment Office for more than three decades. The maps Persily devised reduced population deviations to less than one percentage point and since he drew them free of an intent to benefit a political party, they allowed voters' preferences to translate more efficiently into seats. Persily's maps opened the way for Republican gains.[4] Republicans picked up 27 seats in the House to win a majority and added four seats in the Senate.

With the state legislature and the governorship now in GOP hands, the new ruling party set out to undo the Democratic congressional gerrymander. Georgia joined Texas as the only states to carry out a mid-decade congressional redistricting. In drawing new congressional districts, Republicans' top priority was to bolster the position of Phil Gingrey. The old district had given George Bush 51 percent of the vote in 2000. The new district had cast almost two-thirds of its ballots for Bush; Gingrey has continued to win reelection with comfortable margins.

A second objective was to unseat Jim Marshall. His district also became more Republican. The district in map 5.2 had cast 52 percent of its vote for Bush in

2000; Bush had won the replacement district, now the 8th District, with 58 percent. Map 5.3 shows that the new plan restored the district to a north-south axis that extended from near the Florida border into southeastern metro Atlanta. Republicans had strongly criticized Democrats for their disregard of county lines when drawing districts in 2001. The new map reduced the split counties in the 8th District from five to three. Moreover, it reunited the district's most populous county, Bibb, the home of the city of Macon. Marshall repeated his near death experience from 2002 winning reelection in 2006 with 51 percent of the vote. Had Republicans been willing to split Bibb and pull out the black population and

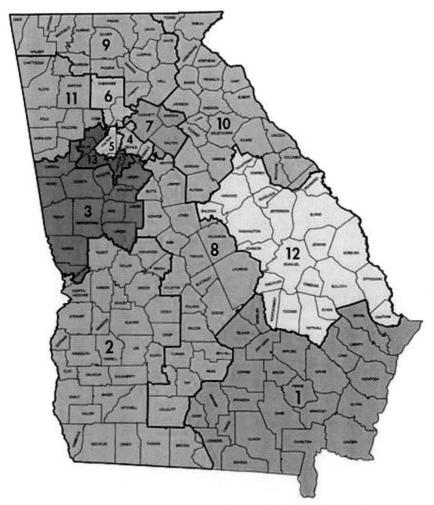

Map 5.3.   2006 Georgia Congressional Districts. Carl Vinson Institute of Government, University of Georgia.

replace it with whites, Marshall would probably have lost.[5] Instead, he held on until 2010 when he faced his most experienced challenger, seven-term House member Austin Scott and lost six percentage points.[6]

A third goal of the new maps sought to unseat John Barrow who had defeated Max Burns in 2004. Barrow's district lost its northern portion including his home in Athens. The new design kept the district largely in South Georgia. It became slightly blacker but also more Republican. This surprising combination resulted from the elimination of white moderates and liberals in Athens and their replacement with much more conservative rural whites. Barrow, like Marshall, also thwarted Republican designs but by an even narrower margin of fewer than 900 votes making him the most marginal Democratic incumbent reelected to the House in 2006.

A fourth result of the new Republican maps made districts generally more compact. The most dramatic change involved the "dead cat on the expressway" 13th District. Its new design consolidated it to the south and west of John Lewis's 5th District.

Unlike the Texas mid-decade redistricting orchestrated by U.S. House Majority Leader Tom DeLay, which resulted in a six-seat GOP pickup, Georgia's efforts did not immediately eliminate any Democratic incumbents. The only change in partisanship during the life of the 2005 map came in 2010 with Marshall's loss.

2011 REDISTRICTING

Governor Nathan Deal continued the practice of recent decades and convened a special session of the General Assembly in the late summer of 2011. As the legislators assembled, Republicans, for the first time, had the opportunity to draw the maps for state legislators. Republicans had continued to make gains in state House elections and several party switches after the 2010 results made obvious that Democrats were not going to become the majority in the near future, Republicans held 116 of the lower chamber's 180 seats. Gains in the Senate had been modest, but 36 of 56 senators assembling in Atlanta to draw new maps were Republican. With a Republican governor heading the executive branch, the GOP was positioned to work its will.

Unlike Democrats a decade earlier, Republicans had an infinite number of options, each of which would result in their continued control of the congressional and state legislative delegations. Their dominance did not mean, however, that Republicans were indifferent to the ways in which lines were drawn. They wanted to add two congressional seats to the eight they held and increase their share in the state legislature to two-thirds. A two-thirds majority would allow the Republicans to amend the state constitution with no need to win any Democratic support.

Each chamber has a committee responsible for reapportionment and redistricting, and since 1971 the legislature has maintained a reapportionment office. The office has a permanent staff which expands in anticipation of the decennial census and then shrinks again once statewide maps have secured approval. During the rest of the decade, a small staff makes minor adjustments to the state maps but also helps local entities that need to redraw council, commission, and school board districts. This office ensures that a trained staff is available to teach the necessary skills to those hired on a temporary basis.

Prior to the 2011 redistricting, the permanent staff worked not for the legislature but rather for the Carl Vinson Institute of Government at the University of Georgia. The services of the staff were available to any legislator, although the close ties between the director and the former speaker of the House led Republicans to question whether the advice was free of partisan bias and whether Republican confidences would be kept. As a consequence, beginning with the 1990 redistricting rounds, Republicans funded a separate effort. The original design with the three majority-black districts challenged in *Miller v. Johnson* came from the Republican-Black Caucus collaboration.[7] In 2001, the Republican effort was largely an academic exercise since they had no input into the design of the maps pushed through by Democrats.

In 2011 with the Republicans now in charge of the legislature, the ties to the University of Georgia were sundered, and the permanent staff of the office was moved onto the legislative payroll. The new director of the Legislative Reapportionment Office was an attorney who had worked in the Legislative Counsel's office. While he had little prior experience in redistricting, some of the existing staffers were proficient using the geographic information system to draw maps.

During the early summer, members of the legislative reapportionment committees held hearings in a dozen locations around the state. Several themes emerged in the course of the hearings. First, those who appeared at the hearings frequently asked that the legislature maintain their communities as a whole and not divide them among districts. Often speakers indicated less concern about whether their community ended up in a Democratic or a Republican district so long as it could be undivided. While the concept of "community of interest" is often difficult to define, many of the speakers seemingly thought of their county as a community of interest.

A second frequent plea, and this one is more naïve than the first, urged the legislators to keep politics out of the process. During his governorship, Sonny Perdue had appointed a blue ribbon commission to explore shifting redistricting in Georgia to an independent commission. The recommendations of that body never received serious consideration in the General Assembly, which meant that politics would undoubtedly play a role in the decisions to be rendered late in the summer of 2011.

Democrats, who anticipated that their desires would be given short shrift by the reapportionment committees, challenged the legislators at the public hearings to "show us the maps!" Technicians in the Legislative Reapportionment Office were meeting with legislators in order to gather information about potential designs, but lines remained fluid during the time of the hearings, which ended some six weeks before the special session.

Prior to the session each chamber adopted a set of principles. Top priority went to equalizing population, and for the congressional districts the goal was that all districts would be within plus or minus 1 percent of the ideal population. For the state legislative chambers, the goal was that population should be as "substantially equal as practicable" in light of other objectives. The second objective was to ensure that the maps comply with the Voting Rights Act (VRA). This was absolutely essential since Georgia is covered by Section 5 of the VRA and therefore must secure federal approval prior to implementing new maps. Although not spelled out in the principles, compliance with the VRA would mean that the maps not be guilty of retrogression. The non-retrogression standard as enunciated by the Supreme Court and reiterated in the guidelines provided by the Department of Justice (DOJ) means that racial minorities must not be left any worse off in the new maps than they were in the benchmark (pre-existing) plan. At a minimum the number of majority-minority districts would have to be maintained in the new maps. Although not necessary to achieve preclearance by DOJ, Georgia would also want to have maps that complied with Section 2 of the VRA. Section 2 requires that a new map should dilute the political influence of racial minorities, and in Georgia that has meant African Americans.

The next objective, and this received no explanation in the guidelines, called upon the committees to adopt plans fully compliant with all aspects of the U.S. and Georgia Constitutions. The fourth objective mandated that districts be contiguous. It specifically barred the practice of point contiguity where a district would be contiguous in the sense that the red or black squares on a checkerboard are contiguous at a point.

Republicans felt that they had been disadvantaged when Democrats drew a number of multi-member districts for the state House. Therefore one of the principles for 2011 banned multi-member districts.

Although not mandating that they be followed, the principles also directed the committees to consider several elements. The first among these was, to the extent possible, avoid dividing county and precincts. Of course, in the need to equalize populations, dividing some counties and precincts would be unavoidable. A second factor at this level called for compactness, although the guidelines did not specify what might constitute compactness. The third element to be considered was communities of interest. Again, the principles contain no definition for what might constitute a community of interest. At a lower level in the hierarchy of concerns came treatment of incumbents. The principles stated that "efforts should be made to avoid the unnecessary pairing of incumbents."

In 2011, Republicans did not have to resort to extraordinary measures in order to maintain and even expand their control of legislative seats. The maps that Republicans produced scored reasonably well in terms of compactness, unlike the maps from a decade earlier. While Republicans, unlike Democrats a decade earlier, did not seize every opportunity to exploit their advantage, they did draw maps that favored their party.

Republican's top priority was to ensure that the new congressional district gained as a result of Georgia's growth would be safely Republican. Since growth had disproportionately occurred in the Atlanta area, the new district would have to go somewhere in North Georgia, but a number of possibilities existed for placement.

Governor Deal had represented the 9th District from 1992 until he resigned to seek the governorship in 2010. His successor, chosen in a special election, came from west of Deal's hometown. In an historic first, both Georgia's governor and lieutenant governor came from Gainesville. The two leaders of the executive branch wanted their home town to anchor Georgia's new district. In his first year as governor, Deal had established excellent relations with Republicans in the General Assembly. The legislature deferred to the popular governor's wishes and made Gainesville the focal point for the new district. However, since Deal had represented the 9th District, he wanted to see that number retained by the new district, so the number 14 was assigned to what had been much of the western area he had represented but now had the individual who had succeeded Deal as its legislator.

The new 9th District has the smallest black population of any district in the state, with African Americans constituting less than 7 percent of the adult population. In the 2010 statewide elections, the new district had demonstrated greater loyalty to the GOP than any other district. Johnny Isakson won reelection to the U.S. Senate with 79 percent of the vote in this district.

A second GOP consideration involved the district in the middle of south Georgia that Austin Scott had taken from Jim Marshall in the previous fall. As shown repeatedly during the previous decade, the 8th District was the most competitive in the state. Republicans hoped to make it securely Republican. In order to secure the Republican grip on the newly acquired 8th District, the new maps shifted the bulk of Bibb County and most of its African Americans westward into Sanford Bishop's 2nd District. This change benefitted both parties. By moving Macon's African American population in to the 2nd District, it gave Bishop a majority black constituency for the first time since the 1996 redistricting. Not only was the new district more than 52 percent black in its total population, it had a narrow black majority among registered voters, an increase of more than 3 percentage points on this dimension. In 2010, nine-term incumbent Bishop had his narrowest brush with defeat holding off state legislator Mike Keown by less than 4,000 votes. Making the district somewhat blacker might well discourage a quality challenge from someone like Keown, and even if that did not obviate a serious challenge, the increased black population should enhance Bishop's reelection prospects. The black voters that shifted from the 8th to the 2nd District reduced the registration in the former from approximately one-third to 27 percent black. Reducing the black concentration rendered the new district approximately 4 percentage points more Republican. For Scott, who comes from the southern end of the district, campaigning will become easier. He picked up seven counties and parts of an eighth near his home. These additions allowed the district to shed its metro-Atlanta counties several hours to the north.

A third objective involved the state's last remaining congressional white Democrat, the 12th District's John Barrow. Prior to 1964, every representative from the five Deep South states had been a Democrat for generations. Now Barrow was the last of that breed that Republicans hoped to drive into extinction. To weaken Barrow,

Republicans removed Savannah's African Americans and pushed the 12th District northward to include all of Richmond County (Augusta) and parts of Augusta's most heavily Republican suburbs in Columbia County (see map 5.4). The new plan reduced the black population concentration from 44 to 35 percent.[8] The partisan change tracked closely with the racial change as the new district became 10 percentage points more Republican and, based on past experience, would give a Republican a comfortable margin. The one element that might save Barrow is his incumbency. Barrow is a tireless campaigner who regularly visits all parts of his district. Moreover, his talented fund-raiser Ashley Jones succeeds in making her boss one of the best

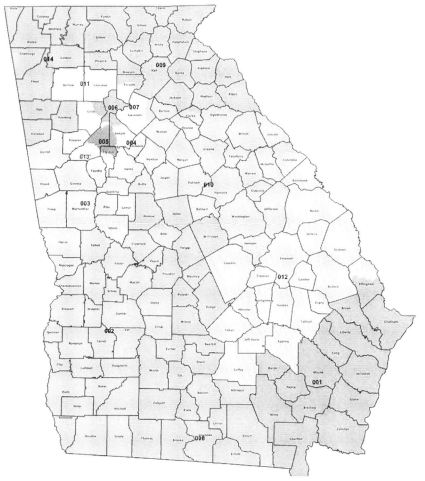

Map 5.4. 2012 Georgia Congressional Districts. Georgia Joint Reapportionment Office, www1.legis.ga.gov/legis/2011_12/house/Committees/reapportionment/gahl-crMaps.html.

funded Georgia legislators. In 2010, despite having only token opposition, Barrow raised almost $2 million. In 2006 after confronting an earlier redistricting that significantly changed his district, Barrow raised almost $2.5 million, substantially more than any other Georgia congressional candidate. With a target of $3 million, it is not surprising that Barrow was victorious in 2012.

A fourth concern, and this was certainly much less significant than the others, involved the 7th District. John Linder had retired after 18 years, and his long-time chief of staff Rob Woodall had succeeded him. The district, in Atlanta's northeast suburbs was becoming increasingly diverse, and Republican strength had been ebbing. Woodall won handily, but some worried that by the end of the decade, the district might become Democratic. In an effort to make the 7th District secure for Republicans for the next decade, it lost the southern part of Gwinnett County, which was becoming increasingly Democratic and moved into Forsyth County. Forsyth is the third most heavily Republican county in the state and in 2010 gave Republican candidates more than 80 percent of the vote.

Since Georgia must pass muster with federal authorities pursuant to Section 5 of the Voting Rights Act, the mapmakers took care to leave the four African American members of Congress no worse off in the new maps. As already noted, the 2nd District became more heavily black as it went about overcoming a population deficit of almost 9 percent. John Lewis's Atlanta district was under-populated by almost 9 percent. To bring the Lewis district up to the needed population, the new plan extended it into northern Clayton County, which has become the state's second most heavily black county, and incorporated more of southwest DeKalb County. In making these additions, the black population increased from 51.5 percent to 60.5 percent. The 4th District represented by Hank Johnson needed a population increase of almost 4 percent. Since it yielded some of its territory to Lewis, the 4th District moved eastward to include all of Rockdale and the western half of Newton County as well as more of southern Gwinnett County. The result of these additions boosted the black population from 57.5 percent to 59 percent. David Scott's 13th District was the one district with a black legislator that was over-populated, and it had to give up 13 percent of its population. In the new configuration, its black percentage dropped from 58.5 percent to 57 percent, but it continued to be strongly Democratic having given more than 60 percent of its votes to Democrats in 2010 statewide elections.

A couple of wrinkles entered the plans that had exclusively political explanations. A last-minute adjustment extended the 1st District into the northeast corner of Lowndes County so that Moody Air Force Base could be retained by Appropriations Committee member Jack Kingston.

Part of the adjustment of John Lewis's district shifted it out of the wealthy in-town Buckhead neighborhood. Most Buckhead residents identified as Republicans, but they had remained in Democrat Lewis's district so that all Republican members of Congress had equal opportunities to seek funding from these well-heeled residents. Tom Price had represented the northern part of Fulton County and coveted Buckhead. However Price had made the strategic mistake of defecting from the gubernatorial campaign of his fellow member of Congress Nathan Deal. When the Deal campaign confronted a whiff of scandal, Price switched his support to Karen Handel. But Deal rode out the questions about ethics and defeated Handel in the Republican runoff. Forgiveness only goes so far, and the governor's supporters were unwilling to allow Price the riches of Buckhead. Moreover giving Price Buckhead would mean that he would represent Deal since it houses the governor's mansion. To thwart their 2010 opponent, Phil Gingrey's 11th District that included two northern suburban counties and then part of Cobb County extended a finger into Fulton to snatch away Buckhead.

Assigning the northeastern corner of the state to the newly designed 9th District forced two other Republican districts to give way. The 10th District, which had stretched from Augusta to the North Carolina line, shifted four or five counties south. The state's smallest county, Clarke, got divided between the 9th and 10th Districts. To make up for losing its northern counties, the 10th District was shoved southward but picked up rural counties with relatively little population. To offset the potential population deficit, the 10th District moved westward to include all of four metropolitan Atlanta counties and parts of three others. The district remained overwhelmingly Republican, but its new design posed the potential that incumbent Paul Broun might face a primary challenge from an Atlanta-area Republican.

The other incumbent Republican dislocated as a result of the creation of the new 9th District, Tom Graves, had won the old 9th District in a special election to succeed Deal. The new plan removed eight counties and a portion of another from what had been the eastern flank of Graves's district. To replace these in the newly christened 14th District, Graves will have to campaign in five counties and a portion of another one in which he is unknown. His new district became much smaller and filled the northwestern corner of Georgia. Despite the change, it remains securely Republican.

Despite some dislocations, the new maps resulted in only one pairing of incumbents. John Barrow, who had moved from Athens when Clarke County was removed from his district in the 2005 redistricting to Savannah, now had to relocate again. The new maps placed his Savannah home in the same district with his old Clarke Central high school classmate Jack Kingston.

In pursuit of the objective to minimize the number of county splits, the map divided 16 counties. Predominantly rural districts had few splits. Six districts, as reported in table 5.1, split only two counties each. The 14th District splits a single county. Four districts reaching into the Atlanta suburbs each split three counties. Two counties, Fulton and Gwinnett, are too large to fit into a single district and therefore had to be split. Fulton ended divided among four districts, while Gwinnett, Cobb, DeKalb, and Henry were divided three ways. In contrast, the 2002 map drawn by Democrats split Gwinnett four ways and split six counties three ways. The 2002 map split 34 of Georgia's 159 counties.

Core retention measures the degree to which a new map disrupts existing relationships between constituents and their legislator. This measure indicates the share

Table 5.1. **Measures for Congressional Districts**

District	Compactness[1]	Core Retention	County Splits
1	.22	68.8	2
2	.31	77.8	2
3	.28	91.1	3
4	.27	66.7	3
5	.37	77.2	3
6	.27	76.8	3
7	.26	78.0	2
8	.16	63.6	2
9	.30	58.4	3
10	.27	37.3	5
11	.28	48.1	2
12	.18	53.2	2
13	.16	84.5	5
14	.31	45.5[2]	1
Average	.26	66.3	

1. Compactness is measured as the Polsby-Popper score.
2. This indicates the share of the population in the 14th District that Tom Graves represented when elected from the old 9th District.

of the population that continues to have the same representative in the new as in the old map. An unchanged district or a district that lost population but gained no one because of over-population would have a score of 100 percent. On average the districts retained about two-thirds of the people who had lived in the old district. At the upper limit, Lynn Westmoreland's 3rd District experienced the least change with 91 percent of the residents remaining the same. The most dramatically transformed, Paul Broun's 10th District, retained little more than a third of its former residents as it shifted south and west.

Often the majority party will see that its legislators keep more of their constituents than do the representatives from the minority party. That did not occur in Georgia. On average, the five districts represented by Democrats retained almost 72 percent of their constituents, while the eight districts with Republicans kept 65.3 percent of their old constituents. Part of the explanation for Democrats doing better than Republicans probably has to do with the Voting Rights Act non-retrogression standard. Each of the four districts represented by an African American retained more constituents than the average for all Republicans with David Scott in the 13th District keeping almost 85 percent of his constituents. The one Democrat who experienced the greatest change, John Barrow, whose career was clearly in the sights of the map makers, retained little more than half of his constituents.

Core retention in the 2011 maps contrasts sharply with the plan drawn a decade earlier by Democrats who desperately tried to follow the traditional practice of protecting their own. The average core retention for the three Democratic incumbents was almost 90 percent, while for the six Republican incumbents in 2001 it was only 72 percent.[9] For the entire map the average core retention was 77.2 percent of the old population.

The average compactness score reported in table 5.1 for the 2011 plan equaled the plan adopted after *Miller v. Johnson* invalidated the affirmative action gerrymander imposed in 1992. The average perimeter to area for the 1996 plan of 0.26 came from a plan drawn by the federal court. In contrast, the average compactness of the districts drawn by Democrats in 2001 was only 0.12. At the low end of the scale for the 2001 plan, one district had a compactness score of 0.03 meaning that if one configured a circle having the same perimeter as the outline of the district, the district would fill only 3 percent of that circle.

If the new districts perform as expected based on past election results, Republicans will sweep everything except the four districts represented by African Americans. John Lewis's 60 percent black district is projected to cast at least three-fourths of its votes for a Democrat. At the other extreme, the 9th District in northeast Georgia would be expected to give almost 80 percent of its votes to a Republican. None of the district is projected to be particularly competitive thus the new Georgia map follows the recent trend of crafting constituencies that tilt overwhelmingly in favor of one party or the other thereby reducing the responsiveness of the design as well as limiting the incentives for incumbents to do anything more than appeal to their committed partisans.

DEMOCRATIC OPPOSITION

As expected, Democrats objected to the GOP configurations. One complaint pointed to the disproportionate advantage Republicans seemed destined to gain from the new maps. Democrats contended that they should have a share of legislatives seats roughly proportional to their share of the electorate. The American electoral system with its single-member districts is not designed for a one-to-one translation of votes into seats. Even a non-partisan districting plan would almost certainly result in the majority party receiving a larger share of seats than its proportion of the votes. This is because the majority party usually wins a disproportionate share of the competitive seats. Indeed a widely accepted measure of bias assumes that the majority party will get a disproportionate share of the seats.[10] In an unbiased map, the advantage given to a majority party would be the same regardless of which party polled most of the votes. Most European systems result in parties getting about the same share of seats as votes, but the design of those systems is entirely different. The European systems have multi-member districts and award seats on the basis of the share of the votes that a party attracts.

Democrats pointed to the 47 percent of the vote won by Barack Obama and used that to argue that they should have majorities in about 47 percent of the districts. Even if one accepted that Democrats should get a share of seats proportional to their performance among voters, 47 percent would be a high point. In the 2010 elections for statewide constitutional officers, no Democratic candidate attracted as much as 44 percent of the vote, and some failed to even break 40 percent. In terms of the congressional maps, a 47 percent share of the congressional seats would result in an 8–6 Republican advantage or an evenly divided delegation. As noted above, Republicans hope that the maps will give them a ten-four advantage and expect to do no worse than win nine seats.

African American legislator Al Williams acknowledged that Republicans could control the process since they had a majority in the legislature, but he thought that they had exceeded their mandate. "I have no problem being in the minority and taking a spanking. But I just didn't want it to be a beat down."[11]

Maps that give one party a disproportionate advantage are not something that the Department of Justice will reject as violative of Section 5 of the VRA. A second argument might, however, have resonated with DOJ. Stacey Abrams, the minority leader in the House, asserted that the Republican objective was to resegregate the state.[12] She claimed that the Republican Party was using redistricting "to silence whites and isolate minorities into enclaves where no racial coalition can exist. This amounts to a resegregation of Georgia into a party of white Republicans and black Democrats, leaving Latinos and Asians to fend for themselves." Abrams called for "integrated political districts [that] proved that we are willing to work not only across the aisle but across the racial spectrum. Society is changing. Georgia cannot afford to be left behind." U.S. Representative John Lewis (D) agreed with Abrams's assessment. "Resegregation—call it what it is. If it walks like a duck, if it quacks like a duck, it's a duck. These maps fail to recognize both the spirit and the letter of the Voting Rights Act," fumed the civil rights icon.[13] The state's leading newspaper, *The Atlanta Journal Constitution*, seemingly agreed with Abrams's claims and headlined one article with: "White Democrat Faces Political Extinction."[14] Abrams elaborated, "Essentially, what's being created is a white Republican Party and black Democratic Party."[15]

A black senator from Atlanta, Vincent Fort, used fiery rhetoric to evoke wrongs from the past when castigating the Republican maps. "A hundred years ago, you used to take away the vote with a whip and a noose. Today you take it away with computers and hard drives and other electronic equipment. It wasn't right then, and it wasn't right now."[16]

The non-retrogression standard used by DOJ when evaluating plans submitted by Section 5 states protects minority legislative seats. Abrams worried that those might be the only Democratic seats under the new maps. With the Republican effort to unseat John Barrow by making his 12th District whiter and more Republican, the potential for the Georgia delegation to have ten white Republicans and four black Democrats was not unrealistic. Her criticisms, however, did not stop with the congressional maps. The Senate map had 18 districts that had histories of voting for Democrats, and of these, 15 were majority black. The plan divided the one rural white Democratic senator's district between two others so that future white Democratic senators might come exclusively from the Atlanta metropolitan area. The new House plan had 56 districts that had voted for Democrats in the past, and of these

49 had black population majorities and 48 were majority black among their registered voters. Democrats worried that with these plans in place, the Democratic Party would be seen as the black party.

Jason Carter, grandson of the former president, led the Democratic forces in the Senate on redistricting. The young senator argued that white Democrats who had secured support from black voters deserved protection under Section 5 of the Voting Rights Act. His logic was that these whites were the candidates of choice of black voters and eliminating them would reduce black political influence. The same argument had been launched in Texas in 2003 in litigation challenging the redistricting plan drawn at the behest of U.S. House Majority Leader Tom DeLay. These claims had proven unavailing in the Texas litigation. Carter characterized his claims as "new legal ground" and indicated his interest in litigating the issue.[17] Since the Department of Justice approved Georgia's maps, if this issue is to be litigated, it may be up to Carter and his law firm to deliver on the threat.

The 2010 election had demonstrated that the lines between Democrat and Republican and black and white had moved ever closer together. Estimates put the share of the white vote going for Democratic candidates running statewide in 2010 at approximately 20 percent. On the other hand, Democrats won 95 percent of the black vote. A party which can attract only one in four or one in five white voters has no hope of winning statewide offices even when attracting 95 percent of the black vote.

Republicans responded to the minority leader's critiques noting that pursuant to Section 5 of the Voting Rights Act, Georgia *must* maintain existing minority districts. Republicans emphasized that in meeting Section 5 obligations they had the same number of majority-black seats in the House as in the benchmark plan, added a majority-black Senate district, and raised the African American population to a majority in an additional congressional district. Anything less, Republicans said would result in the maps not satisfying federal law.

Stacey Abrams believed Republican actions violated the spirit of the VRA. She noted that civil rights legislation "did not seek to shuffle minority voters into enclaves with their own legislators in isolated voting districts. And it surely did not imagine a white party and black party."[18] In response to the criticism that their maps promoted segregation, the chair of the Senate Reapportionment Committee responded, "I'm into following the law."[19]

By bringing part of Phil Gingrey's district into Buckhead, a Republican will represent part of the city of Atlanta for the first time since Fletcher Thompson left the House to run for the Senate in 1972. John Lewis, who had represented Buckhead and the rest of Atlanta since 1987, saw the removal of part of the city from his district as "an affront to the spirit and the letter of the Voting Rights Act. The city of Atlanta should remain whole and attempts to split the city are nothing more than naked partisanships."[20] The Republican whip in the state House responded, "It's important for the city of Atlanta, the capital city of our state, to have strong congressional representation on both sides of the political aisle so our needs and interests are taken care of regardless of who is in power in the White House or Congress."[21]

Some observers saw the 2011 maps as the culmination of a trend begun 20 years earlier. House Minority Leader Abrams acknowledged her party's complicity. "Democrats screwed it up when we had it, and Republicans are screwing it up now."[22] Michael Thurmond chaired the Georgia's Legislative Black Caucus during the 1991–1992 redistricting sessions. He had sought a second majority-black congressional district but opposed the efforts by a minority of the Caucus who demanded and ultimately received at the hands of the Department of Justice a third majority black district.[23] The plan that designed three majority-black districts was christened Max Black since it maximized the number of black seats. After reviewing the 2011 maps, Thurmond recalled, "I knew the Max Black strategy would lead to less influence. I prayed that I was wrong, but it turned out I wasn't."[24]

To achieve the Max Black goals required an unprecedented ignoring of county boundaries and the drawing of the least compact congressional districts the state had ever seen. The legislature, under the demanding eye of DOJ, linked together distant black populations while excising nearby white census blocks in order to boost the black percentage. Ultimately the Supreme Court chastised DOJ attorneys for the bias they displayed in reviewing Georgia's maps and concluded that by forcing the state to consider only race when drawing these districts it violated the Equal Protection Clause of the 14th Amendment.[25] The Supreme Court undid the maps, but traditional respect for county boundaries had been sundered. Ten years later Democrats in their desperate bid to win seats in the face of growing voter affection for the GOP continued splitting counties but guided this time by efforts to separate Democrats from Republicans. In 2011 Democratic critics claimed that Republicans had continued the practice of separating Democrats from Republicans, and since Democratic loyalists had now become predominantly black, this had the effect of separating black from white. A major difference, however, was that the Republican boundaries resulted in far more compact districts, as noted above, than did the lines drawn at the behest of DOJ or by Democrats in 2001.

A consequence of drawing four majority-black districts and ten heavily white districts will likely mean that none of them is competitive at least in the early years of the plan's life. When the results from 2010 elections are imposed on the new districts, ten of them gave Senator Johnny Isakson at least 60 percent of the vote in his reelection bid while in the four majority-black districts Isakson's Democratic opponent won two by landslide margins. In the 2010 gubernatorial contest the Republican (Deal) won nine of the districts with at least 55 percent of the vote, and in a tenth district with a Republican member of Congress, Deal took 54.95 percent of the vote. The four majority-black districts gave the Democratic gubernatorial nominees at least 57 percent of the vote.

PLAN SUBMISSION

Georgia had to secure approval of the maps from federal authorities before using the new districts in the 2012 election. Two paths exist for obtaining approval. The administrative path, which has been most frequently taken by Section 5 jurisdictions, involves submitting the plans to Department of Justice. DOJ then has 60 days to decide whether the plans are retrogressive. The burden of proving that the plans have neither a discriminatory intent nor a discriminatory effect is borne by the submitting jurisdiction.[26]

The alternative approval process, which Georgia pursued in 2001, seeks a declaratory judgment by the district court of the District of Columbia that the plans are not discriminatory. At the trial DOJ serves as the defendant. Therefore DOJ has input into the assessment of the fairness of the plans either way. The difference is that in the judicial approach, DOJ is the opposing party. In the administrative approach, DOJ is both the opponent but also the "judge."

In 2011, Georgia's Republican administration had concerns that it might not receive fair treatment from DOJ, which was in Democratic hands for the first time of a major redistricting. A second concern was that DOJ might prolong the process which could delay the time for qualifying candidates for the 2012 election cycle. Ten years earlier, Democrats had opted for the judicial route in order to deny the Bush Justice Department complete control over the fate of their gerrymander.

While political parties have worried that if the opposition party controlled DOJ it might impact the approval process for their plans, the partisan nature of the plans should not be a consideration. The only issue for DOJ or the court to consider in a Section 5 submission is whether a plan is guilty of retrogression. That is, does the proposal make it less likely that minorities can elect their preferred candidates than under the benchmark plan?

In 2011, Georgia followed five other states and added a new wrinkle to the submission process. The state first filed suit in the District of Columbia; a few days later, Georgia submitted its maps to DOJ.[27] If DOJ responded affirmatively and quickly, the suit would become moot. On the other hand, if DOJ dragged its feet by asking for additional information after receipt of which the agency would have yet another 60 days to consider the plans, or if DOJ objected to one or more of the plans, then the litigation process would already be under way.

Some observers speculated that by doing dual submissions, Georgia and other states threatened the entire Section 5 review process. During the 2006 debate and hearings considering the extension of Section 5 for another 25 years, questions arose about the appropriateness of continuing the involvement of the federal government in what had traditionally been a local or state process. When initially asked to rule on the constitutionality of Section 5, the Supreme Court accepted the extraordinary oversight of requiring federal approval before implementation of state or local actions on the grounds that the obstacles to black participation had been so pervasive and persistent and southern jurisdictions had operated in such bad faith for so long that a major adjustment in federalism was necessary in the short run.[28] The 1965 VRA authorized Section 5 preclearance for only five years. Congress granted extensions in 1970, 1975, 1982, and then most recently in 2006. The basis for the initial coverage of Section 5 had been low participation rates in the 1964 presidential election coupled with the use of literacy tests as preconditions for registering to vote. By 2006, black participation rates in Georgia and the other states subject to Section 5 closely approximated those for whites. Moreover, black participation in Georgia and in most of the other Section 5 states, differed little from that in the rest of the nation and frequently exceeded participation rates for African Americans in states not subject to preclearance.[29] Some have warned Congress that failure to change the basis for requiring Section 5 coverage risked having the provision struck down as unconstitutional.[30] Holding the threat of litigation over DOJ's head by submitting the 2011 plans for judicial review might prompt the agency to approve the plans. To make the threat explicit, Georgia's pleadings in the district court asked that if any part of the plans were found to be in conflict with Section 5 then the court should find Section 5 to be unconstitutional.

PLANS APPROVED

Although numerous individuals asked DOJ to reject the plans, these pleas carried no weight. On December 23, 2011, DOJ approved all three Georgia maps. This marked the first time that Georgia had secured federal approval of the first draft of all of its maps. Undoubtedly many of the criticisms were irrelevant since they complained about the partisan nature of the plans rather than identifying aspects of racial discrimination. Some of the admonitions to contact DOJ noted the partisan nature of the plans.

DOJ approval notwithstanding, Georgia may not be completely in the clear. The litigation threatened by Jason Carter and other Democrats may still take place. Democrats could seek to prove that the Republican plans constitute an actionable partisan gerrymander. However, since no one has ever succeeded in a partisan gerrymandering case, that seems a long shot.

Republicans took care to eliminate one possible line of attack. In the past, plaintiffs have often succeeded when they could show the court a plan that had less population deviation than that adopted by the state. However, since the new map has a range in district populations of only 2 percent, a claim that the plan violates the Equal Protection Clause would be almost impossible.

A more likely approach will be for the challengers to claim that the Republican plans violate Section 2 of the Voting Rights Act. Success under this provision of the VRA requires a showing that the plans unfairly dilute minority political influence. Section 2 differs from Section 5 in that the latter compares the treatment of minorities in a new plan against the benchmark while Section 2 asks whether the political influence of a minority group has been diluted in that minorities have less opportunity to elect their preferences than do other voters. DOJ approval does not inoculate a jurisdiction from a successful Section 2 challenge. A Section 2 challenge in Georgia may be difficult since the state created an additional majority black congressional district. Democrats might argue that since John Barrow has relied upon strong support in the African American community to win his 12th-District seat, reducing the black concentration in that district dilutes black political influence. In 2003, when Texas Republicans redrew that state's congressional districts with an eye toward eliminating the white Democrats in the delegation, opponents argued that the Democrats should be protected under Section 2 because they were the preferred candidates of black and Hispanic voters. Those claims yielded no success in Texas.

If legal challenges to the plan are successful, it would involve drawing new lines prior to 2014. Georgia and a number of other states have in the past had to produce such new maps following a court ruling invalidating the current plan.

NOTES

1. I appreciate the careful reading Bryan Tyson gave an earlier draft of this chapter.

2. On the Max Black redistricting approach imposed on Georgia in 1992, see Charles S. Bullock III, *Redistricting: The Most Political Activity in America* (Lanham, MD: Rowman & Littlefield, 2010), chapter 6; Robert A. Holmes, "Reapportionment Strategies in the 1990s: The Case of Georgia," in Bernard Grofman, ed., *Race and Redistricting in the 1990s* (New York: Agathon, 1998): 191–228.

3. Ronald Keith Gaddie and Charles S. Bullock III, "From *Ashcroft* to *Larios*: Recent Redistricting Lessons from Georgia," *Fordham Urban Law Journal* 34 (April 2007): 997–1048.

4. The maps actually used involved some modification of Persily's proposal. Since he had no information on the location of incumbents' homes, his maps paired many of them while leaving adjacent districts open. Both Democrats and Republicans made proposals to the three-judge panel to unpair incumbents. To the extent that it could easily do so, the court granted those requests.

5. M.V. Hood III, and Seth C. McKee, "Trying to Thread the Needle: The Effects of Redistricting in a Georgia Congressional District," *PS* 42 (October 2009).

6. Charles S. Bullock III and Karen P. Owen, "*Marshall vs. Scott* in Georgia's Eighth Congressional District: The Power of Incumbency Fails," in Randall E. Adkins and David Dulio, eds., *Cases in Congressional Campaigns: Riding the Wave* (New York: Routledge, 2012), 219–38.

7. *Miller v. Johnson*, 515 U.S. 900 (1995).

8. The black share among registered voters declined from 42.5 percent to less than one-third.

9. Georgia had eight incumbent Republicans going into the 2002 election, but as noted previously, the plans drawn by Democrats paired two sets of Republican incumbents. One, Saxby Chambliss, opted to run for the U.S. Senate. In the other pairing John Linder, who brought 34.3 percent of his constituents into the new 7th District, defeated Bob Barr, 18.5 percent of whose former constituents appeared in the new 7th.

10. Andrew Gelman and Gary King, "A Unified Method of Evaluating Electoral Systems and Redistricting Plans," *American Journal of Political Science* 38 (May 1994): 514–54.

11. Errin Haines, "Voting Maps Ok'd over Dem Objections," *Athens Banner Herald* (August 19, 2011): A6.

12. Stacey Abrams, "Integrate, Don't Resegregate," *Atlanta Journal Constitution* (September 8, 2011): A14.

13. Jim Galloway, John Perry, Aaron Gould Sheinin, and Christina Torres, "Revamped Districts Further Polarize," *Atlanta Journal Constitution* (August 28, 2011): A1, A6.

14. Bill Torpy, "White Democrat Faces Political Extinction," *Atlanta Journal Constitution* (August 28, 2011): B1, B7.

15. Blake Aued, "Novel Challenge to Voting Maps," *Athens Banner Herald* (August 27, 2011): A8.

16. Jim Galloway, "Mapping Political History," *Atlanta Journal Constitution* (August 21, 2011): B3.

17. Aaron Gould Sheinin and Kristina Torres, "Week One and Redistricting: What Happened, What's Next," *Atlanta Journal Constitution* (August 21, 2011): B2.

18. Ibid., p. A6.

19. Ibid.

20. Aaron Gould Sheinin and Kristina Torres, "Plans Split Atlanta District," *Atlanta Journal Constitution* (August 23, 2011): A6.

21. Ibid.

22. Blake Aued, "Novel Challenge to Voting Maps," *Athens Banner Herald* (August 27, 2011): A8; see also Galloway, "Mapping Political History."

23. On the efforts of some members of the Legislative Black Caucus to force the crafting of a third majority-black district, see Robert A. Holmes, "Reapportionment Strategies in the 1990s: The Case of Georgia," in Bernard Grofman, ed., *Race and Redistricting in the 1990s* (New York: Agathon, 1998), 191–228.

24. Galloway et al., "Revamped Districts Further Polarize," p. A6.

25. *Miller v. Johnson,* 515 U.S. 900 (1995).

26. *Georgia v. United States,* 411 U.S. 526 (1973).

27. Not every Section 5 state followed the dual submission route. Texas initially submitted plans to DOJ, but before the department rendered a decision, Texas withdrew its plans and submitted them to the District of Columbia Court. The court rejected the congressional plans on the grounds that they did not provide sufficient electoral opportunities for Hispanics.

28. *South Carolina v. Katzenbach,* 383 U.S. 301 (1996).

29. Charles S. Bullock III and Ronald Keith Gaddie, *The Triumph of Voting Rights in the South* (Norman: University of Oklahoma Press, 2009).

30. Ibid.

6

"Fair" Districts in Florida

New Congressional Seats, New Constitutional Standards, Same Old Republican Advantage?

Aubrey Jewett

Population growth and increasing demographic diversity, new voter-approved state constitutional standards designed to curtail gerrymandering by the legislature, and Republican control of state government all affected redistricting in Florida in 2012. Florida gained almost 3 million people in the decade following the 2000 census bringing the state population to about 19 million by 2010. Hispanic growth accounted for more than half of the overall population increase, and Florida's black population grew substantially as well. Growth was most pronounced in Central and Southwest Florida, and Hispanic (mostly Puerto Rican) population growth was particularly robust across the Interstate-4 (I-4) corridor that traverses the middle of the state. Florida's overall population increase resulted in the apportionment of two new congressional seats for the Sunshine State in 2012 and required the Florida legislature to draw district lines for 27 seats rather than the existing 25.

In November 2010, Florida voters passed two amendments to the Florida Constitution giving the legislature guidelines to follow while drawing the new district lines. The amendments (one for legislative and one for congressional redistricting) prohibit the drawing of new district lines with the intent of favoring or disfavoring political parties or incumbents or the intent or result of diminishing minority representation and require districts to be compact and follow existing geographic and political boundaries where feasible. The "Fair Disricts" constitutional amendments were placed on the ballot and promoted by a coalition of non-partisan good government and Democratic affiliated groups who were upset with the overt partisan gerrymandering that occurred after the 2000 census. Republicans seized control of the Florida legislative and executive branches for the first time since Reconstruction in the late 1990s and used the 2002 redistricting to pack blacks and other Democratic supporters into relatively few districts. This helped Republicans maintain control of the legislature and congressional delegation throughout the subsequent decade despite being the minority party in terms of statewide voter registration.

In 2012, with strong majorities in the Florida House and Senate and control of the governor's office, Republicans again completely controlled the redistricting process. GOP legislators managed to draw new congressional district lines that favored their party despite the new constitutional standards and despite the fact that there were half a million more registered Democrats in the state than there were Republicans. GOP legislators maintained that the federal Voting Rights Act (VRA) required no retrogression of current minority voting districts and therefore that standards in the new Florida constitutional amendment referencing minorities must take precedence over the other new standards. Following this logic, they packed minority residents into five existing black and six existing Cuban-Hispanic majority or influence congressional districts and drew a new Puerto Rican-Hispanic leaning district in Central Florida. The three black majority-minority districts all had more than 60 percent Democratic registration and the two black and one Puerto Rican influence districts all had more than 50 percent Democratic registration, leaving surrounding districts more favorable to the GOP. Republican legislators maintain that the Republican advantage did not occur because of intentional partisan or incumbent gerrymandering that would violate Florida's new constitutional amendment, but rather because they followed the letter of the law concerning minority voting rights.

The "Fair Districts" coalition of Democrats and good government groups sued in state court seeking to have the congressional map invalidated and redrawn (the Florida Supreme Court automatically reviews the proposed state House and Senate maps). However the Circuit Court denied the motion for summary judgment, declared the legislatively drawn congressional districts valid on their face, and ruled they could be used without change. And on the same day, the U.S. Department of Justice (DOJ) gave VRA preclearance to both the congressional and legislative maps. While additional lawsuits are ongoing, even if the courts rule in favor of the challengers, it is likely that the new maps will still favor the Republican Party to some degree because of the legal requirement for ethnic and racial gerrymandering to ensure adequate minority representation. Alternative maps proposed by the Democratic Party and a coalition of good government groups do make the congressional districts more evenly divided between the two parties. However they do so in part by reducing the percentage of minority groups in a number of districts below their current levels (including reducing one from over 50 percent black to fewer than 40 percent), and so those maps themselves may violate the VRA. Thus regardless of the outcome of future court battles, Florida Republicans will likely continue to have a partisan advantage in legislative and congressional elections throughout the coming decade based on favorable district composition.

DEMOGRAPHIC TRENDS IN FLORIDA

Florida grew at a rapid pace for the past sixty years with a population increase of 578 percent between 1950 and 2010, although population growth has slowed since the beginning of the Great Recession in 2007.[1] Florida is the 4th largest state and is expected to overtake New York for 3rd place in the coming decade. Florida is also a very diverse state with the highest percentage of senior citizens of any state, the 6th highest percentage of Hispanic residents, and the 11th highest percentage of black residents. Over the last century Florida's population centroid, or exact population center, has shifted south from Jefferson County in the Panhandle to Polk County in Central Florida as more and more people moved to Central and South Florida. Florida is also a very urban state (ranking 6th out of 50 states) with about 85 percent living in an urban area within ten miles of the coast. Florida's population and political culture have often been described as "rootless"[2] since so few of its residents were born in Florida (just 35 percent in 2010—2nd lowest in the country, only greater than Nevada) and since there is a great deal of population churning (during much of the last decade one person moved out of Florida for every two persons that moved in).

Table 6.1 indicates that Florida's overall population grew by 17.6 percent over the decade and that 18,801,310 people lived in the state by 2010. Non-Hispanic white population grew slowly by about 4 percent to almost 11 million and is about 60 percent of Florida's total population (this is down from 65 percent in 2000). Hispanic population grew by 57 percent to over four million and Hispanics make up 22.5 percent of Florida's population (up from 17 percent in 2000). Within the Hispanic community Cubans are the largest subgroup (1.2 million) followed by Puerto Ricans (850,000) and Mexicans (630,000). Cubans have long dominated Hispanic politics in Florida because of their numbers, concentration, shared ideology and easier path to citizenship.[3] However the Puerto Rican and Mexican population grew at a faster rate (76 percent and 73 percent respectively) compared to the Cuban population (45 percent). The Puerto Rican population is beginning to exercise more political clout as their numbers grow and because they have the political advantage over other

Table 6.1. Florida Demographics, 2000 to 2010

Characteristic	2000 (#)	2010 (#)	2010 (%)	2000–2010 % Change
Total Population	15,982,738	18,801,310		17.6
White Non-Hispanic	10,458,509	10,884,722	57.9	4.1
Hispanic	2,682,715	4,223,806	22.5	57.4
Cuban	833,120	1,213,438	6.5	45.6
Puerto Rican	482,027	847,550	4.5	75.8
Mexican	363,925	629,718	3.3	73.0
Black	2,335,505	2,999,862	16.0	28.4
Asian	266,256	454,821	2.4	70.8
Native American	53,541	71,458	.4	33.5

Source: U.S. Census Bureau, American Fact Finder, 2000 and 2010.

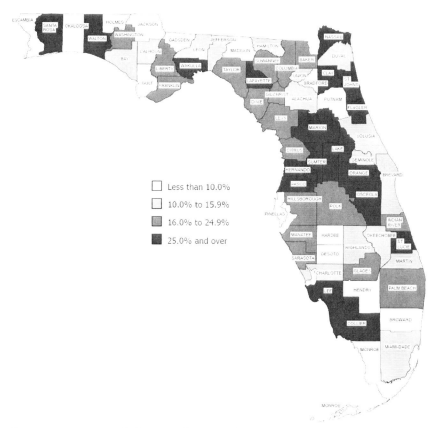

Map 6.1.   County Population Growth Rate in Florida, 2000–2010. Bureau of Economic and Business Research, "Florida Population: Census Summary 2010," April 2011.

Hispanic subgroups of being U.S. citizens. Florida's black population grew by 28 percent to almost three million residents and makes up 16 percent of the Florida population (up from 14.6 percent in 2000). Florida's increasing population and diversity mirror the demographic changes occurring in the United States.

While Florida's overall population grew by almost 3 million people, map 6.1 shows that there were substantial differences in growth rates in different regions and counties in the state. Central Florida was the fastest growing region with 7 counties growing at more than 25 percent including Sumter at 75 percent (8th fastest in the United States) and Osceola at 56 percent. Southwest Florida also grew rapidly (Lee and Collier over 25 percent) as did Northeast Florida with 4 counties over 25 percent including Flagler at 92 percent (3rd fastest in the United States) and St. Johns at 54 percent. Overall the Panhandle region (9 counties at less than 10 percent) and South Central Florida (4 counties at less than 10 percent) grew the slowest. Only 2 counties in Florida actually lost population over the decade: Pinellas on the Gulf Coast lost about 5,000 residents, and Monroe (including Key West) at the tip of Florida lost about 6,500. While Florida's other 65 counties did grow over the decade, 24 counties actually lost some population towards the end of the decade from their peak in 2007. The Great Recession that engulfed Florida, along with declining house prices and increasing unemployment, caused out-migration in these counties for the last several years of the decade.

Table 6.2 displays the ten largest and smallest counties in Florida. The three largest counties are all in Southeast Florida: Miami-Dade, Broward, and Palm Beach. Five of the largest Counties are in Central Florida: Hillsborough, Orange, Pinellas, Polk, and Brevard. Only one of the largest counties is in North Florida: Duval. Conversely, nine of the smallest counties are in the Panhandle. The only exception, Glades, is in South Central Florida.

Florida's growing minority population is also unequally distributed around the state (see table 6.3). By percentage of county residents, blacks are more concentrated in the rural Panhandle in North Florida. However, in terms of sheer population, the largest numbers of blacks live in urban Southeast and Central Florida. Eight of the ten counties with the highest percentage of black residents are in North Florida. Six of these are near Tallahassee, the state capitol: Jackson, Leon, Hamilton, Jefferson, Madison, and Gadsen (which is the only county in Florida with a majority of black residents at 56 percent). However, with the exception of Leon, these counties (and also Union) do not have many residents. In addition to Leon, Panhandle counties with high percentages and large numbers of black residents also include Duval in Northeast Florida and Escambia in the Western Panhandle. Counties with the highest number of black residents cluster in two areas. In Southeast Florida, Miami Dade, Broward, and Palm Beach combined have over 1.2 million black residents. A large number of blacks in this region are immigrants

Table 6.2. Florida's Largest and Smallest Counties by Population

Largest Counties (Mostly South and Central Florida)		Smallest Counties (Mostly North Florida)	
Miami-Dade	2,496,435	Liberty	8,365
Broward	1,748,066	Lafayette	8,870
Palm Beach	1,320,134	Franklin	11,549
Hillsborough	1,229,226	Glades	12,884
Orange	1,145,956	Calhoun	14,625
Pinellas	916,542	Jefferson	14,761
Duval	864,263	Hamilton	14,799
Lee	618,754	Union	15,535
Polk	602,095	Gulf	15,863
Brevard	543,376	Dixie	16,422

Source: U.S. Census Bureau, 2010 census.

Table 6.3.   Florida's Largest Black Population by County

Counties with Highest Percentage (Mostly Rural North Florida)		Counties with Highest Number (Mostly Urban South and Central Florida)	
Gadsen	56.7	Miami-Dade	495,865
Madison	39.4	Broward	492,887
Jefferson	36.7	Duval	266,600
Hamilton	35.3	Orange	255,384
Leon	31.4	Palm Beach	241,177
Duval	30.8	Hillsborough	222,529
Jackson	27.6	Pinellas	103,294
Broward	26.2	Polk	95,359
Escambia	24.2	Leon	86,610
Union	22.9	Escambia	72,146

Source: U.S. Census Bureau, 2010 census.

from Haiti, Jamaica, and other Caribbean Islands. And in Central Florida, along the I-4 Corridor, Orange, Hillsborough, Pinellas, and Polk combined have almost 700,000 black residents. The counties with the lowest percentage of black residents tend to be on the Gulf Coast in the Central and Southwestern parts of the state. Black Floridians, like blacks in most of the country, tend to identify with and vote for the Democratic Party, although blacks from the Caribbean are slightly more likely to be politically independent or Republican.

The ten counties with the greatest number of Hispanics in Florida contain almost 80 percent of the state's total Hispanic population (see table 6.4). Southeast and Central Florida have most of the state's Hispanic population while North Florida has relatively few Hispanic residents. Miami-Dade alone, with 1.6 million Hispanics (65 percent of the county population), has more than 38 percent of the state's total Hispanic population. Miami-Dade, along with Broward and Palm Beach, give Southeast Florida more than 2.3 million Hispanics—more than 50 percent of the state's total Hispanic population. Cuban's are the largest Hispanic subgroup in Florida and are concentrated mainly in Southeast Florida—particularly Miami-Dade which has over 850,000 Cubans who make up more than ⅓ of the total county population. Cubans have traditionally been Republican, although younger Cubans are becoming more politically independent or Democratic. Cubans have dominated Hispanic politics in Florida for some years in terms of voting and office holding. Central Florida also has several counties with large Hispanic populations including Orange, Hillsborough, Osceola (where Hispanics make up over 45 percent of the county population), Polk, and Pinellas which combined have almost 1 million Hispanic residents. Puerto Ricans are the 2nd largest Hispanic subgroup in Florida (and growing faster than the Cuban population) and are clustered in Central Florida, with more than 220,000

Table 6.4. Florida's Largest Hispanic Population by County

County (Sub-group)	Hispanic Population	% of County Population	County (Sub-group)	Hispanic Population	% of County Population
Miami-Dade	1,623,859	65.0	Osceola	122,146	45.5
Cuban	856,007	34.3	Puerto Rican	72,986	27.7
Puerto Rican	92,358	3.7	Mexican	7,381	2.7
Mexican	51,736	2.1	Cuban	5,424	2.0
Broward	438,247	25.1	Lee	113,308	18.3
Cuban	83,713	4.8	Mexican	34,212	5.5
Puerto Rican	75,840	4.3	Puerto Rican	24,503	4.0
Mexican	29,917	1.7	Cuban	20,253	3.3
Orange	308,244	26.9	Polk	106,532	17.7
Puerto Rican	149,557	13.0	Mexican	45,725	7.6
Mexican	36,652	3.2	Puerto Rican	34,825	5.8
Cuban	22,528	2.0	Cuban	6,992	1.2
Hillsborough	306,635	24.9	Pinellas	73,241	8.0
Puerto Rican	91,476	7.4	Mexican	22,093	2.4
Mexican	65,578	5.3	Puerto Rican	21,550	2.4
Cuban	65,451	5.3	Cuban	8,029	.9
Palm Beach	250,823	19	Duval	65,398	7.6
Mexican	49,141	3.7	Puerto Rican	21,634	2.5
Cuban	43,038	3.3	Mexican	14,415	1.7
Puerto Rican	39,529	3.0	Cuban	7,214	.8

Source: U.S. Census Bureau, 2010 census, County Profile of General Demographic Characteristics.

Puerto Ricans living in Orange and Osceola alone. Puerto Ricans in Florida lean Democratic but are considered "in play" by both major political parties. Puerto Ricans are beginning to emerge as a more powerful force in Florida politics in both voting and office holding. Mexican is the 3rd largest Hispanic subgroup in Florida, and these residents tend to be Democratic. But since Floridians of Mexican descent are more widely dispersed and frequently not citizens they have wielded little political power in the state.

A BRIEF HISTORY OF REAPPORTIONMENT
AND REDISTRICTING IN FLORIDA

Previous to 1962, the Florida legislature was malapportioned—that is, there were unequal numbers of people in each district. Each county got at least one seat in the Florida House regardless of population size. Because of Florida's rapid but unequally distributed population growth, this allowed just 18 percent of Florida's population to elect a majority to the state legislature.[4] It gave the Panhandle legislators, called "Pork Choppers," enormous power to bring money and programs to rural communities at the expense of the growing urban and suburban areas.[5] Many attempts were made and many special sessions held in the 1950s and early 1960s to reapportion Florida's electoral districts fairly, but the Pork Choppers in the legislature were able to defeat every meaningful reform. The U.S. Supreme Court decision in *Baker v. Carr* (1962), and the subsequent decisions mandating one-person, one-vote in legislative and congressional districting,[6] had a profound effect on the Florida legislature.[7] Reapportionment broke the grip of the rural North Florida "pork choppers" and redistributed legislative power to Central and South Florida.[8] It allowed African Americans to win state legislative office for the first time since Reconstruction. It brought a new generation of urban Democratic legislators to Tallahassee like Bob Graham who later served as governor. Reapportionment also dramatically increased Republican representation in the Florida House from less than ten members to thirty-nine members in the special election in 1967 that instituted fair reapportionment in Florida under the direction of a federal court[9]—and in the subsequent decades, it helped translate growing Republican strength in Florida's urban and suburban areas into more Republican legislative seats,[10] senate seats, and congressional seats.

In 1972, the issue of multimember districts caused the most contention during redistricting.[11] Florida gained 3 congressional seats through reapportionment (bringing it to 15), but while each congressional district held just one member, Florida House and Senate districts in more urban areas often held more than one. Republicans, Cuban Americans, and Blacks fought for single member districts because it is difficult for minority groups to elect minority legislators in multimember districts. However, the districting plan approved by the legislature included 5 six-member, 5 five-member, and 21 single member districts in the Florida House and 7 three-member, 7 two-member, and 5 single member districts in the Florida

Senate. The Florida Supreme Court upheld the use of multi-member districts despite some reservations and attempts to change the Florida Constitution also failed. Finally however, the adoption of single member districts in the 1982 redistricting helped create a more representative legislative body whose membership more closely mirrored the demographics of the state. Republicans actually lost seats in the 1982 election but then began gaining ground in subsequent elections. But Blacks and Hispanics both gained a number of legislative seats in 1982 as single member districts allowed the creation of districts with larger and more concentrated populations of minority groups. However, there were still no minorities in the congressional delegation (which grew by 4 more seats in 1982 bringing the delegation to 19 members) until Hispanic Republican Ileana Ros-Lehtinen won a special election in South Florida in 1989. Subsequently, in the 1990 midterm elections, Republicans won a majority of the congressional delegation seats (10–9) for the first time in Florida since Reconstruction.

Increased political competition in the state and the lack of minorities in the congressional delegation made redistricting a "hardball sport" in 1992 as members fought over how to create the majority-minority districts required by the 1986 U.S. Supreme Court ruling in *Thornburg v. Gingles*.[12] The legal skirmishing began when Dade County Republican Representative Miguel DeGrandy filed suit in federal court asking the court to draw both legislative and congressional districts to ensure that minority voters, including Hispanics, were given maximum opportunities to elect representatives. Republicans were interested not only in creating Republican-leaning, heavily Cuban-American districts in Miami-Dade County, but also in "packing" Democratic African-American voters into big-city districts in order to give Republican candidates a better opportunity to win in surrounding suburban districts. Black legislators and groups joined forces with Republicans and Hispanics to increase the number of black-majority districts. Despite the disagreements, lawmakers succeeded in adopting a joint resolution creating the House and Senate districts, and the Florida Supreme Court declared these plans constitutional.

However, the U.S. Justice Department objected to the Senate redistricting plan. The legislature was unable to agree on how to fix the problem, and so the Florida Supreme Court redrew it, creating an additional Black district in the Tampa-St. Pete area. This Senate plan and the House plan created by the legislature were reviewed by a three-judge panel from the Federal District Court in the DeGrandy case that had been combined with lawsuits filed by the NAACP and others. The federal judges approved the plan drawn for the Senate but redrew the House boundaries in 31 districts and created five more favorable Hispanic (and thus Republican) districts in South Florida. But the state appealed that decision, and ultimately the U.S. Supreme Court overturned the lower court and reinstated the House plan approved by the state legislature and the Senate plan drawn by the Florida Supreme Court.[13] In the end, the House plan included 13 districts with majority black populations and nine with majority Hispanic population, and the Senate plan included three districts with majority black populations and three with majority Hispanic population.[14]

The creation of these minority access districts helped Republicans take control of the Florida Senate in 1994 and the Florida House in 1996.

The political infighting in the 1992 legislature over congressional redistricting created total gridlock despite the Democratic majority in both the House and Senate and control of the governor's office. The federal district court was obliged to draw the state's congressional district map after the legislature failed to approve a map. It did so by creating three heavily African-American districts, subsequently won by African-American Democrats, and two heavily Hispanic districts, subsequently won by Cuban-American Republicans. Overall, Florida gained 4 more congressional seats after the 1990 census, and Republicans picked up 3 of these new seats for a total of 13 out of 23 seats in the delegation. Florida was a key component of the nationwide Republican victory in the 1994 congressional elections when for the first time in forty years Republicans captured control of the U.S. House of Representatives. The GOP won fifteen seats in Florida in 1994 in part due to the racial gerrymandering that created the districts in 1992. In 1996, a three-judge federal panel ruled that Florida's 3rd Congressional District (extending over 250 miles from Jacksonville to both Orlando and Gainesville in order to create an African-American majority) was unconstitutional based on the U.S. Supreme Court decisions in *Shaw v. Reno* in 1993 and *Miller v Johnson* in 1995.[15] The legislature responded by redrawing congressional districts in northeast Florida in time for the 1996 election. Despite a drop in black voters from 50 percent to 41 percent, African-American Corrine Brown won reelection in District 3 relying heavily on the advantages of incumbency.

Florida redistricting in 2002 brought a new twist: complete Republican control of the process due to strong GOP majorities in both the Florida House and Senate and GOP control of the governor's office and cabinet. Democrats had controlled all previous redistricting since shortly after the Civil War. The GOP-controlled redistricting in Florida in 2002 was based on three guidelines: the constitutional obligation to create districts of relatively equal size based on Florida's 2000 population of 16 million; the civil rights law prohibiting dilution of Black and Hispanic voting strength; and the desire to create as many Republican-leaning districts as possible by packing Democrats together in relatively fewer districts. With the aid of sophisticated software, Republicans were able to bring partisan gerrymandering to new heights (or depths depending on one's point of view).

Florida gained 2 more congressional seats after the 2000 census, and the congressional redistricting plan created one new Republican district in East Central Florida for House Speaker Tom Feeney and one new Republican Cuban district in South Florida for State Senator Mario Diaz-Balart, Chair of the committee in charge of congressional redistricting. The plan also altered Democratic Congresswoman Karen Thurman's district in the Tampa area from moderately Democratic to slightly Republican for State Senator Ginny Brown-Waite. Republicans won all 3 of these seats, kept the 15 seats they already had, and took commanding control of the Florida congressional delegation 18 to 7. Table 6.5 displays Republican effectiveness in achieving their goals. At the congressional level, three black and three Hispanic

Table 6.5.　2002 Florida District Statistics

	Congress (25 Seats)	State House (120 Seats)	State Senate (40 Seats)
Target Population	639,295	133,186	399,559
Range	0%	2.79%	.03%
Black Majority	3	13	3
Hispanic Majority	3	11	3
Republican Majority	2	18	5
Republican Plurality	13	47	15
Democratic Majority	7	38	13
Democratic Plurality	3	17	7

Source: Compiled by the author from data found at www.flsenate.gov/senateredistricting/.

majority districts were drawn. Based on party registration, 2 districts had a Republican majority and 13 had a Republican plurality while 7 districts had a Democratic majority and 3 had a Democratic plurality. Legislative redistricting followed the same strategy as congressional redistricting and produced similar results. Minority districts were created for black Democrats, and white Democrats were packed into a relatively few districts to leave surrounding districts leaning Republican. In South Florida, minority districts were also created for Cuban Republicans. The end result: in a state where Democratic registration actually outpaced Republican registration by 3.5 percentage points, Republicans took an 81–39 seat lead in the Florida House and a 26–14 lead in the Florida Senate.

While the Department of Justice reviewed all of the 2002 redistricting plans, and several interested parties filed lawsuits in state and federal court, in the end, only a small change to three state legislative districts in South Florida was required. However the process did drag on until July less than two weeks before the qualifying deadline for candidates to file papers to run for office. The DOJ objected to a reduction in the number of Hispanics in a Collier County-based House district. House Speaker Tom Feeney took the unusual step of redrawing the map himself rather than calling a special session to try and get the new Florida House map approved without delaying the election timeline. A federal district court three-judge panel accepted the proposed "Speaker's fix" mandating that the legislature adopt the revised map permanently shortly after the 2002 elections and resubmit the plans for final verification (the state Senate and congressional district maps had been approved by the DOJ and the panel of federal judges about two week earlier).[16] While the last-minute alterations and unusual process added drama to the 2002 redistricting cycle, the relatively few changes required were a drastically different result from 1992 when multiple changes were required by the Justice Department, Florida Supreme Court, and various Federal Courts.

REDISTRICTING STANDARDS AND
PROCESS IN THE SUNSHINE STATE

Democrats, some independents, and even a handful of Republicans complained bitterly about the overt partisan and incumbent gerrymandering that occurred in 2002.[17] However, both Florida and federal courts had long held that political gerrymandering may be unfair, but it is not unconstitutional. Thus a coalition of good government and Democratic affiliated groups began an effort to change Florida's Constitution through initiative petition and statewide referendum to make the redistricting process "more fair." The Committee for Fair Elections first tried to take redistricting out of the hands of the Florida Legislature altogether. The Fair Districts group circulated a petition calling for an amendment to the Florida Constitution that would have turned the responsibility over to an independent redistricting commission, similar to the process in place in some other states. The proposal almost made the 2006 ballot but was rejected by the Florida Supreme Court because it did not comply with the constitutional requirement of a single-subject and the ballot summary was misleading.[18]

Somewhat reluctantly, the group abandoned the idea of the independent commission, went back to the drawing board, and crafted two new amendments focused more on setting clear standards than on who would do the drawing. These were referred to as the "Fair Districts" amendments, and both initiatives obtained the necessary number of signatures, cleared Florida Supreme Court review, and then were handily approved by the voters (each got 63 percent "yes" votes) in November 2010. A lawsuit was immediately filed by U.S. Representatives Corrine Brown and Mario Diaz Balart (and later joined by the Florida House under the direction of Republican Speaker Dean Cannon) to block the congressional amendment, arguing it was improperly enacted by voters instead of lawmakers and intruded upon the power of Congress to regulate elections and the legislature's constitutionally delegated power to draw congressional lines. However a federal judge and federal appeals court panel rejected these challenges and upheld the new standards.[19]

One amendment sets the standards for drawing the congressional districts, the other for creating the state legislative districts (Senate and House) although the standards for both are identical (two separate amendments were needed to comply with Florida's single subject rule for initiatives proposing changes to the Florida Constitution). The specific Florida Constitutional standards for drawing congressional redistricting boundaries include:[20]

a.   No apportionment plan or individual district shall be drawn with the intent to favor or disfavor a political party or an incumbent; and districts shall not be drawn with the intent or result of denying or abridging the equal opportunity of racial or language minorities to participate in the political process or to diminish their ability to elect representatives of their choice; and districts shall consist of contiguous territory.

b.   Unless compliance with the standards in this subsection conflicts with the standards in subsection (a) or with federal law, districts shall be as nearly equal in population as is practicable; districts shall be compact; and districts shall, where feasible, utilize existing political and geographical boundaries.

c. The order in which the standards within subsections (a) and (b) of this section are set forth shall not be read to establish any priority of one standard over the other within that subsection.

In addition to these new state standards, Florida must follow federal law as well when crafting its districts. So, for instance, as mentioned earlier, under the *Baker v. Carr* ruling, voting districts must be of equal population size to comply with the one person, one vote standard. The federal Voting Rights Act (VRA) also lays out quite explicit rules that state and local governments must adhere to when engaging in redistricting to protect the voting power of minorities. Section 2 of the VRA applies to all states and localities and helps to ensure that minority voters have an equal opportunity to influence the political process and elect representatives of their choice. Section 5 of the VRA applies only to covered jurisdiction with a history of discrimination and requires those areas to seek preclearance from the Justice Department before adopting any electoral changes including redistricting plans. In Florida, Section 5 affects five counties—Collier, Hardee, Hendry, Hillsborough, and Monroe. But because redistricting plans in one part of the state affect the districts in other parts of the state, preclearance is required for the entire legislative and congressional redistricting plans. In summary, under the VRA, Florida cannot adopt any practice or procedure that would deprive minorities of an effective vote, cannot dilute minority votes, cannot adopt a plan that makes minorities worse off than they were under existing plans (called retrogression), and must seek approval (preclearance) of its plans from the Department of Justice or the Federal Court in Washington, DC, before the plan can go into effect. Section 2 and Section 5 of the VRA have been especially important tools in protecting the voting rights of racial, ethnic, and language minorities in Florida.[21] Florida's growing and diverse minority populations make it more difficult to draw districts that satisfy federal law than is the case in states with less diverse populations.

Since the Fair Districts Amendments are election laws that affect minority voting rights, they also had to receive preclearance from the Department of Justice after they were passed by Florida voters. Outgoing Governor Crist submitted the request for preclearance after the 2010 election. But incoming Governor Scott pulled the request a few days after taking office, leading to Democratic charges of obstruction and a lawsuit that sought to force the governor to put the request back in.[22] Eventually on March 29, 2011, the legislature itself formally submitted the Amendments for preclearance. In the submission, the legislature warned that the Amendments were potentially regressive, and thus supported the preclearance of the new standards only when understood as not constraining its ability to craft minority districts under the VRA:

Properly interpreted, we (the Florida House of Representatives and the Florida Senate) do not believe that the Amendments create roadblocks to the preservation or enhancement of minority voting strength. To avoid retrogression in the position of racial minorities, the

Amendments must be understood to preserve without change the Legislature's prior ability to construct effective minority districts. Moreover, the Voting Rights Provisions ensure that the Amendments in no way constrain the Legislature's discretion to preserve or enhance minority voting strength, and permit any practices or considerations that might be instrumental to that important purpose.[23]

The Fair Districts amendment language received approval from the Department of Justice without comment on May 31, 2011.

The redistricting process in Florida is governed by the state constitution, state statute, and legislative rules. The process can be divided into two parts: the steps leading up to the 60-day legislative session and the steps after legislative enactment. As a preliminary step in 2010, the legislature developed and released a web-based district building application that was made available to the public. In December 2010 Florida received official notification of the apportionment of 27 congressional seats. In March 2011 Florida received the 2010 census data from the U.S. Census Bureau. During the summer of 2011 the legislature hosted 26 public meetings around the state to receive public input to help the legislature in the creation of the new districts. About 5,000 people attended the meetings and over 1,600 spoke. And at the invitation of the legislature over 150 proposed maps were submitted by the public (only 4 maps were submitted by the public in 2002) including 54 complete congressional maps.[24] Members of the Fair Districts Committee and their Democratic supporters criticized the legislature for not presenting legislative proposals for the public to discuss and analyze, for seeming uninterested in what the public was saying, and for rarely speaking at the meetings (a strategy designed to reduce the chance that a legislator might say something that could be used in the expected lawsuits over redistricting).[25] Republican legislators fired back that most critics had failed to submit their own plans that they believed would satisfy the new Fair District standards and that it was appropriate to gather information first so that the public would not think that the legislature had already decided what to do. Finally from October to December 2011 the legislative Redistricting Committees and Subcommittee began reviewing public input and drafting plans.

While the normal 60-day legislative session in Florida runs from March to May, the legislature moved the session to January 10 to March 9 to help ensure that the entire redistricting process would be finished in time for candidate qualifying in June. The processes and timetable for adopting new congressional and legislative lines differ somewhat (see figure 6.1). Once approved as joint resolutions, the legislative plans are sent to the Attorney General who must submit them within 15 days to the Florida Supreme Court for review. The court then has 30 days to approve the plans or require changes. For the congressional plan, once approved as a bill by both houses of the legislature, the governor has 7 or 15 days to sign the plan into law or veto it.[26] Both the legislative and congressional plans must then be submitted for preclearance by the U.S. Department of Justice. Finally, if all goes well, the maps are also cleared of remaining court challenges before the end of May so that qualifying for state or federal elections in Florida can take place June 4 to June 8.

2012: After Legislative Enactment

Legislative (State House and Senate) Redistricting Plans	Congressional Redistricting Plan
Between January 10 to March 9 – Legislature approves Legislative plans	Between January 10 to March 9 – Legislature approves Congressional plan
15 Days – Attorney General submits Legislative plans to FL Supreme Court	7 or 15 Days– Governor signs Congressional plan into law
30 Days – FL Supreme Court upholds the Legislative plans	NO AUTOMATIC COURT REVIEW
60 Days – US DOJ preclears the Legislative plans	60 Days – US DOJ preclears the Congressional plan
June 4 to 8 – Qualifying for state and federal elections in Florida	June 4 to 8 – Qualifying for state and federal elections in Florida

Figure 6.1. Comparison of the Legislative and Congressional Redistricting Process in Florida. Florida House of Representatives, "The Language of Redistricting Key Concepts & Terminology," www.floridaredistricting.org

PASSAGE OF THE 2012 FLORIDA CONGRESSIONAL REDISTRICTING PLAN

Despite the 41 percent to 36 percent Democratic edge in statewide voter registration, Republicans held a supermajority in both the Florida House (81–39) and Senate (28–12) after the 2010 elections. Thus they controlled all facets of the legislative process concerning redistricting in the 2012 session including subcommittees, committees, the calendar, and floor action (and since Governor Scott is also Republican there was no veto threat to the congressional plan either). However, legally according to the Fair Districts Amendments, they could not draw district lines with the *intent* of favoring the Republican Party or incumbents as they had in 2002. And they also had to make the districts more compact and follow political and geographic boundaries where feasible unlike 2002. However, just like 2002, Republicans did have to protect minority voting rights because of the VRA and because of the new Fair Districts Amendments. Given these parameters, GOP legislators devised a strategy to follow these standards and still end up with a partisan advantage in the new redistricting plans that they hoped would withstand review by the DOJ and the legal challenges sure to be filed by their Democratic opponents.

Republicans involved in the redistricting process publically stated over and over again that they were committed to following the new standards and having the most open and transparent redistricting process in the state history.[27] They forbid any discussion concerning incumbents' preferred districts or residences, promised not to meet with congressional lobbyists and did not include member addresses on the maps[28]—a huge change from all previous redistricting efforts in Florida when lobbying by incumbents was rampant and often successful. They forbid any discussion of the partisan makeup of the new districts and did not publically provide data or statistics for party registration or electoral behavior in the new districts (in 2002 this political information was plainly listed online and in hard copy alongside the demographic district information). They also repeatedly stated that minority voting rights would have to take precedence over the other new standards because of federal requirements, and that they would not allow retrogression in existing minority districts or minority vote dilution in any areas of the state with fast growing minority populations.[29] Thus by creating a number of majority-minority, minority influence and minority coalition districts, the surrounding districts were "bleached" and became more Republican. And legally, Republicans claimed that they did not draw the lines with the "intent" of helping their political party, but rather the Republican edge that occurred was simply a result of following the required standards quite faithfully. And since the Fair Districts Amendments only forbid intentional partisan gerrymandering, Republicans felt they had a strong legal case.

The legislature moved quickly to pass the new maps once the legislative session began on January 10. The Senate Redistricting Committee passed senate and congressional maps for consideration by the full chamber on January 11 after voting down a Democratic alternative. The full Senate approved the plans in a bipartisan 34–6 vote on January 18. The House Redistricting Committee passed their house and congressional plans on February 3, and the full chamber approved them later that same day on a party line vote 80–37. After some discussion the Senate agreed to some minor changes requested by the House in its congressional redistricting plan to increase minority strength and reduce the number of counties and cities split in several districts. On February 8 the Florida House voted on final versions of the plans, and on February 9 the final version of the redistricting maps was approved by the Florida Senate: the congressional map CS/SB 1174 by a party line vote 80–37 in the House and a bipartisan 31–7 in the Senate.

On the same day as final passage, the Democratic Party filed suit in state court to invalidate the congressional plan, and a coalition of interest groups who supported the Fair Districts Amendments announced they would file a separate law suit challenging the congressional maps after they were signed into law by Governor Scott. Florida Democratic Party Chairman Rod Smith said the maps "fail to meet the plain meaning of Fair Districts" regarding partisan and incumbent gerrymandering. The coalition, including the League of Women Voters, Common Cause, and the National Council of La Raza, claimed the congressional map was "intentionally enhanced" and accused Republican U.S. Representatives Dan Webster of Winter Garden and Mario Díaz-Balart of Miami of taking "affirmative steps to influence members of the legislature and its staff to 'improve' the composition of their new districts to make them more favorable." It also accused the legislature of "packing artificially high numbers of minorities into certain districts"—singling out the Jacksonville-to-Orlando district of Democratic U.S. Rep. Corrine Brown—to "diminish the influence" of minorities in surrounding districts by rendering them more white and more likely to vote Republican.[30] A week later, Governor Scott signed the new congressional map into law on February 16, and soon after the second lawsuit was filed.

The two lawsuits were combined and heard on an expedited basis in the 2nd Judicial Circuit in Tallahassee. The plaintiffs asked for a summary judgment declaring the new map to be unconstitutional on its face or as an alternative for a temporary injunction maintaining the existing districts until final resolution of all claims. However, on April 30, after reading the motions and responses, hearing the arguments, and weighing the evidence, Judge Terry Lewis denied both requests.[31] In a very detailed response to each of the eight allegations covering a total of 23 out of the 27 districts, Judge Lewis repeatedly stated that there was insufficient evidence to declare any of the disputed districts unconstitutional. He declared that evidence of intentional partisan or incumbent gerrymandering, lack of compactness, or crossing county or city lines could be explained by constitutionally appropriate decisions concerning minority districts or by valid policy choices concerning local geographic boundaries. Judge Lewis went on to add that replacement maps proposed by the plaintiffs would either make minorities worse off (and in several instances lead to retrogression in some of the five Florida counties covered specifically by Section 5 of the VRA) or would be only as or even less compact, or would divide as many or more cities and counties than the legislatively approved districts. Judge Lewis concluded that "the new map appears on its face to be an improvement over the one it replaces."

In addition to the court battle, the state also needed preclearance from the U.S. Department of Justice. The state submitted the congressional and legislative plans in March and sent additional information in late April. A few days later, the Civil Rights Division of the DOJ approved the new proposed congressional and legislative district maps without requiring any changes. In a brief letter to the attorneys representing the state of Florida dated April 30, the same day as Judge Lewis's decision in Tallahassee, the Assistant U.S. Attorney General wrote, "The Attorney General does not interpose any objection to the specified changes."[32] Map 6.2 displays the new congressional districts drawn by the legislature, approved by the governor, and accepted by the 2nd Judicial Circuit of Florida and the DOJ.

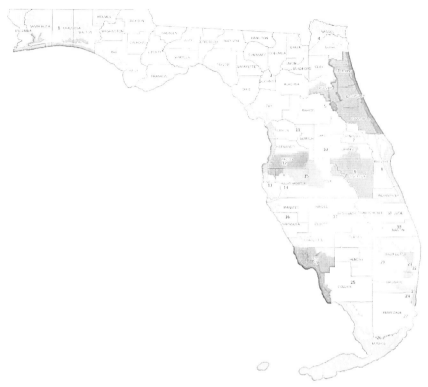

Map 6.2. 2012 Florida Congressional Districts. Florida House of Representatives, www.floridaredistricting.org/.

ASSESSING THE 2012 FLORIDA
CONGRESSIONAL REDISTRICTING PLAN

While the circuit court ruling and Justice Department decision paved the way for the 2012 congressional elections in Florida to be held using the map drawn by the legislature, they did not close the door on future legal challenges. Ultimately the Florida Supreme Court, the federal courts, or the U.S. Justice Department may still determine how well the legislative plan follows all applicable standards and if changes are needed. At the state level, the Florida Supreme Court already required changes to the new Florida Senate districts, although they did accept the House districts without change. And the U.S. Justice Department noted in their letter to Florida that preclearance "does not bar subsequent litigation to enjoin the enforcement of the changes."

The standards to be evaluated include: equal district population size, compactness, contiguity, following geographic and political boundaries where feasible, prohibiting drawing lines with the intent of favoring or disfavoring incumbents, prohibiting drawing lines with the intent of favoring or disfavoring political parties, and ensuring that racial, ethnic, and language minorities have the equal opportunity to participate in the political process and the ability to elect the representatives of their choice.

With a total census population of 18,801,310 and an apportionment of 27 congressional representatives, each new district contains 696,345 or 696,344 people thus meeting the one person, one vote standard – perhaps the only standard that will not be contested in court. According to the staff analysis by the Florida House of Representatives the 2012 districts are more compact and follow political boundaries more faithfully compared to the 2002 districts.[33] The new congressional map reduces the total perimeter, width and height of districts, consistently based on various methods of measurement and reduces the distance and driving time to travel the average district. In addition each of the 27 districts is contiguous. In terms of political boundaries, the new districts reduce the number of Florida's 67 counties split from 30 to 21 and the number of its 411 cities split from 110 to 27. And, given Florida's peninsular shape, virtually every district description also includes a natural geographic boundary such as the Gulf of Mexico, Atlantic Ocean, or river. In terms of overall numbers, it is clear that the new congressional map has more compact districts that split less counties and cities than the previous map. However, because the minority districts required some element of gerrymandering, the minority districts and the surrounding districts are less compact and split more counties and cities than a plan without gerrymandered minority districts. If legal actions continue, it will be up to the courts and the DOJ to sort out if the proper balance between the two has been met.

While intent is difficult to infer from results, the actual status of incumbents (particularly Republican incumbents) in the new congressional maps seems to bolster the legislative contention that the districts were drawn without intent to favor or disfavor incumbents. By one count, almost half of the incumbent legislators were either drawn out of their district, were given a district that is worse for their reelection chances, were drawn into a district with another incumbent, and/or are seeking to run in a different geographic district than the one they are currently in.[34] For instance Republican Representatives Sandy Adams and John Mica were drawn into the same district, decided to run for the same seat, and engaged in a brutal Republican primary where Mica defeated Adams (this would normally be unheard of in a state that gained two seats for members of the majority party). Republican Representatives Rich Nugent and Cliff Stearns were also drawn into the same district but worked out an agreement to run for different seats. However, running in an unfamiliar district, twelve-term incumbent Stearns went on to lose a multi-person primary to Tea-Party backed political newcomer Ted Yoho. South Florida Republican Congressmen Dan Rooney and Alan West both saw their districts become more Democratic, and both decided to run in new districts. Panhandle Republican Steve Southerland and South Florida Hispanic Republican David Rivera both have districts that are slightly more Democratic than before. On the other hand, two Republican members, Dan Webster from Central Florida and Mario Diaz-Balart from South Florida, saw their competitive districts become somewhat safer. Perhaps not surprisingly, the legislature is accused by the Fair District coalition of intentionally seeking to help these two incumbents in violation of the Florida Constitution.

Intent concerning partisanship is also difficult to infer from the results of the maps, but like incumbency, the results may possibly shed some light on partisan intent. On the other hand, both the VRA and new Fair Districts standards make it clear that the actual ability of racial and language minorities to participate equally and elect representatives of their choice is what matters regardless of intent. Of course here there are still unresolved legal questions regarding the amount of minorities that should be placed in a district to satisfy the federal and state requirements. Table 6.6 displays the demographic and political statistics for each new proposed congressional district.[35]

The proposed congressional map has 16 districts out of 27 that have a GOP registration advantage and 11 with a Democratic advantage. Creating a third "toss up" category for districts with less than a 1 percent edge results in a 14 to 10 GOP advantage with 3 toss up districts (15, 18, and 26). As of 2010, the current 25-seat congressional map had a 15 to 10 Republican registration advantage or 13 to 9 with 3 toss ups. The current congressional delegation makeup as of January 2012 is 19 Republicans to 6 Democrats (the GOP had an 18–7 lead during the early part of the decade with Democrats winning 10 seats in 2008 and then losing 4 of those in 2010). When looking at the performance of the proposed districts in statewide elections, 17 out of 27 new districts voted for John McCain over Barack Obama (who won the state by about 2 percent) in the 2008 presidential race in Florida, and 17 out of 27 also voted for Rick Scott over Alex Sink in the 2010 gubernatorial race (won by Scott by about 1 percent). Overall state registration as of January 2012 gives Democrats a 40.5 to 36.15 percentage point lead out of 11.24 million voters.

The proposed congressional maps have 3 black majority seats (Districts 5 in North to Central Florida and 20 and 24 in Southeast Florida) and two black influence seats with at least 20 percent black population (Districts 2 near Tallahassee and 14 near Tampa). There are also three Hispanic majority seats that are predominantly Cuban (Districts 25, 26, and 27 all in the Miami-Broward area of Southeast Florida) and four Hispanic influence seats: three with at least 30 percent of the population (9 in the Orlando area and 23 and 24 in Broward-Palm Beach) and one with at least 20 percent (District 14 in Tampa). Note that District 14 is a minority coalition district with about 25 percent black and 25 percent Hispanic voting age population. Overall, the six majority-minority districts and five of the six minority influence districts more or less emulate what was in place under the previous district plan. The one exception, District 9 in Orange and Osceola, is the first Hispanic influence congressional seat in Central Florida. District 9 has 41 percent Hispanic voting age population, and the dominant Hispanic group in the district is Puerto Rican (about 25 percent of the district), giving voters in that district an excellent opportunity to elect the first Puerto Rican Hispanic to Congress from Florida (however, that opportunity was lost when two Puerto Rican Republicans split the Hispanic vote in the Republican primary allowing a conservative non-Hispanic white candidate Todd

Table 6.6. Demographic and Political Statistics for Florida's 2012 Congressional Districts

District	Voting Age Population			Party Registration			2008 Presidential		2010 Gubernatorial	
	White	Hispanic	Black	Dem	Rep	Other	Obama	McCain	Sink (D)	Scott (R)
1	77.6	4.5	13.2	31.0	50.9	18.1	32.0	66.8	30.3	63.7
2	68.5	4.8	23.8	54.3	31.7	14.0	47.0	51.9	51.6	44.8
3	75.8	7.0	13.3	43.5	38.8	17.7	39.5	59.2	40.4	55.6
4	74.9	6.7	12.9	34.9	45.5	19.6	36.5	62.5	36.1	60.8
5	36.2	11.1	50.1	60.7	21.1	18.1	70.5	28.8	65.4	31.9
6	82.8	5.7	9.0	36.5	40.0	23.4	45.4	53.4	41.4	54.6
7	70.2	17.0	9.0	35.0	39.4	25.6	49.1	49.9	45.7	50.5
8	80.4	7.7	9.1	35.0	43.9	21.1	43.8	54.9	40.4	55.1
9	42.9	41.4	12.4	43.4	28.2	28.3	60.2	39.0	53.0	43.3
10	69.9	14.2	11.1	36.8	40.3	22.8	47.2	52.0	43.8	52.3
11	83.1	7.4	7.7	37.0	42.1	20.9	43.0	55.7	39.5	54.8
12	82.6	9.9	4.3	34.7	40.1	25.2	46.6	52.1	43.4	51.9
13	83.5	7.2	5.3	36.2	38.0	25.8	51.1	47.3	48.5	46.6
14	46.5	25.6	25.6	51.0	25.4	23.6	65.0	34.0	61.0	35.8
15	68.6	15.0	12.7	39.0	38.6	22.4	45.9	52.9	43.7	52.5
16	83.5	8.8	5.8	32.8	43.6	23.5	48.1	50.8	44.1	51.7
17	75.4	14.4	8.4	37.7	40.8	21.6	43.0	55.7	39.4	55.4
18	74.7	12.1	11.1	37.3	38.0	24.7	51.0	48.0	47.3	49.3
19	77.1	14.8	6.5	28.4	47.2	24.5	42.3	56.8	35.4	61.0
20	29.5	18.5	50.0	65.2	14.4	20.4	80.4	19.0	78.1	19.9
21	66.6	18.3	11.2	48.1	26.0	25.9	63.5	35.9	61.4	36.1
22	69.4	17.7	10.3	41.6	32.6	25.8	56.7	42.5	53.3	44.1
23	49.2	36.7	11.0	48.5	25.7	25.8	61.8	37.5	60.1	37.6
24	12.6	33.2	54.9	69.3	11.1	19.6	86.2	13.5	84.8	13.7
25	21.2	70.7	7.7	32.4	40.0	27.5	45.5	53.9	40.7	57.1
26	20.2	68.9	10.0	35.8	36.8	27.4	49.5	49.9	48.8	49.0
27	17.5	75.0	7.7	35.8	38.2	26.0	48.5	50.9	47.5	50.6

Source: The Florida Legislature and the Orlando Sentinel (Thanks to Reporter Aaron Deslatte).

Note: White is non-Hispanic White, Black is all Black including Hispanic Black, and Hispanic is all Hispanic.

Long to finish first and face off against the only announced Democratic candidate in the race: controversial former Congressman Alan Grayson).

Looking at the partisan results of the new congressional districts bolsters the Democratic argument that there must have been some intentional partisan gerrymandering. The spirit of the Fair Districts Amendments suggests that in a state with 500,000 more Democrats than Republicans and a 2008 statewide victory by Democrat Barack Obama there should not be 16-17 congressional districts out of 27 with a Republican edge in partisan registration and/or voting behavior. Conversely Republicans rightly point out that results are not intent, and that one needs to take a broader view to understand why district composition is the way it is. Republicans insist that they needed to make sure there was no retrogression or vote dilution in minority districts and that some existing minority districts needed to be boosted and an additional minority district needed to be created because of minority population growth in certain parts of the state. GOP legislators contend that they accurately followed the Voting Rights Act and the Fair District Amendment itself when drawing the districts and that the end result was simply more Republican districts.

Of course Democrats and the coalition of groups supporting Fair Districts counter that Republicans have gone well beyond what is required in creating minority districts to ensure that minority voters have an equal chance to participate and elect representatives of their choosing. They argue that several of the black majority-minority districts are so packed with black residents that minority voters are actually hurt by the redistricting in violation of the Voting Rights Act and the Fair Districts standards (in essence arguing that black votes are wasted and that blacks are denied the right to have more Democratic representation in Congress from Florida). Democrats also insist that intentionally packing extra Democrats into those minority districts also violates the Fair District standards prohibiting intentional partisan gerrymandering. The three black majority-minority districts have in excess of 60 percent Democratic registration (District 5 with 60.7, District 20 with 65.2 and District 24 with 69.3). The two black influence districts have over 50 percent Democratic registration (District 2 with 54.3 and district 14 with 51). On the flip side only one proposed congressional seat is even 50 percent Republican: District 1 isolated in the Western Panhandle with 50.9 percent. And none of the South Florida majority-minority Hispanic Districts are even over 41 percent Republican (although each has a slight GOP edge in partisan registration). Of course Republicans legislators will counter that black districts contain more Democrats than Cuban-Hispanic districts contain Republicans because about 83 percent of registered Blacks in Florida identify with the Democratic Party while the Florida Hispanic vote is more split between the parties (31 percent of registered Hispanics identify as Republican while 38 percent identify as Democratic).

The Democratic Party and the coalition of groups supporting Fair Districts have developed alternative maps that give the Democratic Party a slight edge in the majority of districts. The Democratic Party-designed map would give the Democrats a 14 to 13 advantage in districts based on voter registration and on voting for Obama in 2008, and the map drawn by the League of Women Voters, Common Cause, and Democracia would also create more Democratic districts. [36] However they accomplish this in part by severely reducing the percent of black voters in the minority district that currently stretches from Jacksonville to Orlando: down to 34 percent or 35 percent in both plans from over 50 percent in both the current district and legislatively proposed district (they also bring the other two black majority districts down to around 50 percent). In addition, the coalition plan does away with the new Hispanic influence district in Central Florida with only 16 percent Hispanic rather than the legislative proposal of 41 percent. As Judge Lewis hinted in his decision upholding the legislatively drawn districts, both of these "solutions" may run afoul of the Voting Rights Act: the large reduction in Black residents in an existing district potentially viewed as unconstitutional retrogression and the lack of a new Hispanic district in a fast growing Hispanic area as a violation of the right of minorities to elect representatives of their choosing.

In the end, after all the challenges have been completed, it seems likely that the new maps will look similar (if not identical) to what the Republican-controlled legislature produced. Although some tweaks may boost Democratic prospects in several districts, Republicans will most likely retain some advantage in a majority of districts for the simple reason that some level of racial gerrymandering is going to be required by the VRA. The Florida Supreme Court is the best hope for Democrats since they will review the maps based on the Fair District standards and the VRA (the federal courts would only be concerned with the VRA if they became involved) and since there are four Democrats on that seven member court. The Florida Supreme Court did require changes to the Florida Senate map, giving Democrats some hope that the court might also make changes to the congressional plan assuming the case reaches Florida's highest court. And even under a map drawn by the Republican legislature, Democrats managed to gain four seats as President Obama did well in the state (going from a 19–6 deficit to a 17–10 one).

The stakes of this redistricting battle are quite high since they will help determine the partisan, racial and ethnic composition of Florida's congressional delegation in the decade ahead and influence the level of satisfaction that Florida voters have with their representation in Congress. And with 27 seats in play, overall majority control of Congress could be affected by the redistricting decisions made in the Sunshine State.

NOTES

1. Data in this section is taken from the 2000 and 2010 U.S. Census. State rankings are taken from the 2011 *Statistical Abstract of the United States*.

2. Tom Fiedler, "A Sense of Rootlessness," in *The Florida Handbook*, 1997–1998, ed. Allen Morris (Tallahassee, FL: Peninsular Press, 1997), 557.

3. Dario Moreno, "Florida's Hispanic Voters," in *Florida Politics: Ten Media Markets, One Powerful State*, eds. Kevin Hill, Susan MacManus, and Dario Moreno (Tallahassee, FL: Florida Institute of Government, 2004), 83–99.

4. Sandra L. Myres, *One Man, One Vote* (Austin, TX: Steck-Vaughn, 1970).

5. Hugh Douglas Price, "Florida: Politics and the 'Pork Choppers.'" In *The Politics of Reapportionment*, ed. Malcolm E. Jewell (Westport, CT: Greenwood Press, 1962).

6. *Baker v. Carr*, 369 U.S. 186 (1962). See also *Reynolds v. Sims*, 377 U.S. 533 (1964) and *Wesberry v. Sanders*, 376 U.S. 1 (1964).

7. Michael Maggioto et al., "The Impact of Reapportionment on Public Policy," *American Politics Quarterly* 13 (January 1985), 101–21.

8. Susan A. MacManus, ed. *Reapportionment and Representation in Florida: A Historical Collection*. (Tampa: University of South Florida, 1991).

9. The legislature attempted to draw district lines to comply with *Baker v. Carr* three times in the early 1960s, but each plan was invalidated by the federal courts. Finally, the federal court took the unusual step of invalidating the results of the fall 1966 elections, hurriedly drew their own district maps complying with one person, one vote, and required special elections in the spring of 1967.

10. Aubrey Jewett, "Republican Strength in a Southern Legislature: The Impact of One Person, One Vote Redistricting in Florida," *American Review of Politic* (Spring 2000), Volume 21: 1–18.

11. Neil Skene, "Reapportionment," in *The Florida Handbook, 2005–2006*, eds. Allen Morris and Joan Perry Morris (Peninsular Publishing Company: Tallahassee, 2005).

12. *Thornburg v Gingles*, 478 U.S. 30 (1986).

13. *Johnson v DeGrandy* 512 US 997 (1994).

14. For a thorough review of all issues affecting redistricting in Florida in 1992 through 2001 see Susan A. MacManus ed., *Mapping Florida's Political Landscape* (Florida Institute of Government Press: Tallahassee, 2001).

15. *Shaw v. Reno* 509 U.S. 630 (1993) and *Miller v. Johnson* 515 U.S. 900 (1995).

16. Joni James, "In Win for GOP-led Legislature, Panel OK's Redistricting Plan," *Miami Herald*, July 10, 2002, accessed February 27, 2012, http://archive.fairvote.org/redistricting/reports/remanual/flnews.htm.

17. Some of the description of requirements and process in this section is taken from Susan A. MacManus, Aubrey Jewett, Thomas R. Dye, and David J. Bonanza, *Politics in Florida*, 3rd ed. (Tallahassee, FL: Florida Institute of Government Press. 2011), 201–208.

18. It was rejected for covering too many subjects (an independent redistricting commission and single-member-districts) and for being misleading (the ballot summary called the commission non-partisan when its membership was actually to be selected in a partisan fashion).

19. See Aaron Deslatte, "Judges Uphold Fair District Standards as Constitutional," *Orlando Sentinel*, January 31, 2012, accessed February 27, 2012, www.orlandosentinel.com/news/politics/os-judges-reject-fair-districts-challenge-20120131,0,5652143.story.

20. *Florida Constitution*, Article III, Section 20.

21. JoNel Newman, "Voting Rights in Florida, 1982–2006: A Report of RenewtheVRA.org," March 2006, accessed February 27, 2012, www.aclufl.org/issues/voting_rights/Florida VRA2.pdf.

22. Dara Kam, "Scott holds up federal approval of redistricting amendments; Democrats outraged," *Palm Beach Post*, January 25, 2011, accessed February 27, 2012, www.palmbeachpost.com/news/state/scott-holds-up-federal-approval-of-redistricting-amendments-1209699.html.

23. Letter from Andy Bardos, special counsel to the Senate president, and George Levesque, general counsel to the Florida House of Representatives, to T. Christian Herren, Jr., chief of the Voting Section, Civil Rights Division, United States Department of Justice (March 29, 2011), 7, accessed February 27, 2012, www.myfloridahouse.gov/Sections/Documents/loaddoc.aspx?DocumentType=Press percent20Release&FileName=257.

24. Florida House of Representatives Staff Analysis of Bill # CS/HB 6005 PCB CRS 12–06, Establishing the Congressional Districts of the State (January 30, 2012), 14–16.

25. Associated Press, "Critics bash Florida lawmakers' redistricting process," *Tampa Tribune*, June 21, 2011, accessed February 27, 2012, www2.tbo.com/news/politics/2011/jun/21/critics-bash-florida-lawmakers-redistricting-proce-ar-238832/.

26. If the legislature is still in session when the bill is sent to the governor's office then the governor must act within a week. If the bill is sent at the end of session and the legislature adjourns, then the governor has 15 days.

27. See the press releases issued by the Florida House and the Florida Senate, February 3, 2012, accessed February 27, 2012, www.myfloridahouse.gov/Sections/HouseNews/preview .aspx?PressReleaseId=496 and www.flsenate.gov/Media/PressRelease/Show/Senators/2010-2012/District26/PressRelease/PressRelease20120210090519959.

28. Mark Mathews, "Members of Congress told not to try to influence new districts," *Orlando Sentinel*, July 9, 2011, accessed February 27, 2012, http://articles.orlandosentinel .com/2011-07-09/news/os-congress-redistricting-lobbying-20110706_1_central-florida -incumbents-congressional-districts-state-lawmakers.

29. The Buzz (from the staff of the *Tampa Bay Times*), "The emerging thinking on 'retrogression;' Florida redistricting's big word," *Tampa Bay Times*, November 28, 2011, accessed February 27, 2012, www.tampabay.com/blogs/the-buzz-florida-politics/content/emerging -thinking-retrogression-florida-redistrictings-big-word.

30. All quotes in this paragraph can be found in Aaron Deslatte and Kathleen Haughney, "Critics immediately challenge lawmakers' redrawn districts," *Orlando Sentinel*, February 9, 2012, accessed February 27, 2012, http://articles.orlandosentinel.com/2012-02-09/news/os -redistricting-passes-legislature-20120209_1_jacksonville-to-orlando-district-congressional -map-redrawn-districts.

31. See Order Denying Motion for Summary Judgment, Judge Terry P. Lewis, In the Circuit Court of the Second Judicial Circuit in and for Leon County, Florida, April 30, 2012. Available at http://censusvalidator.blob.core.windows.net/mydistrictbuilderdata/Legal/Order_Lewis04-30.pdf.

32. The U.S. Justice Department letter granting preclearance to the legislatively drawn maps can be found at http://censusvalidator.blob.core.windows.net/mydistrictbuilderdata/forDOJ/2012.04.30_DOJApproval_HSC.pdf

33. Florida House of Representatives Staff Analysis of Bill # CS/HB 6005 PCB CRS 12-06, Establishing the Congressional Districts of the State. January 30, 2012.

34. Aaron Blake, "Breaking Down the Florida GOP's Redistricting Map," *The Washington Post*, January 26, 2012, accessed February 27, 2012, www.washingtonpost.com/blogs/the-fix/post/breaking-down-the-florida-gops-redistricting-map/2012/01/26/gIQAd CFYTQ_blog.html.

35. Demographic statistics come from The Florida Legislature, "District Summary Population Report for Congressional Plan H000C9047," February 2012, accessed February 27, 2012, www.flsenate.gov/PublishedContent/Session/Redistricting/Plans/H000C9047/H000C9047_pop_sum.pdf. Political statistics come from the *Orlando Sentinel* Interactive Redistricting Map, February 2012, accessed February 27, 2012, www.orlandosentinel.com/news/politics/os-gfx-redistricting-2010-maps,0,6525157.htmlpage.

36. See the *Orlando Sentinel* Interactive Redistricting Map, February 2012, accessed February 27, 2012, www.orlandosentinel.com/news/politics/os-gfx-redistricting-2010-maps,0,6525157 .htmlpage.

7

Congressional Redistricting in Louisiana

Region, Race, Party, and Incumbents

Pearson Cross

Charles Bullock subtitled his recent book on redistricting "The Most Political Activity in America."[1] What is true for America is especially true for Louisiana, where politics is a game played for fun, power, and profit. From its high-minded beginnings in public meetings to its stressful denouement, a short hour before the mandated end of the session, the 2011 congressional redistricting cycle in Louisiana was a primer on the politics of race, party, region, and incumbency. The factor providing urgency and weight to the process was the loss of a seat, resulting from population losses through outmigration, a flat reproductive rate, and the effects of Hurricanes Katrina and Rita. These demographic realities provided the context for the struggle between an emergent GOP majority in both House and Senate, flexing its muscles for the first time since Reconstruction, and the Democratic Party, led by the Black Caucus. At various times during the process, the most important actors were the Black Caucus, the seven incumbent Congressmen, the Governmental Affairs committee chairs in House and Senate, Governor Bobby Jindal, and finally, the individual members of the legislature who argued passionately (and in some cases) persuasively for their vision. Congressional redistricting raised the question central to Louisiana politics, that is, "just who are we anyway," as rednecks, blacks, Cajuns, Francophiles, the oil industry, agriculturalists, fishermen, and urbanites all fought for power and representation. In the end, the most important single factor governing congressional redistricting was regionalism. As the session wound down, the parties joined together to protect incumbents, the rural-urban regional conflict was resolved in favor of the rural parishes, Governor Jindal reversed his no-participation pledge, the Black Caucus promised to bring suit, and two Republican Congressmen from Southern Louisiana were put into the same district, promising a barn-burning congressional race in Southwest Louisiana in 2012.

DEMOGRAPHIC TRENDS

Starting as far back as the 2001 redistricting session, voices prophesying the loss of a congressional seat were a rising chorus in Louisiana, picking up with Hurricanes Katrina and Rita in 2005, and increasing in intensity as other states posted strong population growth.[2] Having lost an eighth seat in the 1991–1992 cycle, Louisianans were familiar with complex entanglements that could ensue as districts were redrawn to take account of demographic changes and the Department of Justice requirements under the Voting Rights Act.[3] Indeed, the consequences of losing a congressional seat seemed so dire to Senator David Vitter and others, including Louisiana Republican Party Chair Roger Villere, that legislation was introduced in Congress to limit the census to counting "citizens" rather than "persons," with the rationale being that states like Texas, California, and Arizona were benefiting unfairly from the large number of illegal aliens within their boundaries.[4] Restricting the census to the counting of citizens rather than persons would, it was argued, increase the chance that Louisiana retain all seven of its congressmen. Appealing for support across the aisle, Chairman Villere argued that counting aliens was "not a Republican problem. It's a problem for the state of Louisiana . . . everybody has a vested interest that our Louisiana voting strength is not diluted."[5] Despite the flood of protest, Louisiana became the only state outside the Northeast or Midwest to lose a congressional district.[6]

Louisiana was recently described as "demographically unique in the decade of the 2000s" and a "national leader" in the category of population.[7] Despite losing a seat in the 2011 apportionment, Louisiana's population grew in real terms. From 2000 to 2010, Louisiana's population grew from 4,205,900 to 4,533,372, a growth rate of 1.4 percent. This rate of growth, however, was considerably slower than that experienced by other states, which grew on average by 9.7 percent in the decade, and even slower when measured against other southern states, where the rate of growth was 14.3 percent. Overall, Louisiana's population growth "over the past 30 years has been almost 2 percent less than the nation's population growth over the past 10 years," explaining quite clearly why Louisiana lost congressional seats in both 1990 and 2010.[8]

There are several explanations for Louisiana's demographic malaise, some short term, others more glacial. In the short term, Hurricanes Katrina and Rita hit Louisiana like a bomb, dispersing populations gathered along the coast and in New Orleans to more inland parishes, and to other cities and states, principally in Texas and Georgia.[9] In 2006, it was reckoned that Louisiana's population had shrunk 5 percent in the year from July 1, 2005, to July 1, 2006, equivalent to around 250,000 people.[10] Population in Orleans Parish fell from a 2000 level of 484,674 to a post-Katrina level of 343,829. Other parishes along the coast were similarly hit by the storms of 2005, Plaquemine fell from 26,757 to 23,043; Cameron from 9,991 to 6,899; and St. Bernard from 67,229 to 35,897.[11] The New Orleans Metro Area had 1,316,512 residents on April 1, 2000. On July 1, 2006, that number had fallen to 987,533 before rebounding to 1,189,981 in July 2009, a net loss of 126,531 people. The 2010 census indicates that New Orleans itself lost 140,845 residents, a drop of 29 percent from 2000.[12]

Out-migration was another factor influencing Louisiana's population. Louisiana lost citizens through negative net migration every year from 1981 through 2009. Once gone, it takes Louisiana a long time to replace lost citizens. For example, a report by demographers Troy Blanchard and Karen Paterson estimated that it would take until July 1, 2010, to return Louisiana's population to the levels prior to Katrina's arrival in August 2005. Taken together, Louisiana's population growth from 2000 to 2009 was an anemic 0.5 percent. This follows on the heels of a previous period between 1985 and 1990, when Louisiana lost 250,654 persons to net out-migration. Blanchard and Paterson estimate total net out-migration during those years to be over 300,000.[13] A Pew Research Center report stated that in 2007, 301,000 persons moved to Louisiana while 572,000 moved out, making it the state with the largest net migration loss that year. Southern Louisiana is clearly the "odd man out" in the South, which, as a region, is expected to grow 42.9 percent between 2000 and 2030, surpassing every other region except the western region, where a growth rate of 45.8 percent is predicted over the period.[14] Equally troubling for Louisiana, the population that is leaving is disproportionately young and educated, leaving behind the elderly, the less educated, and the less able.[15]

Further complicating redistricting in 2011 was the uneven pattern of inter-parish population movements, combined with the general trend of rural out-migration. One report noted that "more than one-third of nonmetro counties lost at least 10 percent of their population through net outmigration over 1988–2008."

Map 7.1. Louisiana's Shifting Population. Public Affairs Research Council of Louisiana.

Many of these counties (parishes) were in Louisiana, and particularly Northern Louisiana. In fact, as map 7.1 illustrates, 18 of 64 Louisiana parishes lost population in absolute terms between 2000 and 2010, not including the 6 additional parishes whose population losses may be attributed, at least in part, to Hurricanes Katrina and Rita (Jefferson, Plaquemines, St. Bernard, Orleans, Cameron, and Iberia). With the exception of Bossier Parish in Northwest Louisiana, and Grant Parish in central Louisiana, the only parishes gaining population of any significance were urban parishes in Southern Louisiana (e.g., Lafayette, Livingston, Ascension, St. Tammany, and Tangipahoa).[16] Thus, while the state as a whole grew slowly (1.4 percent) from 2000 to 2010, the rate of growth in the nine-parish Baton Rouge area was a much more brisk 14 percent.[17] In sum, Louisiana's rural and northern parishes have lost population to the more southern and urban parishes, which are themselves growing more slowly than the United States as a whole, and much more slowly than the rest of the South.

THE REDISTRICTING PROCESS IN LOUISIANA

Louisiana's redistricting process is relatively straightforward but unabashedly political. Louisiana is one of 39 states in which the legislature is responsible for drawing lines for the Congress.[18] Typically, the governor calls a special legislative redistricting session, as in 2001, preferring to keep the brutal and bloody business of redistricting out of the horse-trading that takes place during regular state politics.[19] This session is usually preceded by public meetings held around the state to gain citizen input and to try "to make it open to everybody to participate." As Rick Gallot, Chair of the House and Governmental Affairs Committee put it, "Our goal was to make it an open process."[20] The actual process of drawing the lines is delegated to the Governmental Affairs Committees in the House and Senate where the chairpersons take the lead, although any member of House or Senate can submit a map or plan for redistricting. Louisiana has a partisan legislature, but curiously, committee chairmanships and appointments are divided between the two parties such that both Democrats and Republicans chair important committees, and the formula for seat distribution also varies from committee to committee.[21]

The most important figure in assigning committee seats is the governor, who typically (and informally) lets the legislature know whom he or she would prefer as speaker of the House and president of the Senate.[22] Then, the governor's chosen speaker and president make most of the rest of the selections in consultation with the governor's staff and also the individual members, rewarding and punishing as they see fit.[23] In most cycles, the Legislature takes the preferences of the incumbent congressmen and women into consideration, especially so in years when a seat is lost, vitiating the norm of incumbent protection. Rival bills emerging from the two committees seek support in the other chamber until the governor backs one of the bills, at which point tents are folded and the governor's plan is accepted by a simple majority vote of each chamber.[24] The signature of the governor completes the process in the state. From that point, the legislative act is submitted within 60 days to either the Department of Justice or the U.S. District Court for the District of Columbia for what is known as "preclearance."

Louisiana is one of sixteen states wholly or partially covered by Section 5 of the Voting Rights Act (VRA). The Voting Rights Act was originally passed to prevent southern states (primarily) from discriminating against African Americans by denying them the right to vote, particularly with the use of literacy tests and other barriers to suffrage. Section 5 of the VRA "requires states with histories of discrimination to have changes in their voting laws and redistricting plans approved," either by the Department of Justice or the federal courts.[25] Louisiana is also covered under Section 2 of the VRA, which is aimed at making sure that changes to election law or procedure do not adversely affect the ability of various racial, ethnic, and/or language minorities to elect candidates of their choice.[26] The VRA has been amended four times since 1965, expanded to include new groups (language), and also to eliminate "intent to discriminate" as a necessary trigger for relief.

Louisiana failed to receive preclearance of its districting plans in both 1990 and 2000, in part because of the mixed signals that the Justice Department and the Court were sending on the issue of majority-minority districts. For example, in 1991, seeking to create a second majority-minority district in addition to District 2, Louisiana lawmakers crafted the infamous "Zorro" District, so called because it looked like the mark that Zorro used to make on his victims. In geographical terms, it crossed Louisiana from northwest to northeast, darted down the Mississippi River parishes picking up black voters in Grambling, Monroe, and Alexandria before finishing in the black districts of Baton Rouge and Lafayette. All told, it covered part of 28 parishes and made a mockery of traditional districting principles (e.g., compactness, contiguity). The Zorro district was rejected by the Courts for being racially gerrymandered and thereby "denying white voters their right to equal protection of the laws under the 14th Amendment."[27] Louisiana's 2000 legislative plan was challenged in 2000 as well, "because it reduced the number of minority districts compared to the previous map in effect," or what is called in districting parlance, "retrogression."[28] Given the history of challenges to districting in Louisiana under various sections of the VRA, preclearance and the avoidance of retrogression are both likely to be a significant part of the process for several cycles yet to come.[29]

2001 REDISTRICTING PROCESS

Compared to the 2011 redistricting session, the 2001 session was a miserly affair, conducted in just over a week. The biggest reason for the short session was the terrorist attack on New York on September 11, 2001.[30] Called by Governor Mike Foster and beginning October 8 of 2001, the session lasted a scant 8 days, although long enough for nerves to be rubbed raw. The session's brevity also resulted from the consideration of bills to district the BESE and Supreme Court Districts in committee prior to the formal opening of the session. Appearing before the Governmental Affairs Committees in House and Senate, Representatives Chris John, D-Crowley, and Billy Tauzin, R-Chackbay, presented a draft proposal for redistricting the congressional seats that was endorsed by all six of the returning U.S. Congressmen.[31] This proposal, which was to become the basis for congressional redistricting in 2001, was a status quo document focused on incumbent protection, leaving an estimated 94 percent of all citizens in the same district. What allowed for such marginal adjustment was the slow growth rate in Louisiana and the maintenance of the same number of congressional seats. Between 1990 and 2000, the state's population grew by an anemic 5.9 percent to 4.47 million, requiring the average congressional District to pick up only "about 36,000 more people than in 1990, for a total of about 638,400."[32] Still, voices spoke against the incumbent's apparent fait de accompli. State Senator James David Cain complained, "I thought these districts belonged to the people, but isn't it sad that we got to do these districts like the congressmen want? . . . They're walking a dog and we're following right behind them."[33]

Drama was provided by the Black Caucus, which was disappointed that a second majority-minority district was not given serious consideration. A bill introduced in the House by Black Caucus Chairperson Arthur Morrell, D-New Orleans, would have created a "black-majority district stretching south from the Arkansas line to the Baton Rouge and Lafayette areas."[34] This bill, offered as an Amendment to the plan put forward by the incumbent congressmen, was defeated soundly 71–31, as members, remembering the "Zorro" and "Slash" districts (as well as the court challenges they provoked), sought to avoid legal uncertainty. Evaluating Morrell's doomed plan, 3rd District Congressman Billy Tauzin put it, "That's the kind of district, as you know, that was already considered unconstitutional."[35] In contrast, David Vitter described the incumbent's plan as "straightforward and reasonable . . . I don't think it's terribly controversial in any way."[36] For their part, and, in an apparently inevitable accompaniment to redistricting in Louisiana, the Black Caucus promised to bring a challenge to the plan in the Courts.

Agreeing with the incumbents, the House voted 65–34 and the Senate 21–16 to approve a bill by Representative Peppi Bruneau, R-New Orleans, very much like the original plan submitted by the congressional delegation, although tweaked to keep St. Bernard and Lafayette together. This final plan was estimated to keep 96.8 percent of Louisiana residents in their current districts (see map 7.2).[37]

The 2nd District continued as the only majority minority one, limited to New Orleans and Jefferson parishes and containing 413,782 black residents, or 64.8 percent of the total. The next highest total percentage of black residents in any district was the 5th, at 34.1 percent, following closely by the 4th and 6th Districts at 33.9 percent and 33.6 percent respectively. Perhaps most important for the next redistricting cycle (2011), the vertical north-south alignment of the 4th and 5th Districts was maintained. Needing to pick up about 22,000 residents in the 4th and about 28,000 in the 5th, the two vertical districts expanded south in search of numbers,

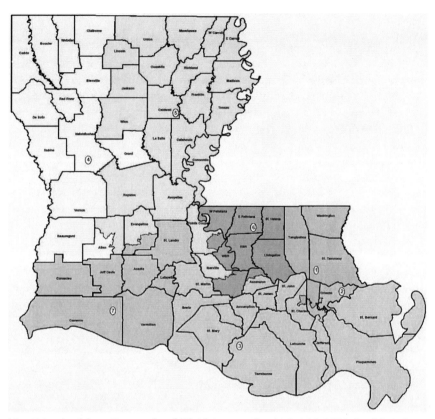

Map 7.2. Louisiana Congressional Districts according to Act 10, 2001. Louisiana State Legislature.

confirming the expectations of Associated Press writer Brett Martel, who said, "[F] or McCrery and Cooksey, who share the entire width of Northern Louisiana, there is nowhere to expand but south, probably into districts now held by [Congressmen] John and Baker."[38]

THE REDISTRICTING PROCESS IN 2011

The Players

The most important players in the 2011 congressional redistricting process were Governor Jindal; the members of House and Senate Governmental Affairs Committees and their chairpersons—Rick Gallot, D-Grambling, and Robert "Bob" Kostelka, R-West Monroe; the Black Caucus; six of the seven incumbent congressmen; and finally, the U.S. Department of Justice (DOJ). There were also a number of prominent businesses and interest groups which weighed in at various points.[39] Each exercised real influence over the shape of the process and the final outcome, although not at the same time or in the same way. Governor Jindal, despite his promise to let the legislature do its job, stayed connected to the process throughout, making his preference for a vertical north-south district plan known and refusing to let the Legislature stray from his vision, which, at the end of the day, was the ruling one. The Legislature, after calling itself into session for the first time, decided to finish the process rather than defer it until the next year.

In his speech marking the opening of the 2011 Legislative Redistricting session on March 21, 2011, Governor Bobby Jindal invoked the spirit of past Louisiana politicians Billy Tauzin and John Breaux, noting that "in our state we have a great tradition of working across party lines" and a "tradition of non-partisanship when it came to putting Louisiana first."[40] He also pledged to stay out of the process saying "We've asked the congressional delegation to come up with its own plan. . . . We'll let the legislature handle (the legislative map)."[41] Prior to the opening of the session, there had been a good bit of maneuvering behind the scenes, although not by the governor himself. The Louisiana Family Forum (LFF), a powerful conservative Christian lobbying organization and advocacy group, was first out of the gate with a controversial redistricting proposal to merge the 2nd and 3rd Districts and "maximiz[e] congressional representation for each Louisiana citizen." Noting that the drawing of congressional lines in Louisiana "have traditionally required more input from various sources, including . . . non-profit organizations and partisan political groups," the LFF argued for broad changes to District 2, the state's only majority-minority district. Given that District 2 had "lost more than 300,000 people from the 2000 census," the LFF maintained that it was the only "logical choice for combination with another district."[42] Although District 2 would remain majority-minority under the LFF's scheme, the proposal was not greeted warmly by the members of the Black Caucus, who resented what they perceived as an effort to undercut black voting rights in Louisiana. "What it comes down to," said Senator J. P. Morrel, D-New Orleans, is "this is purely a political move by . . . a super right wing conservative group" with the "goal to dilute anyone who has a non-neoconservative agenda. That's their goal."[43]

A pre-session meeting in January at the Hunan Dynasty, a Chinese restaurant in Washington, DC, was attended by all seven incumbent congressmen, who listened to a presentation by Louisiana State Senator Bob Kostelka, chairman of the Senate and Governmental Affairs Committee. Senator Kostelka outlined the rules governing redistricting and also presented them with a tentative map of the proposed districts.[44] Reports from this informal meeting early in the process outlined the principal areas of contention that were to arise during the formal session: whether to keep the 4th and 5th Districts in north Louisiana vertical; whether the Louisiana coast should be represented by one, two, or three districts; and finally, what shape should the majority-minority district (2nd) take. The odd man out at the meeting was Congressman Jeff Landry, R-LA 3, whose 2010 election made him the member of the delegation with the least seniority and the member most likely to find his district swallowed by other districts. Working to find a district in which he could run successfully, Landry announced his support for a "coastal district that puts as much of the coast in one congressional district as possible."[45] Echoing the self-interest inherent in the process, Congressman Rodney Alexander, R-LA 5, reported that "most congressional delegation members recommended a plan that keeps two northern districts above Interstate 10," which would make a single coast district unlikely.[46]

Prior to the opening of the session, the joint Governmental Affairs Committees from the House and Senate held nine public meetings around the state. Their purpose was to gain input from Louisiana residents in each region as to what they preferred in the way of districts.[47] The most common theme repeated by residents was a desire that regions and communities be respected and kept together, whether it was Terrebonne and Lafourche, Lake Charles and Lafayette, or some other community in Louisiana, presaging what was to be the most contentious issue raised during the Session.[48] Redistricting in Louisiana in 2011 was a political process that involved a number of important players and raised three principal questions: how to draw a map that respected the integrity of regions and communities while accommodating broad demographic changes; how to achieve the appropriate balance between the desire of incumbents for reelection while reducing the size of the delegation from seven to six; and finally, how to maintain black voting rights and avoid retrogression and federal court challenges.

The Proposals

A number of different plans for redistricting were proposed and considered in committee or by the Legislature during the session. These plans differed in geographical terms and effects as well as in demographic terms. Some plans were introduced with support from the Republican Caucus, others were supported by the Black Caucus and Democrats, others had the support of Governor Bobby Jindal, and still others were favored by one or another of the incumbent congressmen. Some plans were popular in Southern Louisiana, others in Northern Louisiana. Some plans divided parishes and communities long together, others kept them together. Throughout the entire process, the question of which plan would ultimately win was unclear, until the last hour of the session, when Governor Jindal entered the debate armed with a veto threat that helped decide the issue. The single most important factor distinguishing the various plans from one another was their treatment of Northern Louisiana.

Some voices early in the debate called for a horizontal I-20 district, bringing Shreveport and Alexandria together in the same district and extending across the entire northern part of the state. Other voices including Jindal's chief-of-staff, Timmy Teepell, called for maintaining the vertical north-south alignment of 2001, saying "If you look at the state of Louisiana, you're going to have two districts north of the I-10." "The question is: Should they be horizontal or should they be vertical? We believe they should be vertical."[49] Most other questions were secondary to this central question. (Horizontal and vertical alignments are shown in maps 7.3 and 7.4.)

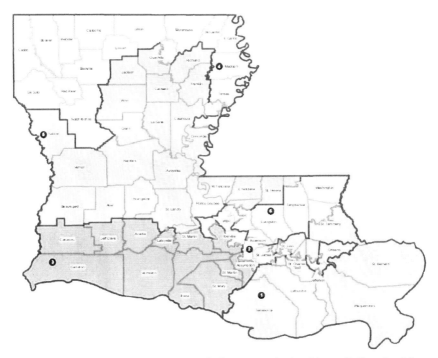

Map 7.3. SB 24 Proposal—A Horizontal Plan Map Submitted by Neil Riser. Louisiana State Legislature.

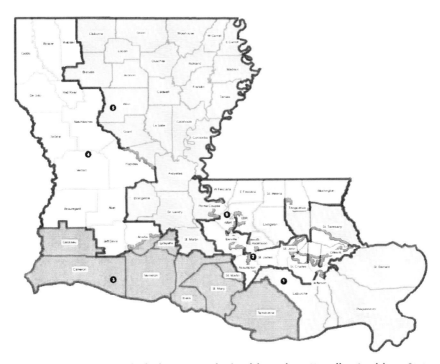

Map 7.4. SB 2—A Vertical Plan Map Submitted by Robert Kostelka. Louisiana State Legislature.

After two weeks of committee hearings, the House had three different bills and the Senate had four. Initially, the smart money favored the vertical district alignment. Maintaining the 4th and 5th Districts in their present form had the backing of six of the seven congressmen; was preferred by the GOP leadership and rank and file membership; was the closest thing to a "status quo" plan; was Governor Bobby Jindal's preferred choice; provided the best chance to preserve the partisan balance in the remaining districts; and was the most popular plan among Northern Louisiana legislators, who had a history of uniting on issues affecting their region.

Several plans introduced were variants of the vertical alignment, two of which were introduced by northern legislators. House Bill 6 (HB6), for example, by Representative Erich Ponti, R-Baton Rouge, was a clear statement of the vertical alignment. In his plan, the 4th and 5th Districts were maintained, although the 5th extended into the Florida parishes.[50] On the Senate side, Bob Kostelka, R-Monroe, introduced Senate Bill 2 (SB2), which was the plan initially agreed to by six of the seven incumbent congressmen at the meeting in Washington. In Kostelka's plan, the 5th District would intrude into Acadiana, grabbing part of St. Martin and Pointe Coupee parishes; Lafayette and Lake Charles would remain together; but Lafourche and Terrebonne would be split. A third vertical plan, Senate Bill 24 (SB24), introduced in the Senate by Neil Riser, R-Columbia, differed from Kostelka's plan mainly by reducing the percentage of black population in the 2nd District and distributing them elsewhere.[51]

One essential difference between the vertical and horizontal plans was their effect on Southern Louisiana districts. As noted above, population losses in Northern Louisiana required the 4th and 5th Districts to search for additional residents further south. With redistricting raising the district ideal to 755,562, the 4th and 5th Districts needed an additional 110,762 and 187,404 persons (respectively) to satisfy the requirements. Those numbers could reached only by encroaching on Acadiana, Baton Rouge, or the Florida parishes. Some early versions of the vertical plans raised the controversial prospect of the 4th District extending all the way from the Arkansas border to the Gulf of Mexico, a distance of some 250 miles. Likewise, the 5th would need to extend deep into Terrebonne and Lafourche parishes, confounding commonly held principles of redistricting. If the vertical, north-south alignment was to win, the effects would be felt in the south, where some residents would find themselves represented by congressmen living five hours away.[52]

The choices were equally stark for Southwest Louisiana. If the vertical plan should be adopted, some part of Acadiana would end up in the 4th District. Other plans would split Terrebonne and Lafourche in the south or divide Baton Rouge, the fastest growing area in the state; still other plans would split Lake Charles and Lafayette. All the vertical north-south plans had wrenching political and regional ramifications for Southern Louisiana, a point keenly felt by legislators from that area. One such legislator, faced with splitting Terrebonne and Lafourche Parishes asked a vertical plan supporter rhetorically, "Did you ever eat any bad gumbo, any bad boudin, anything like that, left you a bad taste in your mouth with the Acadian people?"[53]

Arrayed against the vertical plans were four horizontal plans: two offered in the House (HB3 and HB4) and two in the Senate (SB3 and SB23). Rick Gallot, D-Grambling, introduced HB3 and HB4, both of which divided Northern Louisiana along a horizontal axis, creating in the process a 4th district with a higher percentage of African Americans, making it somewhat more hospitable for Democrats and minorities.[54] HB3 followed this trend while placing Congressmen Boustany and Landry in the same southwest district. Similar but different, HB4 grouped Landry with Congressman Bill Cassidy in the 6th District while maintaining a horizontal north.[55] On the Senate side, Senator Lydia Jackson, D-Shreveport, introduced SB3; and Rob Marrineaux; D-Livonia, introduced SB23, both horizontal plans. Estimates suggest that a horizontal 4th District drawn along the northern border of Louisiana might raise the number of black voters in the district to between 36 and 42 percent, depending on how it was drawn.[56] Despite the fact that no plan making it out of committee created a second majority-minority district, the horizontal plans introduced did raise the possibility of a Democrat, if not an African American, competing in the 4th District. Meeting this challenge head-on, incumbent 4th District Congressman John Fleming, R-Shreveport, denounced it, raising a question that was heard throughout the debate: Was it better for a region to be represented by one or two congressmen, in terms of federal largesse and representation?[57] One writer pointed out that the proposed 5th District created by the horizontal plan would be a 26-parish monster, running "from Richland Parish in the north to French-speaking St. Landry in the heart of Acadiana, to Washington Parish on the southernmost border with Mississippi."[58] Supporters of the horizontal plan argued that culturally and regionally, voters in Shreveport had a great deal more in common with Monroe than they did with French-speaking Cajuns in Acadiana. One proponent compared the horizontal plan invidiously to the vertical plan, which would, he said, yoke "grim denizens of the Bible Belt . . . with jitterbugging Cajuns." Another representative from Southern Louisiana said more succinctly, if less colorfully, what most residents of the 7th District already believed, "We don't share an economy, we don't share hurricanes."[59]

Despite the ongoing effort to change the racial balance in the 4th District, it was going to take a major effort just to put enough African Americans in the 2nd, which was still the only Louisiana majority-minority district. Estimates suggested that after the effects of Katrina and out-migration, the 2nd District would need to pick up 262,210 people to reach the required ideal of 755,562. Of these, 161,000 would need to be black in order to maintain a sufficient majority-minority balance and thereby avoid preclearance problems with the Justice Department.[60] One side effect of the proposed expansion of the 2nd District up-river to Baton Rouge, was that Republican Congressman Bill Cassidy's 6th District would become a friendlier place for him, more conservative ideologically and whiter demographically.[61] Another undeniable effect of all the horizontal plans was that they made redistricting Southern Louisiana easier. A horizontal alignment would allow Lake Charles and Lafayette to remain in the same district, keep Lafourche and Terrebonne united, and reduce the pressure to split Baton Rouge among three separate districts.

Regionalism

As the discussion above reveals, the politics of congressional redistricting in the Louisiana legislature revolved around race, party, region, and incumbency. Of these, the most important factor was region, and the final agreed-upon plan incorporated the most important regional imperatives. It was apparent throughout the session that while a speaker might be motivated by race, party, or incumbency, all sought to cover themselves in the language of region. Thus, as legislators sought to create majority-minority districts or protect incumbents, they used regional justifications to do so. Bob Kostelka, Chairman of the Senate and Governmental Affairs Committee stated his intentions unequivocally prior to the session's start: "I expressly requested this committee chairmanship because I knew we had reapportionment coming up, and I wanted to make sure we kept a northeastern Louisiana congressman. . . . We're one of the poorest regions in the country, and we need all the help we can get."[62] Prior to the Session, it was noted that Kostelka and Gallot, his counterpart in the House—represented essentially the same district in Northeast Louisiana, with Kostelka's Senate District 35 encompassing Gallot's House District 11 seat, predisposing the process toward maintaining a northeastern congressional seat. Kostelka, made no bones about it, stating, "I want to keep [the seat] for Northeast Louisiana. That's not taking it away from anybody else, that's just saying we need our own representative for this part of the state."[63]

Similar sentiments were heard from other parts of Louisiana including the coastal areas. Advocating for his plan which created a single coastal district and kept Terrebonne united with Lafourche Parish, Representative Joe Harrison, R-Gray, argued, "[C]oastal issues have become among the most important for our state and it's time we speak with one voice." Echoing this position and promoting a friendly district at the same time, Congressman Jeff Landry testified to the "tremendous amount of hunger on the coast" for a single district uniting the Louisiana coastline. This sentiment was echoed by Plaquemines Parish President Billy Nungesser who said, "I absolutely believe it's important to get someone who is focused on Southern Louisiana."[64] The fact that a single Louisiana coastal district would give Congressman Jeff Landry the best opportunity to win a second term was dismissed by the congressman who said, "[T]his is not about pitting Landry vs. Boustany, it's about what's best for Louisiana."

Countering Landry's position, Congressman Charles Boustany, LA-7, representing Southwest Louisiana argued, "It would be better to have two or three members fighting for the Louisiana coastline than just one. . . . If you have more than one member fighting for the coastline, you're going to be more effective." Going farther, Boustany accused Landry of trying to "gerrymander a district that would give him a potential seat."[65] Boustany appealed to the Legislature to "hear the voices of the people of Lafayette, Calcasieu, Acadia, Jeff Davis, Vermilion and Cameron and maintain the integrity of the Calcasieu-Lafayette Corridor. . . . The state deserves a map which . . . protects the integrity of Acadiana and coastal Southwest Louisiana."[66]

The appeal to regionalism was also present in the discussion of the horizontal districting plan that would link Shreveport and Monroe and then create a single district across the broad rural middle of Louisiana (as noted above). Rick Gallot, R-Grambling, argued, "What regions have more in common, Shreveport and Lake Charles, Monroe and St. Francisville, or Monroe and Shreveport?"[67] Regionalism also made for strange bedfellows, as Congressman Boustany, understanding the districting advantages offered by supporting the Shreveport-Monroe district, reversed his previous position and incurred the ire of his Republican colleagues. According to a very upset John Fleming, Boustany "called each and every committee member on the Governmental Affairs Committee in the House to urge them to adopt the [horizontal] Jackson plan" that Fleming maintained would "add another Democrat to the House of Representatives."[68]

For his part, Boustany disavowed the importance of the partisan effect, saying, "They should not be putting French-speaking rice farmers and crawfish farmers in [a] Northern Louisiana [district]."[69] Speaking about Senator Lydia Jackson's SB3, which would create two horizontal east-west districts, one of which would have sizable numbers of minority voters, Dan Morrish, R-Jennings, said Jackson's bill "had the most support among his constituents because it keeps the region whole." Or, in other words, keeping Acadiana whole was worth more to Acadians than holding the line against the election of more Democrats elsewhere. Speaking the language of regionalism but against Jackson's plan, Congressman Alexander said, "I don't think it is doing the central part of the state fair where one man or woman has to cover 30 parishes."[70] The fact that his reelection might be imperiled by the creation of such a district was apparently not the central element in Congressman Alexander's opposition. Senator Neil Riser, author of a vertical alignment plan, stated the problem, "There's no perfect plan when we have to go from seven congressmen to six. . . . I understand their concerns, but I've not seen a bill in any form that won't split some parishes and regions."[71]

Race

Race and questions of fairness to minority voters constituted a constant subtext to congressional redistricting but were never the central theme.[72] That being said, the continued existence of Cedric Richmond's majority-minority 2nd District (encompassing Orleans and parts of Jefferson and continuing up the river in search of black residents) was a foregone conclusion in all plans submitted during the legislative session.[73] Speaker Jim Tucker noted that his "first priority is to draw a plan that complies with federal law," while Senate President Chaisson said, "we all have an interest in making sure that our plans get approved."[74]

While there were no challenges to the 2nd District, neither was serious consideration given to plans introduced to draw another majority-minority district to accommodate Louisiana's 32 percent black population. The embarrassments of the 1990s when the "Zorro" and "Slash" districts were undone by Court challenges were remembered all too well and served as a brake on legislative over-reaching. Rick Gallot, for his part, said he found it "impossible to draw a second majority non-white congressional district," although that didn't stop him (as noted above) from trying to reshape the 4th District into an east-west district with some chance thereby of electing a minority office-holder, or at least, a representative more re-sponsive to policy positions supported by minority communities.[75] Thus, the pro-posed east-west district scheme became the repository for the hopes of those who were amenable to the creation of a second minority-majority district but could not find a way to make it happen.

Throughout the process, the legislative Black Caucus raised serious questions about the intentions of the authors and the results of the various maps presented. They fought for a horizontal congressional district in Northern Louisiana and also the creation of additional majority-minority seats in the LA House and Senate. Racial tensions occasionally spilled over during the session, particularly in one con-frontation between Bob Kostelka, Chair of the Senate and Governmental Affairs Committee, and Senator Karen Carter Peterson, a member of the Black Caucus who was supporting the horizontal plan championed by her fellow caucus member Lydia Jackson. Sniping between Kostelka and his colleagues, some of whom were African American, culminated in an outburst in which he "sought to quiet" Sena-tor Peterson, D-New Orleans, addressing her as "little lady." In another exchange, Kostelka peppered Senator Lydia Jackson with questions about her (HB3) plan, ask-ing "How many congressmen have you talked to?" and "What about the governor? Have you heard what he said about my plan?" These exchanges led Senator Peterson to question whether Kostelka "is the right person with the right temperament for this job."[76] While Senate President Chaisson refused to change committee assignments, unconfirmed reports had him taking steps to maintain order for the rest of the Ses-sion. For its part, the Legislative Black Caucus announced plans to ask the Justice Department not to approve the redistricting plans passed by the Legislature, on the grounds that they did not "adequately protect and enhance the voting strength of non-white voters." In a statement the Caucus said, "Despite our efforts, we believe the process was conducted in a manner that diminished minority voters' ability to select a candidate of their choice."[77]

Party

The partisan context of redistricting in Louisiana is odd by most measures, at once partisan and at the same time, not. The curious habit of doling out commit-tee seats and chairs with only passing regard for party has previously been noted as creating a context in which a Democrat chaired the House and Governmental Affairs Committee while a Republican chaired its counterpart in the Senate. As a state, Louisiana had been progressing more slowly than most southern states toward Republican ascendancy, and in fact, up through the 2007 election, both houses of the Legislature were majority Democratic.[78] However, the election of Barack Obama in 2008, followed by the passage of national health care legislation, punctuated by the BP oil spill and the federally-imposed moratorium on new exploration in the Gulf of Mexico, pushed Louisiana out of its gradualist pattern of Republican accommodation and into full red-state status. Thus, at the start of the redistricting process, both houses of the Louisiana Legislature, the governor, all seven statewide elected officials, and six of seven congressmen were Republicans.[79] The fact that this could redound to the GOP's advantage in the redistricting process was noted by Democrat Rick Gallot, who dispassionately observed, "We are in a new environment, to the victors go the spoils."[80]

In terms of party politics, maintaining the status quo with vertical districts (4 and 5) in the north, a single southwest (3) and southeast district, (1) and, a Baton Rouge district (6) provided Republicans with the best chance of limiting the damage of the 2010 apportionment to one inevitable seat. Having previously conquered all the congressional districts but the 2nd, Republicans were faced with the necessity of sacrificing one of their own seats. Thus, the struggle to redistrict congressional seats in Louisiana was only partly partisan, although votes in committee and on the floor often reflected partisan balances.

The most hotly debated partisan divide was over the horizontal versus vertical alignment in Northern Louisiana. As stated above, Democrats—feeling that a second majority-minority district was not possible—sought to remake the 4th District in such a way that it would be more amenable to minorities and Democrats. Although most of the discussion of this issue invoked regionalism and community interest, some observers felt that this was a direct attempt to change the partisan balance in the Louisiana Congressional Delegation. Roger Villere, State Republican Party chairman, released a blistering memo in which he denounced the proposed horizontal district alignment: "Today the Louisiana State Senate passed a congressional redistricting plan that's got Nancy Pelosi celebrating a big victory for liberal democrats in Baton Rouge." Continuing he fulminated, "If the Pelosi-Plan becomes law it will be more likely that Louisiana sends a pro-Pelosi, pro-Obama, tax hiking liberal to Washington. The Pelosi-Plan must be stopped."[81]

Partisan rhetoric aside, it is clear that Democrats saw a horizontal district in northern Louisiana as more friendly to long-term electoral prospects, while Republicans saw the vertical districting as being in their long-term advantage. Votes taken in the House and Senate reflect a clear partisan divide on plans to create a refigured 4th District, with Democrats supporting it and Republicans against it. This general rule, however, was tempered by representatives like Republicans Dan Morrish and Norby Chabert and others who saw the benefits that a horizontal plan might have for keeping communities together in the south. Elsewhere this strict partisan divide was undercut as well by incumbency and regionalism as Congressman Charles Boustany, in particular, defected and began to ally himself with the horizontal plan because it worked to keep his district in Southwest Louisiana whole.[82]

A final partisan controversy concerned the Washington, DC, law firm of Holtzman Vogel hired by Speaker Jim Tucker to assist Louisiana with its filing with the Department of Justice. The firm had "strong ties to the National Republican Committee (NRC)" and members had served as "chief counsel" to the NRC. Objecting to the lack of consultation in selecting the firm, House and Governmental Affairs Chairman and Democrat Rick Gallot pointed out that the process had been considerably less robust than the "nine bids" sought "earlier this year before choosing a new vendor to run the House cafeteria." "Is our food in the cafeteria more important than our compliance with the Voting Rights Act?" Gallot asked.[83] At the end of the day, however, Governor Jindal's veto threat, combined with the frustration of being unable to accomplish the goal that they had set for themselves when they called themselves into session, provided the Legislature with sufficient reason to accept a vertical plan, despite the problems it caused for south Louisiana.[84]

Incumbents

The incumbent congressmen played a role in 2011 very much like the role they played in 2001: that is, they testified before the Legislature on a redistricting plan that a majority supported and were gratified to see a plan very much like the one they favored passed by the Legislature. There were some bumps along the way though. As might be expected, the sacrificial lamb of the redistricting cycle, Jeff Landry, complained bitterly that he "didn't get in some smoke filled room and decide on some principles" of redistricting.[85] Following the pattern of "redistricting speak," in which self-interest is invariably cloaked in the language of region, community, and voter interest, Congressman Boustany, the chief beneficiary of Landry's evisceration, disavowed any self-interest in the process, arguing that he was "interested in helping guide the legislature in drawing a map that looks at historic and economic divisions and current commonalities, [both] cultural and environmental."[86] Not surprisingly, Boustany did not remain loyal to the plan brokered by Senator Kostelka when it appeared that to do so would cost him parts of Calcasieu, Jeff Davis, and Acadia parishes. Explaining Boustany's defection, John Maginnis theorized that while the vertical plan looked feasible from a distance, "no matter how the configuration was drawn and redrawn . . . it poached precincts in Southwestern Louisiana, divided the twin bayou parishes Lafourche and Terrebonne or shaved off the top of the Florida parishes."[87] For a time, Boustany even offered vocal support for Senator Lydia Jackson's SB3, which was one of the most popular horizontal plans.

This betrayal of common principles brokered over Chinese food was greeted with disdain by 4th District Congressman John Fleming, who, coincidentally, had the most to lose from a horizontal scheme. Speaking of Boustany, Fleming said, "In order to perfect one district, he really fouls up the rest. . . . I don't think I can trust anything he said, everything he told me he reneged on."[88] As a whole, the GOP members of the delegation were incredulous that Boustany would potentially "sacrifice another GOP seat in order to create a perfect district for himself when he already had a good one." "I suspect this was [Boustany's] plan all along" said Fleming.[89] With Boustany's defection and the session coming to a climax, five of the six GOP congressmen wrote Governor Jindal and asked that congressional redistricting be put off for a year.[90] Neil Riser, the author of SB24, one of the last two plans standing at the end of the session, took over handling its counterpart from the House, HB6. Taking the floor, Riser implored his colleagues to pass HB6, saying, "If we pass anything else we're voting for a special session."[91] Senator Kostelka stated his objections to postponing the redistricting: "I was opposed to that because to come back to that . . . it would be in the fiscal session and that would have been chaotic . . . and if you didn't do it then you would have to call another special session . . . and if you didn't do it then . . ." and so on.[92] In the end, the request by the incumbent congressmen to postpone the matter was beside the point, as the Louisiana Legislature took matters into their own hands, ultimately passing a north-south plan that satisfied Jindal and made six of seven congressman very happy indeed.

Governor Jindal

Historically, Louisiana's governors exercise great power over the state legislature in a tradition going back at least as far as Huey Long and possibly before.[93] Although Jindal initially disavowed any intention to influence the Legislature's disposition of redistricting, at the same time he said that the only plan acceptable to him would be one that kept vertical districts in the north. The impact of that statement was assessed by 6th District Congressman Bill Cassidy, R-Baton Rouge, who said "the governor clearly has the ability to influence the process and he has chosen to back vertical districts. That has to have an impact." Jindal's impact was felt even more directly when he sent his two top aides, Timmy Teepell and Steven Waguespack, to meet with House Republicans a week after the session opened, reportedly to emphasize the importance of maintaining GOP districts in the House. Surprisingly, given its frequent occurrence, Black Caucus Chairperson, Pat Smith, D-Baton Rouge, said "she was appalled by the governor getting into what is purely a legislative arena."[94] Others were less surprised at Jindal's actions. Rep. John Bel Edwards, D-Amite, for example, opined that Jindal's "public and private statements are rarely in harmony."[95]

In fact, Jindal monitored the process throughout the districting session and maintained pressure at points where he felt it needed guidance. When the Senate was considering a vertical plan by Neil Riser (SB24), for example, Jindal sent a note to all 39 senators urging them to support it. In a short-lived show of independence, the Senate promptly defeated Riser's plan 19–20, and approved Lydia Jackson's SB3 which called for horizontal districts. Not impressed, Jindal delivered an explicit threat to veto any plan that did not create vertical districts. Defending his threat and responding to criticism that he was hampering progress, Jindal said, "It seems to make sense to me, why surprise people?"[96] The fact that Jindal was willing to announce his support for the vertical district alignment and threaten the Legislature with a veto if his wishes were not followed indicates his willingness to intervene for his favored outcome. Jindal's public statements to the contrary, redistricting was guided in the House and Senate by leaders chosen by Jindal, who reached agreement on a plan that was (generally) approved by him in advance. Assessing Jindal's importance to the process, House and Governmental Affairs Chairperson Rick Gallot, D-Grambling, concluded, "I think the main factor was the will of the governor."[97]

OUTCOMES

A report by Public Affairs Research Council (PAR), a Louisiana public interest think tank, expressed the opinion in a report issued prior the redistricting session that "it is likely . . . significant efforts will be made to protect the districts of sitting legislators."[98] That opinion was validated in the districts drawn in the 2011 session. By and large, the districts were drawn to return five Republicans and one Democratic incumbent to office in 2012. Prior to redistricting the 1st, 4th, 6th, and 7th districts were all over the number of persons needed had the number of seats remained at seven, while the 2nd and 3rd had fewer than necessary. The 6th District (Baton Rouge) in particular, which gained residents displaced by Katrina, was 79,874 over. However, no existing district was at the new ideal of 755,562, as required by the loss of a seat. Thus, reassigning the voters to six not seven districts added voters to every remaining district. The largest number of persons added to any district, excluding the entirely revamped 3rd District (previously the 7th), was District 2, which gained 284,072 new persons. Other districts picked up smaller numbers of new voters, including the 6th District, where only 28,064 new persons were needed to meet the ideal.[99] No incumbents ended outside of Cedric Richmond, and Jeff Landry got more than 27.5 percent new voters.[100] Although the 2011 redistricting was not as status-quo as the 2001 redistricting, which kept 96.8 percent of the same voters in each district, by and large, the changes made in 2011 advantaged those already holding office.

In the 1st District, Congressman Steve Scalise was the incumbent with the most radically reshaped district from a geographical standpoint, giving up all of Washington Parish and part of Tangipahoa in Northeast Louisiana while picking up most of the Southeast Louisiana Coastline, specifically St. Bernard and Plaquemines Parishes (entirely) and Jefferson, Lafourche, and Terrebonne (partly).

Even with parts of eight parishes making up the 1st District, it was still the most compact Louisiana district created in 2011 (see map 7.5). Numerically, Congressman Scalise got 207,767 persons who were not in his district previously (27.5 percent). Adding these numbers did not, however, greatly affect the racial and partisan breakdown of his district. In the 2001 districting, white residents totaled 82.6 percent, while black residents totaled 13.2 percent.

In the 2011 districting, white residents totaled 79.2 percent, while black residents totaled 13.8 percent. Thus, the 1st District remained the Louisiana district with the lowest proportion of black voters and the district most likely to elect a Republican.[101]

The 2nd District remained the lone majority-minority district in Louisiana and indeed the only district with an African American population over 36 percent.[102]

Map 7.5.   Final Congressional Districts after 2011 Redistricting. Louisiana State Legislature.

Prior to the 2011 districting, the 2nd was a two-parish district with residents drawn from Orleans (447,223) and Jefferson (191,339) parishes respectively. Covering parts of 11 parishes in its 2011 incarnation, the 2nd District moved up the Mississippi River, capturing residents in St. Charles (33,730), St. John the Baptist (33,564), St. James (22,102), Ascension (20,312), Assumption (7,637), Iberville (23,326), West Baton Rouge (10,626), and finally, East Baton Rouge, where it grabbed 102,184 residents. Slightly over 37 percent of the persons now in the 2nd are new to the district. Racially, the 2nd District has 63.9 percent blacks and 31.2 percent whites, down slightly from the 64.7 percent and 30.2 percent figures in the 2001 redistricting. Very likely the new 2nd will retreat slightly from its D+25 rating, but still should be a safe district for Democrats. The real question for Cedric Richmond, the first-term incumbent facing reelection, is: will a candidate emerge from "up-river," representing East Baton Rouge and the river parishes? If so, the dynamics of politics in this district which have been largely New Orleans-based could change a great deal. Either way it appears to be a safe seat for minority and Democratic candidates.[103]

The 3rd District in Southwest Louisiana is the old 7th District remade, with a few more parishes to the east and a few less to the north. In the 2001 redistricting scheme, Lafayette and Calcasieu Parishes predominated among the eight parishes represented with 190,503 and 183,577 residents respectively. The newly drawn 3rd

District lost Evangeline and St. Landry Parishes to the 4th District, but picked up St. Martin, Iberia, and St. Mary in the East from the prior 3rd District. The old 8-parish 7th District is now, largely, the 10-parish 3rd. The black-white resident ratios remain similar, at 70.5 percent white and 25.6 percent black, respectively, compared to 72.7 percent and 25.3 percent in the old district. This 3rd District will continue to trend conservative with something close to the R+14 of the 7th District previously.[104] What distinguishes the 3rd District from the other five extant Louisiana Districts is the likelihood of a contested seat; Congressman Jeff Landry's home in Iberia was placed into the new 3rd district, making him an unwelcome addition to Congressman Boustany's largely intact district. Landry brought approximately 180,000 residents from the old 3rd into the new 3rd with him, many of whom voted for him by large margins.[105] However, in the new 3rd District they will be faced with the 575,512 persons previously in Boustany's old 7th District, creating an uphill struggle for Landry if he seeks to win the seat. Adding drama to the potential contest, there is no love lost between the Boustany and Landry. In fact, Boustany was a vocal supporter of Landry's rival for the GOP nomination in 2010, former Louisiana House Speaker Hunt Downer.

The 4th District in Northwest Louisiana remained very much the same in 2011, although extending south and east to add new voters. The expanding 4th District covered all or parts of 13 parishes in 2011, and has expanded to all or part of 15 parishes in 2011. The demography of the district remains much the same, with white residents falling slightly from 62.9 percent to 61.1 percent in 2011 and black residents rising slightly from 33.8 percent to 34.8 percent. This district is rated R+11 by Cook, and was, as noted above, the most likely candidate for reshaping into a friendlier district for minority voters and Democrats. Having failed to pass a horizontal plan, this district remains likely to return a Republican to office.[106]

Already the largest district territorially, the 5th District covering northeast Louisiana expanded yet again, to take in 24 of Louisiana's 64 parishes in part or whole. The 5th yielded population to the 4th District in both the north (Union Parish), and in the south (Evangeline, Allen), but gained in the middle of the state, with Grant Parish and, in the Florida parishes, at the expense of the 1st and 6th Districts (West and East Feliciana, St. Helena, Tangipahoa, and Washington Parishes). The 5th District gained 187,404 new residents with the changes. Demographically, the district experienced moderate change, going from 64.1 percent (white) and 34.1 percent (black) voters respectively, to 61.7 percent and 35.8 percent. The 5th District was rated R+14 by Cook, but the increase in minority voters could lower that rating and make the district somewhat more competitive for a Democrat, should one emerge to challenge Rodney Alexander, currently the dean of the Louisiana delegation.[107]

Finally, the 6th District lost what had been a fairly compact shape in the 2001 districting, as the 2nd District bifurcated it in search of minority voters. As drawn in 2011, the 6th wraps almost entirely around the 2nd District, blanketing it north, south, and west, leaving the east as the only unencumbered side. The primary focus of the expansion of the 6th in search of residents was south into Terrebonne and Lafourche Parishes, and southeast into Ascension, Livingston, and St. John Parishes.

The 6th is the district with the most altered demographic profile, as the 2nd District poached minority voters previously in the 6th. White voters in the 6th rose from 63.7 percent in 2001 to 71.4 percent in 2011, while black voters fell from 33.6 percent in 2001 to 23.5 percent in 2011. Of these, 189,610 are new to the district (25.1 percent). These changes increase the conservative cast of the district which was R+10 in 2008, but should rise in 2012, making a democratic challenge to Congressman Bill Cassidy's reelection less likely and successful. Ultimately, Cassidy did not face any Democratic challenger in 2012, instead defeating an independent and a libertarian with almost 80 percent of the vote.

CONCLUSION

Prior to redistricting, the Cook Report noted that Republicans had nearly "run . . . the table on Democrats in the last decade," leaving Republicans with "no more Democrats to target."[108] The congressional redistricting of 2011 did nothing to change that reality. Democrats were not able to breech the wall of opposition created by Republican Governor Jindal, GOP majorities in both houses, and five of the six incumbent congressmen in their quest to reshape one of the five GOP districts and make it more likely for a Democrat or a minority to get elected. Similarly, the Justice Department's preclearance requirement and the specter of court challenges based on retrogression denied Republicans the opportunity to undo the 2nd District and compete for that seat. The winners in the 2011 congressional redistricting process were Governor Bobby Jindal, who entered the debate forcefully and effectively, strengthening his Republican bona fides should he seek further state or national office; Chairman Bob Kostelka, whose planning, vision, and early entry into the process helped determine the outcome; and Northern Louisiana, which despite losing population, retained a congressman in both Northwest and Northeast Louisiana, at the expense of the more populous south Louisiana. The biggest losers were the Black Caucus, which failed to change the reelection dynamics of even one district, and south Louisiana, which suffered the ignominy of seeing its representatives vote to support the governor's plan, rather than for greater representation for the most populous part of the state.[109] Thus, at the end of the 2011 redistricting cycle in Louisiana, there are five safe Republican districts and one safe Democratic district, just about what everyone predicted prior to the process.

NOTES

1. *Redistricting: The Most Political Activity in America* (New York: Rowman & Littlefield Publishers, 2010). William Blair, Louisiana House of Representatives Research Analyst helped with the maps, charts, and numbers. Interviews with Chairmen Rick Gallot and Bob Kostelka provided valuable insight. Comments from Jeff Sadow and John Sutherlin were perceptive and helpful.

2. Looking into the future, House Speaker pro tem Peppi Bruneau, R-New Orleans, whose plan for redistricting eventually prevailed in 2001, predicted that Louisiana was "on the cusp" of losing a congressional seat in 2010. Ed Anderson, "State could lose another seat in Congress," *The Times Picayune*, July 31, 2001. Gerard Shields, "La. Likely to lose congressional seat," *The Advocate*, December 22, 2006.

3. Richard L. Engstrom and Jason F. Kirksey, "Race and Representational Districting in Louisiana," in *Race and Redistricting in the 1990s*, ed. Bernard Grofman (New York: Agathon Press, 1998). In 1991, the attempt to create a second minority district outside New Orleans led to the creation of a district whose perimeter was, at 2,558 miles, the longest and most oddly shaped of any congressional district in the country (p. 229). This district was struck down by the ruling in *Hays v. State of Louisiana* (1993).

4. John S. Baker and Elliot Stonecipher, "Our Unconstitutional Census," *Wall Street Journal*, August 9, 2009. According to the article, California had a noncitizen population of 5,622,422. Based on their calculations, California would lose nine congressmen should the census count only citizens. For further information compare the statements of Charles Kincannon, Director U.S. Census Bureau, and Steven A. Camarota, Director or Research, Center for Immigration Studies in Testimony prepared for the House Subcommittee on Federalism and the Census, December 6, 2005.

5. Quoted in Marsha Shuler, "La. GOP to fight counting of illegals," *Advocate*, August 30, 2009.

6. Frank Newport, "All 10 States Losing Congressional Seats Tilt Democratic," *Gallup .com*, December 27, 2010.

7. Certainly an ironic category in which to be a leader. Troy C. Blanchard, Karen Paterson, 2009 Louisiana Net Migration in National and Historical Context. "Population Update" (No. 1–December 22, 2009) Executive Summary.

8. U.S. census, 2010. Louisiana Public Broadcast Publications, "Redistricting Louisiana." 2011. Prior to the 1980s, Louisiana's brisk growth dovetailed the rest of the southern region, with growth averaging 17.16 percent every ten year increment. Information derived from Frank Hobbs, Nicole Stoops, "Census 2000 Special Report: Demographic Trends in the 20th Century," November 2002.

9. In Louisiana, parishes are the governmental form that in other states are referred to as counties. There are no significant functional differences between the two governmental forms.

10. Penny Brown, "La. Left in dismal situation," *The Advocate*, December 22, 2006.

11. These figures are from the 2010 census, allowing for short-term displacement to subside. Michelle Krupa, "New Orleans' official 2010 census population is 343,829, agency reports," *The Times Picayune*, February 03, 2011.

12. Michelle Krupa, "Minority populations still growing in New Orleans area, but not as fast," *The Times Picayune*, June 13, 2010. LPB, "Redistricting Louisiana."

13. The term "net migration," "refers to the difference between the number of persons migrating into and out of the state." Troy C. Blanchard, Karen Paterson, "Population Update" (No. 1-December 22, 2009) Executive Summary.

14. PEW Research Center, Comings and Goings: Migration Flows in the U.S. (pewsocialtrends.org/2008). Over the long term, Louisiana's population is projected to grow only 7.5 percent between 2000 and 2030, suggesting that the loss of another congressional seat could be in Louisiana's future. U.S. Census Bureau, Population Division, Interim State Population Projections, 2005, April 21, 2005.

15. Penny Brown, "Census: State getting older," *Advocate*, May 30, 2007.

16. Steven Ward, "Northern parishes still losing population," *Advocate*, March 24, 2008.

17. Marsha Shuler, Gerard Shields, Mark Ballard, "Congressional remap bills on agenda," *The Advocate*, April 2, 2011. Further evidence of instate migration is provided by the population of BESE districts, which varied from their ideal of 566,671 residents by a negative 172,000 in the New Orleans area and by a plus 142,000 in the Baton Rouge area. Will Sentell, House Backs 2 Remap Bills," *The Advocate*, March 31, 2011.

18. Bullock, III, p. 9. Besides Congress, the Louisiana legislature is also responsible for drawing district lines for the House and Senate, the Board of Secondary and Elementary Education (BESE), the Public Service Commission, and the Supreme Court.

19. One of the oddities of the 2011 cycle is that it was the first time the Legislature had called itself into session for the purpose of redistricting.

20. Phone Interview, January 19, 2012.

21. One of the telling oddities of the 2011 redistricting session is that the chair of the House Governmental Affairs Committee, Democrat Rick Gallot, shared duties with Republican vice-chair, M. J. "Mert" Smiley Jr., while on the Senate Side, Governmental Affairs Committee chair Republican Robert "Bob" Kostelka shared duties with Democrat vice-chair, David Heitmeier.

22. Blatant contravention of separation of powers is one of the reasons why Louisiana governors enjoy unusual power over the Legislature.

23. There are numerous examples of governors punishing legislators for failing to follow instructions, one of the most recent examples is told in John Maginnis, "What Standing Up to Jindal Gets You," *Advertiser*, January 18, 2012.

24. It is customary for the both the Senate and House to accept each other's districting of their own seats without discussion or amendment.

25. "Redistricting 2010: Reforming the Process of Distributing Political Power," PAR Analysis 317, February, 2009.

26. Section 2 of the VRA now covers all states and prohibits "any state or political subdivision from imposing any voting qualification, standard, practice or procedure that results in the denial or abridgment of any U.S. citizen's right to vote on account of race, color or status as a member of a language minority group." *Redistricting Law 2010*. William Pound, Director, National Conference of State Legislatures, November 2009, p. 54.

27. The Louisiana case was *United States v. Hays*, 515 U.S. 737 (1995). Redistricting Law 2010. The "Zorro" district and other districts drawn to advantage minorities are discussed in a perceptive article by Benjamin Forest, "Mapping Democracy: Racial Identity and the Quandary of Political Representation, *Annals of the Association of American Geographers* 91, no. 1 (2001): 143–66.

28. *Redistricting 2010*, p. 8.

29. Federal courts may start to give greater weight to state legislative decisions, if the recent decision in Texas (*Rick Perry v. Shannon Perez et al.*, 2012) is indicative of future Supreme Court jurisprudence.

30. Jack Wardlaw, "Lawmakers Predict Rapid Redistricting," *Times Picayune*, October 9, 2001.

31. Representative John Cooksey, R-Monroe, did not run for reelection in 2002, seeking a seat in the U.S. Senate instead.

32. Ed Anderson, "State could lose another seat in Congress, *Times Picayune*, July 31, 2001. Actual ideal total was 638,425.

33. Steve Ritea, Laura Maggi, "House District Remap Ok'd," *Times Picayune*, October 16, 2001.

34. Steve Ritea, Jack Wardlaw, "House Approves Congressional Remap; But black members are largely opposed," *Times Picayune*, October 11, 2001.

35. Quoted in John Mercurio, "Between the Lines," *Roll Call*, October 8, 2001.

36. Mercurio, "Between the Lines."

37. Steve Ritea, "Remap Changes Little in New Orleans Area," *Times Picayune*, October 10, 2001.

38. "Figures Present Fewer Redistricting Problems Than Anticipated," Associated Press, January 2001.

39. One group that may have had some influence on the process was led by Glen Post, Century Link CEO, who, along with others from northeast Louisiana, met with Jindal to press for a vertical district alignment.

40. Speech archived at www.votesmart.org.

41. Quoted in Bill Barrow, "Gov. Bobby Jindal does not expect to take lead role in redistricting," *Times Picayune*, January 5, 2011.

42. Louisiana Family Forum Action: 2011 Congressional Re-Districting Report. The LFF's figures and proposals were based on estimates prior to the actual 2010 census. The 2001 Second District began the process with a population of 471,490, or 284,072 less than the new ideal of 755,562. District summary totals provided by Dr. William Blair, Louisiana House demographer.

43. Quoted in Nathan Stubbs, "The Odd Couple," *The Independent*, March 2, 2010. Drawing even more heat was a controversial plan by the LFF partnering with State Senator Elbert Guillory to redistrict the House and Senate, moving majority-minority districts away from New Orleans in an explicit move to undercut the power of the New Orleans delegation.

44. Senator Kostelka reported that "everybody just about, [at the meeting] agreed with what I wanted to do." Interview, January 24, 2012. The map and plan for redistricting presented by Kostelka was created by three University of Louisiana at Monroe professors, working for the Cain group (Dr. John Sutherlin agent), based in Lafayette. Financial records indicate that several of the incumbents underwrote the group's efforts. Jeremy Alford, *Independent*, April 27, 2011.

45. Cook Political Report, March 3, 2011.

46. Deborah Barfield Berry, "Lawmakers push for the boundaries," *News Star*, February 6, 2011.

47. Twenty-nine senators and representatives from the two committees, not counting staff.

48. Interview, Rep. Rick Gallot, January 20, 2011.

49. Marsha Shuler et al., "Congressional Remap," *Advocate*, April 2, 2011.

50. These are eight parishes that were originally part of west Florida and were not included in the Louisiana Purchase. They lie directly under the part of Mississippi that extends over eastern Louisiana.

51. Marsha Shuler, Mark Ballard, "House districts proposed," *Advocate*, March 28, 2011.

52. In particular, those residents of the Florida parishes represented by Rodney Alexander.

53. Rep. Norby Chabert quoted in Jeremy Alford, "Splitsville," *Independent*, April 13, 2011.

54. Depending on how the horizontal districts were drawn, the 4th district ranged from 36 percent black to a high of 42 percent. White residents would be around 54 percent, black voters 42 percent under Gallot's plan creating a district "more racially balanced than any of the current congressional districts." Bill Barrow, "Redistricting is expected to change the way race influences Louisiana politics, *Times Picayune*, March 20, 2011.

55. Another slightly different horizontal plan (HB8) that failed to gain traction was introduced by Republican Joe Harrison, R-Gray, in the House.

56. This was clearly a fall-back position for black legislators, who were not able to convince enough of their colleagues that another majority-minority district could be created without court challenge. One plan to create a second majority-minority district, HB42, was introduced by Michael Jackson, I-Baton Rouge. Jackson's plan was radical, in that it would take in portions of 24 of Louisiana's 64 parishes, and require a major reorganization of the other congressional districts, including taking part of the black voters along the Mississippi River by Baton Rouge slated by most plans to bring the 2nd District up to 755,562. Clearly unwilling to tilt at windmills, Jackson's bill was killed in committee.

57. Both north and south Louisiana considered the question of which is better: one congressman or two? The question seems to have been settled authoritatively by HB6, the bill finally passed.

58. Ed Anderson, Bill Barrow, "Louisiana Senate approves regional, horizontal districts for Congress, *Times Picayune*, April 5, 2011.

59. James Gill, "Redistricting inspires meddling from Gov. Bobby Jindal," *Times Picayune*, April 13, 2011; Senator Dan Morrish, R-Jennings, Interview, KATC.

60. Cook Political report, March 3, 2011. Later census figures had the actual number at 284,072. Had the 2nd District been at or near the new population figure of 755,562, the pressure to draw a new majority-minority district might have been felt more keenly. As it was, the second was continued up along the Mississippi River into Baton Rouge to gather the requisite number of black votes. The most heated debates about race and districts that either advantaged or disadvantaged minorities took place in the context of House and Senate districts. By comparison, the debate about adding a second majority-minority congressional district was muted.

61. "Redistricting Preview: Louisiana," *Cook Political Report*, March 3, 2011.

62. Quoted in Greg Hilburn, "Kostelka, Gallot to Chair Redraw," *News Star*, March 20, 2011.

63. Hilburn, "Kostelka, Gallot to Chair Redraw," quoted in Stephen Largen, "Analyst: Kostelka playing hardball," *News Star*, October 12, 2009. Senator Kostelka said as much in a phone interview, arguing that "I was not for a [single north LA Congressman] because we tried that once before . . ." (interview, January 24, 2012). While the chairs of the redistricting committees in House and Senate were both from northeast Louisiana, the rest of the committee was not. The Senate committee had 9 members, three of whom were from northern Louisiana, while the House committee had 19 members, only 3 of whom were from northern Louisiana.

64. Quoted in Alex Isenstadt, "Would 1 voice be better in Louisiana?" *Politico*, February 3, 2011.

65. Isenstadt, "Would 1 voice be better in Louisiana?" Nugesser may have been rehearsing for his unsuccessful run against Jay Dardenne in the lt. governor's race in the fall 2011 elections.

66. Quoted in Jonathan Tilove, "Redistricting plan sets off fireworks in Louisiana delegation," *Times Picayune*, April 7, 2011.

67. The first four cities would be grouped by a vertical map, Monroe and Shreveport by a horizontal map. Quoted in Hilburn, March 20, 2011.

68. Quoted in Tilove, ibid.

69. Quoted in Shuler, et al., ibid.

70. Quoted in John Maginnis, "LaPolitics Weekly," March 18, 2011.

71. Quoted in Greg Hilburn, Mike Hasten, "State Senate delays vote on Riser's plan to keep a Monroe-based congressional district," *News Star*, April 4, 2011.

72. As noted above, the really bitter battles over racial redistricting took place in the context of House and Senate seats.

73. Leaving aside the Louisiana Family Forum's plan which combined the 2nd and 3rd Districts and died in committee.

74. Quoted in Bill Barrow, "Redistricting," *Times Picayune*, March 20, 2011. Retrogression, or the diminution of minority chances for electing a representative of their choice, particularly through reducing the number of districts, is, of course, the most certain way to prompt a negative review by the Justice Department.

75. Barrow, "Redistricting." Minority voters in Louisiana register to vote in lower numbers, are younger on average than other voters, and turn out to vote at lower rates, which diminishes their power relative to their overall percentage of the population. These realities also problematize the question of what level of minority voters in a district makes it possible for minorities to elect a representative of their own choosing.

76. Bill Barrow and Ed Anderson, "Talks to shape new legislative districts are tinged with race, power," *Times Picayune*, March 22, 2011.

77. Barrow, Anderson, "Jindal signs bill creating new Louisiana congressional legislative districts," *Times Picayune*, April 14, 2011. The Department of Justice did not agree and decided not to bar the new maps at either the congressional or legislative level. Relief, if there were to be any, would have to be sought through the Courts, an option that as of this writing has not been pursued.

78. In Louisiana, state-wide offices and all Legislative seats are contested every four years in odd numbered years (2003, 2007, 2011, etc.). The turn of the "solid south" from blue to red has been well documented. For one view see Aubrey Jewett, "Partisan Change in Southern Legislatures, 1946–1995," *Legislative Studies Quarterly*, August 2001.

79. This Republican ascendancy in the Legislature was sealed not by election for the most part, but by the filling of open seats and the switching of long-time Democrats to the Republican Party. At the state-wide level, three current officeholders (Treasurer John Kennedy, Insurance Commissioner Jim Donelon, and Attorney General Buddy Caldwell) were Democrats before switching to the Republican Party.

80. Barrow, Anderson, "Talks to Shape," March 22, 2011.

81. "Update: Pelosi-Plan Advances in LA Legislature," e-mail alert issued April 5, 2011.

82. Discussed in greater detail immediately below.

83. Apparently an outside attorney was needed because of advice given by House Clerk Alfred "Butch" Speer who would ordinarily handle the issue. Quoted in Jan Moller, "House Speaker Jim Tucker defends hiring GOP law firm," *Times Picayune*, April 15, 2011.

84. The vertical districting most heavily influenced the parishes in north Acadiana which were put into the 4th District (Beauregard, Allen, Evangeline, St. Landry), the 5th District (St. Landry), and those long-term communities which were split, in particular St. Landry split between the 4th, 5th, and 3rd, and Terrebonne and Lafourche split between the 1st and 6th.

85. Quoted in Melinda Deslatte, "Congressional remap dividing LA Delegation," *Victoria Advocate*, February 11, 2011.

86. Quoted in Deslatte, "Congressional remap dividing LA Delegation."

87. "Governor takes map and goes home," *Times Picayune*, April 13, 2011.

88. Tilove, "Redistricting Plan," April 7, 2011. Quoted in Nathan L. Gonzales, "Republicans Ready to Unveil Compromise Map in Louisiana," *Roll Call*, April 7, 2011.

89. Gonzales, "Republicans Ready to Unveil Compromise Map in Louisiana."

90. Boustany excepted.

91. Quoted in "Senate approves congress redistricting," *Advocate*, April 14, 2011.

92. Phone Interview, January 24, 2012.

93. Some trace the history of Louisiana's powerful governor as far back as the royal governors during the French and Spanish period. Wall et al., *Louisiana: A History* 5th ed. (Wheeling, IL: Harlan Davidson, 2008).

94. Quoted in March Ballard, "Jindal aides get involved in redistricting," *Advocate*, March 28, 2011.

95. Ballard, "Jindal aides get involved in redistricting."

96. Quoted in Mark Ballard, Marsha Shuler, "Senate reviews remap after Jindal threat," *Advocate*, April 7, 2011.

97. Interview, January 19, 2012.

98. PAR, "Louisiana Redistricting: A 2011 Progress Report," Publication 327, February, 2011.

99. The 6th District ultimately gained 189,610 new residents as some previously in the 6th District moved to the 2nd and 5th Districts.

100. It was Landry's 3rd District that largely supplied the additional voters necessary to bring the 1st, 6th, and 3rd Districts up to the 755,562 mandate.

101. LA-1 was the District with the highest conservative Partisan Voting Index at R+24 (in 2008). Estimate is based on the percentage that a congressional district votes above the national totals for the Republican or Democratic candidate for president. http://cookpolitical.com

102. The African American population in Louisiana is 32 percent.

103. Barring, of course, an unexpected scandal or disruption of the type that put Republican Joseph Gao into office for one term, 2008–2010.

104. Cook, ibid.

105. 2010 vote totals in the three districts coming over to the newly created 3rd were in favor of Landry 11,550 to 4,427 in St. Martin, 9,464 to 5,155 in St. Mary, and 14,667 to 6,088, over his Democratic opponent Ravi Sangisetty. Jeff Landry won the district by a vote of 63.7 percent versus Sangisetty's 36.2 percent. Louisiana Secretary of State, www.sos.la.gov.

106. Although John Fleming's 2010 reelection margin was solid (63–32 percent) over Democratic challenged David Melville, the slimness of his victory in 2008 over Democrat Paul Carmouche (450 votes) indicated some concern leading into 2012. Fleming, however, did not face a Democratic challenger despite the district going 2 to 1 with regards to Democratic registration.

107. Being the "dean of the delegation" doesn't count for much in Louisiana, where the congressional delegation is fairly young. Rodney Alexander was first elected in 2002 as a Democrat, later changing parties in 2004. Charles Boustany was elected in 2004; Bill Cassidy and John Fleming in 2008; and Cedric Richmond and Jeff Landry in 2010.

108. "Redistricting Preview," Cook Report Online Edition, March 3, 2011.

109. As Rick Gallot, speaking of southern Louisiana legislators, put it, "Although the numerical advantage was in southern Louisiana, none of them were willing to put their cojones on the line." Interview, January 19, 2012.

8

Redistricting in Massachusetts

Shannon Jenkins and Samantha Pettey[1]

When the Massachusetts legislature set out to draw new legislative maps, no one thought it would be easy. With the state's population growth lagging behind most other states in the country, the state was set to lose one congressional seat, and it was up to a committee of state legislators to determine who the odd person out would be. In a Democratic state, with a legislature controlled by the Democratic party and a congressional delegation that consisted entirely of Democrats, determining this was going to be no easy task.

Thus, all eyes turned to Barney Frank; in the aftermath of a bruising 2010 reelection campaign, many assumed that he was ready to throw in the towel.[2] Such an announcement would have diminished the dilemma of the redistricting committee. Instead of nine seats for ten representatives, a timely announcement by Frank would have left nine seats for nine representatives. However, Barney Frank does not often do things simply because others want him to do things; Barney does what Barney wants. So in February of 2011, Frank announced he was in.[3]

Next, speculation emerged that one of the incumbent representatives might challenge Republican Senator Scott Brown.[4] Elected in 2010 to fill out the remainder of Ted Kennedy's Senate term, Sen. Brown would have to stand for reelection a little over two years after he initially won the seat. As a Republican in a highly Democratic state, it was assumed that Brown would be easy pickings. Rep. Michael Capuano, who ran unsuccessfully for the Democratic nomination in the 2010 special election, was seen as the leading contender to challenge Brown.[5] But with Brown sitting on a war chest of over $7 million dollars at the start of the year and fairly high approval ratings,[6] none of the House delegation stepped forward.

Thus, it seemed that there would be no easy way out for the legislative committee tasked with redrawing the congressional maps. The committee began the process by holding hearings throughout the state and meeting with key political actors, both publicly and in private.[7] But then, just days after the maps for the state legislative districts were released and on the eve of the unveiling of the congressional district maps, Rep. John Olver announced that he planned to retire.[8] Political observers in the state thought this move would save the day for the legislative committee, as they were once again back to a position where the number of incumbent representatives equaled the number of seats available.[9] As Sen. Finegold, a member of the redistricting committee said, "There has been a gigantic sigh of relief here in the Statehouse that Congressman Olver has decided to retire because we don't have to have anybody run against each other."[10] It was widely assumed that the maps that were forthcoming would divide Olver's district in Western Massachusetts among the remaining incumbent representatives and would only otherwise tweak the existing district boundaries to stay within required population parameters.[11]

It was to great surprise to many in the state, then, when the new maps were unveiled. Not only were there significant shifts in many of the district lines, but the legislative committee managed to pit two Democratic incumbent representatives, Rep. William Keating and Rep. Steven Lynch, against each other in one district and to create an entirely new district with no sitting incumbent.[12] Luckily for both Keating and Lynch though, Keating happened to own a second home in the newly created district; within hours of the release of the map, Keating announced plans to move permanently into said second home.[13] Once again, Massachusetts was back to nine seats and nine incumbents, if one still counted a sitting representative in an entirely new district as an incumbent. Not for long though. One of the districts most dramatically changed in the new plan was that of Barney Frank. The changes were so significant, in fact, that Frank announced his plans to retire within days of seeing the map, deciding that it would be too much work to seek reelection in such a changed district.[14]

Thus, over the course of the redistricting process, the state went from having ten representatives and nine seats, to nine representatives and nine seats, to eight representatives and nine seats. In a state so dominated by Democrats, the key question has to be then: when faced with the ability to make an easy decision and protect all of the sitting incumbents, why did the committee in charge of redistricting alter the district lines so substantially to the extent it induced one of the most senior members of the state congressional delegation to retire?

The answer lies both in the changing demographics of the state population and the ugly aftermath of the 2000 redistricting cycle. In short, legislators were leery of another lawsuit challenging the results of the redistricting process (the last lawsuit brought down the powerful then Speaker of the House Thomas Finneran); as a result, they drew maps more with an eye to the courts than to the incumbents.

POPULATION CHANGES

When it was announced that Massachusetts would be losing one congressional district, few were surprised. Prior to the 2010 census, the existing districts in Massachusetts were already under ideal by at least 62,000 constituents per district; added up across all ten districts, the amount under the ideal approximately equaled one congressional district.[15] While the population of Massachusetts grew from 2000 to 2010 by 3.1 percent, to reach a total of 6,547,629 people, this growth lagged behind the United States as a whole, which averaged a 9.7 percent growth rate.[16]

Furthermore, as map 8.1 shows, the population growth and loss was not evenly distributed throughout the state nor was it evenly distributed across various demographic groups. As Secretary of State William Galvin noted, in-state population shift would "dictate in large measure where the opportunities for redistricting occur and where the opportunities to spread districts out occur."[17] Thus, the committee in charge of redistricting would need to take this uneven population growth into consideration when drawing new maps.

Generally speaking the areas near the Boston metro area experienced population growth, while the western part of the state and Cape Cod experienced population decline.[18] For example, the largest county in Massachusetts is Middlesex County, which borders Boston and contains about 1.5 million people. Close by is Boston, the state's most populated city, which about 617,000 people call home. While Western Massachusetts has two of the state's largest geographic counties, Berkshire and Franklin, the area has the fewest number of people and has experienced population loss since 2000.[19]

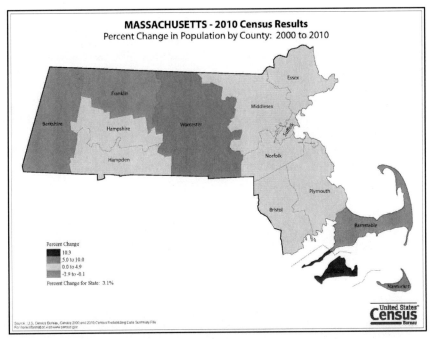

Map 8.1.   Population Change in Massachusetts, 2000–2010. U.S. Census Bureau.

Population loss was particularly acute in Rep. Olver's congressional district which traversed Western Massachusetts and included parts of both Berkshire and Franklin. Barnstable County, located on Cape Cod in southeastern Massachusetts, also showed negative growth by 3 percent. This is part of the 10th Congressional District which was represented by freshman Rep. Keating; his district also included areas of population growth, but the majority of people in the 10th District reside in Barnstable county and parts of Plymouth county, counties that experienced population loss or low growth rates. Thus, population loss was concentrated in the first and tenth congressional districts, so it was assumed that if drastic changes were to be made, the changes would be concentrated in these districts. Of course, changes to congressional districts do not occur in a vacuum, when the boundaries of one district change, so too must the boundaries of another district. Given these population parameters, speculation began to emerge: would the committee consolidate the districts of Olver and Rep. Richard Neal, the other representative with constituents in Western Massachusetts, and force them to run against each other in the primary or would the committee force Keating to face off with another incumbent and if so, who would that be?

In addition to concerns about the geographic distribution of population loss, the committee would need to pay attention to how population change was distributed across various demographic groups. This was particularly true given the lawsuit that stemmed from the 2000 redistricting (see below); this time around, the committee seemed focused on avoiding a similar outcome.[20]

Generally speaking, Massachusetts's population is predominantly white, consisting of about 5.3 million of its total 6.5 million people in 2010.[21] Despite this fact, population growth between 2000 and 2010 in Massachusetts was largely due to the growing minority populations within the state. For example, the total population of black or African Americans grew from 5.4 to 6.6 percent of the population. The percent Asian increased from 3.8 to 5.3, and the total Hispanic population increased from 6.8 to 9.6 percent. The Asian and Hispanic populations swelled by more than 46 percent from 2000 to 2010.[22] Overall, minority populations in the state increased by 36 percent, while the white populations decreased by 4 percent.[23]

In fact, had the Hispanic population in Massachusetts not grown, the state would not have had population growth at all.[24] The majority of this Hispanic population growth occurred in and around central Massachusetts. Worcester County, located in central Massachusetts, had the highest percent increase in population growth; much of this can be attributed to the growth in Hispanic residents. In Springfield, located in Worcester County and the third largest city in the state, Hispanics make up nearly 39 percent of the population in 2010, compared to a Hispanic population of 27.2 percent in 2000.[25] The Hispanic population grew in other regions of the state as well. Holyoke and Chicopee, located in nearby Hampden County, also saw Hispanic population increases from 2000 to 2010. Now, 48.4 percent of the population in Holyoke is Hispanic, and 14.8 percent are Hispanic in Chicopee.[26] Other communities around these areas, such as Montague and Northampton among others, saw about a 5 percent increase in the Hispanic population.[27]

Thus, the committee needed to take particular care in addressing the concerns of the growing minority populations in the state. Much of this concern was focused on the maps for the state house and senate; as these districts are smaller than congressional districts, activists were focused on ensuring that the interests of the growing African American, Asian, and Hispanic populations would be accurately reflected in those maps. In fact, challenges to the 2000 maps focused on the state legislative maps, not the congressional maps. However, this did not mean that the committee could ignore the differences in population growth across different demographic groups when drawing the congressional maps. Of key concern for these maps was the retention of the majority minority status of the 8th Congressional District.[28]

THE REDISTRICTING PROCESS IN MASSACHUSETTS

Redistricting is sometimes seen as the rawest exercise of political power. In Massachusetts, home to the original district that wrought the term "gerrymander," this is undoubtedly true. Over the course of state history, this exercise of power has led to numerous "interesting" looking districts, including the existing 4th Congressional District, represented by Barney Frank (see map 8.2).

In Massachusetts, if there's political power to be wielded, the place to look for the base of that power is in the state legislature. Structurally, the legislature dominates the three branches of government. This is in part a historical legacy; the Massachusetts

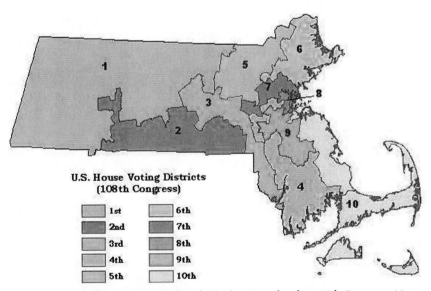

U.S. House Voting Districts (108th Congress)

1st	6th
2nd	7th
3rd	8th
4th	9th
5th	10th

Map 8.2.   Massachusetts Congressional District Maps for the 108th Congress. Massachusetts Office of Geographic Information 2007.

constitution is the only one of the constitutions from the 13 original colonies still in effect[29] and was constructed during a time when the framers were fearful of a strong executive, given their experience with the British crown. Squire and Hamm note that the legislature was powerful in Massachusetts from colonial times; it remains so to this day.[30] Legislative dominance is also due to more contemporary politics. While the state and the legislature are predominantly Democratic and have been for several decades now, Republicans have been successful in state-wide campaigns, as evidenced by the fact that four out of the last five governors have been Republicans.[31] However, Democrats have wielded a veto-proof majority during these periods of Republican governors, so they have gotten used to doing what they want.

In the redistricting process, the Massachusetts Constitution further reinforces this legislative dominance by giving control over the process to the General Court, the formal name of the Massachusetts state legislature. While the Constitution establishes some parameters for the drawing of district lines for the state senate, state house, and governor's council, it is largely silent on the matter of drawing congressional districts, aside from vesting that power in the legislature.

Thus, the legislature has the ability to determine how the legislature will go about drawing the district lines. In 2010, this was achieved by a special joint committee composed of members from both the House and Senate.[32] In 2000, the House established a committee to draw its own version of the maps, which were then submitted to a Senate committee. In all cases, these committees are created by an act of the legislature; the act sets up the charge and the composition of the committee(s). Traditionally, the process of overseeing the establishment and makeup of this committee is dominated by the legislative leaders in the two chambers. While Clucas ranks the institutional power of the Massachusetts House Speaker fairly low as compared to other state house speakers,[33] the fact of the matter is that legislative leaders dominate legislative life in Massachusetts. It is not unheard of for legislators to receive a major bill mere hours before being required to vote on it, and key legislative deals are often hammered out between the speaker, the Senate president, and (sometimes) the governor. Therefore, the extent to which the joint redistricting committee operates independently is generally at the discretion of said legislative leaders. In 2000, as noted in *Black Political Task Force v. Galvin*, House Speaker Thomas Finneran kept "the process on a short leash."[34] While Finneran himself denied any involvement with the redistricting process, the Court cites extensive evidence of Finneran's involvement. This involvement eventually led to Finneran's downfall and provided important lessons for the legislature during the 2010 redistricting process.

2000 REDISTRICTING

If redistricting generally is the rawest exercise of political power, then the 2000 redistricting process in Massachusetts was a textbook example of this exercise of power. Redistricting in the state is typically very partisan, and 2000's mapping was no different, despite the fact that the net number of seats did not change after the 2000 census. Of course, some saw the existing maps as questionable and "convoluted"[35] and in need of revamping, but that did not necessarily mean all politicians in Massachusetts agreed that this was the case. In 2000, Democrats dominated the state legislature, but a Republican, Jane Swift, was governor. However, given that the Democratic majority was veto-proof, Swift's interests did not play much of a role in the 2000 process. Rather, the Democrats, and one Democrat in particular, House Speaker Thomas Finneran, controlled the process. Generally speaking, Finneran wielded his power as speaker heavily, using it to set the agenda for the state house,[36] and to punish those who opposed him.[37] The redistricting process was no exception. He appointed key legislative allies to the committee and hired other allies as staff to the committee.[38] While the committee held five public hearing meetings across the state to listen to public input and concerns on the redistricting process, this appeared to merely be windowing dressing. As the court noted in the subsequent court case about redistricting, Finneran kept the process on a "short leash" and did much of the "heavy lifting" with his staff.[39] Finneran's key concern in doing so was to change the boundaries of his own district to make it more safe, primarily by diluting the growing voting power of minorities there.[40]

Despite the fact that the state legislative maps were Finneran's key concern, he did have a hand in drawing up the House version of the congressional maps as well. In drawing the maps, Finneran noted he had three goals: to create a majority-minority district, to unite communities of interest and to ensure adequate representation for the SouthCoast of the state.[41] The maps produced by the House Redistricting Committee to reflect these goals had the effect of "blindsiding" sitting Representative Marty Meehan, whose district was eliminated in favor of creating the aforementioned southern district.[42] Analysts assumed this was because Meehan was mulling over a run for governor, but Meehan had not yet made a commitment to do so. Rather, some say the House plan may have been Finneran's punishment for Meehan, who had been fighting for campaign finance reform, a proposal Finneran "despised."[43] Under these plans, Meehan would be pitted against incumbent Rep. John Tierney, unusual given the state was not losing a congressional district.[44]

Meehan quickly decided to forgo a run for governor and enlisted the support of Senate Majority Leader Thomas Birmingham.[45] The maps unveiled were the product of the House committee; the Senate, listening to the pleas of Rep. Meehan, produced their own congressional maps, which also created a majority-minority district, but at the same time managed to preserve the districts of all of the sitting incumbents. Gov. Swift joined the party, producing her own version of the congressional maps, as did Republicans in the legislature; given the size of the Democratic majority in the legislature, though, the latter two sets of maps did not figure into the final compromise.[46] Instead, leaders in the legislature worked, sometimes contentiously, to fashion a compromise plan. When legislative leaders unveiled these compromise maps, it turned out that incumbency interests prevailed; rather than radically reshaping district lines in creating a new district, legislators simply tinkered at the edges.[47] While Swift vetoed the

Democratic maps, the legislature quickly overrode her veto,[48] and the "incumbent protection plan" prevailed.[49] Thus, the congressional maps produced by 2000 redistricting were enacted on February 11, 2002, without the governor's signature.

This marked the end of the chapter on the 2000 congressional redistricting, but not the state legislative redistricting as those plans were challenged in state and federal court for violations of the Voting Rights Act.[50] Coalitions of black, Latino, and Asian activists challenged these maps on the grounds they weakened the voting power of their communities. Their goal was to stop Finneran from diluting the voting power of African American neighborhoods in his district by replacing them with predominantly white precincts.[51]

The Black Political Task Force and others challenged the state maps in a civil case due to this unfair representation of minority voters, arguing the districts in the state maps clearly favored white incumbents. Ultimately, a panel of three judges agreed with the plaintiffs and ruled the map unconstitutional as it was in violation of the Voting Rights Act of 1965.[52] The judges ruled the maps weakened black voters in 17 districts around the Boston area and that the black population in the area was significantly large enough to hold a majority in at least one more of the districts than allocated. The courts then gave the state legislature six weeks to redraw the districts while accepting comments from the Black Political Task Force.[53]

Of particular importance in the ruling was the fact that House Speaker Thomas Finneran was footnoted for misleading the court when he testified about his overall involvement in the process.[54] Finneran, under oath, stated that the first time he saw the maps were when they were introduced to the full House for vote.[55] In reality, Finneran worked closely with the committee during the process. For example, only four legislative staffers had access to and proper training for use of the redistricting software, which was only available in the Speaker's office.[56]

Federal prosecutors eventually indicted Finneran in June of 2005 for perjury and obstruction of justice due to his blatant misrepresentation of his participation in the redistricting process. Finneran testified he had not seen the plans, yet the indictment included evidence that showed Finneran's active role in eight meetings about redistricting. Rather than having to serve possible prison time if proven guilty, Finneran pleaded guilty to the obstruction of justice charges and eventually agreed to not run for local, state, or federal office for five years. He also received unsupervised probation for eighteen months and was fined $25,000.[57] Thus, while the congressional maps were not the target of the lawsuit, the 2000 redistricting process was politicized to such an extent that it eventually brought down one of the most powerful politicians in the state of Massachusetts.

2010 REDISTRICTING

Redistricting got its official kick-off in 2009 in Massachusetts, when the House and the Senate voted to support the creation of a special joint committee on redistricting.

Legislation passed by the House and the Senate established the parameters for the committee (21 of 28 members from the House with at least five Republicans across the membership from both chambers) and allowed the committee to hire staff and purchase the necessary technology.[58] Representative Michael Moran and Senator Stanley Rosenberg, as co-chairs of the Committee on Election Laws, would lead the process. Republicans quickly recognized that there was not much chance that their interests would be given much weight in the process, so they took the opportunity to propose that an independent redistricting commission be created to draw district lines, rather than using a legislative committee. That proposal was quickly rejected by Democrats, both in 2009[59] and in 2011.[60]

While Republicans made inroads into the Massachusetts House with the 2010 elections, the Democrats still held majorities in both chambers of the General Court, allowing them to largely do what they wanted during the redistricting process in 2011. In fact, the Democratic majorities were so large (they controlled 90 percent of the seats in the Senate and 80 percent of the seats in the House), they could override any potential veto by the Democratic governor, Deval Patrick. As a result, Patrick was largely left out of the redistricting process, probably much to his liking given the hot potato it had become in 2000.[61]

Because the special redistricting committee that was created in 2009 expired with the end of the 2009–2010 legislative session (before committee members were appointed), the committee needed to be reauthorized in 2011 to officially get to work. So, on February 10, 2011, a joint Senate-House redistricting committee was established by order of the Senate.[62] The House quickly concurred in the beginning of March. The House vote occurred largely along party lines as Republicans voted against the committee after their proposed amendment to create the independent commission was rejected. The order charged the committee with developing legislation for the congressional district maps, along with maps for the state house, state senate, and the governor's council. It also mandated that the committee hold public hearings across the state to receive input from interested parties.[63] Just how seriously the committee was to take this mandate remained to be seen.

Both chambers then appointed members to the special committee in mid-March, which had chairs from both of the chambers. Senator Stanley Rosenberg, a Democrat from Amherst and the president pro tempore of the Senate, was chosen as the Senate chair, while Representative Michael Moran, a Democrat from Brighton (in Boston), was chosen as the House Chair.[64] Sen. Sonia Chang-Diaz, a Democrat from Boston, and Rep. Cheryl Coakley-Rivera, a Democrat from Springfield, were chosen as the Senate and House vice-chairs, respectively. Senators Barry Finegold (D-Andover), Karen Spilka (D-Ashland), James Timilty (D-Walpole), Bruce Tarr (R-Gloucester and the Senate Minority Leader), and Daniel Wold (D-Harwich) filled out the rest of the Senate delegation. House members of the committee included: Demetrius Atsalis (D-Barnstable), Garrett Bradley (D-Hingham), Antonio Cabral (D-New Bedford), Marcos Devers (D-Lawrence), Linda Forry (D-Dorchester, Boston), Paul Frost (R-Auburn), Sean Garbelly (D-Arlington), Anne Gobi (D-Spencer), Patricia

Haddad (D-Somerset), Bradford Hill (R-Ipswich), Bradley Jones (R-North Reading), John Keenan (D-Salem), Stephen Kulik (D-Worthington), Vincent Pedone (D-Worcester), Alice Peisch (D-Wellesley), Elizabeth Poirier (R-North Attleboro), Byron Rushing (D-South End, Boston), and Joseph Wagner (D-Chicopee).

While the Republican membership of the committee from the House came almost entirely from the leadership (Jones was the Minority leader, and Hill and Poirier were the 2nd and 3rd assistant leaders respectively), there were only five Republicans on the entire committee. Therefore, as expected, Republican interests were generally not considered in process; Democratic interests dominated. In a one-party state, the most important cleavages are not between the in-party and out-party, but between different coalitions within the majority party. In Massachusetts, one of the key lines of dispute is between legislators who represent districts in Boston and the surrounding area and legislators from districts outside of the Boston metro area. Past congressional district maps have sometimes reinforced this division, as was the case with the 1993 district maps which split Fall River and New Bedford, two of the ten largest cities in Massachusetts, into separate congressional districts, despite the fact that they share many common interests (as past textile towns) and are close geographically (with less than 10 miles separating them). Nonetheless, the geographic composition of the new redistricting committee seemed fairly well balanced. Although Boston had four legislators on the committee, there were also legislators from the next two largest cities, Worcester and Springfield. Several legislators from the western part of the state were appointed to the committee, as were legislators from the cape, the north shore, and south coast of Massachusetts. Furthermore, there was at least one legislator who represented a town in each of the state's existing congressional districts. However, several of the ten largest cities outside the Boston metro area in the state did not have representatives on the committee, such as Fall River and Lowell, while there were four legislators from Boston alone, including the House chair of the committee. Thus, while the committee may not have been perfectly representative of the state, the composition of the committee appeared to have been established to allow major interests in the state to have a seat at the table.

Legislators quickly got to work at their task, holding their first meeting on March 16. At this meeting, committee members were given background information as part of a presentation from H. Reed Witherby; they learned about key laws and court rulings governing the process and learned the ideal district size in the state in 2011 would be 727,514. This was a significant increase from 2001, when the ideal district size was 634,910. Thus, nearly 100,000 residents had to be added to each congressional district.[65]

In addition to holding 13 public hearings across the state, the chairs and the committee also decided to hold private meetings with interested organizations and with each of the members of the congressional delegation. In fact, the private meetings with the congressional delegation were held prior to the official establishment of the special committee. Chairs Rosenberg and Moran traveled to Western Massachusetts to meet individually with Reps. Neal and Olver in the beginning of February.[66] They also traveled to Washington, DC, to meet with the rest of Massachusetts delegation in mid-February even though the House only voted to reauthorize the committee in March. Rosenberg and Moran argued these meetings were being held to "explain the process," but it was widely understood that these meetings were a chance for each member of the delegation to make their best case for maintaining their district to the chairs of the redistricting committee.[67] In addition, Reps. Capuano and Lynch made a visit to the state capital in June to meet with the chairs and further attempt to influence the process in their favor. In all, the committee chairs met with all members of the congressional delegation at least once and with some members on multiple occasions.[68]

While the content of these meetings was private, there was much speculation about what happened, as many observers were trying to determine who would be left holding the short end of the stick. Representative Tierney was not seen as having particularly close ties to the state legislature. Furthermore, his wife was under a cloud of legal suspicion, having pled guilty to helping her brother file false tax returns for an illegal gambling corporation he ran offshore,[69] which led to speculation that he would either retire or his district would bear the brunt of redistricting. However, given that Tierney's district was tucked into the northeast corner of the state, if his district were to be eliminated and he chose to remain in the race, his district would have to be consolidated with the district of Rep. Ed Markey, one of the senior members of the congressional delegation or with the district of Rep. Nikki Tsongas.[70] While Massachusetts has historically been seen as a liberal state, it has been surprisingly unreceptive to electing women to Congress; aside from Tsongas, only three women have ever served in the House, and no women have ever served in the Senate.[71] Thus, Rep. Tsongas was the only female member of the Massachusetts congressional delegation; in the aftermath of the 2010 special election, where Attorney General Martha Coakley lost the chance to become the second female member of the Massachusetts congressional delegation and the first ever female senator from the state, members of the redistricting committee did not seem particularly eager to force a Democratic primary battle that would include Rep. Tsongas.[72] Thus, Markey, Tierney, and Tsongas appeared to be relatively safe.

Most agreed that Representative Frank, now that he was in, was not in danger of being pitted against another incumbent, although this was not certain. Instead, given the less than compact nature of Frank's existing district and the fact that he lived in the northern most part of the district, it seemed possible that Frank would have his district redrawn to the point where he no longer lived in it.[73] One of the key bases of Frank's electoral strength was in New Bedford, a city on the south coast of the state; Frank's advocacy for the fishing community in the city, an important industry in the city, had made the city the core of his constituency. Frank wanted to maintain this base, but the city was at the southern end of his district; there was clearly a tension, then, in drawing a district for Frank that met districting guidelines and kept both his house and his New Bedford base in it.

Finally, there was speculation about the districts of those congresspersons representing districts where population loss was concentrated. The Western portion of the state was represented by Reps. Olver and Neal; while it seemed to make sense to consolidate these two western districts into one, residents of these districts were already leery of what they saw as the Boston-centric focus of state government and were ready to adamantly defend their right to two congressional districts.[74] Given that the committee was co-chaired by a state senator from the western part of the state (Rosenberg), this outcome seemed likely.[75] The other area where population loss was concentrated was in the Cape. This area was represented by freshman Rep. Keating. At the bottom rung of the congressional delegation ladder, Keating seemed vulnerable, but merging Keating's district with another would also mean that some other representative, higher up on the ladder, would be saddled with a primary battle against an experienced Democrat. The two most likely candidates were seen as Rep. Lynch and Rep. Frank.

The committee also met privately with several organizations, as noted in the letter the chairs of the committee submitted to the legislature.[76] However, the names of all of these organizations were not released to the public. Undoubtedly, these organizations were those who expressed a vested interest in the process and who, it seemed, might be likely to mount a legal challenge if they did not like the outcome of the process. Other groups who were interested in the process were active in trying to influence the maps submitted by the committee. For example, Fair Districts Massachusetts, the New Democracy Coalition, the Massachusetts Black Empowerment for Redistricting, and Common Cause of Massachusetts were all active in proposing their own version of state and congressional district maps to reflect the particular interests of their organization. For instance, the first three organizations were particularly interested in the retention of the 8th district as a majority-minority district in the state, given that most of the state's population could be attributed to growth in minority communities.[77]

Along with these private meetings, the committee held a series of public meetings across the state. According to the committee's letter to the General Court,[78] during this process, they held 13 public hearings across the Commonwealth that were attended by over 4,000 people, heard testimony from over 400 people, and established a website about redistricting that was visited by over 35,000 individuals. Some of the testimony in these hearings did not seem to be particularly useful; as state Rep. Jones noted, some individuals requested that the committee not eliminate a congressional district or that they not change the district boundaries.[79] But mostly, these meetings allowed individuals in regions across the state to make the best case for a variety of arguments, such as having two representatives in Western Massachusetts,[80] consolidating towns that were split in the 2000 redistricting into one district,[81] ensuring towns were not split and not splitting towns from their current congressional representative,[82] among others.[83] In all, the chairs of the committee claimed to have logged 1,254 miles traveling between Boston and the public hearings to ensure adequate public input into the process.[84]

After all of these public hearings and private meetings, the committee set to work on the maps. As opposed to 2000, the legislative leaders in the General Chamber were fairly hands off during this information-gathering and map-drawing process. The committee seemed to have a fair deal of discretion to work independently, and the chairs, along with the committee members, appeared to function as one committee, as opposed to two committees from two different chambers. News accounts during this period rarely mentioned the legislative leaders, House Speaker Robert DeLeo and Senate President Therese Murray. Instead, news stories focused almost exclusively on Moran and Rosenberg (with occasional reports from other members of the committee, particularly the Republican members), and they were almost always described as working together. It appears, then, that the legislative leaders learned their lessons from 2000 and kept their hands off redistricting in this go around.

The state legislative maps were released first, followed by the unveiling of the congressional maps on November 7, 2011. As noted above, the extent to which the districts changed surprised some observers, particularly since Rep. Olver had announced his intentions to retire prior to the unveiling of the maps. Perhaps the committee was already committed to the plan that was unveiled, and it was too late to change the maps when Olver made his announcement. Or perhaps Olver had received word from the committee that his reelection would be made more difficult by forcing him to compete against another incumbent. Regardless of whether either of these is true or if Olver was simply retiring to spend more time with his wife, who was ill, his announcement appeared to have little influence over the maps that were presented. The changes in these maps were called "sweeping," with co-chair Moran noting, "we didn't tinker on the edges here."[85]

In looking at the new maps, there were some clear winners and losers. Among the winners were those advocating for the retention of the majority-minority district. Given that Moran had stated that maintaining the 8th district as a majority-minority district was the committee's "highest priority,"[86] it was little surprise that happened under the new maps. Among the losers were the ten towns that were split into separate congressional districts, including two of the ten largest cities in the state, Cambridge and Fall River. Notably, neither of these cities had representatives on the committee. Other cities split under the new maps were Milton, Boston, Andover, Sudbury, Palmer, Bellingham, Raynham, and Wichendon. Of course, Boston was split so as to maintain two congressional districts for the city, so it would be wrong to include that city on the list of losers. As McMorrow notes, the committee was faced with three options for the city of Boston: one, two, or three districts.[87] The first option, one district for Boston, would have meant pitting two incumbents against each other, while the committee was unwilling to fracture Boston across three districts to fit Cambridge into one. So in the battle of the two largest cities (Boston and Cambridge) in the state, Boston came out ahead.

In the congressional delegation, Frank and Keating were the clear losers. Frank was driven out of Congress by the new maps, while Keating was driven out of his house. Capuano and Lynch's July meeting with the committee seemed to have worked too, as both of those representatives saw changes that strengthened their Democratic base. Of course, Lynch was paired with Keating under the new maps, but given

Keating's quick decision to move (so quick in fact, that one wonders whether the legislative committee knew about Keating's second house and Keating knew what the maps would look like before they emerged) meant that Lynch didn't have to sweat much. Rep. James McGovern's new district would only contain about a third of his current constituents, but it does not appear that McGovern is in any electoral danger from the changes to his district.[88] Tsongas's district did not change much nor did Markey's, so they seemed to be winners as well. Tierney's district changed the least, but given his wife's problems and the fact that his district saw the addition of several Republican strongholds, he could see a serious Republican challenger emerge. It's hard to determine whether Tierney's a winner or loser at this point.[89]

Events unfolded swiftly after the unveiling of the maps. Despite extensive public input prior to the drawing of the maps, no public hearings were held after the plans were revealed, and the public was only given three days in which to comment on the maps. As predicted, complaints emerged from the cities that were split under the new maps, but the General Court seemed not to notice these complaints much. As House committee chair Moran stated, the legislature would vote on the new maps "with or without additional citizen input."[90] And the General Court did, in fact, vote on the new maps without any further citizen input; one could also argue they approved maps without any further legislative input as well. Of the eight amendments offered in the House, only one, that established which precincts in Raynham would be in which congressional district, was adopted. In the Senate, only one of the ten amendments was adopted; as with the accepted House amendment, it established which precincts were in which district, but this time for Andover. Furthermore, the plans were adopted without debate in either chamber.[91] On Novmber 1, 2011, the House voted to approve, and the Senate quickly followed suit on the same day. Governor Patrick then signed the maps into law on the 21st of the same month, appearing to bring the process to a close (see map 8.3).[92]

CONCLUSION

Aside from the winners and losers mentioned above, one could argue that the residents of the state of Massachusetts were also clear winners during the 2010 redistricting process. In the past, turnover in the state's congressional delegation has moved at a glacial pace, at best. Of the ten representatives from Massachusetts, seven of them began their service prior to 2000. But during the 2010 redistricting process, two of those most senior members, Olver and Frank, decided to retire. Now, Frank's 4th District has no sitting incumbent, nor does the newly created 9th District on the south coast. Although one may think of Keating as an incumbent in the latter district, the truth is that this will be a difficult endeavor for him. Already, Bristol County District Attorney Sam Sutter has announced plans to run for the 9th Congressional District seat, challenging Keating in the Democratic primary.[93] Other candidates, potentially from both parties, will surely emerge. Of course, while

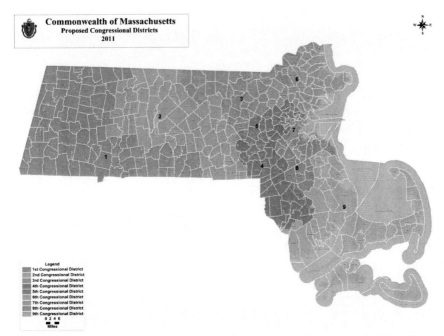

Map 8.3. Massachusetts New Congressional Maps. Massachusetts Special Joint Committee on Redistricting 2011.

the makeup of the delegation will surely change, the question is whether this will be a radical departure from the past. Already, old names are emerging as we move towards the 2012 elections; Joseph Kennedy III, the grandson of Robert Kennedy and the son of former Rep. Joseph Kennedy, has formed an exploratory committee for the 4th Congressional District, hardly a new name on the Massachusetts political scene.[94] Furthermore, the demographic makeup of the congressional delegation seems unlikely to change. The current delegation is dominated by white males (nine of them), and few of the candidates who have emerged to announce either intentions to run or who have formed exploratory committees break this demographic mold.

Interestingly, the one marker of the delegation that may see change is that of its partisan composition. Despite the fact these maps were drawn by a Democratic legislature in a Democratic state, observers seem to agree that these new maps open the door for Republicans to make a return to the ranks of the state House delegation. Rep. Tierney may be vulnerable; his wife's legal problems coupled with the fact that Billerica and Tewksbury, two towns that lean Republican, were added to his district makes him a prime target. In fact, former state Senate minority leader, Richard Tisei, has announced plans to run against Tierney for this seat.[95] In addition, analysts see the newly created 9th District as a potential pickup for the Republicans as the district contains fewer registered Democrats than other regions of the state.[96] Finally, Frank's opponent from 2010, Republican Sean Beilat, appears to be ready to run for that seat again; given that he mounted a credible challenge to Frank in 2010, he will be a serious contender for the seat.[97] Thus, after years of many non-competitive House elections, residents of the state should see at least two to three competitive races in 2012.

The one thing residents needed even more than a shake-up in the congressional delegation was a restoration of trust in the redistricting process. That's not to say the process was not political. But, residents and groups throughout the state reported that the 2010 process was a marked improvement over what happened in 2000. The Massachusetts Common Cause called the process this time around "the most open, transparent, and principled redistricting process ever in Massachusetts."[98] Bruce Bikerstaff and Malia Lazu, two community organizers who were engaged in advocating for a better redistricting process, stated: "Ten years ago, the redistricting process was deeply flawed and led to a successful lawsuit by communities of interest in Boston to block the Commonwealth's final maps. Ten years later, state Rep. Michael Moran and state Sen. Stanley Rosenberg have taken great steps to ensure the spirit of the redistricting process is realized."[99] They called this round of redistricting a "major step forward."

Of course, not everyone is happy about the outcome of the process. As one analyst noted, "It's disturbing that one of the House's sharpest critics of Republican policies [Frank] can be bounced because of lousy redistricting—by his own party."[100] It's probably not possible that redistricting in a state losing a congressional seat will produce an outcome that makes everyone happy. It may not even be possible to do that in a state gaining a congressional seat. But, the redistricting committee went a long way in restoring public confidence in a process that had gone badly off the rails in 2000. Part of this was self-serving; by producing maps that radically changed the composition of the congressional districts in the state, instead of preserving the interests of incumbents at all costs, the committee appears to have successfully avoided the one outcome they dreaded most: a lawsuit. But in serving their own interests, the committee also seems to have done a good job in serving the interests of residents of the state as well. And that's an outcome almost no one would have predicted when this process started.

NOTES

1. The authors would like to thank Matt Sylvain and Jason Wentworth for their research support.

2. Michael Norton and Matt Murphy, "Political calculations begin as census confirms Massachusetts House seat loss," *Dedham Transcript,* December 22, 2010.

3. Laura Crimaldi, "U.S. Rep. Frank to seek re-election," *Boston Herald,* February 3, 2011.

4. Matt Murphy, "Weekly Roundup—Electoral Curveballs," *Statehouse News Service*, October 29, 2011.

5. Michael O'Brien, "Rep. Capuano: Decision by Summer on Challenge to Scott Brown," *The Hill,* January 31, 2011.

6. Hillary Chabot and Christine McConville, "Scott Brown seeing green with $7M," *Boston Herald*, January 31, 2011.

7. Stanley Rosenberg and Michael Moran, "Report of the Joint Special Committee on Redistricting, 2011," www.malegislature.gov/Bills/187/House/H03798 (retrieved January 12, 2012).

8. Chris Cassidy, "Olver to retire, easing redistrict plan decisions," *Boston Herald*, October 27, 2011.

9. Mark Arsenault, "Olver to retire, redistricting may ease," *Boston Globe*, October 27, 2011.

10. Michael Graham, "Tyranny of majority," *Boston Herald*, October 28, 2011.

11. Arsenault, "Olver to retire."

12. David Riley, 2011, "Massachusetts. Lawmakers release plan to reshape congressional seats," *MetroWest Daily News*, November 8, 2011.

13. Frank Phillips and Noah Bierman, "Keating to move from Quincy to Cape, due to redistricting map," *Boston Globe*, November 8, 2011.

14. Dave Wedge, Hillary Chabot, and Natalie Sherman, "Barney Frank blames redistricting in decision to quit," *Boston Herald*, November 28, 2011.

15. Michael P. MacDonald and Micah Altman, "Massachusetts 2010 Census Selected Statistics," *Public Mapping Project 2011*, www.publicmapping.org/resources/state-resources/massachusetts/massachusetts-2010-census-statistics (accessed January 12, 2012).

16. U.S. Census Bureau, "U.S. Census Bureau Delivers Massachusetts' 2010 Census Population Totals, Including First Look at Race and Hispanic Origin Data for Legislative Redistricting," www.census.gov/newsroom/releases/archives/2010_census/cb11-cn104.html (accessed January 12, 2012).

17. Norton and Murphy, "Political calculations."

18. When speaking generally of counties, Dukes and Nantucket counties will be excluded due to geographical differences and drastic population differences as compared to Massachusetts as a whole. The two counties total around 30,000 people and are demographic outliers in Massachusetts. Despite the high positive percentage change in population since 2000 the counties are still vastly different from Massachusetts as a whole (2011 census).

19. U.S. Census Bureau, "U.S. Census Bureau Delivers."

20. Frank Phillips, "Districting Map leaves much intact, GOP raps Democratic plan," *Boston Globe*, December 4, 2011.

21. U.S. Census Bureau, "U.S. Census Bureau Delivers."

22. Priyanka Dayal, "Changing faces; We're growing more ethnically diverse," *Worcester Telegram and Gazette*, April 10, 2011.

23. Dayal, "Changing faces."

24. Elizabeth Roman, "Census 2010: Hispanic Boost in Massachusetts Population," *The Republican*, March 28, 2011.

25. Roman, "Census 2010."

26. Roman, "Census 2010."

27. Roman, "Census 2010."

28. At the start of the redistricting process, some in Massachusetts advocated for the creation of a majority-minority district, including Fair Vote (Nancy Rearson Stewart, "Group proposes splitting South Shore to create a mostly minority congressional district," *Patriot Ledger*, May 12, 2011.) and Senator Scott Brown (Michael Norton, "Rep. Michael Capuano:

District is already majority-minority, and Sen. Brown can tour it," *Masslive.com*, www .masslive.com/news/index.ssf/2011/04/rep_michael_capuano_district_i.html (accessed January 12, 2012). But Massachusetts has had a majority-minority congressional district since the 2000 redistricting; the 8th district is represented by Rep. Michael Capuano.

29. Peverill Squire and Keith Hamm, *101 Chambers: Congress, State Legislatures and the Future of Legislative Studies* (Columbus, OH: The Ohio State University Press, 2005), 20.

30. Squire and Hamm, *101 Chambers*, 20.

31. The Republicans include William Weld, Paul Cellucci, Jane Swift, Mitt Romney; the lone Democrat is current Gov. Deval Patrick. Both Govs. Cellucci and Swift were appointed to the position after Govs. Weld and Cellucci, respectively, resigned to take other positions. Cellucci was eventually elected to the position, whereas Swift was not.

32. Massachusetts is unique in that it not only uses joint committees for special purposes such as these, it also uses them for the regular processing of legislation. So this joint committee arrangement resembles the norm in the legislative process.

33. Richard Clucas, "Principal-Agent Theory and the Power of State House Speakers," *Legislative Studies Quarterly* 26 (2001): 319–38.

34. *Black Political Task Force v. Galvin* 300 F. Supp. 2d 291 (D. Massachusetts. 2004).

35. National Journal Group, "Almanac of American Politics 2008," www3.nationaljournal .com/pubs/almanac/2008/states/ma/ma_cong.htm (accessed January 12, 2012).

36. Raphael Lewis, "Finneran lieutenants eye bid for House speaker," *Boston Globe*, August 14, 2004.

37. Dan Kennedy, "Speaker Tom Finneran faces an effective GOP governor and a growing number of organized political enemies, but he's not heading for the door . . . yet," *The Boston Phoenix*, August 15 23, 2003.

38. Granite State Progress, "Shades of Finneran: A Comparison of NH Speaker of the House Bill O'Brien and His Former Law Partner, Convicted MA House Speaker Thomas Finneran," 2011, www.granitestateprogress.org/news/shades-of-finneran-a-comparison-of-nh-speaker-of -the-house-bill-obrien-and-his-former-law-partner-co.html (accessed January 12, 2012).

39. While the court case dealt with the demographic makeup of the state legislative districts, the role Finneran played in redistricting is relevant as it shows that the make-up of the 2000 committee and indeed the entire process was driven by purely political concerns.

40. Charles Euchner, "State Must Draw Line, But Fairly," *Rappaport Institute for Greater Boston*, November 13, 2003.

41. Rick Klein and Glen Johnson, "No fast help for Meehan on district: Governor, speaker keep their distance," *Boston Globe*, July 26, 2001.

42. Frank Phillips, "Meehan vows fight for district: Gubernatorial bid is out; seeks new House term," *Boston Globe*, July 24, 2001.

43. Phillips, "Meehan vows."

44. Klein and Johnson, "No fast help."

45. Phillips, "Meehan vows."

46. Michael W. Freeman, "Legislature approves new redistricting plan," *Herald News*, December 4, 2001.

47. Phillips, "Meehan vows."

48. John Mercurio, "Between the lines," *Roll Call*, January 21, 2002.

49. National Journal Group, "Almanac of American Politics 2008."

50. Justin Levitt, "All about Redistricting: Massachusetts," 2011, http://redistricting.lls .edu/states-MA.php (retrieved June 11, 2011).

51. Yawu Miller, "Redrawing Political Maps Takes a First Step," *Bay State Banner,* June 19, 2011.

52. *Black Political Task Force* v. *Galvin.*

53. *Black Political Task Force* v. *Galvin.*

54. Phillips, "Meehan vows."

55. Steve Marantz, "Group Urges Finneran Perjury Probe," *Boston Herald,* March 10, 2004.

56. Granite State Progress, "Shades of Finneran."

57. *In the Matter of Thomas M. Finneran.* 2007. 455 Massachusetts. 722.

58. Gintautus Dumcius, "House okays redistricting, reorganization plans," *Belmont Citizen-Herald,* March 6, 2009.

59. Dumcius, "House okays."

60. While this plan received unified support from the Republicans, Democrats both inside and outside the legislature were less than enthusiastic about the plan. Secretary of State Galvin appeared to support the plan, probably not a surprise given that he was named as the defendant in the lawsuit in the 2000 redistricting process, although he claimed later that contrary to Republican assertions, he "consistently opposed plans that would strip the Legislature of its constitutional power" (Kyle Cheney, "Weekly Roundup—Senate Dems Scuttle Independent Redistricting Panel," *Statehouse New Service,* January 20, 2011). Other state Democrats were as mixed in their signals as Galvin. Republicans claimed the plan was supported by Gov. Patrick (Paul Adams, "Adams Supports Independent Redistricting Commission," *Tewksbury Patch,* March 5, 2011), but news accounts during 2011 suggest that Patrick stated that the legislature should keep the redistricting process "at arm's length," but that he wanted to hear from the legislature itself before supporting such a plan ("Patrick: Redistricting should be kept 'at arms' length,'" *Boston Herald,* December 6, 2010).

61. Frank Phillips, "Electoral districts being redrawn," *Boston Globe,* August 19, 2011.

62. Bob Katzen, "Beacon Hill Roll Call: Senate approves redistricting commission," *Beacon Hill Roll Call,* February 11, 2011.

63. Massachusetts General Court, "2011 Special Joint Committee on Redistricting Committee Charge," www.malegislature.gov/District/ContentPage/RedistrictingDocument4 (accessed January 12, 2012).

64. As noted above, the two served as co-chairs of the Elections and Committee, and so were serving as de-facto chairs of the Redistricting Committee prior to the appointment of all of the members in 2011.

65. H. Reed Witherby, "2011 Presentation to the Special Joint Committee on Redistricting: Overview of Redistricting," www.malegislature.gov/District/ContentPage/Redistricting Document2 (accessed January 12, 2012).

66. Steve Brown, "Legislators sound out congressional delegation about redistricting," *90.9 WBUR,* www.masslive.com/news/index.ssf/2011/03/western_massachusetts_could_be.html (accessed January 12, 2012).

67. Noah Bierman, "State legislators go to D.C. to discuss redistricting process," *Boston Globe,* February 20, 2011; Dumcius, "House okays."

68. Murphy, "Weekly Roundup."

69. Stephanie Ebbert, "Congressman Tierney's wife convicted in federal tax fraud case," *Boston Globe,* October 6, 2010.

70. Frank Phillips, "Electoral districts being redrawn."

71. Office of the Clerk, "Women Representatives and Senators by State and Territory, 1917–Present," http://womenincongress.house.gov/historical-data/representatives-senators-by-state.html (accessed January 12, 2012).

72. Frank Phillips, "Electoral districts being redrawn."

73. Frank Phillips, "Electoral districts being redrawn."

74. Dan Ring, "Massachusetts legislators enter new phrase in fight over congressional redistricting," *The Republican,* July 16, 2011.

75. Frank Phillips, "Electoral districts being redrawn."

76. Rosenberg and Moran, "Report of the Joint Special Committee."

77. Yawu Miller, "Groups propose increase in minority voting districts," *Boston Banner*, September 29, 2011.

78. Rosenberg and Moran, "Report of the Joint Special Committee."

79. Paul Feely, "Minority Leader Jones weighs in on redrawing lines," *Daily Times Chronicle,* October 7, 2011.

80. "W. Massachusetts pols: Don't take away Congressional seat," *Boston Globe,* March 26, 2011.

81. Paul Crocetti, "Is there political gamesmanship in Massachusetts Redistricting?" *Herald News,* February 12, 2011.

82. Dumcius, "House okays"; Thor Jourgensen, "Tierney: Keep Lynn in Sixth District," *Daily Item*, May 17, 2011.

83. Robert Preer, "Local leaders fret over shifting districts," *Boston Globe*, September 15, 2011.

84. Ring, "Massachusetts legislators."

85. Phillips and Bierman, "Keating to move."

86. Bob Salsberg, "Advocates seek boost in Massachusetts minority voter clout," *Boston Globe,* October 5, 2011.

87. Paul McMorrow, "Cambridge feels the diss in redistricting," *Commonwealth Magazine,* November 15, 2011.

88. Answer Guy, "Massachusetts Redistricting Analysis," *Daily Kos,* November 14, 2011, www.dailykos.com/story/2011/11/14/1036024/-Massachusetts-Redistricting-Analysis (accessed January 12, 2012).

89. Howie Carr, "Fly 'em to the moonbats," *Boston Herald,* November 13, 2011.

90. Robert I. Rottberg, "Let's have a good look at those redistricting maps," *Boston Globe,* August 6, 2011.

91. Bob Salsberg, "Massachusetts House, Senate approve new district maps," *Boston Globe,* November 1, 2011.

92. As of the publication of this chapter, no lawsuits have been filed against the new congressional district maps, so it appears that the process in Massachusetts has drawn to a close.

93. Matthew Nadler, "Bristol County District Attorney Sam Sutter wants to change the atmosphere in Washington," *Plymouth Daily News,* January 12, 2012.

94. Will Richmond, "Joseph Kennedy III, Marty Farren announce run for 4th Congressional seat," *Taunton Daily Gazette,* January 6, 2012.

95. Phillips and Bierman, "Keating to move."

96. "GOP's Hodgson weighing run in new 9th Congressional district," *Patriot Ledger,* November 8, 2011.

97. Chloe Gotsis, "Sean Beilat tweets about 4th Congressional run," *Newton TAB Blog*, January 4, 2012, http://blogs.wickedlocal.com/newton/2012/01/04/sean-bielat-tweets-about-4th-congressional-run/#axzz1jJyUfDF4 (accessed January 12, 2012).

98. Massachusetts Common Cause, "Redistricting," 2011, www.commoncause.org/site/pp.asp?c=dkLNK1MQIwG&b=4849049 (accessed January 12, 2012).

99. Bruce Bickerstaff and Malia Lazu, "Redistricting and civic engagement—it worked well," *Dorcester Reporter*, November 2, 2011.

100. J. P. Green, "Redistricting debacle dumps Dem warhorse," *Democratic Strategist*, November 30, 2011.

9

Michigan

Republican Domination during a Population Exodus

Michael K. Romano, Todd A. Curry, and John A. Clark

> In our estimation the Republican majority is doing what we probably would do if we were in control.
>
> —Vernon Smith, Democratic State Senator (MI)[1]

It is an uneasy truth in the United States that the process of redistricting after the decennial census is highly politicized and controversial. Critics often complain that the process results in back-alley dealings, "safe seats" in both the state legislature and Congress, and court battles over claims of voter marginalization. The concept of gerrymandering—the redrawing of district lines in order to benefit a particular candidate, interest, or political party—has become ubiquitous in the vocabulary of the public, the media, and politicians as a term used to describe the entire redistricting process instead of particular maps or states. Critics of redistricting generally link the ideal process to the ability of an individual state, and by proxy the United States as a whole, to host free and fair elections for representatives in the state and federal legislature. Low levels of incumbent turnover coupled with high vote margins in elections is tantamount in the eyes of critics to the removal of democracy, since the people's choice is subsumed by the district lines being drawn by their electors. In Michigan, where district lines are decided by the dominant party in the state legislature, the redistricting process has generally been one in which advocacy groups and minority party lawmakers have been shut out of negotiations. With the loss of one congressional seat and a significant drop in the population of the state, the calls for inclusion by these groups resonated strongly during the 2011 cycle.

Following the 2010 census, Michigan was the only state in the Union which lost population, declining over half a percent since 2000, while the nation as a whole gained nearly 10 percent. The bulk of this decline came from the traditionally African American stronghold of Detroit, which witnessed a 25 percent drop in population during the ten years since the previous census. In the wake of this population exodus, Michigan lost one congressional seat. With a majority Republican legislature, a Republican governor, and majority Republican Supreme Court, Democrats were destined to lose; the only question remained to be how much.

Michigan's redistricting process is constrained for two reasons. The first is that, similar to states such as Georgia, Illinois, Texas, and several others, Michigan is home to two minority-majority districts, both located in the Detroit metropolitan area. Due to the high minority population in Detroit, Michigan, has had a tradition of dividing the city in order to increase minority representation in accordance with Section II of the Voting Rights Act. There has been substantial movement and research in the area of racial gerrymandering, both from a representational perspective[2] and from a judicial/legal perspective,[3] which generally finds that the creation of minority-majority districts tends to have a distinct effect on the pool of potential candidates as well as on the likelihood of increasing minority voting in the district. As we will also discuss below, due to the presence of two townships under "covered jurisdiction" in accordance with Section V of the Voting Rights Act, the Michigan legislature must also follow redistricting guidelines that strongly impact the redrawing of districts no matter what party is in control of the process.

The second constraint on the Michigan process is the highly partisan nature of redistricting in the state. Michigan is not alone in this regard; however, the most recent rounds of redistricting in the state have been strongly influenced by party dynamics and electoral peculiarities such as term limits in the state legislature. Unlike racial redistricting, partisan gerrymandering has had less empirical analysis in the literature. The reason for this is due to the problem of identifying partisan gerrymandering empirically in order to test its effect on other aspects of the American political system. One important distinction between racial and partisan gerrymandering has been the ability to "know it when you see it" with regard to the former. Partisan gerrymandering, while no less invidious, is much more difficult to identify and even more complicated to correct for. Justice Sandra Day O'Connor noted in her dissent in *Davis v. Bandemer* (1986)[4] that unlike racial groups, which are easily identifiable, partisan groups behave differently and can fluctuate more easily. Thus, partisan gerrymandering is more difficult to identify and prove from a legal perspective. Likewise, identifying partisan groups in many areas of the United States has largely been based on assumptions about demographic and geographic areas utilizing survey data of a subset of the population, causing examinations of partisan gerrymandering to be generally biased.[5] As we will see below, the Republican dominance in Michigan over the past two redistricting cycles has led to much controversy over the validity of the state's maps. With little opportunity for recourse, state Democratic lawmakers and citizen groups found themselves shut out of the process. The 2011 cycle provided some opportunities for transparency, but in large part offered more of the same from Republicans attempting to shore up support in volatile districts and protect their interests in the state.

Before discussing the current Michigan redistricting process and maps, we begin by describing the legal process and issues with which Michigan must contend. Along with this, we examine the previous rounds of redistricting historically, making note of how these cycles affected the process overall. Afterward, we assess the demographic trends and changes that have occurred in Michigan since the previous round of re-districting to get a sense of what factors the legislature had to deal with during the redistricting process. Finally, we will examine the 2011 process and its likely impact on congressional elections in the decade to come.

THE PROCESS OF REDISTRICTING IN MICHIGAN

Baker v. Carr (1962),[6] *Reynolds v. Sims* (1964),[7] and the Voting Rights Act (VRA) of 1965 provided much of the institutional inertia that has come to dominate the process of redistricting in Michigan. Beyond the limits of "one person, one vote," Michigan has to contend with not only Section II of the VRA (which concerns the dilution of a minority group's voting power and applies to all states) but also the more strict requirements under Section V. Two Michigan townships (Clyde and Buena Vista) fall under the description of "covered jurisdiction" as described in Section V.[8] Section V requires that the state submit the redistricting plans to either the Department of Justice or the U.S. District Court for the District of Columbia for pre-approval to ensure that the plans are nondiscriminatory concerning the minority communities of those locales.[9]

In addition to the need to comply with the following practices, Michigan map-makers over the past five census cycles have had to contest with a gradual but steady decline in the number of seats allocated for their congressional delegation. In 1960, Michigan had 18 seats in the U.S. House of Representatives. In the 1970 census Michigan lost 1 seat. This trend has continued in every following census, leaving the state with just 14 seats in the United States House of Representatives following the 2010 census. Since the *Baker v. Carr* (1962) decision, the redrawing of congressional districts has been left to the state legislature, allowing the majority party to control the process.[10] For a 40-year period, Democrats in the state legislature controlled the redistricting process; however in 2001 the Republicans had their first chance to redraw the lines.

The Michigan Redistricting Process in 2001

While Michigan had a 7 percent population gain in the 1990s, it was not enough to keep pace with the changes nationally. Michigan lost one seat, giving the new Republican majority legislature a chance to not only make certain districts easier or more difficult for incumbents, but also the chance to delete a district entirely. Considering this was the Republicans first chance to draw districts, how the process was going to unfold was a mystery. Ultimately, the process the Republicans used in 2001 was neither public nor transparent.

Democrats and public interest groups charged that the 2001 redistricting process was done in overt secrecy with the meetings open only to Republican Party officials and legislative leaders. The Democrats and the public were kept largely in the dark concerning the shape of the districts, despite numerous calls for public forums and hearings. The maps for the legislative and congressional districts were not made available to them until immediately prior to the vote. This led one observer to proclaim that "the process and outcome demonstrate that redistricting in Michigan in 2001 was an exercise in which one party chose the constituencies it preferred for its members in ways that limit the ability of the citizens of Michigan to play meaningful roles in determining the makeup of their congressional delegation or their state legislature."[11]

Strengthening Republicans in 2001

One goal of the redistricting plan was to help bolster Republican representation in the Michigan congressional delegation. Mapmakers attempted to make the 8th District, represented by freshman Republican Congressman Mike Rogers, a safer seat. In 2000, Rogers won the seat by only 111 votes. Following the redistricting, which added two solidly Republican counties to the 8th District while removing a section of Washtenaw County that was mostly Democratic, Rogers won the 2002 election with 69 percent of the vote.

Also, the Republicans redrew two districts, the 10th and the 11th, in order to establish new safer seats. The 10th District was drawn in the "thumb" region of Michigan for Candice Miller, the outgoing secretary of state. This district included much of what had been Democratic whip David Bonior's congressional district, effectively drawing him out of office.[12] Miller easily won the 2002 election with 64 percent of the vote. The 11th District was tailor-made for term-limited state Senator Thad McCotter and drawn to include sections of Oakland County and Wayne County, which were previous strongholds of support during his time in the state Senate. McCotter, who was also the vice chair of the Senate Reapportionment Committee, won his 2002 election with 59 percent.

The six Republican incumbents witnessed little change to their constituencies and all were easily reelected in 2002. Only two representatives, Dave Camp and Joe Knollenberg, saw moderate changes to their districts. Camp's district was redrawn in such a fashion that saw his geographic constituency change. Compared with his previous district however, the new 4th District was virtually the same in relationship to demographics and partisan affiliation. Knollenberg's new district retained a sizable portion of his previous district but also included a significant section of Oakland County. Having to campaign to different constituents proved a non-issue and Knollenberg easily won in 2002 with 59 percent of the vote.

Targeting Democrats in 2001

A second goal of the Republican redistricting effort was to make life hard for Democratic candidates. Three districts were drawn to make incumbent Democrats face off against each other. Following the 2002 election, three Democrats were no longer in congressional office: Jim Barcia, David Bonior, and Lynn Rivers. Each of their districts were moved and redrawn in a fashion that if they had chosen to run, they would have had to challenge other Democrats. Only Lynn Rivers chose to challenge a sitting incumbent, John Dingle, during the primary. Dingle won by 20 points over Rivers in the primary, and went on to win reelection in the general election as well. While the Republicans modified the two minority-majority districts in Detroit, they did so in fashion that only took into account population loss. Ultimately, John Conyers and Carolyn Cheeks-Kilpatrick, the two representatives from Detroit, easily won re-election in 2002.

While there was a legal challenge to the Republican redistricting plan in 2001, the odds were stacked against the Democrats. Michigan Democrats charged that the redistricting plans ran afoul of a 1996 statue commonly known as the Apol standards.[13] The Apol standards, the Democrats argued, stated that district lines had to be drawn in such a fashion that minimized the number of county and municipal boundary breaks, which the Republican plan did not do. The statute, which had been amended in 1999 to give the Michigan Supreme Court original and exclusive jurisdiction, was relatively silent on whether it applied to just state legislative districts or also congressional districts.[14] The Supreme Court, in a 6–1 decision, claimed that the Apol standards were meant to apply solely to state legislative districts and furthermore, it was entirely at the discretion of the state Republicans to follow them. This ultimately ended the legal challenge and solidified the new districts.

In the aftermath of the 2001 redistricting process, the payoff for Republicans in the 2002 elections was evident. In 2001 the congressional delegation was 9 to 7 in favor of the Democrats; after November 2002 it was 9 to 6 Republican. The Republicans showed skill in creating safe Republican districts while overpacking Democratic districts. In 2002, the average Republican victor garnered around 66 percent of the vote, while Democrats averaged 82 percent. While redistricting left the Democrats disadvantaged concerning the number of seats they held, the districts as constituted were overly safe. Even accounting for population movement, it seemed unlikely that either party would have any difficulty remaining in those seats for the following ten years. Nevertheless, Democrats were able to knock off two Republican incumbents in 2008. After one of the seats reverted to Republicans and a formerly Democratic seat changed parties, the partisan makeup of Michigan's delegation remains the same in 2011.

DEMOGRAPHIC TRENDS FROM 2000 TO 2010[15]

Between 2000 and 2010, the state of Michigan experienced two major demographic changes that helped to shape the 2011 redistricting process. First and most notably, Michigan lost a portion of its population, the only state in the 2010 census to drop in population since 2000. Second, while the overall population of Michigan was in decline, the minority population of the state grew from 21.4 percent in 2000 to 23.4 percent in 2010. Unlike previous years, however, the minority population is more dispersed geographically, with many moving away from the Detroit area into the suburbs. Detroit is still a central hub for residents in the state, minority or otherwise, but this geographic dispersion helped Republican lawmakers focus their attention on the highly Democratic Detroit areas when redrawing the district maps, clustering those districts together while providing a better safety net for volatile districts in the western part of the state.

Population Decline

Michigan has been a site of substantial decline in recent years. Poor economic conditions coupled with a struggling auto industry have caused a portion of the state's population to either disperse from the larger cities, or leave the state all together. The 2010 census reported a population decline of 55,183 (approximately –0.6 percent) from 2000. With a total population of 9,883,640, Michigan remained the eighth most populous state in the nation; however the steady decline over the past four reapportionment cycles relative to other states has caused the state to consistently lose seats in Congress. With its fourteen seats, Michigan's ideal population for each district was approximately 705,974.

Utilizing data from the most recent census, table 9.1 shows the current deviations from the ideal point in the last two rounds of redistricting. What becomes most apparent is that, while many of the post–2001 districts still fall close to their ideals, the loss of a single representative seat causes all but the 8th and 10th Districts to

Table 9.1.   District Breakdowns of Population by 2001 and 2011 Ideal Points

District	Total Pop. (2011)	2001 Ideal Point	Deviation	2011 Ideal Point	Deviation
Congressional District 1	650,222	662,588	–12,366	705,974	–55,752
Congressional District 2	698,831	662,588	36,243	705,974	–7,143
Congressional District 3	694,695	662,588	32,107	705,974	–11,279
Congressional District 4	686,378	662,588	23,790	705,974	–19,596
Congressional District 5	635,129	662,588	–27,459	705,974	–70,845
Congressional District 6	671,883	662,588	9,295	705,974	–34,091
Congressional District 7	676,899	662,588	14,311	705,974	–29,075
Congressional District 8	707,572	662,588	44,984	705,974	1,598
Congressional District 9	657,590	662,588	–4,998	705,974	–48,384
Congressional District 10	719,712	662,588	57,124	705,974	13,738
Congressional District 11	695,888	662,588	33,300	705,974	–10,086
Congressional District 12	636,601	662,588	–25,987	705,974	–69,373
Congressional District 13	519,570	662,588	–143,018	705,974	–186,404
Congressional District 14	550,465	662,588	–112,123	705,974	–155,509
Congressional District 15	682,205	662,588	19,617	705,974	–23,769

fall drastically below the current ideal point for the post–2010 census. The two districts, held currently by Republicans Mike Rogers and Candice Miller respectively, were the sites of some focus during the 2001 round of redistricting as mentioned in the previous section, which may account for them maintaining a larger portion of their population. As table 9.1 reveals, the areas with the largest population shifts in Michigan have been the 13th and 14th Districts, which encompass the Detroit metro area and its surrounding suburbs. The western parts of the state, however, have experienced less population attrition, with many districts maintaining levels close to the 2001 ideal point.

While district sizes have shifted tremendously between 2001 and 2011, most Michiganders continue to live on the east side of the state; however their movement from the central locus of Detroit has started to scatter some of the population westward. The southeastern counties of Wayne, Oakland, and Macomb comprise approximately 39 percent of the state's total population in 2010. The total population of all three counties combined (3,863,924) is enough to fill five of Michigan's fourteen congressional seats, with 334,054 people to spare (almost half of a sixth district). The current populations of Wayne, Oakland, and Macomb, while still the highest in the state, are down from the previous census data, when the counties comprised 40.7 percent of the population (4,043,646). The most drastic decline in population, in terms of relative magnitude, has been Wayne County, with a decrease in population of 11.7 percent between 2001 and 2011.

At the center of the overall population decline in Wayne County, and Michigan in general, has been the mass exodus from the state's most populous city: Detroit. With a total population of 713,777 (7.22 percent of the state's population) the city itself could make up one of the fourteen congressional districts allotted to Michigan during the reapportionment process, if not for the tradition in the city of containing minority-majority districts. While the speed of the decline over the past decade has been slow, much of the migration that has occurred within the state comes from citizens leaving the city and moving to the surrounding suburbs. The most significant factor, however, is individuals moving out of the state all together. Table 9.2 shows the general migration out of Detroit to other areas from 2005 to 2009. The major source of the population decline is evident in the migration of almost one-third of departing Detroit residents to other states, including Ohio, Florida, and California. Within the state, the largest shift in population from Detroit has been to the suburbs

Table 9.2. Principal Domestic Migration Flows into and out from Detroit, 2005–2009

Rank	Destination of Migrants from Detroit	Percent
1	Other States	30.4%
2	Wayne County (Excluding Detroit)	24.2%
3	Oakland County	17.8%
4	Macomb County	14.6%
5	Other Counties	13.1%

of Wayne County, where the city is located, with almost one-fourth of those leaving the city heading for the surrounding suburbs. The next largest destinations, Oakland and Macomb Counties, both lie to the northeast of Wayne County and together account for approximately one-third of the total migration from the city. Finally, 4.1 percent of the city's population migrated to other Michigan counties, primarily relocating to the central part of the state near the capital of Lansing and Michigan's second largest city of Grand Rapids.

With the immense amount of migration from the state, the issue of brain drain—the large-scale emigration of highly trained and intelligent people from a region—has become a predominant question for many in Michigan. Over the past decade, the extent of immigration to Michigan for individuals with some college education or more has been on a substantial downward trend, decreasing from 7.5 percent between 2000 and 2004, to 3.7 percent by 2010. Meanwhile, the amount of emigration out of the state for individuals with the same level of educational attainment rose to its highest in 2006 (9.3 percent), returning to 7.4 percent the following year and hitting a plateau since that time. According to the most recent census data, the level of emigration for individuals ages twenty-five or older with some college education was approximately 6.6 percent (see figure 9.1).

Based on the data presented, we conclude that this trend in educational migration is indicative of transitory patterns in educational attainment, with individuals entering the state for a short period of time for educational purposes, and leaving the state after they have completed their degree. As figure 9.2 reveals, the net migration of individuals with a bachelor's degree or better accounts for the starkest decline over the ten-year period. Individuals reporting at least a postsecondary education trend in a similar fashion, declining over time and leveling off by 2009.

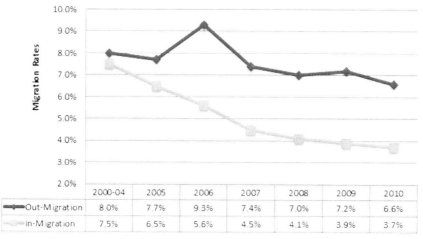

	2000–04	2005	2006	2007	2008	2009	2010
Out-Migration	8.0%	7.7%	9.3%	7.4%	7.0%	7.2%	6.6%
In-Migration	7.5%	6.5%	5.6%	4.5%	4.1%	3.9%	3.7%

Figure 9.1.   Domestic Migration Flows for People Age +25 with Some College or More. Created by the author.

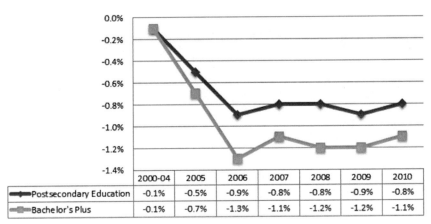

	2000-04	2005	2006	2007	2008	2009	2010
◆ Postsecondary Education	-0.1%	-0.5%	-0.9%	-0.8%	-0.8%	-0.9%	-0.8%
■ Bachelor's Plus	-0.1%	-0.7%	-1.3%	-1.1%	-1.2%	-1.2%	-1.1%

Figure 9.2. Net Migration Rates for People with Post-Secondary, Bachelor's Degree, or Higher: Michigan, 2000–2010.

Minority Growth

Whereas Michigan's population on the whole has suffered from consistent declines over the past ten years, the minority population in the state has seen considerable growth. On the whole, the minority population in Michigan grew to 23.4 percent of the total population in 2010 (2,312,772), up from 21.4 percent in 2000. This growth was primarily due to an influx of Hispanic or Latino residents into the state, which counteracted a slight decline in the state's African American population from 2000 to 2010. Overall, Michigan's Hispanic population grew an estimated 34.7 percent, going from 323,877 (approximately 3.3 percent) in 2000 to 436,358 (approximately 4.4 percent) in 2010. The black population, on the other hand, experienced a minor decline from 2000 to 2010, with a decrease of approximately 5.0 percent.

Table 9.3 breaks down minority populations by district based on total population in order to demonstrate more clearly how Michigan's minority populations are dispersed. According to the 1965 Voting Rights Act (VRA), states are prohibited from drawing district maps in a manner that may dilute the voting power of racial or ethnic minorities. As discussed in the previous section, Michigan must follow both Section II and Section V of the VRA when drawing district maps. Specifically, map-makers must account for the significance of Michigan's largest minority population, African Americans, who made up 14.1 percent of the overall population in 2010. Michigan's Hispanic population, which accounted for approximately 4 percent overall, was not significant enough to garner major attention during the redistricting process, with the highest concentration of Hispanic residents living in Michigan's former 13th District and accounting for 10.45 percent of that district's population. African Americans made up 60.5 percent of Michigan's total minority population in 2010, with the largest concentrations of residents living in the former 13th and 14th District, which subsume most of the Detroit metropolitan area. In 2010, the 13th

Table 9.3.   Minority Populations by Congressional District

District	Total Population	Total Black Population	Total Hispanic Population	% Black Population	% Hispanic Population
Totals	9,883,640	1,400,362	436,358	14.17%	4.41%
C.D. 1	650,222	7,877	7,907	1.21%	1.22%
C.D. 2	698,831	32,894	46,194	4.71%	6.61%
C.D. 3	694,695	60,949	59,823	8.77%	8.61%
C.D. 4	686,378	18,323	21,207	2.67%	3.09%
C.D. 5	635,129	119,552	27,598	18.82%	4.35%
C.D. 6	671,883	59,783	34,646	8.90%	5.16%
C.D. 7	676,899	40,115	28,544	5.93%	4.22%
C.D. 8	707,572	37,744	32,341	5.33%	4.57%
C.D. 9	657,590	76,223	27,214	11.59%	4.14%
C.D. 10	719,712	20,922	20,256	2.91%	2.81%
C.D. 11	695,888	64,849	20,726	9.32%	2.98%
C.D. 12	636,601	134,694	12,788	21.16%	2.01%
C.D. 13	519,570	306,339	54,312	58.96%	10.45%
C.D. 14	550,465	325,975	14,826	59.22%	2.69%
C.D. 15	682,205	94,123	27,976	13.80%	4.10%

District was home to 306,339 black residents (approximately 58.96 percent of that district's population), while the 14th was home to 325,975 black residents (59.22 percent of the district's population). On average, not including the Detroit districts, the African American population within each district hovered around 8.86 percent, while the Hispanic population in all districts was an estimated 4.47 percent.

Due to its high volume of citizens and despite the amount of migration out of the city, Detroit is generally the central focus of controversy during the redistricting process as Republicans and Democrats argue over the best way to divide the city in order to provide the most equitable distribution of citizens while still accounting for recognized "communities of interest" within the city's boundaries. The minority population within the city saw a decrease of approximately 25 percent, causing some nervousness among Democrats concerned about the future of the two minority-majority districts that encompass the city's limits. The primary reason for this decrease, however, was due to extensive migration of the minority population in Detroit into other parts of the state, causing a slightly more scattered picture of the population than in the 2000 census. Some suburban areas surrounding Detroit saw extensive increases in their minority populations. The cities of Warren and Eastpointe, which lie north of Detroit proper, saw triple digit growth in the African American population; growing 496 percent and 260 percent respectively. Minority populations saw similar growth percentages on the western side of the state as well. In Michigan's 3rd District, which encompasses Michigan's second largest city of Grand Rapids (population 188,040), the population of African Americans grew between 80 percent (in the city of Kentwood) and 49 percent (in the city of Wyoming). Similarly, Michigan's Hispanic population saw triple digit increases in growth in the 3rd District, with an estimated 109 percent in Wyoming and 135 percent in Kentwood.

THE MICHIGAN REDISTRICTING PROCESS IN 2010

The contours of the political process to redraw Michigan's congressional district were shaped in the 2010 elections. Republicans won back the governorship for the first time since 2002 and captured large majorities in both chambers of the state legislature.[16] Republicans also picked up two congressional seats as former Rep. Tim Walberg recaptured the seat he lost in 2008 to Democrat Mark Shauer and Dan Benishek won an open seat that had been held by Democrat Bart Stupak. Their victories in 2010 gave GOP lawmakers two more incumbents to protect—and two less Democrats to punish—in the redistricting process.

State legislators in Michigan can serve a maximum of three two-year House terms and two four-year Senate terms. Previous research indicates that term limits can affect the redistricting process at the state legislative level. With fewer incumbents to protect, mapmakers are freer to draw district boundaries that maximize party goals rather than help current officeholders retain their seats.[17] Term limits do not extend to members of the U.S. Congress where incumbents expect their interests to be protected. There is another way in which term limits affect congressional elections, though. Because they cannot make a career in the current position, term-limited state legislators are often less willing to wait until a higher office becomes open. When district lines are drawn to create safe seats, there is an incentive to challenge incumbent members of their own party in primaries.

The chairs of the state House and Senate redistricting committees were new to the legislature since the previous round of redistricting. State Senator Joe Hune, chair of the Senate Redistricting Committee, stated that the process would be "bipartisan, fair and open" compared to ten years earlier. "Whatever the criteria is this time, I'm sure I'll take a heck of a lot of grief," he said. "But it will be a fair plan."[18] Openness and fairness are terms that are open to interpretation, but there is little evidence of bipartisanship in the drawing of congressional district lines. Detroit area Democrats did have some input into the state Senate districts, however. The Wayne County portion of the Democratic map was incorporated into the Republican plan although the Democrats' statewide map was rejected.[19]

As in 2001, the process was essentially closed. There was little public discussion of specific plans or the process generally. A brief window on the process opened when news leaked regarding a meeting of Republican leaders to review proposed maps. Among those reported to be in attendance at the Washington, DC, meeting were all nine Republican members of the state's congressional delegation and their chiefs of staff, state legislative leaders, and representatives of the attorney general's office and Michigan Chamber of Commerce.[20]

The congressional redistricting plan was released by state legislative leaders on June 17, 2011. It was approved by the state House six days later on a near party-line vote. The Senate approved the plan on June 29. Governor Rick Snyder signed the legislation on August 9, 2011.

One difference from the previous decade was the ability of ambitious state legislators to serve their own electoral ambitions. As previously noted, in 2001 Thaddeus

McCotter, then a member of the Senate Redistricting Committee, helped map out a district in suburban Detroit to which he first was elected in 2002 and has held ever since. The situation worked differently for one legislator ten years later. State Representative Marty Knollenberg, a member of the House Redistricting Committee, announced plans to challenge Democratic incumbent Gary Peters in 2012. Knollenberg's father held the seat for sixteen years before losing to Peters in 2008. The timing seemed good since term limits prevented Knollenberg from returning to the state House. However, when the maps were released Knollenberg's residence was in a different district. He chose to run for Oakland County treasurer instead.

Advocacy Groups Respond to Gerrymandering

In reaction to the veil of secrecy that covered the 2001 Michigan redistricting process, several advocacy groups attempted to put pressure on the legislature to provide a more transparent, open process in which the public had larger sway on the final proposed plan. These groups initiated campaigns across Michigan and several other Midwest and Western states, most notably Illinois, Arizona, Wisconsin, Minnesota, and Ohio, all in attempts to provide a "public option" for the redistricting plan. Mary Wilson, national president of the League of Women Voters, argued that such efforts would revitalize the process, stating that, "Historically, transparency has been absent in the process used by officials to design and carry out redistricting in the states. . . . Members of the public must be able to see and participate in this process. Redistricting should foster the democratic principle of allowing voters to choose their elected officials rather than be a process in which we allow our elected officials to 'choose their constituents.'"[21] In Michigan, the initiative was supported by minority Democratic lawmakers who were in danger of losing power in both the state legislature and Congress. Kate Segal, D-Battle Creek, stated that the redistricting process itself should be changed to a citizen-led routine, echoing the arguments of Wilson and other groups, and that public hearings should be held on the proposed plans in order to gather citizen feedback.[22]

Most of the groups involved in redistricting campaigns focused their attention on attempts at constitutional reform and revisions of redistricting law in order to achieve a more open process. Draw the Line Midwest, in collaboration with the Brennan Center for Justice in New York and several other groups scattered throughout the Midwest, focused on attempting to draw attention to the political nature of the redistricting process in Michigan by campaigning in the local media in hopes that public attention would increase the level of scrutiny. The group's campaign released several opinion pieces in Michigan newspapers throughout the redistricting process in which they laid out their wishes for redistricting reform, among them the call for public posting and public hearings on maps, a provision for citizen-drawn maps, and written justification for district lines for each proposed district.[23] Similarly, the Michigan Citizens' Research Council outlined several reforms and lobbied the state legislature for constitutional reform, specifically focusing on the re-creation of a redistricting commission, increasing transparency, and providing more protection to communities of interest. One of the more extensive projects, the Michigan Citizens' Redistricting Competition sponsored by the Michigan Center for Election Law and Administration (MCELA), provided open source software to citizens and asked them to draw the district lines. The competition, which lasted from May 2 to 23, 2011, received 200 entries, with the top 20 being chosen by a panel of judges and then submitted to the state legislature, who had agreed to take the maps under consideration. In the end, however, the citizen-drawn maps were not clearly represented in the final proposed plan. Jocelyn Benson, founder and CEO of the MCELA, stated in an interview after the redistricting plan was signed into law that, "the Congressional District map is arguably the most oddly shaped in Michigan's history, with districts swirling around Southeast Michigan like colors in a Willy Wonka lollipop."[24]

The Maps

Map 9.1 shows the newly drawn districts, which take into account the population loss after the 2010 census.[25] The goal for Republican mapmakers in 2001 was to move their party from a minority of the state's congressional delegation into a majority. Having done so, their more modest goal in 2011 was to protect their majority. A secondary goal was to make life difficult for the Democratic incumbents. They were successful on both counts.

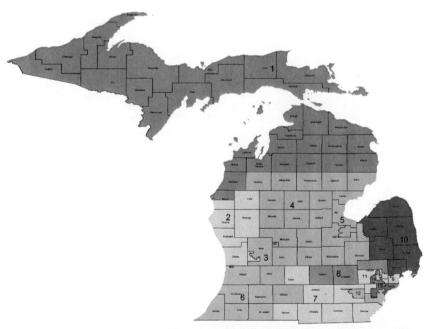

Map 9.1.   2011 Michigan Congressional Districts. Michigan House of Representatives.

Republican Districts

Of the nine districts controlled by Republicans going into redistricting, two were held by Democrats prior to the 2010 elections. Shoring up these districts was a top priority. In the process, most Republican districts were made more compact, and none were renumbered following the loss of one seat to reapportionment. In contrast, none of the districts held by Democrats was made more compact, and only one Democratic seat retains its number as in the previous Congress.

The 1st District includes all of Michigan's upper peninsula and much of the top of the lower peninsula. Republican Dan Benishek was a political novice before capturing the seat left open by the retirement of Democratic Representative Bart Stupak. The original district extended as far to the south and east as Bay County. The new district moved west and north, absorbing counties from the former 2nd and 4th Districts. Though still sprawling, it is somewhat more compact than it was.

Michigan's 7th District elected different candidates in each election between 2004 and 2010. Following Republican Nick Smith's retirement, the seat was held by fellow Republicans Joe Schwarz and Tim Walberg for one term each. Mark Shauer, a Democrat, defeated Walberg in 2008 before losing a rematch in 2010. The new district no longer contains Calhoun County (Battle Creek). It extends east into Monroe County and picked up additional precincts from Washtenaw County, although not the college towns of Ann Arbor and Ypsilanti. Monroe County was only slightly more Republican than Calhoun in past elections. The main reason this change helps Walberg is that Battle Creek is the home of Schwarz and Schauer, both considered potential challengers to Walberg. Schwarz was recruited by the Democratic Congressional Campaign Committee to switch parties and challenge Walberg, but opted to stay out of the race.

Other districts had to be adjusted to accommodate these changes. The most significant impact was felt by the 3rd District, which absorbed Calhoun County from the 7th. The district is represented by Justin Amash, a freshman Republican. The addition of Democratic-leaning Battle Creek should make the district somewhat more competitive. Amash's chances of reelection got decidedly stronger, however, when Shauer decided not to run in the district.

Democratic Districts

The population loss in Detroit coupled with Republican control of the process made the southeast corner of the state an obvious choice to absorb the loss of a U.S. House seat. Mapmakers were constrained by the desire to shore up Republican incumbents and the need to maintain the state's two districts with African American majorities. With all six Democratic incumbents concentrated in a single corner of the state, though, the question was which—not whether—Democrats would lose a seat.

Most observers expected the districts held by Sander Levin (12th) and Gary Peters (9th) to be consolidated. The two Democrats live a short distance from one another in Oakland County. Levin is the brother of Michigan's senior U.S. senator, Carl Levin, and is the top Democrat on the powerful Ways and Means Committee. Peters was first elected in the Obama wave of 2008 and narrowly won reelection in 2010. The new 9th District overlaps more with Levin's district. It curls around the city of Bloomfield Hills, territory currently represented by Peters.

The population decline in Detroit meant that the two districts with majorities of African American residents, both represented by Democrats, would need to expand considerably. John Conyers (14th District) was first elected to the U.S. House in the large Democratic class of 1964. Hansen Clarke (13th district) was first elected in 2010. The old districts ran mostly north–south. The new districts run east-west. Conyers decided to run in the new 13th District which contains more of his current district (although not his residence). Clarke switched to the 14th District, even though he lives in the new 13th District.

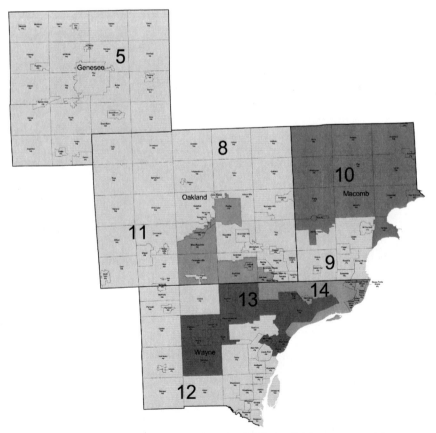

Map 9.2. 2011 Metro Detroit Congressional Districts. Michigan House of Representatives.

The 14th District deserves special attention for its creative design. An inset of the Detroit area districts is presented in map 9.2. Starting in downtown Detroit, the 14th District heads north and east along the lakeshore before shifting sharply west at the corner of Wayne County. It straddles the border between Wayne and Oakland Counties before moving north to Pontiac. A small sliver is carved out so that the city of Farmington can be in the more Republican 11th district. The 14th has been called "a true monstrosity" and "a land of opposites" by political observers. "Traveling the new oddly shaped 14th Congressional District is a tour of Metro Detroit's most disparate communities," wrote one journalist.[26] Although the district has a slight African American majority, there are other blocs of voters, including Hispanics, Arab Americans, and wealthy Republicans.

How complex are these district boundaries? To give an example, one could drive along I-75 from the Pontiac Silverdome (former home of the Detroit Lions) to Ford Field (the Lions current stadium)—a distance of about 30 miles—and change congressional districts six times. There are places where one can drive straight north from the southern edge of Wayne County to the northern edge of adjacent Oakland County and change districts a dozen times, yet there are only six districts that include these two counties.

The new district lines led to competitive primaries in at least two Democratic districts. Representative Gary Peters's residence was placed in the new 9th District along with fellow incumbent Sander Levin. Rather than challenge Levin in the primary, however, Peters chose to run in the new 14th District. He faces a showdown with Representative Hansen Clarke and at least two other candidates. John Conyers also faces a primary challenge in the new 13th District. Conyers' challenger is Bert Johnson, a state senator who, like Conyers, does not live in the district.

In addition to these changes, the district represented by John Dingell was renumbered from the 15th to the 12th. Dingell's district became more Democratic when parts of Detroit were added to replace Monroe County and the parts of Washtenaw County that became part of the 7th District. The 5th District retains its number and the economically depressed region around Flint and Saginaw. It now extends north around Lake Huron into counties that formerly were part of the 1st District. Democratic incumbent Dale Kildee is retiring, so this district is the only truly open seat in the state in 2012.

CONCLUSION

Following the November elections in 2012 the congressional delegation for the state of Michigan consisted of nine Republicans and five Democrats. Of these nine Republicans, all were incumbents. One Democrat retired (Dale Kildee), two Democratic incumbents (Gary Peters and Hansen Clarke) faced off in a primary with two other candidates, and another incumbent (John Conyers) faced a stiff primary challenge from a state Senator, the Michigan Democratic delegation had as few as two incumbents returning, John Dingle and Sandy Levin. The party will still soon have to face the retirement of three of its incumbents. Dingle, originally elected in 1954, and Conyers, originally elected in 1964, have both signaled that their careers will soon come to a close. Levin, the most junior of the three, has *only* served since 1983. All three are over 80 years old.

How would things have been different if Democrats had controlled the redistricting process? From one perspective, it is unlikely that Democratic legislators would have preferred an open process if it reduced their ability to accomplish their party's goals. The districts themselves would be different, though. We doubt that a Democratic map would flip as many seats as Republicans did a decade ago, but we are certain that Democratic incumbents would feel more comfortable and Republicans less so, and several safe Republican seats would be more competitive. Under the right electoral circumstances, those competitive districts could shift the balance of power back to the Democrats. Thus, the party labels would change, by the process remains the same. The story left to be told in the upcoming years will likely be one of Republican stability while the Democrats remain in a state of flux.

NOTES

1. *Journal of the Michigan Senate*, October 28, 1999.

2. David Canon, *Race, Redistricting and Representation: The Unintended Consequences of Black Majority Districts* (Chicago, IL: University of Chicago Press, 2002); Katherine Tate, "Black Opinion on the Legitimacy of Racial Redistricting and Minority-Majority Districts," *The American Political Science Review*, 1 (2004): 45–56.

3. Christopher M. Burke, *The Appearance of Equality: Racial Gerrymandering, Redistricting and the Supreme Court* (Westport, CT: Greenwood Publishing Group, 1999); Tinsley E. Yarbrough, *Race and Redistricting: The Shaw-Cromartie Cases* (Lawrence, KS: University Press of Kansas, 2002).

4. *Davis v. Bandemer*, 478 U.S. 30 (1986).

5. Mark E. Rush, *Does Redistricting Make a Difference? Partisan Representation and Electoral Behavior* (Baltimore, MD: Johns Hopkins University Press, 1993).

6. *Baker v. Carr*, 369 U.S. 186 (1962).

7. *Reynolds v. Sims*, 377 U.S. 533 (1964).

8. Covered jurisdictions, as defined by Section V of the VRA, are townships, counties, or states which have exhibited a significant history of discrimination against minority voters.

9. The fate of Section V of the Voting Rights Act is unclear, as the United States Supreme Court in *Northwest Austin Municipal Utility District No. 1 v. Holder* (2009) stated that the time may come soon in the future to consider the constitutionality of preclearance.

10. Redistricting of the state legislative districts was left to a bipartisan commission from 1963 through 1990. This commission consistently deadlocked, which meant the Michigan Supreme Court drew the districts. Currently, the legislature is responsible for redistricting the state legislative districts as well as congressional districts.

11. John R. Chamberlin, "The Republicans Take Control: The 2001 Redistricting in Michigan," in *Redistricting in the New Millennium*, ed. Peter F. Galderisi (Lanham, MD: Lexington Books, 2005).

12. David Bonior decided to run for governor, finishing third in the Democratic primary.

13. The Apol standards are a collection of laws, named after Bernie Apol, who served as a special master for the Michigan Supreme Court during two rounds of redistricting. The standards go beyond the regulations of the VRA, taking into account continuity with local jurisdictional boundaries and compactness.

14. When the statute was amended in 1999, the state legislation had a Republican majority, as did the Michigan Supreme Court.

15. All data utilized in this section come from the Michigan secretary of state's office and the office of the Michigan State Legislature, and is reflective of the data published by the U.S. Census Bureau.

16. State senators in Michigan do not serve staggered terms, so the entire chamber was up for election in 2010.

17. Brian F. Schaffner, Michael W. Wagner, and Jonathan Winburn, "Incumbents Out, Party In? Term Limits and Partisan Redistricting in State Legislatures," *State Politics & Policy Quarterly* 4 (2004): 396–414.

18. Susan J. Demas and John Bebow, "Redrawing Michigan," Center for Michigan, February 2011, 16–18.

19. Karen Bouffard, "Senate approves district changes," *Detroit News*, June 24, 2011.

20. Nathan Hurst, Marisa Schultz, and David Shepardson, "GOP draft plan targets Peters, Levin," *Detroit News*, May 28, 2011.

21. News Release, League of Women Voters: www.lwv.org/AM/Template.cfm?Section= Redistricting&TEMPLATE=/CM/ContentDisplay.cfm&CONTENTID=13907.

22. *Battle Creek Enquirer*, "Fair or partisan? Battles under way to remap voting districts," April 24, 2011.

23. *Lansing State Journal*, "Reiser, Caldwell: Michigan must fix its broken redistricting process," April 18, 2011. Also see: *Michigan State News*, "Michigan needs an open-door policy on redistricting," April 22, 2011.

24. *LegalNews.com*, "Asked and Answered: Jocelyn Benson Discusses Redistricting," October 17, 2011.

25. The authors would like to thank Mike Vatter, computer coordinator for the Michigan Senate Democratic Office, for his assistance in procuring the district maps included in this chapter.

26. Jack Lessenberry, "Redistricting Woes," Michigan Public Radio, June 20, 2011; Marisa Schultz, "New 14th District: A Land of Opposites," *Detroit News*, August 4, 2011.

10

Redistricting in Arizona

An Independent Process Challenged by Partisan Politics

Frederic I. Solop and Ajang A. Salkhi

Redistricting is like a blank canvas. Responsible officials come together to draw new congressional and legislative district boundaries every ten years. Sometimes officials have to create new congressional districts or reduce the number of districts in a state. Though shaped by existing rules and regulations, the process always begins anew. The canvas is metaphorically blank at the start of the process, yet the picture that develops inevitably reflects cleavages and conflicts that characterize policy making in the state. Such is the case with the 2010 redistricting process in Arizona.

As explained in this chapter, Arizona is one of seven states that place the power of redistricting in the hands of an independent body. Arizona voters sent a clear message in 2000 that they no longer wanted the redistricting process controlled by partisan politics. Ironically, the greatest fears of Arizona voters have been realized in the latest round of redistricting politics. While an Arizona Independent Redistricting Commission (AIRC) labored to develop new congressional and legislative maps, the process became immersed in the nastiest of partisan politics. Partisans used all the tools at their disposal to derail the work of the Arizona Independent Redistricting Commission. The power of the executive and legislative branches of government was brought to bear against the work of the AIRC. Only the judicial branch protected the independence of the process and allowed the AIRC to effectively complete their mission. In the end, the blank canvas was full. New districts were drafted, and the partisan conflicts colored the outcomes.

DEMOGRAPHIC TRENDS

The story of redistricting in Arizona (and the other forty-nine states) begins with an understanding of changing state demographics. According to the U.S. Census

Bureau, the state of Arizona had 6,392,017 residents as of April 1, 2010, making it 16th in population among the 50 states.[1] A decade earlier, Arizona ranked 24th in population. Between 2000 and 2010, Arizona's growth rate was second only to Nevada, with the addition of over 1.2 million residents. Arizona experienced a 24.5 percent population gain for the decade, while the nation experienced an average 9.7 percent growth rate during the same period.[2]

Over the past two decades, Arizona's growth trajectory propelled the state toward being allocated new congressional seats. Due to reapportionment, the state's congressional delegation grew from six to eight in 2001, and from eight to nine in 2011. The task of redrawing congressional districts following the 2010 census was particularly challenging as population growth had not been evenly experienced across the entire state. While one county grew by 109 percent between 2000 and 2010 (Pinal County), another county lost 1.3 percent of its population (Greenlee County).

Arizona's population has historically been concentrated among a very small number of urban areas. Sixty percent of the state's population, or 3.8 million people, live within Maricopa County, one of fifteen counties in the state. Maricopa County includes Phoenix, the fifth largest city in the nation with 1.4 million people or 22 percent of all people living in Arizona. The second largest county is Pima County. Pima County includes Tucson with a population of just under one million people (980,263). Pinal County, the fastest growing county in Arizona, contains 375,770 residents. Pinal County is situated between Maricopa and Pima Counties, making this area of the state the most populous corridor.

Another challenge to redrawing congressional district boundaries is the diversity of the Arizona population. According to 2010 census data, 57.8 percent of the Arizona population is white, non-Hispanic, compared to 63.7 percent nationally.[3] Hispanics are the largest minority population and also the fastest growing segment of the population making up 29.6 percent of the state population. This demographic group experienced a 25.3 percent growth rate between 2000 and 2010.[4] The state population also incudes Native Americans (4.6 percent), blacks/African Americans (4.1 percent), and Asians (2.8 percent).[5]

Finally, it is important to situate redistricting within a political context. After the 2010 election cycle, Arizona proved to be a solidly Republican state. All statewide elected offices were held by Republicans (governor, secretary of state, attorney general, state treasurer, superintendent of public instruction, and state mine inspector). Republicans dominated the state legislature by holding a supermajority of seats in both houses (21 Republican seats and 9 Democratic seats in the Senate; 40 Republican seats and 20 Democrats seats in the House of Representatives). Republicans also controlled 5 of 8 congressional seats. Voter registration favors Republicans[6], although Independents are the fastest growing segment of the electorate.[7] While public opinion trends more centrist, the policy agenda is conservative. Arizona is known for instituting policies that constrain the lives of undocumented workers; having tough, no-holds-barred County Sheriffs (e.g., Maricopa County Sheriff Joe Arpaio; Pinal County Sheriff Paul Babeu), and having limited state government constrained by fiscal crisis (i.e., rising costs of operation coupled with declining revenues).

Rapid growth, population diversity, and uneven development presented unique challenges to redistricting in Arizona. Situated within a highly charged, partisan environment, the redistricting process was ripe for raising questions, concerns, and second guessing. Tasked with creating competitive congressional districts while maintaining similarly situated "communities of interest," redistricting in Arizona was challenging, conflict-ridden, and eventful.

THE REDISTRICTING PROCESS

Arizona is one of seven states in having independent redistricting commissions.[8] The other six states are California, Hawaii, Idaho, Iowa, New Jersey, and Washington. The goal of an independent redistricting process is to eliminate the suggestion that partisan legislators control the redistricting process to perpetuate the power of their respective political parties. The evidence as to whether independent redistricting in Arizona leads to healthier processes is scant as we only have one data point—redistricting after the 2000 census—to examine for evidence. It is fair to say that the rhetoric of impartiality dominates the conversation in independent redistricting states and there is great intention to make nonpartisan redistricting processes work. At the same time, there are limits. Independent redistricting commissions do not operate in a vacuum. They work within a broader political context and are exposed, if not shaped, by the winds of partisan politics in their states and the nation as a whole.[9] Lastly, it is vital to understand that redistricting will never produce perfect results, as even the most subtle of changes to a precinct can have significant (and sometimes unintended) political ramifications. As a result, political parties advocate for district boundaries deemed beneficial to their long-term interests.

In November 2000, Arizona voters voted to amend the state constitution (56 percent to 44 percent) to say that redistricting would no longer be controlled by the state legislature or the governor.[10] The proposition called for formation of a five person commission to redraw district boundaries every ten years.[11] In addition, redistricting in Arizona would continue to follow all of the dictates of processes established by the U.S. Constitution. No more than two persons serving on the Arizona Independent Redistricting Commission (AIRC) are allowed to be from the same political party. One commission member must be independent and not registered with any political party at the time of appointment.[12] Applicants are required to meet specific criteria including geographic representation of the state, political affiliation (Democrats, Republicans, Independents), and lack of political employment or activity.[13] The first four members are selected by the four caucus leaders from the State Legislature. Once selected, the four commissioners choose the fifth member of the commission, an Independent, from the applicant pool. The Independent member of the Commission plays the role of Commission chair.[14]

The Constitutional amendment goes on to prescribe that the Arizona Independent Redistricting Commission be conducted in four phases. Commission members are instructed to first constitute equally populated districts in "a grid like pattern."

This is phase one of the redistricting process. In phase two, districts are to be altered to meet six established goals: compliance with the U.S. Constitution, population equality, compactness and contiguity, keep communities of interest together, follow geographic boundaries, and create competitive districts whenever possible.[15] Following the initial establishment of districts, the draft plan must be submitted to the public for a thirty-day review period. The AIRC is then responsible for distilling feedback and establishing final maps. Final maps will then be submitted to the Arizona Secretary of State and the U.S. Justice Department for "preclearance," as Arizona remains included, according to the Voting Rights of 1965, among a list of states that must have changes to election laws scrutinized by the federal government prior to implementation.[16]

OVERVIEW OF THE 2000 REDISTRICTING PROCESS

The first Arizona Independent Redistricting Commission was constituted in 2001. Recent population growth translated into an increased allocation of congressional seats—from six to eight. At the time, Republicans dominated the state, holding the governor's seat, controlling a supermajority of state Senate seats, and having five of six congressional seats.[17] Democrats hoped that an independent redistricting process would bring better results for the Party than a process controlled by partisan Republicans.[18] In addition, the process began with much optimism as the memory of redistricting in the 1990s was not so pleasant and not so distant. Democrats and Republicans squabbled over competing plans in the previous decade, a third-party intervenor brought another plan into the mix, and the courts ultimately decided which plan the state would follow in 1993.[19]

Not surprisingly, the Arizona redistricting process during the first decade of the twenty-first century did not rise to meet prevailing expectations. Hispanics were outraged from the start when the five selected commission members were all white.[20] Democrats were unhappy with the first round of maps developed by the AIRC[21] and threatened to bring the issue to the courts.[22] Their major concern was the number of safe legislative seats given to Republicans.[23] Ironically, despite early resistance to call for an independent redistricting process, Republicans fared better than Democrats in the initial process of developing new legislative districts.[24] Submission of proposed maps to the Justice Department with a request for preclearance was made in January 2002.[25] The process of receiving preclearance was then substantially delayed by two factors. First, the Justice Department asked the AIRC to provide additional data about Latino voters.[26] Second, an error was discovered in the way Election Data Services—a consulting company hired to help draw state maps—combined active and inactive voters in its calculations.[27]

Concerns about new boundaries not being in place by the 2002 election cycle were realized when the Justice Department rejected Commission maps in May as diluting minority voting strength.[28] Once preclearance was granted on February

10, 2003, the Democratic Party, the Navajo Nation, Hopi Tribe, and Flagstaff City Government filed a separate lawsuit in Maricopa County State Superior Court alleging AIRC failure to create enough competitive districts and failure to protect the interests of minority groups and communities of interest.[29] Following a series of legal wrangling, a Superior Court Judge made a finding in January 2004 that legislative and congressional maps developed by the AIRC were unconstitutional as the commission failed to give adequate consideration to creating competitive districts.[30] Furthermore, the judge said that the maps could not be used in the 2004 election cycle.[31] Though unhappy with the process, the AIRC developed new maps that were subsequently accepted by a Superior Court Judge in mid-April 2004.[32]

In 2004, Arizona Secretary of State Jan Brewer filed a lawsuit arguing that there was not enough time to implement newly drawn districts for the upcoming election.[33] The Arizona Court of Appeals agreed with this logic and in May 2004 decided that it was too late to apply the newly drawn maps for the 2004 election cycle.[34] The court later sent the maps to the Superior Court with additional instructions on how to review the constitutionality of the maps.[35] The Superior Court, applying a new test, again found that the Arizona Independent Redistricting Commission failed to adequately consider the goal of competitiveness when developing the maps.[36] The AIRC appealed this decision and won. In April 2008, the Arizona Court of Appeals found that the AIRC did adequately consider the goal of competitiveness in their deliberations.[37] The issue then went to the Arizona Supreme Court for review. The Supreme Court in May 2009 essentially agreed with the Court of Appeals that the AIRC redistricting plan was constitutional.[38] The Supreme Court sent the issue back to a trial court with instructions to accept the AIRC maps,[39] thus ending the redistricting process first initiated in 2001. After much legal wrangling, the process concluded within a year and a half of the next redistricting cycle getting started. This series of events framed the context within which the 2010–2011 redistricting process would eventually play out.

THE 2010–2011 REDISTRICTING PROCESS

Formation of the Arizona Independent Redistricting Commission

The 2010–2011 Arizona redistricting process began as prescribed in voter supported Proposition 106. The Commission on Appellate Court Appointments began creating a pool of twenty-five eligible applicants in late 2010. Not unexpectedly, controversy beset the process almost immediately. Arizona House Speaker Kirk Adams and a conservative organization accused a member of the Commission on Appellate Court Appointments for criticizing a potential applicant as unqualified on the basis of religious faith, as expressed in the applicant's application.[40] The commission member denied this accusation, but resigned from the Commission to avoid becoming a distraction from future Commission work.[41] Other commission members said the candidate was eliminated from the final list simply because there were other, more well qualified candidates to select, not because of religious conviction. In retrospect, the first salvos of partisanship were lobbed into the Arizona redistricting process from the start, and a pattern of partisan intervention into a nonpartisan, independent process was established.

Soon after this initial incident, House Speaker Kirk Adams and Senate President-Elect Russell Pearce, both Republicans, raised objections to the list of candidates and tried to have three people dropped from the applicant pool.[42] The Commission on Appellate Court Appointments rebuffed the two powerful lawmakers with a 4–9 vote in favor of keeping the current list of candidates, but not without prompting two Commission members to publicly raise their concerns about attempts to tamper with an Independent process. One Commission member said, "There is no greater intrusion in the process than to have two top Republican leaders intervene."[43] Another Commission member said, "I hope the people of Arizona are watching this and looking out for the dirty rotten politics."[44]

Senators Adams and Pearce continued pressing their objections to the presence of three people on the list of twenty-five potential nominees produced by the Commission on Appellate Court Appointments. After finding no support from the Commission itself, the two Republican leaders brought their objections to the Arizona Supreme Court. They argued that the redistricting law forbids former office holders from being AIRC nominees and two potential nominees, Mark Schnepf and Steve Sossaman, should be disqualified because they held seats on public irrigation boards.[45] The lawmakers argued that a third nominee, Paul Bender, served as a tribal judge and was also ineligible to serve on the Arizona Independent Redistricting Commission.[46] The Court agreed that Schnepf and Sossaman should be removed from the list of nominees, but that Bender should be allowed to stay on the list.[47] The court also mandated that the Commission needed to immediately add two replacements to the list of nominees.[48] By the end of the week the Court decision was issued, the Commission added two new Republicans to the list of twenty-five AIRC nominees.[49]

Arizona Independent Redistricting Commission appointments began the following week. Kirk Adams, Republican House speaker, was the first to pick a member of the commission. His appointment had to be made by January 31.[50] Adams selected Scott Freeman, a Phoenix Attorney and registered Republican, to sit on the Commission.[51] Soon after making the appointment, Adams resigned to run for an open seat in the United States House of Representatives that became vacant once Representative Jeff Flake announced his candidacy for the United States Senate.

House Minority Leader Chad Campbell was next to choose. Campbell selected José Manuel Herrera, a Democrat, an accountant, and a resident of Phoenix to service on the Commission.[52] Republican Senate President Russell Pearce was scheduled to make the next Commission appointment. Despite nine Republicans continuing to stand on the nomination list, Russell Pearce's options were limited. Proposition 106 requires that no more than two AIRC members will reside in the same county and the first two selected Commissioners reside in Maricopa County.[53] This left

Rick Stertz, a Pima County (Tucson area) Republican, and Betty White, also from Pima County, eligible to be selected.[54] Concerns soon emerged as to whether Stertz accurately completed his nomination application by failing to disclose federal tax concerns and tax liens against him.[55] Despite these questions, Pearce selected Stertz to sit on the AIRC. Senate minority leader David Schapira made the next appointment to the Redistricting Commission.[56] Schapira selected Linda McNulty, a lawyer from Tucson to sit on the panel.[57]

The four commissioners (two Democrats and two Republicans) were sworn into office on February 24, 2011.[58] Their first task was to select an Independent nominee to serve as the fifth member of the Commission and to chair Commission proceedings. The nomination list developed by the Commission on Appellate Court Appointments included five Independent nominees. Each of the nominees had a thirty-minute interview with the group of appointed Commissioners, and a decision was made on March 1, 2011, in executive session to hire Colleen Mathis, to serve as the fifth member of the Arizona Independent Redistricting Commission.[59] Mathis lives in Pima County, Arizona, and works in the field of health care at the University of Arizona.[60]

Immediately following Colleen Mathis's appointment in March, questions started being raised as to whether Mathis purposely failed to report information about her husband on her application to serve on the AIRC. Despite the allegation, Colleen Mathis had been openly discussing her husband having a career in politics. In a May 15, 2011, *Arizona Republic* article, Colleen mentions her husband Chris having previously worked as a congressional staff member for Republicans Chuck Hagel (Nebraska) and Bob Michell (Illinois).[61] But questions emerged about Mathis failing to disclose her husband's employment as a campaign treasurer for a two-term Democratic congresswoman. Mathis responded immediately arguing that her failure to disclose this information was an oversight on her part and not meant to deceive anyone.[62] She would willingly amend her application to include this information.

The Commission Begins Working

Once the Arizona Independent Redistricting Commission was constituted, members established an ambitious timeline and began undertaking the momentous task of redrawing legislative and congressional districts. The starting place for the redistricting process was the 2010 census information, which was made available to states in March 2011. At the same time, organized forces were aligning to influence the process. Democrats and members of the newly constituted Arizona Competitive Districts Coalition, a nonprofit organization working to create a larger number of competitive legislative districts, sought to bring greater alignment between the newly known demographics of Arizona voters and partisan control of seats in the legislature. While Democrats constituted 32 percent of the registered population in the state and Republicans 36 percent, the Coalition pointed out that Democrats only held 9 of 30 State Senate seats.[63] FAIR Trust, a legal trust exempt from campaign finance laws, played an active role trying to influence redistricting on behalf of a group of incumbent Republican legislators and congressional representatives.[64]

Commission members embarked upon an ambitious tour of Arizona, holding town-hall-style meetings, and listening to the redistricting-related concerns of residents and local political leaders alike. One of the first decisions made by the AIRC involved hiring an executive director. After an extensive interview process, the Commission selected Ray Bladine, former Phoenix deputy city manager, for the position on April 20, 2011.[65] After moving beyond the hiring of an executive director and computer support personnel, and defining record-keeping processes and procedures, the Commission turned to hiring two staff attorneys to support the work of the AIRC. The Commission had several well-qualified applicants for the position. Once Commission members reviewed credentials and interviewed candidates from a short list of law firms, the Commission selected two firms to represent their work, one Democratic and one Republican.

Arizona's Independent Redistricting Commission voted 3–2 to contract for Democratic counsel with Osborne Maledon whose team will be headed up by former state Solicitor General Mary O'Grady; and for Republican counsel with Ballard Spahr LLP, led by former chief counsel to Arizona Gov. Jan Brewer, Joe Kanefield.[66] The Commission vote consisted of Mathis, the Independent Commission chair, siding with the two Democrats on a 3–2 vote.[67]

The Commission moved on to hiring a consulting firm to help produce draft maps. Although several firms responded to the Commission's request for proposals, two consulting firms were shortlisted for serious consideration. Republicans on the AIRC favored hiring National Demographics Corporation, the firm previously hired to work with the AIRC in the previous round of redistricting.[68] The two AIRC Democrats and Independent chair Colleen Mathis supported hiring Strategic Telemetry.[69] This firm had a reputation for supporting Democratic Party candidates including Barack Obama in 2008 and John Kerry in 2004, although the firm had worked for Mayor Michael Bloomberg in New York City. Despite concerns about Democratic Party bias, Strategic Telemetry was hired with a 3–2 vote. In retrospect, the headline of an Associated Press article reporting on this decision was a harbinger of what lay ahead: "Arizona Redistricting Embroiled in Politics Early."[70]

Republican leaders in Arizona were incensed about the decision to hire Strategic Telemetry and they began raising serious objections about how the vote was conducted. Christian Palmer of the *Arizona Capitol Times* conducted an independent investigation into issues being raised and confirmed the following:

1. Up to June 29, 2011, the Commission spent 34 of 74 meeting hours in executive session.
2. The procurement file documenting the process of how seven applicant mapping firms were narrowed to four and then to one was "incomplete" with important scoring sheets and other materials missing.

3. The Commission's relationship with the State Procurement Office was inexplicably severed after the RFP for mapping firms was distributed. The original RFP informed applicant firms that they would need to abide to State Procurement Office rules.

4. The two Commission Democrats and the Independent Chair each gave Strategic Telemetry perfect scores of 700 points out of 700. They also scored the firm preferred by Commission Republicans much lower.[71]

Republican State Attorney General Tom Horne announced on July 21, 2011, that he was opening an investigation into the decision-making process that led to the hiring of Strategic Telemetry.[72] He also expressed concern about the missing scoring sheets as a potential violation of state law.[73] At the same time, Tea Party activists in Arizona and state Senator Frank Antenori (a candidate for the 2nd Congressional District as of January 2012) began calling for Colleen Mathis to resign her position on the AIRC.[74] Representative Terri Proud, a Republican from Tucson, began circulating a petition calling for the state legislature to repeal the 2000 vote which wrest control of redistricting in the hands of an independent commission.[75] AIRC Commissioners immediately came to Mathis's defense: "She's a true Independent, and she has the toughest job on the commission. Tougher than mine, that's for sure," said Democratic Commissioner Jose Herrera. "I support her. . . . I'm confident she's trying to do the right thing. And I want to try to help her as much as I can," said Republican Commissioner Scott Freeman.[76]

Horne's investigation continued throughout August. During this time, he interviewed the two Republican Commissioner members and reviewed available documents. On September 7, 2011, Horne filed a petition in Maricopa County Superior Court, asking that the Court order Independent Chairperson Mathis and the two Democratic AIRC Commissioners to cooperate with the process.[77] Horne believed that serial conversations took place among Commission members outside the purview of public observation and that a decision to hire Strategic Telemetry skirted around Arizona's open meeting laws.[78] On the other hand, commission attorneys argued in an earlier letter that the attorney general's investigation lacked reasonable cause and that the attorney general's power to enforce state open meeting laws did not apply to the AIRC.[79] A hearing was set for October 3.[80]

Mapping

Against this backdrop of political wrangling, public accusations, and investigations, the Arizona Independent Redistricting Commission began diving deeply into the mapping process. The task facing the AIRC was overwhelming. At the congressional level, most of the population growth of the last ten years fell within the Phoenix area, spanning Congressional Districts 2 and 6 (see map 10.1).[81]

While, logically, a new 9th Congressional District would draw constituents from Districts 2 and 6, the Commission had other interests to balance, including ensuring

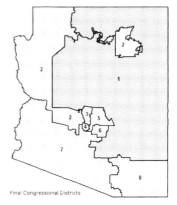

**Map 10.1.   2001 Arizona Congressional Districts.
Arizona Independent Redistricting Commission,
http://2001.azredistricting.org/.**

minority representation, maintaining communities of interest, and compliance with the federal Voting Rights Act.[82]

The Arizona Independent Redistricting Commission initiated a series of public outreach meetings in late July 2011. According to Public Information Officer Stuart Robinson, fifteen public meetings were held around the state across seventeen days.[83] Robinson distinguished these public meetings as different from "commission meetings" held in different locations around the state earlier in the process.[84] During these sessions, public officials and members of the public were allowed to raise concerns about how legislative and congressional districts should be drawn, which communities actually share similar interests, and how the values of representation, competetiveness, and fairness should be balanced. These sessions also offered a soapbox for organized interests (e.g., the Arizona Tea Party, FAIR Trust) and disgruntled public officials (e.g., Republic State Representative Terri Proud) to criticize the work of the AIRC and to influence public opinion.[85] In one recruiting message, Tea Party organizers used the following language:

> [Arizona Independent Redistricting Commission members have] a definite liberal/
> progressive bias for chopping our State up into revised districts that would water down
> our ability to elect representatives who subscribe to our conservative, Constitutional, less
> government, free-market, secure borders principles and positions.[86]

Despite the growing controversy, Strategic Telemetry went to work in the middle of August developing two congressional district grid maps for the Arizona Independent Redistricting Commission.[87] The mapping group presented two optional starting points to the AIRC. Option one was focused toward accommodating urban needs, specifically the growing population of Phoenix suburban areas, and option two was oriented toward keeping rural areas together.[88] After public discussion and open debate, the AIRC selected option two as their starting point for continued work.[89] Rau reported that Commissioners expressed interest in tweaking the map to reflect personal concerns, including having only two congressional districts border

Mexico (Commissioner Herrera); having four districts border Mexico (Commissioner Stertz); not dividing any county across more than two congressional districts (Commissioner Freeman); and, trying to cluster larger communities along the western border into one "River" district (Commissioner Herrera).[90] Rau also reported that communities across the state had been weighing in with their mapping preferences. Public involvement included 2,000 people attending recent commission meetings, 530 people addressing the AIRC at meetings, and more than 2,000 written comments submitted.[91]

On August 25, 2011, a new wrinkle was introduced into the redistricting process. Attorney General Tom Horne filed suit in federal court in an attempt to block application of the Voting Rights Act provision that requires federal preclearance of any changes made to Arizona election law.[92] Eric Holder, the U.S. attorney general, responded by saying he would vigorously defend the constitutionality of the Voting Rights Act.[93]

Two days after the Attorney General filed this lawsuit, two prominent (former) Democratic leaders in the state had an opinion piece published in the *Arizona Republic*, the statewide newspaper. Terry Goddard (former Phoenix mayor, former Arizona attorney general, and former gubernatorial candidate) and Paul Johnson (former Phoenix mayor) commented:

> Arizona's Independent Redistricting Commission has the important task of redrawing our legislative and congressional boundaries under guidelines established by voters when they passed Proposition 106 nearly a dozen years ago.
>
> Unfortunately, from the moment the current commission began its work, it has been under attack by a highly partisan coalition that is throwing roadblocks in its path. . . . We call on Attorney General Horne to end his part in the intimidation campaign and allow the commission to focus on the important duties entrusted to it by Arizona voters.[94]

The partisan bickering made national news. The *New York Times* published an article on September 3, 2011, titled "Arizona Redistricting Panel Is under Attack, Even Before Its Work Is Done."[95] This article outlined the nature and extent of political conflicts taking place in the state around redistricting, including Republican efforts to oust Colleen Mathis from her position as AIRC chair and repeated denunciations of the AIRC by Tea Party supporters at public meetings. The article reported that Attorney General Tom Horne would be filing a legal motion within the week to compel Mathis and the two panel Democrats to cooperate with his investigation into how the decision to hire Strategic Telemetry was made.[96]

The bickering was taken to a new level when Attorney General Horne accused Colleen Mathis of knowingly destroying documents involved in selection of the mapping company. The information behind this accusation was ascribed to Republican Commissioner Stertz in an interview conducted as part of the Horne investigation.[97] Ray Bladine, AIRC executive director, immediately responded, saying, "No documents that should have been kept under procurement code were destroyed."[98] Republican efforts to stifle the work of the AIRC were met by newly mobilized Democratic opposition. On September 8, Luis Heredia, Executive Director of the Arizona Democratic Party, filed a lawsuit claiming that Republican Commissioner Rick Stertz knowingly falsified information on his application to be on the Commission.[99] The Commission subsequently voted to pay for individual lawyers to support Mathis and the Democratic Commissioners as they respond to Horne's multiple legal filings.[100]

The Arizona Independent Redistricting Commission began meeting almost every day, either in Phoenix, Casa Grande, or Tucson. Meetings were open to the public. Discussions were meaningful and substantive. Agenda topics included how to best incorporate prisoners into redistricting plans, developing a definition of "competiveness," considering how many districts should border Mexico, and discussion of how Native Americans can best be included in the process.[101] In an article titled "Ariz. redistricting panelists argue over criteria," Associated Press reporter Paul Davenport reminded readers that "besides communities of interest, competitiveness, minority voting rights and local government boundaries, the other constitutionally mandated criteria that the commission must consider are equal populations and geographic features.[102]

Chairperson Mathis integrated the many concerns being raised and proposed a consensus congressional district map on September 26, 2011.[103] This map featured two rural districts, one on each side of the state, three districts touching the border with Mexico, and four, yet to be drawn, districts in the Phoenix area.[104] The map, according to Mathis, included two competitive districts, two districts that favor Democrats, and two districts favoring Republicans.[105] On September 27, the Commission voted 5–0 to adopt this map as the working map for continued discussions.[106] Soon after, the AIRC developed the initial concept by including one minority-oriented district going from Southwest Phoenix to Central Phoenix and another competitive district running north-south from Northeast Phoenix through Tempe.[107] Democrats raised immediate concerns to what Mathis labeled the "donut" plan. They claimed that the plan did not propose the most competitive districts possible, the plan was protective of incumbent legislators, and the plan was generally supportive of Republican interests.[108]

Following a weekend of minor tinkering, the AIRC presented new maps on October 3 (see map 10.2). Commissioners disagreed about the value of the maps. One Commissioner complained that once the maps were distributed, the Commission was being asked to immediately adopt the maps and submit them to the public for a thirty-day review.[109] By the end of the day, the Commission adopted the maps on another divided vote with the two Democrats and the Commission Chair voting for adoption of the maps, one Republican Commissioner voting against the maps, and one Republican Commissioner abstaining from the vote.[110]

According to press reports, of the nine congressional districts proposed by the new maps, four are considered strongly Republican, two are strongly Democratic, and three are potentially competitive for both political parties.[111] Although incumbency had never been a topic of conversation, all incumbent Representatives would be in their own districts with no two incumbents having to face off against one another.[112]

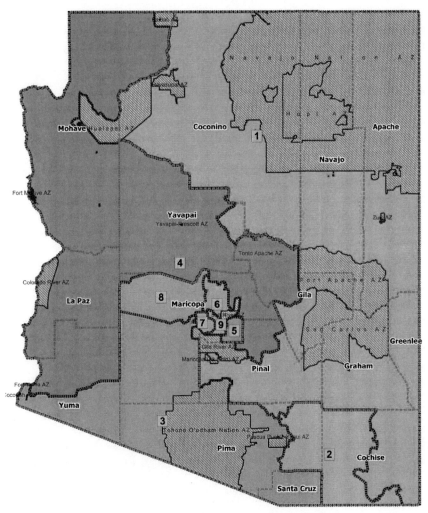

Map 10.2. 2010 Redistricting First Draft Arizona Congressional Districts. Arizona Independent Redistricting Commission, http://www.azredistricting.org.

However, some observers suggested that two incumbent representatives, Ben Quayle and David Schweikert, may choose to compete against each other, rather than one of them taking chances in the more competitive 9th congressional district.[113]

The Thirty-Day Review Period

Adoption of the draft maps now launched a thirty-day public review period. Not surprisingly, a new round of analysis and critique began immediately. Dan Nowicki of the *Arizona Republic* reported on who wins and who loses under the proposed maps, along with speculation about how the 2012 congressional elections would be affected.[114] Nowicki suggested that Republicans might be disadvantaged as they held five seats prior to redistricting, but only four districts are considered as favoring Republicans under the new system.[115] Republican Representative Paul Gosar would be placed in a district that would have a higher proportion of Democrats than in the past and would consequently be a more competitive district.[116] Other potential candidates would have to begin adjusting potential campaign strategies as district lines were not expected to deviate much from the proposed maps.[117] The conventional wisdom was that the new maps favor Democrats, giving them a competitive opportunity to win four or five congressional districts in the upcoming elections.[118]

Republican Governor Jan Brewer was incensed. To properly capture the depths of her anger, we quote at length from a press release distributed from the governor's office:

> The IRC proposal is simply gerrymandering at its worst. This unaccountable, unelected Commission has misused its authority to draw a congressional map that is every Democrat's dream. In doing so, they've violated their bedrock legal requirements to maintain districts that protect communities of interest and are geographically compact. . . . Allegations have been rampant throughout the redistricting process that the IRC has violated the law, from its refusal to cooperate with a state investigation, to its disregard of procurement procedures and Arizona's Open Meeting Law. . . . I've held my tongue, waiting for the results of the Arizona Attorney General's investigation and hoping the IRC would put forward a fair proposal consistent with the requirements set forth in the Arizona Constitution. This map dashes those hopes and I'll be silent no longer. Arizona voters are owed a redistricting process that is lawful and transparent. The Arizona Constitution mandates that IRC members conduct redistricting in an honest, independent and impartial fashion, upholding public confidence in the integrity of the redistricting process. . . . Based on this proposal and the IRC's prior behavior, it seems clear the commission is bent on awarding to the Democratic Party control of congressional districts that it could not win on Election Day. This is nothing less than neglect of duty and gross misconduct.[119]

Amidst a cacophonous uproar of Republican discontent, the AIRC came together on October 10 to adopt a draft map of legislative districts. The final vote in favor of adoption was 4–1 with Republican Commissioner Stertz voting against adoption.[120] This vote came just in time as the AIRC was committed to participating in thirty public meetings around the state beginning the next day. This next round of meetings was designed to give the public an opportunity to comment on the adopted congressional and legislative district maps.[121]

Many points of view were registered in these Commission meetings. Some people expressed support for AIRC redistricting efforts, while others lobbied for changing the maps one way or another. Some people used the opportunity to lambast Commission members for having a Democratic bias and being completely out of touch with reality.[122] Simultaneous to the Commission hosting public meetings, Republican members of the state legislature sought to create a platform of their own for commenting on Commission proceedings. Billed as a "fact-finding" opportunity, Republican leadership established a joint House-Senate Committee to hear testimony and formulate recommendations for the AIRC. This was not a bipartisan effort. Democrats appointed to the committee believed this process was partisan and boycotted the committee hearings.[123]

Republican attacks against the AIRC escalated substantially on October 26 when Arizona Governor Jan Brewer sent a letter to AIRC chair Colleen Mathis and a second letter to all five Commissioners.[124] The letter to Mathis provided detailed commentary on the proposed maps. This was information that commissioners could digest as they deliberated upon all feedback received during the thirty-day public comment period. The letter to all commissioners contained serious accusations about the work of the Commission. The governor defined this letter as "written notice of allegations that you have committed substantial neglect of duty and gross misconduct in office while serving on the Independent Redistricting Commission (IRC)." The governor outlined a series of allegations, including violations of constitutional requirements of beginning with a "grid-like pattern," privileging competitiveness over other considerations when drawing up district boundaries, engaging in gerrymandering, refusing to cooperate with an Attorney General investigation, pre-arranged voting in violation of open meeting standards, and procurement violations when selecting vendors.[125] She required each Commissioner to respond directly to these allegations within five days.[126]

Democratic leadership in the Arizona state legislature responded immediately, saying "The Attorney General, the Republican Legislature and now the governor are abusing their public offices for partisan gain."[127] Louis Heredia, head of the state Democratic Party, said Brewer was "drunk with power" and described the situation as "a brazen power grab that would rival any in Arizona history."[128]

Meanwhile, two other significant developments occurred in the interim between Governor Brewer issuing her letter of allegations and the time Commissioner responses were due. On October 28, a Maricopa Superior Court Judge issued a response to Attorney General Horne's case seeking to require AIRC Commissioner participation in a legal investigation involving possible violation of Arizona open meeting laws.[129] The judge removed Horne from the suit.[130] Because Horne initially trained AIRC on open-meeting rules, the judge determined that the lawsuit was a conflict of interest.[131] Horne indicated that the Maricopa County Attorney's office would resume the suit.[132] On the next day, the Commission voted 3–2 to fund individual attorneys to represent commissioners as they respond to allegations raised by Attorney General Tom Horne and Governor Jan Brewer.[133]

In addition to Mary O'Grady, the Commission lawyer, filing a response to the governor's allegations, each Commissioner responded in time to meet the October 31 deadline.[134] Paul Davenport summarized the essence of all responses:

> O'Grady wrote that Brewer's accusations "disregards the principles" embodied in the 2000 ballot measures approved by Arizona voters to take redistricting out of the hands of the governor and the Legislature.
>
> In her own letter, commission chair Colleen Mathis, an independent, said she was "personally devastated" by the accusations. She joined in the commission's response but

also separately denied any wrongdoing in the procurement process for the commission's hiring of mapping consultants. . . . O'Grady said Brewer had no basis to consider removing commissioners because of alleged open-meeting law violations. That issue is for the courts to resolve, the attorney said.[135]

One day after receiving written responses from Commission members, the governor, acting through Arizona's Secretary of State, Ken Bennett, sent a letter of impeachment to Chairperson Colleen Mathis. Bennett executed the impeachment letter because Governor Brewer was on a national speaking tour promoting her newly published book.[136] The letter accused Mathis of "a failure to apply the Arizona Constitution's redistricting provisions in an honest, independent and impartial fashion, and a failure to uphold public confidence in the integrity of the redistricting process."[137] According to the letter, "the foregoing constitutes neglect of duty or gross misconduct in office."[138] The remedy? "Accordingly, I hereby remove you as the fifth member of the Arizona Independent Redistricting Commission and as its chair. This removal will be effective immediately upon concurrence of two-thirds of the Arizona Senate."[139]

The Arizona state Senate met that evening to consider Governor Brewer's letter. Within one half hour of meeting,[140] the Senate voted 21–6, to remove Mathis from office.[141] All twenty-one Senate Republicans voted for removal, six Democratic Senators voted against removal, and another three Democrats did not attend the session and were therefore unable to cast a vote.[142]

The AIRC immediately responded by filing a request with the Maricopa County Superior Court asking for a temporary restraining order to stop the removal of Colleen Mathis from her position.[143] Without the restraining order, the Arizona Commission on Appellate Court Appointments would have thirty days to develop a list of three nominees for Commission chair; remaining Commission members would then need to select a chairperson from the list within fourteen days.[144] The Commission also filed papers in the Arizona Supreme Court and Arizona Superior Court asking that Mathis's removal be reversed.[145]

Arizona Democrats responded immediately to Mathis's removal from office. Andrew Cherny, Democratic Party Executive Director and congressional candidate in the Tempe-based 9th congressional district, claimed this situation was, "a historic abuse of power without parallel in modern American history."[146] Arizona House (Democratic) Minority Leader Chad Campbell said, "The governor and legislature have sunk to a new low with this special session. The blatant bullying, intimidation and partisanship they have inflicted on the citizen members of the Independent Redistricting Commission is abhorrent. They should be ashamed of themselves."[147] Senate (Democratic) Minority Leader David Schapira commented, "There was no basis for the removal of Chairwoman Mathis except pure partisan politics. . . . Now, we have a witch hunt coordinated by a governor, secretary of state, attorney general, Republican Congressional delegation and Republican legislators with a predetermined outcome. It's a disgrace."[148] Arizona Democrats threatened to file a lawsuit asking the Maricopa Superior Court to reverse the governor's finding of 'gross misconduct.'[149]

Against the backdrop of judicial, executive, and legislative maneuvering, the AIRC continued to hold public hearings on the draft maps. Simultaneously, the Commission on Appellate Court Appointments commenced the process of seeking applications for a new Independent chairperson.[150] November 9 was the close of the thirty-day, public comment period. The Arizona State Supreme Court ruled on November 8 that Mathis's request to be temporarily reinstated as AIRC chair, prior to a final ruling on the issues scheduled for November 17, was turned down.[151]

Applications for the now vacant position of Commission chair were due November 15. Nineteen people applied for the position.[152] A screening panel was charged with narrowing the list down to five, with interviews scheduled for November 28.[153] However, this process was halted on November 15, 2011, when the Arizona Supreme Court issued a ruling against Governor Brewer. The Court found that Governor Brewer "does not demonstrate 'substantial neglect of duty, gross misconduct in office or inability to discharge the duties of office.'"[154] The Supreme Court reinstated Colleen Mathis to her position as chair of the Arizona Independent Redistricting Commission.

The governor's immediate response was to say her attorneys are studying the court finding and she is considering whether there is another way to remove Mathis from office.[155] Howard Fischer, a veteran Arizona journalist, reported that Republicans were considering a ballot question asking voters to overturn their original support for an independent redistricting process.[156] The governor, working with the State Senate, moved forward four days later and filed two motions with the Arizona State Supreme Court. They asked the Court to reconsider its earlier ruling barring the governor from removing Mathis from office.[157] While considering this merits of this request, the governor and the State Senate asked that the Court bar Mathis from resuming the duties of her office.

Two days later, the Arizona Supreme Court clarified its earlier ruling by stating that the Court's decision was made on substantive, not procedural grounds.[158] The issues raised by the governor did not constitute gross misconduct or negligence of office, especially when the governor questioned the nature of maps that are only in draft stage.[159] Further, the Court said, the governor was unable to provide evidence that the state's open meeting regulations were violated.[160] The Court also stated that the decision would not be revisited. At this moment, the Commission needed to resume its work with Mathis at the helm, following the Thanksgiving break. The commission had much work ahead processing all comments presented during the thirty-day public comment period.

The AIRC resumed work after Thanksgiving with Stategic Telemetry presenting a summary of public comments and minor adjustments made to the draft legislative districts. On December 9, the Maricopa County Superior Court handed another win to the AIRC. The Court, responding to the attorney general's earlier case regarding violation of open meeting laws, said the state Open Meeting Law does not apply to the work of the AIRC. Further, the Court said AIRC had legal immunity from such considerations and that investigations by the state attorney general and Maricopa County attorney's office must cease.[161]

This was followed by the AIRC actively deciding not to release transcripts from closed executive sessions.[162] In a 3–2 vote, with the two Republican Commissioners voting for release of the transcripts, the AIRC decided to wait to release the transcripts until an anticipated appeal of the recent Court decision is completed.[163]

Finally, on Tuesday, December 20, 2011, the Arizona Independent Redistricting Commission voted to approve a congressional district map for Arizona (see map 10.3).[164]

The new map reflected several changes added to the draft map approved earlier in the fall. Changes included: having two districts border Mexico rather than three;

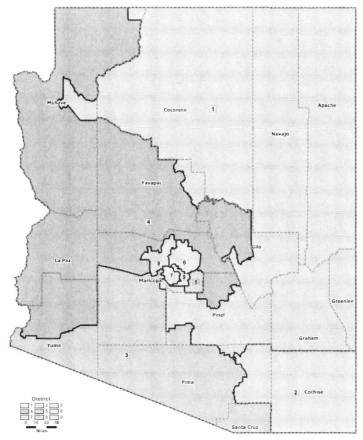

Map 10.3. 2010 Final Congressional District Arizona Map Submitted for Preclearance. Arizona Independent Redistricting Commission, http:// www.azredistricting.org.

moving conservative-leaning Prescott out of CD-1 thereby making the district more competitive; moving Fountain Hills from a rural district to an urban district and thereby keeping incumbent Representatives Quayle and Schweikert in separate districts; keeping Cochise County together; and, putting northern Tucson bedroom communities into rural CD-1 rather than be in the same district with Tucson.[165]

The vote for adopting the "tentative final" congressional district map was 3–2.[166] Predictably, the two Democrats on the Commission and the Commission chair voted in favor of the congressional map, and the two Republicans on the panel opposed its adoption.[167] As Howard Fischer explained, the new congressional district map creates four districts with a Republican advantage, two districts with a Democratic advantage, and three competitive districts.[168] The Commissioners now submitted the tentative, final congressional map to Dr. Gary King for an analysis of racial impacts. That analysis came in after the New Year began. Following the analysis, no changes were made to the congressional map. The AIRC gave final approval to the congressional map on January 17, 2012.[169] AIRC chair and the two Commission Democrats voted in favor of adopting the congressional map, and the two Commission Republicans voted against adopting the new congressional map.[170] The congressional map was certified and submitted to the U.S. Department of Justice for preclearance, as prescribed under the Voting Rights Act.

CONCLUSION

In 2000, Arizona voters sent a clear message that they were unhappy with partisan politics as usual. Forever more, the power to establish new congressional and legislative districts every ten years, would be placed in the hands of an independent commission, rather than in the hands of biased officials. Unfortunately, the independent redistricting process in 2010 to 2012 became an invitation to partisans to work even harder to influence the formation of new political boundaries. The full power of the state legislature and governor's office came to bear on the process, and, yet, the Arizona Independent Redistricting Commission resisted this pressure. The tenor of the process was sad and dispiriting, and left citizens with a tainted understanding of how politics works in the state. As Abbey Livingston of *Roll Call* said, "The Arizona redistricting process has become one of the nastiest and most litigious of the year."[171]

Republicans continue to claim they are disadvantaged by the AIRC maps, but the jury is out. Assuming Justice Department approval and administration of the new political boundaries, the true impact of new maps on the political landscape in Arizona will only be known after a couple of election cycles are played out.

Anticipating that the new maps will be approved, there was immediate jockeying for future advantage. Representative Gosar, from CD-1, announced that he would be running for office from the newly constituted CD-4 within days of the AIRC approving the new maps.[172] Other CD-1 candidates include former Representative Ann Kirkpatrick and political activist Wenona Benally Baldenego running as Democrats, while former State Senator Jonathan Paton is seeking the Republican nomination. Others may join the race. Representative Gabrielle Giffords resigned her congressional seat on January 23 to dedicate all her energy to recuperating from a gunshot wound to the head sustained in January 2011. The current CD-8 is identified as CD-2 under the new maps, and Gifford's resignation led to much interest and speculation about a successor. Republicans are optimistic about their chances to win the district in a special election, giving them an advantage heading into the 2012 election.[173] Giffords's 2010 rival, Jesse Kelly, announced that he will run for the seat, as have State Senator Frank Antenori and University of Arizona Sports Announcer David Sitton.

In CD-3, Rep. Grijalva is facing a challenge from within the Democratic Party, as former State Senator Amanda Aguirre is running in this likely Democratic seat. While in CD-4, Rep. Gosar will compete against Sheriff Paul Babeau from Pinal County[174] and State Senator Ron Gould. As previously mentioned in CD-5, former State House Speaker Kirk Adams quickly announced his candidacy. He will be challenged by former Representative Matt Salmon in this reliably Republican seat. In CD-6, Rep. Schweikert announced his intentions, but we still await Rep. Quayle, as many believe this could be an intraparty contest. Finally, in CD-9, joining former State Senate Minority Leader David Schapira and Andrei Cherny as candidates for the seat, is now former State Senator Krysten Sinema. She recently resigned her position in the State Senate to run in this competitive, yet Democratic-leaning open seat.

As in all states in the nation, the Arizona redistricting process was highly visible and of great importance to the future of political relationships. New districts were forged in a highly contentious atmosphere where partisan forces engaged in a prolonged attack against the work of independent commissioners. In fact, the final outcome of the process may still be in question as predominant Arizona Republicans are seeking to challenge the maps in the courts, through a ballot initiative, or both. Andrew Tobin, Arizona speaker of the House, in fact, developed his own congressional and legislative district maps outside of the public process and is seeking to have the legislature authorize a special election asking voters for an up or down vote on substituting his maps for the AIRC maps.[175]

Partisan interference with the work of Arizona's Independent Redistricting Commission has been an affront to the public interest in having a transparent, balanced, redistricting process. Unfortunately, from a macro perspective, the politics surrounding redistricting in Arizona are nothing more than a reflection of politics practiced in other realms of state policy-making. In the short run, however, the public interest prevailed. Against the blustery winds of contention, AIRC commissioners stood steadfast and completed their mission to produce new congressional and legislative maps for the state.

NOTES

1. "U.S. Census Bureau Delivers Arizona's 2010 Census Population Totals, Including First Look at Race and Hispanic Origin Data for Legislative Redistricting," *U.S. Census Bureau,*

March 10, 2011, http://2010.census.gov/news/releases/operations/cb11-cn76.html (accessed October 20, 2011).

2. "Arizona grows but at slower rate," *U.S. News and World Report*, undated, www.usa today.com/news/nation/census/profile/AZ (accessed October 20, 2011).

3. "State and County Quick Facts, Arizona," *U.S. Census Bureau*, date not provided, http://quickfacts.census.gov/qfd/states/04000.html (accessed January 19, 2012).

4. "Arizona's Economy: Important Results for Arizona from the 2010 Census," *Eller School of Management*, March 2011, http://azeconomy.eller.arizona.edu/AZE11q1/Important_results_ for_Arizona_from_Census_2010.asp (accessed October 20, 2011).

5. "State and County Quick Facts," date not provided.

6. According to Arizona Secretary of State figures as of January 2011 (start of the re-districting process), voter registration was 36 percent Republican, 32 percent Democrat, and 32 percent Independent, www.azsos.gov/election/voterreg/2011-01-01.pdf (accessed on November 8, 2011).

7. "Joanne Ingram, Report: Arizona Independents growing in voters but not unified," *Yuma Sun*, August 30, 2011, www.yumasun.com/articles/political-72591-independents-voters.html (accessed November 8, 2011).

8. "2012 Cook Political Report Redistricting Outlook," *Cook Political Report*, undated, http://cookpolitical.com/node/10516 (accessed January 19, 2012).

9. Josh Goodman, "Why redistricting commissions aren't immune from politics," *State-line*, January 27, 2012, www.stateline.org/live/details/story?contentId=627668 (accessed January 30, 2012).

10. "Arizona Secretary of State, State of Arizona Official Canvas: 2000 General Election," *State of Arizona*, www.azsos.gov/election/2000/General/Canvass2000GE.pdf (accessed January 20, 2012.

11. Joseph Kanefield and Mary O'Grady, "Arizona Independent Redistricting Commission Legal Overview," *Arizona Independent Redistricting Commission*, July 8, 2011, www.az redistricting.org/docs/Meeting-Info/AZ-Independent-Redistricting-Commission-Legal -Overview-070811.pdf (accessed November 7, 2011).

12. Ibid.

13. "Arizona Senate Research Staff, Issue Brief: Arizona Redistricting and Reapportion-ment," *Arizona Senate*, November 30, 2009, www.azleg.gov/briefs/Senate/REAPPORTION-MENT AND REDISTRICTING.pdf (accessed November 14, 2011).

14. Ibid.

15. Kanefield and O'Grady, ibid.

16. Kanefield and O'Grady, ibid.

17. Redistricting in Arizona, *BallotPedia*, undated, http://ballotpedia.org/wiki/index.php/ Redistricting_in_Arizona (accessed November 11, 2011).

18. Associated Press, "Arizona Democrats May Gain Clout from Remapping," *Los Angeles Times*, December 30, 2000, http://articles.latimes.com/2000/dec/30/news/mn-6522 (ac-cessed November 10, 2011).

19. "Arizona Redistricting 2000," *FairVote: Voting and Democracy Research Center*, undated, http://archive.fairvote.org/index.php?page=292 (accessed November 10, 2011).

20. *BallotPedia*, ibid.

21. Chip Scutari, "Redistricting Map Finished; New boundaries don't please all," *Ari-zona Republic*, October 13, 2001, http://archive.fairvote.org/redistricting/reports/remanual/ aznews3.htm (accessed November 11, 2011).

22. *BallotPedia*, ibid.

23. Robbie Sherwood and Chip Scutari, "Redistrict Process Was Still Political; Dems may try legal challenge," *Arizona Republic*, October 15, 2001, http://archive.fairvote.org/redistricting/reports/remanual/aznews3.htm (accessed November 11, 2011).

24. Ibid.

25. *BallotPedia*, ibid.

26. Chip Scutari, "Redistricting process has new setback: Justice Department seeks more information," *Arizona Republic*, March 5, 2002, http://archive.fairvote.org/redistricting/reports/remanual/aznews.htm (accessed November 11, 2011).

27. Chip Scutari and Robbie Sherwood, "Errors could affect new legislative boundaries, election," *Arizona Republic*, April 26, 2002, http://archive.fairvote.org/redistricting/reports/remanual/aznews.htm (accessed November 11, 2011).

28. Howard Fisher, "Redistricting Lines Rejected; New plan needed by next week for federal review," *Arizona Daily Star*, May 21, 2002. http://archive.fairvote.org/redistricting/reports/remanual/aznews.htm (accessed November 11, 2011).

29. "Redistricting—9 heavily minority, 19 GOP, 11 Democratic—OK'd, Tucson Citizen," February 18, 2003, http://archive.fairvote.org/redistricting/reports/remanual/aznews.htm (accessed November 11, 2011).

30. Paul Davenport, "Arizona Map Ruled Unconstitutional," *Associate Press*, January 16, 2004, http://archive.fairvote.org/redistricting/reports/remanual/aznews.htm-setback (accessed November 11, 2011).

31. Davenport, "Arizona Map Ruled Unconstitutional."

32. Paul Davenport, "Judge OKs Arizona legislative district map," *Associated Press*, April 16, 2004), http://archive.fairvote.org/redistricting/reports/remanual/aznews.htm-setback (accessed November 11, 2011).

33. Paul Davenport, "Time now a factor in redistricting, Dems urge haste; some say it's too late," *Associated Press*, May 1, 2004, http://archive.fairvote.org/redistricting/reports/remanual/aznews.htm-setback (accessed November 11, 2011).

34. Arizona State Senate Research Staff, ibid.

35. Arizona State Senate Research Staff, ibid.

36. Arizona State Senate Research Staff, ibid.

37. Arizona State Senate Research Staff, ibid.

38. Arizona State Senate Research Staff, ibid.

39. Arizona State Senate Research Staff, ibid.

40. Howard Fischer, "Selection of redistricting panel stirs controversy," *East Valley Tribune*, December 13, 2010, www.eastvalleytribune.com/arizona/politics/article_7969dfee-06e8-11e0-b560-001cc4c002e0.html (accessed November 14, 2011).

41. Fox10, "Panel Member Quits Amid Redistricting Controversy," *My Fox Phoenix*, December 14, 2010, www.myfoxphoenix.com/dpp/news/politics/state_politics/panel-member-quits-redistricting-controversy-apx-12142010 (accessed November 14, 2011).

42. Fox10, ibid; Mary Jo Pitzl, "Arizona redistricting process: Panel rebuffs Pearce, Adams," *Arizona Republic,* December 30, 2010, www.azcentral.com/news/articles/2010/12/29/20101229arizona-redistricting-panel-disqualify-request-decision29-ON.html (accessed November 8, 2011).

43. Pitzl, December 30, 2010, ibid.

44. Pitzl, December 30, 2010, ibid.

45. Mary Jo Pitzl, "State's high court rules on redistricting nominees," *Arizona Republic*, January 20, 2011, www.azcentral.com/news/election/azelections/articles/2011/01/19/20110

119arizona-redistricting-supreme-court-ruling.html (accessed November 15, 2011); Howard Fischer, "State's high court keeps 1 on redistricting list, ousts 2," *East Valley Tribune*, January 19, 2011, http://www.eastvalleytribune.com/arizona/politics/article_43800960-241d-11e0-8c59 -001cc4c03286.html (accessed November 15, 2011).

46. Pitzl, January 20, 2011, ibid.; Fischer, January 19, 2011, ibid.

47. Pitzl, January 20, 2011, ibid.; Fischer, January 19, 2011, ibid.

48. Pitzl, January 20, 2011, ibid.; Fischer, January 19, 2011, ibid.

49. Mary Jo Pitzl, "2 added to list of GOP redistricting nominees," *Arizona Republic*, January 22, 2011, www.azcentral.com/arizonarepublic/local/articles/2011/01/22/20110122ar izona percent27s-independent-redistricting-commission-candidates.html (accessed November 16, 2011).

50. Pitzl, January 22, 2011, ibid.

51. Rhonda Bodfield, "Pueblo Politics: House speaker names first redistricting pick," *Arizona Daily Star*, January 31, 2011, http://azstarnet.com/news/blogs/pueblo-politics/article_078f55b8 -2d7e-11e0-9262-001cc4c03286.html?mode=story (accessed November 16, 2011).

52. Mary Jo Pitzl, "New members on redistrict panel," *Arizona Republic,* February 3, 2011, www.azcentral.com/arizonarepublic/local/articles/2011/02/03/20110203arizona-redistrict -panel-new-members.html (accessed November 16, 2911).

53. Mary Jo Pitzl, "Arizona redistrict hopeful kept mum on liens," *Arizona Republic*, February 4, 2011, www.azcentral.com/arizonarepublic/local/articles/2011/02/04/20110204arizona -redistrict-candidate-rick-stertz.html (accessed November 17, 2011).

54. Pitzl, ibid.

55. Pitzl, ibid.

56. Mary Jo Pitzl, "Pearce picks Stertz for redistricting panel," *Arizona Republic*, February 9, 2011, www.azcentral.com/news/election/azelections/articles/2011/02/09/20110209arizona -redistricting-panel-stertz-pearce.html (accessed November 17, 2011).

57. "Tucsonan named to AZ redistricting commission," *KVOA*, February 15, 2011, www .kvoa.com/news/tucsonan-named-to-az-redistricting-commission (accessed November 17, 2011).

58. Steve Muratore, "When all was said and done, not all was said or done," *The Arizona Egalitarian*, February 24, 2011, http://stevemuratore.blogspot.com/2011/02/when-all-was-said -and-done-not-all-was.html (accessed November 9, 2011).

59. Steve Muratore, "It depends on what the meaning of the word 'IS' is!" *The Arizona Egalitarian*, March 1, 2011, http://stevemuratore.blogspot.com/2011/03/it-depends-on-what -meaning-of-word-is.html (accessed November 9, 2011).

60. Commissioners, *Arizona Independent Redistricting Commission*, undated, http://az redistricting.org/About-IRC/Commissioners.asp (accessed November 25, 2011).

61. Mary Jo Pitzl, "Mathis: Engage voters in redistricting plan," *Arizona Republic*, May 15, 2011, www.azcentral.com/arizonarepublic/local/articles/2011/05/15/20110515arizona -redistricting-political.html (accessed November 9, 2011).

62. Evan Wyloge, "Arizona's redistricting chairwoman admits to inaccuracies in her application," *Resource Library,* July 8, 2011, http://findarticles.com/p/news-articles/arizona -capitol-times/mi_8079/is_20110708/arizonas-redistricting-chairwoman-admits-inaccuracies/ ai_n57838971 (accessed November 9, 2011).

63. Rhonda Bodfield, "Political redistricting panel poised to start work," *Arizona Daily Star*, February 27, 2011, http://azstarnet.com/news/local/govt-and-politics/elections/article_ bdf7ef05-99e2-5818-91e3-a0e0ef2d7368.html?mode=story (accessed November 23, 2011).

64. Evan Wyloge, "FAIR game? How GOP politicians are trying to secretly influence the IRC," *Arizona Capitol Times*, October 31, 2011, http://azcapitoltimes.com/news/2011/10/31/fair-game (accessed January 21, 2011).

65. Steve Muratore, "Arizona Redistricting-Progress in the Works," *Arizona Egalitarian*, April 20, 2011, http://stevemuratore.blogspot.com/2011/04/arizona-redistricting-progress-in-works.html (accessed November 29, 2011).

66. Steve Muratore, "Redistricting—Legal Council Chosen," *Arizona Egalitarian*, May 13, 2011, http://stevemuratore.blogspot.com/2011/05/redistricting-legal-counsel-chosen.html (accessed November 30, 2011).

67. Steve Muratore, ibid.

68. Evan Wyloge, "Redistricting panel hires D.C.-based, Democratically connected mapping firm," *Arizona Capitol Times*, June 29, 2011, http://azcapitoltimes.com/news/2011/06/29/redistricting-panel-hires-dc-based-democratically-connected-mapping-firm (accessed November 7, 2011).

69. Wyloge, ibid.

70. Associated Press, "Arizona Redistricting Embroiled in Politics Early," *KTAR*, July 9, 2011, http://www.ktar.com/?nid=6&sid=1432440 (accessed November 7, 2011).

71. Christian Palmer, "What we're not IRC-ing: Map-drawing panel spends half its time meeting behind closed doors," *Arizona Capitol Times*, June 15, 2011, http://findarticles.com/p/news-articles/arizona-capitol-times/mi_8079/is_20110715/irc-ing-arizonas-map-drawing/ai_n57875996/?tag=content;col1 (accessed November 29, 2011).

72. Stephen Lemons, "Tea Party Calls for Redistricting Chair's Head: Republican and Democratic Commissioners Support Her (w/Addendum)," *New Times Blogs*, July 22, 2011, http://blogs.phoenixnewtimes.com/bastard/2011/07/tea_party_calls_for_redistrict.php (accessed November 9, 2011).

73. Jim Small, "Attorney General Tom Horne announces redistricting commission investigation," *Arizona Capitol Times*, July 21, 2011, http://azcapitoltimes.com/news/2011/07/21/attorney-general-tom-horne-announces-redistricting-commission-investigation (accessed December 1, 2011).

74. Lemons, July 22, 2011.

75. Small, July 21, 2011.

76. Lemons, July 22, 2011.

77. Paul Davenport, "Horne asks court to order IRC's cooperation with probe," *Arizona Capitol Times*, September 7, 2011, http://azcapitoltimes.com/news/2011/09/07/horne-asks-court-to-order-ircs-cooperation-with-probe (accessed November 30, 2011).

78. Davenport, ibid.

79. Davenport, ibid.

80. Davenport, ibid.

81. Ronald J. Hansen and Dan Nowicki, "Phoenix area's edge suburbs drive redistricting," *Arizona Republic*, August 5, 2011, www.azcentral.com/community/gilbert/articles/2011/08/05/20110805phoenix-area-edge-suburbs-drive-redistricting.html (accessed December 1, 2011).

82. Hansen and Nowicki, ibid.

83. Stuart Robinson, conversation with Steve Muratore as reported in the *Arizona Egalitarian*, July 24, 2011, http://stevemuratore.blogspot.com/2011/07/redistricting-yuma-hearing-and-more.html (accessed December 1, 2011).

84. Robinson, ibid.

85. See Arizona Equalitarian archives (July–August 2011).

86. Steve Muratore, "Redistricting—Prescott/Cottonwood hearing and more UP-DATED," *The Arizona Egalitarian*, July 29, 2011, http://stevemuratore.blogspot.com/2011/07/redistricting-prescottcottonwood.html (accessed December 2, 2011).

87. Alia Beard Rau, "Arizona redistricting commission picks a starting map," *Arizona Republic*, August 19, 2011, www.azcentral.com/news/election/azelections/articles/2011/08/18/20110818arizona-redistricting-panel-starting-map.html (accessed December 1, 2011).

88. Rau, ibid.

89. Rau, ibid.

90. Rau, ibid.

91. Rau, ibid.

92. Dylan Smith, "AG Horne sues over Voting Rights Act review," *Tucson Sentinal*, August 25, 2011, www.tucsonsentinel.com/local/report/082511_horne_redistricting/ag-horne-sues-over-voting-rights-act-review (accessed December 4, 2011).

93. Smith, ibid.

94. Terry Goddard and Paul Johnson, "Goddard and Johnson: Stop attacking redistricting commission," *Arizona Republic*, August 27, 2011, www.azcentral.com/arizonarepublic/opinions/articles/2011/08/27/20110827goddard27-redistricting-commission.html (accessed December 5, 2011).

95. Mark Lacey, "Arizona Redistricting Panel Is Under Attack, Even Before Its Work Is Done," *New York Times*, September 3, 2011, www.nytimes.com/2011/09/04/us/04redistrict.html?_r=3&pagewanted=1&hp (accessed December 5, 2011).

96. Lacey, ibid.

97. Evan Wyloge, "Horne: Redistricting commissioner claims chairwoman destroyed documents," *Arizona Capitol Times*, September 7, 2011, http://azcapitoltimes.com/news/2011/09/07/horne-redistricting-commissioner-claims-chairwoman-destroyed-documents (accessed December 5, 2011); Paul Davenport, "Redistricting officials face new allegations," *Arizona Capitol Times*, September 8, 2011, http://azcapitoltimes.com/news/2011/09/08/redistricting-officials-face-new-allegations (accessed December 5, 2011).

98. Wyloge, September 7, 2011.

99. Paul Davenport, "September 8, 2011; Steve Muratore, Redistricting—shredded wheat, er, documents? UPDATED," *Arizona Egalitarian*, September 8, 2011, http://stevemuratore.blogspot.com/2011/09/redistricting-shredded-wheat-er.html (accessed December 5, 2011).

100. Steve Muratore, "Redistricting—the plot thickens," *Arizona Egalitarian*, September 9, 2011, http://stevemuratore.blogspot.com/2011/09/redistricting-plot-thickens.html (accessed December 5, 2011).

101. Mary Jo Pitzl, "Navajos seek tribal-dominated district in Arizona," *Arizona Republic*, September 16, 2011, www.azcentral.com/arizonarepublic/local/articles/2011/09/15/20110915arizona-redistricting-navajos-seek-tribal-dominated.html (accessed December 5, 2011).

102. Paul Davenport, "Ariz. redistricting panelists argue over criteria," *Houston Chronicle*, September 22, 2011, www.chron.com/news/article/Ariz-redistricting-panelists-argue-over-criteria-2184481.php (accessed December 5, 2011).

103. Paul Davenport, "State: Commission chair proposes congressional map," *Daily Courier*, September 26, 2011, www.dcourier.com/Main.asp?SectionID=1&SubSectionID=1&ArticleID=98396 (accessed December 5, 2011).

104. Davenport, ibid.

105. Evan Wyloge, "Redistricting commission approves 'donut' map; Dems call it rotten," *Arizona Capitol Times*, September 29, 2011, http://azcapitoltimes.com/news/2011/09/29/redistricting-commission's-approves-'donut'-map-dems-call-it-rotten (accessed December 5, 2011).

106. Steve Muratore, "Redistricting—disturbing developments UPDATED," *The Arizona Egalitarian*, September 27, 2011, http://stevemuratore.blogspot.com/2011/09/redistricting-disturbing-developments.html (accessed December 5, 2011).

107. Mary Jo Pitzl, "Tentative Arizona congressional map emerges," *Arizona Republic*, September 30, 2011, www.azcentral.com/arizonarepublic/local/articles/2011/09/29/20110929arizona-redistricting-tentative-congressional-map-emerges.html (accessed December 5, 2011).

108. Wyloge, September 29, 2011, ibid.

109. Mary Jo Pitzl, "Arizona redistricting commission proposes new map," *Arizona Republic*, October 4, 2011. www.azcentral.com/news/election/azelections/articles/2011/10/03/20111003arizona-redistricting-new-map-proposed.html (accessed December 7, 2011).

110. Mary Jo Pitzl, ibid.

111. Mary Jo Pitzl, ibid.

112. Mary Jo Pitzl, ibid.

113. Joah Lederman, "Gov. Brewer threatens impeachment for Arizona redistricting panel," *The Hill*, October 27, 2011, http://thehill.com/blogs/ballot-box/redistricting/190345-gov-brewer-threatens-impeachment-for-ariz-redistricting-panel (accessed December 8, 2011).

114. Dan Nowicki, "New Ariz. congressional map may alter races for Congress," *Arizona Republic*, October 5, 2011, www.azcentral.com/news/election/azelections/articles/2011/10/05/20111005arizona-new-map-may-alter-congress-races.html (accessed December 7, 2011).

115. Dan Nowicki, ibid.

116. Dan Nowicki, ibid.

117. Dan Nowicki, ibid.

118. Aaron Blake, "Redistricting draft map in Arizona favors Democrats," *Washington Post*, October 4, 2011, www.washingtonpost.com/blogs/the-fix/post/redistricting-draft-map-in-arizona-favors-democrats/2011/10/04/gIQAI33YLL_blog.html (accessed December 5, 2011).

119. Jan Brewer, "Governor Brewer: Redistricting Commission Has Botched Process," *Governor Jan Brewer Website*, October 5, 2011, http://azgovernor.gov/dms/upload/PR_100511_IRC.pdf (accessed December 7, 2011).

120. Steve Muratore, "Redistricting—amazing cooperation," *Arizona Egalitarian*, October 10, 2011, http://stevemuratore.blogspot.com/2011/10/redistricting-amazing-cooperation.html (accessed December 7, 2011).

121. The schedule of meetings is available at www.azredistricting.org/docs/Meeting-Info/Public-Hearings-2nd-Round.pdf (accessed December 7, 2011).

122. See *Arizona Egalitarian* October postings for descriptions of events taking place at specific meetings.

123. Paul Davenport, "Ariz. legislators seeking voice on redistricting," *Deseret News*, October 21, 2011, www.deseretnews.com/article/700190337/Ariz-legislators-seeking-voice-on-redistricting.html?pg=1 (accessed December 8, 2011).

124. Both letters are dated October 26, 2011, and available on Governor Jan Brewer's website, www.azgovernor.gov/Newsroom/Gov_PR.asp (accessed December 8, 2011).

125. Jeremy Duda, "Brewer takes first step in removal of redistricting commissioners," *Arizona Capitol Times*, October 26, 2011, http://azcapitoltimes.com/news/2011/10/26/brewer-takes-first-step-in-removal-of-redistricting-commissioners (accessed December 8, 2011).

126. Duda, ibid.

127. Steve Muratore, "Redistricting—Brewer threatens AIRC, takes tea party bait UP-DATED," *Arizona Egalitarian,* October 26, 2011, http://stevemuratore.blogspot.com/2011/10/redistricting-brewer-threatens-airc.html (accessed December 8, 2011).

128. Abby Livingston, "Arizona Governor Starts Impeachment Process against Redistricting Panel," *Roll Call,* October 26, 2011, www.rollcall.com/news/arizona_governor_jan_brewer_starts_impeachment_against_redistricting_panel-209840-1.html?utm_source=twitterfeed&utm_medium=twitter (accessed December 8, 2011).

129. Mary Jo Pitzl, "Judge ousts Arizona attorney general from redistricting case," *Arizona Republic,* October 29, 2011, www.azcentral.com/news/articles/2011/10/28/20111028arizona-redistricting-ruline-horne-out-of-commission.html (accessed December 8, 2011).

130. Pitzl, ibid.

131. Mary Jo Pitzl, ibid.

132. Mary Jo Pitzl, ibid.

133. Mary Jo Pitzl, "3 Arizona redistricting commission members hire legal counsel," *Arizona Republic,* October 30, 2011, www.azcentral.com/news/articles/2011/10/30/20111030arizona-redistrict-commission-members-hire-legal-counsel.html (accessed December 8, 2011).

134. Response letters can be found at the *Arizona Egalitarian* blog entry for October 31, 2011, http://stevemuratore.blogspot.com/2011/10/redistricting-lege-committee-whitewash.html (accessed on December 8, 2011).

135. Paul Davenport, "Ariz. legislative panel: Redistricting maps flawed," *RealClearPolitics,* October 31, 2011, www.realclearpolitics.com/news/ap/politics/2011/Oct/31/ariz__legislative_panel__redistricting_maps_flawed.html (accessed December 9, 2011).

136. Howard Fischer, "Brewer on tour: Carps on Obama, liberal media," *Verde Independent,* October 13, 2011, http://verdenews.com/Main.asp?SectionID=1&SubSectionID=1&ArticleID=44282 (accessed November 3, 2011).

137. Letter signed by Ken Bennett on behalf of Governor Jan Brewer, November 1, 2011, http://azgovernor.gov/dms/upload/PR_110111_LetterIRCChairwoman.pdf. Note: Governor Brewer was out of the state conducting a two-week book tour at the time the letter was distributed.

138. Letter signed by Ken Bennett.

139. Letter signed by Ken Bennett.

140. Abby Livingston, "Arizona Governor Removes Mapmaker," *Roll Call,* November 1, 2011, www.rollcall.com/news/arizona_special_session_hash_out_redistricting_shakeup-209952-1.html?utm_source=twitterfeed&utm_medium=twitter (accessed December 9, 2011).

141. Jessica Taylor, "Ariz. Senate Votes to Remove Independent Redistricting Chair," *Hotline On Call,* November 1, 2011, http://hotlineoncall.nationaljournal.com/archives/2011/11/brewer-preparin.php (accessed December 9, 2011).

142. Steve Muratore, "Redistricting—Senate floor session is a SHAM," *Arizona Egalitarian,* November 1, 2011, http://stevemuratore.blogspot.com/2011/11/redistricting-senate-floor-session-is.html (accessed December 9, 2011).

143. Alex Isenstadt, "Colleen Mathis impeached by Jan Brewer, Arizona Senate," *Politico,* November 2, 2011, www.politico.com/news/stories/1111/67408.html (accessed December 9, 2011).

144. Abby Livingston, "Arizona Governor Removes Mapmaker," *Roll Call,* November 1, 2011, www.rollcall.com/news/arizona_special_session_hash_out_redistricting_shakeup-209952-1.html?utm_source=twitterfeed&utm_medium=twitter (accessed December 9, 2011).

145. Abby Livingston and Jonathan Strong, "Arizona Map in Flux after Mathis Impeachment," *Roll Call*, November 2, 2001, www.rollcall.com/news/Map-in-Flux-After-Mathis -Impeachment-209982-1.html?utm_source=twitterfeed&utm_medium=twitter (accessed December 9, 2011).

146. Livingston and Strong, ibid.

147. Press Release, "Response from the Arizona Democratic Party to the Tea-Publican Abuse of Power," *Blog for Arizona*, November 2011, www.blogforarizona.com/blog/2011/11/ response-from-the-arizona-democratic-party-to-tea-publican-abuse-of-power.html (accessed December 9, 2011).

148. Press Release, ibid.

149. Jessica Taylor, "Ariz. Senate Votes to Remove Independent Redistricting Chair," *Hotline On Call*, November 1, 2011, http://hotlineoncall.nationaljournal.com/archives/2011/11/ brewer-preparin.php (accessed December 9, 2011).

150. Mary Jo Pitzl, "Brewer, GOP blasted over Arizona redistrict panel ouster," *Arizona Republic*, November 3, 2011, www.azcentral.com/news/articles/2011/11/03/20111103brewer -gop-blasted-redistrict-panel-ouster.html (accessed December 9, 2011).

151. Abby Livingston, "Arizona Court Blocks Temporary Return of Booted Redistricting Chief," *Roll Call*, November 8, 2011, www.rollcall.com/news/arizona_court_blocks_tempo rary_return_of_booted_redistricting_chief-210149-1.html (accessed December 9, 2011).

152. Howard Fischer, "19 apply for Mathis' seat on redistricting commission," *East Valley Tribune*, November 15, 2011, www.eastvalleytribune.com/arizona/politics/article_ae504936 -1007-11e1-a5b1-001cc4c03286.html (accessed December 10, 2011).

153. Fischer, ibid.

154. Mary Jo Pitzl, "Court orders reinstatement of redistricting official," *Arizona Republic*, November 18, 2011, www.azcentral.com/news/election/azelections/articles/2011/11/17/2011 1117arizona-court-hears-challenge-redistricting-ouster.html (accessed December 10, 2011).

155. Howard Fischer, "Brewer may attempt to fire redistricting chair again," *East Valley Tribune*, November 18, 2011, www.eastvalleytribune.com/arizona/article_c4e267ac-1245 -11e1-a064-001cc4c03286.html (accessed December 10, 2011).

156. Fischer, ibid.

157. Abby Livingston, "Arizona Legal Battle Continues over Redistricting Chief," *Roll Call*, November 21, 2011, www.rollcall.com/news/arizona_legal_battle_redistricting_chief_ continues-210512-1.html (accessed December 10, 2011).

158. Paul Davenport, "Arizona high court explains redistricting ruling," *RealClearPolitics*, November 23, 2011, www.realclearpolitics.com/news/ap/politics/2011/Nov/23/arizona_ high_court_explains_redistricting_ruling.html (accessed December 10, 2011).

159. Davenport, ibid.

160. Davenport, ibid.

161. Paul Davenport, "Open meeting probe of redistricting panel barred," *Tri Valley Central*, December 9, 2011, http://hosted.ap.org/dynamic/stories/A/AZ_ARIZONA_RE DISTRICTING_AZOL-?SITE=AZCAS&SECTION=STATE&TEMPLATE=DEFAULT (accessed December 10, 2011).

162. Paul Davenport, "Arizona redistricting panel won't unseal transcripts," *Arizona Republic*, December 15, 2011, www.azcentral.com/news/election/azelections/articles/2011/12/15/2011 1215arizona-redistricting-panel-wont-unseal-transcripts.html (accessed January 3, 2011).

163. Davenport, ibid.

164. Mary Jo Pitzl, "Arizona Redistrict panel turns in new map," *Arizona Republic*, December 20, 2011, www.azcentral.com/arizonarepublic/news/articles/2011/12/20/20111220 arizona-redistrict-panel-turns-new-map.html (accessed January 3, 2011).

165. Pitzl, ibid.

166. Howard Fischer, "Redistrict Panel OK's Map; Republicans Unhappy," *Arizona Daily Star*, December 21, 2011, http://azstarnet.com/news/local/redistrict-panel-oks-map-gop -unhappy/article_21787fb5-bd31-5664-b5d9-9ccba71af57d.html?mode=story(accessed January 24, 2011).

167. Fischer, ibid.

168. Fischer, ibid.

169. Howard Fischer, "Redistricting Commission Finalizes Arizona Political Maps," *East Valley Tribune*, January 17, 2011, www.eastvalleytribune.com/arizona/article_b81fbd78 -4146-11e1-ad6f-001871e3ce6c.html?utm_source=twitterfeed&utm_medium=twitter (accessed January 24, 2011).

170. Fischer, ibid.

171. Abby Livingston, "Arizona Legal Battle Continues over Redistricting Chief," *Roll Call*, November 21, 2011, www.rollcall.com/news/arizona_legal_battle_redistricting_chief_ continues-210512-1.html (accessed December 10, 2011).

172. Teri Walker, "IRC Approves Redistricting Maps," *Arizona Journal*, January 25, 2012, www.azjournal.com/2012/01/25/irc-approves-redistricting-maps (accessed January 25, 2012).

173. Associated Press, "Giffords's decision to resign sets stage for free-for-all with high stakes in House race," *Washington Post*, January 23, 2011, www.washingtonpost.com/politics/ campaigns/giffords-resignation-from-congress-opens-up-race-triggers-messy-elections-amid -redistricting/2012/01/22/gIQAMTCWJQ_story.html (accessed January 25, 2011).

174. Josh Lederman, "Two in Arizona Make House Runs Official," *The Hill*, January 4, 2011, http://thehill.com/blogs/ballot-box/house-races/202419-2-in-arizona-make-house -runs-official (accessed January 25, 2011).

175. Mary Jo Pitzl, "Andy Tobin Seeks Public Vote on His Redistricting Plan," *Tucson Citizen*, January 27, 2012, http://tucsoncitizen.com/arizona-news/2012/01/27/andy-tobin -seeks-public-vote-on-his-redistricting-plan (accessed February 1, 2012).

11

Carving Lines in the Cascades

Redistricting Washington[1]

Kevin Pirch

For many people, the thought of Washington State conjures up images of the Space Needle, Microsoft, and Starbucks. It might be fish being thrown at Pike Place Market or a music scene that dominated the 1990s. However, Washington State is much more than any of those images. Tucked in the northwest corner of the nation, Washington State has been described as two separate states divided by the Cascade Mountains which run from the Canadian border through the state to Oregon. Known as the "Cascade Curtain," this mountain range not only creates an imposing physical barrier for the state, but also an ideological and socioeconomic divide as well.

The west side of the state is, by far, the more populated part of the state. Anchored by the Seattle-Tacoma metropolitan area, 5.3 million of the state's 6.7 million residents live on the western side of the Cascades. Although rural areas do exist on this side of the state, most people live in the cities and suburbs of the four most populous counties—King, Pierce, Thurston, and Snohomish—that make up the greater Seattle area around Puget Sound or in the Portland, Oregon, suburbs of Clark County. This area is known for having a populous with higher than average levels of education and income, and an economy which is built upon technology including Microsoft and Amazon.com, aerospace, including Boeing, and other skilled industries. While this side of the state is often described as being politically liberal with a tendency to support Democratic Party candidates and causes, it is important to note that it is not uniformly Democratic. This is especially true in southwestern Washington and in the Seattle exurbs and near military bases where Republicans have traditionally done well.

In contrast to the densely populated western portion of the state, eastern Washington accounts for only approximately one-fifth of the state's population. While home to state's second largest city, Spokane, and the fast growing Tri-Cities region, this part of the state is generally known for agriculture and natural resources. While internationally known for the production of fruits and wheat, this area also is home to numerous vineyards and other crops, while energy production from the numerous hydroelectric dams on the Columbia River and its tributaries and an ever-increasing number of wind farms employs thousands. Just as the west side of the state has a reputation for being politically liberal, Eastern Washington is known for its support of Republican causes and candidates—although, as in Western Washington, this is probably more of a function of population density, as densely populated Spokane tends to support Democrats and more rural western parts of the state have supported Republicans. However, one thing that has united almost all parts of Washington has been the growth in population during the first decade of the twenty-first century.

The ten years between the 2001 and 2011 redistricting were yet another, in a long series of decades which has seen tremendous growth in the population of the Evergreen State. During those ten years, almost one million new residents called Washington State home. Because of this, Washington gained a tenth congressional seat in the 2011 reapportionment, which was the first time the state had gained a seat since the 1980 census. All told, there were 6,724,540 people who resided in Washington State, according to the 2010 census. Although the median age of Washington State residents is remarkably similar to the nation as a whole—Washington State's is 37.3 years, compared to 37.2 for the nation, in many other regards Washington State residents differ from the nation. First, Washington State is less ethnically diverse than the United States. Only 3.6 percent of the population of the state identifies as African American, and 11.2 percent of the population stated they were Hispanic, both of which were fewer than the nation as a whole. However, there were greater percentages of Asian and Pacific Islanders in the state compared to the entire nation.

While the population of the state increased by nearly one million people, that increase was not seen throughout the entire state. As is often the case, the population increased dramatically in some parts of the state, while in other areas it increased at a much slower pace, or even declined. In Washington State, the areas with the most substantial amounts of population growth were the exurban areas south, north, and west of the Seattle-Tacoma metropolitan area, as well as the exurban areas in southern Washington in the Portland, Oregon, metropolitan area. The final area of the five fastest growing areas of the state was in south-central area surrounding the Tri-Cities of Pasco, Richland, and Kennewick as well as Walla Walla, Washington, which became a haven for retirees as well as burgeoning wine and agriculture industries. Among the areas of slowest growth were places which already had high densities and were built out, such as the central parts of Tacoma and Spokane, as well as the interior suburbs of Seattle, such as Shoreline.

WASHINGTON STATE LAW

A Brief History of the Redistricting Commission

While the federal courts have, in the main, argued these practices are constitutional, the state of Washington has created laws designed to prevent some of the most egregious abuses from occurring. Prior to 1990s, Washington State empowered the state legislature to draw the boundaries of the state's districts, as many other states do. However, the attempt at redistricting following the 1980 census was an exceptionally difficult endeavor. The first proposal was vetoed by Governor John Spellman primarily because it divided the city of Spokane into two different congressional districts.[2] The second redistricting proposal was invalidated by the federal court over issues of malapportionment, due to a difference of more than 1 percent of the population between the 4th and 8th Congressional Districts.[3] This second plan also caused concerns among some in the public because it placed Everett in the same congressional district as Seattle, leaving many in Snohomish County to believe their representation would be muted by the more populous city.[4]

Because of these issues, an increasing number of elected officials and citizens called for an independent commission to draw the political boundaries in the state. One proposal for the independent commission came from Secretary of State Ralph Munro who advocated for the Commission to begin in 1984 to draw the 1980 boundaries. The Commission would be composed of a member selected by the governor, another member would be selected from the party that did not occupy the governor's mansion, a third member would be selected from the party controlling the legislature, another member would be selected from the party which was in the minority in the legislature, and these four would select the final member of the commission. In addition, the Commission was to be tasked with drawing the lines to prevent districts from straddling the Cascade Mountains, or uniting the northern part of Puget Sound with Seattle and ensure the boundaries would not dilute the voting power of minorities.[5] While that specific proposal was not adopted, the Washington State legislature and the voters approved an amendment to the Constitution creating an independent commission to draw the legislative boundaries in November 1983.

Starting with the 1990 redistricting, Washington State has employed a five member redistricting body. The Commission is composed of four members, one of whom is selected from the two largest political parties in both houses of the state legislature. (While the law does not say it explicitly, the practical effect is that House Democrats and House Republicans each pick a member while Senate Democrats and Senate Republicans select the other two.) These four members then select a non-voting chair to govern the work. In the current redistricting process, the Commission must complete work by January 30, 2012, and turn the plan over to the legislature for possible amendment—passage of the plan a requires a two-thirds affirmative vote of both houses by February 10, although if the legislature does not act, the plan becomes law. If at least three of the voting members cannot come to an agreement, however, the process of redistricting is handed over to the state Supreme Court, which must create a plan by March 1, 2012, in this round.

Using the data from the decennial census, these commissioners and their staff are tasked with redrawing the state's congressional and legislative districts. In addition, the law requires the Commission follow certain guidelines when crafting these boundaries. First, following the federal Court's rulings, the districts must have as equal population as possible (excluding nonresident military personnel). These boundaries are also to follow already created political boundaries as much as possible in an attempt at keeping political communities whole. For example, boundaries should follow county or municipal boundaries as much as possible, and cities should be represented by as few legislators as possible. In practical terms, this directive should prevent cracking a political group and diluting their power as much as possible. Additionally, these legislative districts are intended to be as compact and contiguous as possible to discourage large, meandering districts which might be used to punish or reward various political groups through cracking their political power. As an extreme example, consider a district which covered Queen Anne Hill in Seattle, parts of the suburbs of eastern King County, and parts of Ellensburg and Yakima. Finally, districts must be made as politically competitive as possible.

While all three of the goals (beyond the federally mandated rule of equal population) are designed to decrease the opportunity for partisans to gerrymander the state's districts, it is important to note that these three goals might be difficult to simultaneously establish and might, on occasion, even be contradictory. For example, in recent decades the people in the United States have begun to politically self-segregate themselves. While the causes of this phenomenon are debatable, the implications of this are that Democrats tend to cluster in Democratic-leaning neighborhoods, while Republicans tend to reside more in Republican-leaning neighborhoods. Consequently, it might be difficult to make districts that are compact and follow previously established political boundaries that are also politically competitive. If that is the case, in many instances the Commission must be forced to choose between creating a politically competitive district which might cross those boundaries and might not be exceptionally compact, or have a compact boundary which is less competitive. Moreover, because the population in certain parts of the state, especially in eastern Washington, is less dense than in more urban parts of western Washington, traditional connotations of "compact" might not apply. Because of the requirement of equal population, some compact districts might encompass thousands of square miles and be larger than some states. While these three directives might be contradictory, or at least challenging, it is what the Commission is tasked to do, and because of that it is important to evaluate the Commission's work on these three aspects of redistricting.

Competitive Elections

One of the directives to the redistricting commission is to attempt to make elections as competitive as possible. There are a number of reasons why this might be considered advantageous for redistricting. First, creating competitive elections, by definition, means that partisan gerrymandering has been kept to a minimum. In districts where both major parties have an equal chance of winning an election, it is doubtful that either cracking or packing has occurred. Second, there is a possibility that in districts where elected officials believe they are immune from electoral competition from the other party, those representatives might become less attentive to their constituents. Simply put, more competitive elections should lead to more responsive officials. Finally, there is some evidence that more competitive elections produce more centrist candidates who would be able to create compromises with other parties and produce results which might be more acceptable to a larger segment of the electorate.

However, competitive elections throughout Washington State might be more difficult than making nine (now ten) congressional districts and forty-nine legislative districts each have a relatively equal number of Democrats and Republicans. First, it is impossible to know how voters will vote for various candidates over the following decade. In addition, in Washington, like most states, one political party tends to outperform the other party. If one party tends to get tens of thousands of votes statewide more than the other party, it would be impossible to make all of the districts equally competitive. Couple this with the fact that people tend to self-segregate based in part on their party affiliation, competitiveness is, at best, a challenge for redistricting.

Rather than attempting to make each district equal in partisan strength, another way to measure the competitiveness of each district is to examine how partisan the district is compared to the state as a whole. One way to measure this is to use the Cook Partisan Voting Index (PVI), which explores how much support the major party candidates receive in a district compared to what those same candidates receive on average in the entire state.[6] Using results from the November elections in 2004 and 2008, we find six of the nine Washington congressional districts have a positive PVI, meaning they are more Democratic than the state as a whole, while the two districts which represent eastern Washington are more Republican than the state average. Only one, the 3rd Congressional District in southwestern Washington, is even with the state average. Nationally, Washington's 7th District was the twenty-first most Democratic congressional district in the country, with a PVI of D+31 while the 4th Congressional District was the eighty-fifth most Republican district in the nation with a PVI of R+13. The rest of the congressional districts have a PVI which is less than 10, indicating that while the Democrats do have an advantage, especially in most of western Washington, the PVI for congressional districts is generally within the normal range of the national average (see table 11.1).

Like the congressional districts, the state's legislative districts also are relatively competitive, when evaluated by the PVI. Of the forty-nine legislative districts, thirty-five have a PVI of fewer than 10, and six have a PVI of less than 1. These most competitive districts were situated around the Seattle suburbs and the Olympic peninsula. In those legislative districts with very large PVIs, it appears to be more of a result of people living with politically like-minded individuals rather than any type of partisan gerrymandering. For example, the five most Democratic districts according to the PVI are all found in the city of Seattle, while the five most Republican districts are found in Eastern Washington centered around the Tri-Cities, Yakima, and the northeastern corner of the state (see map 11.1).

Table 11.1. Washington State Congressional PVI for Last Two Presidential Votes

District Number	2004 President's Vote	2008 President's Vote	Average	PVI	Rank
	%	%	%		
1	56	62	59.0	D 9	321
2	51	56	53.5	D 3	269
3	48	53	50.5	EVEN	242
4	36	40	38.0	R 13	85
5	41	46	43.5	R 7	148
6	53	57	55.0	D 5	288
7	79	84	81.5	D 31	414
8	51	57	54.0	D 3	268
9	53	58	55.5	D 5	286

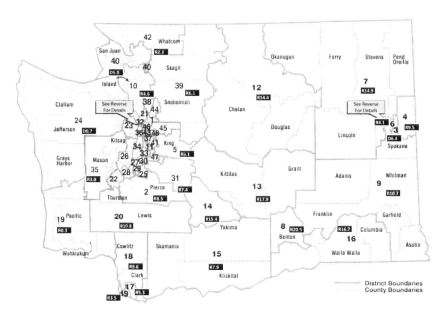

Map 11.1. Statewide Legislative Districts and Their Average Partisan Voting Index from the 2004 and 2008 Gubernatorial Elections. Washington State Redistricting Commission.

Compactness

For over a century, it has been understood that one of the primary ways to prevent gerrymandering is through the creation of compact districts. By definition, gerrymandering requires creating oddly shaped districts to either keep politically like-minded individuals together or splitting them apart. In either case, these districts become geometric oddities, which could in the extreme, be over a hundred miles long but only as wide as a highway median in some areas. To combat this type of oddly shaped district, the state of Washington has encouraged the Commission to keep districts as compact as possible. However, while a popular conception of compactness is having a small area, this might not be practically possible when districts are required to have equal population and populations are less dense in rural areas. Because of this, other ways of measuring density need to be explored rather than simply measuring the size of the district.

One way to measure the compactness of a district is to compare its size to another geometric shape. Geometrically speaking, the most compact shape possible is a circle—there is no other shape which can have as large an area compared to the size of its perimeter. So one way to measure the compactness of a district is to compare the area of the district to the size of the smallest possible circle which surrounds the district. The more of area of the circle which is contained in the district, the more compact the district is; while if there is a large amount of area in the circle which is not found in the circle, the less compact the district is. As these outlying areas increase, the compactness of the district decreases. Districts which have a higher percentage are considered to be more compact, while those with a smaller percentage—regardless of their actual size—are considered to be less compact. What this measurement tends to find is that districts which are created from odd, many angled shapes, and those which tend to be exceptionally narrow and long are found to be less compact than those districts which resemble shapes with fewer angles and corners.[7] For example, a circle encompassing all parts of Washington's 9th Congressional District (from Renton to Rainier) would also contain parts of Kitsap County, Tacoma, and unincorporated Pierce County. This means that the vast majority of the land which would be in that encompassing circle would fall outside of the area in the district. The most compact district, according to this metric, is the 8th Congressional District whose shape has no truly circuitous patterns and roughly resembles a rectangle. Using data from the U.S. Census Bureau, it is possible to measure the compactness of congressional districts. However, because no data exists for the size of legislative districts, this measure cannot be used to evaluate state legislative districts.

First, it is apparent that there are dramatic differences in the size of congressional districts in the state of Washington where the smallest district is the 7th Congressional District which is, essentially, the City of Seattle and Vashon Island and is about 115 square miles. The largest is the 5th District at about 22,000 square miles, which is approximately the size of West Virginia (see table 11.2).

Table 11.2.   Compactness of New Washington Congressional Districts

Congressional District	Land Area	Circular Area	Compactness Ratio
	square miles	*square miles*	
CD 1	439.21	2,340.21	18.77
CD 2	6,565.33	16,277.76	40.33
CD 3	7,515.38	15,386.00	48.85
CD 4	19,015.49	41,013.78	46.45
CD 5	22,863.97	72,145.70	31.65
CD 6	6,781.44	17,662.50	38.39
CD 7	141.31	890.74	15.86
CD 8	2,579.22	4,450.67	57.95
CD 9	607.71	4,221.94	14.39

However, somewhat counterintuitively, the most compact districts according to this metric are the larger, rural districts while the more urban districts are less compact. This is due in large part to the provision of following previously created boundaries when creating districts. Some congressional districts on the west side are oddly shaped because the cities which they encompass are oddly shaped. In addition, the geometric shape of the state creates areas which might make districts less compact, as using this metric could create the appearance of a less compact district because the district must include geographically diverse areas such as distant islands or peninsulas.

Following Existing Boundaries

The final directive to the commission along with creating politically competitive districts and making compact legislative boundaries is to follow previously created political boundaries. If a legislative district follows the boundaries of other political entities such as counties or cities, it is less likely that the process of drawing these boundaries would be used for political benefits. In addition, by following these boundaries, elected officials would be more likely to represent politically homogenous groups, which facilitates in representation. However, because the law requires legislative districts to have equal population, following already established boundaries is not always possible.

Generally speaking, the 2001 redistricting commission followed previously created political boundaries, notably county boundaries, especially outside of the Puget Sound region. In Eastern Washington, county lines divide the 4th and 5th Congressional Districts almost universally except for a small portion of Adams County which is excluded from the 5th District and a portion of Skamania County which is included in the 4th District. Similarly, the 2nd District also follows county or international boundaries, except when it gets close to the greater Seattle area, where it dissects both the cities of Monroe and Everett. The 3rd District also follows county lines until it enters the Olympia region where the 3rd and 9th split both Lacy and Olympia. Inside the more populated Seattle metropolitan area, boundaries are less likely to follow established political boundaries, as the counties might be too populated to follow county lines, and cities too underpopulated to merit their own member of Congress. Because of this, the 1st, 2nd, 6th, 8th, and 9th Districts are less likely to follow those boundaries than in other parts of the state, and the affected cities and counties are divided among multiple members of Congress.

This pattern also remains generally true when examining the current legislative districts in the state of Washington. While in less urban areas the legislative districts do tend to follow county lines and other political and natural boundaries (such as rivers), in urban areas it is again often the case that legislative boundaries split some cities in half and in many cases creates districts where parts of many cities and unincorporated counties are represented.

THOUGHTS ON THE 2001 REDISTRICTING

Often when people examine the quality of the job in redistricting, people tend to compare the results of the redistricting process to some idealized abstract. However, because of legal and geographic realities, comparing the process to an unattainable, theoretical goal is incorrect. Not only is it intellectually inappropriate not to acknowledge the constraints on the redistricting process, it can also provide a disservice to the electorate.

If people believe the political process is corrupted through gerrymandering and that elections are predetermined because of the redistricting process, they are likely to become more cynical and less trusting of the political process. These feelings of distrust and detachment from government have been shown to be a cause in some people's decision to not vote. Simply put, feelings that the redistricting process is designed to promote political parties or candidates, or are in some other way not benefiting the citizens of the state, could provide an incentive for some people to not vote.

This does not mean that political considerations do not occur and that elected officials and political parties try to influence the process. There are an infinite number of ways the redistricting process could redraw the lines and it would be naïve to argue that politics does not play a role in the process. However, it could be seriously damaging to the body politic if the public takes the mind-set that redistricting creates the environment where "elected officials selected their voters, not voters selecting their elected officials" when that is not the case.

Modern redistricting commissions must ensure that all legislative districts have an exactly equal population, and, in Washington State, must also be compact and follow previously created political boundaries as much as possible. Because of these requirements, and the technology which allows the mapping to become more exacting, gerrymandering in a manner seen in other states or other times is more difficult than many people might believe.

There were during the 2001 redistricting, as in all redistricting processes, a number of changes at both the congressional and legislative levels as the population changed. At the congressional level the most noticeable changes in the 2001 redistricting was the shrinking—in geographic terms—of the 3rd Congressional District centered in Southeast Washington and the 2nd Congressional District which extends from the north Seattle suburbs to the Canadian border. Because shrinking the size of a legislative district is a result of increased population density (since all districts must have equal population), this is consistent with the increased population growth in those two areas in the 1990s. The decreased size in terms of land area in the 3rd and 2nd, caused, in effect, the other congressional districts in western Washington to increase in geographic size. On the eastern side of the Cascades, the 5th Congressional District received Okanagan County from the 4th Congressional District, and the 4th Congressional District expanded into part of Skamania County and took all of Klickitat County.

With regards to the Washington State legislature's boundaries, like the congressional districts, all of the boundaries were required to shift to allow for equal population. In Eastern Washington, the 4th District expanded to encompass all of northeast Spokane County, and the 9th District gained the two most south eastern counties in the state: Asotin and Garfield. But the most dramatic changes occurred in Western Washington. In Southeastern Washington, the 17th District went from covering all of Skamania County and most of southeastern Clark County to covering only some—but not all—of the Vancouver suburbs. Again, this is in keeping with the exceptional growth in southeastern Washington during the 1990s. Likewise, there were significant changes in the northern part of Puget Sound. There the 42nd District lost eastern Whatcom County as the area around Bellingham increased in population and the 39th District collected eastern Skagit and Whatcom counties. As a result of this, the 40th Legislative District became perhaps the most circuitous district in the state as it encompassed Anacortes, San Juan County, and then also incorporates Mount Vernon and Burlington by following a small strip of land between two parallel roads (one of them being District Line Road) to connect these two land masses in one contiguous area.

However, generally speaking, the 2001 redistricting process produced congressional districts which were compact, and when they were not compact, it could be argued that lack of compactness was due to geographic limitations rather than actions of the commission. In total the average compactness ratio for Washington State congressional districts was 34.74. While there is no agreed upon metric about what is an acceptable level of compactness, many of Washington's congressional districts would seemingly pass a reasonable test of compactness. Moreover, some of the less compact districts are so because natural impediments—oceans, Puget Sound, and islands—or political boundaries—Oregon or Canada, for instance—make perfectly compact districts impossible.

In addition, by some measurements there is a good deal of competitiveness involved in many legislative elections. Like compactness, there are many ways to measure political competition and no agreed upon metric to measure competitiveness in a world where the electorate is not 50 percent Democrats and 50 percent

Republicans. Of the 49 legislative districts, in 23 of them, the governor's races in the past decade were decided by an average of less than 10 percentage points, and 20 of the legislative districts tended to support Democratic gubernatorial candidates while 29 supported Republicans. Again, considering that people tend to live with people who share common political ideas, and creating compact political districts prohibits making unusually large districts, there is a degree of political competition in Washington State.

Finally, in many places where the lines were redrawn in 2001, there is an attempt to follow previously created political boundaries. When congressional districts were redrawn, there were instances where county lines were honored. For instance, the 5th Congressional District included all of Okanagan County and the 6th Congressional District got all of Gray's Harbor County. Similarly, this also occurred in instances in the legislature where changes, especially in less populated areas, were done on county lines. While drawing boundaries is constricted by other restrictions, such as equal population, it is important to note that political and natural boundaries are respected.

THE 2011 REDISTRICTING

From the time the census data came out indicating that Washington State would receive another seat in the U.S. House of Representatives and the malapportionment report on how much each district would have to be reconfigured, one thing stood out: for the first time, one of Washington State's congressional districts would have to cross the Cascade Mountains uniting the politically diverse views of the state. As required by statute, the caucuses of both legislative chambers selected a person to serve on the legislative redistricting committee. For the Republican Party, the Senate selected former U.S. Senator Slade Gorton, who had also served as the state's Attorney General and a member of the state House of Representatives. In addition, after his term as Senator, Gorton served on the 9/11 Commission, the National War Powers Commission, and the National Commission of Federal Election Reform. While the House Republicans selected Tom Huff, a former member of the state House of Representatives and the founding chair of the Washington Retail Association.

Among the Democrats, the Senate chose Tim Ceis, a former deputy mayor of Seattle who had also served in multiple positions in the King County government—which is home to Seattle, many of its suburbs, and over a quarter of the state's total population. The House of Representatives selected Dean Foster, a former staff member for the House, aide to former Governor Booth Gardner, and the only member of the commission who had served on the 2001 redistricting commission. While there were no noticeable complaints about the commission members who were chosen or their qualifications, there was concern about the lack of diversity on the commission. Noticeably, all of the members of the Commission were white men from Western Washington, which caused some people to argue that the nonvoting commission chair should be a woman or from Eastern

Washington.[8] Perhaps because of this, Dr. Lura Powell, an analytical chemist and former director of the Pacific Northwest National Laboratory and resident of Eastern Washington was selected as the nonvoting commission chair.

Beginning on January 18, 2011, the Commission began meeting in Olympia to start drafting the maps for the new districts which had to be approved by the legislature in one year's time. During the next twelve months, the commission took to the road to get input from all parts of the state in 18 separate meetings throughout the summer before the four commissioners released their initial proposals in mid-September. Because Washington State was gaining a congressional seat and one member of the state's congressional delegation was retiring to run for governor, there was less pressure on the Commission to protect congressional incumbents.

Those initial proposals were generally greeted with some satisfaction among voters and interest groups and a little trepidation with some elected officials. Of the four initial proposals, three of the maps created a "minority-majority" congressional district in Western Washington around the Seattle area, while the fourth member had a district with a minority population of more than 40 percent.[9] Moreover, all of the initial proposals, save Gorton's, were relatively similar in answering the question of where the congressional district would cross the Cascade Mountains. For both the Democrats' proposals and Huff's map, the 8th Congressional District would stretch from the far eastern suburbs of Seattle, over the mountains to incorporate the two adjacent counties of Chelan and Kittitas. These two counties had the advantage of possessing relatively large population centers as well as being economically and culturally more connected to Western Washington. The proximity of these two counties to Seattle made them not only reliant on agriculture, but also on tourism catering to western Washingtonians.

The trepidation found among some political actors was found in the Commission's drawing of the forty-nine state legislative districts. Here, the four commissioners adroitly drew lines to maximize their party's fortunes while reminding the opposing party's elected officials their incumbency advantages could be whipped away by moving the lines on a map. For example, in one of the Democrats' proposals, the Senate Republican floor leader's home would have been drawn into the same district as the Senate Minority Leader (who was also a Republican). Meanwhile, Republicans drew lines to crack a reliably Democratic Spokane legislative district into four separate districts and placed the Democratic Senate majority leader into a Republican leaning district. However, most observers took these initial proposals as more places to begin negotiations and reminders of the power of redistricting, rather than solid commitments to change the maps.

The disparities between the legislative maps and a desire for each party to create an advantage in the newest congressional district did begin to bog the Commission down as the autumn unfolded. Both sides presented draft maps the following month in October, which remained equally far apart in terms of compromises, and concern began to grow that they would not be able to accomplish their task by the required January deadline. In an attempt to expedite the process, the Commissioners agreed to begin meeting as bipartisan subcommittees to draw the legislative districts—focusing first on the Westside of the state, one team would begin at the Canadian border heading south and begin drawing compromise maps for legislative districts, while the other team would start at the Oregon border and draw compromise boundaries while working their way north. The two groups would then meet in the populous middle at the Pierce and King county line, in the middle of the Seattle-Tacoma metropolitan area. Because thirty-eight of the state's forty-nine legislative districts are found on the west side of the state, the most intensive work of the Commission was in drawing those lines. While the focus continued on the west side of the state, which drew the ire of many eastern Washingtonians, the fact remained that the bulk of the population, districts, and boundaries were hundreds of miles away over the Cascades.

By all accounts the Commissioners continued meeting in their bipartisan subcommittees through the month of November and missed their self-imposed deadline of the end of November to complete their maps. Those maps, which were finally released on December 16, 2011, were striking because not all of the legislative incumbents were protected: one senator and four members of the state House were drawn out of their districts and displaced.[10] After finishing those western legislative districts, the Commission spent the final two weeks before their legally imposed deadline on the Eastern Washington legislative districts and the congressional districts. The fact that the commission would only spend two weeks on those maps was met with consternation among the public, especially among eastern Washingtonians who felt that a commission populated with Western Washington residents were neglecting them.[11] Like the Western Washington legislative districts, the Commission broke into bipartisan subgroups with Commissioners Gorton and Ceis focused on the congressional maps while the other two focused on the legislative districts.

Then, twelve days later, on December 28, the two commissioners released their proposed map for the new ten congressional districts. As initially proposed by three of the Commissioners, the major crossing of the Cascade Mountains occurred in central part of the state as Kittitas and Chelan counties' 110,000 residents were united with a district made up primarily of the far eastern suburbs of Seattle and Tacoma. Meanwhile, the new 10th Congressional District was centered on Olympia, the state's capital, and southern Puget Sound. The other major change of the Washington State congressional map was the movement of the 1st Congressional District. There, the district was moved from the northern Seattle suburbs, Bainbridge Island, and part of the Olympic Peninsula, to the northern Cascades and the far northwestern part of the state to the Canadian border, as well as grabbing some of the wealthiest suburbs of Seattle. While a major change in the district, this was less of a political challenge for the Commission, as the incumbent Congressman, Jay Inslee, had retired his seat to run for governor.

Finally, on January 1, 2012, at 9:55 p.m., just two hours and five minutes before their deadline, the four commissioners approved the redistricting of the state's forty-nine legislative districts and ten congressional districts. The state legislature, as required, approved the maps on February 7, with a 95–0 vote in the state House

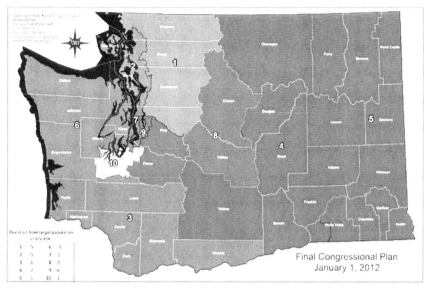

Map 11.2.   New Washington Congressional Districts. Washington State Redistricting Commission.

of Representatives and a 44–4 vote in the Senate. The next day, the plan was challenged in court by John Milem, a Vancouver, Washington, resident who stated that the new maps divided too many cities and reduced political competition rather than encouraging it.[12] Milem, who attended all of the commission's meetings, argued that the legislative and congressional districts, in many regards, became less politically competitive and could have been drawn to keep communities more intact. One month later, the Washington State Supreme Court ruled that the boundaries would stay intact for the 2012 elections (see map 11.2).

RESULTS OF THE 2011 REDISTRICTING

While much of the Washington State Redistricting Commission's focus remained on the state's legislative boundaries, there were significant implications for the congressional districts as well. First, as part of the redistricting, the state's first "minority-majority" district was created with the 9th Congressional District which covers the southern and southwestern Seattle suburbs. Additionally, the four bipartisan commissioners were able to find another thing which they could all agree upon: incumbency protection, as most political observers consider the lines drawn to keep those seats safe. Or, as one reporter explained after the December 28 maps were released: "Washington's eight U.S. House members seeking re-election in 2012 all found something nice in their stockings this week. The state Redistricting Commission unveiled maps that insulate the four Democrats and four Republicans from having to worry much about being unseated by the opposing party."[13] In fact, most political observers believe that Washington's redistricting has created four safe Republican seats, five safe Democratic seats, and one competitive one.

What stood out most among the congressional redistricting was how little attention was formally paid to it by the Commission. The initially individual maps of three of the Commission members look remarkably similar to the second, and final, map which was released three months later. This is probably due to the embarrassment of riches which befell the Commission. First, by gaining a seat, the Commission did not have to face the battle other states experienced which lost seats; each incumbent member could be protected from being drawn out of a district. Additionally, the retirement of one member of Congress allowed for increased flexibility in drawing the seats. With no entrenched political power residing in the 1st Congressional District, the Commission could freely alter that district and move it to a different part of the state. Finally, because much of Washington State has become increasingly politically homogenous at the level of congressional districts (for example, eastern and southwestern Washington tend to support Republicans, while Seattle and many of the interior suburbs support Democrats), drawing these safe districts became a much easier exercise.

This could not be the case for the state's legislative districts which is why so much time was focused on them. Rather than containing about 674,500 people as the congressional districts do, the state's legislative districts will contain only about 137,000 residents. Because of this many small pockets of voters who might not be able to influence the outcome in a congressional district could greatly impact the outcome in legislative districts. Moreover, because the population of exurban areas which tended to support Republicans grew at a much larger rate than the urban Democratic strongholds, there was a significant, if quiet battle playing out for control of the Washington State legislature playing out during much of the Commission's meetings. As these legislative districts get moved to reflect this change, it is probably likely that the Republicans, who have found few opportunities to control the statehouse, might become closer to realizing that chance after the redistricting.

NOTES

1. Portions of this chapter originally appeared in "The Redistricting Process in Washington State" published by the Institute for Public Policy and Economic Analysis at Eastern Washington University. Used with permission of the Institute.

2. Dave Workman, "Redistricting Panel Proposed," *Spokesman Review*, November 3, 1981.

3. Mary Cronin, "Congressional Redistricting Issue Could Stall Legislatures," *Lewiston Morning Tribune*, January 11, 1983, 9.

4. Associated Press, "Outside Commission Sought for Redistricting," *Lewiston Morning Tribune*, January 12, 1983, 24.

5. Workman, "Redistricting Panel Proposed."

6. On the congressional level, the Partisan Vote Index is calculated by determining the average percent of vote the Democratic presidential nominee received in the past two elections in the entire state compared to the percent of the vote the Democratic nominee received, on average, in a specific congressional district; the state PVI tracks the same information, but uses gubernatorial election results and state legislative districts rather than federal election data. So, for example, if a district had a PVI of +5, that would mean that it is 5 percent more Democratic than the state as a whole, while a PVI of -10 would mean it is 10 percent more Republican than the state as a whole.

7. The specific way of measuring the compactness of the district is to first bisect a line between the two furthest points in the district, which becomes the center of the circle encompassing the entire district. The area of the circle is then found ($A=\pi r^2$), and then the size of the district is divided by the size of the circle.

8. Editorial Board, "Washington's Redistricting Commission Should Include a Member from the Eastside of the State," *Seattle Times*, January 10, 2011.

9. Jim Camden, "Political Maps Unveiled," *Spokesman Review*, September 14, 2011.

10. Andrew Garber, "Some Shuffles, Few Ruffles in State Districting," *Seattle Times*, December 16, 2011.

11. Editorial, "Editorial: East Side in the Dark on Details of Redistricting," *Spokesman Review*, December 12, 2011.

12. Jim Camden, "Redistricting Plan Challenged," *Spokesman Review*, February 9, 2012.

13. Jordan Schrader, "Redistricting Maps Help Lawmakers," *Olympian*, December 31, 2011.

12

Missouri

Show Me . . . Again and Again!

Rickert Althaus, Jeremy D. Walling, and William J. Miller

Missouri, "The Show-Me State," was once again unable to complete its decennial congressional redistricting process on the first attempt. Instead, it required a gubernatorial veto, a legislative override, multiple lawsuits, the involvement of multiple courts, and almost a second round of mapmaking. In this way, the 2011–2012 process resembled some of the recent decades' experiences. The "re-run" nature of the process and the multiple required attempts to eventually finalize a map had a certain familiarity to those watching the process unfold.

MISSOURI POLITICAL CULTURE AND DEMOGRAPHICS

Missouri is in many ways a "typical" state when it comes to government and politics. In fact, it had such a bellwether record for presidential elections during the twentieth century that the *Economist* once called it "America's Focus Group."[1] Some of its apparent representativeness may have been due to the happenstance of its location in the center of the country. It was long said that Kansas City looked to the west, and that St. Louis looked to the east. In addition to that mix of western ranching and eastern industry was the Bootheel culture of the old south and the row-crop agriculture of the Midwest. The diversity of its economy may have had something to do with the diversity, and therefore representativeness, of its culture and politics.

Despite its long-standing reputation of being politically representative of the broader populace, Missouri appears to be trending a bit more Republican, with that party holding a veto-proof majority in the state Senate and not quite that same majority in the state House. Six of the nine U.S. Representatives in 2012 were Republicans, as was one of the U.S. Senators, and two of the six statewide elected executive officials. In the 2008 presidential election, the state went for John McCain, though by a margin of one-tenth of one percent. This was only the second time in a hundred years that Missouri didn't vote for the winning presidential candidate.

The 2010 census figures disclose that the demographic makeup of the Missouri population is more white (by 10.4 percent), less Hispanic/Latino (by 12.8 percent), and less Asian (by 3.2 percent) than the U.S. total. Even so, the demographic profile of the state has become somewhat more "representative" since the 2000 census.[2]

The 2010 census also showed that the population of the state, while increasing since 2000, did not keep pace with the rate of increase of the total U.S. population. Relatively speaking, then, the state fell behind, and did so sufficiently that it was necessary for the state's U.S. House of Representatives delegation to drop from nine members to eight.

Interestingly, Missouri just barely missed out on retaining nine seats. According to the Census Bureau's calculations, of the states that lost seats, Missouri would have had the highest priority for keeping the seat it eventually lost.[3]

The process used to draw congressional districts in Missouri is fairly typical, as will be described below. In addition, the political and legal fighting that accompanied the process during this cycle, compounded by the necessity of losing a district, was also fairly typical.

WHO DOES CONGRESSIONAL REDISTRICTING?

Missouri uses a fairly traditional method for congressional redistricting. The state constitution (Article III, Section 45) requires that congressional districts be established by the state legislature. This is accomplished by the usual legislative process, with bills being introduced in each chamber, one version being ultimately agreed to by both houses, and that bill being sent to the governor for his or her approval or veto. If the governor approves the plan, or if it is enacted over a veto, the description of each congressional district (including whole counties, or for portions of a county, the relevant tract blocks or voting districts) eventually is placed in a separate section of Chapter 128 of the Revised Statutes of Missouri.

WHAT IS REQUIRED OF A
CONGRESSIONAL REDISTRICTING PLAN?

Section 45 of Article III of the Missouri Constitution requires that congressional districts "shall be composed of contiguous territory as compact and as nearly equal in population as may be."

Equality

The federal courts have spoken over the years about how equal the population of congressional districts must be in order to meet constitutional standards. The first major case addressing this principle was the landmark 1964 Supreme Court case of *Wesberry v. Sanders*.[4] *Wesberry* involved congressional districts in Georgia, where the most populous district contained three times as many people as the least populous district. The Court struck down those districts, saying, "as nearly as is practicable, one man's vote in a congressional election is to be worth as much as another's."[5]

In 1969, the Court gave further guidance on how equal the population of congressional districts must be. In a challenge to the Missouri congressional districts of the time, the Court held that "the 'as nearly as practicable' standard requires that the State make a good-faith effort to achieve precise mathematical equality."[6]

In a 1983 case involving New Jersey congressional districts, the Court reiterated its insistence on equality. It said, "Adopting any standard other than population equality . . . would subtly erode the Constitution's ideal of equal representation. If state legislators knew that a certain *de minimis* level of population differences was acceptable, they would doubtless strive to achieve that level rather than equality."[7]

It is clear, therefore, that the Supreme Court requires redistricting entities to aim for absolute equality of population between congressional districts. (The Court has tolerated more inequality in state legislative and other non-congressional districts.) Equality is a simple mathematical concept that is easily grasped, and the equality standard doesn't appear to have been a difficult hurdle for many states in their recent rounds of redistricting.

Whether the Missouri Constitution's standard of "as nearly equal in population as may be" means exactly the same thing as "as nearly as practicable" is unknown, and from a practical standpoint, irrelevant. Because of the principle of federal supremacy, the U.S. Supreme Court's definition will prevail.

Compactness

There has been less agreement about how to evaluate the compactness of a congressional district, though the topic has been vigorously debated in the academic literature. Scholars have proposed multiple methods of measuring compactness, but have been unable to agree on one. To some, it seems as if each method could conceivably be used to justify districts that to the layperson would be obviously undesirable.[8] Others who have taken up the topic have concluded that compactness measures should only be used within a state and not between states, and that ideally, multiple measures should be used.[9]

The courts seem to have encountered compactness as an issue primarily when being asked to address partisan or racial gerrymandering. This appears logical, because many times redistricting bodies have stretched or manipulated district boundaries in order to concentrate or dilute voters of certain ethnicities or partisan preferences. Districts that have boundaries that are stretched or otherwise convoluted are less likely to appear to be compact.

Though the Supreme Court has addressed partisan and racial gerrymandering, and on some of those occasions mentioned the issue of compactness, it has not established a standard for measuring compactness. In fact, the Court has noted that a strict compactness requirement could have the possible consequence of "packing" political party adherents into a district,[10] which to some might look like a partisan gerrymander.

As a result, with no clear guidance on how compact districts must be in order to be "compact," states appear to have a certain amount of immunity against charges that their congressional districts are not sufficiently compact. Some have gone so far as to say that "compactness is in the eye of the beholder."[11]

IF AN AGREEMENT CAN'T BE REACHED: THE LESSON FROM THE 1980 CENSUS

The state constitution and statutes are both silent about what is to be done if the regular legislative process does not yield a map. In the recent past, federal law and federal courts have resolved the matter.

Following the 1980 census, the state was told that it was to lose a House seat, shrinking the delegation from ten to nine. Throughout its 1981 session, the Democrat-controlled state legislature struggled with the question of which congressional district would be lost. Some Democratic legislators wanted to keep three districts in the St. Louis metropolitan area, but some of the rural members (many of whom were also Democrats) felt that because St. Louis city proper had actually lost population, it should be divided up between two remaining St. Louis-area districts. Racial interests entered into the political equation, as well, because the incumbent in the city-dominated district was the delegation's sole African-American, Representative William (Bill) Clay.

When the legislative session ended in June without agreement on a map, lawsuits were filed in both of the federal district courts of the state, asking for a judicial remedy. Ultimately those suits were consolidated in the western district court (because the office of Secretary of State James Kirkpatrick, the main defendant, was located in Jefferson City, in the western district).

A three-judge panel was convened under federal statute (discussed below), consisting of one judge from each of the two district courts, and a third judge from the court of appeals of the eighth circuit. The panel asserted jurisdiction based upon the principles of a "federal question" and of "deprivation of constitutional rights."

In the meantime, Missouri Governor Kit Bond called the legislature into special session to see if it could agree on a map. The federal court took no further action on the lawsuit while the session, which ran from November 6 to December 17, was underway. The result of the special session was the same as the regular session held that spring: no agreement could be reached.

On January 7, 1982, the court issued its opinion in *Shayer v. Kirkpatrick*,[12] and the appendix of the opinion was the court-ordered redistricting plan. The court's map maintained the three St. Louis-area congressional districts, and instead eliminated a district with a Republican incumbent in south-central Missouri, carving it up and assigning portions to neighboring districts.

PERCEIVED PARTISANSHIP IN JUDICIAL REDISTRICTING[13]

In its opinion, the court rejected the possibility that the state simply hold at-large elections for the House delegation. To reach this decision, the court had to reconcile two apparently contradictory federal statutes. A 1929 statute (2 U.S.C. § 2a[c][5]) stated, "Until a state is redistricted . . . if there is a decrease in the number of Representatives . . . they shall be elected from the State at large."

On the other hand, a 1967 statute (2 U.S.C. § 2c) said "there shall be established by law a number of districts equal to the number of Representatives to which such State is so entitled, and Representatives shall be elected only from districts so established." The court held that the latter statute implicitly repealed the former provision. The U.S. Supreme Court upheld an appeal of the *Shayer* case later that year.[14]

In a 2003 case from Mississippi,[15] the Supreme Court upheld a federal court redistricting plan (also involving the loss of a House seat) where the state had no viable alternative. The opinion of the Court stated that the at-large provisions of the 1929 statute could apply *only* if "the state legislature, and state and federal courts, have all failed to redistrict."[16] Some of the Justices who concurred in upholding the lower court's plan, however, felt that at-large elections could *never* be used, and that the 1967 statute did in fact repeal the 1929 provision.

It appears as if the Supreme Court has not provided further clarification on the inherent tension between the two statutes since its 2003 case, nor have those statutes been legislatively modified by Congress. Therefore, it seems safe to say that the reasoning of the *Shayer* case remains in effect: that when a state is unable to establish required congressional districts, the federal courts can and will.

WHAT HAPPENED FOLLOWING THE 1990 CENSUS?

In 1991, the redistricting process proceeded about as smoothly as can be imagined, given that the map drawing in Missouri is done by the legislature and requires the approval of the governor. For this cycle, a Republican was in the Governor's Mansion, and the Democrats controlled the state legislature. The Democratic margin in the Senate was a "veto-proof" 23 to 11, but the party's advantage in the House was only 98 to 65. This meant that it would have been unlikely for the Democrats to be able to engineer an override of the Republican governor's veto, should one have come to pass. That created an environment in which cooperation between the parties was essential if redistricting by a judicial panel was to be avoided: neither party could force its will on the other.

Another factor that made the redistricting process less contentious during this cycle was that the size of the congressional delegation was to remain the same. Therefore, there were no major concerns about which party's incumbent would have that district eliminated.

The balance of power between the legislative and executive branches, combined with the fact that the number of congressional districts was not to change, made for a rather placid outcome. The "Missouri Congressional Redistricting Act (SB 369),"[17] sponsored by Senator Roger Wilson, was passed by both chambers on May 16. Governor John Ashcroft signed the bill on July 8, and those districts governed the congressional elections of the following year.

WHAT HAPPENED FOLLOWING THE 2000 CENSUS?

There was a close political party split in the Missouri Senate at the beginning of the 2001 legislative session. In fact, because of three vacancies[18] in the thirty-four-member body, neither political party held the constitutional majority of eighteen seats. On the first day of the session, the Republicans held sixteen seats, the Democrats held fifteen, and the Democratic lieutenant governor presided. With this even split of power, the parties agreed to a formal power-sharing agreement under which a Democrat was named president pro tempore, and a Republican was designated co-president pro tempore.

Because of this close party split and uncertainty over which party would eventually control the Senate, the decennial congressional redistricting got off to slow start. It appeared possible that the legislature would be too evenly divided to be able to accomplish the task, and that once again, a panel of federal judges might be called upon to design a map of the congressional districts. To head this off, the incumbent members of Congress, who were obviously interested in whatever map might result, negotiated their own fates.

A compromise map was eventually agreed to by representatives of eight of the nine members of the congressional delegation. At least in part because the plan had the backing of all but one of those most directly affected, both houses of the state legislature adopted it with about two days left in the legislative session, and the governor signed the bill. Though some observers thought that there might be a legal challenge to the new congressional map for partisan reasons, none emerged, and those congressional districts remained in force for the rest of the decade. Those districts can be seen in map 12.1.

WHAT HAPPENED FOLLOWING THE 2010 CENSUS?

The events of the 2011 to 2012 round of congressional redistricting in Missouri are fairly straightforward. The politics that underlay those events are a bit more complex and are explained in a separate section below.

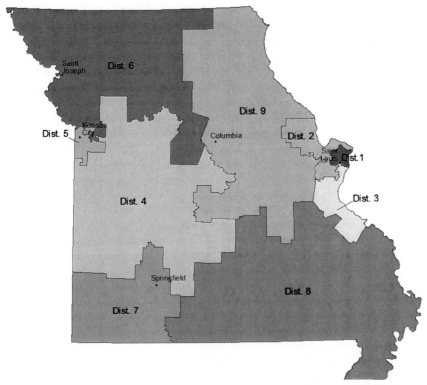

Map 12.1. Previous Missouri Congressional Districts. Missouri General Assembly.

By the end of 2010, it was known which states would be gaining, losing, or keeping the same number of House seats for the next decade. On December 21, the Census Bureau delivered the apportionment counts to President Obama, ten days before the statutory deadline.[19] Though Missourians knew that the state would be losing a representative, not much progress could occur on the actual redistricting until the more detailed census information was received by the state.

On January 13, 2011, a "placeholder" bill (HB 193) was introduced in the House by Representative John Diehl, the chair of the Special Standing Committee on Redistricting. This bill had no substantive content, but consisted of one sentence saying that it was the "basic format" for dividing the state into eight congressional districts. The bill was "read" a second time, and on January 20 it was referred to the Committee, where it awaited the data and the process that would lead to its being fleshed out.

On February 24, 2011, the Census Bureau released a more detailed report[20] to Missouri officials that enabled the redistricting process to begin in earnest. The House redistricting committee held two days of hearings in early March, and two more in late March and early April. On April 5, the Committee held a brief public hearing, then met in executive session, and then voted to adopt a committee substitute for HB 193 that contained the actual content of the new congressional districts, describing each from the county level down to the census blocks. That same day, the House Rules Committee, also chaired by Rep. Diehl, met and approved the substitute bill. Later that afternoon, Chair Diehl reported on the floor that both the Redistricting Committee and the Rules Committee recommended that the substitute bill "do pass."

On the next day, April 6, the House approved the substitute bill the requisite three times, and sent it on to the Senate, where it was also "read" for the first time on that day. Over the next week, the bill was referred to the Senate Select Committee on Redistricting (chaired by Senator Scott Rupp [R]), which held a hearing on it and then voted to send it on to the full Senate with a "do pass" recommendation. On the floor of the Senate, Sen. Rupp offered a Senate substitute for the House committee substitute, and the Senate's substitute was adopted. The main difference between the House and Senate versions had to do with the treatment of Jefferson County, a Democrat-leaning ring county south of St. Louis. There was also some concern about St. Charles County, a strong Republican western St. Louis suburban area, and some additional differences over some of the southwest Missouri counties.[21]

On April 13, the Senate substitute was approved in its third reading, and was sent on to the House. The following day, the House decided not to adopt the Senate version, and it called on the Senate to either concur with the House version or agree to meet in a conference committee. It took the Senate almost a week to agree to confer.[22] During that time, a meeting was held between the House and Senate leadership and the three incumbent Republican U.S. representatives from the districts surrounding the St. Louis area.[23] The *St. Louis Post-Dispatch* reported[24] that the three incumbents supported the House plan. It took the House and Senate conferees a week to agree on a solution, which was described by Speaker of the House Steve Tilley (R) as being a middle ground.[25] Both the House and Senate gave final approval to the conference committee report on April 27, 2011, and the "Conference Committee Substitute for the Senate Substitute for the House Committee Substitute for House Bill 193" was signed by the leaders of both chambers and delivered to the governor that night.

Governor Jay Nixon (D) reviewed the bill for two days, and issued a veto of it on April 30. His veto message asserted that the map did "not adequately protect the interests of all Missourians."[26] The timing of the veto was sufficient for the legislature to take additional action, either by revising the map or by overriding the veto, before the mandatory end of the session. On May 4, both chambers voted to override the veto, and the bill was sent on to the Secretary of State.

As discussed below, the legislative map did away with one of the two Democratic districts in the St. Louis area. The one that remained was a "majority-minority" district, with African Americans making up a fraction of a percentage point less than 50 percent of the population, but about 6 percent more than whites.[27] The racial factor is an important one for at least partially explaining the override, because the final version of the congressional district map included two safe districts, one in St. Louis and one in Kansas City. The incumbents in both of those districts were African Americans.

At the time of the override votes in early May, the Republican majority in the House was 105–55, with 3 vacancies. An override required 107 votes. Those voting to override included all 105 Republicans plus 4 African American Democrats, two each from the St. Louis and Kansas City areas. The 44 "no" votes all came from Democrats (and 7 Democrats were absent with leave).[28] It is unknown what might have happened if all of the House Democrats had voted together to sustain the governor's veto. Possible scenarios might have included a special legislative session being called to complete the redistricting, or districts might have ended up being drawn by federal judges, as they were following the 1980 census. What is certain, however, is that by voting with the Republicans, these Democrats helped approve a plan with two safe urban districts whose seats were currently filled with popular African Americans.

Most observers had predicted an easy override vote in the Senate, where Republicans held a veto-proof 26–8 majority. With a full complement of members, only 23 votes were needed to overturn the governor's veto. The 27 "aye" votes included those from three Democratic Senators, all from the Kansas City metropolitan area, and the 7 votes against included two rural Republicans. It appears less likely that racial issues explain these crossover votes, and perhaps more likely that they reflect a mix of motives. Nonetheless, an African American newspaper in St. Louis credited the successful override to "critical support from African American Democratic legislators."[29]

The override of the governor's veto marked the end of the legislative phase of redistricting, but it marked the beginning of the judicial phase. Both Democrats and Republicans found something to dislike about the adopted map. Under that map, Democrats were most likely going to be able to hold only one-fourth of the state's congressional seats, even though the state's electorate is much more closely divided. Most of the Democratic objections centered on the disappearance of one of the three St. Louis area districts. Republicans, on the other hand, were more likely to object to the Kansas City district, which though heavily Democratic, had been stretched significantly more eastward into more conservative rural areas.

These partisan concerns may have been the main motivating factor for those who had objections to the new map, but legal grounds would be necessary in order to successfully challenge the map in court. As explained above, the two essential criteria for congressional districts in Missouri are equality and compactness. Because the congressional districts were undeniably equal, the remaining route for a challenge was that they were insufficiently compact. That argument was the main one underlying the briefs and court opinions that were written over the months to follow. The new districts can be seen in map 12.2. The judicial activity is summarized in the following box:

September 23, 2011: Democrats filed suit in Cole County Circuit Court (Jefferson City) challenging the map (*Kenneth Pearson et al. v. Chris Koster et al*).[30]

November 22, 2011: Republicans filed suit in the same court, specifically challenging the districts in the western part of the state (*Stan McClatchey et al. v. Robin Carnahan*).[31]

December 12, 2011: Cole County Circuit Judge Dan Green rejected legal challenges of both the Democrats and the Republicans, and dismissed both cases for failure to state a claim.

December 13, 2011: The Democrats in the *Pearson* case appealed to the Missouri Supreme Court,[32] and the following day, the Republicans in the *McClatchey* case did as well.[33]

January 12, 2012: The Missouri Supreme Court heard both cases, and in its opinion, the Court sent the cases back to the original trial court to have it determine whether the districts were "compact." It ordered the trial court judgment to be reached no later than February 3, in case another round of redistricting were to be necessary.

February 3, 2012: The Cole County Circuit Court upheld the map, declaring that the plaintiffs had not proven their case that the districts were insufficiently compact. The decision was largely based on the January 17 Missouri Supreme Court opinion that said that "[T]hese maps could be drawn in multiple ways, all of which might meet the constitutional requirements," and that "compactness and numerical equality cannot be achieved with absolute precision."[34]

February 16, 2012: The Missouri Supreme Court heard the appeals from both the Democrats and Republicans that the trial court erred in determining compactness. The Court's deliberations continued past the March 27 deadline for candidate filing.

May 25, 2012: The Missouri Supreme Court upheld the congressional map, saying that the lower court did not err, and that the standard "does not require absolute precision in compactness."[35]

Map 12.2. New Missouri Congressional Districts. Missouri General Assembly.

"F*** YOU!" THE POLITICS AND EFFECTS OF THE POST–2010 REDISTRICTING

Politics

The large Republican majorities in both houses of the state legislature essentially preordained that it was going to be a Democrat-held congressional district that was going to disappear as a result of the redistricting. Prior to that, there were three Democrats in the congressional delegation, one in the Kansas City area and two in the St. Louis area. From a practical standpoint, it was going to be much easier to make one of the St. Louis districts disappear than to eliminate the Kansas City district.

With that given, most of the suspense surrounded the question of which St. Louis incumbent was going to lose his district. Both seats were held by sons of powerful, well-known politicians. In the 1st District, William Lacy Clay Jr. (known as "Lacy"), served in the seat that his father, William Lacy Clay Sr. (known as "Bill"), had held for over thirty years. The 3rd District was held by John Russell ("Russ") Carnahan, the son of a two-term governor and the grandson of a seven-term congressman from southeast Missouri.

The demographics of the two districts were important in the redistricting decisions. As of the 2010 census date, the 1st District was 49.8 percent African American, and 46.9 percent white, while the 3rd District was 9.1 percent African American and 85.7 percent white.[36] A redistricting body that chose to eliminate the heavily-minority 1st District might be alleged to be diluting the voting strength of African-Americans, and might run afoul of provisions of the 1965 Voting Rights Act.

As the redistricting process played out in the Missouri legislature and it became apparent that the 3rd District was the one that was going to be eliminated, Carnahan reportedly approached Clay on the floor of the House to ask for his help in opposing the Republican plan. When Clay refused, Carnahan responded, "F*** you! Thanks for your help!"[37]

The remaining St. Louis-area Representative, six-term Republican Todd Akin of the 2nd District, announced several weeks later that he would not run for re-election to the House, but would instead run for the U.S. Senate. This gave Carnahan an opportunity to run for that open seat, albeit in a district with a 53 percent Republican majority.[38]

This might not have been an insurmountable hurdle. His voting record could be described as moderate; according to the *National Journal*, Carnahan was the 139th most liberal member of the House in 2011.[39] He also had a reputation of bipartisanship in Congress.[40] Also a strength, his name recognition was almost universal: in addition to his late father Mel being a two-term governor, his mother Jean served two years as an appointed U.S. senator, and his sister Robin served two terms as Missouri secretary of state. Nonetheless, only a small portion of his old district was to be included within the boundaries of the new 2nd District (though that could also have been said about the new 1st, 3rd, and 8th Districts). So, rather than choosing to run in the 2nd District, where he would probably have easily won the nomination and the general election would have been the larger hurdle, Carnahan decided to run against Clay in the 1st District, where the primary winner would be expected to have an easy time of it in the general election.

Effects

Carnahan's decision guaranteed the Democrats the loss of a seat, most probably leaving them with only two: one in St. Louis and one in Kansas City. It also split traditional Democratic supporters, with unions and local government officials on both sides of the race. It also raised racial issues within the Democratic coalition. Carnahan and his family had long had strong support among African-American voters in Missouri, but Lacy Clay's father had been the first African-American member of Congress from Missouri.[41] Some analysts felt that hurt feelings from a divisive primary battle could have the potential to affect turnout in November, and therefore have an impact on the fate of other statewide Democratic candidates, including incumbent U.S. Senator Claire McCaskill.

It is clear, then, that the 2011–2012 redistricting in Missouri would at the very least have an impact on the partisan makeup of the 2013–2015 House delegation, which would most likely have a 6–2 Republican advantage. Whether the effects of the Carnahan-Clay primary race would have spillover effects on other general election races would remain to be seen.

There could be other longer-term effects that result, as well. Some observers of Missouri politics have found that when a party controls a congressional seat, the party can use that platform to expand and firm up the party strength at the lower levels, such as in the state legislature or county offices.[42] A congressional incumbent can give the party higher visibility, can attract or energize or endorse party candidates for those other offices, and by raising money, can help the election chances of those candidates. A popular incumbent can also make the party more attractive to potential voters, who might then be more willing to consider candidates of that party for other elected positions.

Because there will most likely be one less Democratic House member from Missouri, that means that there will be one less incumbent to foster and support Democratic candidates at the lower levels. That could potentially mean fewer lower-level Democratic office-holders gaining seasoning and credibility to run for higher offices. Over the long term, such a scenario could even further Missouri's possible shift from a swing state to a Republican-leaning one.

THE FUTURE OF CONGRESSIONAL
REDISTRICTING IN MISSOURI

Some have wondered about the prospects of Missouri moving away from the traditional legislative method of redistricting and adopting some other method. For example, Missouri has for decades used bipartisan commissions to redraw district maps for both houses of the state legislature. However, if the standard for success for a redistricting effort is that the responsible body effectively completes its task in the time allotted and that its plan does not draw a serious court challenge from either party, then the Missouri experience with these commissions has not been entirely successful.

It was a 1966 amendment to the state Constitution that required the use of bipartisan commissions to draw state legislative districts. In the five decennial redistricting cycles that have taken place since that time, not once have both the House and Senate commissions been able to produce maps that subsequently went into effect. In some cases, the House commission was successful, and in some cases, the Senate commission was successful, but in each of these redistricting cycles, state appellate court judges eventually drew the map for at least one legislative body, and on two occasions, both. With that mixed record over recent decades, it does not seem that adopting the bipartisan commission method of redrawing congressional districts would guarantee success for that process, either.

Some observers of the most recent round of congressional redistricting in Missouri have expressed interest in the state adopting the Iowa method of redistricting. The

Iowa plan has districts drawn by a nonpartisan (instead of bipartisan) body, considering only the numbers of people in each district and supposedly not considering the partisan or other political ramifications of the map. The major newspapers in both Kansas City and St. Louis have editorially endorsed such an idea for the Missouri congressional redistricting process.[43]

Such an idea has not seemed to get much traction beyond the newspapers' editorial boards. Early in the 2011 legislative session, Missouri Representative Jeanne Kirkton (D) introduced a resolution to propose a state constitutional amendment that would have gone even further than the Iowa plan.[44] Whereas in Iowa the proposed districts must eventually be approved by both the legislature and the governor, the Kirkton amendment would have kept the entire redistricting process out of the hands of elected officials. It called for the position of a state demographer to be created, and for that person (or office?) to develop the maps for the congressional districts and the state legislative districts, which would then go directly to the Missouri Secretary of State for implementation. The suggested amendment language included directions for the establishment of districts, and even included a definition of, and formulas for calculating "compactness" of districts.

It appears that no companion measure to the Kirkton resolution was introduced in the state Senate. In the House, it was referred to the Special Standing Committee on Redistricting, and no hearings were held on it. During the 2012 session, Rep. Kirkton did not reintroduce her resolution.

Missouri House Speaker Pro Tem and later Republican candidate for Missouri Secretary of State Shane Schoeller announced in November 2011 his interest in utilizing the Iowa plan for drawing the districts for the state legislature.[45] (Apparently he did not intend that the Iowa plan be used for congressional districts.) No Iowa plan component was included in any of the election-related legislation he introduced in the 2012 session. In fact, it appears that, apart from the 2011 Kirkton resolution, in neither 2011 nor 2012 did any member of either legislative chamber introduce legislation that would change away from the customary legislative drawing of congressional districts.

Missouri is not known for policy innovation—it is the "Show-Me State," after all. For the legislature to become convinced to adopt another method of redistricting, the members would have to be convinced ("shown") that the new method would be better. The conventional method was sufficient to allow the heavy Republican majorities in the legislature to expand the party's majority in the state's congressional delegation. The Iowa plan might not have had the same result. It would therefore seem counterintuitive to expect the legislative majority to be interested in the near term in adopting a plan that would potentially lessen its influence.

Missouri does have a frequently-used citizen initiative process that can be used to propose either state constitutional amendments or state statutes. It is conceivable that a group or coalition of groups could put together an Iowa-type proposal and circulate petitions to put the matter on the ballot directly. However, it is unclear how much the controversy of the 2011–2012 congressional redistricting was of concern to Missouri voters as it was taking place. It is also unclear how willing citizens' groups would be to put the effort and expense into a petition drive to address an issue that is nine years in the future, in order to avoid a repeat of this cycle's controversy, the electoral outcome of which perhaps half or more of the state's voters might not have found objectionable.

Those who are most likely to object to the "politics" of the redistricting process are probably those who end up on its short end—in other words, those who support the minority party or who have an objective (maintaining a fully rural district, or including a particular county or city in one district rather than another, for example) that was not advanced by the plan that was approved. Clearly, the current method of legislative drawing of Missouri congressional districts is "political." Finding a different method of redistricting that minimizes the "politics" of the process is a tall order. Even when the districts were drawn by federal judges following the 1980 census, some Missourians saw "politics." The bipartisan commission method of drawing Missouri state legislative districts has had failures that can be attributed to "politics,"[46] so adopting that method for congressional districts will not eliminate "politics." Even the Iowa plan depends on the legislature and the governor agreeing to the map drawn by the nonpartisan body. It is not hard to imagine a scenario where "political" concerns could enter into that approval process. The one method discussed in this chapter that most isolates the process from the "politics" of elected officials is the Kirkton proposal and the "politics" of adopting and implementing such a proposal might prove to be too high a hurdle to ever come about.

What can we expect for the future of congressional redistricting in Missouri? Given the status quo in the state legislature, in the absence of an initiative effort, it seems unlikely that Missouri will change its redistricting process in the near future. That means it will continue to use the traditional legislative process to draw the state's congressional districts, and it will continue to experience the traditional consequences of that process. Change will only come about *if* a sufficient number of those in the "Show-Me State" feel that they have been adequately "shown" a better way.

NOTES

1. *The Economist*, September 23, 2000, 31.
2. U.S. Census Bureau, "State and County Quick Facts" for 2010 data, and "Demographic Profiles: National Summaries by Geography" for 2000 data.
3. U.S. Census Bureau, "Priority Values for 2010 Census."
4. *Wesberry v. Sanders*, 376 U.S. 1 (1964).
5. *Wesberry v. Sanders*.
6. *Kirkpatrick v. Preisler*, 394 U.S. 526 (1969).
7. *Karcher v. Daggett*, 462 U.S. 725 (1983).
8. H. P. Young, "Measuring the Compactness of Legislative Districts," *Legislative Studies Quarterly* 13, 1 (February 1988): 105–15.

9. Richard Niemi, Bernard Grofman, Carl Carlucci, and Thomas Hoefeller, "Measuring Compactness and the Role of a Compactness Standard in a Test for Partisan and Racial Gerrymandering," *Journal of Politics* 52, 4 (November 1990): 1155–81.

10. *Vieth v. Jubelirer*, 541 U.S. 267 (2004).

11. Three examples include: Plaintiff's brief in *Jefferson County Commission v. Tennan* (2012); attorney Miguel De Grandy, quoted by Andrew Abramson in "Black Leader's Map Idea for West Palm Beach's Redistrict Plan Stirs Legal Concerns," *Palm Beach Post*, Aug. 20, 2011; "Renewing the Temporary Provisions of the Voting Rights Act: Legislative Options after *Lulac v. Perry*," Senate Hearing 109–823, Hearing before the Subcommittee on the Constitution, Civil Rights and Property Rights of the Senate Judiciary Committee, July 13, 2006, 417.

12. 541 F.Supp. 922 (1982).

13. Paul W. Adams, *Missouri Times*, January 4, 1982, 6.

14. *Schatzle v. Kirkpatrick*, 456 U.S. 966 (1982).

15. *Branch v. Smith*, 538 U.S. 254 (2003).

16. *Branch v. Smith*.

17. The bill was actually: CCS HCS SS SS SB 369.

18. William (Lacy) Clay (D) had been elected to Congress from the 1st District, Sam Graves (R) had been elected to Congress from the 6th District, and Joe Maxwell (D) had been elected lieutenant governor.

19. Census Bureau press release CB10-CN.93.

20. Census Bureau press release CB11-CN.49.

21. "Missouri Senate Approves New Congressional Map," Senate press release, April 14, 2011.

22. It did so on April 20, 2011.

23. Todd Akin of the 2nd District, Jo Ann Emerson of the 8th District, and Blaine Luetkemeyer of the 9th District

24. Rebecca Berg, "Senate Breaks Redistricting Logjam, Sends Maps to Conference Committee," *St. Louis Post-Dispatch*, April 20, 2011.

25. Rebecca Berg, "Apparent Redistricting Compromise Reached, House and Senate to Vote on Proposal," *St. Louis Post-Dispatch*, April 27, 2011.

26. Jay Nixon, veto message of April 30, 2011, as printed in May 2, 2011, *Journal of the House*, May 2, 2011, 1739.

27. Kevin McDermott and Nicholas J. C. Pistor, "Race Has Role in Carnahan, Clay Contest," *St. Louis Post-Dispatch*, July 22, 2012, A1.

28. *Journal of the House*, May 4, 2011, 1807.

29. "The Growing Isolation of Russ Carnahan," *St. Louis American*, January 12, 2012.

30. 11AC-CC00624.

31. 11AC-CC00752.

32. SC 92200.

33. SC 92203.

34. Court's opinion in the combined cases of SC 92200 and SC 92203.

35. Court's opinion in the combined cases of SC 92317 and SC 92326.

36. McDermott and Pistor, "Race Has Role." U.S. Census Bureau website reports similar figures for the 3rd District, but a higher percentage of African Americans for the 1st District.

37. Reported by www.politico.com, April 19, 2011.

38. "The Growing Isolation of Russ Carnahan," *St. Louis American*, January 12, 2012, updated January 18, 2012.

39. "A Congress Divided," *National Journal's* 2011 Vote Ratings," *National Journal*, February 23, 2012.

40. Bill Lambrecht, "1 Seat, 2 Incumbents," *St. Louis Post-Dispatch*, July 16, 2012, A1.

41. McDermott and Pistor, "Race has Role."

42. Brian Smentkowski, Rickert Althaus, and Peter J. Bergerson, "Emerson Defeats Heckemeyer in Missouri's Eighth District Race," in *The Roads to Congress 1998*, ed. Robert Dewhirst and Sunil Ahuja (Wadsworth/Thompson Learning: Belmont CA, 2000).

43. *Kansas City Star*, "Redistricting Can Be Heavenly—Just Ask Iowa," April 23, 2011; *St. Louis Post-Dispatch*, "Map Quest," April 26, 2011, A10.

44. House Joint Resolution No. 19, introduced February 9, 2011.

45. Chris Blank, "State Rep. Proposes Election Reforms, Voter Photo ID Requirement," *Associated Press*, November 3, 2011.

46. During the 2011–2012 legislative redistricting cycle, the governor chose to appoint a new second commission after a state judicial panel drew a map because the initial commission was unable to agree to a map, and the judicial map was struck down.

13

Congressional Redistricting in New Jersey

Brigid Callahan Harrison

New Jersey, like nearly every state in 2011, faced the prospect of redistricting—the process of redrawing the boundary lines of congressional districts to ensure that each person is equally represented in the U.S. House of Representatives. Occurring after reapportionment, redistricting enables states to achieve the principle of "one person—one vote" by configuring districts of equal population. According to the 2010 U.S. census, the state's overall growth rate of 4.5 percent was not enough to stave off a cut to the number of members representing the state in the U.S. House of Representatives. In 2011, the reapportionment process determined that New Jersey would lose one seat of its thirteen seats in the House of Representatives.

NEW JERSEY'S POPULATION, DEMOGRAPHIC TRENDS AND REDISTRICTING

The country's most densely-populated state boasted 377,500 new residents in the decade between the 2000 and 2010 censuses. New Jersey's overall population increased from 8.4 to 8.8 million, retaining its status as the nation's eleventh most populous state, according to Census Bureau figures.

And so, while New Jersey did not meet the fate of neighboring New York and nearby Ohio in losing two seats, it joined Pennsylvania, Illinois, Iowa, Louisiana, Massachusetts, Michigan, and Missouri who each lost one. It certainly could not keep pace with the high rates of growth seen in the southern and western portions of the United States. The comparatively slow growth rate (compared to the average U.S. population rate growth of 10 percent between 2000 and 2010) meant that New Jersey's House delegation would shrink for the third time since 1980, having lost one in both the 1980 and 1990 reapportionment process. (The state retained its seats in 1970 and 2000.)

Geographically, the nature of the changes between the state's 21 counties and 566 municipalities also influenced the redistricting process. While many coastal towns—41 of 49 oceanside towns (from Cape May at the southern tip to Sea Bright in Monmouth County at New Jersey's eastern shoulder) lost population as a result of the housing bubble bursting, their inland counterparts retained population or grew between 2000 and 2010.[1] In particular, southern New Jersey saw the greatest population growth—continuing a trend stemming back to 1980—which provides a degree of protection for the congressional districts in the southern part of the state, and the members who serve in them. For example, Ocean and Gloucester counties saw their populations increase by 13 percent each, the largest percentages of growth in New Jersey. Much of the growth in southern New Jersey comes about as a result of the sluggish economy during much of the 2000–2010 decade: because housing prices are lower on average in the southern portion of the state, many southern counties and towns saw their populations increase as commuters sought cheaper homes. Much of New Jersey's population growth also came in suburban communities, with Ocean County in particular attracting many new residents, primarily because of affordable "over 55" housing developments in this coastal south Jersey county.

But between 2000 and 2010, New Jersey's cities were able to reverse a trend of declining population. The state's largest city, Newark, showed a 1 percent population increase, gaining about 7,000 people and growing from 247,546 in 2000 to 277,140 in 2010. This was the first measurable growth seen since 1980. Newark's growth came despite the overall decline in population in its surrounding environ, Essex County, which dropped by 1 percent. Newark's growth offered a degree of protection for its congressional district in the 2011 redistricting process. Nearby Jersey City, the state's second largest city, is seeing redevelopment and gentrification as young urban professionals are choosing it as a cost-friendly alternative to Manhattan (easily reachable on a PATH train), and it saw a 3 percent population increase between 2000 and 2010.

New Jersey's redistricting process also was influenced by the state's increasing diversity. In 2010, about 1.5 million New Jerseyans identified themselves as Hispanic or Latino, an increase of about 438,000, representing a 39 percent increase from 2000. The growth is part of a long-term trend for New Jersey, which has traditionally attracted large numbers of Hispanic immigrants. While decades ago Hispanics immigrated to New Jersey from Cuba and Puerto Rico, today there is a great diversity in the heritage of New Jersey's Latino population, and newer immigrants are likely to hail from Mexico, and South and Central American nations. They are now the dominant minority group in the state.

New Jersey also saw increasing diversity among other racial and ethnic groups. 14 percent of the state's population identifies itself as African American, totaling about 1.2 million residents, a 6 percent increase in 10 years. The state's Asian American population increased by 2 percent between 2000 and 2010, growing from 6 to 8 percent. And almost a quarter of a million New Jerseyans identified themselves as multiracial.

OVERVIEW OF THE
REDISTRICTING PROCESS IN NEW JERSEY

In New Jersey, the congressional redistricting process is structured according to a New Jersey State Constitutional Amendment, which was passed by voters in 1995. According to the amendment, redistricting occurs through a bi-partisan Redistricting Commission, which is created for such purpose after reapportionment occurs. The state provides for two separate—though similar—structures for state legislative redistricting and congressional redistricting, and state legislative redistricting precedes congressional redistricting as the boundaries of legislative maps are required in the spring of years ending in 1, in order to facilitate the state's odd-year election cycle. Congressional redistricting follows, taking place in the fall and winter of years ending in 1.

In New Jersey, the Congressional Redistricting Commission is composed of 13 members. Twelve are partisan members: 2 are appointed by the Assembly speaker and 2 by the State Senate president; 2 also are appointed by the Assembly minority leader and 2 by the Senate minority leader. In addition, the state chairs of the two political parties whose candidates for governor received the largest and second largest number of votes in the most recent gubernatorial election appoint 2 members each.

The 13th member—the tie-breaker—is selected by a majority vote of the 12 partisan members. The state Constitution mandates that the 13th member be selected July 15 of years ending in 1. The only qualifications specified are that the individual be a resident of New Jersey for 5 years, and that the appointee has not held party or public office in those five years. If there is a stalemate and the partisan appointees cannot reach a consensus on a 13th member, they must notify the New Jersey State Supreme Court, and in doing so, must provide the Court with the names of the two highest vote-getters from among those considered by the 12 partisan Redistricting Commission members. One of the two top vote-getters—"the more qualified" candidate when considering "education and occupational experience, prior public service in government or otherwise and demonstrated ability to represent the best interest of the people of this State" is then selected by a majority vote of the full State Supreme Court. The 13th member's selection must be certified by the Court to the secretary of state by August 15.

In 2011, the State Supreme Court did not need to decide, as the partisan members of the Redistricting Commission selected John J. Farmer Jr. as the 13th member. John Farmer is the Dean of the Rutgers University Law School, a position he has served in since 2009. Prior to his career at Rutgers, he had been appointed in 1997 by Republican Governor Christine Todd Whitman as chief counsel to the governor. He had previously served as her deputy chief counsel and assistant counsel. Farmer also had served as attorney general for the State of Jersey in the Whitman administration. When former New Jersey Governor Tom Kean (R) and former Indiana Congressman Lee Hamilton (D-IN-09) were tapped to co-chair the 9/11 Commission (the "National Commission on Terrorist Attacks Upon the United States"), Farmer was selected as senior counsel to the Commission. He also served as counsel to Alan Rosenthal, the tie-breaking member of the New Jersey State Legislative Redistricting Commission, which had reconfigured New Jersey's state legislative districts earlier in 2011. As the 13th member of the Commission, Farmer served as its chair. (Each of the partisan delegations also selects a chair of their delegation.)

According to the state Constitution, the Redistricting Commission must conduct its organizational meeting no later than the Wednesday after the first Monday in September of each year ending in 1.[2] In 2011, that meeting took place on September 6, 2011, in the State House Annex in Trenton.[3]

The State Constitution also requires the Commission to hold at least three public hearings in different parts of the State.[4] The public hearings in 2011 were conducted on September 22 in Camden, which is in South Jersey;[5] and on October 11 in New Brunswick[6] in central New Jersey, and in Newark[7] in North Jersey. The State Constitution charges the Commission with reviewing written district plans submitted by members of the public, "subject to the constraints of time and convenience"[8] of the Commission.

While Commission meetings other than the public hearings may be closed to the public, the final meeting at which the redistricting map is adopted must be an open public meeting, and requires at least 24 hours public notice. This meeting occurred on December 23 in 2011, in the State House Annex,[9] nearly a month before the Commission was required to submit a Redistricting Plan on January 17, 2012. If no plan was able to garner a majority of seven votes from the Commission, the top two district plans receiving the largest number of votes (each more than five) would be submitted to the New Jersey Supreme Court, which would select a plan.

PRINCIPLES GUIDING NEW JERSEY'S 2011 CONGRESSIONAL REDISTRICTING PROCESS

The New Jersey State Constitution does not provide any guidance or standards to be used by the Redistricting Commission during the congressional redistricting process (it does do so for state legislative redistricting). Nonetheless, the process for congressional redistricting is constrained by federal guidelines stemming from U.S. constitutional provisions, federal statutes (including the Voting Rights Act of 1965), and state and federal court rulings.

Derived from these sources came six standards that were applied during the 2011 redistricting process. These standards included:

- Equal Distribution of Population Within Districts in the State
- Geographical Contiguity
- Geographical Compactness
- Protection of Incumbent Members of Congress

- Protection of Communities of Interest
- Protection of Minority-Majority Districts

Federal standards require equal populations in congressional districts within a state.[10] (States with only one member of the House of Representatives will obviously vary in populations.) The principle stated in *Wesberry v. Sanders* that "one man's vote in a congressional election is to be worth as much as another's,"[11] or "one person one vote," has subsequently been strictly interpreted so as to disallow much deviation in district size whatsoever. Though the Supreme Court has said that small deviations in district population size could occur in order to facilitate other redistricting goals, including "making districts compact, respecting municipal boundaries, preserving the cores of prior districts, and avoiding contests between incumbent Representatives,"[12] the Court has placed a strict standard on deviations, resulting in congressional districts with essentially even populations.[13]

With regard to contiguity, the desirable goal is to create a district in which it is possible to get from any one point in the district to any other without having to leave the district to do so. Contiguity is not a federally-mandated criterion for redistricting, but is a factor in New Jersey's redistricting process, as it is in many other states.

Another important though not overreaching standard in New Jersey's congressional redistricting process is compactness. The 2001 map chosen by that year's Redistricting Commission resulted in some of the least compact congressional districts, yet compactness was still a guiding principle in 2011. There are differing scholarly perspectives in measuring compactness, though most compare the geometric shape of a district to a perfectly compact geometric shape. One such measure, the Reock measure, compares the area of a district with that of the smallest circle that can encapsulate the district.[14] The Convex Hull is a similar paradigm, though the encapsulating figure is a comparative measure of the area of a district in terms of the smallest convex polygon that can enclose it (instead of a circle). Both of these measures fail to take into account the shape of districts – and sometimes score oddly shaped but densely packed districts similar to those with regular shapes. Another model, the Polsby-Popper measure compares the area of a congressional district with the area of a circle with the same perimeter as the district.[15] Similarly, the Schwartzberg measure compares the perimeter of the district to the circumference of the circle whose area is equal to the area of the district. But these two models are particularly problematic in a state such as New Jersey, which has irregular borders created by the Atlantic Ocean on the east, and the Delaware River in the west. Districts bordering these irregular geographic boundaries (nearly all in the state) would score relatively low when compared to districts in western states with more regular geographic borders.

No matter how compactness is measured, however, it is viewed as a desirable goal for both constituents and their representatives, as it increases the likelihood that constituents will share communities of interest borne of their geographic proximity that can be better represented by their elected House members (not to mention the fact that it cuts down on travel time within the district for the representatives). Thus compactness was a desirable though not stringent goal for the 2011 Redistricting Commission, and was secondary to other redistricting principles.

One of these principles recognized by both congressional and state legislative redistricting commissions in New Jersey is incumbent protection. While the U.S. Supreme Court has recognized a narrow interpretation[16] in protecting "incumbents from contests with each other,"[17] New Jersey has traditionally applied this criteria rather strongly, going so far as to adopt a minimally-altered redistricting plan submitted by the congressional delegation in 2001. While protection of individual incumbent members of Congress is an immediate goal, in New Jersey incumbency protection has applied to the individual members as well as their parties, so that, should an individual member of Congress leave office, his or her party would be well-positioned to maintain the seat based on the partisan composition of the district. In 2011, this criterion was, of course, difficult to adhere to because of the loss of a congressional seat, which, in the absence of a retirement, necessarily forced competition between at least two incumbents.

There were varying perceptions of "communities of interest" in the 2011 congressional redistricting process in New Jersey. The most common interpretation centered on the desire of racial and ethics groups to be consolidated so as to maximize their potentiality at demographic representation in Congress. Such was a common theme among advocates for Hispanic and Latino communities, African American communities, and Asian American communities.[18] In other instances, municipal elected officials advocated either for keeping their entire municipality in one district (municipal splits into multiple districts were a common outcome of the 2001 map), or remaining in their current district.[19] Finally, another view of communities of interest centered on the differences in outlook and culture between New Jersey's urban communities versus the state's suburban and rural communities.

A very important consideration in New Jersey's redistricting process was the protection of racial and ethnic minority populations as cohesive demographic constituencies in two of New Jersey's congressional districts. New Jersey's 10th Congressional District is one of 27 in the nation in which African Americans constitute a majority of the population. In keeping with the 1982 amendments to the Voting Rights Act which prevent the dilution of minority populations for the purpose of representation, New Jersey's 10th Congressional District, which is about 57 percent African American, was regarded as a district that would be protected from being cracked, or broken up into several adjacent districts. The 10th, which is comprised primarily of Newark but also parts of Jersey City and other neighboring towns, has met the federally mandated standards guiding the creation of majority-minority districts: the 10th is comprised of a large demographic group in a compact setting and it consists of a cohesive voting bloc—a community of interest. Thus, despite the fact that the 10th was one of the least populated congressional districts in the state, the odds of it being dissolved into other districts in 2011 were quite slim.

And while the 13th Congressional District—once represented by now-U.S. Senator Robert Menendez (D-NJ), and now represented by Congressman Albio Sires

(D-NJ13)—is not technically a majority-minority district, the plurality of Hispanics/Latinos in the district (who constitute 48 percent of the district's population), the significant increase in the state's Latino population in the decade between 2000 and 2010, and the strong organization among Latino activists in the state, including during the congressional redistricting process, meant that New Jersey's 13th Congressional District, while necessarily changing in numeric designation (because of the loss of one House seat) would not change in a manner that would dilute the district's Hispanic and Latino populations.

THE CONTEXT FOR 2011:
THE 2000 REDISTRICTING PROCESS

On October 26, 2001, the New Jersey Redistricting Commission approved a new map of New Jersey's congressional districts. The decision, which was rendered nearly three months before the state constitutional deadline, was easier than 2011 as New Jersey had maintained all of its 13 seats in the House of Representatives.[20] The map that was chosen by the Commission mirrored the map submitted by the bipartisan congressional delegation.[21] It rendered most congressional districts even in population, with an ideal size of 647,258, but the districts were drawn to be even less competitive than they already were,[22] and 90 percent of New Jerseyans kept their same representative.[23]

In 2001, the Redistricting Commission was chaired by Rutgers University Political Science Professor Alan Rosenthal, whose academic work has centered on the priority of stability in the process of redistricting legislatures.[24] To that end, Rosenthal's preferences were rationalized by proponents of the incumbent-centered redistricting plan, who asserted that New Jersey's best interest would be served by protecting incumbent members of Congress who were more likely to secure key committee chairmanships and other benefits of seniority doled out by congressional leaders.

The plan was criticized on several fronts. First, some argued that, by so strongly protecting incumbents, the plan squashed competition, thus eliminating the watchdog function performed by competitive elections. It was also feared that lack of competitive elections would have a deleterious impact on voter turnout.

Other criticisms of the 2001 map centered on its incumbent-centered gerrymandering, which caused other principles of redistricting to be violated. Several of New Jersey's congressional districts formed after the 2000 census were rated in the bottom quintile for compactness. In particular, the 16th, the 12th, and the 13th districts were criticized for their lack of compactness and lack of contiguity.[25] The 6th district, represented since 1993 by Rep. Frank Pallone, was perhaps a great-grandson of Elbridge Gerry's iconic gerrymander. It hugged the coast through the neck of the state, and ventured inland to chisel out portions of four counties. It included 40 municipalities, though 6 of these towns were sliced apart, with parts of some towns falling into the 12th District. Represented by Congressman Rush Holt since 1999, the 12th District straddled the state from the Atlantic Ocean across to Pennsylvania. It included parts of five counties, and 44 municipalities, 7 of which are divided into other districts. The 13th district, represented since 2006 by Rep. Albio Sires, is a near minority-majority district with a 48 percent Hispanic population. As drawn in the 2001 map, it spanned four counties and 17 municipalities, 7 of which were divided into other congressional districts. The 13th was a noncontiguous district, with parts of the district being separated by the 10th Congressional District.

The principles of compactness and contiguity gave way to the principle of incumbency protection in 2001, but party composition also mattered that year. In 2001, New Jersey was a solidly Democratic state: it had a Democratic governor, a Democratically controlled state legislature, and both U.S. Senators were Democrats. Thus the congressional breakdown of 7 House seats being held by Democrats (the 1st, the 6th, the 8th, the 9th, the 10th, the 12th, and the 13th) while 6 were held by Republicans (the 2nd, the 3rd, the 4th, the 5th, the 7th, and the 11th) was not widely challenged, and thus it remained in the 2001 plan (see map 13.1).

REDISTRICTING NEW JERSEY, 2011

The issue of which party was the majority party in the state would be a consideration in the 2011 congressional redistricting process. Redistricting in New Jersey is a partisan affair, and congressional redistricting differed from 2001 primarily because of the emergence of Republican Governor Chris Christie.

Christie had won election in 2009, defeating Democrat Jon Corzine, despite the fact that Corzine had outspent Christie $23.6 million to Christie's $8.8 million. The tough-talking Christie then emerged as a *tour de force* on the national political scene, and was frequently described in 2010 as a potential Republican presidential candidate. He enjoyed strong popularity in New Jersey. And so in 2011, Republicans cited Christie's election as evidence of the changing tide of partisan allegiances in the state. They also argued that despite the fact that Democrats held a majority of members of the House of Representatives from New Jersey, the six New Jersey House Republicans had garnered more votes than the Democrats in 2010's midterm elections. Republicans painted these trends as evidence of a new swelling tide of Republicanism in the Garden State.

Whether one agrees with Chris Christie's politics or not, he is widely recognized a masterful politician who surrounds himself with brilliant political strategists. Since his arrival on the political scene, he has snatched victory after victory from the Democrats. And so it was surprising to many that one of the few political blunders of his administration came in the state legislative redistricting process, which precedes congressional redistricting in years ending in 1. When the state was faced with the prospect of redistricting state legislative districts early in 2011, the Republican team agreed with the Democrats and appointed Alan Rosenthal (who had chaired 2001's congressional redistricting) the tie-breaking nonpartisan

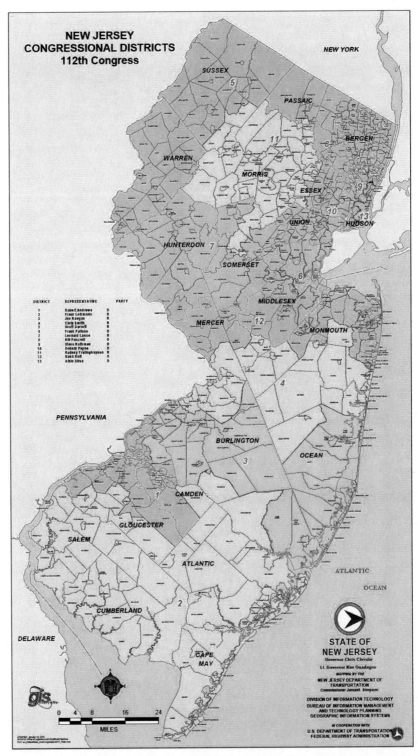

Map 13.1. New Jersey Congressional Districts, 2002–2011. New Jersey Department of Transportation.

member on the Commission. In that process, Rosenthal, to the dismay of Christie and his Republican allies, chose the Democratic map, which preserved incumbency (or "stability in legislatures" as Rosenthal terms it in academic writings).[26] Preserving stability, or incumbency, essentially meant preserving Democratic majorities in the State Senate and State Assembly. In the end, redistricting meant essentially no change in legislative composition, and the sole district of forty that was alleged to have become competitive after redistricting remained in the hands of the Democratic incumbent despite a strong Christie-endorsed challenge from a county legislator in 2011.[27]

It was in this context that congressional redistricting took place. But the issue of whether New Jersey is a Democratic or a Republican state had a bit more resonance in the context of congressional elections. And this point became particularly important because losing one seat necessarily meant sacrificing one of the incumbent legislators, or at least forcing an incumbent-on-incumbent battle. Democrats argued that New Jersey's long track record of voting for Democratic presidential candidates, governors, U.S. senators, and Democratic majorities in both houses of the state legislature is indicative of the state's status as a blue state. "New Jersey is a Democratic state. Clearly a majority of the representatives should be Democratic because that represents how people vote in the state over the long run," said Democratic State Chairman John Wisniewski, an assemblyman from Middlesex County. "You can take snapshots of individual elections . . . but in the long run, New Jersey is Democratic."[28]

While party played an important role in statewide congressional redistricting decisions, individual members of the House of Representatives were, of course, vested in their own careers and the composition of their own districts. So on a more parochial level, the redistricting process was an every-man-for-himself affair (New Jersey currently sends no women to Congress), and individual members of New Jersey's congressional delegation were vested in the composition of the Redistricting Commission. They lobbied legislative and party leaders for the appointment of commissioners who would look out for congress members' individual interests.

As described above, twelve of the Redistricting Commission members are appointed on a partisan basis. In 2011, the leaders within each party appeared to have collaborated within their caucuses and chosen a slate of six delegates, rather than having individual leaders select their allocated two appointees. According to State Party Chairman John Wisniewski, "The speaker, Senate president and myself worked collaboratively to pick commissioners to represent the people and geography of the state of New Jersey."[29] Republican Chairman Sam Raia stated, "Selecting members to redraw New Jersey's congressional districts is a deliberative process and after careful consideration, we have nominated citizens that represent the rich communities and divergent views that make our state great. We went through great lengths to identify a panel of individuals that will bring a wide variety of skills to the process and we are confident that these men and women will provide thoughtful and prudent insight to the redistricting process."[30]

COMMISSION MEMBERS

In 2011, the Commission was comprised of the members listed in table 13.1.

The most influential members were those elected to chair their party's delegation. These included Republican political strategist Mike DuHaime, and Democrat Joseph Roberts Jr. was widely credited with crafting Governor Christie's "David versus Goliath" victory over Jon Corzine. He is affiliated with Mercury, a consulting group that advises politicians and Fortune 500 companies. DuHaime was Governor Christie's point man on the commission, though all of the appointees were Christie loyalists.

The other Republican Commissioners included:

- Caroline Casagrande, a Republican member of the General Assembly who has represented parts of Monmouth and Ocean counties since 2008. Casagrande was the youngest woman ever elected to New Jersey's General Assembly.
- Sherine El-Abd of Passaic County, a former deputy director for the state Division on Women where she focused on civil rights and minority affairs. She is also the former director of the Egyptian American Business Association, and she served on the Steering Committee for Bush-Cheney 2004.
- The Rev. Aubrey Fenton, a former Burlington County freeholder director, who is pastor at Abundant Life Fellowship.
- Eric Jaso, an attorney, who worked as an assistant U.S. attorney under Chris Christie when was New Jersey's U.S. attorney. Jaso holds leadership positions in the Hispanic Bar Association of New Jersey and the Hispanic National Bar Association.
- Susan Sheppard, a former teacher who was elected to the Cape May County Board of Chosen Freeholders in 2010, and has served as a trustee of Ocean City Free Public Library.

Table 13.1. New Jersey Redistricting Commission Members

John J. Farmer, Jr. (Chairman)	
Democratic Members	**Republican Members**
Joseph Roberts, Jr. (Delegation Chairman)	Michael DuHaime (Delegation Chairman)
Michael Baker (Delegation Vice-chair)	Caroline Casagrande
Nilsa Cruz-Perez	Sherine El-Abd
Edward Farmer	Aubrey Fenton
Jeannine Frisby LaRue	Eric Jaso
Philip Thigpen	M. Susan Sheppard

Joe Roberts, the Democrat's chair, retired from the General Assembly in 2010, having been elected in 1987 and serving first as Democratic majority leader and then being elected twice as the Assembly speaker.

The Democratic Commissioners included:

- Michael Baker, who served a short stint in the State Assembly, and was a member of the East Brunswick Township Council. He is an attorney in private practice, whose specialization is farmland and open space preservation.
- Nilsa Cruz-Perez, the first Hispanic woman to serve in the Assembly. She represented part of South Jersey's Camden and Gloucester counties from 1995 until 2010. She is a former sergeant in the U.S. army.
- Edward Farmer, the chairman of the Passaic County Community College Board of Trustees. He is CEO and president of Millennium Strategies, a political consulting firm. He is no relation to John J. Farmer Jr., the chairman of the Commission.
- Jeannine Frisby LaRue, who was deputy chief of staff to former Gov. Jon S. Corzine, and also served as vice president of public affairs for Rutgers University. She currently is senior vice president at the Kaufman Zita Group.
- Philip Thigpen, who is the chairman of the Essex County Democratic party, which he has chaired since 2001. He also has served on the Essex County Freeholder Board and was an East Orange councilman.

Roberts and several other commissioners were widely viewed as serving as protectors for individual congressional incumbents with whom they had political alliances. Roberts is an ally of Congressman Rob Andrews (D-NJ01). Republican Cape May Freeholder Susan Sheppard was a strong backer of Rep. Frank LoBiondo (R-NJ02) (though LoBiondo had comparatively little need for protection given the disproportionate growth that occurred in some areas of his congressional district). Fenton is a political ally of Congressman Jon Runyan (R-NJ03), the newest member of New Jersey's congressional delegation. Edward Farmer had served as Congressman William Pascrell's (D-NJ09) Chief of Staff. And the Commission Chairman, John Farmer, was viewed as seeking to protect Rep. Leonard Lance (R-NJ07), as many in the statehouse said that the two were friends, though there were no public statements to that effect made by either man.[31]

THE PROCESS

Following the organizational meeting, the Redistricting Commission hosted the three public hearings required by the New Jersey State Constitution. These meetings were sparsely attended, attracting on average about 30 attendees each. Most of the testimony consisted of advocates for various racial and ethnic groups within the state advocating for their "communities of interest." For example, Jerry Vattamala, an attorney with the Asian American Legal Defense and Education Fund, urged the commission to consolidate Asian Americans' voting power, as previous maps had diluted the Asian American vote by dividing Asian communities into various districts. "Asian American communities of interest should be kept whole," he said. "The time to correct this injustice is now."[32]

For the deliberations, the Commission met in several rooms at the Heldrich Hotel in New Brunswick. The Democrats' strategy was based in the idea that New Jersey is a Democratic state. Citing the fact that George H. W. Bush was the last Republican presidential candidate carrying the state, the Democrats sought to have the redistricting process result in partisan gerrymandered districts where Democrats would have strong advantages in six districts and a slight edge in one of them. They initially proposed doing this by changing the 3rd Congressional District and making it more Democratic. Though historically a Republican seat, the late Democratic Rep. John Adler managed to capture the seat for the Democrats relying on President Obama's coattails in 2008. He lost to former Philadelphia Eagles offensive tackle Jon Runyan (R-NJ03) in 2010, and died in April 2011 of a staph infection associated with treatment for a coronary ailment.

But the microlevel politics of the Commission itself had some bearing on what the final maps would come to look like. Many observers asserted that the members with allegiances to specific members—Runyan and Pascrell in particular—were, on the surface, effective in their attempts to guard their congress members. Others contended that while not protected by one of the partisan members, Congressman Leonard Lance (R-NJ07) was afforded important protection as the Commission members viewed Commission Chair John Farmer as predisposed to protecting Lance's 7th, a leaning-Republican district that could have been reconfigured into a competitive or leaning-Democratic district.

In the first meeting of the Commission on December 19, Chairman Farmer guided the Democratic and Republican delegations by urging them to submit maps that would alter the political landscape in northern New Jersey. He later explained his rational asserting that because the districts in the north were underpopulated, these were the districts that would need to be configured. The 10th District (represented by Democratic Rep. Donald Payne until his death in 2012) and the 13th District (represented by Democratic Congressman Albio Sires) were both considered to be essentially safe as the 10th is a majority-minority district, and the 13th is nearly one. Thus, remaining on the table were the 5th (represented by Republican Scott Garrett), the 7th (represented by Republican Leonard Lance), the 8th (represented by Democrat Bill Pascrell), and the 9th (represented by Democrat Steve Rothman). In the end, the largest source of contention between the two sides was how to configure the three adjacent districts in North Jersey that were not majority-minority districts that had seen the slowest population growth or even some loss.

The battle centered on the 5th, a swath of a district that spans New Jersey's northwestern-most border with Pennsylvania, across the top of the state including some of the sparsely populated areas of North Jersey to the more densely populated and tony suburbs in eastern Bergen County across the Hudson River from Manhattan, where some of the state's most affluent residents live. The district currently is represented by Congressman Scott Garrett, the most conservative member of the state's congressional delegation, a politician who is often seen as being out of step with the liberal-to-moderate Republicans usually found in New Jersey politics. Democrats sought to make the 5th a fair-fight district, where Congressman Steve Rothman of the old 9th district, a policy-oriented liberal who has served in Congress since 1996 would battle it out with Garrett in an even-steven district.

In the first meeting, Farmer also urged what he called an "open process," that is, that the Democratic and Republican teams should revise their submissions from the maps that each team had submitted rather than creating new surprise maps. In their initial submissions, predictably each team proposed an intraparty fight between incumbents from the opposing party. The Democrats proposed a matchup between Garrett and Lance, while the Republicans argued for a Pascrell-Rothman fight.

By December 21, it was clear that the districts most impacted would be Republican Garrett's 5th and Democratic Rothman's 8th—though the question that remained was whether the new configuration of the districts would make it a Republican-leaning district or a fair-fight competitive district.

On December 22, just one day before the final map would be decided, the Democrats threw a Hail Mary pass and proposed the fair-fight district in the 5th, while maintaining the status quo in the 3rd (leaving it, essentially a Republican district, though perhaps competitive given the right circumstances), while the Republicans proposed a plan that, while physically moving Rothman and his home town of Englewood into the 9th, would configure the 5th giving Garrett or any other Republican running there in the future a 4 percent partisan edge. This would force Rothman into the position of running a bruising and expensive campaign against Garrett, or moving to the 8th Congressional District and challenging U.S. Rep. Bill Pascrell (D-NJ08), a friend and colleague of Rothman's.

THE DECISION AND THE AFTERMATH

In the end, Chairman Farmer chose the Republican map, which differed only from the Democrats' in that it removed a Democratic strong-hold (Cherry Hill) from Runyan's 3rd District, somewhat divided some of the Asian American communities that sought consolidation in the 5th, and it rendered the 5th a substantially Republican district.

The map was perceived as a political victory for Gov. Christie, and also for his strategist Michael DuHaime, who had chaired the Republican delegation. Steve Rothman was faced with the prospect of challenging Garrett in a now Republican district where Garrett would enjoy a 4 percent partisan advantage, and one in which many of his former constituents no longer lived (having been redistricted into the

old 8th District, represented by Bill Pascrell). Many Democrats relished the prospect of a Garrett-Rothman matchup, and the Democratic Congressional Campaign
Committee reportedly promised Rothman up to $2 million in campaign funding if
he challenged Garrett, with $1 million to be paid upfront and additional funding to
follow if the Rothman campaign gained traction.[33]

But in the end, the prospect of challenging Garrett (and then running for re-
election in a lower-turnout off year election in 2014) proved too daunting. On
December 27, Rothman announced that he would challenge Democratic colleague
Bill Pascrell in a June 2012 primary. The two share nearly identical voting records in
Congress, though differ in personal style. Rothman tends toward the refined policy-
wonk, Pascrell is a savvy retail politician. Among their few differences are their ages
(Rothman is 59, Pascrell is 75) and their religions (Pascrell is Catholic, Rothman is
Jewish). Their race marks one of 13 incumbent-on-incumbent races resulting from
redistricting nationally (see map 13.2).

EFFECTS AND IMPLICATIONS

In the immediate aftermath of the decision, some Democrats were accused of having sour grapes (they tried to stall the final vote on the map when it was revealed
that Farmer had selected the Republican map, and then complained that the process
failed to give the public the opportunity to react to the map, though they had agreed
to the process before the map was chosen). The longer-term impact of the decision
was a net decrease in the number of Democratic members of the U.S. House of
Representatives from New Jersey, and a bruising and expensive primary battle that
pitted like-minded colleagues against each other.

On the whole, key criticisms centered on the lack of competitiveness that is generated by partisan-gerrymandered districts, though many recognize that the stability
generated by this lack of competitiveness provides more value in Congress (which
has a greater norm of seniority) than in the state legislature. Another criticism is
that some racial and ethnic minority populations (particularly Asian Americans in
Bergen) are diluted, but other groups (including Latinos and African Americans)
are satisfied that the two majority-minority districts are preserved,[34] and that racial
and ethnic populations are not cracked in other districts, so that these populations
constitute important constituent groups in non-majority-minority districts.

But many view the new map as an improvement over the 2001 map, especially in
terms of communities of interest and compactness. For example, the 2011 map split
14 municipalities into differing congressional districts, whereas the 2001 map had
carved up 29, several into three different districts. The map also is regarded as more
geographically compact than its 2001 counterpart. Finally, the new map offers stronger protection for incumbents, particularly for Representatives Runyan (R-NJ03),
Garrett (R-NJ05), Lance (R-NJ07), and Holt (D-NJ12, now 11).

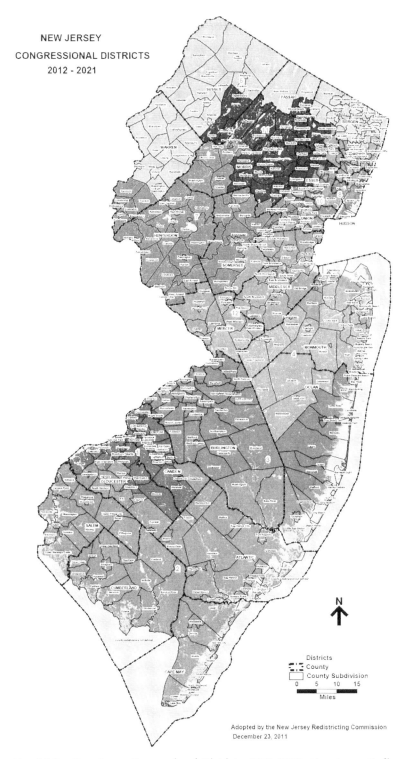

Map 13.2.   New Jersey Congressional Districts, 2012–2021. New Jersey Redistricting Commission.

NOTES

1. "Census results show N.J. Shore town populations are shrinking," *Star-Ledger*, May 12, 2011, www.nj.com/news/index.ssf/2011/05/census_results_show_nj_shore_to.html.

2. http://njredistrictingcommission.org/constitutionbylaws.asp.

3. The Redistricting Commission's Organizational meeting agenda is available at www.njredistrictingcommission.org//Documents/09-06-11%20REDC%20Complete.pdf and a transcript of its meeting is available at www.njredistrictingcommission.org//Documents/09-06-11%20REDC%20Complete.pdf.

4. http://njredistrictingcommission.org/constitutionbylaws.asp.

5. A transcript of this meeting is available at www.njredistrictingcommission.org//Documents/09-22-11%20REDC%20Complete%20_2_.pdf.

6. A transcript of this meeting is available at www.njredistrictingcommission.org//Documents/10-11-11%20REDC%20Complete%20pnf.pdf.

7. A transcript of this meeting is available at www.njredistrictingcommission.org//Documents/10-11-11%20REDC%20Complete%20_2_.pdf.

8. http://njredistrictingcommission.org/constitutionbylaws.asp.

9. A transcript of this meeting is available at www.njredistrictingcommission.org//Documents/12-23-11%20REDC%20title%20pnf.pdf.

10. In *Wesberry v. Sanders,* 376 U.S. 1 (1964) the Supreme Court held that a congressional plan with a 19-person total range of deviation was unconstitutional because the state's justification (preserving split boundaries) could be more closely achieved by alternative plans with a smaller deviation, and because the justification was not the actual cause of deviation in the first place).

11. *Wesberry v. Sanders,* 376 U.S. 1 (1964).

12. *Karcher v. Daggett,* 462 U.S. 725, 734 (1983).

13. In *State ex rel. Stephan v. Graves,* 796 F. Supp. 468 (D. Kan. 1992), the Supreme Court ruled that a redistricting plan with a population deviation of 0.94 percent was unconstitutional because it failed to achieve population equality, stating that maintenance of county borders did not justify the population deviation. In *Vieth v. Jubelirer,* 541 U.S. 267 (2004) the Court rejected a Pennsylvania congressional redistricting plan with a deviation of 19 people because the state could preserve split boundaries using plans that would result in smaller deviation, and the rationale for the deviation was not in fact the origin of the deviation.

14. Ernest C. Reock, "A Note: Measuring Compactness as a Requirement of Legislative Apportionment," *Midwest Journal of Political Science* 5 (1961): 70–74.

15. Daniel D. Polsby and Robert D. Popper, "The Third Criterion: Compactness as a Procedural Safeguard against Partisan Gerrymandering," *Yale Law and Policy Review* 9 (1991): 301–53.

16. *Johnson v. Miller,* 922 F. Supp. 1556 (S.D. Ga. 1995), in which the Court describes the protection of incumbents as "inherently more political than factors such as communities of interest and compactness," and so therefore it we "subordinated [protection of incumbents] to the other considerations."

17. *Abrams v. Johnson,* 521 U.S. 74, 84 (1997).

18. Matt Friedman, "Racial, ethnic representation dominates talk at N.J. congressional redistricting hearing," October 11, 2011. www.nj.com/news/index.ssf/2011/10/racial_ethnic_representation_d.html.

19. Friedman, ibid.

20. "New Jersey District Map Still Helps Incumbents," *New York Times*, October 27, 2001, www.nytimes.com/2001/10/27/nyregion/new-jersey-district-map-still-helps-incumbents.html.

21. Ron Marsico. "Incumbents like new congressional map," *Star-Ledger*, October, 2001, http://archive.fairvote.org/redistricting/reports/remanual/njnews.htm#incumbents.

22. Michael Symons, "Rep. Holt's seat safer," *Asbury Park Press*, October, 2001, p. 3A.

23. *Op. Cit.* Marsico, http://archive.fairvote.org/redistricting/reports/remanual/njnews .htm#incumbents.

24. Alan Rosenthal, *Legislative Life* (Harper and Row, 1981); *Governors and Legislatures* (CQ Press, 1990); *The Decline of Representative Democracy* (CQ Press 1998).

25. "Redistricting the Nation, Top 10," www.redistrictingthenation.com/top10.aspx.

26. Alan Rosenthal, *Republic on Trial: The Case for Representative Democracy*, with John Hibbing, Burdett Loomis, and Karl Kurtz (CQ Press, 2002).

27. Karen Sudol, "Gordon defeats Driscoll, Republicans concede in 38th District," *Bergen Record*, November 8, 2011, www.northjersey.com/news/DISTRICT_38.html.

28. Matt Friedman, "Census 2010: Slower population growth causes N.J. to lose seat in U.S. House," *Star-Ledger*, December 21, 2010, www.nj.com/news/index.ssf/2010/12/census_2010_ slow_population_gr.html.

29. Max Pizarro, "Congressional Commission to hold organizational meeting this afternoon," *PolitickerNJ*, September 6, 2011, www.politickernj.com/50713/congressional -commission-hold-organizational-meeting.

30. Max Pizarro, "DuHaime, others, picked for Republican redistricting team," *PolitickerNJ*, June 15, 2011, www.politickernj.com/back_room/duhaime-lead-republican-redistricting-team.

31. Darryl R. Isherwood, "Winners and Losers: Congressional redistricting edition," *PolitickerNJ*, December 27, 2011, www.politickernj.com/53485/winners-and-losers-congres sional-redistricting-edition.

32. Friedman, Matt. "Racial, ethnic representation dominates talk at N.J. congressio- nal redistricting hearing," *Star-Ledger*, www.nj.com/news/index.ssf/2011/10/racial_ethnic_ representation_d.html.

33. Darryl R. Isherwood, "DCCC offered Rothman $1 million to challenge Garrett," *PolitickerNJ*, December 29, 2011, www.politickernj.com/53499/dccc-offered-rothman -1-million-challenge-garrett.

34. "Congressional redistricting hammering at the Heldrich puts 5 and 9 at ground zero," *PolitickerNJ*, December 21, 2011, www.politickernj.com/53427/congressional-redistricting -hammering-heldrich-puts-5-and-9-ground-zero.

14

Lone Star Lines

The Battle over Redistricting in Texas

Jason P. Casellas and Alvaro Jose Corral

In 2011, all eyes were on the Lone Star state as it once again faced a difficult and contentious redistricting process. A decade ago Texas made international headlines when Democratic members of the state legislature fled across state lines on two occasions to avoid casting votes on what they considered to be an extra-legal (if not, illegal), mid-decade gerrymander orchestrated by then Majority Leader U.S. Rep. Tom DeLay, R-Texas. This time around, the reapportionment process yielded four new seats to the state's congressional delegation, the largest gain of any state. Because of this significant gain, it was inevitable that litigation and controversy would ensue in order to determine who would benefit from these new districts.

In stark contrast to most parts of the country, the economic boom characterized by some as the "Texas miracle," drew people and capital alike to the Lone Star state throughout the Aughts. As the U.S. economy struggled to create jobs during the recovery process following the economic recession of 2008, one report estimated that Texas alone was responsible for half of the jobs created in the United States between June 2009 and June 2011.[1] Because of Texas's low tax and low regulation environment, many businesses have relocated to the state.

Immigrants from around the world and Americans from across the country were drawn to Texas for many reasons. Throughout the decade Austin cemented itself as one of the nation's leading high-tech hubs joining the ranks of Silicon Valley. The oil and gas industry along the state's gulf coast continued to be a strong segment of the Texas economy as well. Meanwhile, robust trade with Mexico contributed to a booming Texas border economy from El Paso to Brownsville. Since 2000 when Latinos surpassed African Americans as the largest minority group in the United States, demographers have predicted Latinos to reach a quarter of the population by 2025. Texas has been at the forefront of that growth and is quickly becoming the microcosm of America's not so distant future. In Texas, Latinos now make up nearly

40 percent of the state's population, although a large proportion are undocumented thus delaying the group's burgeoning political influence.

Politically, the stakes are high. With a U.S. House of Representatives already firmly in Republican control, and with the hopes of reaching a majority in the Senate, Republicans set their sights on Texas, a state that has voted for every Republican nominee for president since 1968, as it would surely be an integral part to their political strategy. Republicans had also attained a supermajority in the state legislature as a result of the 2010 elections thus making it easier for legislators to draw districts protecting and expanding their influence.

Legislators in Texas, as in other states where legislatures are responsible for drawing districts, consider many factors when drawing new districts. First and foremost, partisanship is a key variable such that the party in control of the legislature will attempt to draw as many districts as possible that will help them keep their majority. Another important factor is incumbent protection. Incumbents will attempt to draw districts that will make it even easier for them to win re-election. Obviously, incumbents in the majority party will have the advantage in this process, but even incumbents in the minority party have some influence, and will make deals with the majority to protect their districts. Even members of the U.S. Congress attempt to intervene so that their districts will be more favorable in the next election. This can include promises to key leaders in the state legislature that they will support their possible re-election bids or attempts to move up the political ladder.

At issue, however, was how the Republican-controlled legislature, with a powerful ally in Gov. Rick Perry, now the longest serving governor in the state's history, would walk the fine line between protecting his party's incumbents while adequately reflecting the undeniable growth of the state's non-White population, led largely by Latinos. Unlike many other states, Texas is subject to Section 5 of the Voting Rights Act, which requires preclearance of the new lines by the Department of Justice or the DC Federal District Court. For the first time since the Voting Rights Act was signed into law, the Democratic Party controls the Justice Department. Texas Attorney General Greg Abbott has defended the legislature by arguing that Section 5 preclearance discriminates against Texas and is a violation of the Tenth Amendment.

SETTING THE STAGE: THE 2010 CENSUS

Texas demographer Steve Murdoch recently stated that "it's basically over for Anglos" referring to the demographic trends of the state. The changing complexion of the Texas electorate is in many ways the story of the redistricting process. In the last decade Texas grew by 20 percent to 25 million residents. The number of Texas Latinos increased from 6.7 million to approximately 9.5 million, or 41 percent,[2] which accounts for nearly one-fifth (18.7 percent) of the entire Latino population in the United States.[3] Latinos alone were responsible for 65 percent of the state's total growth. Of the top ten places with 100,000 people that are the most Latino, four are in Texas. The city of Laredo boasts a 96 percent Latino population, the second highest of any other place behind only East L.A., California. All in all, 51 of the 254 Texas counties are majority Latino.[4]

Although Latinos are in many ways central to the growth, other racial and ethnic minority groups have increased across the board in the state. African Americans saw a population gain of 523,000, while the white population grew by 465,000. The Asian American population also grew by 71 percent and now comprises 3.8 percent of the state.

The number of Latinos in a state proved in many ways determinative in the 2010 reapportionment process. Latinos average 15.2 percent of the voter eligible population (VEP) in states gaining seats while the same figure in states losing seats is 5.4 percent. The figures of the resident population tell a similar story as states losing seats have an average of 8.4 percent of their resident population Latinos, while states gaining seats have nearly triple the amount of Latino residents (23.6 percent).[5] This suggests that much of the population growth in the United States is driven by Latinos rather than increased birth rates among native born Anglos.

In Texas, Latinos account for one-in-four (25.5 percent) of the state's eligible voters and 36.9 percent of the state's population.[6] Although Latinos make up 38 percent of the Texas population, they only comprise a third (33 percent) of the voting age population (VAP). Some 43 percent of Texas Latinos are eligible to vote, but after taking into account voter registration, they are no more than a quarter of the Texas electorate.[7] It is also important to consider Texas's voter turnout, which by all estimates is the most abysmal in the country. In 2010, Texas ranked 50th in turnout among eligible voters.[8] On the other hand, voter registration figures for Black and Anglo populations in Texas are nearly identical (73.7 percent and 72.4 percent, respectively) as well as turnout figures (64.9 percent and 64.7 percent, respectively) in 2008.[9] Asians and Latinos are another story entirely. While 67 percent of Texas Latinos are registered to vote, only 45.7 percent of Asians in Texas are registered. In regards to turnout, only one-third of Asians in Texas voted in 2008, while the same figure for Latinos was 55 percent.[10]

One explanation for the low rate of Latino turnout is illustrated by the age breakdown of voter-eligible population as Latino eligible voters are younger than Anglo and Black eligible voters. In 2010, a full 31 percent of Hispanic eligible voters are between the ages of 18–29 compared to 19 percent of white, and 26 percent of black, and 21 percent of Asian eligible voters.[11] This means that the largest reservoir of Latino voting strength in Texas lies in the population least likely to turn out.

Immediately following the release of the U.S. census figures in February 2011, groups on both sides of the aisle filed suit against any maps produced on the basis of the figures. In the case of *Teuber et al. v. State of Texas et al*, brought forth by Tea Party Activists, the plaintiffs argued against any redistricting map based upon census counts that included undocumented citizens. In February 2011, attorney Jose Garza of the Mexican American Legislative Caucus argued for the defendants in *Teuber*, and ultimately was able to get the case dismissed.

For their part, minority groups challenged census counts as well, specifically the accuracy of figures from the Rio Grande Valley. In the suit filed on April 5, Jose Garza cited the Census Bureau's decision to forego the use of "mail-out, mail-in" counting strategy in *colonias* as the principle reason why the bureau could not secure a complete count of Latinos. The MALC placed the undercount figure along the border region between 4 percent and 8 percent of the actual population. According to the plaintiffs, undercounts meant that districts such as D-15 in Hidalgo County were overpopulated to the tune of +12 percent, while D-28, also encompassing parts of Hidalgo County, had a deviation of about +22 percent.[12] Such undercounts, the legislators argue, could have significant effects on the creation of state legislative districts, as well as congressional districts.

Latino groups hoping for a two- or three-seat gain in descriptive representation face an uphill battle as Republicans in the state legislature would surely seek to protect their party's incumbents. Nina Perales, of the Mexican American Legal Defense and Education Fund (MALDEF), called for two of the new congressional districts to be Latino majority districts. Perales argued that because of Latino population growth the legislature was obligated under the Voting Rights Act, to draw two districts in which the Latino-favored candidate could be elected.

Despite demographic figures in their favor, Latinos have had a tough time being elected to office in Texas due to historical and institutional factors. As Casellas (2011) has argued, the state legislative institutional design makes an important difference in terms of Latino representation.[13] Casellas (2011) notes that a hypothetical 50 percent Latino citizen district has a 53 percent chance of electing a Latino, while a hypothetical 50 percent Latino population (citizen and noncitizen) district has merely a 31 percent chance of electing a Latino. Also, Texas lacks term-limits, which bodes poorly for amateur Latino office-seekers as the incumbent re-election rates are high.

THE TEXAS PROCESS

The Texas State Legislature differs from other legislative bodies in that it is in many respects a "citizen" legislature, meeting for only 140 days every two years. The legislature is tasked with drawing congressional lines in the first session following the decennial census. All electoral changes in Texas are subject to preclearance by the Justice Department or the District of Columbia Federal District Court as stipulated by Section 5 of the Voting Rights Act. Like many other southern states subject to preclearance, Texas has a history of disenfranchising African Americans and other minorities. One tool particularly favored in Texas was the "white primary," originally established to explicitly prohibit non-whites (African Americans primarily, but also Mexican Americans in south Texas) from joining the Democratic Party or participating in its primary elections. Although the Supreme Court later ruled such primaries unconstitutional, the legacy of voter disenfranchisement continues in more subtle ways.

In terms of minority representation, the state of Texas has to comply with the Voting Rights Act of 1965, its subsequent amendments, and developed case law. In particular, legislators cannot dilute the minority vote as they draw the new districts, as this would trigger a section 2 violation. All states are subject to section 2, which prohibits the disenfranchisement of voting rights. Minority voters must have the ability to elect candidates of choice, who may or may not be minority. Under section 2, however, minorities must be sufficiently large to vote as a bloc and an adjacent white majority must also vote as a bloc against the minority community's preferred candidate. This makes it more difficult for litigants to prove a section 2 violation. Additionally, existing majority-minority districts cannot be eliminated as this would amount to retrogression. With Texas's additional four seats, however, the legislature did not attempt to eliminate any majority-minority districts. The crux of the debate was over the additional four seats in the U.S. House and how many of those should be majority-minority.

Legislatures have to be careful not to use race or ethnicity as the sole criterion in drawing districts. This is unconstitutional according to existing case law much in the same way college administrators can only use race or ethnicity as one of many factors when deciding college admissions. The court has used the term "totality of circumstances" to refer to the process whereby new legislative districts are assessed. The Court has also ruled that this process might yield outcomes whereby majority-minority districts might not be the only way to improve minority representation. Coalitional districts might advance the interests of minority voters in more positive ways than majority-minority districts, dependent on the circumstances. This conundrum has led Latino civil rights groups to disagree about the current 25th Congressional District, situated in Austin. Some Latino groups argue that the coalitional district with roughly a third white, Latino, and black population should be protected because the interests of minorities are well represented by the white congressman, Lloyd Doggett. However, other groups argue that new majority-minority districts should be created so that minority candidates can be elected, rather than white Democrats. This inevitably leads to the debate between descriptive and substantive representation. Descriptive representation involves someone with shared demographic characteristics representing a constituency, while substantive representation involves the interests of constituents regardless of the race of the representative.

THE REDISTRICTING PROCESS IN 2000

Perhaps one of the central features of modern Texas politics has been the resurgence of the Republican Party in the state since the early 1990s. The redistricting process of 1991 would prove to be the last decade-long installment of maps drawn by a Democratic majority. The Republican delegation to the U.S. House of Representatives grew from two in 1974 to twenty-three by 2010.[14] In fact, no Democrat has won statewide since 1994.

The Texas redistricting process following the previous reapportionment was a long and hard fought battle that began in 2001 and did not end until 2006. The first attempt to redistrict was fruitless as the legislature could not agree to a map and Governor Perry refused to call a special session. The failure of the Texas Legislature to settle congressional lines in the first legislative session following the 2000 reapportionment brought about a court-drawn map that the burgeoning Republican Party felt did not reflect its political clout. After wresting the majority from the Democrats in the 2002 elections, Republicans in the State House at the behest of Congressman Tom DeLay boldly asserted the legislature's constitutional duty to approve a map born from the halls in Austin not a courtroom.

Republicans pointed to a history of partisan gerrymandering under the Democrats who held a majority in the State House since Reconstruction. They reasoned that the 1991 map had been so partisan that ten years later, despite the fact that the Texas electorate was voting 55 percent for Republicans in statewide races, Democrats remained in control of two-thirds of the seats in the Texas House. Viewing these plans as a power-grab, Democrats fled the state on two occasions (Democratic House members to Ardmore, Oklahoma, and Democratic Senators to Albuquerque, New Mexico) in order to break quorum so that the redistricting could not proceed. The so-called "flying D's" made national headlines as Republican leaders in Texas attempted to enlist Texas state troopers to return the renegade Democrats to Austin.

After months of wrangling, Republicans proved victorious, but spectators to the process agreed that three special sessions and breaking thirty years of the Senate's two-thirds rule tradition had left the state with a toxic political climate. Not all parts of the map persisted until the end of the decade. In a 5–4 decision the U.S. Supreme Court ruled in *LULAC v. Perry* (2006) that the Latino population in former U.S. Rep. Henry Bonilla's district had undergone sufficient retrogression and was found in violation of the Voting Rights Act. As a remedy, the court redrew U.S. Rep. Lloyd Doggett's (D-Austin) district from the Rio Grande Valley to Austin and consolidated it around the Austin area.

FROM THE CAPITOL TO THE COURTS: THE 2011 TEXAS REDISTRICTING PROCESS

At the outset of the 2010 redistricting process Republicans held all of the statewide elected offices, as well as a supermajority in the Texas House—101 of the 150 members of the State House are Republican, while the Senate was divided with 19 Republicans and 12 Democrats. Republican Governor Rick Perry was re-elected to an unprecedented third term in 2010 defeating former Houston Mayor Bill White. Absent from the process this time was former House Majority Leader Tom DeLay who in November 2010 was convicted of felony money laundering that occurred a month prior to the Republican's 2002 takeover of the Texas House.

The year 2010 was also notable for minority representation as Texas elected two new Latino Republicans to the U.S. House (Bill Flores and Francisco "Quico" Canseco). In addition, five new Latino Republicans were elected to the Texas House. State Rep. Aaron Pena of Edinburg later switched to the Republican Party, raising the number of Latino Republicans in the State House to a record of six. They join 25 Latino Democrats for a total of 31 Latinos in the lower chamber. In the State Senate, there are 7 Latino Democrats in the 31-member chamber.

With Democrats facing an uphill battle despite demographics in their favor following the news of reapportionment, Gov. Perry declared that he wanted three of the new four seats to be Republican. Latino civil rights groups, on the other hand, believed minorities were worthy of larger gains by way of more Latino-majority districts. Anglo Democrats found themselves as the most politically vulnerable under all potential outcomes. That is, if Republican legislators or civil rights groups triumphed, gains for either party would come at the expense of Anglo Democrats. Indeed, at the outset of the 2003 redistricting process led by Tom DeLay and the Republicans in Texas House, there were ten Anglo Democrats in the congressional delegation. After being heavily targeted by the maps produced by 2010 only two Anglo Democrats remained standing—Doggett and Gene Green of Houston.

As the 82nd legislative session commenced in January 2011, the two figures in charge of the redistricting process were State Sen. Ken Seliger (R-Amarillo) with his position as chair of Senate Redistricting Committee and State Rep. Burt Solomons (R-Carrollton)—chair of the House Redistricting Committee.

For their part, minority groups led by the Texas Latino Redistricting Taskforce (TLRT) released a proposal with two new Latino-majority districts to add to the seven Latino-majority districts—a number not increased since 1991. Of the two new Latino-majority districts, TLRT agreed that one should be a fourth district in South Texas and a new district that would represent Latinos in the Dallas area, now totaling 1 million. Their ally in the House would be State Rep. Marc Veasey (D-Fort Worth) whose "Fair Texas Plan" reflected minority growth in the state. Veasey's plan, which was ultimately defeated, would have set up 14 districts in which a Democrat is favored, 13 of which would be predominantly minority. The other 22 districts would favor Republicans.

On May 26, final day of the legislative session, Gov. Perry called for a special session to begin. Under the Texas constitution, special sessions ordered by the governor are limited to 30 days. Days before the special session was to begin, the Latino Redistricting Task Force gave the legislature a grade of "F" for failing to create enough Latino-opportunity districts to reflect the community's growth in the state. Members of the Task Force include Mexican American Legal Defense and Education Fund (MALDEF), the League of United Latin American Citizens (LULAC), the GI Forum, the Mexican-American Bar Association, and the Southwest Voter Registration and Education Project (SWVRI). Former LULAC president Hector Flores expressed a frustration lived a decade before by stating that the latest redistricting process "smacks of déjà vu." In response to the maps championed by Republicans, U.S. Reps.

Gene Green (D-Houston) and Sheila Jackson Lee (D-Houston) came out aggressively in opposition stating that the one proposed minority district would surely fail judicial scrutiny. Others, like Rep. Green were in favor of a Latino-majority district in Houston. Indeed, State Rep. Carol Alvarado (D) proposed the Houston district in the amendment process.

The special session commenced on May 31, and by June 9 the House Redistricting Committee sent their plan out of committee with an 11–5 party-line vote. During the committee meeting, changes were made to only North and South Texas (see map 14.1). The author of the map, Rep. Solomons, reduced Latino voting strength in U.S. Rep. Francisco "Quico" Canseco's district 23 in anticipation of a potential rematch in 2012 with former U.S. Rep. Ciro Rodriguez (D-San Antonio). The justification that was given for the dilution of Latino voting strength in Canseco's district was that it would bolster Latinos elsewhere. Solomons stated that shifting Latinos from Canseco's district and from the newly created D-35 stemmed from concerns expressed by U.S. Rep. Charlie Gonzalez's (D) constituents in San Antonio. Charlie Gonzalez, son of the legendary Henry B. Gonzalez who represented San Antonio for 37 years, took his father's seat in 1998 and was considered by many to have such a firm grip on the seat that fewer Latinos in his district would do little to endanger his prospects for reelection. In somewhat surprising news, however, Gonzalez announced that he would not seek re-election. This led State Rep. Joaquin Castro, D-San Antonio, to change his political plans and run for Gonzalez's seat in order to avoid a bruising Democratic primary with Doggett in the newly created district 35. The second area tinkered with during the special session was North Texas where precincts from Tarrant and Denton counties were altered to the benefit of U.S. Rep. Kay Granger (R-Fort Worth). Final Passage of Senate Bill 4 in the House came on June 15, 2011, with a 20–12 party-line vote.

In more than 400 pages of emails released later by a federal judge in August, Republicans suffered from infighting throughout the process. In one email dated in late May, U.S. Rep. Lamar Smith, R-San Antonio, wrote to his lawyer that he would be willing to swap part of his district to help newly elected Republican Canseco's district be more Republican. In the email, Smith asks, "Would it help Quico on the margin if I gave him 3k more in Bexar (either GOP or Hispanics) and took Edwards [County] in exchange?" U.S. Reps. Joe Barton, R-Ennis, and Smith, each championing different plans, engaged in tense exchanges during delegation meetings. Barton critiqued Smith's version of CD 20 because Latino vote dilution would likely be used against Republicans by the San Antonio court. In the end, the swap was not made, but Canseco's district was redrawn to be more Republican, and therefore less Latino.

The Solomons-Seliger Republican plan carved out a new Latino-majority district (D-35, seemingly named for the interstate corridor that runs between San Antonio and Austin) did so by siphoning Latino voters from Rep. Charlie Gonzalez's San Antonio district. The campaign for district 35 was to be the manifestation (distillation) of the principle dynamics of current Texas politics determinative of the state's political future. Lloyd Doggett, a perennial target of Republicans at

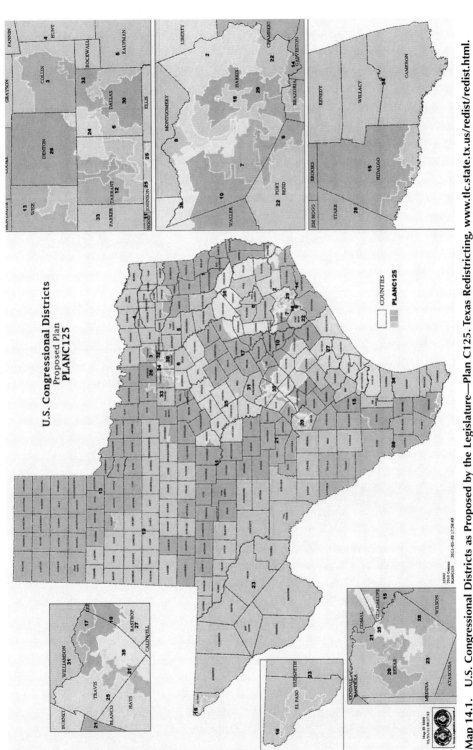

Map 14.1. U.S. Congressional Districts as Proposed by the Legislature—Plan C125. Texas Redistricting, www.tlc.state.tx.us/redist/redist.html.

every redistricting turn, and one of Governor Perry's staunchest critics, was by 2011 the last of a dying breed—an Anglo Democrat. Although Democrats throughout the state viewed Doggett favorably, for many Latinos Doggett represented their frustration with President Obama and the Democratic Party more broadly for the administration's failure to address immigration reform. With Doggett drawn out of his Austin-based district and into a heavily-Latino district capturing major parts of San Antonio, Joaquin Castro, twin brother of San Antonio Mayor Julian Castro, was provided the ideal opportunity to make his jump from local politics to the national spotlight. Doggett on the other hand would most likely face a difficult contest for D-25 stretching from Austin north to the Dallas area.

Indeed, Travis County (where Austin is located) was one of most gerrymandered areas as the state's plan increased the number of districts in the county from 3 to 5, none of which were anchored in Travis County. Republicans in the legislature thought that this would be the best way to force white Democrat Lloyd Doggett into a difficult re-election race. The Voting Rights Act only protects racial and ethnic minorities, not white liberal "minorities" in Austin. Bexar County (San Antonio) was also split into five districts; however, one of the districts was wholly in the county.

Litigation over the legislature's maps played out on two fronts. The first venue was a DC federal district court as Attorney General Greg Abbott (R) asserted the state's statutory right under Section 5 to seek judicial preclearance rather than administrative preclearance by the Department of Justice (DOJ) when he filed in court on July 18. On Monday, September 19, the Justice Department filed in court against the Texas congressional map and the map of the Texas House districts, which they found to be in violation of the Voting Rights Act because the maps would not "maintain or increase the ability of minority voters to elect their candidates of choice." The maps for the Texas state senate and school districts, meanwhile, were not found to be in violation.

Midway through the process of preclearance, accusations of delay were directed at both sides. Opponents of the legislature's maps accused Abbott's office of purposely choosing the slower route of administrative preclearance by seeking a declaratory judgment by a DC Court. The state's defense rested on the grounds of their experience with DOJ as the state sought administrative preclearance for the state's Voter ID law. Abbott pointed to repeated instances in which the DOJ requested additional information despite the state's willingness to provide any and all information forthrightly.

On November 8, the DC district court denied summary judgment on the maps stating that the State of Texas "used an improper standard or methodology to determine which districts afford minority voters the ability to elect their preferred candidates of choice." This decision effectively forced the lower federal district court to deal with the drawing of districts in accordance with the Voting Rights Act.

A three-judge federal panel in San Antonio was therefore tasked with providing an interim map that corrected for malapportionment. The panel then was faced with deciding which map should be used as the basis for the new lines. The three-judge panel in San Antonio reasoned that it should redraw district lines according to those used in the most recent election, 2010, rather than on the basis of the map passed by the state Legislature because it had not yet been precleared. Indeed, the state pointed to previous case law, specifically *Abrams v. Johnson* (1997), to argue that whenever possible, courts should defer to the legislative branch, an argument that the U.S. Supreme Court would later accept. By using the 2010 lines the court produced a map that was less favorable to Republicans. Had the court paid deference to the legislature's proposal instead, the interim map would have been less favorable but probably more palatable to Republicans.

On November 18, 2011, the San Antonio court released its map. The court's map restored Travis County to only three districts. Comparisons between the map produced by the legislature (Plan C 125) and the court-ordered interim map (Plan C 220) show that 24 of the 36 districts in the court's map include two-thirds or more of the state's original district. Indeed, in 9 districts the court maintained 90 percent or more of the same district from the state's map (see map 14.2). Nevertheless, the state of Texas still objected to the court-drawn maps as not consistent with the will and intent of the legislature.

On Friday, December 9, 2011, the U.S. Supreme Court blocked the interim maps drawn by the San Antonio federal court from implementation but did not stay the filing period. Following the stay on the interim maps by the Supreme Court, local precincts throughout Texas wondered how they would schedule elections in time for the March 6 primaries. One option was to split the primary elections, but many feared that would result in voter fatigue and be a costly burden on taxpayers. Meanwhile, incumbents and challengers alike had to meet filing deadlines for some yet-to-be-determined-districts. Ultimately, the elections were moved to April 3, although this date is still tentative, depending on the outcome of litigation.

In 2009, Texas also found itself at the center of the debate relating to the Voting Rights Act with *Northwest Austin Municipal Utility District No. 1 v. Holder*. In that case the court granted the district the right to avoid preclearance as they sought to move a polling place from a garage to a school. In an 8–1 decision, the court ruled that the municipality could "bail out" of its Section 5 preclearance requirement. Writing for the majority, Chief Justice John Roberts stated that "things have changed in the South," suggesting that progress on racial issues would soon render the VRA unnecessary. Others point to the election of President Barack Obama as *prima facie* evidence that whites were willing to vote for African American candidates. Just weeks before the high court would hear the Texas redistricting case, Attorney General Eric H. Holder Jr. gave a speech in fierce defense of the VRA at the Lyndon B. Johnson Presidential Library just blocks away from the Texas capitol.

On January 9 the U.S. Supreme Court heard the Texas redistricting cases. The three cases before the Supreme Court justices were *Perry v. Perez*, concerning the Texas House; *Perry v. Davis*, on redistricting the State Senate; and *Perry v. Perez*, on the U.S. House of Representatives. The Supreme Court began hearing oral arguments on January 9. In the background lay the federal district court, which

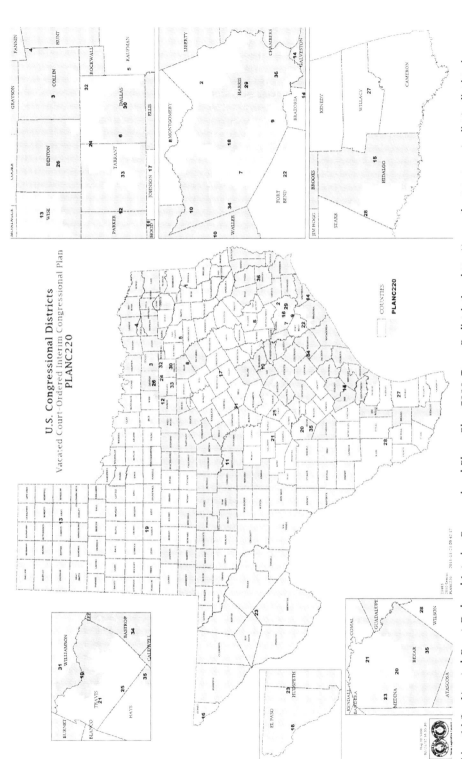

Map 14.2.   Vacated Court-Ordered Interim Congressional Plan—Plan C220. Texas Redistricting, http://www.tlc.state.tx.us/redist/redist.html.

scheduled to hear the Texas case (*Texas v. U.S.*) between January 17 and 26. Though few expected the high court to use the Texas case to dismantle Section 5 completely, many believed they would continue to cast doubt on the relevance of the pre-clearance requirement.

In a brief preceding the Supreme Court's hearing of the case, the state of Texas made clear what it believed to be the only two options facing the court—either order the use of the state's plans in lieu of the lower court's interim maps or find Section 5 of the VRA unconstitutional. The state in its brief made repeated claims about the intrusive nature of preclearance and how it curtails the state's sovereignty. Perhaps the state's strongest claim is that the nature of administrative preclearance can be gamed in such a way that obtaining preclearance judicially through a DC court in a timely manner is overly difficult or too burdensome. Central to the state's argument is that the DOJ is permitted to delay the process by requesting additional filing information by the state at any time and withholding a ruling based on clerical matters.

Each side seemed to have prior case law in their favor. The crux of the state's argument rested on the court's decision in *Upham v. Seamon* (1982) that courts should defer to legislative maps whenever possible. In that case, the Justice Department did not grant preclearance to the congressional map produced by the legislature following the 1980 census due to the configuration of two South Texas districts. In addition to adjustments for the two South Texas districts the court redrew lines in Dallas County. On appeal, the Supreme Court held that the district court overstepped its bounds by modifying a state plan beyond those districts initially found to be in violation. For their part, minority groups cite *Lopez v. Monterey County*, in which the court ruled that a map that had not been precleared could not be used on an interim basis.

In late January 2012, the U.S. Supreme Court ultimately ruled by remanding the case back to the San Antonio three-judge panel, effectively choosing a third option in lieu of the state's purported two options. The Court sided with Abbott in a sense by arguing that the three-judge panel should have used the legislature's maps as the starting point, rather than the 2010 maps. At this point, the problem is whether the three-judge panel will have sufficient time to deliver a map that will withstand additional judicial scrutiny in time for the primary in early April 2012. Some have suggested a split primary, although the state opposes this for budgetary reasons as well as the additional burden on voters. The three-judge panel has negotiated with attorneys from the MALC and the state to come up with a plan that has bipartisan support.

On February 15, 2012, minority groups and the Attorney General reached an agreement on the Texas Senate districts (see map 14.3). Sen. Wendy Davis (D-Fort Worth) agreed to the map because it essentially gave her a district that was a substantial improvement over the Republican legislature map. Texas has only 31 senate districts, which are larger in population than U.S. House districts, making it more difficult to gerrymander given this reality.

Remaining in limbo as of February 21, 2012, are the State House and U.S. House districts. Minority groups such as MALDEF and LULAC argue that not enough districts in the State House reflect the strong Latino population growth

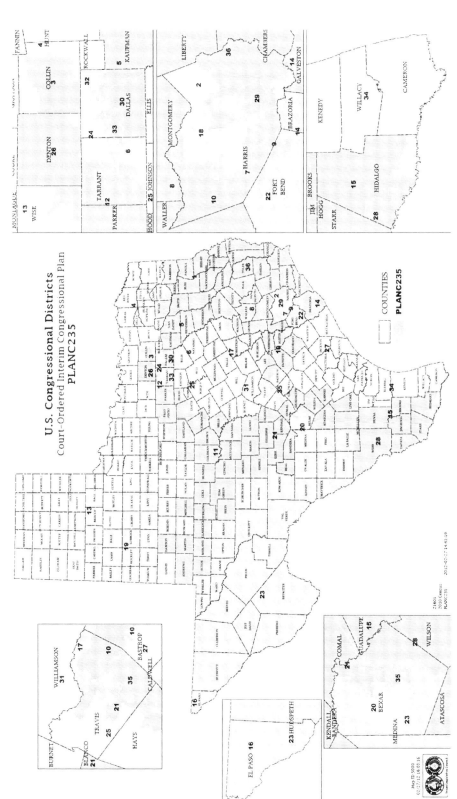

U.S. Congressional Districts
Court-Ordered Interim Congressional Plan
PLANC235

Map 14.3. Court-Ordered Interim Congressional Plan—Plan C235. Texas Redistricting, http://www.tlc.state.tx.us/redist/redist.html.

in the past ten years. Because the state is currently waiting for the higher courts to rule on both Section 2 and Section 5 lawsuits, the Texas primary, originally scheduled for March, has been pushed back to May 29, at the earliest. This had important implications for the U.S. Senate primary, an open seat race where Lt. Gov. David Dewhurst was upset by former state solicitor general and Tea Party favorite Ted Cruz for the Republican nomination. And more importantly, the state's Republican voters had to wait to cast their votes for the Republican presidential nomination, causing the nation's most populous Republican state to have less impact in selecting who became the Republican standard bearer in November 2012.

IMPACT AND EFFECTS

If political competition stiffens and demographic trends in favor of Democrats continue, control in the Texas legislature may flip back and forth between the parties throughout the next decade. Given the history of redistricting and the dangerous precedent of mid-decade redistricting, legislative majorities may attempt to redistrict any time they regain a majority. At the same time, the future of the Voting Rights Act and Section 5 is very much in doubt. Chief Justice Roberts and others on the court have signaled possible disagreement with the provision and its future. Texas has made clear, with much more clarity than ever before, that they oppose Section 5 as a violation of state sovereignty. The attorney general's argument is that Texas should not be held to a different standard than other states not subject to preclearance. A variant of the argument that Section 5 should either apply everywhere or nowhere seems to be gaining traction in many circles. Section 2, however, applies nationwide, and is probably on firmer legal ground. Not all of the lawsuits in Texas fall under Section 5. Some allege section 2 violations of abridging the rights of minorities, Hispanics in particular.

State Senator Jeff Wentworth (R-San Antonio) has proposed an independent redistricting commission for Texas. His proposal, modeled on Arizona and California, would in theory take the politics out of redistricting. As we have seen with Arizona, however, Gov. Jan Brewer (R) objected to the chair of the Independent commission for favoring a map that benefited Democrats. The Arizona State Senate ultimately removed the chair. Wentworth's proposal has not gained much support in the legislature. This is no doubt because legislators want to have control over the process that determines the districts they will represent.

Texas redistricting is as contentious in 2012 as it was in the early 2000s. With the margin so tight in the U.S. House of Representatives, both political parties are trying to use whatever tools at their disposal to influence the process. Republicans have the upper hand because they control the legislature and the governorship. However, the Voting Rights Act prevents them from disenfranchising minority voters, who are the remaining Democrats in the state. This will lead to tension and conflict, but it still remains the case that the bulk of the population growth in Texas in the last ten years has been due to Hispanics. This will change Texas politics in the years to come, and will affect how Texas redistricts in the future.

NOTES

1. The Dallas Fed found that Texas was responsible for 261,700, or 49.9 percent of the jobs created in the United States between June 2009 and June 2011.

2. Nationally, the Latino population grew by 43 percent between 2000 and 2010.

3. The Hispanic Population: 2010. 2010 Census Briefs. Issued 2011. By Sharon R. Ennis, Merarys Rios-Vargas, and Nora G. Albert.

4. Ibid.

5. Pew Hispanic Center, "The 2010 Congressional Reapportionment and Latinos," January 5, 2011.

6. Ibid.

7. Ibid., table 2.

8. Michael P. McDonald, "2010 General Election Turnout Rates," *United States Elections Project*. Accessed December 20, 2011.

9. League of Women Voters of Texas, 2011. Letter from Karen Nichlson president, LWV-Texas addressed to Chris Herren of Justice Department concerning SB 14 of Texas Legislature. Letter dated August 18, 2011.

10. Ibid.

11. Pew Hispanic Center, "The Latino Electorate in 2010: More Voters, More Non-Voters," April 26, 2011.

12. *MALC v. Perry.*

13. Jason Casellas, *Latino Representation in State Houses and Congress* (New York: Cambridge University Press, 2011).

14. Texas Politics Project, University of Texas at Austin.

15

Redistricting Congressional Districts in Ohio

An Example of a Partisan Process with Long-Lasting Consequences

Mark Salling

In this chapter we empirically examine how the congressional redistricting process and its election outcomes in Ohio are influenced by elections for state offices. This is a story of how partisan state politics largely determines who represents Ohioans in the federal Congress and how that influence can and does distort the proportional representation of the electorate. Ohioans have little understanding of how their votes for three state offices prior to each decennial census limits their ability to select a representational state legislature and how that ultimately affects how well represented their party preferences are for their congressional delegation.

Remarkably, the influence those three state office holders have on congressional outcomes extends into, not one, but two decades beyond their election. Through greater nonpartisan fair elections interest groups and media scrutiny, the public's understanding of and concern for the process has been increased with the most recent round of redistricting in the state. Yet, the state's congressional landscape is again set for the next decade and beyond—unless reformers can rally enough public opinion and force a major change before 2021.

OHIO'S DEMOGRAPHIC TRENDS

An overview of the state's demographic landscape provides a backdrop to an understanding of Ohio's congressional boundaries and representation, as concentrations of urban and minority populations guide some boundary decisions and provide opportunities to pack voters into districts that give advantage to partisan interests.

Overall Population Growth

Ohio achieved statehood in 1803 as the 17th state in the union. Its current status as the seventh most populous state (with more than 11.5 million persons) is largely attributed to its industrial growth in the 1800s and first half of the twentieth century. Steady growth accelerated in the early decades of the twentieth century as industrial jobs drew migrants from more rural states and immigrants from Europe.

Population grew by almost 60 percent from 1900 to 1930 (see figure 15.1). After slowed growth in the Great Depression years of the 1930s (showing only a 3.9 percent increase), population growth took off again after World War II. The migration of African Americans from the rural South and the growth of the baby boomer population in the late 1940s, 1950s, and early 1960s contributed to faster population growth in Ohio than in most other states during that period (see figure 15.2).

However, since 1970 the state's population growth has tapered off considerably as its manufacturing base has lost its earlier competitive advantages over national and international competitors and the migration into the state and its industrial centers has now all but stopped. Today Ohio's population growth is sustained by its natural growth—more births than deaths—rather than by migrants to the state. The state has been a net loser in migration since the 1970s and has not kept pace with national growth rates.[1]

Geographic Distribution of the Population

Ohio's population is largely urban. In 2000 more than 77 percent of the population lived in areas classified as urban, and 64.4 percent were in urbanized areas.[2]

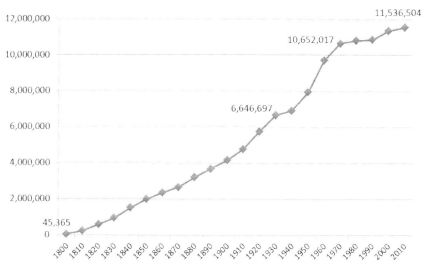

Figure 15.1.   Ohio's Population Growth. U.S. Census Data.

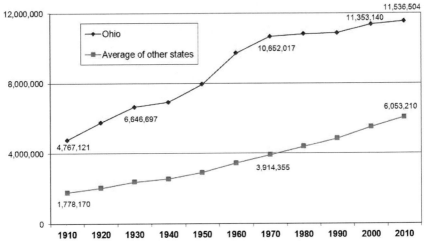

Figure 15.2. Ohio's Population, 1910 to 2010 Compared to the Average of Other States. U.S. Census Data.

Ohio's largest cities include Columbus (787,033), Cleveland (396,815), Cincinnati (296,943), Toledo (287,208), Akron (199,110), and Dayton (141,527).

Many of the state's cities are within metropolitan areas of considerably larger populations, however (see map 15.1). The Cleveland-Elyria-Mentor, Ohio Metro Area had 2,077,240 persons, 18 percent of the state, in the 2010 census. The Columbus and Cincinnati metro areas were also over a million in population, and the Dayton, Akron, and Toledo metro areas exceeded 500,000 persons. Almost half (48 percent) of the state's population lives in one of the largest three metro areas, and more than 80 percent of the state's population lives in one of the state's sixteen metropolitan areas. Urban sprawl and the loss of in-migration to replace households leaving inner city neighborhoods for newer suburban housing have reduced the high densities of urban places that were common fifty years ago. Cleveland's population fell by almost 17 percent, from 478,403 to 396,815, from 2000 to 2010; Cincinnati lost more than 10 percent, from 331,285 to 296,943.

The Largest Minorities: Blacks and Hispanics

In terms of population size, in the 2010 census African Americans (1,407,681) and Hispanics/Latinos (354,674) were Ohio's major minorities. Asians were the next largest group with 192,233 persons.[3] African Americans comprised 12.2 percent of the state's population; the Hispanic or Latino percentage was 3.1 percent. The state was 97.9 percent white in the 2010 census.

The state's African American population is largely concentrated in the largest cities. They are a majority (53 percent) of the population in Cleveland, and one of the state's congressional districts (mostly found on Cleveland's east side) has been

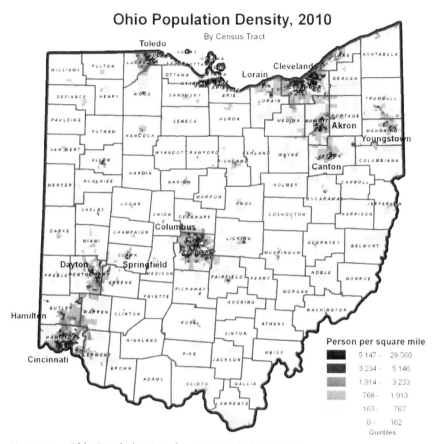

Map 15.1.   Ohio Population Density, 2010. U.S. Census Data.

represented by an African American since the 1960s. The loss of approximately 31,000 (13 percent) in the Black population in Cleveland since 2000, however, is forcing a significant change in that district's boundaries in order to meet the requirements of the Voting Rights Act of 1965 (see discussion below). The Hispanic/Latino population, in addition to their urban concentrations, is also found in rural, agricultural communities, particularly in northeast Ohio and Lake County to the east of Cleveland.

APPORTIONMENT: POPULATION AND THE NUMBER OF CONGRESSIONAL SEATS

The decennial census is used to apportion congressional representation among the states. The number of seats each state is assigned is approximately proportional to

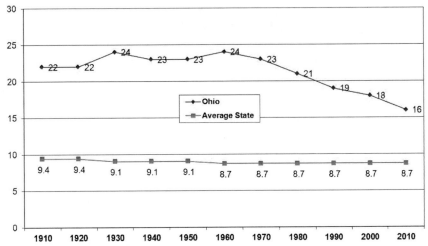

Figure 15.3. Ohio's Congressional Seats Compared to the Average for All States. Created by the author.

its population.[4] A large population in Ohio has meant a large share of congressional seats in the House of Representatives. But with Ohio's population growth lagging behind that of other states in recent decades the proportion of congressional seats has declined (see figure 15.3).

In 1930 and again in 1960, Ohio had 24 of the 435 congressional districts in the House of Representatives.[5] Starting in 1970 Ohio saw continued losses in representation up to and including the 2010 census results. From highs above 5 percent of the population until 1970, to 3.74 percent in 2010, Ohio was among a handful of states that lost two seats—from 18 to 16, as a result of the most recent census.

DRAWING CONGRESSIONAL BOUNDARIES

The process of apportionment sets the number of congressional seats for each state, but within each state the geography of district boundaries is largely up to each state. While each state does it its own way, the process is almost always driven by partisan politics and a political party in control can skew the results heavily in its favor—one could say beyond the will of the people. The process of redistricting is critical to partisan political control, and partisan political control is critical to redistricting. Ohio provides a good example.

The Congressional Redistricting Process

Congressional districts in Ohio are created by an act of the Ohio legislature—known as the General Assembly—every ten years following the decennial census.[6] A simple majority in both the Ohio House and Senate of the General Assembly and the signature of the governor are required, though the General Assembly can override a governor's veto with a three-fifths majority in both bodies. The law will stand if the governor fails to act within ten days.[7]

Outside of who draws districts, the state's constitution says little about how the congressional boundaries are to be drawn.[8] Neither does the U.S. Constitution. However, the U.S. Supreme Court has identified various criteria based on the Fourteenth and Fifteenth Amendments to the U.S. Constitution. The Supreme Court has required that "absolute population equality be the paramount objective of apportionment" in establishing congressional districts.[9] So congressional districts must be as equal in population as practicable.

Additionally, provisions of the Voting Rights Act of 1965 must be met. These provisions prohibit states and political subdivisions from denying or abridging the right to vote on the basis of race, color, or status as a member of a language minority group.[10] Districting plans also cannot dilute the voting strength of certain minorities. Some practices that have been questioned under the act include the packing of minority voters into a limited number of districts and the fracturing of minority voting strength by dividing minority voters into a number of districts.[11]

Where possible, the courts have ruled that protected minorities must be provided with one or more districts in which they are a majority. A majority-minority district is a congressional or other election district in which the majority of the constituents are racial or ethnic minorities (white non-Hispanics). Ohio has one majority-minority district, and the new congressional map scheduled for the 2012 elections will also have one.

Nationally, state or federal court challenges to congressional redistricting plans have resulted in some decisions that support principles such as compactness, contiguity, preservation of political subdivisions or communities of interest, and representational fairness. These concepts are further discussed below. While some states have established a process for adopting congressional district plans that consider these principles, and some provide for the districts to be drawn by a nonpartisan board or commission, Ohio continues to let political partisanship, within limits of population equality and the Voting Rights Act, guide the process.

HOW POLITICAL PARTISANSHIP GUIDES CONGRESSIONAL REDISTRICTING

Because congressional districts are drawn by the state legislature, control of both houses of the General Assembly by one party offers opportunity for that party to create congressional districts in its favor. But how does a political party attain a strong majority in the state legislature so that it can create a favorable congressional plan? The answer is in having a majority in the state's Apportionment Board.

The Apportionment Board

In Ohio the state legislature is divided into two chambers, the House with 99 districts and the Senate with 33 districts. The boundaries for these districts are drawn by an Apportionment Board.[12,13] The Board was established by an Ohio Constitutional amendment in 1967 and its first redistricting war in the 1972 elections. The Apportionment Board is made up of five elected officials: governor, auditor of state, secretary of state, one person chosen by the speaker of the House of Representatives and the leader in the Senate of the political party of which the speaker of the House is a member, and one person chosen by the legislative leaders in the two houses of the major political party of which the speaker of the House is not a member. In other words, it is made up of one member each from the two major political parties and three state offices.

The Apportionment Board is convened every ten years and meets between August 1 and October 1 in each year ending in the numeral "1." Thus, whichever political party wins two of the three state offices prior to the year of the census controls the redistricting of the state's legislative boundaries.[14]

If the state legislative districts can be drawn to a significant advantage for one party, and that helps it hold a majority over time, the subsequent congressional districting can also be drawn to that party's advantage ten years later. The partisan effect of redistricting state legislative boundaries must last to the next decade, overcoming changes in the electorate and other factors that could lead to shifts in their political preferences. That provides motivation for the party that draws the state legislative districts to do as much as possible to give itself a strong boundary advantage.

There are some limits to what partisanship alone can do. The state's constitution provides some requirements for redistricting the state legislature and it is useful to consider what they are.

Requirements for General Assembly Districts

Unlike with congressional districts, the Ohio Constitution establishes requirements that General Assembly district plans must meet. These include population equality, compactness, and contiguousness of territory.[15] Where possible, districts must be composed of whole counties and, if counties must be split by district boundaries, they must keep government units whole. Preference is given, in order, to counties, townships, municipal corporations, and city wards. Senate districts are composed of three contiguous House districts. Counties should not be split by Senate districts where possible and must have as many Senate districts as population size will warrant.

Population equality is based on the "ratio of representation" or target population, which is determined by dividing the population of the state by 99 for House districts, and by 33 for Senate districts. The target populations for redistricting the 2012 General Assembly are 116,530 in the House and 349,591 in the Senate. The population of each district generally must be within five percent (95 percent to

105 percent) of the applicable targets. If a county contains a population of between ten percent (90 percent to 110 percent) for the House, reasonable effort must be made to create a House district consisting of the whole county. The population of the Senate districts must be within five percent (95 percent to 105 percent) of the Senate's target population.

As with congressional districts, the U.S. Supreme Court has ruled that the Equal Protection Clause of the Fourteenth Amendment to the U.S. Constitution applies to state legislative districting plans as well. Thus although state legislative plans may have a wider population variance between districts than congressional plans, the districts still must have substantial equality of population.

These requirements do not include principles of competitiveness or proportional representation among major political parties. They do not speak to giving the electorate choices. Packing as many voters of one party into few districts or dividing them into small numbers across multiple districts is not a matter of consideration under the current rules. Thus state legislative districts can be, and have been, drawn to favor the political party that controls the Apportionment Board. And these advantages can and do last for the ten years necessary to provide advantage to the party in the congressional redistricting process.

REPRESENTATIONAL FAIRNESS AND COMPETITIVENESS

Data tell us that partisan control over redistricting Ohio's state legislature leads to a disproportionate share of wins for the party in the legislature and subsequently in congressional seats. What does "disproportionate share" mean? In this context, a disproportionate share of election wins for one party means that more elections are won by one political party than what might be expected from the proportion of votes for that party.

A disproportionate share gives rise to the concept of representational fairness in elections, which says that the fairness of an election is measurable by the number of seats won by a party or group of candidates compared to the proportion of votes received by that party or group. A "fair" election requires that these proportions— votes received and seats won—are relatively similar.[16] According to this principle, if political party A receives 70 percent of the vote for congressional races in the state, it "should" win close to 70 percent of the seats.

How has Ohio done in regard to representational fairness? First we look at the state legislature since its political composition influences congressional redistricting.

Representational Fairness in the State Legislature

Figures 15.4 and 15.5 show how the percentage of votes for candidates from the two major political parties in the Ohio House and Senate do not necessarily indicate the number of such offices won by those parties.[17]

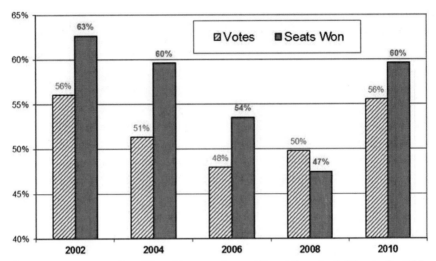

Figure 15.4. Percent Republican Votes vs. Percent Republican Seats Won in the Ohio House. Created by the author.

Clearly, a disproportionate number of Republican candidates—the party in control of the Apportionment Board in 2001—won their seats in the state legislature throughout the decade. In the 2002 election, with 56 percent of the votes statewide for Republican candidates, Republican candidates for the House won 63 percent of the seats. If the distribution of wins were proportionate to the statewide preference for Republican and Democratic candidates, the Republicans would have won seven

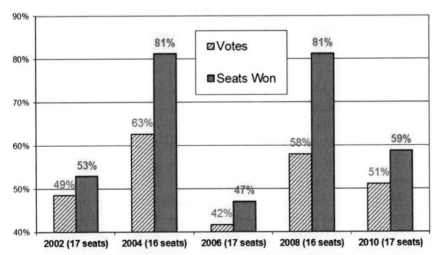

Figure 15.5. Percent Republican Votes vs. Percent Republican Seats Won in the Ohio Senate. Created by the author.

fewer seats and the Democrats seven more. One could reasonably attribute seven seats won by Republican candidates to how the boundaries were drawn in 2001 by the Apportionment Board.

The advantage lasted almost without interruption throughout the decade. With barely 51 percent of the vote in 2004, Republicans won 60 percent of the races. Most remarkably, in the 2006 election Republican candidates won a majority (56 percent) of the elections with only 42 percent of the votes. It would be difficult to attribute this discrepancy to anything other than the advantage that district geography provided the Republicans. These boundary effects are not insurmountable when strong political factors come into play. The effect of the Obama presidential candidacy carried the Democrats to two more wins that the statewide votes would have warranted in the 2008 elections. But in 2010, the Republican slate again won a disproportionate number of races given the votes they received. By the end of the decade, the strong Republican majority in the state's House of Representatives was largely due to the work of the Republican controlled Apportionment Board in 2001. Overall in the decade Republicans won 22 more seats in the House than their statewide votes would indicate.

In the Senate, the same pattern can be observed. With fewer than half of the votes statewide, Republican candidates still won a majority of elections in 2002. The disparity was greater in the 2004 election. They fell only one short of a majority of wins in the 2006 elections with only 42 percent of the states' votes. In the 2008 election they won three seats more than their statewide vote share (despite the Democratic presidential win in 2008), and overall in the decade eight more seats were won by Republicans than one might expect based on the voter's preferences for the candidates of the two parties.

The impact of the Republican controlled 2001 Apportionment Board was to put many more Republicans in the General Assembly than the proportion of votes earned by Republican candidates. By 2011, the state legislature—both chambers— was under control of a majority of Republicans. Those representatives then drew the state's congressional boundaries.[18]

Impact on Congressional Outcomes

Figure 15.6 illustrates the eventual impact of a partisan Apportionment Board on congressional election outcomes. Until 1972, the Republican Party held a majority in both chambers of the General Assembly. With a three-to-two majority on the Apportionment Board in 1971, Democrats took majority control of the formerly Republican controlled House in the 1972 election and of the formerly Republican controlled Senate in the 1974 election. Congressional districts at that time were drawn by the Republican control of both chambers of the General Assembly in 1971, and their impact on keeping Republicans in Congress lasted throughout that decade, even though the effects declined over time. A large majority of the congressional seats of the 1970s were won by Republicans.

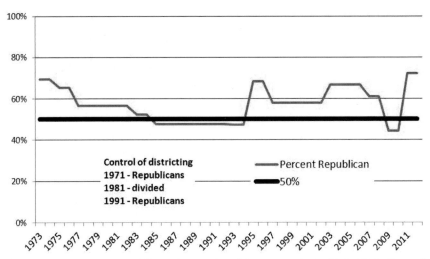

Figure 15.6. Percent Republican Congressional Representatives, 1973–2012. Created by the author.

Democratic control of the House was maintained through the 1980s, though Republicans gained temporary control again in 1980 for a brief time. The emergence of a Democratic majority in the state legislature in the 1970s, and thus their political strength in the congressional districting process in 1981, led to a more balanced split in seats won by both parties from 1982 through 1994. From 1962 through 1970, Republicans had won 72 percent of the congressional races; in the 1980s, after the effects of the politically balanced redistricting in 1971, they won 49 percent of the seats (see figure 15.6).

This analysis suggests a causal, but lagged effect of a partisan Apportionment Board on congressional election outcomes. State legislative districts are drawn by the Apportionment Board to favor one party over another, and that legislature then skews the political composition of the congressional seats in the following decade.

Of course redistricting is not the only factor affecting the shares of congressional seats won by each political party. The winds of change in the preferences of the electorate are often created by economic trends, heightened social issues, and political scandal. Nevertheless, the impact of drawing election districts to one party's advantage is extremely clear in these data. The Republican-dominated Apportionment Board of 1991 created a General Assembly that set the congressional boundary landscape in 2001.

When Ohio voters elected Republicans to be the governor, secretary of state, and state auditor again in 1998, they gave Republicans four of the five positions on the Reapportionment Board. That helped the Republicans maintain a majority in both houses of the state legislature in elections from 2002 through 2006. The Democrats barely took control of the state house in 2008, but lost it again in 2010.

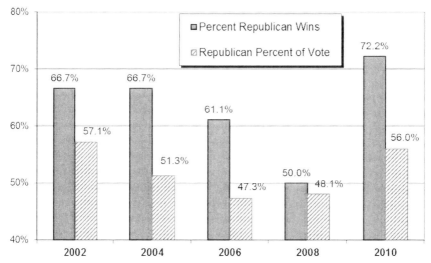

Figure 15.7.   Republican Congressional Wins and Percentage of Vote in Ohio. Created by the author.

So the Republicans drew the state's congressional districts that went into effect in 2002. Since then, the Republicans have been able to win more seats in Congress than their share of the state's voters might suggest (see figure 15.7). In 2002, Republican candidates for Congress won two-thirds (12) of the races, though they attained only 57 percent of the votes statewide. In 2004, they again won two-thirds of the 18 seats, while receiving only a little more than half (51 percent) of the votes in the state's congressional voting. In 2006, they won more than 60 percent (11) of the races, while actually getting less than half (48 percent) of the votes for congressional seats in Ohio.

For the only time in the decade, in 2008 the parties shared equally in congressional wins, accurately reflecting the state's roughly 50/50 preference for Republican and Democratic candidates that year. But in the 2010 election Republicans won more than 72 percent (13) of the 18 seats while receiving 56 percent of the votes.

The discrepancy between seats won and percent of the total vote is a measure of representational fairness, which is a concept advocated by nonpartisan fair election organizations and seems only logical as a goal in a democracy. The discrepancy is the result of partisan control of redistricting, starting with the Apportionment Board.

Noncompetiveness

In addition to the effect of partisan redistricting on representational fairness, districts drawn in 2001 were largely noncompetitive, strongly favoring one party over the other. Democrats were packed in relatively few districts and spread too thin to have much impact on election outcomes. The noncompetitiveness of the overall districting plan is seen in the fact that throughout the elections of 2002 to 2010, 14 of the 18 districts saw no change in the party winning the congressional seat. Two of the

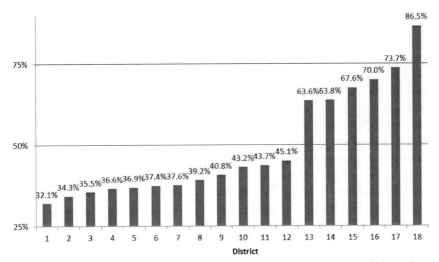

Figure 15.8. Percentage of Votes for Democratic Congressional Candidates from 2002–2010, by District. Created by the author.

four districts that saw a change in party during the decade resulted from Democrats winning in the Obama tidal wave of 2008, and one was won by the Republicans in their huge 2010 comeback election.

Competitive districts can be defined as those in which the votes for the losing candidate are within five (or alternatively ten) percent of a fifty percent split with the winner. When all the congressional votes for the two major parties are added for the five election years and we consider a range of five percent around a fifty percent split in votes for the two parties, 6 of the 18 congressional districts favored Democratic candidates, 11 favored Republicans, and 1 could be called competitive. Figure 15.8 clearly shows the packing of democratic voting in five districts (all with more than 63 percent of the votes going for Democratic candidates) and the relatively few districts in the competitive range.

To be clear, this is an issue of fair and competitive elections. As far as we know, the Republicans have done nothing more than what the Democrats may have done if they had been in the clear majority in 2011.

The Losing Electorate

The losers resulting from partisan redistricting were not only the Democratic candidates and their party, but the many voters—Democratic and Republican voters alike—who cast ballots in districts in which the political outcome was largely already determined by who drew the district boundaries. A commonly stated complaint about partisan redistricting is that the politicians pick their voters rather than the voters picking their politicians. Voters lose their right to have an equal say in who runs their government.

The democratic principle of "one person, one vote" was articulated in the United States Supreme Court (*Reynolds v. Sims*, 377 U.S. 533 [1964]), and though it spoke of equality of population in each district, the underlying objective was to create the opportunity for every person's vote to be as close in importance as anyone else's vote.[19]

Representational fairness and competitiveness of districts come at the issue of one person, one vote from different directions. The former is measured by the relationship between the partisan results and partisan votes statewide (or in a municipality in the case of a ward districting plan). Competitiveness can be measured for each district, asking how balanced the party affiliations are within the district, though one can also assess the number of competitive districts that a statewide districting plan produces. We have seen that the plan drawn in 2001 in Ohio has produced both representationally unfair districts and an overwhelmingly large proportion of noncompetitive districts.

To assess the effect on voters, we can count the number of votes in these elections that were, in hindsight, unnecessary—wasted—in achieving the outcomes of the elections. The most competitive district is one in which the outcome is decided by one vote. For discussion here we consider competitive elections those that result in a percentage distribution of votes for the two major parties to be between 40 and 60 percent. That is, the votes for the two parties are within 20 percent of each other. Using that criterion, among the average of 4,226,403 votes for Democratic and Republic congressional candidates in the five elections from 2002 to 2010, an average of 829,808 votes were cast for losing candidates in noncompetitive elections. Almost one in five votes in the state (19.6 percent) was wasted because votes were for losing candidates who had little chance of winning their elections. One could also say that many of the votes for winning candidates in those districts were also unnecessary. But at least those voters were rewarded by getting a representative of their choice.

OUTCOMES OF THE RECENT ROUND OF REDISTRICTING AND THE LONG-TERM PROSPECTIVE

With the most recent election, the voters again chose Republicans to control the Reapportionment Board and the state legislature, and thus the political landscape well into the next decade. Though there is no known research on the issue, it is this writer's opinion that relatively few voters in the state know that their votes for at least two of the offices—secretary of state and state auditor—prior to the decennial census have anything to do with the drawing of legislative districts. Nevertheless, the Republican-dominated state legislature drew new congressional districts in 2011 that are again highly noncompetitive and will, all other things being equal, result in a Republican-heavy congressional delegation for Ohio for the next decade.

As noted earlier, Ohio lost two congressional seats as a result of the 2010 census, down from 18 to 16. The Republican mapmakers were able to pit two incumbent Democrats, Marcie Kaptur and Dennis Kucinich, against each other in the primary, thus taking care of one of the lost seats. The other lost seat will be realized through putting incumbent Democrat Betty Sutton up against incumbent Republican Jim Renacci, whom they thought would be able to win in a newly constructed district 16 that leans heavily Republican. Apparently the Republican Party thought the 2010 election results were solid enough Republican to attain an election victory for Renacci. A little more than 53 percent of the 2010 congressional votes in that new district went to Republican candidates, better than the 42 percent for Democrats. However, combining the 2008 and 2010 election results shows the percentages to be much closer—50 percent versus 48 percent, respectively. Not surprisingly, polls showed a very close race, but ultimately Renacci was able to defeat Sutton by four points, showing that map makers did not misjudge the outcome.[20]

Nevertheless, 5 of the new 16 districts, made by the Republican-controlled state legislature and signed into law by the Republican governor, are strongly Republican-leaning, with more than 60 percent of the combined Democrat and Republican votes in those elections going to Republican candidates for Congress. Three others mildly lean Republican with 55 to 60 percent of the votes going for Republican congressional candidates. Four of the 16 are strongly Democratic-leaning districts, and one is mildly Democratic-leaning. Three of the districts had more than 65 percent of the electorate voting for Democrats in the combined 2008 and 2010 congressional races, demonstrating the packing of Democratic voters in a few districts. Only one district had more than 65 percent Republican voters in those two elections. That leaves three that can be said to be competitive, where roughly half (45 to 55 percent) of the votes were for either party.[21]

Meanwhile, the new state legislative districts, drawn again by a Republican majority on the Apportionment Board (having won all the state offices on the Board in 2011), give the Republicans strong and disproportionate advantage over the Democrats. In the House, there are 46 Republican-leaning districts (using aggregated 2008 and 2010 House elections and a 5 percent competitive range), 37 Democrat-leaning districts, and 16 that are competitive. In the Senate, the numbers are 20, 9, and 4, respectively. Thus only 16 percent of the House districts and 12 percent of the Senate districts are competitive.

If the Republicans can continue to capitalize on the geographic advantages in the state legislature for this coming decade, until 2021, they will be in a good position (especially if they also have the governorship) to again design congressional districts to their favor starting with the 2022 elections. Much can happen between now and then, but the current configuration of legislative boundaries is a known and important factor in predicting the future ten years from now.

Added to the importance that geography (favorable districts) provides is the advantage of incumbency. Preferable districts for the party in control of redistricting lead to incumbents who are difficult to defeat by challengers. This perpetuates the disproportionate share of election wins for the party that sets the political landscape at the beginning of the decade in Ohio.[22]

That is, unless the partisan process is changed.

Challenges

Redistricting in Ohio was and still is hotly challenged by both the Ohio Democratic Party and nonpartisan, fair elections groups.

In 2005, a coalition of political and fair elections groups proposed a series of changes to the state's redistricting process, including establishing a bipartisan commission to do the job.[23] Called "Reform Ohio Now," the coalition was successful in putting their proposals on the fall 2005 ballot. But largely because its proposals were too complex for the public to understand and accept, voters rejected it by a wide margin. It provided for proposed plans to be submitted by the public, scored using a fixed formula, and a winner selected. Scores were based on criteria for compactness, statewide partisan balance (representational fairness), and competitive districts among others. Composition on the commission was limited to persons with virtually no partisan association. Survey research after the election concluded that, despite its defeat, voters support the underlying principles of redistricting reform.[24]

Following defeat of Reform Ohio Now, then Ohio House Majority Leader Jon Husted (Republican) proposed changes to the redistricting process for congressional districts. Ohio House Joint Resolution 13 was introduced in May 2006 and included replacing the Apportionment Board with a less partisan Ohio Apportionment Commission.[25] The Commission would consist of seven members, four of which must be appointed by the leaders in the General Assembly, and three of which must be appointed unanimously by the first four. It set forth objectives that included maximizing the number of competitive districts. The resolution did not receive enough support in the Ohio House and Senate to make it to the ballot for voters to consider.

In 2009, Husted, then a senator and candidate for Ohio Secretary of State, continued to champion redistricting reform. There was also interest on the Democratic side. Senate Joint Resolution 5 would have changed the makeup of the Apportionment Board to make it less partisan, provided for it to redistrict both congressional and state legislative districts, and given priority to compactness, keeping communities together, and competitive districts. In the spring of 2010, the Ohio House passed House Joint Resolution 15, which was designed to reform how districts of the Ohio General Assembly are drawn though congressional districts would still be drawn by the legislature. The House resolution provided for an open and public competition to draw legislative state districts and a strictly formulaic selection of a plan based on specific criteria.[26]

The two sides could not reconcile differences in these two reform proposals, and the issue never made it to the ballot. The redistricting process went unchanged in 2011. Despite these setbacks to reform in the legislature, public interest groups at both the national and state levels kept the pressure on to produce a fairer, less partisan process.

In 2009, then Ohio secretary of state, Jennifer Brunner (Democrat), held a competition to test the feasibility of a formula-based process to select a "fair" congressional district plan using a public participation process.[27] The project tested the notion that persons with access through the Internet to software and data and some limited training could create a districting plan that achieved a number of goals concerning criteria thought to contribute to a fair districting plan. It was assumed that a "good" redistricting process would seek to preserve Ohio communities, promote political competition, result in an accurate reflection of the political leanings of the electorate, and provide an open and transparent process. Each criterion was assigned different weight. Compactness and commonalities of interest were deemed to be twice as important as competitiveness and representational fairness. The purpose was to enable stakeholders, as represented by public interest groups, grassroots community organizations, or any citizen, to participate in testing a decision-making process that would affect the political geography of the state and therefore the political outcomes of many future elections.

The competition began on April 10, 2009, and concluded on May 11, 2009. Though some eighty user accounts were requested, only fourteen plans were submitted. Three were disqualified because they did not meet all of the threshold conditions concerning a majority-minority district, equal population, and contiguity.

One of the winning plans (three were selected) had the following characteristics:

- nine Republican-leaning and nine Democratic-leaning districts,
- eleven competitive districts,
- twenty county fragments, and
- the sixth highest compactness ratio.

For comparison, the current congressional plan for the state (also shown in figure 15.1) has these characteristics:

- a partisan split of likely representation, with thirteen Republican-leaning and five Democratic-leaning districts,
- seven competitive districts,
- forty-four county fragments, and
- a compactness score lower than all of the submitted plans.

According to these criteria, the winning plans were superior to the current congressional district plan. In fact, even the worst-scoring plan submitted in the competition was quantitatively "better" than the redistricting plan implemented in 2001. The competition was judged by the SOS, its partners, and others to be successful, though it was also recognized that improvements would be necessary should a similar redistricting process be put into practice for the state.

Despite these conclusions and the proposals for reform put forth by both Democratic and Republican leaders, the state legislature did not change the existing process. Apparently both parties thought they could win the Apportionment Board and the state legislature in the 2010 elections. The Democrats horribly misjudged both of those outcomes. Failing to see legislation changing the process, fair elections interest groups hoped they could alter the partisanship through public pressure.

Of particular note is the work of the Midwest Democracy Network, which describes itself as

> an alliance of more than 25 nonprofit, nonpartisan civic engagement organizations dedicated to improving the condition of democracy in Illinois, Indiana, Michigan, Minnesota, Ohio and Wisconsin. Some partners are state-based advocacy groups and some are national research and policy institutions; some focus on specific reform issues, while others work on a broader democracy agenda. Several academics also participate in the Network.
>
> Nonetheless, all participants in the Network share the belief that our fundamental democratic values and principles—especially those that speak to honesty, fairness, transparency, accountability, citizen participation, competition, respect for constitutional rights and the rule of law, and the public's need for reliable information—must be continuously reinforced and fiercely protected against those who see politics as a means to promote narrow interests rather than the common good.[28]

The organization provided resources, including an Internet-based districting software system, for public competitions in each of its target states to demonstrate and publicize how better, more democratic state legislative and congressional district plans could be constructed. In Ohio the project included 25 supporting organizations led by the League of Women Voters and Ohio Citizen Action.[29]

The Ohio competition resulted in 53 submitted and evaluated plans using a scoring that placed value on competitive and compact districts, with few splits of counties and communities, and a balanced partisan share of likely election winners. The Midwest Democracy Network compared the legislature's plan with the plans submitted in its competition. The congressional plan that the state legislature approved in September (HB 319) was heavily skewed to favor Republicans and scored last when compared to the citizen-submitted plans.

HB 319 included 65 county fragments, divided 27 counties, split 7 counties into 3 or more districts, included only 2 competitive districts (within 20 percent in previous vote shares), and had no highly competitive districts (within 10 percent). Republicans were favored in 12 of the 16 districts. By comparison, the winning plan submitted by a citizen included 21 county fragments, divided 9 counties, split 2 counties into 3 or more districts, had 11 competitive and 8 highly competitive districts, resulted in an equal partisan split, and was 35 percent more compact than HB 319 (see maps 15.2 and 15.3).

When the initial congressional districting plan was passed by the majority Republican legislature, Ohio Democratic leaders threatened to raise enough petition signatures to put the plan to a referendum. That created the possibility that the spring primary election would have to be delayed, and if a compromise was not reached, the legislature's plan may have been put to a vote in the coming year.[30] The legislature avoided that when the congressional plan was slightly modified in December 2011. The revised plan accommodated and won the support of the state's legislative Black Caucus by keeping some urban neighborhoods together, also enhancing concentrations of African Americans in those districts.[31] It was enough support to stop the referendum movement.

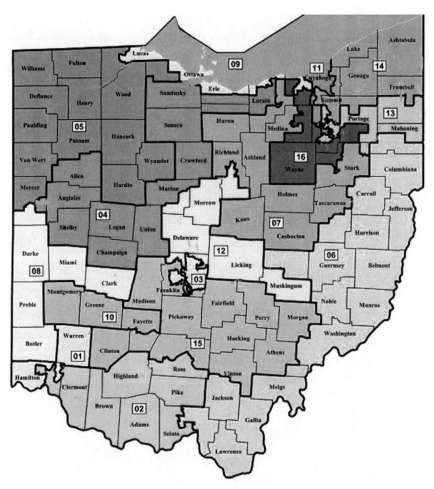

Map 15.2. Ohio 2002–2012 Congressional Districts. Legislative Task Force on Redistricting.

As to whether is it likely that the state's congressional plan can be changed now, the Ohio Legislative Services Commission points out:

> It is not entirely clear under what circumstances a state may redraw congressional districts between censuses. Plans must be redrawn if a districting plan is determined to be unconstitutional. And in 2006, the U.S. Supreme Court permitted the Texas Legislature to redraw, in the middle of the decade, a districting plan that had been adopted by a federal court. The Supreme Court did not determine, however, whether a legislature may draw a new redistricting plan mid-decade if the prior plan was adopted by the legislature. Thus, it is uncertain whether states may redraw their own legislatively enacted plans prior to the next census.[32]

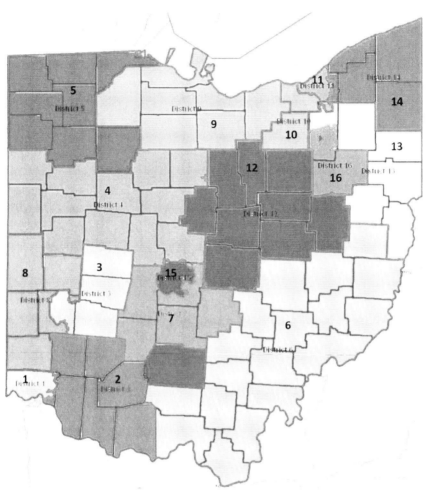

Map 15.3.   Ohio Enacted Congressional Districts for 2012–2022. Legislative Task Force on Redistricting.

THE FUTURE

While the congressional districting plan is set to be implemented for the 2012 elections, a court challenge to the state legislative districting plan by the Ohio Democratic Party was filed in early January 2012.[33] Unless there is a successful challenge to the congressional plan, the soonest that a significant change to the state legislative districts would have on congressional districts would be for the 2022 elections.

Probably the best hope for a less partisan and one-sided congressional boundary plan in the next decade and beyond is in changing the state's constitution. Secretary of State Jon Husted, a Republican member of the Apportionment Board, has again called for a revision to the redistricting process.[34] There is some hope and expectation that the newly formed Ohio Constitutional Modernization Commission will take up the issue.

Importantly, the issue has reached a much more elevated public awareness than ever, and the pressure for change will likely be kept on by fair elections advocates, not to mention the Democrats who know that it is so important to their future.

NOTES

1. The Census Bureau estimated that Ohio had a net migration of -247,751 persons and a net natural growth of 389,121 persons between 2000 and 2009. See Table 4. Cumulative Estimates of the Components of Resident Population Change for the United States, Regions, States, and Puerto Rico: April 1, 2000, to July 1, 2009 (NST-EST2009-04), Source: U.S. Census Bureau, Population Division, release date: December 2009. IRS estimates show a domestic net migration loss of -511,263 in the 1980s. See "State Migration Flows to and From Ohio: 1980-2010 (xls) (updated 12-16-11)," Policy, Research & Strategic Planning Office, Ohio Dept. of Development (JH, 7/09) from data from the Internal Service (IRS), Department of Commerce, U.S. Census Bureau.

2. Urban areas include both urbanized areas and urban clusters in the 2000 census. An urban cluster is "a densely settled area that has a census population of 2,500 to 49,999." An urbanized area is "a densely settled area that has a census population of at least 50,000. www.census.gov/dmd/www/glossary.html#U. See also Demographic Profile: 2000, Technical Documentation, 2000 Census of Population and Housing, U.S. Department of Commerce, U.S. Census Bureau, Issued August 2002 (Revised). Data on urban population from the 2010 census are not available at this writing.

3. The one race categories are used here.

4. The federal census determines the population as of April 1, in each year ending in the numeral "0." Within a week after the opening of Congress the following year of the census, the president must report the census counts, and the number of congressional representatives to which each state is entitled, to the Congress. See United States Code (U.S.C.) § 2a, www .law.cornell.edu/uscode/2/2a.shtml and http://uscode.house.gov/download/pls/02C1.txt.

5. The number of congressional districts increased from 433 to 435 in 1930 due to the addition of Arizona and New Mexico to statehood. The Reapportionment Act of 1911 set the number at 433, but at 435 when Arizona and New Mexico would reach statehood. See www .census.gov/history/pdf/1910_Apportionment.pdf.

6. The way congressional district plans are enacted by the General Assembly is codified in section 3521.01 of the Revised Code. See www.legislature.state.oh.us/BillText129/129_ HB_369_EN_N.pdf.

7. See www.legislature.state.oh.us/organizational.cfm.

8. A good description of reapportionment and redistricting in Ohio is provided by "Adopting General Assembly and Congressional Districts," by Lynda J. Jacobsen, *Members Only*, Volume 129, Issue 1, revised July 15, 2011, Ohio Legislative Services Commission, www.lsc .state.oh.us/membersonly/129Congressionaldistricts.pdf.

9. *Karcher v. Daggett*, 462 U.S. 725, 732 (1983).

10. Public Law No. 89-110 (codified as amended at 42 U.S.C. §§ 1971, 1973 to 1973bb-1). Voting Rights Act of 1965 at http://library.clerk.house.gov/reference-files/PPL_Voting RightsAct_1965.pdf. See also "Geometry and Geography: Racial Gerrymandering and the Voting Rights Act," by Howard M. Shapiro, *Yale Law Review*, Vol. 94, No. 1, November 1984, pp. 189-208, www.jstor.org/pss/796320.

11. *Redistricting Law 2010*, National Conference of State Legislatures, September 29, 2009, www.sos.state.oh.us/sos/upload/reshape/RedistrictingLaw2010.pdf.

12. Section 1 of Article XI of the Ohio Constitution, www.sos.state.oh.us/sos/upload/publications/election/Constitution.pdf.

13. The Apportionment Board is misnamed. Apportionment determines the number of districts; districting determines their geographic boundaries. Since the Apportionment Board does not determine the number of state legislative districts, but does draw their boundaries, it should be named the General Assembly Districting Board.

14. If the Ohio Supreme Court or the U.S. Supreme Court invalidates the General Assembly district plan, the Apportionment Board must meet to determine a new district plan using the provisions of Article XI that remain effective.

15. The boundary of each district must be a single, nonintersecting, continuous line.

16. We present this definition based on consultation with several sources, including http://en.wikipedia.org/wiki/Proportional_representation, http://www.historylearningsite.co.uk/proportional_representation.htm, http://www.fairvote.org/choice-voting-proportional-represen tation#.TyR6cVxST7E, and http://www.democracy-building.info/voting-systems.html.

17. Election data in this analysis are from the election pages of the Ohio secretary of state's website at www.sos.state.oh.us/sos/elections/Research/electResultsMain.aspx.

18. Of course, the legislators themselves don't generally literally draw the district boundaries. Staff and consultants are put to that task, with party leaders and other members guiding the process and making decisions.

19. The *Reynolds v. Sims* case was about state legislative districts, but the principle of "one person, one vote" was extended to congressional districts in *Wesberry v. Sanders, 376* U.S. 1 (1964).

20. See "Rep. Betty Sutton to challenge Rep. Jim Renacci for Congress," by Sabrina Eaton, *The Plain Dealer*, December 07, 2011, www.cleveland.com/open/index.ssf/2011/12/rep_betty_sutton_to_challenge.html.

21. We use the combined results of the 2008 and 2010 elections in measuring competitiveness. The 2008 election was generally tilted toward Democratic candidates, largely due to the popularity of Obama on the national scene, while the 2010 election saw a major shift toward Republicans. While the favorable 2008 political climate for the Democrats may have been short-lived, there is also no assurance that the 2010 Republican landslide will be a long-term trend. Swings such as these can mislead pundits and planners. It should also be pointed out that the percentages reported in this section are approximate and based on using precinct-level election results assigned to the new districts based on the geographic centroid on the precinct.

22. The substantial advantages of incumbency are well documented. See: 1) John R. Alford, and David W. Brady, 1993, "Personal and Partisan Advantage in U.S. Congressional Elections, 1846–1990," in *Congress Reconsidered*, 5th ed., edited by Lawrence C. Dodd and Bruce I. Oppenheimer, Washington, DC: *Congressional Quarterly*; and 2) Robert S. Erikson, "The Advantage of Incumbency in Congressional Elections," *Polity*, Vol. 3, No. 3, spring 1971, pp. 395–405, www.jstor.org/stable/3234117.

23. See: 1) "Common Sense Reforms for Ohio," Common Cause, Washington, DC. www .commoncause.org/site/pp.asp?c=dkLNK1MQIwG&b=880499; 2) Dale A. Oesterle, "Ohio's Dramatic Citizen Initiative: Reform Ohio Now," *Election Law & Moritz*, The Ohio State University, October 11, 2005, http://moritzlaw.osu.edu/electionlaw/comments/2005/051011.php; and 3) Justin Levitt and Kahlil Williams, "Analysis of Ohio Redistricting Reform Proposals," Brennan Center for Justice, Washington, DC, http://brennan.3cdn.net/91ba3aebb92ae728b2_ fqm6bxb8w.pdf.

24. See "Building a National Redistricting Reform Movement," Redistricting Conference Report, of the League of Women Voters, the Campaign Legal Center, and Council for Excellence in Government, Salt Lake City, April, 2006, www.americansforredistrictingreform.org/ html/documents/SLCRedistrictingReportFINAL.pdf.

25. H. J. R. 13, 126th General Assembly, introduced by Representative Richard L. DeWine, Bill Analysis, Ohio Legislative Services Commission, http://lsc.state.oh.us/analyses/ analysis126.nsf/c68a7e88e02f43a985256dad004e48aa/ddcf66b54f0ee0cc8525716b005097 23?OpenDocument.

26. See: 1) "Redistricting Reform Comparison," www.ohiocitizen.org/money/redistrict/ comparison.pdf, linked from *Money in Politics*, Ohio Citizen Action, 2009, www.ohiocitizen .org/money/redistrict.html; and 2) Mark Naymik, "Redistricting proposals abound in Ohio," *The Plain Dealer*, Cleveland.com, March 23, 2009, www.cleveland.com/news/plaindealer/ index.ssf?/base/cuyahoga/1237797110279300.xml&coll=2.

27. See Mark Salling, "Public Participation Geographic Information Systems for Redistricting: A Case Study in Ohio," *Journal of the Urban and Regional Information Systems Association*, Vol. 23: Issue 1, 2011, pp. 33–40, www.urisa.org/files/2011%20URISA%20Journal%20 Vol%2023%20Issue%201_1.pdf.

28. See www.midwestdemocracynetwork.org/index.php/about_the_network.

29. It should also be pointed out that Secretary of State Jon Husted also established an Internet site where citizens could suggest state legislative district boundaries.

30. Sabrina Eaton, "Ohio Supreme Court orders secretary of state to consider referendum vote on new Ohio Congressional maps," *The Plain Dealer*, Cleveland.com, October 14, 2011, www.cleveland.com/open/index.ssf/2011/10/ohio_supreme_court_orders_refe.html. A running and relatively up-to-date summary of the redistricting situation in Ohio is found at http://ballotpedia.org/wiki/index.php/Redistricting_in_Ohio.

31. See Aaron Marshall, "Ohio lawmakers reach deal on congressional redistricting and single primary election (updated)," *The Plain Dealer*, Cleveland.com, December 15, 2011, www.cleveland.com/open/index.ssf/2011/12/ohio_lawmakers_could_be_close.html.

32. Page 4 of Lynda J. Jacobsen, *Members Only*, Volume 129, Issue 1, revised July 15, 2011, Ohio Legislative Services Commission, www.lsc.state.oh.us/membersonly/129Congressional districts.pdf.

33. Sandy Fitzgerald, "Ohio Democrats Sue over Redistricting Map," Newsmax, January 2, 2012. www.newsmax.com/TheWire/Ohio-redistricting-lawsuit/2012/01/06/id/423216.

34. Jim Siegel, "Husted says he's ready to help lawmakers find new map process," *The Columbus Dispatch*, January 11, 2012, www.dispatchpolitics.com/content/blogs/the-daily -briefing/2012/01/1-11-12-husted-redistrict.html.

16

Raw Political Power, Gerrymandering, and the Illusion of Fairness

The Pennsylvania Redistricting Process, 2001 and 2011[1]

Harry C. "Neil" Strine IV

"Controversial" and "gerrymandered" are the best words used to describe the results of Pennsylvania's congressional redistricting process in 2001 and in 2011. The process probably would not have been as controversial during these cycles had Pennsylvania not lost seats in Congress. However, the past two redistricting cycles in Pennsylvania have resulted in a loss of three members of the House of Representatives—two following the 2000 census and the loss of one seat after the 2010 census. On December 14, 2011, the Pennsylvania State Senate passed Senate Bill 1249, "an act apportioning this commonwealth into congressional districts in conformity with constitutional requirements; providing for the nomination and election of congressmen; and requiring publication of notice of the establishment of congressional districts following the federal decennial census" by a 26–24 margin. The Pennsylvania House of Representatives passed Senate Bill 1249 on December 20, 2011, and Governor Tom Corbett signed the bill into law as Act 131 on December 22, 2011, officially establishing 18 congressional districts in the Commonwealth of Pennsylvania.

Newspapers and political critics from Pennsylvania and around the country did not wait for House passage to criticize Pennsylvania's congressional redistricting bill. Dr. Terry Madonna, an expert on Pennsylvania politics and political science professor at Franklin and Marshall College in Lancaster, Pennsylvania, made a remarkable assessment of the new 2012 redistricting law in the Sunday, December 18 edition of the online version of the *Harrisburg Patriot-News*. Dr. Madonna called the new congressional redistricting law "the most gerrymandered map I've seen in modern history in our state. . . . I'm not suggesting that we ever had bizarre looking districts before; but we never had this many."[2] The online news source newsworks.org, an affiliate of the Wilmington PBS radio station WHYY, reported on December 8, 2011, that "Pennsylvania is something of a poster child for partisan gerrymandering. One survey, by the Philadelphia-based data mapping firm

Azavea, concluded the state's current congressional map is the second-most gerry-mandered in the nation."[3] The headline of an article from Real Clear Politics.com stated "In Pennsylvania, the Gerrymander of the Decade?" in which the author, Sean Trende, took Pennsylvania lawmakers to task for taking a state with a 2–3 percentage point Democratic voter advantage and creating 12 out of 18 congressional districts that are more Republican than the rest of the country. The *Harrisburg Patriot-News* Editorial Board chose "PA Congressional map is ridiculous and we will live with it for the next 10 years" as its editorial headline in the Thursday, December 15, 2011, edition of Pennlive.com.[4] The loss of two congressional seats in Pennsylvania following the 2000 census was just as controversial, perhaps more so, than the latest round of congressional redistricting.

The 2001 congressional redistricting process in Pennsylvania resulted in a federal court case that made it all the way to the United States Supreme Court. The Supreme Court case, *Vieth v. Jubelirer* (2004), included registered Democratic voters Norma Jean and Richard Vieth and Susan Furey who claimed that the 2000 Pennsylvania redistricting law, Act 1, establishing the new congressional districts, violated the one-person, one vote concept in Article 1, Section 2 of the Constitution, the Equal Protection Clause, the Privileges and Immunities Clause, and the Freedom of Association.

2010 STATE DEMOGRAPHIC TRENDS

Since the 2000 congressional redistricting, the population in Pennsylvania has shifted to the East. Southwestern Pennsylvania, including Pittsburgh, has lost residents while central Pennsylvania and the Lehigh Valley have grown in numbers. The Philadelphia area has remained relatively unchanged. Each of the 18 new congressional districts will have a population of about 705,688 people. According to Thomas Fitzgerald, writing for the March 16, 2011, edition of the *Philadelphia Inquirer*, "Four of the five existing districts with the lowest population numbers statewide are in the West: the 14th represented by Democrat Mike Doyle; the 12th, home to Democrat Mark Critz; and the 4th, home to Democrat Jason Altmire. Republican Mike Kelly's Third district, in Northwestern Pennsylvania, also shrank. Democrat Chaka Fattah's Philadelphia-based 2nd District has the third lowest population numbers in the state."[5] The fastest growing congressional districts include Jim Gerlach in the 6th, Joseph Pitts in the 16th, and Todd Platts in the 19th Congressional District.[6]

The 2010 census figures for Pennsylvania confirm these population trends within the Commonwealth. The city of Philadelphia has a population of 1,526,006 and grew by a scant 0.6 percent since 2000. Pittsburgh, with a population of 305,704, witnessed a population reduction of 8.6 percent, and Erie, a city with almost 102,000 residents declined in population by 1.6 percent. While the Western part of the state saw population declines, the cities in the East such as Allentown and Reading, saw population increases of 10.7 percent and 8.5 percent respectfully.

FORMAL REDISTRICTING PROCESS WITHIN THE STATE

Pennsylvania's redistricting process is no different than passing any other piece of legislation. Following the decennial federal census, the Commonwealth is provided with their number of House districts from the federal government. According to the Pennsylvania Redistricting Website, "Congressional redistricting plans have historically been referred to each chamber's state government committee." When the government committees agree on a redistricting plan, the bill must be passed through the Pennsylvania House of Representatives and the Pennsylvania Senate and then signed into law by the governor. The state legislative redistricting process, by contrast, is specifically outlined by Article 2, Section 17 of the Pennsylvania Constitution. Article 2, Section 17 requires a five person "Legislative Reapportionment Commission" consisting of the four caucus chairpersons in the General Assembly plus a chairperson to be selected by these leaders or by the Pennsylvania Supreme Court.[7] This commission-style state legislative redistricting process has been in effect since 1968. Ivey DeJesus, writing for pennlive.com, the online version of the *Harrisburg Patriot-News*, noted on January 29, 2012, "The congressional redistricting happened much more swiftly than the General Assembly's, and with much less transparency."[8] Outside of the federal requirements for congressional districts, the Commonwealth of Pennsylvania does not have a formal process any different than the passing of a regular piece of legislation. The General Assembly is not required to hold any public hearings, form a nonpartisan commission, or take any special action for congressional redistricting. Pennsylvania does not make any attempt to keep congressional redistricting from becoming a political power show. The majority party in control of the Pennsylvania government has a "carte blanche" in drawing congressional districts.

Each of the four caucuses in the Pennsylvania state government—the House Republicans, House Democrats, Senate Republicans, and Senate Democrats—all maintained Redistricting Offices in the Capitol Building for both the 2001 and 2011 redistricting processes. Each redistricting office was headed by a political appointee, and their office coordinated all activities in regarding the redistricting process.

DISCUSSION OF HOW THE PROCESS WENT IN THE WAKE OF THE 2000 CENSUS

The 2001 redistricting process in Pennsylvania gained national attention. Following the 2000 election in which George W. Bush won the White House and Republicans captured control of both houses of Congress, the Republicans had a tenuous 11-seat advantage in the House of Representatives—222–211. Thomas Edsall, in a January 6, 2002, issue of the *Washington Post* reported that "NRCC Chairman Thomas M. Davis III (VA) and Karl Rove, senior adviser to President Bush, pressed the Pennsylvania legislators to approve a plan with the most Republican gains as part of the effort to retain GOP control of the House."[9] According to the same article, the

Pennsylvania redistricting plan in 2000 was expected to change the congressional delegation from an 11–10 majority to a 13–6 majority.

Given these national conditions, Pennsylvania was especially critical because the Commonwealth would lose 2 seats following the 2000 census, but both the Pennsylvania governor and General Assembly were in Republican hands. The Republicans controlling the Pennsylvania legislature, and thus, the new congressional map, sought to redraw the congressional districts that would attempt to maintain the precarious 11-seat majority for the Republican Party in the United States House of Representatives.

As stated previously, the 2001 redistricting process in Pennsylvania resulted in a federal court case that made its way to the United States Supreme Court in the 2004 case of *Vieth v. Jubelirer*. This federal court case began in the United States District Court for the Middle District of Pennsylvania in Harrisburg as *Vieth v. Commonwealth of Pennsylvania*. The District Court decision provided the background of the case.

On November 16, 2001, Senators Brightbill and Lemmond, both Republican members of the chamber, introduced Pennsylvania Senate Bill no. 1200. Members of the Democratic minority, State Senators Mellow, O'Pake, Wagner, Musto, Kasunic, Fumo, and Stout, introduced a competing redistricting bill, Senate Bill no. 1241. In December 2001, the Pennsylvania State Senate considered amendments to the Republican-backed redistricting bill, and eventually passed Senate Bill no. 1200. The redistricting plan that passed the Pennsylvania State Senate contained a population deviation of 24 people between the most and least populated congressional districts in the state. The Federal District Court for the Middle District of Pennsylvania reported further facts of the case in their per curiam opinion:

> After an amendment by the House of Representatives, that chamber passed Senate Bill 1200 on December 12, 2001. The version of Senate Bill no. 1200 that passed the House had a total population deviation of nineteen persons. It also maintained two minority-majority districts in the Philadelphia area, created one open seat in the Southeastern part of the Commonwealth and paired two Democratic incumbents in the same district. One Democratic Incumbent was paired against one Republican incumbent. The Senate refused to concur in the amendments to Senate Bill 1200 offered by the House of Representatives. A Conference Committee was appointed and a plan was eventually devised that contained a nineteen person deviation. This Conference Committee Report on Senate Bill no. 1200 was passed by the Senate on January 3, 2002 and by the House of Representatives on the same day.[10]

Governor Mark Schweiker signed Senate Bill 1200 (Act1) into law on January 7, 2002, establishing Pennsylvania's new congressional districts as per the results of the 2000 census. As reported by the *Washington Post*, the Federal District Court noted the conversations occurring between officials at the federal level with the state lawmakers in Harrisburg after the impasse between the Pennsylvania State House and the Pennsylvania State Senate in December 2001:

In the meantime, prominent national figures in the Republican party—such as congressional Speaker of the House Dennis Hastert, Congressman Thomas R. Davis III, United States Senator Rick Santorum, and Karl Rove, political consultant to current President George W. Bush—began pressuring Governor Schweiker, a Republican, and the Republican members of the General Assembly to adopt the Senate redistricting plan as a punitive measure against Democrats for having enacted apparently pro-Democrat redistricting plans in other states. . . . In the process, they effectively ignored all members of the General Assembly, including members of the Conference Committee appointed to resolve the impasse between the competing plans.[11]

The plaintiffs in this case, Richard and Norma Jean Vieth, both lived in Lebanon County, in a portion of the county that would fall into the new congressional district, district no. 16. The other plaintiff, Susan Furey, lived in the 13th Congressional District, but was now in the new 6th Congressional District according to Act 1. The plaintiffs sued because the 19 congressional districts did not have equal population. According to the Federal District Court for the Middle District of Pennsylvania, equal division of Pennsylvania's 12,281,054 population over 19 districts equals 646,371 or 646,372 people per district. Under Act 1 signed by Governor Schweiker, the population of congressional districts 1, 2, and 17 would have a population of 646,361 and the new 7th Congressional District would have a population of 646,380, a difference of 19 people. The Court found Act 1 unconstitutional because the legislature had considered a plan that provided for no deviation in population. House Democratic Leader, William DeWeese, was quoted as saying, "Any third grader with five minutes to spare could look at the Republican reapportionment map and know that somebody was up to no good."[12]

Justice Antonin Scalia noted that the Plaintiffs complained that the Pennsylvania General Assembly passed a redistricting law in which "prominent national figures in the Republican Party pressured the general assembly to adopt a partisan redistricting plan as a punitive measure against Democrats for having enacted pro-Democrat redistricting plans elsewhere."[13] The Federal District Court for the Middle District of Pennsylvania only found the 2000 redistricting law unconstitutional because it violated the one-man, one-vote principle "because it was possible to create districts with smaller differences" in population from one another. The United States Supreme Court decided not to intervene in this case.[14]

On April 9, 2002, Representatives Perzel and Ryan introduced House Bill no. 2545 to amend Act no. 1 to conform with the Federal District Court decision for the Middle District of Pennsylvania. The Pennsylvania General Assembly later passed a law to remedy the uneven populations in each of the congressional districts in response to the Federal District Court's decision. The law became Act 34 of 2002, and it served as the controlling legislation for Pennsylvania's congressional districts from 2002 through 2011. Aside from the obvious national political implications of the 2001 Pennsylvania redistricting, the reaction from newspapers, pundits, and others was less than flattering for the new congressional districts drawn by the legislature in 2001.

Although the Republican-dominated Pennsylvania legislature set up a 12–7 edge in favor of the Republicans following the 2002 redistricting, this advantage did not last long. After the 2006 and 2008 congressional elections, the Pennsylvania delegation to the U.S. House of Representatives flipped to a 12–7 advantage for the Democrats. Republicans regained their five-seat majority in the delegation following the 2010 midterm elections. Thomas Fitzgerald in the *Philadelphia Inquirer* summed up the calculated strategy of redistricting the best, "It just goes to show, experts say, that redistricting is unpredictable, subject to many variables."[15]

AN EXAMINATION OF THE
2011 CONGRESSIONAL REDISTRICTING PROCESS

The 2011 Pennsylvania congressional redistricting process began on March 9, 2011, when the United States Census Bureau released the Pennsylvania population data to the state legislature. The 2011 process was, at least from the perspective of Republican state lawmakers, one of the most transparent redistricting procedures in Pennsylvania's history. On August 18, 2011, the office of Senator Dominic Pileggi, the Senate Republican majority leader, issued a press release announcing the launch of the first-ever Pennsylvania redistricting website that would provide the public with information on both state and congressional redistricting. Senator Pileggi's news release declares, "I hope this website leads to greater public involvement in the redistricting process. It's a great tool to contact the Commission, learn the basics of redistricting, and stay informed as the Legislative Reapportionment Commission's work progresses."[16] Furthermore, Pileggi claims that Pennsylvania's redistricting website is just one of many actions the legislature has taken in recent years to be more open to the public. "This is another step forward in our ongoing effort to change the culture of Pennsylvania state government. In recent years, we have rewritten the Right-To-Know Law and created an office of Open Records, created a searchable e-library of state contracts, strengthened the Sunshine Law, and passed a law creating an online database for the state budget."[17] The redistricting website contains valuable information for Pennsylvania residents and any other interested observer. The website contains regular updates on the redistricting process, including dates and times of public hearings, links to census data and redistricting court decisions, as well as links to interactive maps outlining the 1991, 2001, and 2011 congressional districts in Pennsylvania. Users may, for example, click on the Pennsylvania map and then have the website overlay the 2011 district lines on top of the 2001 lines and the 1991 congressional district boundaries. This tool allows anyone to see how the shape of each Pennsylvania congressional district has changed over the past three congressional redistricting procedures, 1991, 2001, and 2011. In addition to viewing the congressional districts, users may choose to add county, municipal, and school district boundaries to the map to determine the extent to which the congressional districts follow these political subdivisions. The website is also a clearinghouse for all of the available data used to draw the district lines. Anyone with the appropriate software may download the various state, census, and other data used by the state to draw the district boundaries from the website. For example, anyone interested in viewing geographic and/or geospatial maps may do so from this website. Finally, the text of all appropriate redistricting legislation since 1991 is accessible from this helpful website.

It is important to note, however, that the redistricting website was released on August 18, 2011, almost three months after the first legislative hearing on congressional redistricting and more than two months after the final state legislative hearing in Harrisburg. However, the dates for the joint State Senate and House Government legislative hearings were posted on the Pennsylvania House Government Committee's website. Unless the residents of Pennsylvania were specifically looking for this website, which was not easy to find, they would not know these legislative hearings were being held. It is unlikely that many Pennsylvanians would know which committee or committees would be responsible for drawing the congressional districts in the first place.

The Pennsylvania State Senate Government Committee and the Pennsylvania House Government Committee held a total of three joint hearings in 2011 to get public input in the redrawing of congressional lines following the 2010 census. The joint hearings took place on May 12, 2011 at the Philadelphia Convention Center, on June 9 at the Cranberry Township Municipal Building, near Pittsburgh; and on June 14, 2011, in Harrisburg at the North Office Building on the Capitol complex. The Senate and House government committees traveled to the eastern and western portions of the Commonwealth for public input on how the Commonwealth should draw the 18 congressional district lines. As discussed earlier, the Pennsylvania redistricting process is purely political in nature, yet the theme of the testimony from the joint hearings, from both the legislators and the witnesses, was that this needs to be a fair and impartial process. It is interesting to note that no public hearings were held during the 2001 redistricting process. The Republican leaders of the government committees, members of the majority party, especially stressed the need for transparency, fairness, and balance in their public statements.

In his opening comments at the Philadelphia hearing, Senator Charles T. McIlhinney, the Republican chairman of the Senate Government Committee, stated, "It's never an easy thing to do, to draw lines on a map, but we want to do this in as most open and transparent manner as possible. And with that in mind, we are going to embark on a number of these hearings, have input from interested parties, from individual citizens across Pennsylvania, take that information that we gather and then proceed to attempt to draw fair and balanced maps for our congressional districts in Pennsylvania. And at the end of the testimony, we're also going to open this up for public comment, if anybody who wanted to make a few comments concerning what the process should be when we draw the maps."[18] Similarly, Representative Daryl Metcalfe, the Republican chairman of the House Government Committee, appealed for fairness and transparency in his opening statement as well. "Ultimately our objective is to make sure that the product will be one that's legal, and one that's fair. It's reassuring that we have one vote for one person. So I look forward to the testimony that we're going to hear this morning, and we'll hear over the next two hearings."[19] Most, if not all of the hearing witnesses appealed to the idea of fairness and equality in the drawing of the district lines. The other members of the Joint House and Senate Committee present at the May 12 hearing included Representative Tim Brigs, Senator Andrew Dinniman, Representative Glenn R. Grell, Representative Marcia M. Hahn, Representative Jerry Knowles, Representative T. Mark Mustio, Representative Jerry Stern, and Senator Tina Tartaglione.

A total of seven witnesses testified at the May 12, 2011, hearing representing a variety of public interests: The League of Women Voters of Pennsylvania, Kitchen Table Patriots, the American Civil Liberties Union of Pennsylvania, the Philadelphia Jewish Voice, the City of Philadelphia Commission on Human Relations, and a representative from the Asian Pacific American Bar Association. The hearing itself only lasted about 45 minutes. The witnesses addressed a wide variety of concerns and made several suggestions to the members of the Joint Government Committee. Lora Lavin, the vice president for Issues and Action for the League of Women Voters of Pennsylvania, took the opportunity of her testimony to push the lawmakers for reform of the process. Lavin stated that the League of Women Voters supported any redistricting reform that would not "remain under the control of incumbent legislators and the legislative leadership."[20] More specifically, the League of Women Voters called for specific changes such as requiring districts to be compact and contiguous, providing public access to computer software that citizens could use on their own to come up with proposed maps, make data available to the public on the Internet that will be used to draft the redistricting plans, and make all communications between the mapmakers and outside parties public regarding any plan. To discourage gerrymandering, Ms. Lavin suggested that the committee avoid the use of party identification, voting histories, and location of any incumbent officials to draw the district lines. The League of Women Voters, as a nonpartisan organization, stressed fairness and balance to draw the lines. At the conclusion of Ms. Lavin's testimony there was discussion among the committee about the use of computer programs to draw congressional districts that would eliminate party bias.

The second witness was Anastasia Przybylski of the grassroots organization, Kitchen Table Patriots. Just before delivering her opening statement, Ms. Przybylski informed the panel that an Internet redistricting game was available on the Internet, at the redistrictinggame.com. Ms. Przybylski noted, "It's a game to show how convoluted this redistricng can be. Like if you want to make it more Republican or more Democratic, you can make your own maps. And anyway, it was actually fun." Przybylski approached the redistricting process as a concerned member of the community about how the redistricting process in Pennsylvania will turn out:

> I got involved with politics in early 2009 and I thought I could make a difference, and since then I've knocked on more doors, made more phone calls, and put up more signs than I could have ever imagined, which brings me here today to testify about the redis-

tricting process. Can I really make a difference, or is the process rigged? . . . For years, the manipulation of district lines has occurred to pack districts with like-minded voters, or dilute the voting power of one group or another. This has undermined the very spirit of a fair democratic election. These tactics harm the very electoral process, and undermine our Constitution. Voters should select their representatives, not the other way around.

The third witness at the hearing was Andy Hoover, the Legislative Director for the American Civil Liberties Union of Pennsylvania. Hoover reminded the committee about their responsibilities under the Federal Voting Rights Act and the Fourteenth Amendment's equal protection clause and "one person, one vote principle." The primary concern of the American Civil Liberties Union of Pennsylvania, according to Hoover, is to ensure "minority representation" and "transparency in the process." During an exchange with the joint committee Hoover reinforced the suggestion that was made by the previous witnesses to utilize technology as a way to make the redistricting process as fair as possible.

A representative from the *Philadelphia Jewish Voice*—an online volunteer, non-profit newspaper—appeared as the fourth witness before the panel. As with the previous witnesses, Dr. Daniel Loeb testified against gerrymandering district lines. "Unfortunately, we have grown used to a system of gerrymandering, which turns democracy upside-down so that it is politicians who choose the voters strategically in order to advance their own personal interests, rather than the other way around." Loeb indicated that the *Philadelphia Jewish Voice*, the League of Women Voters of Pennsylvania, and other groups were planning to hold a redistricting competition like those held in other states where members of the public may submit proposed congressional maps using various computer programs such as Azavea's "District Builder." Loeb informed the committee, again, that programs such as "The Redistricting Game.Com," "Dave's Redistricting App," and "Azavea's District Builder" would allow public input into the redistricting process. The entries would be judged based on "impartial and numerical criteria, measuring equality, continuity, integrity, competitiveness, proportionality, and compactness."

It is important to note that during the exchange with Dr. Loeb of the *Philadelphia Jewish Voice*, Senator Charles T. McIlhinney made a key statement regarding gerrymandering and the general process of redistricting. In responding to the fact that Pennsylvania's congressional delegation had a majority of Republicans despite having 4.1 million registered Democrats versus 3 million registered Republicans in Pennsylvania, McIlhinney explained that things change. "But I also want to point out that that last map was drawn by a Republican controlled legislature when they had a majority of Republicans, and a few years after that it flipped, there was a majority of Democratic Congressmen in Pennsylvania, which flipped back again. So just because you're drawing data and we should simply draw for Democrats and Republicans, people change." Following Dr. Loeb's testimony, Senator McIlhinney recognized Kay Yu, the chairperson of the Commission on Human Relations for the city of Philadelphia, for attending the hearing; however, she did not provide any public testimony.

The sixth witness to appear before the Joint House and Senate Government Committee in Philadelphia was Don Adams, who was associated with the Independence Hall Tea Party Association, representing tea party members from Pennsylvania, New Jersey, and Delaware. It is worth noting that Mr. Adams was the only witness at the Philadelphia hearing to recognize the *political* nature of the PA redistricting process. "We don't expect you to draw perfect districts or perfect boundaries. We realize that this is a serious business and it's a matter that does involve political inclinations and proclivities."[21] Furthermore, Adams suggests that the Republicans do have the advantage in this round of redistricting and that the district map will reflect this advantage. Having made this point, however, Adams implored the committee to avoid drawing "outrageous" districts like the current district that covers Johnstown, Pennsylvania. According to Adams, Congressman Critz's district "almost looks like—kind of like a constellation of stars or a solar system, whatever, but it's a mess, and we think that should be avoided."[22] The final witness at the Philadelphia hearing, Stella Tsai, is a litigation partner at a Philadelphia law firm who appeared as the president of the Asian Pacific Bar Association. Tsai reminded the panel that the Asian American population is one of the fastest growing groups in Pennsylvania and in Philadelphia, in particular, and should not be splintered in the new congressional districts. According to Tsai, the Supreme Court decision of *Miller v. Johnson* "requires that you have several factors in redistricting, including communities of interest" such as the Asian American population.[23]

The second hearing of the Joint Senate and House State Government Committee took place at the Cranberry Township Municipal Building in Cranberry Township, Pennsylvania (near Pittsburgh), on Thursday, June 9, 2011, and featured 14 witnesses. Five of the 14 witnesses were current county commissioners representing five counties in western Pennsylvania. The witness list also included a representative from a Tea Party organization, Dave Battaglia, the Director of Taxpayers United for Representation Now (TURN), a Republican committeeperson from Armstrong County, and other interested private citizens.

In addition to the House and Senate chairs, seven members of the State House of Representatives attended the hearing, including Representatives George Dunbar, Eli Evankovitch, Matt Gabler, Glenn R. Grell, Seth Grove, Timothy Krieger, and Brad Roae. This second hearing began very similarly as the Philadelphia hearing with both Representative Metcalfe and Senator McIlhinney stressing their efforts to make the process of drawing new district lines as transparent and fair as possible. After Representative Metcalfe's opening statement, Senator McIlhinney defended the process:

> A lot of criticism has been thrown our way of how we do this process, but we're really making a true, honest effort to be very public and forthcoming with this process. At the end of the day, lines are drawn on a map and everybody is not happy, but we're trying to do this in a process that you can clearly see how we're doing, put it together as best as possible, knowing full well that we're not going to make everyone happy at the end of the day. But we're endeavoring to do it, and I'm excited to continue this process.[24]

The first two witnesses at the western Pennsylvania hearing were experts on the redistricting process. Dr. Michael McDonald, Associate Professor at George Mason University and Non-Resident Senior Fellow at the Brookings Institution, and Dr. Jennifer Nicoll Victor, Assistant Professor of Political Science at the University of Pittsburgh, discussed the legal and technical requirements of redistricting.

McDonald, who had also been a redistricting consultant for 7 states since the 1980s, addressed the panel via Skype technology from George Mason University. He is also a researcher for "The Public Mapping Project," which is an organization that encourages public participation in redistricting projects. More specifically, publicmapping.org allows the public to use the same data and tools that state legislatures have to draw districts. McDonald stressed the importance of public participation in the process in his testimony:

> Because when the public is shut out of this process, and when their representational needs are not met, there are actually some very important detrimental effects that can happen to democracy when the public is not represented very well by a redistricting plan. We know on the academic side that when districts are splitting up communities, when they're splitting political boundaries, we know that we have lower turnout because people don't know their representatives as well, they have lower name recognition, and as I said, leads to other detrimental effects.[25]

Dr. McDonald also warned the panel of legislators not to divide a community or political subdivision into too many pieces because it makes it difficult for that community to request assistance from their legislator. In California, according to McDonald, one community was divided into five different districts, and none of the elected officials "felt like they actually represented it," and so the community did not get the economic development they were hoping for because none of the representatives felt like they were the "advocate" for that specific community.[26]

The second witness at the Cranberry Township meeting was Dr. Jennifer Nicoll Victor, assistant professor in the Department of Political Science at the University of Pittsburgh. Dr. Victor reviewed the two main constitutional and statutory requirements district maps must satisfy. First, according to the Supreme Court in its 1964 case, *Wesberry v. Sanders*, congressional districts must have equal populations "to the extent practicable." Secondly, according to the Voting Rights Act of 1965, "race cannot be the predominant factor in the shape of a district, unless the state can show a compelling reason to do so."[27] Victor also spoke about how districts should be contiguous, compact, and preserve political and geographic boundaries of communities. Dr. Victor indicated in her testimony that the most important factors in drawing congressional lines are to have equal population in each district and to have a standard threshold for compactness.

In her exchange with Representative Matt Gabler, Dr. Victor explained that she had no evidence that computer-drawn maps are any better than human-drawn maps and that ultimately the political climate of a state will determine whether

the congressional map will be challenged in court. Professor Victor is the only witness in the Cranberry Township hearing to acknowledge that the legislature will
ultimately draw a map based on politics and was the second witness in the first two
hearings to recognize this idea:

> Redistricting is a political process. Those who would come to you and say take the poli-
> tics out of this process, I would say there is no way to do that. It is impossible to make
> redistricting an apolitical process. You are a political body, you are drawing lines that
> affect another political body. There is no way to take the politics out of this process. So
> that being said, I think it's most important to make the process as absolutely transparent
> as possible, do nothing in secret, do everything in the public, make every stage as open
> as possible, and that way the steps that you follow and the outcome that you produce is
> less likely to be challenged.[28]

While the May 12 Joint Hearing in Philadelphia could be characterized as a forum
for interest groups with testimony from The League of Women Voters, the American
Civil Liberty Association, and others, the Cranberry Township hearing featured significant number of county commissioners from western Pennsylvania as witnesses.
This is significant because, as mentioned above, western Pennsylvania had lost the
most population since the 2000 census and would most likely be the area of the
Commonwealth to see the biggest changes in the congressional districts. In order to
eliminate a congressional district, the state legislature would need to take population
from one district and add some of the population from another district. The western
counties, due to their population loss, would be most susceptible to the addition of
or the subtraction of municipalities in order to have a roughly equal population in
each congressional district. One or more commissioners from Armstrong, Butler,
Lawrence, Warren, and Indiana counties lined up at the microphone to urge fairness,
and, most importantly, to avoid dividing the western counties and municipalities
between different members of Congress.

Commissioner James Kennedy from Butler County strongly recommended that
since Butler County was one of the fastest growing counties, the state legislature
needs to keep the entire county within the same congressional district. Commissioner Steve Craig of Lawrence County made the same argument as James Kennedy in terms of keeping Lawrence County as one unit in a new congressional
district. Craig noted how Lawrence County provides free office space to their congressman and this office is open two to three days per week to provide services to
their citizens, especially to the elderly with Social Security and Veterans' benefits.
More specifically, according to Craig, "Should the county be divided up into two
or more districts, it is highly unlikely that this level of service could be provided.
Our situation today is ideal. We ask that you do everything in your power to allow
the residents of Lawrence County to continue the high levels of service that they
have become accustomed to."[29]

Rodney Ruddock, chairman of the Indiana County Board of Commissioners, and
John Bortz, a Warren County Commissioner, both testified that having multiple

members of Congress is workable for their counties. Ruddock testified that "Indiana County has well-served congressional representation from both District 9 and District 12. Presently, Congressman Bill Shuster and Congressman Mark Critz are equally committed to serving the constituents of the county, oftentimes beyond their defined district boundaries."[30] Ruddock later qualifies his statement by encouraging the members of the Joint Committee to avoid drawing a congressional boundary down the center line of Main Street, such as the current situation in Indiana, Pennsylvania, where the center line of Philadelphia Street, the main street in town, is the dividing line between the 9th and 12th districts. Bortz supported the division of his county, if necessary, and pointed to the success of having more than one representative defend the interests of the Allegheny National Forest that is partially in Warren County.

John Eggleston, the chairman of the Warren County Board of Commissioners, provided the most interesting testimony at the Cranberry Township hearing, approaching the redistricting process from a much different perspective than his fellow county commissioners. Eggleston acknowledges the "cynicism and apathy that has affected the voting process throughout this country over the last few decades" with voter turnout around 20 percent. Further, Eggleston argues that there is also apathy and cynicism toward the whole political system, including at the local levels of government. Any gerrymandering by the state legislature will simply increase the levels of cynicism and apathy among the people:

> Every time someone bends the political process to gain an advantage or hamper someone else's chances for success, the whole process is hurt. That is one of the reasons I would hope there is little or no gerrymandering involved in this process. There are too many people already who have little or no faith in the system and use that as an excuse to not get involved in the process. We've all heard the common refrains: My vote doesn't count; the system is rigged; it doesn't matter, the politicians are just going to do whatever they want. Every time anything happens that puts a blemish on political leaders or the process itself, it also contributes to apathy and cynicism that in my mind represent a far greater threat to our way of life than al-Qaida ever will.[31]

Eggleston's second point is that gerrymandering does not necessarily predict which party's candidate will win the election due to the rise of the independent voter and it also depends on the quality of the candidate:

> The days of gerrymandering a district for a particular result are past us, as election after election proves. The days when almost all the voters automatically pulled the party lever have gone the way of the dodo bird. There will always be those voters that automatically pull the party lever, but it seems that number gets smaller and smaller each election. The point is that having credible, effective candidate will always be the best way to win an election. . . . I believe that the modern voter has made the process of gerrymandering outdated and unnecessary.[32]

Finally, Commissioner Eggleston testified that having two members of Congress for Warren County was actually beneficial because, "What we discovered is that as long as we have good congressmen or women and their staffs are effective, we actually have twice as many advocates for things that affect all of the county."[33]

The final witness at this hearing was Dave Battaglia, a Republican candidate for Armstrong County Commissioner who is also a member of the Indiana Armstrong Patriots, a tea party group. Battaglia urged the committee to place Armstrong County in just one congressional district. Mr. Battaglia highlighted the irregularity of how the 12th and 3rd Congressional Districts are divided in Armstrong County in his testimony before the panel:

> If you're coming on 28 North from Pittsburgh and you merge onto the 422 East exit ramp and enter onto 422, you will be in Buffalo Township, and you will be in the 3rd Congressional District. After two miles, you enter Manor Township and will be in the 12th Congressional District. And as you travel another 3 miles, you will enter Kittanning Township and be in the 3rd Congressional District. After you travel another 5 miles, you will be in Plum Creek Township and back in the 12th Congressional District. So, in the span of 10 miles, and never leaving one roadway, US 422, you've changed congressional districts four times. The 12th District clearly is drawn as irregular as any district in the United States.[34]

The Cranberry Township hearing concluded at 12:52 p.m., lasting about two hours, the longest of the three joint hearings held by the State Senate and House committees. The Cranberry Township hearing also included the most witnesses of any of the three hearings.

The third and final joint hearing for the state's congressional redistricting process took place at 9 AM on June 14, 2011, in Hearing Room no. 1 of the North Office Building on the Capitol grounds in Harrisburg, central Pennsylvania. A total of three witnesses appeared before the Joint committee, including Barry Kauffman, executive director of Common Cause Pennsylvania and two private citizens. One of the private citizens, the last witness in the hearing, testified on the matter of redistricting the state legislature rather than congressional redistricting. This final hearing lasted just 47 minutes.

Barry Kauffman's testimony was largely critical of the Pennsylvania congressional redistricting method. Kauffman, the first witness at the hearing, slammed the Pennsylvania redistricting practices of both the legislature and the courts:

> Pennsylvania is notable for both the ingenuity devoted to the creation of painfully convoluted legislative districts at the congressional and state legislative levels, and for the unwillingness of the Commonwealth's courts to respond favorably to the citizens' complaints about apparent gerrymandering. Arguably, the most recent Supreme Court decision regarding Pennsylvania's congressional districts, *Vieth v. Jubelirer* of 2004, potentially made the process worse than it already was by explicitly declaring that the redistricting process is currently nonjusticiable because of the lack of clear standards that would permit a determination of unacceptably political levels of gerrymandering.[35]

According to Mr. Kauffman, Common Cause does not support redistricting through the normal legislative process in the states. "Common Cause believes that this is a bad idea in that it both exposes legislators to pressure from federal politicians and involves the legislators in potential conflicts of interest as a result of voting on the form of districts in which they plan to run themselves someday."[36] Instead, redistricting should be conducted by an independent commission and include as much public participation as possible. Kauffman also noted that Pennsylvania needs to do a better job of respecting political subdivisions, such as county, township, and municipal boundaries. Kauffman outlines three main reasons why political subdivisions need to be respected. First, people need to know who their elected officials are and to be able to contact them. When people know who their legislator is, they are more likely to turn out to vote on Election Day. The second reason is because a politician will be less likely to pay attention to the needs of a small section of a town or borough than to the other, larger parts of the district. Finally, according to Kauffman, the more fractured districts make it more expensive and difficult for challengers to campaign, thus lessening the competitive nature of elections. As with other witnesses at the two previous hearings, Kauffman called on the legislature to utilize the various technologies available to help draw the legislative districts.

The second witness, Amanda Holt, a resident of Upper Macungie in Lehigh County near Allentown, testified that her voting precinct was separated from the township, the entire county, and was placed in a different congressional district. She urged the panel to keep "existing political subdivisions united" so that the people have "the strongest representation possible."[37] Ms. Holt presented her redistricting plan to the committee to deal with this issue. Representative Metcalfe and Senator McIlhinney appreciated Ms. Holt's concern for the issue. McIlhinney remarked, "First of all, I want to thank you and commend you for your involvement and getting involved. This is the exact type of testimony we're looking for today."[38]

Several themes emerged from the three Joint Hearings held by the House and Senate Government committees during May and June of 2011. First, both the hearing witnesses and the members of the Senate and House committees appealed in their statements for the need to have transparency, fairness, and equality in the process. Second, the overriding concern among the witnesses, of course, was to avoid gerrymandering at all costs within a state, according to Azavea, that is the second-most gerrymandered state in the country, behind only Georgia. Senator McIlhinney and other members of the Joint Committee repeatedly told the witnesses and the audiences at these hearings that this would be a difficult process and that they would do their best to draw a fair map. Senator McIlhinney and Representative Metcalfe appeared very sincere in the hearing rooms about their wish to make the redistricting process as transparent and as fair as possible. The third main idea running through these hearings was maintaining the integrity of the political subdivisions and racial groups within the Commonwealth. Finally, witnesses in each of the three hearings appealed to the joint committee to utilize computer technology in order to draw districts that were compact, contiguous, and have equal populations without regard to political party identification. No further public hearings were held regarding the Pennsylvania redistricting process. The proposed map passed by the Pennsylvania Senate was not published for public feedback prior to Senate action.

On June 23, 2011, the Pennsylvania Senate approved Senate Resolution 148 (SR 148), a concurrent resolution, to use the population data adopted by the Legislative Reapportionment Commission for congressional redistricting in Pennsylvania. The same Senate Resolution was adopted unanimously by the Pennsylvania House of Representatives by a 196–0 vote on June 26, 2011. This resolution makes the U.S. census data submitted to Pennsylvania the official population statistics for use in the Pennsylvania redistricting process. Senators Pileggi, Scarnatti, and McIlhinney sponsored Senate Bill no. 1249 which was referred to the Senate State Government Committee on September 14, 2011. This piece of legislation was passed by the State Senate on December 14, 2011, and reported to the House State Government Committee on the same day. The Pennsylvania House of Representatives passed Senate Bill no. 1249 on December 20, 2011, and then it was signed by the governor on December 22, 2011. At the time of writing this chapter there has not been any legal challenge to Pennsylvania's newly redrawn congressional district map (see maps 16.1 and 16.2).

AN ASSESSMENT OF THE EFFECTS
OF THE 2010 REDISTRICTING PROCESS

There have been several quantitative assessments of the 2010 Redistricting in Pennsylvania. Real Clear Politics examined the old and new district lines based on the two-party vote for President Obama in the 2008 presidential election (see tables 16.1 and 16.2). Trende notes, "The basic idea that guided the Republicans was this:

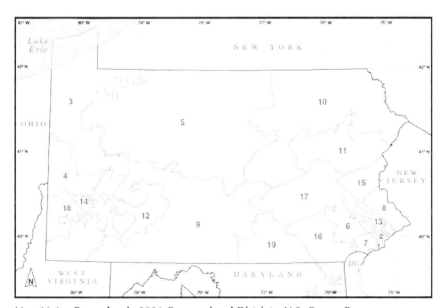

Map 16.1. Pennsylvania 2001 Congressional Districts. U.S. Census Bureau.

Proposed Congressional Districts

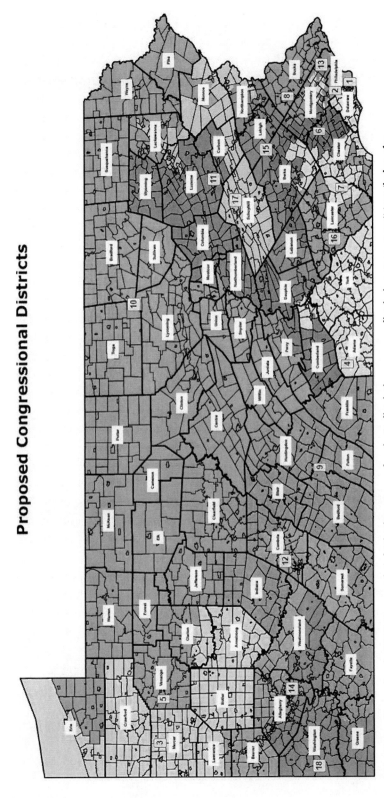

Map 16.2. Pennsylvania 2012 Congressional Districts. Pennsylvania Redistricting, www.redistricting.state.pa.us/Maps/index.cfm.

Table 16.1. Obama 2-Party Vote % under Old and New Pennsylvania Lines

District	Representative	New Obama %	Old Obama%	Shift in O 2PV
1	Brady (Dem.)	79.5%	88.2%	−8.7%
2	Fattah (Dem.)	91.1%	90.4%	.6%
3	Kelly (Rep.)	46.8%	50.0%	−3.2%
4 (old 19th)	Platts (Rep.)	45.6%	43.1%	2.5%
5	Thompson (Rep.)	48.0%	44.7%	3.3%
6	Gerlach (Rep.)	53.4%	58.4%	−4.9%
7	Meehan (Rep.)	51.8%	56.4%	−4.6%
8	Fitzpatrick (Rep.)	53.8%	54.5%	−.7%
9	Shuster (Rep.)	41.5%	35.9%	5.6%
10	Marino (Rep.)	42.9%	45.7%	−2.8%
11	Barletta (Rep.)	47.7%	57.5%	−9.8%
12	Critz (Dem.)	45.2%	49.8%	−4.6%
(old 4th)	Altmire (Dem.)	45.2%	44.7%	.5%
13	Schwartz (Dem.)	66.0%	59.1%	6.9%
14	Doyle (Dem.)	67.8%	70.7%	−2.9%
15	Dent (Rep.)	52.8%	56.3%	−3.5%
16	Pitts (Rep.)	50.6%	48.2%	2.4%
17	Holden (Dem.)	57.5%	48.3%	9.2%
18	Murphy (Rep.)	44.2%	44.6%	−.3%

Take the five extremely vulnerable Republicans, and push them all into Republican leaning districts" (with the exception of Michael Fitzpatrick, whose district becomes only a point or so more Republican due to geographic constraints).[39]

Azavea, a Philadelphia, Pennsylvania, firm specializing in geographic data and geo-spatial analysis, conducted an independent study of the new congressional districts in Pennsylvania following the 2011 redistricting process (see table 16.3). They found that Pennsylvania has the least compact districts in the nation. Eric Boehm of the *PA Independent* reported on December 21, 2011, that Azavea does not use the term

Table 16.2. Obama 2-Party Vote % under Old and New Pennsylvania Lines

	60% +O	57%– 59% O	54%– 56% O	51%– 53% O	52%M– 50% O	53% +M
Old Lines	4	3 (2 Rep.)	3 (3 Rep.)	0	4 (2 Dem.)	6 (1 Dem.)
New Lines	4	1	1 (1 Rep.)	4	2	6 (1 Dem.)

gerrymander "because it implies political intention behind drawing the districts. Instead, they measure 'compactness' on an objective scale." More precisely, Azavea uses the Polsby-Popper measure which "scores the ratio of a district's area compared with a theoretical circle, the same circumference as the district's perimeter. Essentially, it measures the degree to which a district is indented against what the district would look like if it was expanded to be a perfect circle." The more indentations a district has in its borders, the lower its Polsby-popper compactness score. A Polsby-Popper score of zero means the district is not compact at all whereas a compact score of 1 means the district is perfectly compact.

The average score for compactness following the 2011 Pennsylvania redistricting is lower than, or less compact than the 2001 score. Azavea, as reported by

Table 16.3. Comparison of the Compactness of the Pennsylvania Congressional Districts, Using Polsby-Popper Scores

District	Adopted 2001 Redistricting Plan	Adopted 2011 Redistricting Plan	Proposed 2011 Democratic (Minority) Redistricting Plan
1	.067	.080	.08
2	.159	.385	.23
3	.136	.211	.22
4 (old 19th)	.221	.407	.15
5	.211	.271	.28
6	.082	.082	.11
7	.177	.041	.14
8	.333	.365	.35
9	.110	.138	.16
10	.175	.146	.13
11	.262	.136	.23
12	.050	.098	.22
13	.097	.076	.22
14	.098	.114	.18
15	.193	.145	.25
16	.241	.129	.13
17	.257	.084	.14
18	.058	.169	.31
19	.387	N/A	N/A
Average Score	**.174**	**.171**	**.20**

Boehm,[10] found that Pennsylvania's 7th Congressional District is tied with North Carolina's 1st Congressional District for the top fourth least-compact district in the nation with a Polsby-Popper score of .041. Pennsylvania's 7th Congressional District is represented by Patrick Meehan.

CONCLUSION

Pennsylvania is one of the most gerrymandered states in the country. The evidence is quite clear that a legislative district map that follows the route of a regular piece of legislation will have the same negative characteristics as any other legislation passed by a state or federal government. The law will include winners and losers. It is especially important for Democrats and Republicans to gain majority status in Pennsylvania following each decennial census so that they may control the state's representation in Washington, DC. During the 2011 redistricting process in Pennsylvania, the Senate and House Government Committees, the subgroups responsible for drawing legislative districts held three public hearings throughout the Commonwealth. The public statements of the Senate and House Committee chairs would lead the observer to believe that there was a serious effort to make Pennsylvania's process transparent and as fair as possible. The statements seemed genuine, and perhaps these leaders were genuine in their desire for a transparent and fair process. However, the fact of the matter is that despite the public statements made by members of the committees and despite the well-intentioned testimony of the witnesses, at the end of the day Pennsylvania adopted a partisan political map, at least as measured by independent statistical analyses. It has been this way for a long time.

NOTES

1. I wish to thank Mr. Bill Schaller of the GOP House Redistricting Office for his assistance.

2. Charles Thompson, "Congressional Redistricting Puts PA Congressmen at a Distance," *Harrisburg Patriot-News*, December 18, 2011.

3. Dave Davies, "PA Congressional Districts Sure to Generate Controversy," *WHYY*, December 8, 2011, www.newsworks.org/index.php/local/item/31020-pa-congressional-districts -sure-to-generate-controversy (accessed February 15, 2012).

4. Pennlive.com, "Pa. Congressional Map is Ridiculous and We Will Live with it for the Next 10 Years," www.pennlive.com/editorials/index.ssf/2011/12/pa_congressional_map_is_ ridicu.html (accessed February 12, 2012).

5. Thomas Fitzgerald, "Redistricting Battle Begins: With PA Set to Lose One House Seat, Republicans are Starting to Consider which One to Drop," *Philadelphia Inquirer,* March 16, 2011, A1.

6. Fitzgerald, "Redistricting Battle Begins."

7. "Pennsylvania Redistricting: The Legislative Guide to Redistricting in Pennsylvania," www.redistricting.state.pa.us/index.cfm (accessed February 12, 2012).

8. Ivey Dejesus, "Pennsylvania's Newly Adopted Congressional Redistricting Plan Is Riddled with Shortcomings, Critics Say," pennlive.com, January 29, 2012, www.pennlive .com/midstate/index.ssf/2012/01/pennsylvanias_newly-adopted_co.html (accessed February 12, 2012).

9. Thomas Edsall, "Republicans Gain in Pennsylvania's Redistricting Plan," *Washington Post*, January 6, 2002, A4.

10. *Vieth v. Jubelirer*, 2004, 541 U.S. 267.

11. *Vieth v. Jubelirer*, 2004, 541 U.S. 267.

12. Associated Press, "PA Redistricting Plan Overturned," April 8, 2002.

13. *Vieth v. Jubelirer*, 2004, 541 U.S. 267.

14. *Vieth v. Jubelirer*, 2004, 541 U.S. 267.

15. Fitzgerald, 2011.

16. Senator Pileggi.com, "Press Release," August 18, 2011, www.senatorpileggi.com/ press/2011/0811/081811.htm (accessed February 17, 2012).

17. Senator Pileggi.com, "Press Release."

18. Hearing Transcript, May 12, 2011, 3.

19. Hearing Transcript, May 12, 2011, 3.

20. Hearing Transcript, May 12, 2011.

21. Hearing Transcript, May 12, 2011, 43.

22. Hearing Transcript, May 12, 2011, 43.

23. Hearing Transcript, May 12, 2011, 47.

24. Hearing Transcript, May 12, 2011, 55.

25. Hearing Transcript, May 12, 2011, 60.

26. Hearing Transcript, May 12, 2011, 61.

27. Hearing Transcript, May 12, 2011, 69.

28. Hearing Transcript, May 12, 2011, 78.

29. Hearing Transcript, May 12, 2011, 87.

30. Hearing Transcript, May 12, 2011, 94.

31. Hearing Transcript, May 12, 2011, 90.

32. Hearing Transcript, May 12, 2011, 91.

33. Hearing Transcript, May 12, 2011, 92.

34. Hearing Transcript, May 12, 2011, 120.

35. Hearing Transcript, May 12, 2011, 128–29.

36. Hearing Transcript, May 12, 2011, 130.

37. Hearing Transcript, May 12, 2011, 140.

38. Hearing Transcript, May 12, 2011, 143.

39. Sean Trende, "In Pennsylvania, the Gerrymander of the Decade?" RealClearPolitics .org, December 14, 2012, www.realclearpolitics.com/articles/2011/12/14/in_pennsylvania_ the_gerrymander_of_the_decade_112404.html (accessed February 12, 2012).

40. Eric Boehm, "Some of PA's Districts All over the Congressional Map," paindependent .com, December 21, 2011, http://paindependent.com/2011/12/some-of-pas-districts-all-over -the-congressional-map/ (accessed February 13, 2012).

17

Redistricting in Iowa 2011

Timothy M. Hagle

STATE DEMOGRAPHIC TRENDS FROM THE 2010 CENSUS

The 1900 census found that Iowa's population passed 2 million for the first time. The United States population in 1900 was a bit over 76 million. Iowa did not pass 3 million until 2010. The U.S. population in 2010 was nearly 310 million. Since 1900 Iowa went from 11 congressional districts to 4 (see figure 17.1). Iowa simply did not grow fast enough to maintain its number of congressional districts.[1]

The chart shows the stark contrast in the rate of growth between Iowa and the United States as a whole. Iowa's population growth was relatively flat during this entire period while the U.S. population grew dramatically. In terms of percentage increases, Iowa's population only grew more than 5 percent in any decennial period twice (7.46 percent for the 1920 census year and 5.11 for 2000), and it even shrank

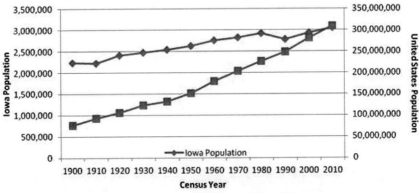

Figure 17.1. Iowa and United States Population Growth, 1900–2010. U.S. census data.

for two periods (1910 and 1980). During the same 1900-to-2010 period, U.S. growth was above double-digits in all but two decennial periods (6.78 percent for the 1940 census year and 8.91 percent for 1990).

When membership in the U.S. House of Representatives was fixed at 435 in 1912, the number of congressional districts (CDs) for each state became a zero-sum game. States that grew faster gained seats at the expense of those that grew more slowly or lost population. Iowa kept its 11 CDs until after the 1930 census when the number dropped to 9. Iowa lost additional CDs in the years following the censuses of 1940, 1960, 1970, and 1990. Following the 2000 census Iowa was lucky to have not lost another congressional seat. Even so, it seemed clear that Iowa would likely lose a seat following the next census, and this was confirmed when the 2010 census data were released.

Reasons for Iowa's slower growth are undoubtedly varied. Iowa is largely known as an agricultural state, though it does have its share of manufacturing and service sector jobs. During Iowa Caucus seasons reporters often note that Iowa's population is older than the national average. This is certainly true as figures for the 2010 census report that 14.9 percent of Iowans are 65 years of age or older, while nationally that group makes up only 13.0 percent of the population. On the other hand, Iowa's percentage of persons under 18 years old is 23.9 which is nearly the same as the U.S. percentage of 24.0. One contributing factor that may help to explain these figures is what is known in the state as "brain drain." More specifically, graduates of Iowa's colleges and universities often feel the need to leave the state to seek higher-paying jobs. Although some return to Iowa later in life to raise a family, the effect contributes to Iowa being below the national average in the 18- to 64-year-old category.

OVERVIEW OF THE REDISTRICTING PROCESS IN IOWA[2]

Like many other states, Iowa revised its redistricting process following the Unites States Supreme Court's decisions in *Baker v. Carr* (1962), *Wesberry v. Sanders* (1964), and *Reynolds v. Sims* (1964).[3] The Supreme Court's decision in *Wesberry* required that U.S. congressional districts be based on population,[4] and in 1968 Iowa amended its constitution to require that state legislative districts also be based on population. The amendments also specified a timeline for the redistricting procedure and a review process:[5]

All dates refer to the calendar year following the decennial census.

February 15   Temporary Redistricting Advisory Commission members must be selected.

April 1   Legislative Services Agency must submit a proposed redistricting plan to the General Assembly.

September 1   The General Assembly must complete the apportionment process.

September 15   If an apportionment plan does not become law by this date, the Iowa Supreme Court shall apportion the state into appropriate districts.

December 31   The Iowa Supreme Court's apportionment plan must be completed.

The redistricting plan adopted by the Iowa General Assembly following the 1970 census contained variations in population among state legislative districts that were challenged in court and ultimately struck down by the Iowa Supreme Court as being contrary to the Iowa Constitution.[6] In accordance with the Iowa Constitution,[7] the Iowa Supreme Court then redrew the district lines,[8] and those districts were used during the 1970s.

In 1980 the Iowa General Assembly passed more specific procedures for legislative redistricting and gave the Legislative Service Bureau the primary responsibility for drawing proposed congressional and state legislative districts.[9] The Legislative Service Bureau (renamed the Legislative Services Agency in 2003[10]) is "a nonpartisan bill drafting agency of the [Iowa] General Assembly."[11] In 1981 the third plan submitted by the LSB was approved by the General Assembly without amendment. In 1991 the first plan was accepted, in 2001 it was the second plan, and in 2011 it was the first plan again.

Equality of population in the various districts is the primary criterion for redistricting. The basic approach is to divide a state's population by the number of congressional or state legislative districts to arrive at an "ideal" population for a district. The next step is to determine how much each proposed district deviates from that ideal to find the range (greatest differences above and below the ideal) and the mean of the deviations. A key factor here is how those measures vary as one works down from Iowa's four congressional districts to its 50 state Senate districts to its 100 state House of Representatives districts. For state offices, the state constitution says the following:

Article III. Of the Distribution of Powers

Senate and House of Representatives—limitation. SEC. 34. The Senate shall be composed of not more than fifty and the House of Representatives of not more than one hundred members. Senators and representatives shall be elected from districts established by law. Each district so established shall be of compact and contiguous territory. The state shall be apportioned into senatorial and representative districts on the basis of population. The general assembly may provide by law for factors in addition to population, not in conflict with the Constitution of the United States, which may be considered in the apportioning of senatorial districts. No law so adopted shall permit the establishment of senatorial districts whereby a majority of the members of the Senate shall represent less than 40 percent of the population of the state as shown by the most recent United States decennial census.

Senators and representatives—number and districts. SEC. 35. The general assembly shall in 1971 and in each year immediately following the United States decennial census determine the number of senators and representatives to be elected to the general assembly and establish senatorial and representative districts. The general assembly shall complete the apportionment prior to September 1 of the year so required. If the apportionment fails to become law prior to September 15 of such year, the supreme court shall cause the state to be apportioned into senatorial and representative districts to comply with the requirements of the constitution prior to December 31 of such year. The reapportioning authority shall, where necessary in establishing senatorial districts, shorten the term of any senator prior to completion of the term. Any senator whose term is so terminated shall not be compensated for the uncompleted part of the term.

Review by supreme court. SEC. 36. Upon verified application by any qualified elector, the supreme court shall review an apportionment plan adopted by the general assembly which has been enacted into law. Should the supreme court determine such plan does not comply with the requirements of the constitution, the court shall within ninety days adopt or cause to be adopted an apportionment plan which shall so comply. The supreme court shall have original jurisdiction of all litigation questioning the apportionment of the general assembly or any apportionment plan adopted by the general assembly.

An additional measurement related to population is a determination of the smallest percentage of Iowa residents who may be represented by a majority of districts. In particular, the Iowa Constitution requires that a plan cannot be adopted such that a majority of the members of the state Senate represent less than 40 percent of the population of the state.[12] As a practical matter, this requirement means that the 26 smallest proposed Senate districts must represent more than 40 percent of the population. Although that seems easy, it means that the total deviation of those 26 districts must be less than 10 percent, or an average variation of slightly less than only 0.39 percent.

The U.S. Supreme Court did not prohibit consideration of factors other than population in how states draw their congressional and state legislative districts. To that end, the Iowa Constitution specifically indicates that districts should be "compact and contiguous" and that other factors, not in conflict with the U.S. Constitution, may be considered.[13]

The Iowa Code specifies seven criteria to be used by the Legislative Services Agency in drafting a proposed redistricting plan.[14] They are as follows:

1. Population. Congressional and state legislative districts shall be as equal as practicable to the ideal population for such districts. Variations may occur only as necessary to comply with one or more of the other listed standards. In addition, no district can vary from the ideal by more than 1 percent, unless it is specifically to comply with another standard.
2. Political boundaries. District boundaries shall coincide with the political boundaries of the state. The number of cities and counties divided between districts shall be as small as possible.
3. Convenient contiguous territory. Areas that meet only at corners are not considered contiguous.
4. Reasonable compactness. Districts must be reasonably compact. This includes consideration of length and width (such that the two measures are as equal as possible) and perimeter.
5. Political parties, incumbents, and group demographics. Districts cannot be drawn to purposefully favor either political party or any incumbent legislator

(state or congressional). Districts also cannot be drawn to augment or dilute the voting strength of any language or racial minority group.
6. Minimize electoral confusion. Each "representative district" (i.e., a district of a member of the Iowa House of Representatives) must lie wholly within a single senatorial district (i.e., the district of a member of the Iowa Senate). If possible Senate and representative districts must be wholly within a single congressional district, but the prior standards take precedence to this one.

Using these criteria, the LSA drafts a proposal to be delivered to the Iowa General Assembly no later than April 1 of each year ending in 1 (i.e., in April of the year following the decennial census).[15]

At approximately the same time the LSA is preparing its initial plan, a Temporary Redistricting Advisory Commission (TRAC) is established. The TRAC is composed of five members. One member of the TRAC is chosen by each of the following four elected officials: the majority and minority floor leaders in the state Senate, the majority and minority floor leaders in the state House of Representatives. The fifth member is chosen by a vote of three of the four other members of the TRAC and the fifth member serves as chairperson. The TRAC members must be in place no later than February 15 of the year ending in 1.[16]

Once the Legislative Services Agency delivers a proposed redistricting plan to the General Assembly, the TRAC must schedule three public hearings in different geographic regions of the state as "expeditiously as reasonably possible."[17] Following these hearings, the TRAC prepares a report summarizing the testimony and information received at the hearings. This report is submitted to the General Assembly no more than 14 days after the initial redistricting plan is delivered to the General Assembly.[18]

After the TRAC report is submitted to the General Assembly, one of the state legislative chambers must bring the proposed plan up for a vote expeditiously, but no sooner than three days following the report's submission. If the first chamber passes the plan, the other chamber must bring it up for a vote in an expeditious manner. Only corrective amendments to the proposed plan are allowed.[19]

If the proposed plan is not enacted,[20] the rejecting body must transmit reasons for the rejection to the LSA. The LSA must then prepare a second plan taking into consideration those reasons. The second proposed plan must be submitted to the General Assembly within 35 days of the rejection of the first proposed plan. The General Assembly must then vote on the second proposal no sooner than seven days after receiving it. Like the first proposal, only corrective amendments are allowed. TRAC is not required to hold public hearings on the second proposal.[21]

If the second proposed plan is not enacted, the rejecting body must again transmit reasons to the LSA. The LSA must then prepare a third plan taking into consideration the reasons for the rejection. The third proposed plan must be submitted to the General Assembly within 35 days of the rejection of the second proposed plan.

As with the second proposal, TRAC is not required to hold public hearings, and the General Assembly may vote on the third plan no sooner than seven days after receiving it. Unlike the first two proposals, the third proposed plan may be amended just like any other bill.[22]

If the Iowa legislature fails to pass a redistricting plan by the required September 1 deadline, the Iowa Supreme Court then has until December 31 to develop its own plan.[23] In addition, if a plan approved by the General Assembly is challenged and struck down by the Iowa Supreme Court, the Court has 90 days to adopt an appropriate plan.[24]

OVERVIEW OF THE 2001 REDISTRICTING PROCESS IN IOWA

Census data for 1990 showed that Iowa lost nearly 5 percent of its population over the prior ten years.[25] As a result, Iowa lost one of its Congressional seats. (See map 17.1 for the congressional districts approved following the 1990 census.) Census data for 2000 showed that Iowa gained back the lost population and at 2,926,324 was slightly above the 1980 figure. Although this growth rate was well below the national average of approximately 12 percent, it was enough to keep Iowa from losing an additional congressional seat. Despite the relative stability of the Iowa population as a whole, population movement within the state from rural to urban areas ensured that the redistricting process would still be interesting.

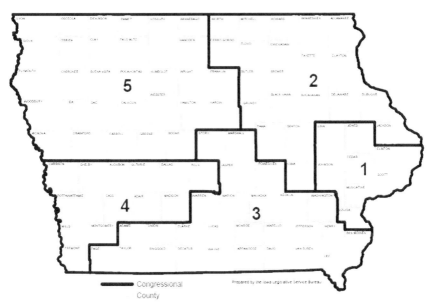

Map 17.1.   Iowa Congressional Districts Effective Beginning with the Elections in 1992 for the 103rd Congress. Iowa Legislative Service Bureau, www.legis.iowa.gov/DOCS/ Resources/Redist/91Congress.pdf.

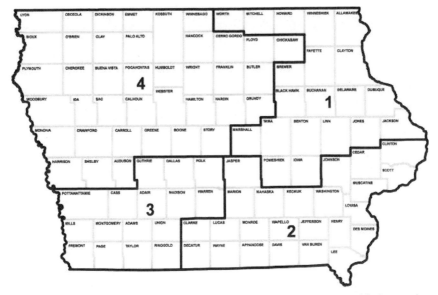

Map 17.2. Proposed Congressional Districts, March 3, 2011. Iowa Legislative Service Bureau, www.legis.iowa.gov/DOCS/Resources/Redist/April2001Report.pdf.

The Legislative Service Bureau (LSB)[26] submitted its proposed redistricting plan in April 2001. (See map 17.2.) Following the constitutional and legislative guidelines indicated in the previous section, state legislative leaders selected the initial four members of the TRAC, who then selected the fifth member. The TRAC scheduled public hearings in three locations across the state: Sioux City (west), Des Moines (central), and Iowa City (eastern). Following the hearings, the TRAC prepared its report to the General Assembly, which contained short summaries of comments from members of the public as well as its own conclusions.[27]

Although proposed redistricting plans submitted by the LSB are based on non-partisan criteria, political activity can become a part of the process during the TRAC hearings and its final report. Democrats and Republicans will often have an opinion whether a particular proposed plan benefits or hurts their party. All members of a particular party may not agree on the pros and cons of any plan, but party leaders will often encourage activists to attend the public hearings to voice their (the activists') thoughts about a particular proposal.[28]

The 2001 TRAC report listed the name and home city of each member of the public who offered comments, as well as a short summary of those comments. The TRAC then characterized the testimony as being either in favor of the plan (+) or against it (–). If one is familiar with the political activists in a particular area, one can see a pattern in the testimony such that Democrats generally approved of the plan and Republicans generally opposed it. Most comments in favor of the plan noted that it was "fair" and that the process should continue to be "nonpartisan." Those against the plan often expressed concern about the lack of an urban/rural mix in the districts compared to the plan adopted in 1991. Several also complained that the population variance among the districts was too great. One liberal Democrat, who several years later became a county supervisor, expressed concern that two growing eastern Iowa counties with economic ties (Linn and Johnson) would be placed in separate congressional districts.

Upon consideration of the testimony received at the public hearings as well as its own analysis of the plan, the TRAC voted three to two to advise rejection of the plan. The "majority" decision does not contain specifics as to the reason for the recommendation to reject the proposal. One member of the majority, however, submitted an additional statement that outlined in some detail his reasoning (which was likely similar to the other two members of the majority).[29] He made three basic points. First, he noted that although the district deviations (congressional, state Senate, and state House) were within statutory limits, they were very close to those upper limits and much higher than the plans adopted in 1981 and 1991. Second, he noted that a politically neutral process does not necessarily guarantee neutral results, and it appeared that one party (the Democrats) saw a great advantage to the proposal. Third, he noted that business and economic interests might be better served if the same elected officials represented particular areas. He noted that although the LSB could not take some of these concerns into consideration when drafting the proposal, the TRAC and the General Assembly could.

A Minority Report (also part of the TRAC report) was submitted by one of the two members who voted to recommend approval of the proposal.[30] The essence of this report was that the proposal met constitutional and statutory requirements and that no proposal would be perfect. This member noted that many of those attending the public hearings did so at the behest of one or the other of the two political parties and largely followed scripted talking points. She noted that the LSB could not take various political factors into consideration when drafting its proposal and suggested that the TRAC should not either. The other member of the minority also submitted comments which mainly echoed the comments in the Minority Report.[31]

Two main differences emerge from the reports and additional comments from the TRAC members. First, although all acknowledged that the population deviations were within constitutional and statutory requirements, even though they were higher than the prior two plans, the majority felt the plan should have smaller deviations while the minority felt the proposal was good enough. Second, the minority wanted the TRAC (and likely the General Assembly) to only consider the nonpartisan criteria indicated in the statute, while the majority was willing to consider additional factors (some political, some not). One can take these positions at face value, but one could also wonder whether they were merely proxies for the political advantage or disadvantage perceived by the two political parties.

After consideration of the TRAC report the Republican-controlled Iowa Senate voted to reject the proposal.[32] In doing so, it emphasized that the LSB should draft a new plan that did a better job of minimizing the population deviations among districts. In particular, it requested that the new proposal at a minimum matched the deviations in congressional and state legislative districts from the current (1991) plan. The Senate also suggested that minimizing population deviations was more important than compactness. In addition, the Senate suggested that the LSB strive to develop a plan that considered urban and rural interests to the extent consistent with the Iowa Code.[33]

The LSB submitted a second proposal on June 1, 2001.[34] (See map 17.3.) In addition to the usual details of the proposed redistricting plan, the proposal included specific responses to the state Senate's concerns regarding the first proposal. Not surprisingly, the LSB indicated that certain concerns were beyond their statutory authority to consider (e.g., consideration of urban-rural interests).[35] The criterion that the LSB could address was population equity among the districts. As indicated previously, one member of the TRAC specifically noted that although the first plan was within constitutional and statutory requirements, the population disparities among the districts were much greater than those in the plans adopted in 1981 or 1991. The second LSB plan dramatically reduced the district deviations. Whereas the first plan had an overall 0.08 percent population variance[36] among the congressional districts, the overall variance in the second plan was only 0.023 percent. That figure was not only well below that of the first plan, but about half of the 1991 (0.05 percent) and 1981 (0.045 percent) plans.[37] The improvement for the state Senate and House of Representative districts was not as dramatic, but the second LSB plan did reduce the overall deviations among the state Senate districts to only slightly above those of the

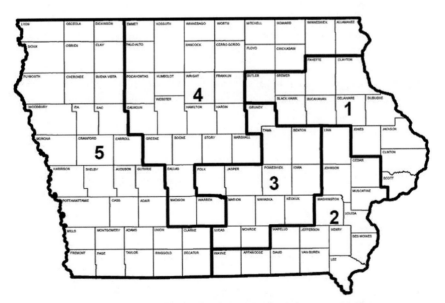

Map 17.3. Proposed Congressional Districts, June 2011. Iowa Legislative Service Bureau, www.legis.iowa.gov/DOCS/Resources/Redist/2001/June2001Report.pdf.

1991 plan (1.46 percent compared to 1.45 percent). The overall deviations in the state house of representative districts were reduced to a level below the 1991 plan (1.89 percent compared to 1.97 percent).[38]

To achieve these reductions in the population deviations among the various districts, LSB had to relax its concern with other factors, such as compactness. This can be seen most clearly when considering maps of the congressional districts for the two plans (maps 17.2 and 17.3). The congressional districts in the first plan were of a more compact and regular shape. In contrast, we see that after removing populous Linn County, the 1st CD had to be extended several counties to the west. The 2nd CD went from a fairly compact shape in the first plan to a right angle in the second (though this kept the Linn-Johnson County business "corridor" in one district). The 4th CD of the second plan has the most unusual shape in that it begins in the very northeast corner of the state, heads west to central Iowa, and then south to hook around Polk County (Iowa's most populous county containing the state capital of Des Moines). Despite the shapes of the CDs being more irregular than in the first plan, other statistics associated with the CDs in the second plan were similar to those of the first plan, and sometimes near those of the 1991 plan.[39]

The TRAC is not required to hold hearings or submit a report for a second (or third) proposal. Despite the lack of a formal mechanism for public input on the second plan, members of the General Assembly no doubt sought and received comments on the second plan from their constituents and other interested parties. The dramatic improvement in the population variances among the districts removed that as a potential criticism of the second proposed plan. The inclusion of Linn and Johnson Counties in a single CD also satisfied those who wanted them represented by a single Congress member because of their linked and growing business interests. Even to the extent that the General Assembly could pay more attention to political and other factors, focus on such other concerns that were clearly outside the constitutional or statutory authority of LSB would have seemed overly political. As a result, on June 19, 2001, the Iowa House of Representatives passed the second plan by a vote of 78–18, and the Senate passed the plan by a vote of 37–13. The plan was signed into law by Governor Tom Vilsack on June 22, 2001.[40]

THE 2011 REDISTRICTING PROCESS IN IOWA

It came as no particular surprise that Iowa lost a congressional seat following the 2010 census. The lost seat increased interest in the redistricting process given that it would mean, barring retirements, that at least two incumbents would be placed in the same congressional district.[41] Some even speculated that the loss of a congressional seat would be a severe test of Iowa's nonpartisan and generally politics-free redistricting process.[42] Regardless of such speculation, once data was received from the U.S. Census Bureau the (now renamed) Legislative Services Agency (LSA) began its task of drafting a plan for the redistricting of Iowa congressional and state legislative districts.

Prior to the release of the LSA proposal, Iowans had an opportunity to try their hand at redistricting the congressional districts by using an application located on the website for the state's leading newspaper, the *Des Moines Register*.[43] The rules for the "redistricting game" were a basic version of those followed by the LSA: counties could not be split between congressional districts, counties in the same CD had to be contiguous (only touching corners was not good enough), and the population in each of the four CDs could not deviate more than 1 percent from the ideal of 761,589. Readers who came up with what they thought was a good map could save it and send it to the *Register*, which might post it online.

The application certainly was not as sophisticated as the software used by the LSA, nor did it include all the criteria considered by the agency, but it did give Iowans an opportunity to think about and explore the possibilities for how the new districts would be drawn. At the very least, the application likely gave many users a greater appreciation for how difficult it is to make sure that the new districts not deviate more than the required 1 percent from the ideal.[44]

The LSA's proposed plan was released on March 31, 2011.[45] The first thing most noticed about the plan was that the portion dealing with the new congressional districts set up not one but two incumbent-versus-incumbent matchups. (See map 17.4.) Republicans Steve King and Tom Latham were both located in the proposed 4th Congressional District (Sac and Story Counties), while Democrats Bruce Braley and Dave Loebsack were in the proposed 1st CD (Black Hawk and Linn Counties).

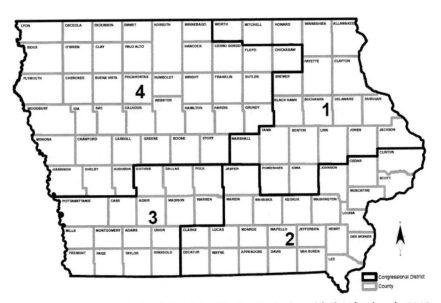

Map 17.4. Iowa Congressional Districts Effective Beginning with the Elections in 2012 for the 113th U.S. Congress. Iowa Legislative Service Bureau, www.legis.iowa.gov/ DOCS/Resources/Redist/2011/2011-03-31/CongressStatewide8x11.pdf.

That left Iowa's fifth incumbent, Democrat Leonard Boswell, alone in the proposed 3rd CD with the 2nd CD open.

The pair of Democrats quickly solved their conflict when Loebsack indicated that he would move a few miles south from Linn to Johnson County should the proposed plan be approved.[46] This made sense as the proposed 2nd CD contained all but one of the counties Loebsack was currently representing.

The solution for the pair of Republicans was less clear. The proposed 4th CD contained roughly the same number of counties currently represented by both King and Latham. When first elected to Congress in 1996, Latham represented Iowa's 5th CD (refer to map 17.1). Thus, Latham had, at one time or another, represented all but a handful of counties in the proposed 4th CD. It seemed, therefore, that it might be more logical for King to move to the new 3rd CD. Although the very conservative King had represented 12 of the 16 counties in the proposed 3rd CD, it was likely that he would have more trouble in Iowa's most populous county, Polk, and the three nearby counties that were also included in that new CD. This was particularly so given that he would be facing the incumbent Boswell who was currently represent-ing Polk County and had represented five other counties in the proposed 3rd CD in the 1990s. A more practical reason for King to resist moving was simply that his construction business was not one that could be easily moved or run from a distance. The conflict was resolved when Latham announced that he would move to the new 3rd CD and challenge Boswell for the seat.[47]

The second thing that stood out in the LSA plan was how small the population deviations were. This was particularly true for the congressional districts where the mean deviation among the four districts was only 29.25 persons or a mere 0.00384 mean deviation percentage. This figure was less than half the 0.00803 percent of the plan adopted in 2001 and less than one-fifth of the 0.02 percent from the 1991 plan.[48] Although the mean deviations for the state Senate[49] and House of Representatives[50] districts were slightly greater than those of the 2001 plan, it seemed unlikely that anyone opposed to the plan would be able to use population deviations as a justification.

Prior to the release of the LSA proposal, members of the TRAC were selected.[51] As noted previously, the statutory requirement is for the TRAC to hold three public meetings in different areas of the state, but it held four meetings located in Council Bluffs (west), Bettendorf (east), Cedar Rapids (east), and Des Moines (central). Comments on the proposal were also sent directly to the LSA and to the TRAC via the web. These comments were also summarized or included in the TRAC report.

Contrary to the first proposal in 2001, the 2011 proposal did not seem to gener-ate as much opposition. Based on the number of citizen comments summarized in the TRAC report there seemed to be fewer citizens offering comments on the plan at the meetings. The majority of the comments in opposition to the plan concerned very specific aspects of it. These included, for example, concerns that the campus of St. Ambrose University in Davenport, Iowa, would be split between two proposed House districts, which would be confusing to student voters. The largest number of comments in opposition to the proposal were related to the fact that Pottawattamie County on Iowa's western border and its largest city, Council Bluffs, would no longer be part of Representative King's district.[52]

Despite the various comments in opposition to the proposal, few seemed to raise complaints specifically related to the criteria that the LSA is allowed to consider. Moreover, many comments dealt with concerns related to political factors that the LSA is specifically prohibited from considering. As a result, the TRAC voted unanimously to approve the proposed plan. No members wrote additional clarifying statements.

On April 14, 2011, House File 682 (the bill embodying the proposed redistricting plan) was passed by the Iowa House of Representatives on a vote of 90–7 and the Iowa Senate on a vote of 48–1. The bill was signed into law by Governor Terry Branstad on April 19, 2011.[53]

EFFECTS AND IMPLICATIONS OF THE
2011 REDISTRICTING PROCESS IN IOWA

Despite the relative ease and apparent lack of political machinations involving Iowa's 2011 redistricting process, there are certainly political implications at both the congressional and state legislative levels.

As described previously, the loss of a congressional seat seemed likely to provide some additional drama to the process. When the LSA proposal was released, many were somewhat surprised that the plan potentially set up two intraparty, incumbent-versus-incumbent contests while leaving another district open. Both intraparty conflicts were resolved relatively quickly, and Iowa will face only one incumbent-versus-incumbent race in the 2012 general election.

There was, however, one additional complication. Christie Vilsack is the former First Lady of Iowa, and her husband, former Governor Tom Vilsack (D), currently (as of 2011) serves as the Secretary of Agriculture in the Obama administration. After eight years as Iowa's First Lady, in addition to all her other activities, Vilsack is quite well known in the state. Before the redistricting process began, Vilsack expressed an interest in running for office. The problem was in deciding where.

Vilsack's hometown is in Mt. Pleasant, Iowa, which is located in Henry County in the southeast portion of the state. That county is in the new 2nd CD. The new 2nd CD was initially open because current Representatives Bruce Braley and Dave Loebsack were both placed in the new 1st CD. As previously noted, Loebsack quickly indicated that he would relocate to Johnson County to stay in the new 2nd CD. The new 2nd CD seemed the most favorable to Democrats (based on active voter registrations[54]) and would provide the best opportunity for Vilsack to win, but it would mean challenging an incumbent of her own party in a primary. Although some do not consider Loebsack a strong incumbent, it seemed clear that party officials (at both state and national levels) would not look kindly on such an unforced intraparty contest in a year that was shaping up to be a difficult one for Democrats.[55]

The new district that seemed the next most favorable to Democrats was the new 1st CD. Again, however, an incumbent Democrat (Braley) already resides in this district. Braley's 2010 victory was extremely narrow, only about 1 percent, but he is considered a possible rising star in Iowa Democratic politics, if not nationally, and as with Loebsack party leaders would not want him challenged unnecessarily.

The new 3rd CD seemed a possibility. Although it also had an incumbent Democrat, Leonard Boswell, there seemed a reasonable possibility that he would retire. If party leaders approached Boswell with the retirement suggestion, he was certainly having none of it. He indicated even before the LSA proposal was released that he planned to run for reelection regardless of a challenge by Vilsack.[56] In addition, Boswell would likely be the strongest of the three incumbent Iowa Democrats, so a challenge to him seemed out of the question.

That left only the new 4th CD, the most Republican-leaning of the four (again, based on active voter registrations). The Republican incumbent for that district, Steve King, is known for being a strong conservative. His base is in the heavily-Republican northwest portion of the state. The new 4th CD leans a bit less to Republicans than the old 5th CD he previously represented, but it still seems to be the district most likely to go for a Republican congressional candidate. With no U.S. Senate seat up in 2012 in Iowa, nor any statewide races, challenging King in the new 4th CD seemed Vilsack's only opportunity to run for high-level office in 2012.

Vilsack chose Ames, Iowa, in Story County (in the central part of the state) as her new home base. Vilsack will likely have strong support in Story County, home to Iowa State University, but many believe she will still have an uphill battle against King. Not surprisingly, others disagree. Some argue that King has had weak opponents in his previous reelection bids and would have more trouble against a well-known and well-funded opponent, as Vilsack will surely be. In addition, the Democratic Congressional Campaign Committee showed support for Vilsack by placing her race against King in their "Red to Blue" list.[57] This signals that the DCCC is willing to put substantial resources into the race based on the assumption Vilsack has a good chance to turn the seat from Republican to Democrat. In contrast, as of January 2012, the Center for American Politics shows the new 4th CD as "leaning" Republican, but the new 3rd CD, with the Boswell-Latham matchup, as a toss-up.[58] Given that the other two Iowa congressional races are only rated as leaning for the incumbent Democrats,[59] it seems all Iowa's congressional races will be hard fought and closely watched.[60]

The 2011 redistricting process in Iowa also had a substantial effect on the state legislature. In preparing its redistricting proposal, the LSA cannot take into consideration political parties, incumbents, or where they reside. That usually means the proposals are more likely to pit incumbents against each other than those of other states. The 2011 plan proved no exception.

The Iowa Senate is divided into 50 districts. Each Senate district is divided into two House districts, creating a House of Representatives of 100 members. When the LSA proposal was released, many quickly examined it to determine which state legislators would be thrown into the same districts. Of the 50 incumbent state senators, 14 were placed in a district with one or more other incumbents. Three were districts with at least one incumbent from the other party. One district paired two Democrats and three districts paired Republicans (and one of those had three incumbent Republicans). Of the 100 incumbent state representatives, 27 were placed into a district with one or more other incumbents. Only one district had at least one incumbent from each party. Three districts paired Democrats and nine paired Republicans.

The much larger number of Republican pairings initially made many Republican state legislators uneasy about the proposal. Republicans had just retaken the Iowa House following the 2010 election and pitting incumbents against each other in 2012 would make it more difficult for them to retain control. Although Democrats retained control of the Iowa Senate by the narrowest of margins following the 2010 elections (26–24), Republicans hoped to gain control there as well in 2012, and the three pairs of Republican incumbents did not help their cause.

Another problem for several legislators was that the political composition of their new district did not favor them. The most extreme example was for Iowa Senate President Jack Kibbie (D). His old Senate district had a voter registration advantage of 788 Democrats, but his new district had an advantage for Republicans of 8,722.[61] (Kibbie was also paired with a Republican incumbent and, at 81, he decided to retire.) More generally, voter registration in 16 of 100 House districts and 12 of 50 Senate districts was against at least one incumbent. Republicans did worse than Democrats in the House districts as 14 had voter registration in their new district against them, whereas this occurred for only 6 Democrats. In the new Senate districts 9 Republicans and 7 Democrats were in districts that leaned to the opposing party.[62]

A third problem facing some state legislators was that their districts generally grew geographically. Iowa's modest population growth largely occurred because of growth in the cities. Democrats representing urban districts often saw their districts shrink geographically as the population became more concentrated. As a result, their new districts often contained a large proportion of people they previously represented. In contrast, Republicans representing more rural districts generally saw their new districts grow geographically. This often meant that a significant portion of their new districts contained people they had not previously represented, thus reducing their incumbency advantage.

It was clear to everyone that the LSA's proposed redistricting plan favored Democrats. The advantage was not intentional on the part of the LSA given the nonpartisan criteria the LSA had to abide by, but simply the luck of the draw. The problem for Republicans was that the population deviations in the plan were so small that they would have a hard time opposing the plan on some other basis. Iowa law does not require that the General Assembly be nonpartisan in its consideration of a redistricting proposal, but the tradition in Iowa is that they are. At the very least, those opposing the plan generally need to do so based on one or more of the criteria that LSA must follow in drafting proposals.

A second problem for Republicans in the General Assembly was that there was no guarantee that a second proposal would be any better for them.[63] Again, the intrastate population movement from rural to urban areas meant that it would always be more likely for Republican incumbents to be placed in the same district as the rural districts grew geographically. As a result, only a few Republicans opposed passage in either chamber.

Since passage of the plan, several officeholders of both parties have decided to retire. Sometimes this occurred when incumbents would have been paired against each other (in a primary or general election). Sometimes this occurred when an incumbent was in a substantially changed district. Regardless of the reason why, such turnover likely helps to keep the focus of state legislators on their constituents. Moreover, as one Iowa blogger put it, the turnover and open seats created by redistricting provide "golden opportunities to elect outstanding individuals who may not otherwise run against an incumbent."[64]

NOTES

1. Data in this section are drawn from U.S. census data found in various locations on the U.S. census website: www.census.gov.

2. In large measure, information in this section is a condensation of Ed Cook, *Redistricting in Iowa* (2007), which can be viewed on the web at www.legis.iowa.gov/DOCS/Central/Guides/redist.pdf.

3. *Baker v. Carr*, 369 U.S. 186 (1962); *Wesberry v. Sanders*, 376 U.S. 1 (1964); *Reynolds v. Sims*, 377 U.S. 533 (1964).

4. *Wesberry* at 7-8.

5. Iowa Constitution, Article III, Sections 34–36.

6. *In re Legislative Districting*, 193 NW2d 784 (1972); followed by supplementary opinions at 196 NW2d 209 (1972) and 199 NW2d 614 (1972).

7. Iowa Constitution, Article III, Section 36.

8. 196 NW2d 209 (1972), with corrections at 199 NW2d 614 (1972).

9. 1980 Iowa Acts, ch. 1021.

10. 2003 Iowa Acts, ch. 35.

11. Cook at 2.

12. Iowa Constitution, Article III, Section 34.

13. Iowa Constitution, Article III, Section 34.

14. Iowa Code, Section 42.4.

15. The April 1 deadline is based on the assumption that the census data necessary to draft the redistricting proposal is received by February 15. If the data is received after February 15, the April 1 deadline is extended by the same number of days. Iowa Code, Section 42.3(1).

16. Iowa Code, Section 42.5(1).

17. Iowa Code, Section 42.6(3).

18. Iowa Code, Section 42.6(3)(b).

19. Iowa Code, Section 42.3(1)(a).

20. The plan is submitted as a bill that must be passed by each chamber and signed by the governor.

21. Iowa Code, Section 42.3(2).

22. Iowa Code, Section 42.3(3).

23. Iowa Constitution, Article III, Section 35.

24. Iowa Constitution, Article III, Section 36.

25. All references to census data come from the United States Census Bureau and can be viewed at various locations on its website: www.census.gov.

26. As a reminder, the Legislative Service Bureau was renamed the Legislative Services Agency in 2003.

27. Report of the Temporary Redistricting Advisory Commission to the General Assembly, April 25, 2001. Viewed at www.legis.iowa.gov/DOCS/GA/78GA/Interim/2000/comminfo/trac/report.htm. The plan is in HTML format without pagination, so I will not provide page citations for further references to it.

28. I speak from personal knowledge as I attended and gave testimony at the Iowa City hearing.

29. Additional Concurring Comments by Mr. Lance D. Ehmcke, Report of the Temporary Redistricting Advisory Commission to the General Assembly, April 25, 2001. Viewed at www.legis.iowa.gov/DOCS/GA/78GA/Interim/2000/comminfo/trac/report.htm.

30. Minority Report by Ms. Gwendolyn Jo McCarty, Report of the Temporary Redistricting Advisory Commission to the General Assembly, April 25, 2001. Viewed at www.legis.iowa.gov/DOCS/GA/78GA/Interim/2000/comminfo/trac/report.htm.

31. Additional Comments from Mr. Joseph O'Hern, Report of the Temporary Redistricting Advisory Commission to the General Assembly, April 25, 2001. Viewed at www.legis.iowa.gov/DOCS/GA/78GA/Interim/2000/comminfo/trac/report.htm.

32. The vote was 21 for, 27 against, and 2 absent or not voting. Senate File 540, Senate Journal (Iowa), p. 1449; failed May 2, 2001.

33. Senate Resolution 50, Senate Journal (Iowa), p. 1497; first reading May 3, 2001.

34. Legislative Service Bureau, "Second Redistricting Plan," June 1, 2001. Viewed on the web at www.legis.iowa.gov/DOCS/Resources/Redist/2001/June2001Report.pdf.

35. Id. at 5.

36. The overall population variance is the range from how much the smallest district varies below the ideal to how much the largest district varies above.

37. Id. at Table 8; TRAC Report of April 25, 2001.

38. Id. at Table 9.

39. Id. at Table 8.

40. The Iowa General Assembly is normally in session from January to May and had to be called into an extraordinary session to vote on the second plan. The votes were on House File 758; Senate Journal, Tuesday, June 19, 2001.

41. Although Iowa did not lose a seat following the 2000 census, two sets of incumbent Congress members were initially placed together in the adopted 2001 plan. Two of them then relocated to stay with the majority of counties in their reformed districts. Rep. Jim Leach (R) moved from Scott to Johnson County to represent the new 2nd CD, and Rep. Leonard Boswell (D) moved from Decatur to Polk County to represent the new 3rd CD. Both were reelected in their reformed districts.

42. Associated Press (via RealClearPolitics.com), "Iowa's politics-free redistricting faces test," February 12, 2011. Viewed at www.realclearpolitics.com/news/ap/politics/2011/Feb/12/iowa_s_politics_free_redistricting_faces_test.html.

43. As I write this, the application is still available at http://data.desmoinesregister.com/dmr/iowa-census/redistricting-game.

44. For those who may be interested, a second tab on the application contains information on the history of redistricting in Iowa. This portion of the application contains a graph of Iowa's population along with a map showing the various CD lines as Iowa started with 2 CDs, increased to 11, then slowly fell to its current 4.

45. Legislative Services Agency, "First Redistricting Plan," March 31, 2011. Viewed on the web at www.legis.iowa.gov/DOCS/Resources/Redist/2011/2011-03-31/Plan1_Report.pdf.

46. James Q. Lynch, "Loebsack plans to move to avoid contest with Braley, however Latham-King match-up possible," *The Gazette* (Cedar Rapids, Iowa), March 31, 2011. Viewed on the web at thegazette.com/2011/03/31/loebsack-plans-to-move-to-avoid-contest-with-braley-however-latham-king-match-up-possible.

47. Unlike Loebsack, Latham waited until the proposed plan was passed by the Iowa House and Senate before he made his announcement. See "Latham Announces Move to New 3rd District," KCRG.com (Cedar Rapids, Iowa, TV station's website), April 15, 2011. Viewed on the web at www.kcrg.com/news/politics/Latham-Announces-Move-to-New-3rd-District-119922909.html.

48. Legislative Services Agency, "First Redistricting Plan," March 31, 2011, at 12, table 1.

49. Id. at 14, table 2.

50. Id. at 18, table 3.

51. One member, Lance Ehmcke, had served on the 2001 TRAC. He had been in the majority that advised rejection of the first proposal.

52. "Report of the Temporary Redistricting Advisory Commission," April 11, 2011. Viewed on the web at www.legis.iowa.gov/DOCS/Resources/Redist/2011/2011-03-31/1104XR-First%20Report.pdf.

53. Legislative Services Agency, "Congressional and Legislative Redistricting Plan Enacted," 2011. Viewed on the web at www.legis.iowa.gov/DOCS/Resources/Redist/2011/2011-03-31/Updates/04-19-2011%20-%20Redistricting%20Plan%20Enacted.pdf.

54. Iowa Secretary of State voter registration totals as of February 2, 2012. Viewed on the web at sos.iowa.gov/elections/pdf/VRStatsArchive/2012/CongJan12.pdf.

55. See, Alex Isenstadt, "Christie Vilsack likely to take on Steve King," *Politico.com*, April 11, 2011. Viewed on the web at www.politico.com/news/stories/0411/53367.html.

56. James Q. Lynch, "Boswell not worried over potential Christie Vilsack challenge," *Quad-City Times*, April 19, 2011. Viewed on the web at qctimes.com/news/state-and-regional/iowa/boswell-not-worried-over-potential-christie-vilsack-challenge/article_fcf2670e-6acb-11e0-82f1-001cc4c002e0.html.

57. DCCC website. Viewed on the web on January 30, 2012, at dccc.org/pages/redtoblue.

58. Center for American Politics, "Sabato's Crystal Ball." Viewed on the web on January 30, 2012, at www.centerforpolitics.org/crystalball/articles/category/2012-house.

59. Id.

60. See, for example, Bret Hayworth, "Politically SpeaKing: Steve King anticipates Fourth District race could be "dirtiest" in Iowa history," *Sioux City Journal*, January 30, 2012. Viewed on the web at www.siouxcityjournal.com/blogs/politically_speaking/politically-speaking-steve-king-anticipates-the-district-race-could-be/article_6dce46dc-051d-55cc-80fa-59d74eeba022.html.

61. Jason Clayworth, "Elected officials ponder new maps' numbers," *Des Moines Register*, April 16, 2011. Viewed on April 17, 2011, on the web at www.desmoinesregister.com/article/20110417/NEWS10/104170332/Elected-officials-ponder-new-maps-numbers (now behind a paywall).

62. Id.

63. See, for example, Mike Glover, "Leaders leaning toward backing redistricting plan," Associated Press via *Times-Republican* (Iowa), April 6, 2011. Viewed on the web at http://times republican.com/page/content.detail/id/134442/Leaders-leaning-toward-backing-redistricting -plan.html?isap=1&nav=5013.

64. Craig Robinson, "The New Legislative Maps Brings [*sic*] New Opportunities and Tough Decisions," *Iowa Republican*, May 10, 2011. Viewed on the web at theiowarepublican .com/2011/the-new-legislative-maps-brings-new-opportunities-and-tough-decisions.

18

Drawing Congressional Districts in Illinois

Always Political, Not Always Partisan

Kent Redfield

The last decade has not been kind to Illinois, politically or economically. Two former governors have been convicted of felonies committed while in office and sentenced to prison (Republican George Ryan, 1998–2002, and Democrat Rod Blagojevich, 2003–2009), further strengthening Illinois's reputation as one of, if not the most, corrupt states in the nation. The near collapse of the national economy in 2008 only added to the state's on-going budget crisis of falling revenues, billions of unpaid bills, and staggering unfunded public pension liabilities. Illinois employment rate was higher at the end of 2011 (9.8 percent) than at the beginning and more than a point above the national average. In January of 2012 more than $8 billion in unpaid bills to vendors, healthcare providers, social service providers and local governments were still outstanding.[1] A temporary income tax increase enacted in the 2010 lame-duck session of the legislature and budget cuts for the fiscal years of 2011 and 2012 have provided a little breathing room. But the long-term prospects for fixing Illinois's budget problems are dim, given the escalating cost of Medicaid and pension funding and the weakness of the state's revenue structure. All of this has made Illinois the poster child in the national media for corrupt, incompetent state government.[2]

In spite of all of this, Illinois remains the economic and political powerhouse of the Midwest. As a state, Illinois ranks fifth with 12,831,000 residents. With a gross domestic product of $630.54 billion in 2009, its economy is the nation's fourth largest. If Illinois were a separate country it would have the seventeenth largest economy in the world. It is a state of great economic diversity. Illinois is an international center of finance and trade. It is home to 31 Fortune 500 companies. With O'Hare Airport (fourth busiest in the world), the intersection of six major U.S. and Canadian railroads in Chicago, and the state's location in the interstate highway system, Illinois plays a central role in the U.S. transportation system. Its manufacturing value-added production was fourth in the nation in 2009. Illinois is also a key agricultural state which annually ranks second nationally in corn and soybean production and fourth in hog production. In 2008 Illinois had the four-teenth highest per capita income among states.[3]

In 2011 the governor of Illinois signed a redistricting plan for Illinois's eighteen congressional districts. A three-judge panel from the U.S. District Court upheld that plan in December of 2011. But they also characterized it as "a blatant political move to increase the number of Democratic congressional seats."[4] Ten years earlier, a dif-ferent Illinois governor signed a congressional redistricting map into law. That map was designed to protect the seats of 19 incumbent congressmen by creating nine safe Republican districts, nine safe Democratic districts, and one potentially competitive but strongly Republican-leaning district. Congressional redistricting is a function of demographics and politics, constrained by constitutional standards and the processes and traditions of each state. Illinois is a strongly Democratic-leaning state with a dominant tradition of highly pragmatic and partisan, but not highly ideological, politics. Illinois politics did not change dramatically between 2001 and 2011. Nei-ther did the formal process for congressional redistricting. The demographic changes that took place between 2000 and 2010 in Illinois were in large part a continuation of the changes that took place between 1990 and 2000. The stark difference in the outcome between the process in 2011 from the outcome in 2001 is a function of opportunity and political priorities, not demographic changes.

THE CHANGING DEMOGRAPHICS OF ILLINOIS[5]

Like other upper Midwest states, Illinois's population growth continues to lag behind the national average. In 2010 Illinois's population was 12,830,632. Between 1990 and 2000 Illinois grew at a rate of 8.7 percent, adding 989,000 residents, while the nation grew by 13.2 percent during the same time period. Illinois grew by only 3.3 percent during the past decade, an increase of 412,000. During this time the na-tion's population increased by 9.7 percent. In the zero-sum game of apportioning congressional seats, Illinois has been a consistent loser over the past 60 years. During that time only the 1970 census did not result in the loss of a congressional seat for Illinois. The size of the Illinois delegation has gone from 26 seats prior to the 1950 census to the current number of 18 seats after the 2010 census. In both 2001 and 2011 the task of congressional redistricting in Illinois was complicated by the loss of another congressional seat.

The racial profile of Illinois in 2010 closely mirrors the national breakdown. Non-Hispanic whites make up 63.7 percent of the populations of both Illinois and the nation as a whole. At 14.5 percent, the percentage of blacks is slightly higher than the 12.6 percent of the entire country. The percentage of Hispanics in Illinois is slightly lower than the national percentage, 15.8 percent to 16.3 percent. The Asian portion of the population of Illinois is almost identical to the national percentage, 4.6 percent to 4.8 percent. Illinois was once considered a microcosm or a bellwether for the country because of its racial and economic diversity, urban, suburban, and rural mix, and its political competitiveness. This is no longer the case politically since no Republican candidate for president has carried Illinois since 1988.

In the early part of the twentieth century Illinois was characterized as consisting of two socio-economic and political regions—Chicago and downstate. The suburbanization of Cook County outside of Chicago and the five counties immediately surrounding Cook County and the rapid increase in population and economic growth of these areas gave rise in the late 1960s to a three region characterization of Illinois—Chicago, the collar counties (the suburban 5½), and downstate. Continued suburban development has extended the concept of the "collar counties" beyond the original five counties surrounding Cook County while suburban Cook County is now consists of older suburbs populated with voters who have provided reliable democratic majorities in local, state, and national elections for the past decade. However, a modified three part regional perspective is still a useful analytical frame for examining the demographics and the politics of Illinois. Chicago/Suburban Cook County constitutes one region, although it is sometimes helpful to treat them separately. The six counties immediately around Cook County—DuPage, Kane, Kendal, Lake, McHenry, and Will—constitute a second region—the collar counties. The remaining 95 Illinois counties make up downstate. A single designation of those 95 counties as "downstate" blurs a great amount of variation among those counties, just as speaking of "Chicago" as a single entity hides important demographic, economic, and political distinctions among the city's neighborhoods and communities. But the analytical constructs of Chicago/Suburban Cook County, the collar counties, and downstate have great value in explaining the demographic changes and political considerations that shaped congressional redistricting in Illinois in 2001 and 2011.

Within the 95 downstate counties, the 10 largest counties are Madison, St. Clair, Rock Island, Winnebago, Peoria, Tazewell, McClean, Champaign, Sangamon, and Macon. Madison and St. Clair counties locate in the Metro East area across the Mississippi from St Louis. Belleville is the largest city in St. Clair County. Rock Island County is located in the quad-city area across the Mississippi River from Davenport, Iowa. Rock Island and Moline are the two largest Illinois cities in the area. Winnebago County is located along Illinois northern border with Wisconsin. Its largest city is Rockford. The rest of the largest downstate counties are two bands across the central portion of the state. The northern band consists of Peoria, Tazewell, McClean, and Champaign Counties and the southern band of Sangamon and Macon counties. The primary cities in these central counties are Peoria, Bloomington/Normal, Champaign/Urbana, Decatur, and Springfield. Of these 10 largest downstate counties only McClean and Champaign Counties experienced significant growth between 2000 and 2010.

A 2010 overall snapshot of Illinois's total population and racial makeup does not reveal the significant patterns and variation which shaped congressional redistricting in 2001and 2010. An examination of population and race by region over time is much more informative. Between 1990 and 2000 downstate Illinois grew by 144,000, the collar county area grew by 573,000, suburban Cook County gained 160,000, and Chicago gained 112,000. Between 2000 and 2010 downstate Illinois grew by 127,000, the collar county area grew by 468,000, suburban Cook County gained 18,000, and Chicago lost more than 200,000. In 1990 downstate's share of the state's population was 36.1 percent, the collar county region's was 19.2 percent, suburban Cook's was 20.3 percent, and Chicago's was 24.4 percent. By 2010 the collar county region's share of the state's population had increase by 6 percent to 25.2 percent. The shares of the other three regions all declined. Chicago fell 3.4 percent to 21.0 percent, downstate decreased almost 2 percent to 34.3 percent, and suburban Cook County fell by .8 percent to 19.5 percent. All things being equal, population pressures from the last two decades should shift congressional districts toward the collar county area and away from Chicago and downstate. However, in politics, things are rarely equal.

Because significant differences exist between the partisan voting behaviors of white, black, Hispanic, and Asian voters in Illinois, increases and decreases in the racial makeup of the state or regions in the state will have significant implications for drawing congressional district maps if the goal is to maximize the advantage of one party over the other. Between 1990 and 2000, the number of non-Hispanic whites in Illinois declined by over 126,000. Between 2000 and 2010 the decline was more than 256,000. Between 1990 and 2010 the percentage of non-Hispanic whites decreased from 74.8 percent of the state's population to 63.7 percent. Between 1990 and 2000, the number of blacks in Illinois increased by over 206,000. Between 2000 and 2010 the total decreased slightly (15,000). In 1990 blacks accounted for 14.8 percent of the state's population. By 2010 the percentage had fallen slightly to 14.5 percent. Between 1990 and 2000, the number of Hispanics in Illinois increased by over 506,000. Between 2000 and 2010 the increase was 415,000. Between 1990 and 2010 the percentage of Hispanics increased from 7.9 percent of the state's population to 15.8 percent. Between 1990 and 2000, the number of Asians in Illinois increased by over 138,000. Between 2000 and 2010 the increase was 167,000. Between 1990 and 2010 the percentage of Asians increased from 2.5 percent of the state's population to 4.6 percent.

While white voters in the state as a whole lean Republican, black and Hispanic voters are strongly Democratic. Asian voters lean Democratic. A relative increase or decrease in groups who tend to favor one party's candidates over the others can be a strong strategic factor in drawing new congressional districts. This is particularly true if those increases or decreases are concentrated in a specific region in the state.

The downstate region of Illinois has been relatively stagnant over the past two decades when compared to the rest of the state. The residents of the region are predominantly white. The percentage of white non-Hispanic residents was 84 percent in 2010, down from 88 percent in 2000 and 91 percent in 1990. The modest population growth that occurred in the region over the past two decades came from small increases in minority populations who are concentrated in large and medium-sized downstate cities. In 2010, 9 percent of downstate residents were black, and 5 percent were Hispanic.

Chicago gained over 110,000 residents between 1990 and 2000 and then lost almost 200,000 residents between 2000 and 2010. The number of non-white Hispanic residents in Chicago declined steadily between 1990 and 2010, falling from 1,056,000 in 1990 to 855,000 in 2010. The number of black residents remained at slightly more than a million from 1990 to 2000 and then declined by more than 180,000 between 2000 and 2010. A significant factor in that decline appears to be an out-migration of blacks to areas outside the state, particularly the south.[6] The decline in black and white residents was partially offset by a steady increase in Hispanic and Asian residents. In 2010 Chicago was 33 percent black, 32 percent white, 29 percent Hispanic, and 6 percent Asian. This is a significant change from 1990, when the breakdown was 39 percent black, 38 percent white, 20 percent Hispanic, and 3 percent Asian.

Suburban Cook County had a steady, modest growth over the past two decades, adding more than 225,000 residents since 1990. However, the racial profile of the region has changed dramatically. In 1990 the region was 80 percent white, 10 percent black, 6 percent Hispanic, and 4 percent Asian. By 2000, the percent of white residents had declined to 68 percent while the percent of blacks had increased to 14 percent and Hispanics to 13 percent. In 2010, suburban Cook County was 58 percent white, 16 percent black, 19 percent Hispanic, and 6 percent Asian.

The collar county region is the fastest growing region in the state, adding almost a million residents since 1990. While the racial makeup of the region has not shifted as dramatically as Suburban Cook County, it has changed significantly. The percentage of white residents has dropped from 85 percent in 1990 to 78 percent in 2000 to 70 percent in 2010. At the same time the percent of Hispanic voters has increased significantly, going from 7 percent in 1990 to 12 percent in 2000 and 18 percent in 2010. The Asian population has doubled in the past to decade and stood at 6 percent in 2010. The percent of black residents in the region has increased only slightly from 5 percent in 1990 to 6 percent in 2010.

THE POLITICAL DEMOGRAPHICS OF ILLINOIS[7]

The reality of the regional differences in Illinois politics is clearly demonstrated in a public opinion poll published by the *Chicago Tribune* in early February of 2012.[8] Overall the president's approval rating in Illinois was 53 percent approve and 40 percent disapprove. Those overall numbers mask stark differences between the regions of Illinois. In Chicago the president's ratings were 82 percent approve and 16 percent disapprove. In suburban Cook County the numbers were 63 percent approve and 30 percent disapprove. In the traditional 5 collar counties the numbers were 48 percent approve and 44 percent disapprove. In downstate the numbers were 36 percent approve and 56 percent disapprove. Residents of Chicago and downstate were at polar opposites, while residents of suburban Cook strongly supported the president and the residents of the collar county region were split in their assessment.

Redistricting is a process which combines population with geography. Congressional districts are geographically defined territories. When political attitudes and voting behavior varies by geographic region, they create opportunities and challenges for those who draw the district boundaries. In the hands of a partisan mapmaker those opportunities and challenges can translate into significant partisan advantages and disadvantages.

In 1978 Colby and Green wrote an article for *Illinois Issues* declaring that "Downstate holds the key to Victory."[9] They argued that the voting power of Democrats in Chicago and Republicans in the suburban Cook County and the surrounding collar counties were equal and that statewide elections would be won in the competitive arena of the remaining downstate counties. The downstate region was a battleground in statewide election during the next 20 years. But over the past two decades downstate has become more and more Republican in its voting patterns. No Democratic candidate for governor has carried downstate in any of the last six elections. In 2010 Democrat Pat Quinn won the race for governor, but lost downstate by 349,000 votes. President Obama carried the downstate region of his home state in 2008, but President Bush carried the region in 2000 and 2004. In the only two elections for U.S. Senate in the last two decades where the Republicans fielded a strong candidate (1998 and 2010), downstate went Republican by 328,000 and 360,000 votes. In 2010 with the entire House up for election and running under a map drawn by the Democrats in 2001, the Democrats picked up one suburban seat, lost one suburban seat, and lost five downstate seats. This is a continuation of a decade-long pattern of the Democrats picking up seats in the legislature in the suburbs and losing seats downstate. In 2010 a Republican candidate easily won a downstate district crafted in 2001 to reelect a Democratic incumbent. There are areas of continuing democratic strength in the downstate region which can be drawn together into congressional districts that favor Democrats. However, when faced with a choice in 2001 between the interest of Chicago and downstate, the leaders of the Democratic Party choose to eliminate a downstate Democratic district in the new congressional map. The new congressional map crafted in 2011 by the Democrats is designed to hold on to two downstate democratic districts while trying to create gains for the Democrats in the collar county region. Clearly the Democrats who drew the 2011 congressional map did not see the future of the Democratic Party in downstate Illinois.

Chicago has maintained its power in Illinois politics by delivering consistently large Democratic majorities in spite of almost no population growth between 1990 and 2000 and a significant loss of population between 2000 and 2010. In each of the past three races for governor, the Democratic candidate has won Chicago by more than 400,000 votes. That margin is more than 150,000 votes greater than the average Democratic margin for the previous three gubernatorial elections. Even allowing for the home state popularity of President Obama, the trend line for the margin of victory from Chicago for Democratic candidates for president has been steadily upward. However, these voting outcomes in statewide elections do not counterbalance relative losses in population by Chicago in regard to other regions of the state. When undertaking redistricting under the rule of one man-one vote, a Chicago with a declining population that is becoming increasingly more Democratic presents a target for a Republican mapmaker who would be happy to pack Democratic voters into supermajority districts located as much as possible within the boundaries of the city. The political demographics of Chicago are also a challenge for a Democratic mapmaker who wants to maintain the same number of congressional districts anchored in Chicago.

In the 2002 general election Democratic gubernatorial candidate Rod Blagojevich won suburban Cook County by more than 50,000 votes. This was the first time in modern Illinois political history stretching back to the pre-suburban early post-war era that a Democrat candidate for governor had done so. In 2006 and 2010 the Democratic candidates for governor won the region by more than 100,000 votes. Democratic candidates for president have won suburban Cook County by comfortable margins since 1992. The only time in the past 30 years that a Republican candidate for the U.S. Senate candidate carried the region was 1998, and then the margin was 13,000 votes. Suburban Cook County has gone from being a key part of the suburban base of the Illinois Republican party during the 1970s and the 1980s to more and more a dependable part of the base of the Illinois Democratic Party over the past 20 years. Chicago's one time political rival has become its partner. In 2010 the Democratic candidate for governor won Chicago and suburban Cook County by 900,000 votes while the Democratic candidate for the U.S. Senate won the region by 898,000 votes.

Over the past 40 years political power in the Republican Party in Illinois has shifted from downstate to the collar counties. When the Republicans gained control over both chambers of the state legislature in 1992, the new house speaker and senate president were both from collar county districts. This was a first for the modern era in Illinois politics. Suburban legislators continue to have majorities in both Republican caucuses. Most of the population growth in the state of the past two decades has been centered in the collar counties. Republican political power in the collar counties is formidable. No Democratic candidate for governor or president in the past 20 years, with the exception of President Obama in 2008, has carried the region. While the Republican Party dominates elections in the collar counties, voting patterns in the region have become less Republican and more competitive. The increased racial diversity of the collar county region has had a strong political effect, as has outmigration from Chicago and the older suburbs close to Chicago. Even with the 2001 congressional map designed to protect incumbents, the Democrats won one collar county region seat in 2006 from a Republican incumbent and captured two open seats anchored in the region in 2008 that had previously been held by Republicans. All three seats switched back to the Republican candidates in 2010.

THE CONGRESSIONAL
REDISTRICTING PROCESS IN ILLINOIS

Of the 44 states with more than one congressional district, there are 20 where their state constitutions impose no requirements or specific criteria for drawing congressional districts. Illinois is one of those 20 states. The drafters of the 1970 Illinois State Constitution created a unique hybrid process for redistricting the state legislature, combining the legislative process with a deadline with the fallback of an eight-member redistricting commission if the legislature and governor fail to act by the deadline. This commission also has a deadline and a fallback provision for adding a ninth member by random selection if the commission fails to act by the deadline. This method of redistricting has proven very controversial. Rather than encourage compromise as the framers intended, it resulted in a winner-take-all redistricting lottery in 1980, 1990, and 2000. But on the matter of congressional redistricting, the 1970 state constitution is silent.

A new law was adopted by Illinois in the spring of 2011(PA 96-1541) to provide additional criteria for the redistricting of the state legislature and set up a committee structure and procedures for developing the maps for state legislative districts. These provisions do not apply to congressional redistricting. However, the congressional maps that were adopted by the legislature in 2011 were considered and approved by the House and Senate committees created by the new law.

The formal process of congressional redistricting in Illinois traditionally takes one of two paths. The first is that the legislature and the governor will agree on a new map which becomes law. The new map will inevitably be challenged in the Federal Courts by partisan groups who believe they have been unfairly disadvantaged by the new map, or by minority groups who believe the new maps do not provide them the opportunity to be represented in proportion to their population numbers. These groups will sue the Illinois State Board of Election (SBE), who is charged with administering the new law. According to 28 US Code subsec. 2284(a), these suits will be heard in federal district court before a three-judge panel as required by federal law for cases involving challenges to the appointment of congressional districts or the appointment of any statewide legislative body.

If the legislature and the governor fail to enact a new congressional district map, the process goes down the second path. Absent the creation a new map, the SBE will proceed to administer the upcoming primary and general election under the old congressional district map. At that point multiple parties will sue the SBE in federal district court. These suits will ask the Court to enjoin the SBE and to adopt a new map (designed by the party bringing suit) to replace the old map for the upcoming primary and general election. The same federal law applies to this situation, and a three-judge panel will be created to hear the case.

ILLINOIS CONGRESSIONAL REDISTRICTING IN 2001

Leading up to release of the 2000 census data in the spring of 2001, there was concern and uncertainty in the minds of those most interested in congressional redistricting, the 20 incumbent congressmen. It was not clear whether or not Illinois population growth would allow it to retain 20 seats in Congress. If not, one of the incumbents would not be returning to Congress. Faced with losing a seat, the next question is where? The population trends from the previous two census reports suggested that Chicago and downstate Illinois would both suffer relative losses in relation to the collar county area.

There were three findings in the 2000 census data with major implications for congressional redistricting in Illinois. The first was not a surprise. Illinois would lose a seat in the 2001 apportionment of congressional seats because of its relatively slow overall growth for the previous decade. The other two findings were surprises. First Chicago gained population during the decade, more than 110,000. Between 1980 and 1990 Chicago's population has declined by more than 215,000, and some loss of population for the 2000 census seemed likely. The combined population gain for Chicago and suburban Cook County, while not large, was twice that of the downstate region. The second surprise was the increase in Hispanic residents in particular and minority residents in general in the collar counties. More than 52 percent of the population gain in the collar counties between 1990 and 2000 came from Hispanics, blacks, and Asians.

Congressional redistricting was not a primary concern of those in control of state government in the spring of 2001. With the legislature controlled by the Democrats and a Republican in the governor's office, the prospect was for another long drawn out process for redistricting the state legislature. In 1981 and 1991 a partisan split between the legislature and the governor's office had resulted in the formation of a bipartisan eight-member redistricting commission as required by the state constitution. Both times the commission failed to reach an agreement by August 10. Once this deadline was passed, a ninth member was added by drawing a name from two names submitted by the State Supreme Court as representative of the two parties. This had to be completed by September 5. The newly constituted nine-member commission had to produce a map by October 5. This was followed with lawsuits by partisan groups and minority groups in both state and federal court. All of this took place against the Illinois election calendar which requires those seeking state or federal office to file nominating petitions by early December so that Illinois's general primary can be held in March. When the state legislative redistricting process plays out this way over more than nine months, it consumes all the time, resources, and energy that the legislative leaders and political party officials can muster. Against this backdrop, congressional redistricting took a backseat in the legislature, particularly when party control of state government was split and a legislative resolution of either state or congressional redistricting seemed unlikely. State legislative redistricting in 2001 did repeat the process of 1981 and 1991. Congressional redistricting, however, took a different path.

In 2001 the Democratic legislature passed a congressional redistricting bill which the Republican governor signed into law in June. The proposed map represented an agreement between 19 of the 20 incumbent congressmen. Why would they enter into an agreement? Why would the legislature and the governor defer to them and ratify the agreement? The answer to the first question lies in the content of the agreement.

After the 1992 election, Democrats held 12 of the 20 congressional seats in Illinois. In the wave election of 1994 Republicans pick up a seat in a suburban district. In 1996 Richard Durban, a longtime incumbent from a downstate congressional district, ran for an open U.S. Senate seat. His congressional seat was won by a Republican, leaving the congressional delegation split 10–10. In 1998 and 2000 there were no close congressional elections in either the primary or the general elections. All of the incumbents were expected to seek reelection in 2002, depending on the outcome of redistricting. The demographic data from the 2000 census showed a general stability in Chicago and suburban Cook County. The growth in minority populations in the region could result in political shifts in terms of who was elected from safe Democratic districts. The greater concern among the incumbents from the Chicago region was that the number of districts from Chicago could be reduced by a winner-take-all court decision. A map drafted by Republican interests could pack Democratic votes into Chicago by significantly reducing the overlapping of Chicago districts into suburban Cook County.

Chicago's population in 2000 was slightly more than 2,896,000. To comply with the equal population requirement, each of Illinois's 19 new districts would have to have approximately 654,000 residents. Dividing those two population numbers yields 4.4 districts. It would have been difficult to maintain 3 black and 1 Hispanic district in Chicago without overlapping into suburban Cook County. But packing Democratic votes inside Chicago would have reduced the total number of Chicago districts while creating more options to overlap Republican districts anchored in the collar counties into suburban Cook County. This kind of math had to be sobering for the seven incumbent congressmen who had Chicago addresses for their principal district offices.

The 2010 demographic data was certainly reassuring for the six incumbent congressmen representing the collar county region. The region was not in danger of losing seats. However, the data clearly showed growing concentrations of racial minorities who could be expected to be generally less supportive of Republican candidates. The six incumbent Republican congressmen from the collar counties could see short-term mischief and long-term danger from a map drawn to maximize Democratic advantage in the region. The state legislative maps drawn in 2001 and 2011 and the congressional map drawn in 2011 by the Democratic legislative leaders, when they had complete control of the process, demonstrated that such concerns were well founded.

The incumbent Democratic congressmen from Chicago and the incumbent Republican congressmen from collar counties could all see danger in maps drawn to maximize the election advantage of the opposite party. They could all see the value of having more favorable districts that would discourage both primary and general election opposition. The picture downstate was shaped by the demographic and political trends of the preceding decade and simple three-man coalition strategy. In 2001 there were four incumbent Republicans and three incumbent Democrats representing downstate districts. As noted earlier, the political demographics of the downstate Illinois region have shifted from a Republican-leaning but competitive region in the 1970s and 1980s to a solidly Republican region with areas of Democratic strength. The population demographics favored the loss of a congressional seat from downstate although it would have been possible to reduce the number of Chicago districts. In 2000 Republican votes in the downstate region were widely dispersed in comparison to Democratic votes which were concentrated in urban areas and a few sparsely populated counties in deep southern Illinois. If the number of downstate districts were reduced from seven to six, there were a number of options for creating Republican districts in the downstate region and only a few for creating Democratic districts. The danger of being the odd man out was greater for the three downstate Democratic congressmen than for the four Republican congressmen.

In retrospect, congressional redistricting in Illinois in 2011 could have played out in a number of ways. One option would have been for Democratic interests, led by the incumbent Democratic congressmen to propose an aggressive Democratic map which eliminated a Republican district in the downstate region and constructed Democratic-leaning districts in the collar counties with the intent of picking up Democratic seats. Republican interest, led by the incumbent Republican congressmen, would have proposed an aggressive Republican map which eliminated a Democratic district downstate, packed Democratic votes into Chicago districts, and constructed Republican-leaning districts in suburban Cook County which overlapped into the collar counties with the intent of picking up Republican seats. Both sides would have ultimately taken their chances in federal court. The other option was for the competing interest to strike a deal to preserve the status quo, or at least most of it. This is what happened.

Negotiations between Republican congressman Dennis Hastert, the speaker of the House, and Democratic Chicago congressman and long-time Chicago ward committeeman William Lipinski produced an agreement to draw a map to protect the reelection chances of 19 incumbent Illinois congressmen and essentially eliminate the downstate district represented by incumbent Democratic congressmen David Phelps.[10] The proposed map retained the strength of those districts which had been considered safe and made all of the remaining districts less competitive. The agreement appealed to the narrow self-interest of the congressmen representing Chicago and collar county districts and the four Republicans representing downstate districts.

For the three Democrats representing downstate districts, the situation was a classic case of odd man out. One downstate Democratic congressman Jerry Costello, represented a district anchored in the Democratic-leaning Metro East area and had been a member of congress since 1992. The population and political demographics of the Metro East area would have made it difficult to put Costello at risk without creating risks for an incumbent Republican congressman or pairing him up with Congressman Phelps. Congressman Phelps represented a largely rural district stretching from the southern tip of Illinois to Decatur, the one urban area of any size in the district located at its far northern end. Neither Costello nor Phelps would have agreed to a map that put them in the same district. The third Democratic downstate congressman, Lane Evans, represented a district anchored in the Quad City area and had been a member of Congress since 1982. The Democratic base of Evans's district was not as strong as Costello's, but putting Evans at risk would have made the seats of the surrounding Republican congressmen less safe. Ultimately the deal offered to Costello and Evans probably came down to demographics and seniority. Evans had been in Congress since 1982 and Costello since 1992. Both had stronger ties to the other members of the Illinois legislature than did Phelps.

With the 18 incumbents on board, the next step was to sell the agreement to the leaders of the four party caucuses in the legislature controlled by the Democrats and the Republican governor. A general reason for the legislature and the governor to ratify the agreement was to get the issue off the table, particularly if it is not your highest priority. Time (and resources) not spent on congressional redistricting, either during the session or during the long court battle that would have been the likely result of failed negotiation in the legislature, is time available for working on legislative redistricting, the state budget, and policy issues. For the Republican legislative leaders and the Republican governor there was little downside to a plan advanced by the senior Republican member of the Illinois congressional delegation that would eliminate a seat held by a Democrat and protect all the Republican incumbents. For the two Democratic leaders who were both from Chicago the decision was more difficult. The plan generated resistance from downstate Democrats in both democratic caucuses. There was push back from the newspapers in southern Illinois that the Democratic leaders in the Senate were protecting Chicago's interest rather than the overall interest of the Democratic Party. While either Democrat leader could have blocked the plan, they ultimately backed it and turned it into legislation which created a district designed to achieve the political goals of the map while meeting constitutional criteria. In the end a strong majority of the Democrats in the legislature supported the plan along with the Republican members.

The mechanics of redistricting involves combining census data with political data down to the precinct level in order to construct districts which achieve political goals while meeting constitutional criteria. This is a complex and expensive task in terms of software and database construction and management. In addition to the science dimension there is also an art dimension. Deciding which elections and which demographic data to include and how to weight them in constructing voting models is a very difficult, often intuitive task. In Illinois the legislature provides resources to the political caucuses to prepare for the redistricting task. While the legislative leaders' first priority is maps for the state legislature, the same groundwork needed to prepare for constructing state legislative maps was also applied to constructing congressional maps. National congressional election committees for the two political parties are also active in gathering and analyzing census and election data. Advances in data sets, database technology, and software have made it easier for groups and individuals to analyze census and political data. But the focal point for the mechanics of redistricting in Illinois is the redistricting staff and operations put together by the four legislative leaders.

It is almost impossible to overstate how powerful the legislative leaders in general, and the Democratic leaders in particular, are in the Illinois legislature. Over the past 40 years power has become more and more centralized, particularly under longtime Speaker Michael Madigan. The speaker and Senate president control the legislative process and all of the staff in Springfield. They also control the financing of targeted legislative races and actually run most of the campaigns in these races through campaign organizations made up of partisan legislative staffers on leave of absence from their jobs with the legislature. With redistricting, as with most issues, the Democrat legislative leaders are the most important actors. While the governor in Illinois can be a counterbalance to the legislative leaders, this was not the case in 2011. The incumbent governor was already succumbing to a political scandal. In the summer he would announce he would not seek reelection. In 2011, there would be a newly elected Democratic governor. But he was weakened by an ongoing budget crisis and the general perception he was ineffective.

The 2001 Illinois congressional map is the kind of sweetheart, incumbent protection map that results from letting representatives choose their constituent rather than having constituents choose their representatives (see maps 18.1 and 18.2).

All of the 19 incumbents who agreed to the new maps were reelected in 2002. In the downstate region, Congressman Phelps's former district was spilt among four other districts. His home in Eldorado was connected by a corridor to the 15th District, which had been extended south more than 125 miles by a narrow band along the Illinois-Indiana border. Had he chosen to run the 15th District against the incumbent Republican congressman, his home would have been more than 250 miles from its northern border. A small part of Phelps's district was placed in Congressman Costello's expanded 12th District, which, while a safe Democratic district, was a poor election option for Phelps. The majority of territory from Phelps's old district was joined to the new 19th, which was represented by Republican Congressman John Shimkus. Phelps chose to run against Shimkus and lost a close election.

The two remaining downstate districts represented by Republicans (the 16th and 18th) were easily expanded to meet the population requirement. Creating a safe Democratic district for Congressmen Evans presented a much greater challenge. The new 16th is a partisan gerrymander to behold. It retains its old urban center in the Quad Cities, moves south along the western quarter of central Illinois, narrows as it stretches south along the Mississippi River. It then moves east picking up large portions of two traditionally Democratic-leaning counties and then splits into two corridors. One continues east into traditional Democratic areas, while the other swings north, runs through the center of Springfield, the state capitol, in a block-wide corridor, expands to pick up the black population on the eastside of Springfield, and then runs along I-72 to pick up most of the City of Decatur. The district wraps around the 18th district with a corridor less than 5 miles wide connecting the upper and lower portions of the district on the east. A line draw from two largest population centers in the district, the Quad Cities and

ILLINOIS CONGRESSIONAL DISTRICTS

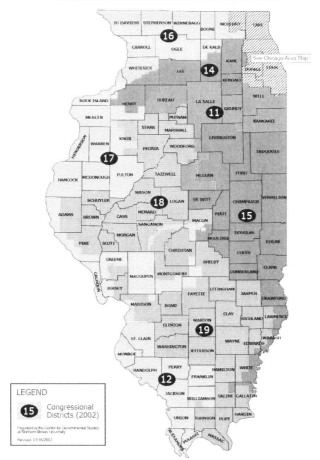

Map 18.1.   2002 Illinois Congressional Districts. Center for Governmental Studies at Northern Illinois University.

Decatur, would cover a distance of more than 150 miles, but would be contained almost entirely in the 18th District, not the 17th. A written description of the district really does not do it justice.

Protecting incumbent Chicago congressmen limited the option of adjusting collar county districts eastward into suburban Cook County. Two districts that had been extended into the downstate area were further expanded by the 2001 map, adding territory and some population. The 14th was extended 50 miles further west across the northern part of the state, picking up Republican voters from rural counties while retaining its core in the western suburbs in Kane County. The 11th, still anchored in the south suburbs of Will County, was shifted out of Cook County and

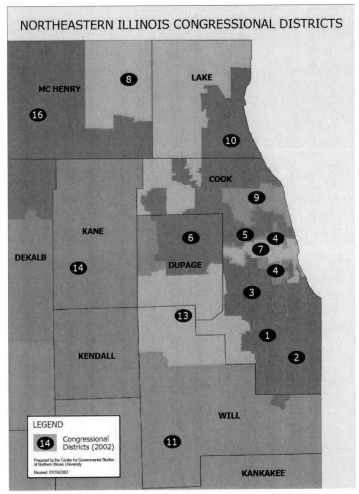

Map 18.2. 2002 Northeast Illinois Congressional Districts. Center for Governmental Studies at Northern Illinois University.

pushed south and west. It was further extended by drawing a corridor 50 miles south from its 1991 border to pick up Republican voters in the Bloomington/Normal area. The population of the southwestern suburban 13th District had grown sufficiently for it to retain the general boundaries from the 1991 map. The core of the district was in DuPage and Will Counties with a portion in suburban Cook. The western suburban 6th District shifted west slightly with DuPage County as its core with a portion in Cook County. The 8th District expanded further west by adding territory from McHenry County and moved further into Lake County on the east while losing Cook County territory to the south. Under the 2001 map a large majority lived in Lake County. The 10th District shifted slightly by moving its northern border in

Lake County south and moving its western border further west in Cook County. A majority of its voters still lived in Cook County.

The changes to the seven Chicago region districts under the 2001 map reflected the population changes that had taken place during the past decade. The western boundary of the 9th congressional district move westward further into Cook County. Under the 1991 map a majority of the voters in the district lived in Chicago. Under the 2001 map a majority were located in Cook County. The Chicago-based 4th, 5th, and 7th Districts retained their essential location and shape. The 3rd District was expanded further west into southwestern Cook County. A majority of its voters were located in Cook County outside Chicago under both the 1991 and 2001 maps. Reflecting the movement of minority populations into southern and southwestern Cook County, the 1st District expanded further into the southwest suburbs, and the 2nd District moved further south into suburban Cook County. While the great majority of the voters in the 1st District lived in Chicago under both maps, more voters in the 2nd District lived in Cook County than in Chicago under the 2001 map.

While the map was designed to elect 10 Republicans and 9 Democrats, its performance over the decade illustrates the limitations of mapmaking. Safe districts are safe, all things being equal. But when it comes to campaigns, candidates, and events in any given election cycle, all things are rarely equal. In 2002 all the incumbents won reelection. In 2004 a Democratic candidate upset a longtime Republican incumbent in a suburban district by convincing voters that the incumbent has lost interest in the district. In 2006 a Democratic candidate won an open suburban seat formerly held by a Republican. In 2008 a Democratic candidate won a third suburban district which became open when the Republican incumbent resigned after a scandal. In 2010 the Democrat incumbents in those three suburban districts lost, along with a Democrat incumbent in a downstate district. While maps are important, they are not determinate.

ILLINOIS CONGRESSIONAL REDISTRICTING IN 2011

The outcome of the 2011 congressional redistricting in Illinois was probably decided on February 2, 2010. On that date State Senator Bill Brady defeated State Senator Kirk Dillard for the Republican nomination for governor by 193 votes. Democratic Governor Pat Quinn had barely survived a challenge from State Comptroller Dan Hynes in the Democratic primary. Illinois was mired in a post-Blagojevich fiscal crisis, and Governor Quinn's approval rating had been declining steadily. With favorable legislative district maps drawn by the Democrats in 2001, only one-third of the state Senate seats up for election, and powerful Speaker Michael Madigan's political organization gearing up for the fall election, the Democrats were expected to retain control of both chambers of the state legislature, which they did. Before the primary the reelection prospects for Governor Quinn, who had been the lieutenant governor before Blagojevich's impeachment and removal from office, looked dismal, even if he survived the primary.

However, on November 2, 2010, Quinn defeated Brady by 31,834 votes out of the 3.46 million cast. By choosing Brady, a downstate social conservative over Dillard, a less conservative candidate from the collar counties, the Republicans selected the weaker candidate. Brady lost the election by underperforming among moderate Republicans and independent voters in the collar counties, while Quinn's margin in Chicago and Cook County overcame Brady's margin downstate. For the first time since the reapportionment revolution of the 1960s one party would control both the state legislature and the governor's office. The Democrats had the power to enact a new congressional map into law without any input from the Republicans. As expected, Illinois lost a seat in the reapportionment of Congress following the 2010 census. The Democrats would have to draw a new map with 18 districts.

In a year when Democrats in congress and in state elections did not fare well, the Democrats in Illinois did well in Illinois, retaining control of both chambers of the legislature and reelecting a governor, secretary of state, and attorney general. The one group of Democrats that did not fare well on election night in Illinois were Democratic candidates for Congress. After the 2008 election Democrats held a 12 to 7 margin. Four Democratic incumbents were defeated in the 2010 election, giving the Republicans an 11 to 8 margin. The remaining Democrats were seven incumbents from safe districts in Chicago or Cook County districts and an incumbent from a safe district located in the downstate metro east area. Any map drafted by the Democrats would retain these districts as safe seats. While it's never good to lose four incumbents, the irony of the situation is that the Democrats could now draw a map designed to maximize the number of potential Democrat seats without being concerned about the need to protect incumbents and with incumbents who would not be overly concerned about reasonable adjustments in their districts.

Within input from the staff of the Democratic Congressional Campaign Committee and incumbent Democratic congressmen, the legislative redistricting staff undertook the task of creating a new congressional district map for Illinois. As noted above, the key actors in the process were the two Democratic legislative leaders, House Speaker Michael Madigan and Senate President John Cullerton. Drawing a new congressional map involved three interrelated tasks. The first was to draw districts for the seven incumbent Chicago congressmen. The major complicating factor was whether the new census data would make it possible or necessary to create a second Hispanic district in Chicago. The second was to create some districts within the collar county region that would elect Democrats. The third was to maintain a safe district for the Democratic incumbent in the metro east area while creating a second downstate district that would be likely to elect a Democrat. Each of these is a part that fits together into a whole. An adjustment in one proposed district can have a cascading impact on other proposed districts.

The 2011 map creates seven safe Democratic districts in and around Chicago; the 9th, 5th, 4th, 7th, 3rd, 1st, and 2nd (see map 18.3). The total is the same as under the 2001 map in spite of the fact that Chicago lost significant population during the

**Map 18.3.   2011 Illinois Statewide Congressional Districts. Illinois
Redistricting,   http://ilhousedems.com/redistricting/2011-maps/
Legislative_Districts_Public_Act/Statewide_PA970006.pdf.**

last decade and suburban Cook County's population was essentially flat (see map
18.4). The key was carefully extending some of these districts into the collar county
area while retaining their partisan identity. All of the incumbent congressmen from
the old districts are running in 2010. The only serious primary challenge in the region
is occurring in the 2nd District.

The 9th District continues to be a suburban Cook County district which overlaps
into Chicago. The 2011 map moved the district father west into parts of Wheeling
and Elk Grove Townships and further north in New Trier and Northfield Townships
(see map 18.5). The anchor of the district remains the city of Evanston and the Rogers Park area of Chicago. The new 9th District also includes the home of Republican
Congressman Dold from the old 10th District, who is not running in this district.

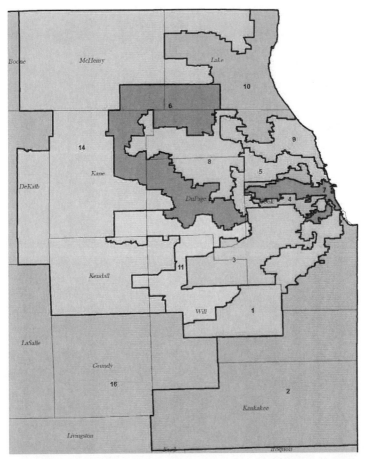

**Map 18.4. 2011 Cook and Collar County Congressional Districts.
Illinois Redistricting, www.ilhousedems.com/redistricting/2011-maps/
Congressional_Proposed_Districts_PDFS/CDCookCollarPA.pdf.**

The 5th District lies to the south of the 9th. This Chicago district stretches west from the Chicago Loop into the north side of Chicago and includes O'Hare Airport. Under the 2011 map territory, the western edge of the district now reaches south into DuPage County before swinging back to pick an area in the western suburbs of Cook County.

To the south of the 5th District is the northern half of the Hispanic 4th District which wraps around the 7th District in an elongated "C" shape. The voting age population of the district is 66 percent Hispanic and 26 percent white. The two halves of the district are still connected on the west by a band along the Tri-state Tollway (I-294). The major adjustment in the 2011 maps is a widening to the connector band to add more residents to the district.

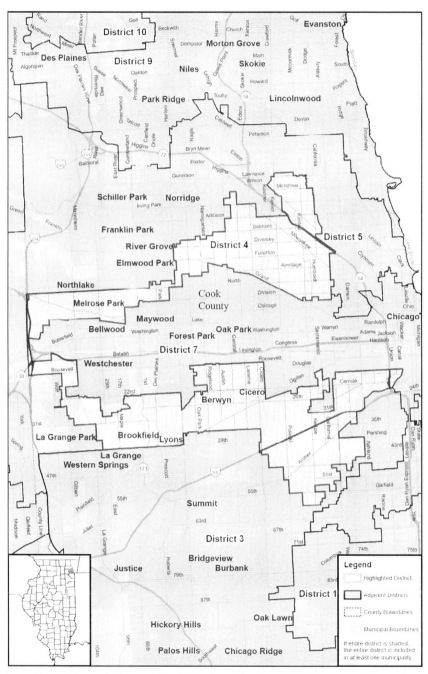

Map 18.5. 2011 4th Congressional District. Illinois Redistricting, www.ilhousedems
.com/redistricting/.

The 7th District is a majority black district sandwiched between the two halves of the 4th District. It runs from the Chicago lakefront west along the Eisenhower Expressway to the western border of Cook County. It also extends south of downtown into the southwest side of Chicago. The 2011 map expanded the southern part of the district further southwest. It has a 50 percent Black and 11 percent Hispanic voting age population.

The 3rd District was significantly changed by the 2011 map. It was expanded south and west into Lemont and Orland townships in far southwestern Cook County and then west into Will County. It still retains some areas in Chicago, but is a much more suburban district than under the 2001 map. Its voting age population is 66 percent white and 25 percent Hispanic.

The 1st Congressional District is anchored in the south side of Chicago. The 2011 map extends the district to the southwest into Will County with the geographic territory of the district split between Cook and Will County. It is a majority black district with 52 percent of the voting age population being black and 37 percent white.

The 2nd District is the third majority-black Chicago district. It is anchored in the far south side of Chicago, but now extends much further south through the eastern half of Will County into Kankakee County. Under the 2011 map it is a black majority district with a voting age population of 54 percent black, 33 percent white, and 11 percent Hispanic. The incumbent from the old 2nd District, Congressman Jesse Jackson, was challenged in the primary by former Congressman Debbie Halverson, who represented the southern part of the district before losing her seat in 2010. Jackson was able to hold off Halverson and win the general election but later resigned his seat due to personal health concerns.

The 2011 map creates 5 districts in the collar county region: the 14th, 10th, 6th, 8th, and 11th. This is a reduction of one from the 2001 map. This was accomplished primarily by packing Republican votes into districts in the region. Under the 2001 map, districts anchored in the suburbs were extended out into downstate areas. Of itself, making the district lost by Illinois to reapportionment a Republican district from the collar county area would have been a significant partisan achievement. But the Democratic mapmakers had even more ambitious goals in the collar county region.

The heart of the new 14th District is the same as the old 14th, Kane and Kendal Counties. The old 14th ran west of Kane and Kendal Counties across portions of five largely rural downstate counties. That portion of the district except for an expanded portion of DeKalb County was eliminated by the 2011 map. The new 14th District runs north from Kane County and picks up most of McHenry County, incorporating territory previously located in the old 16th and 18th Districts. The new 14th then runs east into Lake County picking up areas that were located in the old 10th District. This district is strongly Republican. It contains the home of two incumbent Republican Congressmen, Randy Hultgren (14th) and Joe Walsh (8th). After flirting with running against Hultgren in the new 14th in the primary, Walsh chose to run in the open 8th. This district was designed to pack Republican votes, and it should be a solid Republican district throughout the decade.

The old 10th District was a very competitive district located in far northern Cook County and the eastern half of Lake County along the shore of Lake Michigan. The new 10th has much of the same territory as the old, but it is more Democratic. The district was extended to the Wisconsin Border on the north and to the east through the center of Lake County to the county's western border. Republican-leaning areas of Cook County formerly in the district were shifted into the strongly Republican 6th District. The far southern part of the district in Cook County which contains the home of the Republican incumbent Robert Dold was shifted into the 9th District. Congressman Dold chose to run in his old district rather than the more Democratic-leaning 9th. The voting age population of the district is 65 percent white, 18 percent Hispanic, and 10 percent Asian.

The new 6th District was drawn to pack as many Republican votes as possible into a very safe district. The old 6th was a compact district covering about 40 percent of DuPage County and extending into the northwestern part of Cook County. The new district has a "C" shape with the upper portion reaching into McHenry County and running east into portions of Cook and Lake Counties. The bottom portion runs south from the southeast corner of McHenry County through a portion of Kane County and then runs southeast through a large part of DuPage County. Overall the district shifts west and north with the new 8th District lying between the upper and lower portion of the new 6th. The district contains the homes of two incumbent Republican members of Congress. Congressman Peter Roskam will represent the district in the next congress. Congresswoman Judy Biggert is running in the new 11th District.

Most of the old 8th District is now part of the new 14th and 10th Districts. The new 8th includes the city of Elgin in Kane County on its western boundary. From there the district extends east into Cook County and south into DuPage County, picking up areas of Democratic strength. Its voting age population is 61 percent white, 22 percent Hispanic, and 12 percent Asian. This is a Democratic-leaning district which reflects the impact of demographic changes that have occurred in the collar county region over the past two decades. The winner of the Democratic primary will face off in the fall against Republican Congressman Joe Walsh, who declined to challenge Republican Congressman Roskam in the 6th District.

The final new collar county region district is the 11th. The new 11th has a portion to the north of I-55 that picks up the southern part of DuPage County from the old 13th District and extends east to pick up the southeast corner of Kane County containing the city of Aurora from the old 14th District. The portion to the south and east of I-55 picks up territory in Will County from the old 11th District running north and south along I-80 including the city of Joliet. The voting age population of the district is 60 percent white, 22 percent Hispanic, and 11 percent black. The district leans Democrat. Incumbent Republican Congresswoman Judy Biggert from the old 13th District is running in the district, as is former Democratic Congressman Bill Foster, who represented the old 14th District in 2009–2010.

Under the 2001 map, six congressional districts were anchored in the collar county region. Four of those districts elected a Republican five times during the decade, one elected a Republican four times, and one elected a Republican three times. The 2011 map drawn by the Democratic leaders in the legislature created five districts anchored in the collar county region. Based on the past voting behavior of the precincts, the Democrat mapmakers expect that two districts (6th and 14th) will be safe Republican seats and three (10th, 8th, and 11th) will go Democratic. While the seat loss to redistricting cannot be counted as a pick up for the Illinois Democrats, the 2011 map could result in a loss of four seats for the Illinois Republicans in the collar county area. Such an outcome would be partially attributable to demographic changes in the region; the major factor would be aggressive, creative mapmaking.

The 2011 map creates six districts in the downstate region; the 16th, 17th, 18th, 13th, 16th, and 12th. The goals of the map were to protect the incumbent Democratic congressman in the 12th District and draw a district around the old 17th District that would elect a second Democrat from the region. Creating a third district that was potentially Democrat friendly was a secondary concern.

The old 17th District was an incumbent-protection gerrymander drawn to protect a Democrat in 2001. The base of the district was in the Quad Cities area. With the 2011 agreement to protect all incumbents (except one) and the presence of Republican incumbents in districts to the north and east, the options for adding Democratic voters to the district were limited in 2011. This oddly shaped district trended less Democratic during the decade. In 2010 the incumbent Democrat in the district lost badly. With the Democrats in control of redistricting in 2011 there were options that were not available in 2011. The new 17th District retains the core of the Quad Cities. It is extended north and then east along the Wisconsin border picking up territory from the old 16th District, the most important of which is the city of Rockford in Winnebago County. The new district extends further west into Tazewell and Peoria County to pick up the city of Peoria. The southern part of the old 17th District was shifted into the new 18th District. Incumbent Republican Congressman Bobby Schilling is running in the district, but based on its voting history, the district should strongly favor a Democrat.

The old 16th District was an east-to-west district. Its northern boundary stretched along most of Illinois's border with Wisconsin. Much of its territory was shifted into the new 17th District to the west and the new 14th District to the east. The new 16th District extends south from the Wisconsin border picking up new parts of DeKalb County and three other counties from the old 14th District. It then swings further south and east, picking up two counties from the old 11th District and three counties from the old 15th District, ending at the Indiana border. This is a very Republican district. The Republican incumbent from the old 16th District, Don Manzullo, and the Republican incumbent from the old 11th District, Adam Kinzinger, are running the Republican primary. Manzullo was first elected to Congress in 1992. Kinzinger was elected in 2010. The winner of the Republican primary will be elected in the November general election.

The primary change in the new 18th District from the old 18th District was the shift of the city of Peoria to the 17th District. To compensate for the population loss, the district was extended to the east to pick up territory from the old 11th District and the north and south to pick up territory from the old 17th District. The changes make the district an even safer Republican district. The home of the incumbent congressman from the old 18th District, Congressman Aaron Schock, was in Peoria. He is running in the new 18th and will be elected in the fall to Congress.

The new 15th District shifted significantly southward, losing four counties on the north to the new 14th District and territory to the west to the new 13th District, but gaining all or part of a dozen counties to the south from the old 19th District. The new 15th is less urban and even more Republican than the old 15th. The Republican incumbent, Congressman Tim Johnson, no longer lives in the district because the Champaign/Urbana area was shifted west into the new 13th District. While the home of incumbent John Schimkus from the old 19th District is in the new 12th District, he is running in the new 15th, which contains a significant portion of his old district. Johnson is running in the new 13th District.

The new 13th District is basically a new district without an incumbent congressman. It starts in the north with the Bloomington/Normal area in McClean County, the home of Illinois State University. This territory was in the old 11th District. It extends to the south and west to pick up the Champaign/Urbana area, home of the University of Illinois from the old 15th District and runs west to pick up Decatur and Springfield from the old 17th District. It then swings south and west, picking up four counties from the old 17th and 19th Districts. The district leans Republican, but has a very unfocused identity. As noted above, incumbent Republican congressman Tim Johnson is running in the district.

The new 12th District is largely the old 12th District. The only change is the new 12th picked up one county and part of another from the old 19th District. The district in located in the far southwestern part of the state. Its core is the Metro East area. It also contains traditional Democratic counties from deep southern Illinois. It would be considered a safe Democratic district if the long-time Democratic incumbent, Jerry Costello, had not announced his retirement in the fall of 2011. Without a Democratic candidate who is a good fit for the district, this district could be a tossup short-term and even more problematic if the political trends of the last decade continue in the downstate region.

The 2011 map was challenged in federal courts by a Republican-backed citizens group. Eight of the nine incumbent Republican congressmen from Illinois joined in the suit. The map was challenged as violating the Voting Rights Act by diluting the voting strength of Hispanic residents in Chicago and for violating the constitutional rights of Republican voters by diluting their voting strength with a partisan gerrymander. The Federal Court upheld the map, dismissing both claims. The Court did take judicial notice of the partisan intent of the map, calling it a "blatant political move to increase the number of Democratic congressional seats." Consistent with other recent federal court rulings, the three-judge panel could not find either a sufficient standard for accessing the alleged harm to Republican voters or a workable remedy for addressing such harm. The 2011 map was a partisan gerrymander, but a constitutionally permissible partisan gerrymander.

MAPMAKING IN ILLINOIS

The 2011 congressional district map has the potential to be a huge plus for Democrats in Illinois and nationally. The messy thing about elections, however, is that you have put forward candidates and let citizens vote. In a good year the Democrats should win 12 of the 18 seats in the Illinois congressional delegation. In a bad year they should do no worse than a 9–9 split. Given the demographic changes and political trends over the past two decades, the map illustrates what can be achieved when one party is given complete control over the process with no limitations on maximizing partisan advantage. Redistricting is a means to an end for achieving policy goals. But elections and representation are also ends in and of themselves. The legitimacy of the process depends on citizens engaging the process and believing that they are connected to their representatives. Most voters, if they think about redistricting at all, want redistricting to provide representation in the sense that they want to feel that there is someone in congress or the legislature who understands them and their issues and stands up for them. When congressional or legislative districts fragment the geographic entities that citizens identify with—neighborhoods, communities, cities, counties, or regions—it makes it harder for citizens to see their congressman or legislator as someone "we" have sent to Washington or the state capitol to represent "us."

In contrast to the partisan driven outcome of 2011, the process that produced the 2001 congressional district map was one of bipartisan compromise and accommodation. Unfortunately, the object of the process was the self-preservation of elected officials. Given the massive conflicts of interests for those drawing the maps, the excesses and distortions of the outcome were too predictable.

It is possible to admire the technical expertise and strategic skill of those who master the art of redistricting. The politics and inside maneuvering of redistricting are always great theater. The application of the constitutional rights to the political process is a constantly evolving, human attempt to connect abstract principle with practice. The problem is that the whole of redistricting almost always seems to be less than the sum of the parts. It is not clear that congressional redistricting or redistricting in general is making self-government work better or even work at all. At least not in Illinois.

NOTES

1. *The Illinois State Comptroller's Quarterly,* Edition 4 (Springfield, Illinois: State of Illinois, 2012).

2. *The Illinois State Comptroller's Quarterly; State of Illinois FY 2013 Budget Road Map,* the Institute for Illinois's Fiscal Sustainability at the Civic Federation, January 30, 2012, www.civicfed.org; "The large tax increase just enacted falls short of closing the state's enormous budget gap," Fiscal Fallout No. 5, Fiscal Futures Project, Institute for Government and Public Affairs, University of Illinois, January 18, 2011, http://igpa.uillinois.edu/.

3. See the "About Illinois" section of the State of Illinois official website, www.illinois.gov.

4. *Committee for a Fair and Balanced Map et al. v. Illinois State Board of Elections et al.,* Case no. 1:11-CV-5065, United States District Court Northern District of Illinois, Eastern Division.

5. Census data for 1990, 2000, and 2010, U.S. Census State and County Quick Facts, http://quickfacts.census.gov/qfd/states/17000.html; The Chicago Community Trust, "What Does the 2010 Census Tell Us about Metropolitan Chicago?" www.cct.org.

6. Chicago Community Trust, "What Does the 2010 Census Tell Us."

7. Kent D. Redfield, "Elections," in *Illinois Politics: A Citizens Guide*, eds. James D. Nowlan, Samuel K. Gove, and Richard J. Winkel (University of Illinois Press: Urbana and Chicago, 2010); Illinois State Board of Elections, "Results of 2010 general primary" and "Results of 2010 general election," www.elections.state.il.us/.

8. "Illinois Is Friendly Territory of the President," *Chicago Tribune*, February 9, 2012.

9. Peter W. Colby and Paul Michael Green, "Burgeoning Suburban Power, Shrinking Chicago Power: Downstate Holds the Key to Victory," *Illinois Issues* (Feburary 1978).

10. John S. Jackson and Lourenk Prozesky, "Redistricting in Illinois (2005)," *Simon Review* (Occasional Papers of the Paul Simon Public Policy Institute), Paper 2, April 2005.

19

New York Redistricting in Action

Legislative Inaction and Judicial Enaction

Russell C. Weaver and Joshua J. Dyck

As the Brennan Center for Justice notes in a follow-up to its 2004 report on the New York State (NYS) legislative process, "[i]t has become vogue to attach the phrase 'most dysfunctional' to any discussion about the [NYS] Legislature."[1] Statewide polls show that, "vogueness" notwithstanding, approximately 83 percent of New York voters would tend to agree that the phrase applies.[2] To observers, in action and inaction, the partisans of the Democratic-controlled Assembly and the Republican-controlled Senate seemingly perpetuate policies that "hobble the sincere efforts of a number of rank-and-file legislators to represent the best interests of their constituents and the state as a whole."[3]

Recently U.S. Magistrate Judge Roanne Mann joined this conversation, opining that a "dysfunctional state legislature" has "yet again" necessitated judicial intervention into New York's post-censal congressional redistricting process.[4] The words "yet again" from Judge Mann's opinion offer some insight into New York's modern congressional redistricting history. The current round of remapping marks the fourth consecutive decade during which NYS legislators failed to reconfigure the statewide political landscape in a timely fashion, thereby inciting involvement of the courts.[5] Indeed, the remap was only completed when a federal three-judge panel imposed Judge Mann's recommended plan on the state—just three months ahead of its congressional primary elections.

Here we survey the 2012 congressional redistricting developments in NYS with a particular focus on three themes: the State's (1) *redistricting needs* based on absolute and relative demographic changes between 2000 and 2010; (2) *redistricting process*, in terms of its function and dysfunction; and (3) *redistricting outcomes*, their adherence to legal and traditional redistricting criteria, and implications for the future of redistricting in NYS. Insofar as our goals are to describe the needs, operation, and outcomes of New York's congressional redistricting, it is a convenient approach to

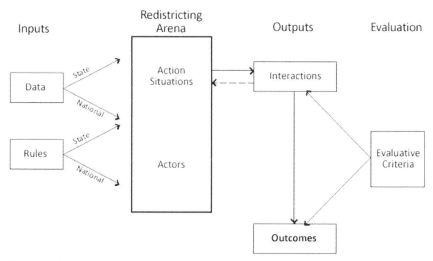

Figure 19.1.   Framework of the Chapter. Created by the author.

divide the chapter into reflections on the process's inputs and outputs. Consistent with this approach, the discussion that follows is organized as a narrow, descriptive application of the IAD framework developed by Ostrom.[6]

First, we recount the historical and contemporary demographic changes that led to the modern population geographies of NYS. We then compare New York's population growth from 2000 to 2010 with national averages for the same time period (see figure 19.1). Such comparisons are made necessary by the fact that intercensal population changes in NYS relative to the nation determine the State's share of the fixed number of members in the U.S. House of Representatives. In this sense, a distinction is made between *reapportionment* and *redistricting*. These concepts are contextualized in a manner that communicates New York's 2012 redistricting needs. Next, we examine the power to redistrict in NYS. We define the relevant rules and actors involved in the process and identify how the interactions of these elements are well-suited for legislative disunity and, ultimately, the need for judicial intervention. Finally, we comment on the outputs of the process, including the court-imposed congressional plan and several procedural reforms that have been proposed to reshape the state's redistricting arena.

INPUTS TO THE NYS REDISTRICTING PROCESS

Population Data

Since 1940 the U.S. Census Bureau has recorded only one drop in New York's statewide population, which occurred between 1970 and 1980. The general trend in NYS, however, has been one of growth. In fact, during the ten-year period leading

Table 19.1. New York State Population, 1940–2010

Census	Population
1940	13,479,142
1950	14,830,192
1960	16,782,304
1970	18,236,967
1980	17,558,072
1990	17,990,455
2000	18,976,457
2010	19,378,102

up to the 2010 census, the number of residents in NYS for the first time surpassed 19 million (table 19.1), maintaining the state's rank as the third most populous in the United States.[7]

The uptick in New York's population from 1980 onward has been relatively unbalanced from an intrastate perspective (see map 19.1). Specifically, much of the state's recent growth has occurred in the nine counties traditionally considered to constitute "downstate" New York.[8] This is evidenced by the steady southeasterly movement of the state's population-weighted mean center during the past three decades (figure 19.2).

According to the latest census, this geographically uneven growth continued into the present decade, albeit at less pronounced rates than in the previous two redistricting cycles. Explicitly, upstate New York grew by 105,233 residents (1.5 percent), compared to a 296,412-person (2.5 percent) increase in the downstate region. For illustrative purposes this imbalance is exaggerated by the cartogram in map 19.2, which shows

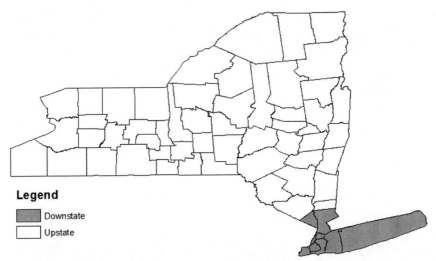

Legend

Downstate

Upstate

Map 19.1.   New York State Regions. Created by the author.

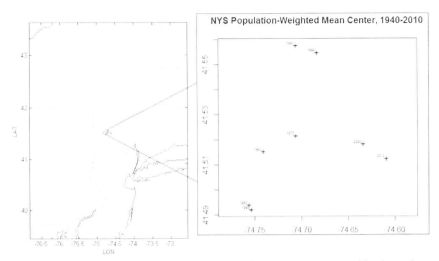

Figure 19.2.   New York State Population-Weighted Mean Center. Created by the author.

generally that: (a) western upstate, most notably in Buffalo and Erie County, was the one region of NYS to lose population during the decade; (b) northern, central, and eastern upstate experienced net gains, though at lesser rates than downstate; (c) the upstate counties adjacent to downstate all grew moderately; and (d) the downstate counties collectively, driven principally by growth in Suffolk County, gained the most

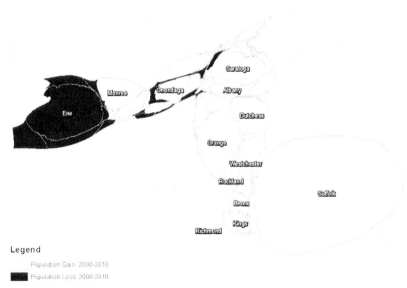

Map 19.2.   Cartogram Showing County Populations Gained and Lost. Created by the author.

population. It will be shown later in the chapter that these relative share shifts have important implications for the state's redistricting outcomes.

Redistricting, Reapportionment, and District Criteria

So far the term "redistricting" has been used loosely to describe the act of remapping New York's congressional districts in response to changing population conditions. Here a few distinctions and more precise definitions will allow for further elucidation of the needs, challenges, and complexity of the situation.

Except for temporary increases in the late 1950s to accommodate the annexations of Alaska and Hawaii to the United States, the size of the lower chamber in the U.S. Congress has been legislatively fixed at 435 members since 1911.[9] While the total number of members is constant, the number of legislators in any one state is adjustable and depends on the state's decennially reported population. Particularly, members of the House of Representatives are allocated to states by a specific formula every ten years following the release of updated census data. Each state is first assigned one member to ensure minimum representation. Subsequently, the remaining 385 seats are apportioned by calculating "priority values" for each state, such that the state with the largest priority value for seat 51 is assigned seat 51, and so on. The priority value for a seat is a function of a given state's population and its current and next potential seat numbers.[10] The purpose of allocating seats in this manner is to apportion representatives to each state proportionally to the state's population relative to the country as a whole. For example, in 1940 NYS accounted for approximately 10 percent of the U.S. population; accordingly, the state was apportioned 45 representatives, or roughly 10 percent of the lower chamber of Congress.

The act of proportionally allocating representatives to states in this manner is known as *reapportionment*. Reapportionment thus entails utilizing updated census data to reassign the 435 members of the U.S. House of Representatives to the states. Underlying this action is the notion that a given state can lose representation without losing population. For example, suppose that there are nine legislative seats in a country with three states: A, B, and C. In period 1 all states have populations of 100, and each state therefore receives one third, or three, of the available seats. In period 2 the population distribution is as follows: A–150; B–250; C–800. All states have grown. However, C's growth far outpaced that of the other two states. State C now accounts for two-thirds of the population. After reapportionment, and under a rule of proportional representation, C then receives two-thirds (or six) of the available representatives. Similarly, A receives one representative and B receives two. Hence the quantity of legislative seats in A and B *decreases* despite *increases* to their populations.

This narrative of growing population accompanied by shrinking representation has characterized the political demographics of NYS since 1940. As depicted in table 19.1, the population of NYS increased by 44 percent over the past seventy years. During the same time period, however, the State's representation in the U.S. House

Table 19.2. Number of Seats in the U.S. House
of Representatives, 1940–2010

Census	New York	Texas	Florida
1940	45	21	6
1950	43	22	8
1960	41	23	12
1970	39	24	15
1980	34	27	19
1990	31	30	23
2000	29	32	25
2010	27	36	27

decreased by 40 percent, from 45 to 27 members (table 19.2). The reason is that, like in the simplified example from above, New York's population growth has fallen behind that of other states such as Florida and Texas (figure 19.3).

In the sense that there are a fixed number of seats in the House of Representatives, the quantity of members available to any given state can be thought of as a rivalrous good. Put differently, as more seats are allocated to any one state, fewer are available to the remaining 49 states. Thus as high-growth states increase in absolute and relative population, they begin to take congressional seats away from their slow-growth or shrinking counterparts. Because of the rapidity with which states like Florida and Texas have grown in the past several decades, their proportional shares of the U.S. population, and by extension of the House of Representatives, have increased relative to New York and other states with below-average growth rates (figure 19.4).

The cumulative result of the processes at work in figures 19.3 and 19.4 is that, for the seventh consecutive decade, the State must erase multiple congressional districts

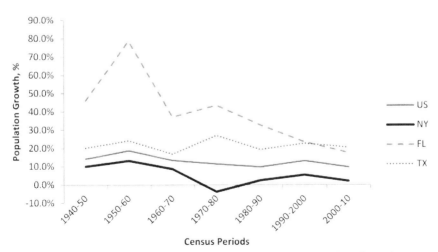

Figure 19.3.   Comparative Population Growth Percentages. Created by the author.

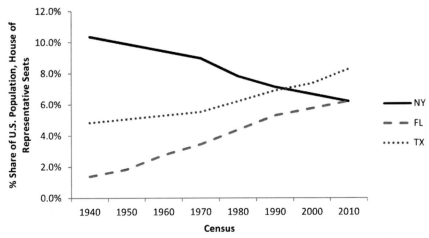

Figure 19.4. Proportional Share of U.S. House of Representatives. Created by the author.

from its political landscape. Whereas initial precensal projections estimated that only one district/member would be the victim of reapportionment,[11] the official 2010 census priority values revealed that growth in the State was even slower than expected.[12] As a consequence, the NYS delegation in the House of Representatives will decrease from 29 to 27 members in 2012.

Clearly, if a state is required to reduce the number of congressional districts within its boundaries, then its existing legislative maps become invalid. Furthermore, a host of statutes and Supreme Court decisions direct states to "make a good-faith effort to achieve precise mathematical equality" of district populations.[13,14,15] The reasoning for this mandate is that, as demographic change occurs nonuniformly within a state (e.g., as in map 19.2), legislative districts tend to become *malapportioned* or not sufficiently equal in population. When single-member districts are not equal in this respect, the weight of any individual vote is affected. Thus, the principle of "one person, one vote" is violated.[16]

Based on New York's 2010 population count and the 27 House seats that were allocated to it, the ideal district size moving forward is 717,707 or 717,708 residents.[17] Relative to this benchmark all of the erstwhile 29 districts in the state are underpopulated, meaning that they are all malapportioned.[18] Given the equal population constraint noted above, the implication is that none of the existing NYS congressional districts can remain wholly intact. Hence it is necessary not only to adjust the *number* of districts as a result of reapportionment. But it is also a fundamental obligation to reconfigure their *boundaries* through the act of redistricting.

Thus the first input to New York's 2012 congressional remap project—2010 U.S. census data—uncovers the dual needs of the state. *Reapportionment* of legislative representatives calls for the elimination of two congressional seats in NYS; and the presence of malapportioned districts tasks the state with *redistricting*, or redrawing its congressional map to achieve a roughly equal distribution of district populations. In performing the latter task, however, population equality is not the sole factor that influences how boundaries are to be drawn. Aside from the "one person, one vote" criterion, a jurisdiction is additionally compelled to produce a redistricting plan that: (a) does not have a retrogressive purpose or effect with respect to minority voting efficacy, nor does it intentionally or unintentionally dilute minority voting strength;[19] (b) features geographically compact districts;[20] (c) ensures that all districts are contiguous;[21] (d) respects political subdivisions;[22] and (e) preserves communities of interest.[23] Taken together these provisions represent the legal and "traditional" criteria used to evaluate redistricting proposals.[24] They are also often seen as the guiding principles that are, at all stages in the process, to enter into the decision calculus of any individual who is given redistricting responsibilities. With this statement we have intimated a pressing question: *who redistricts in New York?* To answer this question, we turn to the state-specific rules of redistricting.

General State Redistricting Rules

The final paragraph of the preceding section identified the foremost legal and "traditional" criteria that set nationally applicable parameters within which state redistricting plans must operate. Beyond those general criteria, however, states are granted considerable discretion with respect to the ways in which they redistrict. Through its laws or constitution, each state effectually establishes its own rules related to who draws political boundaries and how the redistricting process is to function.[25] Two prototypical methods are widely recognized in the literature to this end: (1) legislative redistricting and (2) redistricting by commission.[26] Although these methods are fundamentally different, they are not exactly mutually exclusive. As it will be shown, rather than being categorically separated, the two methods can be thought of as the two ends of a continuum.[27]

Broadly, legislative redistricting involves entrusting a state's lawmakers with the responsibility to adopt redrawn political districts, and it is the more common of the two general methods noted above.[28] As the Brennan Center notes, there are both pros and cons to this strategy; and both sides of the debate are particularly attentive to the observation that legislators who are authorized to oversee congressional redistricting also tend to oversee sub-federal redistricting, including for the state legislative seats that they themselves occupy.[29] This is seen by many as a conflict of interest,[30] in that it enables "incumbency protection" or "bipartisan" gerrymandering—a situation in which incumbent legislators from both major parties collude to approve state districts that are mutually favorable to their reelection chances, thereby minimizing electoral competition and guaranteeing each party a certain number of seats.[31] On the other hand, it has been argued that permitting state legislators to control their own redistricting destinies is appropriate; for legislators are ultimately accountable to the electorates around which their districts are drawn.[32] Presumably the state legislators would arrange for a similar bipartisan agreement at the federal level to protect their parties' share of the state's congressional seats.

The second general method, redistricting by commission, vests the power to redistrict in a committee that does not consist of a full state legislature.[33] Bates identifies three classes of commissions.[34] First, *primary commissions* are granted sole authority to redistrict. The plans drafted by primary commissions are binding and not subject to legislative amendment or executive veto. Second, *backup commissions* are deployed in some states that use legislative redistricting, but only in the event that state legislators reach an impasse during their proceedings. If the legislative redistricting process fails in these states, backup commission plans become binding. Finally, *advisory commissions* create nonbinding proposals intended to advise lawmakers during the otherwise legislative redistricting process. Advisory commissions have no legal redistricting authority, nor are they granted such authority if the legislative process reaches a stalemate.

Accounting for these differences in methods and commissions, a ten-point classification system of state redistricting rules has been proposed that includes various forms of hybrid legislative-commission institutions.[35] The system considers not only the method of redistricting (i.e., legislative or commission), but also the membership of commissions in states that use them. Briefly, redistricting rules range from 1 (least politicized, where states have primary commissions composed of an equal number of members from both parties and a nonpolitical tiebreaker) to 10 (most politicized, where legislators have total control of the process and the legislative plan is subject to executive veto). New York belongs to category 9 in this framework, making its rules some of the most "politicized" and least "independent" in the nation.

Redistricting Rules in NYS

New York's current redistricting institutions are characterized by "exclusive legislative responsibility . . . but the task is assigned to a legislative committee."[36] Stated in terms of the above discussion, NYS has an advisory commission with no legal authority. The legislature ultimately adopts a redistricting plan, and the legislative plan is subject to executive veto. Nevertheless, a 1978 state law established the Legislative Task Force on Demographic Research and Reapportionment ("LATFOR") to act in an advisory capacity, especially with respect to drafting initial proposals and maps.[37] More specifically, LATFOR is a six-member committee empaneled to "compile and analyze data, conduct research for and make reports and recommendations to the legislature" regarding decennial redistricting. The State Assembly and Senate majority leaders each select one citizen-member, and the majority and minority leaders of both houses each select one legislator-member from their respective chamber and party.[38]

While LATFOR then drafts somewhat independent redistricting plans without including the full state legislature per se, its recommendations are not binding on the state. Moreover, the advisory commission is far from what the classification considers to be "independent," as its six members include four legislators and two individuals appointed by legislators.[39] As previously mentioned, one issue with legislative redistricting is that it is controlled by incumbent politicians. Politicians have often been characterized as single-minded seekers of re-election, and thus their preferences to get re-elected are often central to redistricting.[40] Along these lines, Levitt observes that LATFOR, by the very nature of its membership selection, is "heavily influenced by the . . . legislative leadership."[41] For this reason, LATFOR recommendations tendentially reflect legislator preferences, thus representing little more than incumbent-friendly plans presented by a pseudo-independent entity. Research by Seabrook also supports this point, noting that unified partisan control of the redistricting process often produces short-lived benefits given that parties have an interest in minimizing wasted votes so they can maximize the number of seats won.[42] Therefore, we expect the greatest level of incumbent protection when both parties have veto power of the redistricting process.

"Politicized" redistricting institutions of this type have the potential to "exacerbate partisanship in broader political contexts."[43] New York's redistricting has been characterized by a specific kind of politicization given the long-standing divide between the upper and lower houses of the state legislature. Therefore, both partisan bickering and inertia contribute to the public perception that the redistricting process in New York is badly in need of reform.[44] Consequently, the 2012 redistricting process has seen an influx of citizen and nongovernmental actors attempting to influence the process and its outcomes. In the next section several of these actors are introduced, as the focus turns to key players and interactions in the NYS redistricting arena.

INSIDE THE NYS CONGRESSIONAL REDISTRICTING ARENA

The next two sections of this chapter shift attention to the operation and outcomes of the 2012 NYS redistricting process, offering comparisons to the previous round of redistricting where appropriate. We begin by quickly surveying the relevant actors involved in the process, followed by an examination of the rule-player interactions (refer to figure 19.1).

Key Players

LATFOR and the NYS Legislature

Owing to the fact that NYS uses legislative redistricting with an advisory commission, both the legislators and the appointed commission members are unquestionably principal actors in the state's redistricting arena. The compositions of both houses in the New York legislature as well as of LATFOR are presented in table 19.3, together with the partisan share of the state's congressional seats.

Table 19.3. Partisan Control of Legislative Houses in NYS following 2010 Elections

	Total Members	Democrat	Republican
NYS Senate	62	29	32*
NYS Assembly	150	96*	49
LATFOR	4†	2	2
U.S. House	29	21*	8
Governor		*	

*Indicates partisan control;
†Citizen-members (2) excluded

Table 19.3 shows that the NYS government is split on partisan lines, with Democrats controlling the governor's office and the Assembly and Republicans controlling the Senate. Because the legislative houses are divided, LATFOR is equally split between Democrats and Republicans with no tiebreakers. McDonald observes that divided government can lead to a breakdown in legislative redistricting.[45] Seabrook notes further that, even with unified partisan control, it is especially difficult to produce an effective gerrymander when a state is losing seats.[46] That the current round of NYS congressional redistricting was only finalized with the implementation of a court-drawn plan supports this claim. In fact, due to prolonged partisan disagreement over state legislative redistricting issues, neither the NYS legislature nor LATFOR even put forward a congressional redistricting plan.[47] As a result, the only congressional district alternatives were offered by citizens, good government groups, and the courts.

The Governor

First-term Governor Andrew Cuomo was sworn into office on January 1, 2011, after being elected during the 2010 state cycle. Throughout his gubernatorial campaign, the former NYS attorney general stressed that "Cleaning up Albany" was his top priority. Included in this broad issue set was a proposal for redistricting reform, as Cuomo called the extant legislative redistricting process "antithetical to fair and accountable representation."[48] Less than two months into his term, Cuomo presented the "Redistricting Reform Act of 2011" to his colleagues in the legislature. Under the proposal, redistricting authority would shift from the legislature to an independent commission. The commission would be composed of 11 members selected in the following manner. First, the governor receives four appointees. Next, the legislative leaders receive one appointee each, bringing the total appointed membership to eight (4 gubernatorial appointees + 4 legislative appointees). From there, the group of eight collectively nominates 40 potential members. The pool of nominees must include 15 Democrats, 15 Republicans, and 10 individuals with no party affiliation. Finally, the eight members vote to elect three additional members from the 40-person nominee pool. None of the 11 members may be within four years from having served as an elected official, a party official, a lobbyist, or a staff member of any of the above. Such a commission would approach the "most depoliticized" end of the classification system described earlier. However, more than a year after its introduction, the bill remains held up in Senate and Assembly committees.

Despite the lack of legislative action on his Redistricting Reform Act, Cuomo wielded significant influence in the present NYS redistricting arena. Namely, he has the power to veto any legislatively adopted plan—a power he vowed to exercise for any proposal, state or congressional, that did not first pass through an independent committee.[49] The legislature's inability to produce a plan to redraw congressional lines prevented him from having to exercise that power for federal redistricting. The same cannot be said for the eventual state legislative districting compromise.[50] However, the governor wielded extraordinary power to control the agenda, even though the legislature had a first-move advantage. We characterize his ability to steer the redistricting outcome by what has been termed "veto-bargaining."

Citizens and Public Interest Groups

Relative to previous cycles of redistricting, citizens and activist groups seemed to be especially visible and participatory throughout the process this time around. While there is not a single reason for this, possible explanations include the attention paid to redistricting by the gubernatorial campaign of Andrew Cuomo (see above) and the stalwart statewide redistricting reform campaign spearheaded by former New York City Mayor Ed Koch. In early 2010 Koch formed a coalition called "New York Uprising" dedicated to bringing independent redistricting to NYS. The Uprising spent the entire 2010 election cycle traveling the state, urging candidates for state office to sign a pledge that committed them to supporting legislation calling for independent, transparent redistricting. Candidates who signed Koch's pledge were honored by the Uprising as "Heroes of Reform," while candidates who refused to sign were criticized by the ex-Mayor as "Enemies of Reform." Koch went from city to city holding press conferences to inform voters which candidates were "Heroes" and which were "Enemies." In all over 350 "Heroes" signed the Uprising's pledge, 138 of whom were elected to office. Koch's efforts almost certainly increased public attention to redistricting ills in NYS.

A second influential group, ReShape New York, drafted a lengthy report detailing the historical abuses of legislative redistricting in NYS and outlining paths to reform.[51] The organization represents a collaboration of three main organizations: (1) Citizens Union of the City of New York; (2) New York Public Interest Research Group; and (3) The League of Women Voters of NYS. Like Koch (who, incidentally, is a co-chair of ReshapeNY), the coalition publicly lobbied for independent and transparent redistricting in NYS.

Finally, both Common Cause New York and several independent NYS citizens generated their own redistricting maps, which were submitted to LATFOR during public hearings and comment periods. Whereas not all of the citizen-drawn maps were complete, the Common Cause plan comprehensively develops 27 congressional districts that adhere to all legal and traditional redistricting criteria. Common Cause's proposal was praised by several media outlets, including the *New York Daily News*, the *New York Times*, and *Newsday*.[52] The organization claims that its maps "provide an example of what can and should be done to achieve fair, non-politicized districts." To some extent the courts agreed, as the final judicially-imposed plan adopts several of the Common Cause principles and suggestions.

The Department of Justice

Under Section 5 of the Voting Rights Act, states and other jurisdictions that have demonstrable histories of "diminishing the ability of citizens to elect their preferred candidates" must seek federal approval, or *preclearance*, for any proposed changes to, inter alia, their legislative district boundaries.[53] Section 5 is designed to prevent retrogression with respect to minority voting efficacy. In NYS, three "downstate" counties—Bronx, Kings, and New York—are covered by these provisions. For this reason, any NYS redistricting plan that alters the legislative boundaries in one or more of these three counties must be reviewed and approved by the Department of Justice (DOJ). If the DOJ finds that a redistricting plan is consistent with a retrogressive purpose or effect in one of the covered jurisdictions, then it can object to the proposal.

In this regard, the DOJ is a silent player in the NYS redistricting arena. Unlike citizens and interest groups, the DOJ does not lobby elected officials, nor does it publicly campaign on behalf of certain plans or for reforms to state redistricting processes. Instead, the organization simply waits to receive plan submissions, and it then approves or disapproves of redistricting proposals based on their (non)compliance with the Voting Rights Act. Thus, the DOJ does not expressly play a role in designing NYS redistricting alternatives; but its presence in the redistricting arena has the effect of forcing other redistricting players to consider likely DOJ interpretations of boundary changes—particularly those impacting minority communities.

Members of Congress and Lobbyists

Like state-level politicians, incumbent members of Congress act as single-minded seekers of re-election. Not unexpectedly, they therefore attempt to influence the state legislators who are responsible for drawing federal legislative boundaries. Recognizing that New York was due to lose two seats to reapportionment, at least six members of the NYS congressional delegation hired firms to lobby state legislators in attempts to protect their interests.[54]

The set of members of Congress who employed lobbyists is fairly unsurprising. Consider again the unofficial, but well-known, upstate-downstate divide pictured in map 19.1, and the intrastate population share shifts in map 19.2. From the 2010 census data, the nine-county territory of downstate New York currently accounts for

12,268,815 (63.3 percent) of the state's overall population. By extension, upstate represents 36.7 percent of the population, or 7,109,287 residents. This is nearly identical to the regional breakdown recorded in the 2000 census, which was at 63.1 percent-36.9 percent in favor of downstate. Under a rule of proportional representation, these figures imply that downstate should receive 17 of the state's 27 congressional seats with the remaining 10 going to upstate. The existing 29-district split is 18-11, thus implying that reapportionment will cost each region one legislative district (map 19.3).

Now recall that western [upstate] New York was the one region of the state which decreased in net population between 2000 and 2010 (refer to map 19.2). Perhaps anticipating that this regional decline would place their districts on the reapportionment chopping block, Reps. Higgins (27), Hochul (26), and Hanna (25) all contracted with lobbyists to fight for their redistricting interests in the state capital. Higgins, who represents most of Buffalo and Erie County, predictably paid out the most money.[55]

Similarly, with downstate's share of representatives expected to decrease from 18 to 17, three New York City-area members of Congress hired firms to influence the Albany lawmakers. Possibly because of the growth in eastern downstate, especially in Long Island and Suffolk County, it was Reps. Engel (17), Crowley (7), and McCarthy (4)—who represent relatively western areas of downstate—that looked to lobbyists for assistance.

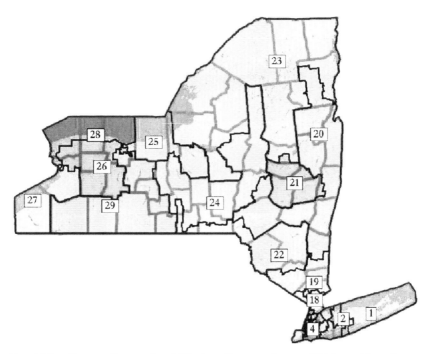

Map 19.3.   Current Congressional Districts. *Favors v. Cuomo* **(2012; see Mann Report and Recommendations).**

The Plaintiffs

As we have already noted, the NYS legislature and LATFOR failed to produce a congressional redistricting plan in 2012. Indeed, the inter-partisan disagreement over state legislative districts brought about a situation in which neither side was willing to move onto congressional redistricting until the state issues were settled; neither side, however, was prepared to settle the state issues. In response to the evident gridlock, several NYS registered voters filed a lawsuit against the state calling for Hon. Judge Irizarry to appoint an independent Special Master to take over the redistricting efforts.[56]

Among their complaints, the plaintiffs alleged that NYS redistricting is little more than an exercise in "partisan self-dealing and incumbent protection," acknowledging the shared interests of LATFOR and the legislative leadership. Additionally the plaintiffs observed that the governor's vow to veto any redistricting plan not generated by an independent commission, coupled with LATFOR's nonindependence, would lead to an "electoral disaster" if districts were not in place in time for the 2012 election cycle. Consistent with this observation, in early February 2012 the timeline for New York's congressional primary elections was advanced to comply with the requirements of the Uniformed and Overseas Citizens Absentee Voting Act of 1986, causing the candidacy petitioning period to begin on March 20, 2012.[57] As a result of the increasing urgency, the plaintiffs' requests were met with swift court action.

The Courts

Approximately three months subsequent to the plaintiffs' initial complaint, Judge Irizarry convened a three-judge panel which appointed Hon. U.S. Magistrate Judge Roanne Mann to the Special Master post, authorizing her to hire an expert consultant and proceed with drafting a recommended congressional redistricting plan. Judge Mann was appointed on February 21 and asked to have a draft proposal available for presentation at a March 5 public hearing. During the public hearing, competing alternatives from the State legislature's partisan caucuses were presented alongside the initial draft by Judge Mann and her expert consultant, Professor Nathaniel Persily. Public comments were recorded prior to, during, and after the public hearing. Factoring the public input into their proposal, Mann and Persily redrafted their congressional maps and submitted a "Report and Recommendation" on March 12, 2012. What LATFOR failed for more than a year to achieve, the courts completed in less than three weeks.

Interaction of Players and Operation of the Process

To some extent the details of this section have already been articulated, but here we take the opportunity to highlight the significant tensions which led to the outcomes that will be discussed in Section 4.

Inter-Partisan Conflict

Given that the NYS government and LATFOR are divided on partisan lines, legislative redistricting is well-suited for conflict. For several decades it has been an unofficial practice of LATFOR to draw state legislative districts prior to remapping the state's congressional landscape. This time around was no exception. Disagreement over redrawing the state's senatorial districts was likely the reason for the extended delay and eventual abdication of duty with respect to congressional redistricting.

As of early 2012, Republicans held a slim 32-30 majority in the NYS Senate. It is notable that one of the members of the Senate's majority Republican caucus was a lifelong Democrat who switched his affiliation to the GOP in 2010 and won an upset victory in a highly Democratic upstate district.[58] In the event that the upset victory did not occur, the Senate would have split 31–31 with a Democratic lieutenant governor having the tiebreaking vote. Thus, in addition to seeking a redistricting plan that would retain Republican control of this particular seat,[59] the Republican leadership fought to strengthen its majority by creating a 63rd Senate district in GOP-friendly territory.[60] Expectedly, Democrats strongly opposed these efforts and called on LATFOR to "go back to the drawing board."[61] Because LATFOR is equally comprised of Democrats and Republicans, progress on the Senate districts eventually stalled over this issue. Rather than moving onto congressional redistricting in light of the state Senate stalemate, LATFOR and the legislature elected to remain in a state of uncompromising equilibrium and interpartisan discord. This impasse prompted the aforementioned lawsuit asking the court to step in and take control of the process.

Judicial Involvement

As was the case ten years prior, a federal three-judge panel eventually came to preside over the current NYS congressional redistricting process. In a further parallel to the 2002 cycle, the panel of judges appointed a special master to draft a congressional districting proposal. While there was still time for LATFOR and the legislature to reach internal compromises and proffer a unified plan, the convening of the three-judge panel appeared to place the process firmly in control of the courts. For that reason, LATFOR essentially put up its white flag on the congressional issue and instead redoubled its state-level efforts. Meanwhile, the partisan legislative factions did generate congressional proposals, but none of them received bipartisan or judicial support.

With the courts assuming a primary role, the influence of lobbyists and members of Congress in the NYS redistricting arena was therefore substantially weakened. The same could be said for the NYS legislature and LATFOR. By contrast, the courts, through their special master and consulting expert, placed significant weight on public input, accepting more than two dozen complete and partial proposals and over 400 comments from party and nonparty members of the public.[62] Among the party plans were four submissions by members of the Senate and Assembly leadership, which were all rejected by the court's expert as "attempting to gain partisan advan-

tage."[63] On the other side of things, the final recommendation of the courts, prepared after the public comment period closed, adopted several facets of the complete
proposal submitted by the nonpartisan organization Common Cause New York.

Finally, court-involvement served to remove the governor and the Department of
Justice from the redistricting arena. To wit, the governor does not have veto power
over court-drawn plans, nor are such plans subject to Section 5 of the Voting Rights
Act.[64] Hence, in the absence of an appeal to a higher venue, judicial imposition of
a court-drawn plan renders the process finalized. In this case, the three-judge panel
ordered NYS to adopt the final recommendations of the special master just one week
after they were presented, and less than four weeks after the three-judge panel was
convened. Organizations such as Common Cause New York and other good government groups praised the final plan "for its compact, common-sense districts."[65]

OUTCOMES AND EVALUATION

Aligning with initial expectations, the court-imposed congressional plan drawn by
Special Master Magistrate Judge Roanne Mann and consulting expert Nathaniel
Persily features 10 districts upstate and 17 seats downstate (map 19.4), where upstate

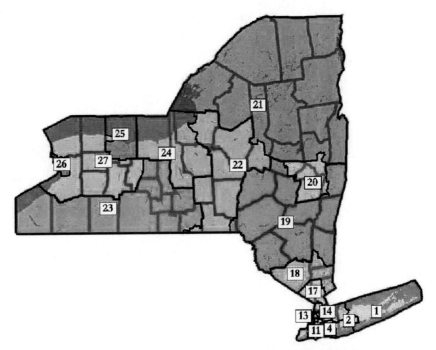

Map 19.4. District Plan Drawn by Special Master Magistrate Judge Roanne Mann.
Favors v. Cuomo **(2012; see Mann Report and Recommendations)**

and downstate are defined in map 19.1. As such, the plan provides each region with representation proportional to its share of the State's population. Here we briefly introduce the plan, henceforth referred to as the "Adopted Plan," and discuss how well it satisfies the goals set forth by the three-judge panel.

Plan Performance

One week after appointing Judge Mann to the Special Master post, the federal three-judge panel issued an Order of Referral[66] which outlined the criteria that Mann and Persily were to follow in drafting the Adopted Plan. As in Section 2.2.1, these criteria explicitly included: (1) equal populations; (2) compliance with the Voting Rights Act so as to avoid diluting minority voting efficacy or producing a retrogressive effect; (3) compactness of districts; (4) contiguity of districts; (5) respect for political subdivisions; and (6) preservation of communities of common interest (ibid.). We now look at the Adopted Plan in terms of each of these items.

Population Equality

Recall that dividing New York's population of 19,378,102 residents by the 27 congressional seats apportioned to the State implies that the ideal district size is either 717,707 or 717,708 constituents. Accounting for the remainder from this division, the precise ideal aggregate redistricting plan features 14 districts with 717,707 residents and 13 districts with 717,708 residents. The Adopted Plan achieves this objective, thereby complying with the "one person, one vote" criterion. In formal terms, the Adopted Plan provides for "zero population deviation."

Racial and Ethnic Minority Considerations

Unlike state- or commission-generated proposals, court-drawn redistricting plans are not subject to Section 5 of the Voting Rights Act. Hence, even though downstate New York contains three Section 5 "covered jurisdictions," the Adopted Plan is not necessarily subject to Department of Justice review. In effect, it is presupposed that plans drafted by court-appointed special masters will comport with all sections of the Voting Rights Act.

It is manifest in both the descriptions that accompany the Adopted Plan[67] and the observable plan outcomes that this presupposition is valid for the present case. Take, for instance, the racial makeup of the existing 29 congressional districts that were created in the previous round of redistricting. Of the 29 districts, 20 featured majority Anglo Voting Age Populations (VAPs), and 9 had majority non-white VAPs.[68] Among the 9 so-called "majority-minority" districts, 3 had majority African American VAPs, and 1 created a majority Hispanic VAP. Relative to these existing conditions, the Adopted Plan decreases the number of Anglo majority VAP districts to 18 and retains the 9 "majority-minority" districts. Hence minority voting strength

Table 19.4. Racial VAP Characteristics of the Adopted Plan

VAP	Seats in Adopted Plan	Seats in Existing Plan
Anglo	18 (–2)	20
African American	3 (—)	3
Hispanic	2 (+1)	1
Total Majority-Minority	9 (—)	9
Total Districts	27 (–2)	29
Change	The total number of districts decreased by two through reapportionment. Both of the eliminated districts were majority Anglo.	

VAP	Share in 2010	Share in 2000
Anglo	60.4%	64.4%
African American	15.2%	14.8%
Hispanic	16.2%	13.8%
Minority	39.6%	35.6%
Total VAP	15,053,173	14,286,530
Change	Over the 10-year period, minority share of statewide VAP increased by 4% relative to Anglos.	

is not diluted, retrogression is a nonfactor,[69] and the decreasing Anglo share of total VAP is met with a decreasing number of Anglo majority districts (table 19.4).

District Compactness

Using eight standard compactness metrics, the Adopted Plan can be shown to outperform the existing districts, as well as the districts in the legislative leadership proposals, in all but one instance.[70] In addition, as map 19.4 makes clear, the Adopted Plan generally draws districts that are regularly shaped and that have comparatively smoother edges than the existing districts (e.g., consider, among others, Districts 28, 20, and 22 in map 19.3).

District Contiguity

All of the 27 districts from the Adopted Plan are contiguous.

Political Subdivisions

Political subdivisions refer to governing jurisdictions below the state level, such as counties, cities, towns, and villages. The unevenness of intrastate population frequently causes redistricting plans to split political subdivisions between multiple congressional districts in order to achieve population equality. For practical purposes in terms of building strategic constituent-government and intergovernmental relationships, it can occasionally be problematic and confusing when proximate areas within the same political subdivisions are represented by more than one Member of Congress. With this in mind, the Adopted Plan sets out to minimize the number of political subdivisions that are split into multiple congressional districts. The existing 29 congressional districts in NYS divide 26 counties and 80 towns. By contrast, the Adopted Plan splits only 20 counties and 75 towns, thereby outperforming the status quo in both of these categories.

Communities of Interest

Communities of interest are less precisely defined than political subdivisions, and their preservation tends to be thought of as the most elusive of the redistricting goals (e.g., Arrington 2010). Communities of interest might be defined in terms of, for example, race/ethnicity, economic status, shared transportation networks and infrastructure, mutual values, or some other commonality. It is not clear exactly what should constitute such a community or how one ought to be delineated cartographically.

The Adopted Plan attempts to operationalize communities of interest geographically, drawing districts that unify "widely recognized" spatial territories such as the North Country, Southern Tier, and Hudson Valley. Additionally, the Adopted Plan separates East and West Manhattan, and it is one of the few proposals to place the Harlem neighborhood of New York City into a single congressional district. In this regard the Adopted Plan, where it was possible for the special master and consulting expert to identify communities of interest, minimized the extent to which such communities are split between districts.

Other Concerns

Both Judge Mann and Professor Persily note in the supplemental documents they submitted to the court[71] that two other considerations factored into their recommendations. First, the Adopted Plan considered the notion of "core constituencies." To assess the "core" of a district, the Adopted Plan examines the between-district shifts in Voting Age Population (VAP). More precisely, the special master and consulting expert overlay the existing district boundaries onto the boundaries in their Adopted Plan. This enables them to compute two quantities: (1) the VAP within an existing district that remains in that district in the Adopted Plan; and (2) the VAP within an existing district that shifts to a new district in the Adopted Plan. Using this methodology, it is shown that 20 of the 27 Adopted districts preserve at least 50 percent of the districts' "core" VAPs.

Secondly, the Adopted Plan considers, but ex ante excludes, protecting incumbency as a valid redistricting criterion. Specifically, the Adopted Plan does not avoid placing more than one incumbent legislator into a single district; but it also does not do so purposefully to influence electoral outcomes.[72] If multiple incumbents are emplaced into a single district, it is so that the Adopted Plan can adhere to the six legal and traditional redistricting criteria set forth above.

Plan Criticisms

Two days after the Adopted Plan was submitted to the court for consideration, members of the Senate Republican caucus (one of whom was also a LATFOR member and the other is the current majority leader) filed a formal objection with the three-judge panel. The basis of this objection (henceforth called the "Senate Majority objection") was a claim that the Adopted Plan "disregards traditional redistricting principles." Specifically, the Senate Majority objection cites the unnecessary pairing of incumbents in single districts as tantamount to a violation of traditional principles which results in "undermining political fairness."

In the opinion that accompanied the Adopted Plan, Judge Mann addressed this issue directly. Namely, upon consideration of all the arguments submitted during the public comment period in favor of incumbency protection, Judge Mann reasoned that "the creation of a redistricting plan that ignored incumbency would enhance both the reality and appearance of judicial impartiality." Accordingly, neither Judge Mann nor Professor Persily requested or received data that would communicate the home addresses of incumbent members of Congress. Somewhat bitingly, Mann further opines that had the NYS legislature fulfilled its constitutional duties and offered its own redistricting plan, "judicial deference [to the incumbency issue] would be paid."

Apart from the overt, politically-motivated criticisms from the Senate Majority caucus, the overall reception of the Adopted Plan was favorable, particularly with the good government organizations described above. As an example, Common Cause New York referred to the Adopted Plan as a "vast improvement over the self-serving interests of the Legislature."[73]

IMPLICATIONS

Earlier we highlighted the merits of the Adopted Plan and noted that the 27 court-redrawn congressional districts in NYS closely adhere to all of the legal and traditional redistricting principles set forth by the federal three-judge panel. In that regard one could feasibly argue that the 2012 congressional redistricting process in New York, for all intents and purposes, concluded successfully. Yet the greater portion of this chapter implies that the State's redistricting institution is far from praiseworthy. Indeed, the interpartisan conflict, attempted influence through lobbyists, legislative impasse, abdication of duty, and eventual court takeover all illustrate exactly how far NYS redistricting lies from the "depoliticized" and "independent" end of the classification system. Furthermore, that the current remapping project represents the fourth consecutive instance of "unwelcomed" judicial intervention into the NYS redistricting,[74] the need for system-wide reform has become increasingly evident. To that end, several proposals have been advanced to overhaul the NYS redistricting arena. We choose to key in on four of the more influential of these alternatives—one with executive office origin, one from within the legislature, and two calls for amendments to the State constitution (table 19.5).

Table 19.5. Proposed Redistricting Reforms in New York

Primary Sponsor	Type of Action Proposed	Membership and Method
Sen. Valesky (D)	Legislation	• 11 total commission members • 8 appointed by the legislative leadership (2 by each leader) • Remaining 3 are elected by 8 appointees • All commission members come from a 40-person nomination pool (15 D, 15 R, 15 neither D nor R) • Nomination pool is created by 8 individuals appointed by the legislative leaders, none of whom also serve on the independent commission (2 by each leader) • Nominees must have a regional and racial/ethnic balance • No members or nominees can be past (within 2 years) or current: elected officials, party leaders, lobbyists, or relatives or staff members of any of the above • **Method**: REMAINS LEGISLATIVE
Gov. Cuomo (D)	Legislation	• Commission membership is the same as in the Valesky proposal • Nomination pool has the same size and composition as the Valesky proposal; but appointees to the nominating committee are not all from the legislative leaders: 4 are appointed by the governor and 4 are appointed by the legislative leadership (1 by each leader) • **Method**: REMAINS LEGISLATIVE
Sen. Bonacic (R)	Constitutional Amendment	• 5 total members • 4 appointed by the legislative leadership (1 by each leader) • 5th member is elected by the 4 appointees; the elected member serves as Chair • No members can be past or current elected or party officials • **Method**: CREATES PRIMARY COMMISSION
Assm. Silver (D)* Sen. Skelos (R)*	Constitutional Amendment†	• 10 total commission members • 8 appointed by legislative leadership (2 by each leader) • Remaining 2 are elected by the 8 appointees—neither of the elected members can be a voter from the two major parties • No members can be past (within 3 years) or current elected or party officials, lobbyists, or staff members or relatives of any of the above • **Method**: REMAINS LEGISLATIVE

*Indicates member of house leadership; † Indicates proposal enacted.

Institutional Reform

Table 19.5 summarizes four of the more well-known redistricting reform propos-als in NYS, all of which have been introduced to the legislature since late 2010. What is noteworthy about most of the proposals is that, while all call for the establishment of a redistricting commission, many of them appear to create an artificial tension between commission independence and commission politicization—with most trad-ing off politicization for nonindependence. Recall that the redistricting institution classification system consists of ten categories that range from 1 (most independent, least politicized) to 10 (least independent, most politicized). Here "independence" refers to the degree of legal authority granted to the commission. The most indepen-dent commissions are therefore those (a) with primary authority to redistrict and (b) whose plans are binding on the state. "Politicization" refers to the membership of the commission and, specifically, whether or not there is a nonpolitical tiebreaking member. Commissions having such a member are said to be relatively depoliticized.

In table 19.5 it is clear that all proposals attempt to involve nonpartisans while simultaneously precluding "insiders" such as lobbyists and ex-politicians from participating in the process. Accordingly, all of the proposed reforms are relatively depoliticized. At the same time, however, observers should be aware that three of the four proposals—including the one that was enacted—still vest final authority in the legislature. That is, the NYS legislature retains the power to vote down plans gener-ated by the depoliticized commissions from the Valesky, Cuomo, and the adopted Silver-Skelos proposals. While each of these reforms do provide second- and third-chance opportunities for their respective commissions to redraw districts in the event of legislative disapproval, once the commission options are exhausted the lawmakers are authorized to change district boundaries and advance their own amended pro-posal. As we have seen, legislative redistricting, especially in NYS, can often result in inert states of interpartisan conflict.

The only reform from table 19.5 that targets both politicization *and* independence is the Bonacic proposal for a constitutional amendment. The Bonacic amendment would create a primary commission with binding redistricting authority. Further-more, the chair of the commission must be elected by the four appointed members, none of whom may be past or current elected or party officials. It is of course reason-able to assume that the four appointees will do well to represent the partisan interests of their appointers in the legislative leadership. Nonetheless, the fact that the four appointees must elect a chairperson with at least three votes presumably implies that there will be a fairly nonpartisan (or, at minimum, a bipartisan) tiebreaking vote. Taking this into account, the Bonacic proposal is relatively depoliticized; and it is the most independent of the four reforms. This should not be interpreted as the authors endorsing the Bonacic proposal. Rather, we simply recognize that the tenets of the Bonacic amendment most closely adhere to the "independence" and "depoliticized" criteria. Regardless of this observation, it was the Silver-Skelos proposal that won the favor of both houses and the governor.

Moving Forward

The final entry in table 19.5, a bipartisan proposal for a state constitutional amendment, was passed by both legislative houses and signed by the governor just three days after the special master submitted her congressional plan to the three-judge panel. Not coincidentally, passage of the amendment occurred on the same day that Governor Cuomo signed into law the legislature's state redistricting proposal, which includes the controversial 63rd Senate district discussed earlier. In exchange for the governor's signature, the legislative houses agreed to pass the redistricting overhaul. Thus, the governor reneged on his vow to veto any redistricting alternative that did not come from an independent redistricting commission. Despite this setback, agreeing to the state legislative redistricting plan enabled Cuomo to follow through on a campaign promise: to oversee sweeping redistricting reform.

Whether the Silver-Skelos amendment will embody sweeping reform is still uncertain. The deal between the governor and the legislature means that districts created by a bipartisan redistricting process that put a premium on incumbent protection will remain in place for the next ten years. Contrary to the hopes and efforts of Ed Koch's New York Uprising and other good government groups, there was no movement to increase independence or transparency in New York's redistricting efforts during the 2012 remapping cycle.[75]

Reform was once again delayed. Moreover, because of the nature of constitutional change in NYS, the Silver-Skelos amendment cannot be fully implemented until it is passed by a second legislature and approved of by voters in a General Election.[76] Hence at least one more year will pass until New Yorkers are assured that their State's redistricting institution will undergo much awaited change.

But are the adopted reforms in line with the desires of NYS voters? One could cynically speculate that by concentrating reform efforts on depoliticizing the NYS redistricting institution instead of increasing its independence, legislators have sewn together a convenient camouflage. It is true that the Silver-Skelos amendment sets very well-specified limits on commission participation (table 19.5). Generally, individuals are required to be several degrees removed from elected officials, party officials, and lobbyists in order to serve on the committee. This fact gives a certain air of independence to the Silver-Skelos amendment, in that commission members cannot be directly affiliated with legislators. With polls showing that more than four-fifths of NYS voters support independent redistricting,[77] this strategy is outwardly responsive to constituent demands. But as we have stressed throughout this chapter, *independence* of a commission is perhaps better judged by its *authority*. The fact that the Silver-Skelos amendment protects legislative control of the process should call into question what effect, if any, the reform will have on future iterations of redistricting in NYS. Much like LATFOR, the proposed commission consists of an even number of members, thereby creating an environment ripe for gridlock. Furthermore, while membership of the new commission will be relatively depoliticized and include two nonpartisans, the lack of independence measured by binding legal authority might well render it impotent and incapable of advancing a workable redistricting plan that attends to self-interested legislative preferences. To the extent that these are valid concerns, the amendment will effectively establish a new scapegoat for future redistricting inertia. Should the commission fail in 2020 to generate a timely, nonpartisan redistricting proposal that passes through both legislative houses, it will, like LATFOR before it, be the subject of increasing public scrutiny and criticism, as lawmakers look on and attempt to deny their own culpability.

Given that the opportunity to significantly reform the NYS redistricting institution for 2012 has expired, the rush to a reform for 2020 may seem somewhat inexplicable. However, it fits quite well with John Kingdon's notion of policy windows being open for a very short amount of time.[78] Ultimately, if this reform is enacted, it is not clear how effective it will be, given that power is still vested in the legislature. Nor is it clear how the public will react to the reform. Some scholars have demonstrated that public opinion about redistricting is not especially well-formed,[79] and others have argued that the even the most egregious gerrymandering plans do not have lasting effects on creating advantages in partisan representation.[80] However, it has also become increasingly clear that the public is concerned with the role of process, fairness, and efficiency in politics.[81] Therefore, even if redistricting outcomes will not ostensibly change our politics, there may still be severe consequences for how the public views the legitimacy of the system. It remains to be seen if New York's movement towards reform has the kind of teeth to produce a process that gains the respect of the public and reform-oriented groups. Given that gridlock is still the likely outcome, we are not optimistic that both the internal and external reputation of New York's legislature as being the "most dysfunctional" is likely to change anytime soon.

NOTES

1. Brennan Center for Justice, "Still Broken: New York State Legislative Reform: 2008 Update" (New York: New York University School of Law, 2008).

2. Quinnipiac University, "New York State Is Dysfunctional, 83% of Voters Say, Quinnipiac University Poll Finds; Candidates Should Pledge to Fix District Lines," Quinnipiac University Polling Institute, June 2010.

3. Brennan Center for Justice, "Still Broken."

4. *Favors v. Cuomo*, No. 1:11-cv-05632 E.D.N.Y. (2012); see also Mann Report and Recommendations.

5. *Flateau v. Anderson*, 537 F.Supp. 257, 261 (S.D.N.Y). (1982); *Puerto Rican Legal Defense and Education Fund v. Gantt*, 796 F. Supp. 677 (E.D. N.Y.). (1992); *Rodriguez v. Pataki*, No. 02-618 (S.D.N.Y.). (2002).

6. Elinor Ostrom, "Institutional Rational Choice: An Assessment of the Institutional Analysis and Development Framework," in *Theories of the Policy Process*, 2/e, ed. Paul A. Sabatier (Cambridge, MA: Westview Press, 2001), 21–64.

7. U.S. Census Bureau, 2010 census of the Population. California was the most populous state in 2010, followed by Texas.

8. Robin Blakely-Armitage, Scott Sanders, Joe Francis, and Jan Vink, "2011 State of Upstate New York Initiative" (Ithaca, NY: Cornell University Community & Regional Development Institute, 2011).

9. Kristin D. Burnett, "Congressional Apportionment," 2010 Census Briefs, No. C2010BR-08 (Washington, DC: United States).

10. A priority value is computed as a given state's population divided by "the geometric mean of its current (n-1) and next (n) potential seat number" (Burnett 2011).

11. Charles S. Bullock, *Redistricting: The Most Political Activity in America* (Lanham, MD: Rowman & Littlefield, 2010); Brennan Center for Justice, *A Citizen's Guide to Redistricting* (New York: New York University School of Law, 2010).

12. Based on the priority values, there would need to be 438 total seats in the House of Representatives for New York to receive a 28th seat.

13. *Kirkpatrick v. Preisler*, 394 U.S. 526. (1969).

14. See also: Article I, Section 2, of the United States Constitution; *Reynolds v. Sims*, 377 U.S. 533. (1964); *Wesberry v. Sanders*, 376 U.S. 1. (1964); *Gray v. Sanders*, 372 U.S. 368. (1963).

15. In this matter the Court has indicated a strong preference for strict equality, having ruled against congressional plans that deviate from the ideal population by less than 1 percent (e.g., *Karcher v. Daggett*, 462 U.S. 725. (1983). Here "ideal" refers to the district population realized when a state's population is divided by the number of congressional seats that have been apportioned to it.

16. *Gray v. Sanders*.

17. 19,378,102 residents/27 seats = 717,707.48 ; see note 6.

18. *Favors v. Cuomo*.

19. *Favors v. Cuomo* 2012, *Voting Rights Act of 1965*, 4 U.S.C. Sec.1973. (1965); Bullock, *Redistricting*.

20. Richard L. Morrill, "Political Redistricting and Geographic Theory," Washington, DC: Association of American Geographers, 1981; Micah Altman, "Traditional Districting Principles: Judicial Myths v. Reality," *Social Science History* 22 (1998): 159–200.

21. Morrill, "Political Redistricting"; Bullock, *Redistricting*.

22. *Favors v. Cuomo*.

23. Bullock, *Redistricting*; Theodore S. Arrington, "Redistricting in the U.S.: A Review of Scholarship and Plan for Future Research," *The Forum* 8, 2 (2010): Article 7.

24. Altman, "Traditional Districting"; Jason Barabas and Jennifer Jerit, "Redistricting Principles and Racial Representation," *State Politics and Policy Quarterly* 4, 4 (2004): 415–35; *Miller v. Johnson*, 515 U.S. 900. (1995).

25. Bullock, *Redistricting*; Michael P. McDonald, "A Comparative Analysis of U.S. State Redistricting Institutions," *State Politics and Policy Quarterly* 4, 4 (2004): 371–96.

26. McDonald, "A Comparative Analysis"; Brennan Center for Justice, *A Citizen's Guide*; Bullock, *Redistricting*.

27. David G. Oedel, Allen K. Lynch, Sean E. Mulholland, and Neil T. Edwards, "Does the Introduction of Independent Redistricting Reduce Congressional Partisanship?" *Villanova Law Review* 54 (2009): 57–90.

28. McDonald, "A Comparative Analysis"; Bullock, *Redistricting*.

29. Brennan Center for Justice, *A Citizen's Guide*.

30. Citizens Union of the City of New York, "Reshaping New York: Ending the Rigged Process of Partisan Gerrymandering with an Impartial and Independent Redistricting Process," A Citizens Union Report (New York: Citizens Union Foundation, 2011).

31. Justin Buchler, "The Inevitability of Gerrymandering: Winners and Losers under Alternative Approaches to Redistricting," *Duke Journal of Constitutional Law and Public Policy* 5 (2010): 17–36.

32. Brennan Center for Justice, *A Citizen's Guide.*

33. McDonald, "A Comparative Analysis"; Brennan Center for Justice, "Still Broken."

34. Ryan P. Bates, "Congressional Authority to Require State Adoption of Independent Redistricting," *Duke Law Journal* 55 (2005): 333–71.

35. Oedel, Lynch, Mulholland, and Edwards, "Does the Introduction."

36. Oedel, Lynch, Mulholland, and Edwards, "Does the Introduction."

37. NY Legis, Law 83-m.

38. NY Legis, Law 83-m.

39. New York State Law 1978.

40. McDonald, "A Comparative Analysis."

41. Justin Levitt, "Justin Levitt before the New York State Public Bar Association Committee on Attorneys in Public Service," Focus on the Legislature: Reform and Renewal (New York: New York University School of Law, January 26, 2010).

42. Nicholas R. Seabrook, "The Limits of Partisan Gerrymandering: Looking Ahead to the 2010 Congressional Redistricting Cycle," *The Forum* 8, 2 (2010).

43. Oedel, Lynch, Mulholland, and Edwards, "Does the Introduction."

44. Quinnipiac University, "Support for Independent Redistricting Inches Up, Qunnipiac University New York State Poll Finds; Voters Support Vegas-Style Casinos 2-1," Quinnipiac University Polling Institute, December 21, 2011.

45. McDonald, "A Comparative Analysis."

46. Seabrook, "The Limits of Partisan Gerrymandering."

47. Colby Hamilton, "Congressional Plan Finalized by Federal Judge—Updated," *The Empire*, March 13, 2012.

48. Andrew Cuomo, "The New NY Agenda: A Plan for Action," Cuomo 2010, www.andrewcuomo.com/system/storage/6/34/9/378/acbookfinal.pdf (accessed March 12, 2012).

49. Capital Tonight, "In No Uncertain Terms, Cuomo Promises LATFOR Veto (Update)," *The Capitol Pressroom*, September 30, 2011 (Albany, NY: YNN).

50. The Associated Press, "Cuomo to sign NY Legislature's redistricting plan," March 15, 2012.

51. Citizens Union of the City of New York, "Reshaping New York."

52. Citizens Redistricting Committee, "Common Cause/NY Urges Court to Reject Incumbency Protection as Factor in Redistricting," Common Cause NY, March 5, 2012, www.citizenredistrictny.org/2012/03/common-causeny-urges-court-to-reject-incumbency-protection-as-a-factor-in-redistricting/ (accessed March 12, 2012).

53. *Voting Rights Act*, 1965.

54. New York Public Interest Research Group, "Lobbying in the First 10 Months of 2011" (New York: NYPIRG, 2011).

55. New York Public Interest Research Group, "Lobbying in the First 10 Months."

56. *Favors v. Cuomo*, 2012.

57. *United States of America v. New York*, 10-CV-1214 (N.D.N.Y.). (2012).

58. Robert J. McCarthy and Tom Precious, "At Long Last, Grisanti Is Winner with Historic Flair," *The Buffalo News*, November 30, 2010.

59. Timothy M. Kennedy, "Senator Kennedy Calls Redistricting Proposal Political Gerrymandering, Urges LATFOR to Head Back to the Drawing Boards," Press release from the

Office of NYS Senator Timothy M. Kennedy, February 16, 2012, www.nysenate.gov/press
-release/senator-kennedy-calls-redistricting-proposal-political-gerrymandering-urges-latfor
-hea (accessed March 12, 2012); Andrew C. White, "New York State Senate Proposed Maps
(updated)," *Daily Kos*, January 27, 2012:, www.dailykos.com/story/2012/01/27/1059070/
-New-York-State-Senate-Proposed-Maps-updated- (accessed March 12, 2012).

60. White, "New York State Senate Proposed."

61. Kennedy, "Senator Kennedy Calls Redistricting Proposal."

62. *Favors v. Cuomo*, 2012.

63. *Favors v. Cuomo*, 2012.

64. *Favors v. Cuomo*, 2012.

65. Thomas Kaplan, "New Congressional Lines Imposed by Federal Court," *New York Times*, March 19, 2012.

66. *Favors v. Cuomo*, 2012.

67. *Favors v. Cuomo*, 2012.

68. Here VAP is the number of individuals of a particular group who are 18 years of age or older, and it is used as a proxy for the universe of eligible voters. VAP is regularly used to approximate voting strength in Voting Rights Act cases.

69. *Favors v. Cuomo*, 2012.

70. *Favors v. Cuomo*, 2012.

71. *Favors v. Cuomo*, 2012.

72. *Favors v. Cuomo*, 2012.

73. Citizens Redistricting Committee, "Common Cause/NY."

74. *Favors v. Cuomo*, 2012.

75. This statement should not be confounded with the idea that the court's involvement was not independent or transparent. Here we are referring to the internal efforts of NYS.

76. "New York State—Constitutional Amendments," in *Zimmerman's Research Guide*, LexisNexis.

77. Quinnipiac University, "Support for Independent Redistricting."

78. John W. Kingdon, *Agendas, Alternatives and Public Policy*, 2nd Edition (New York: Longman, 2003).

79. Costas Panagopolous, "Public Knowledge and Attitudes and Redistricting Institutions" (paper presented at the Baldy Center for Politics and Policy Conference "Major Developments in Redistricting," Buffalo, NY, October 14, 2011).

80. Seabrook, "The Limits of Partisan Gerrymandering."

81. John R. Hibbing and Elizabeth Theiss-Morse, *Stealth Democracy: Americans' Beliefs about How Government Should Work* (Cambridge: Cambridge University Press, 2002).

20

Why Redistricting Matters

Political Decisions and Policy Impacts

William J. Miller

After reading the preceding chapters, it should be evident that each state handles congressional redistricting in its own way. Given the depth of the analyses you have been exposed to throughout the case studies, I will try to not belabor any points and instead utilize these final pages to draw on a few trends and assess how redistricting impacted recent elections.

As we discussed earlier, redistricting is important. District lines play a large role in determining politics in Congress. After all, members only are able to serve when elected by their constituents.

MISCONCEPTIONS

To begin an analysis of the recent redistricting efforts, we can start with a discussion regarding publicly held misconceptions regarding redistricting. First, many citizens have begun to question whether computers could not do a more effective and efficient job at drawing lines. With citizens being able to examine computer-based models and practice drawing the lines, it appears relatively easy. Yet the computer removes the human element that our country was founded on. Without having the human element, it will be difficult to control for many of the variables that mapmakers try to remember when drawing currently. In larger states, the technology actually hasn't shown to be capable of drawing lines that account for more than a few basic criteria.

Second, many have started to look at Iowa as the model of how to redistrict. The use of a nonpartisan bureau to draw lines for the legislature to modify seems to bring in the best of both worlds: nonpartisan efforts to design and a human, political element for matters of ratification. Yet success in Iowa does not necessarily mean the process would go as smoothly in other areas. Perhaps the legislature has more restraint in Iowa. Or maybe Iowa's relative demographic homogeneity makes the entire process less difficult for those tasked with drawing the lines.

Third, there is a belief that if line drawers were to entirely ignore all partisan data (like voting or registration patterns), then the process would be neutral and fair. It seems clear that those tasked with redistricting are not able to ignore such information, but even if they could, it would not automatically lead to neutrality or fairness. Every decision on where to draw a line, however, has a clear partisan effect.

Fourth, many reformers have pushed reverently for lines to be drawn in all states by a nonpartisan body. But as we have read earlier, even this method remains to be quite political. Further, there is no overarching reason why commission members need to be nonpartisan. Individuals who are simply independent can make the same decisions based on the ideal of independence. Partisanship does not, in this case, seem to matter as much as independence.

LOOKING AT THE DECENNIAL REDISTRICTING EFFORT

In the lead-up to the recent redistricting efforts, scholars and pundits raised a series of questions regarding how the process would ultimately play out. One of the most regularly asked questions centered on whether Republicans were even more in control in 2010 than they had been in 2000. After President Obama's election in 2008, many Democrats hoped that his leadership would help foster in waves of state-level politicians in subsequent elections, aiding their efforts to turn the country blue. But, as the 2010 midterm elections ultimately showed, Republicans were able to successfully mitigate such a result. Overall, however, Republicans country-wide were not dramatically better in 2010 than they were in 2000 (even with the 2010 tidal wave of red that swept across the country). Yet it goes without saying that in both years Republicans were better positioned nation-wide than Democrats.

Another important trend noted by many was the increase in electoral volatility from the late 1990s to 2010. While re-election rates have remained relatively stable for members of the United States House of Representatives, districts that used to be safe are less likely to be so today. In fact, it is becoming more difficult to label any district as being truly safe with the volatility within American politics and parties. This volatility leads to incumbents wanting to make their districts even safer, diluting party power in surrounding districts in almost all cases.

If we flip back to the state of Republicans during this redistricting cycle, a major issue was the idea of optimal partisan gerrymandering. In many of the states examined, Republicans already held a hefty majority of congressional seats—such a majority that it is questionable whether the Party can actually gain further seats. If they are unable to gain seats, it could lead to tension within the Republican Party and between incumbents from the party. In other regions, however, Republicans will find themselves being able to shift congressional delegations in their favor.

The Voting Rights Act was predicted to have a significant impact on the 2010 redistricting efforts. First, Democrats control the Department of Justice for the first time during redistricting since the Voting Rights Act was passed in the 1960s. As a result, many representatives in the South who would otherwise be in danger are very likely to be protected. Democratic districts will be protected as a Democratic Department of Justice seems highly unlikely or unwilling to dilute the voting power of their own party in Congress. Taken together, all of these discussions impacted redistricting in various states during the decennial census redistricting.

A key aspect of the most recent redistricting efforts in the United States was the dramatic increase in public participation in the process. With technology increasing in a seemingly exponential manner, it is of little surprise that it has been used by citizens and pundits to experiment with the redistricting process. Online databases and tools allow common citizens to have a go at trying to do the job that seemingly cripples state legislatures across the country once every decade. Ohio and Virginia both held open competitions where citizens were able to design their best maps and have them considered during the actual process.

Broad participation is new. As a result, it is not necessarily easy to determine whether it has a positive or negative impact (if any at all). California and Arizona have both instilled citizens' commissions that are required to listen to public feedback. And Florida is beginning to organize an online map submission system whereby citizens could send successful map designs directly to state legislators.

REDISTRICTING AND THE 2012 ELECTION CYCLE

As bad as 2010 was for House Democrats, 2012 had the potential to be even worse. As discussed above, Republicans didn't have a lot of exposure, since most of their gains were in red territory. More importantly, Republicans controlled more seats in redistricting than they have since the states began regular decennial redistricting in 1972. To understand what impact redistricting truly had on governance, we need to examine cursory results from the 2012 election season to help paint a clear picture.

As we consider the following, understand the following scenario: Consider a district where the Democratic candidate in 2012 won with 51 percent of the vote, while the Republican candidate received 49 percent. If the territory in the newly drawn district historically gave Republican candidates about 5 percent less of the vote than the old district, it is likely that the Republican candidate would have won under the old district lines. Therefore, our analysis would estimate that redistricting likely changed which party won the election in 2012 from Republican to Democratic. The most telling statistic may be that redistricting can be credited for 25 House districts being won by a party that would not have otherwise been predicted to do so. For Republicans, this means they won roughly six more seats in 2012 than they would have if older lines had been utilized. In areas where Republicans were able to draw the lines, the party won eleven more seats than they would have under old lines—including five that had been Democratic for the previous election cycle. In all, nine seats flipped from Republican to Democrat; eight from Democratic to Republican; Republicans maintained control of eight states they were expected to lose otherwise; and Democrats held one seat they would have likely lost. Ultimately, Democrats gained a single net seat thanks to redistricting.

Where Republicans were especially successful in redistricting was in guaranteeing support for vulnerable party incumbents. By protecting six incumbents who could have otherwise lost, the Republican Party maintained six seats in the 2012 election. Six different types of authorities controlled the redistricting process: Republican legislature and governor; Democratic legislature and governor; independent commissions; a politician commission; a state or federal court; or a state legislature and governor with split control between Republicans and Democrats. In the earlier chapters, you were exposed to variants of each. Republican legislators and governors drew the lines for 173 of 435 seats and ultimately won 11 more than they would have previously (5 flipped districts and 6 saved). The Republican candidates won 53 percent of the vote and 72 percent of the seats in these districts. Likewise, 44 districts were drawn by Democratic legislators and governors. In these areas, their party was able to win 56 percent of the vote and 71 percent of the seats.

In all, 79 members of Congress were scheduled to not return to the House of Representatives at the conclusion of the last session. Just more than half of them are not returning due to redistricting in some part. Many opted to not seek re-election or lost in a primary, but of the 26 who made it to Election Day, 19 were sank by redistricting issues.

CONCLUSION

The goal of this book was to introduce the numerous variations of how states choose to draw their congressional district lines. While there are some federal requirements, most of what states do falls back on their own decisions and state laws. And regardless of how much local bodies try to argue the opposite from time to time, redistricting is messy and problematic—yet still very important. I have attempted in this brief concluding chapter to not stretch the scope of the book beyond describing processes. But I hope what has become abundantly clear is that redistricting is different in every location. And that's acceptable; different methods for different people and places. In the end, however, we must realize that whoever wins the election just prior to redistricting will hold more influence and sway—at least for a few years, anyway.

Index

About the Editors

William J. Miller is assistant professor of public administration at Flagler College in St. Augustine, Florida. He received his doctorate in 2010 in public administration and urban studies from The University of Akron along with a master's degree in applied politics (campaign management and polling). He had previously earned his BA from the Ohio University Honors Tutorial College and an MA in political science also from Ohio. He is the editor of *Tea Party Effects on 2010 U.S. Senate Elections: Stuck in the Middle to Lose* (2012), *Taking Sides: Clashing Views on Public Administration & Policy* (2012), *The Battle to Face Obama: The 2012 Republican Nomination and the Future of the Republican Party* (forthcoming), *The Tea Party in 2012: The Party Rolls On* (forthcoming), and *Handbook on Teaching and Learning in Political Science and International Relations* (forthcoming). His research appears in *Journal of Political Science Education, Journal of Political Marketing, Studies in Conflict & Terrorism, International Studies Quarterly, Nonproliferation Review, Afro-Americans in New York Life and History, Journal of South Asian and Middle Eastern Studies, American Behavioral Scientist, PS: Political Science and Politics* and *Journal of Common Market Studies.*

Jeremy D. Walling is associate professor of political science at Southeast Missouri State University. He received his PhD in 2005 from the University of Kansas and his MPA from Missouri State University in 1998. He studies American national institutions, state politics and intergovernmental relations, and public administration ethics and accountability. He was co-editor (with William J. Miller) of *Tea Party Effects on 2010 U.S. Senate Elections: Stuck in the Middle to Lose* and *Taking Sides: Clashing Views in Public Administration and Policy.* Book chapters have been published in *The Battle to Face Obama: The 2012 Republican Nomination, Teaching Politics Beyond the Book*, and *The Constitutionalism of American States.* His work has also appeared in *The Handbook of Administrative Ethics* and *Public Personnel Management*, both with H. George Frederickson.

About the Contributors

Rickert Althaus has been on the political science faculty at Southeast Missouri State University since 1980, where he teaches national and state government and public administration and public policy. His writing has focused on public administration, agricultural policy, and Missouri state government.

Adam R. Brown is an assistant professor of political science at Brigham Young University and a research fellow with the university's Center for the Study of Elections and Democracy. He earned his master's and doctorate degrees in political science from the University of California, San Diego. He has published work dealing with state elections, gubernatorial approval, federalism, state politics, and the political uses of information technology in several of the discipline's journals.

Charles S. Bullock III is the Richard B. Russell Professor of political science and Josiah Meigs Distinguished Teaching Professor at the University of Georgia. His most recent books include *Redistricting: The Most Political Activity in America*, the fourth edition of *The New Politics of the Old South* (co-edited with Mark Rozell), *Key States, High Stakes: Sarah Palin, the Tea Party and the 2010 Elections*, and *The Triumph of Voting Rights in the South* (co-authored with Keith Gaddie) winner of the V. O. Key Award as the best book published on Southern Politics in 2009. His research has been funded by the National Science Foundation, National Institutes of Education, American Enterprise Institute, and the Pew Charitable Trusts. He has been involved with statewide redistricting litigation in Arkansas, Florida, Georgia, Illinois, Louisiana, Maryland, Mississippi, New Mexico, North Carolina, Oklahoma, South Carolina, Texas, Virginia, and Wisconsin.

Jason P. Casellas is assistant professor of government, a faculty associate of the Center for Mexican American Studies, and the associate director of the Irma Rangel

Public Policy Institute at the University of Texas at Austin. He specializes in American politics, with specific research and teaching interests in Latino politics, legislative politics, and state and local politics. He is the author of *Latino Representation in State Houses and Congress.* He is the recipient of numerous fellowships and awards, including a Princeton President's Fellowship, an American Political Science Association Fellowship, a Ford Motor Company Fellowship, the Samuel DuBois Cook Postdoctoral Fellowship at Duke University, and a United States Studies Centre Postdoctoral Fellowship at the University of Sydney (Australia).

John A. Clark is professor and chair of the department of political science at Western Michigan University. He received his PhD from The Ohio State University. His research focuses on political parties, elections, and legislative politics in the United States. He is co-editor of *Southern Political Party Activists: Patterns of Conflict and Change, 1991–2001* (2004) and *Party Organization and Activism in the American South* (1998).

Alvaro Jose Corral is a graduate student at the department of government at the University of Texas at Austin. His interests include Latino Politics and the study of the intersection between race and ethnicity and public policies including immigration and education. He received his BA in political science at UT-Austin. Corral was born in Mexicali, Mexico, and raised in the Rio Grande Valley in the city of McAllen, Texas.

Pearson Cross currently serves as head of the political science department at the University of Louisiana at Lafayette. His principal areas of teaching are state and local politics, Southern politics, and Louisiana politics. He is a regular commentator on Louisiana politics on national, local, and statewide media. Dr. Cross received his BA from San Francisco State University in 1985 and his PhD from Brandeis University in Massachusetts in 1997. His dissertation was titled "Collective Action in Colonial America."

Todd A. Curry earned his doctorate in political science from Western Michigan University in December 2012. His research focuses on tenure, replacement, and policy congruence in State Courts of Last Resort. He is currently examining the nature of substantive representation across the various methods of selection used to staff state Supreme Courts.

David F. Damore is an associate professor in the department of political science at the University of Nevada, Las Vegas (UNLV) where he teaches undergraduate and graduate courses in American Politics and Research Methods. Dr. Damore's research, which has been published in outlets such as *The Journal of Politics, Political Research Quarterly*, and *Political Behavior*, focuses on the study of campaigns and elections and public policy at the state and national levels. His present research assesses how direct democracy is used as a tool of policy making in the American states, and he is beginning work on a book-length manuscript examining the political economy of Nevada's geography. In addition to his position at UNLV, Dr. Damore is a nonresident senior fellow in the Brookings Institution's Governance Studies Program, a key vote advisor to Project Vote Smart, a contributing analyst for Latino Decisions, and he regularly comments on Nevada governmental and political issues for local, national, and international media outlets. Dr. Damore earned his PhD from the University of California, Davis (2000), his MA from the University of Georgia (1995), and his BA from the University of California, San Diego (1992)—all in political science.

Joshua J. Dyck is associate professor of political science and co-director of the Center for Public Opinion at the University of Massachusetts, Lowell. Dyck studies American politics, with a focus on public opinion, voting behavior, and state politics. Much of his research is motivated by the interplay between public opinion and different social and institutional settings, examining the way that democratic citizens react to democratic environments and political institutions. His research has appeared in many leading scholarly journals including *The Journal of Politics, Public Opinion Quarterly, Political Research Quarterly, Social Science Quarterly, Electoral Studies*, and *American Politics Research*. He also is the co-editor of *The Guide to State Politics and Policy*, CQ Press/Sage (2013).

Timothy M. Hagle is associate professor of political science at the University of Iowa. He teaches courses on constitutional law, the judicial system, and public administration. He received BS and BA degrees from Michigan State University (1978), his JD from Thomas M. Cooley Law School (1982), and his MA (1985) and PhD (1988) degrees from Michigan State University. He was appointed by President George W. Bush to serve on the Permanent Committee for the Oliver Wendall Holmes Devise (2002–2009). He also served two years in the Department of Justice (2005–2007) as chief of staff first in the Office for Victims of Crime and then the National Institute of Justice. His current research focuses on American political practice (including the Iowa Caucuses) and agenda setting on the U.S. Supreme Court during the Vinson and Warren Court periods.

Brigid Callahan Harrison is professor of political science and law at Montclair State University. She is the author of *American Democracy Now, A More Perfect Union* (2010) *Power and Society*, and *Women in American Politics* (2003), and various journal articles. Harrison is a frequent commentator in print and electronic media on U.S. politics, providing regular political analysis to FOX News; to local affiliates of ABC, NBC, and CBS; and to various NPR radio programs, including NPR News. She writes a weekly column on New Jersey politics in the Sunday editions of the *Bergen Record,* and her editorials have appeared in the *New York Times, USA Today,* and the *Star-Ledger.* Harrison's research interests include Congress and the presidency, and American public opinion. She is an expert on the politics of the Millennial Generation. She received her BA from The Richard Stockton College of New Jersey, her MA from Rutgers, The State University of New Jersey, and her PhD from Temple University, where she was a national MENSA graduate fellow.

Scott H. Huffmon, PhD, is a professor of political science and founder and director of the Social and Behavioral Research Lab at Winthrop University where he also directs the Winthrop Poll. He joined Winthrop University in 2001 and went on to win the university's Outstanding Junior Professor award in 2004. In 2009, he was awarded a Fulbright to serve as a Lecturer at the University of Debrecen, Hungary, where he taught politics of the American South, state and local government in the United States, and American government for the North American Studies Department and the Political Science Department. His teaching and research interests include American politics, public opinion, Southern politics, religion and politics, survey research, methodology, political parties, campaigns and elections, and state and local politics. His commentary on poll results, South Carolina politics, and southern and national politics in general have been featured in national and international news outlets including CNN, MSNBC, Fox News, NBC Nightly News, ABC News, *New York Times*, *Wall Street Journal*, *Washington Post*, *LA Times*, *Miami Herald*, Politico.com, News Hour (PBS), NPR, BBC, AFP (Agence France-Presse), Tokyo Broadcasting System, and more.

Shannon Jenkins is an associate professor of political science at the University of Massachusetts Dartmouth, specializing in U.S. state politics, women and politics, and public policy. Her research focuses on decision making in state legislatures, with a specific focus on the role of political organizations and gender in shaping outputs in these institutions. Her research has appeared in journals such as *Legislative Studies Quarterly*, *Political Research Quarterly*, *State Politics and Policy Quarterly*, and *Social Science Quarterly*.

Aubrey Jewett received his PhD from Florida State University. He is currently associate professor of political science at the University of Central Florida. His main research and teaching interests are in American national, state, and local politics with a special emphasis on Florida. Professor Jewett has published two books, several book chapters, and numerous research articles in refereed political science journals. In September 2002 Professor Jewett received the Leon Weaver Award for his study of ballot invalidation in Florida during the 2000 presidential election. He authored the chapter on Central Florida politics in the edited volume *Florida Politics: Ten Media Markets, One Powerful State*. He is co-author of *Politics in Florida*, third edition and *Political Rules of the Road*. Professor Jewett has helped to bring in over $1 million of external funding to UCF. He has won multiple awards for teaching and advising excellence and professional service. Professor Jewett was also selected and served as an American Political Science Association Congressional Fellow.

Christopher N. Lawrence (PhD, University of Mississippi, 2003) is currently assistant professor of political science at Middle Georgia State College in Macon,

Georgia. His research primarily focuses on public opinion and voting behavior in the United States and other democracies. His published research has also investigated shirking in the U.S. Congress, institutional design in emerging democracies, and improving political science pedagogy using technology.

Samantha Pettey is a PhD candidate at the University of North Texas focusing on American politics and research methodology. Specifically, her research interests include political psychology, state and local politics, and women in politics with a focus on candidate emergence.

Kevin Pirch is an associate professor in the department of government at Eastern Washington University. His research focus is on voting behavior—particularly regarding Washington State's vote-by-mail system, political parties, and Washington State government. His research has been published in *PS: Political Science and Politics*, *American Review of Politics*, and *Social Science Quarterly*.

Kent Redfield is a professor emeritus of political studies at the University of Illinois—Springfield (UIS). He has research appointments with the Center for State Policy and Leadership at UIS and the University of Illinois's Institute of Government and Public Affairs. Dr. Redfield has a BA in political science from the University of Utah and an MA and PhD in political science from the University of Washington (Seattle). Prior to joining UIS in 1979 Dr. Redfield worked for four years as a member of the research/appropriations staff for the speaker of the Illinois General Assembly. His primary assignment with the legislature was staffing the House's local government committees. Dr. Redfield's research and teaching interests are primarily in the areas of money and politics, Illinois politics, and local government politics and administration.

Michael K. Romano is a Western Michigan University PhD candidate actively exploring the intersections of media, politics, and communication in the political science department. His focus is on the U.S. media as the Fourth Estate, congressional communication strategies, the development of online political discourse, and the relationship between the press and political actors in the United States. His dissertation project examines the strategic utilization of the local press outlets by members of Congress, and how representatives manipulate and control media narratives in order to maintain a sense of representativeness in their constituencies.

Ajang A. Salkhi is a PhD student in the department of politics and international affairs at Northern Arizona University. He holds a master's degree in political science from San Francisco State University. Ajang's academic work focuses on American politics and Iran, with primary interests in U.S. voting behavior and congressional elections.

Mark Salling, senior fellow, Maxine Goodman Levin College of Urban Affairs, Cleveland State University, directs the college's Northern Ohio Data and Information

Service. Dr. Salling manages a team of researchers, GIS specialists, and students involved in data dissemination, demographic analysis, and GIS applications. He is an affiliated scholar with the university's Center for Election Integrity and also serves as research director of The Center for Community Solutions in Cleveland, conducting applied research on social and health issues. He has taught courses on GIS, urban geography, research methods, and demography. He holds a PhD in geography from Kent State University, an MA in geography from the University of Cincinnati, and is a certified GIS professional (GISP).

Frederic I. Solop is a professor in the department of politics and international affairs at Northern Arizona University. Dr. Solop chaired the politics and international affairs department from 2008 to 2011. Between 1997 and 2008, Dr. Solop directed the Social Research Laboratory at Northern Arizona University where he served as principal investigator for over 350 federal, state, and local research projects. His primary areas of research and publication include American politics, elections, social movements, public opinion, and digital democracy. He has been studying and writing about Arizona politics since first moving to the state in 1990. Dr. Solop regularly provides commentary to the media on politics and public policy issues in Arizona.

Harry C. "Neil" Strine IV is an associate professor, director of forensics, and chair of the political science department at Bloomsburg University of Pennsylvania. His research interests include congressional committee hearings, judicial politics, and the presidency. He has published research in the *Journal of Black Studies*, the *KB Journal* (online), the *Encyclopedia of American Government and Civics* (Facts on File), *Governing America: Major Policies and Decisions of Federal, State, and Local Government* (Facts on File), and a book chapter for *The Legacy of the George W. Bush Presidency* (Cambridge Scholars Publishing).

Russell C. Weaver holds a PhD in geography and an MA in economics from The State University of New York at Buffalo. His academic research focuses the interaction of land use, politics, and public policy. He has held senior level positions on the legislative staffs of local and state elected officials in western New York, and he was appointed to the 2011 redistricting commission for the city of Buffalo. Russell currently serves as the in-house social scientist for a voting rights organization in Washington, DC, where he analyzes redistricting proposals and conducts empirical research on group voting behavior.